A Defence of the Midland/LMS Class 4 0-6-0
- also why frames cracked and axleboxes ran hot

In preparation:-

An Introduction to the Locomotive Boiler
- General Performance Characteristics

By the same author:-

An Introduction to Large-lap Valves and their Use on the LMS

Midland Railway built Class 4 0-6-0 N° 3859 seen here in photographic livery soon after the Grouping

A Defence of the Midland/LMS Class 4 0-6-0
- also why frames cracked and axleboxes ran hot

A P Tester BSc CEng MIMarE

Crimson Lake

First published 2011 by:-

Crimson Lake
6 High Street
Aberystwyth
SY23 1JG

© Crimson Lake and A P Tester 2011

ISBN 978 0 9570779 0 4

All rights reserved. No part of this publication may be reproduced, stored in a retrieval system or transmitted in any form or by any means, electronic, mechanical, photocopying, recording or otherwise, without the publisher's prior written permission.

The author discussing 'Big Goods' details at Keighley in the company of N° 43924

Preface

Margot Asquith once accused Lloyd George of not being able to see a belt without wanting to punch below it. Maybe it is present day followers of the wily Welsh Wizard who are unable to see a 'Big Goods' without making some derogatory remark or other - usually a reference to small axleboxes or short-lap valves or poor steaming.

Well there is no denying, as bald statements of fact, the truth of these observations, but what appears to have been overlooked by these critics is that some or all of these same comments could have been directed to any number of other large 0-6-0s of the twentieth century. Furthermore the class was considered by some professional railwaymen to have been a successful, even most useful creation.

This book therefore attempts to provide a defence of the Midland/LMS Standard Class 4 0-6-0, for the author is sceptical about explanations that *all* agree on. C C Pounder, winner of the 1959 Denny Medal with his paper *Human Problems in Marine Engineering*, opined in it that engineers sometimes form their opinions from a mixture of emotion, impression, prejudice, irrationalities, idiosyncrasies, fancies and whims with often only a small part composed of reason.

Conscious of this, in this defence he has tried to put reason above all of the others, but is not so inhuman himself to think that he has not in turn displayed instances of those same weaknesses!

The reader will notice that a high proportion of the photographs illustrate members of the class running on the London Extension of the quondam Midland Railway, particularly in the vicinity of Elstree. The author offers no apology for this, Elstree was where he gained his infant nurture, and he hopes the reader will overlook this indulgence. Likewise, he also hopes that professional stress-men, materials scientists and tribologists will excuse the simplifications he has introduced into what are sophisticated and complicated subjects. Partly this has been prompted by his own gaps, but also to try and give a flavour of contemporary knowledge.

Finally, in this the centennial year of the introduction of the first two examples of the class, he is rather amused to record that the very first locomotive to be rescued for preservation from Woodham Brothers' scrapyard in Barry, was a 'Big Goods', Nº 43924 - someone had the right priorities!

Adrian Tester
Aberystwyth
September 2011

Acknowledgements

Producing this work would have been impossible without access to information, the author therefore wishes to express his thanks to the librarians, archivists and staff at the Institution of Civil Engineers, Institution of Mechanical Engineers, the National Railway Museum, Birmingham and Aberystwyth public libraries.

Thanks are also due for the assistance provided by several fellow members of the Midland Railway Society and the LMS Society who kindly assisted in providing information, photographs etc., but he would particularly like to single out Ralph Ingham, David Hunt and Ian Howard who read this book during its draft stages and each made several helpful comments.

Thanks are also due to Duncan Ballard, Chris Jeffries, Bob Meanley, Eric Riley and Edward Talbot who kindly responded to questions.

The views and opinions expressed in this book are however the author's interpretation, likewise any errors of fact or understanding are his responsibility alone.

The drawings and diagrams have been prepared by the author who also provided about one-half of the photographs from his collection although most of them came originally from the late Derek Wynche. He wishes to thank the following who kindly contributed the remainder:-

I Bowland (Rail 37) - figure 38
D Hunt collection - figures 1, 9, 37, 74, 78, 90, 99 & 103
R Ingham - figure 98
J Jennison - figures 10 & 14
H N Twells - author's picture

Contents

		Page
Chapter 1	Background	1
Chapter 2	Multiplication and Modification	9
Chapter 3	Frames and Cracks	33
	Appendix 3.1 - Some Notes Concerning Crack Development	94
Chapter 4	Axleboxes, Bearing Metals and Lubricants	97
	Appendix 4.1 - Estimating the Oil Delivery from Pad Lubrication	176
Chapter 5	Comparisons, Steaming and Performance	179
	Appendix 5.1 - Accuracy of 4MT 2-6-0 Test Bulletin Results	264
	Appendix 5.2 - Boiler Proportions and Performance	266
Chapter 6	Some Final Thoughts and Summary	271

List of Tables

		Page
I	Coal Consumption Tests October 1913 – Time-table of Engine Working	4
II	Coal Consumption Tests - October 1913	5
III	Ten-year Average of Annual Mileage, Coal Consumption and Repair Costs for Selected LMS Goods Engines	12
IV	Repair Mileages for Selected LMS Locomotive Classes – 1939	14
V	Availability, Miles Run, Coal per Mile and Weekdays Out-of-Service for Tender Goods Engines – Western Division of the LMS Year Ending 31st December 1932	16
VI	Comparison in Availability and Productivity for a Selection of Tender Goods Engines – 1955 and 1956	18
VII	Comparison in Availability and Productivity for a Selection of Tender Goods Engines – 1957	19
VIII	Comparison in Availability and Productivity for a Selection of Tender Goods Engines – 1958	20
IX	A Comparison in Maximum Bending Moments for a Selection of Locomotive Frames	42
X	LMS Passenger Tender Engine Frame Cracks	58
XI	LMS Goods Tender Engine & Tank Engine Frame Cracks	59
XII	Particulars of Class 5 Frames	60
XIII	Class 5 4-6-0 Mixed Traffic Engines	62
XIV	Class 8 2-8-0 Goods Engines	63
XV	N° 4 Class Goods Engines	64
XVI	Good and Bad Orders, N° 4 Class Goods Engines	64
XVII	Measured Frame Stresses in Class 5 4-6-0 N° 5088	67
XVIII	Stresses Measured in Horn Gap and Horn Stay for a Steady Load of Forty Tons Applied Across the Gap	69
XIX	Stresses Measured in Horn Gap and Horn Stay for a Steady Load of Forty Tons Applied Across the Gap – I Loco E Results	70
XX	Positions Most Affected by Cracking - LMS Standard Classes	76
XXI	Frame Cracks in Ex-Midland Engines	77
XXII	Frame Cracks in Ex-Lancashire & Yorkshire Engines	78
XXIII	Frame Cracks in Northern Division Non-Standard Engines	79
XXIV	Piston and Bearing Loads for a Selection of Inside Cylinder Locomotives	98
XXV	Hot Box Performance Record of the ex-LNWR G1 and G2 0-8-0 Classes During the Period 1942-1946	99
XXVI	Sample Friction Values Obtained by Mr Beauchamp Tower – Lubricant Rape Oil, Journal Speed 150 rpm	107
XXVII	Record of a Journal Bearing Test - 1929	110
XXVIII	Record of Brinell Hardness Tests on Tin, Antimony & Copper Alloys	122

XXIX	Record of Compressive Tests on Tin, Antimony & Copper Alloys - 1899	122
XXX	Composition and Mechanical Properties of LMS Bearing Alloys	125
XXXI	LMS Locomotive Axlebox Clearances	135
XXXII	Timken Machine Oil Film Strength Results	156
XXXIII	Percentage of Rape Oil Used in Railway Lubricating Oils	157
XXXIV	Details of Lubricating Oils Used on the LMS – 1944	158
XXXV	Specification Nº 659 – Lubricating Oils for Locomotives (Mineral)	161
XXXVI	Specification Nº 660 – Lubricating Oils for Locomotives (Compounded)	161
XXXVII	Variation in the Delivery of Different Oils by Syphons Comprising Different Numbers of Strands	166
XXXVIII	Goods Derived Income as a Percentage of Gross Income	181
XXXIX	Working Costs as a Percentage of Gross Income	181
XL	LMS Class 4 Replacement Development Chronology - *Locomotive Panorama*	189
XLI	A Comparison between Contemporary Six- and Eight-Coupled Locomotives	190
XLII	Mr Bulleid's Locomotive Performance Analysis	191
XLIII	Improvements in Steaming Capacity with Single Chimneys Following Testing Station Investigations - Post 1948	192
XLIV	Performance Comparison between LMS Standard Class 7 0-8-0 and ex-LNWR G2 0-8-0 - Brent-Toton	193
XLV	Comparison in Goods Engine Performance LMS/BR Toton – Brent Up Loaded Mineral Trains	194
XLVI	Approximate Best Thermal Efficiencies of Various Steam Locomotives	197
XLVII	Toton - Brent Trials – Engine Performance on Grades 1925	200
XLVIII	Toton - Brent Trials - Engine Performance on Grades 1928	201
XLIX	Performance Data Obtained from Class 4 0-6-0 Nº 4542 Using Mobile Test Unit Nº 1 - 1939	222
L	Comparison Between ex-LMS Class 4F 0-6-0 and WD Austerity Class 8F 2-8-0	225
LI	8.00 pm (Saturdays excepted) Class 'D' Freight Trains Huskisson - Rowsley	227
LII	1.10 am pm (Mondays excepted) Class 'D' Freight Trains Rowsley - Walton	229
LIII	Sample LMS Dynamometer Car Tests Toton - Brent Up Loaded Coal Trains – Short-lap Engines	230
LIV	Sample LMS Dynamometer Car Tests Toton - Brent Up Loaded Coal Trains – Large-lap Engines	231
LV	Summary of the Various Drawbar Horsepower Calculations Derived From Short-Lap Engines Used on Toton–Brent Coal Trains	233
LVI	Summary of the Various Drawbar Horsepower Calculations Derived From Large-Lap Engines Used on Toton–Brent Coal Trains	234
LVII	Summary of the Relative Locomotive Loadings - Toton–Brent Coal Trains	235
LVIII	Comparison Between Recorded and Estimated DHP Figures	238
LIX	Maximum Evaporation Rates - G7s Boiler	241
LX	Performance Analysis of Class 4MT 2-6-0 Nº 43094	247
LXI	Performance Analysis of Class 4 0-6-0 Nº 44030 with Standard Tubes and Modified Draughting	248

LXII	Predicted Performance of a Hypothetical Rebuilding of a Standard Class 4 Goods	252
LIII	Comparison in Boiler Proportions and Performance at their Front End Draughting Limits	268

List of Figures

		Page
1	Nº 3835 in Midland days	3
2	Nº 4433 hauling pre-war express goods	6
3	Mileages recorded by ex-LMS Class 8 2-8-0s and Class 4 0-6-0s	15
4	Nº 4260 under construction	21
5	Building and withdrawal profiles for classes 4F 0-6-0 and 4MT 2-6-0	22
6	Locomotive annual running costs	23
7	Nº 3976 fitted with exhaust steam injector	24
8	By-pass and air-valve performance indicator diagrams - Midland Railway	28
9	Nº 3895 in early LMS days	30
10	View of the upper portions of the rocker arms - Class 4 Nº 4027	31
11	Traction forces in a locomotive frame	35
12	Another view of Nº 4260 under construction	36
13	How tractive effort is exerted	37
14	View of the right-hand trailing horns of Class 4 0-6-0 Nº 3924	42
15	Horn guides and hornblocks fitted to LMS Class 5 4-6-0s	43
16	Development of a fatigue crack under repeated application of load	49
17	An S-N diagram plotted from the results of completely reversed axial fatigue tests	50
18	Stress trajectories in a uniformly loaded in tension (a) without and (b) with a crack	51
19	Stress concentration in a bar uniformly loaded in tension (a) without and (b) with a fillet radius	51
20	Stress concentration in a infinite plate with differing alignment of an elliptical hole	52
21	Calculated stress concentration contours near the tip of an elliptical crack	52
22	Practical stress distribution near a circular hole in an infinite plate	53
23	Theoretical stress concentration factors for a rectangular hole in an infinite plate	54
24	Notch sensitivity as a function of notch radius for various strength steels	55
25	View of Class 4F Nº 44232 slung from overhead crane	56
26	Stresses recorded in the fuselage skin at the top and bottom corners of the port escape hatch - *Comet I*	57
27	Record of crack growth at the port forward escape hatch (bottom forward corner) - *Comet I*	57
28	Location and number of frame cracks recorded on early LMS Class 5 4-6-0s	60
29	Comparison of cracks - Class 5 4-6-0	62
30	Frame cracks - Class 8 2-8-0	63
31	Nº 4 Class Goods engines - frame cracks, & works where engines built	65
32	De Forest strain gauges - Class 5 4-6-0 Nº 5088	66

33	Sample frame stresses recorded on LMS Class 5 N° 5088	68
34	Strain gauge positions on dummy Class 5 frame	69
35	Fatigue fracture in an American locomotive bar frame	71
36	Photoelastic analysis of the stress concentrations in a GWR 'King' horn gap	72
37	LMS Class 4 N° 4286 under the shearlegs with its trailing coupled wheels run out	81
38	View of the underside of preserved Class 4 0-6-0 N° 44422	82
39	Number of frame cracks from new - 'Royal Scot' class	85
40	Cracks recorded in BR 'Britannia' Class 4-6-2 N° 70007 *Coeur de Lion* in six months	89
41	Diagram of the horizontal stresses in a Class 5 frame plate obtained by relaxation	91
42	BR Class 7 horn designs	92
43	The unloaded regions adjoining the crack flanks	94
44	The Griffith fracture energy balance	95
45	Midland Railway manganese bronze driving axlebox	103
46	LMS 'Stanier' steel axlebox with pressed in brass	104
47	Beauchamp Tower's experiments on the pressure distribution in a partial bearing	107
48	Formation of the hydrodynamic oil film in a clearance bearing	108
49	Theoretical consideration of journal bearing performance	109
50	Record of a journal bearing test - 1929	110
51	Effect of oiliness on the coefficient of friction	111
52	Characteristic curve for a forced oil-circulation ball bearing	112
53	Modified Stribeck curve for a plain journal	113
54	Effect of surface finish on the coefficient of friction	114
55	Micrograph of ARLE N° 1 tin-antimony-copper white metal	121
56	Compressive strengths of the alloys of tin, antimony and copper	123
57	Creep tests on LMS standard bearing metals	124
58	Compressive tests - IRS bearing metals	124
59	Hardness - temperature curves for a selection of IRS white metals	124
60	Partial bearing	129
61	Bedding the axleboxes of 'Big Goods' 0-6-0s in N° 2 Bay of Derby Erecting Shop in 1929	130
62	Clearances of brasses for LMS locomotive axleboxes	132
63	Surface profiles	133
64	Wear pattern in an axlebox brass	136
65	Wear observed in a Midland loose brass axlebox	138
66	In service wear observed in Standard Class 4 0-6-0 driving axleboxes	139
67	Effects of rotating load and half-speed load vector	140
68	Axlebox temperature-time relationship - GIP Railway, India	142
69	Influence of speed on axlebox equilibrium temperature - GIP Railway, India	143
70	Calculated individual component forces acting on locomotive axleboxes	145
71	Calculated horizontal forces acting on locomotive axleboxes	145

72	Calculation of individual forces acting on an axlebox	146
73	Vector and polar diagrams of the forces acting on axleboxes at 15 mph	147
74	N° 44578 built at Derby in 1939 demonstrates that it has its cranks positioned *á le Stroudley*, and is believed to be left-hand crank lead	150
75	The mechanism of boundary lubrication	152
76	Temperature - viscosity relationship	154
77	Influence of viscosity on bearing performance	155
78	Left-hand drive Class 4 0-6-0 N° 4526 on the down slow passing through Mill Hill	160
79	Pressure distribution in a fitted bearing - Professor Goodman	163
80	Effect the location of oil grooves has on bearing load capacity	164
81	Syphoning experiments	167
82	Crank axle fitted with a roller bearing axlebox	175
83	Diagram of an axlebox	176
84	Typical oil film pressure and temperature curves for waste packed and Isothermos axleboxes	177
85	A National Isothermos journal box	178
86	Locomotive performance - speed against tractive effort	179
87	Examples of Mr Coleman's 0-6-0 replacement proposals for the Standard Class 4	188
88	N° 4405 heading north on the down slow passes under the footbridge immediately north of Elstree station	198
89	Example of the variation in isentrpoic efficiency - LMS Class 4MT 2-6-0 N° 43094	198
90	Former Midland Class 4 0-6-0s N° 3945 and 3946 with the ex-L&YR dynamometer carriage photographed on one of their runs - probably February 1928.	199
91	Class 4 0-6-0, variation in drawbar horsepower and pull with speed	202
92	LMS predicted performance curves for Class 4 0-6-0 & G2 0-8-0 - Rugby Testing Station	203
93	Actual evaporation comparisons WD Classes 2-8-0 and 2-10-0 when burning different coals	208
94	'Big Goods' N° 44030 seen here much earlier in its career as LMS N° 4030 probably not that many years after building in Derby in December 1924.	211
95	Original Midland Railway and LMS short chimney draughting designs	211
96	Later LMS long and short chimney draughting designs	212
97	British Railways modified draughting designs	212
98	Replacement petticoat pipe fitted to Standard 4 N° 43924 - June 2011	213
99	'Big Goods' N° 44203, the other engine tested on the Crewe - Holyhead line.	213
100	Relative sizes of common points in the steam circuit for a selection of locomotives	215
101	Drawbar water and coal consumption - Class 4MT Mogul N° 43094.	218
102	Standard 4 N° 4542, seen here in LMS days.	220
103	Class 4F 0-6-0 N° 44481, the locomotive which took part in the Class 'D' express goods train trials between Rowsley-Peak Forest and Cheadle Heath-Peak Forest in November 1959.	223
104	Variation in steam temperature with time - WAGR Class Fs 4-8-0	224

105	Class 'D' freight train operation Huskisson - Rowsley - dynamometer record over the section Cheadle Heath to Peak Forest made on the second run - Engine N° 44481.	226
106	Class 'D' freight train operation Rowsley - Walton - dynamometer record over the section Cheadle Heath to Peak Forest made on the last run - Engine N° 44481.	228
107	Drawbar steam and coal consumption - WD Class 8F 2-8-0 N° 90464	236
108	Drawbar steam and coal consumption - WD Class 8F 2-10-0 N° 90772	237
109	Boiler efficiency comparison between 4MT 2-6-0 and 4F 0-6-0	240
110	Actual evaporation comparison between 4MT 2-6-0 and 4F 0-6-0	242
111	Comparison in boiler superheat and tube exit temperatures.	243
112	'Big Goods' N° 43937 late in its career photographed with one of its nominal replacements Class 4MT 2-6-0 N° 43156 alongside.	243
113	Variation in smokebox vacuum with steam rate - Class 4F 0-6-0.	244
114	Variation in back pressure with steam rate - 4MT 2-6-0 and 4F 0-6-0	244
115	Variation in drawbar horsepower with steam rate at constant speed of 33 mph.	245
116	Variation in specific drawbar steam consumption - LMS Classes 4 0-6-0 and 4MT 2-6-0 also WD Classes 2-8-0 and 2-10-0	246
117	Variation in isentropic efficiency - LMS Class 4 0-6-0 & 4MT 2-6-0	249
118	Pressure drops through exhaust system for various steam flow rates shewing the contribution made by the various portions	251
119	Predicted superheat temperature and back pressure curves for the 'Big Goods' with original draughting system	256
120	Variation in coal consumption against drawbar horsepower whilst running at a constant speed of 60 miles per hour - Class 4MT 2-6-0 N° 43094	265

Chapter One

Background

Introduction

The Midland Railway/LMS Standard Class 4 0-6-0 has gained an unenviable reputation amongst the locomotive cognoscenti for being a particularly feeble design, or as one of that group wrote:-

"Back in the 1970s when Michael Edwardes took over as chairman of British Leyland he said that the company had become the lame-duck that all lame-ducks are measured by. Perhaps the 4F fits the same description as far as the British steam locomotive is concerned."

One does wonder quite why this particular class has been so singled out for such criticism, after all there were several other similar designs produced in this realm with large diameter inside cylinders. Whilst the 'Big Goods' may not have been of the very finest hopefully it will become apparent that it was far more effective, than perhaps its most vociferous critic[1], would have us believe:-

"As I look back, the affection in which the class 4 0-6-0 Freight was held by the Motive Power heirarchy *(sic)* was quite remarkable. To Anderson, his henchmen, and his immediate successors, it was perfection, and no less than 565 of them were built under L.M.S. auspices, some of them as late as 1941 well towards the end of the Stanier regime. And yet it was a poor engine really. Its steaming was always capricious, and it was distinctly sluggish on excursion and other passenger duties. Its old fashioned valve events produced only moderate fuel economy, whilst, as mentioned above, fractured frames and hot boxes were too frequent. Its deficiencies stemmed mainly from its inherent design and there was little which could be done to it by way of modification or rebuilding, other than by improving the valve events, which was never attempted."

Taken together these would represent a serious criticism of any locomotive design, but particularly so when they refer to a class that numbered 772 examples, built over a period of 30 years under the aegis of three notable Chief Mechanical Engineers. Notwithstanding whatever demands the Motive Power Superintendent James Anderson had made for further Standard Class 4 0-6-0s, if their performance had *really* been as singularly dire as some would have us believe, then surely those three locomotive engineers were tantamount to being negligent of their duties in not providing the operating people with a better engine for hauling the company's trains. A charge that becomes even more important when it is considered the Standard Freight was not only the single most numerous locomotive class owned by the LMS, but also in round figures it represented 10 per cent of the company's locomotive stock. However, we must remember that the Class 4, like all LMS locomotive classes, had in effect to serve two masters each possessing differing criteria by which they judged the success of a design. The Chief Mechanical Engineer's staff, being responsible for the repairs in main workshops wanted engines that would run high mileages between intermediate and general repairs thereby maximizing workshop capacity, while the designers in his team wanted the opportunity to practice their skills designing engines that would do just that. Conversely, the operating people wanted optimally sized locomotives that would haul their trains with reliability and without fuss.

During the nineteenth century, the Locomotive Superintendent held virtually absolute power over all mechanical engineering matters within his department. He provided locomotives, and sometimes rolling stock as well, to meet the demands of the Operating Department whilst complying with the constraints imposed by the Chief Civil Engineer. He was also required to maintain all of the equipment in his care in good order – later demonstrating that responsibility by signing every year the Ministry of Transport Certificate confirming this was indeed the case. All these diverse duties had to be achieved within the

---

1 Mr E S Cox *Chronicles of Steam* Ian Allan London 1967 p37.

finances made available by the directors. However, during the twentieth century, along with renaming the post 'Chief Mechanical Engineer' there was a tendency to erode or devolve some of his powers. For example in 1909, inspired by American practice, the Midland diluted his role by creating a separate Motive Power Department, which assumed responsibility for the work of the running sheds and the enginemen, duly recorded in the board minutes:-

> "The General Manager reported with regard to the Locomotive Department and after full discussion, it was Resolved that the control of that part of the Locomotive Department known as the Locomotive Running Department be transferred to the Traffic Department."

Following Mountford[2] Deeley's resignation, who did not agree with this dilution of his power, Henry Fowler was promoted from Works Manager to become the first Chief Mechanical Engineer and Mr L C Geach was made Superintendent of Motive Power, both with effect from 1st January 1910. The Superintendent of Motive Power was responsible to the Chief Mechanical Engineer, for maintaining the engines to the latter's requirements, and to the Operating Department for working the trains according to the timetable, or as Sir William Stanier described it in 1947[3]:-

> "It is the responsibility of the chief mechanical engineer to supply engines of the correct type to meet the requirements of the chief operating manager, and of the chief operating manager to allocate those engines so that the correct type of engine will be used to do the work required, and it is the superintendent of motive power's duty to see that these engines are maintained in good mechanical condition to work the trains, manned by well-trained and responsible enginemen at the time they are required."

Thus on the LMS, since this structure was adopted by the new entity, the Operating Department was responsible for the use, stabling, manning and day-to-day servicing of the locomotive stock, while the CME designed and manufactured engines and heavy repaired them in accordance with the requirements specified by the operating authorities. This arrangement of necessity meant that an integral part of the Operating Department was its Motive Power Section, staffed by experienced and expert locomotive engineers. Thus although the Motive Power Section held no design remit, some of its engineers, such as James Anderson, possessed considerable design ability and experience, so if the CME's department ever had difficulty in coming up with the goods[4], he was more than able to assist!

The structure used by the LMS was not universal, although something similar was presumably present on the LNER when, following its formation and against Sir Nigel Gresley's advice, the running sheds were transferred to the Traffic Superintendent. On the Southern management of the Locomotive Running Department was astutely vested in a chief officer who was independent of and not subservient to either the operating or technical interests. An arrangement that seems to have avoided much of the strife that appeared on the LMS. On the Great Western locomotive running remained within the CME's remit even if it sometimes might have appeared semi-autonomous.

From Mr Cox's comments, quoted at the beginning of this chapter, we may summarize the main criticisms usually levelled at the Standard Class 4 were that it was:-

---

2 Although normally referred to by enthusiasts as Richard Deeley, he appears to have preferred his second Christian name Mountford.

3 Lt-Col H Rudgard *Organisation and Carrying-Out of Examinations and Repairs of Locomotives at Running Sheds in Relationship to Locomotive Performance and Availability* I Loco E Paper 464 January 1947.

4 Mr Anderson retired at the end of 1932 and was replaced as Superintendent of Motive Power by David Chalmers Urie, the last Locomotive Superintendent of the Highland Railway. He was a son of Robert Urie of the L&SWR and was far from enamoured by William Stanier's earliest designs because of the problems they caused his department. Mr Thornley recorded Mr Urie suggested that as many as possible of the new Classes 5 and 5X should be stored during the 1936-37 winter under cover at main workshops, also the 'Jubilees' on the Central Division be put aside and replaced by ex-L&YR Class 8 4-6-0s! In fact storage of 'Jubilees' had started as early as January 1935 and continued with varying numbers and durations until September 1939. Furthermore Mr Urie was able in September 1935 to have all the 'Patriots' on the Midland Division bar three, transferred to the Western Division in exchange for a similar number of 'Jubilees' to work the new 115min Euston-Birmingham service, due simply to the unreliability of the 'Jubilees'. As Mr Cox ruefully wrote in *Locomotive Panorama Vol I*:-

> "whereas Anderson used to chastise our department with whips, Urie was apt to chastise it with scorpions."

With this opinion of the latest products of the Chief Mechanical Engineer's department, no wonder the Operating Department wanted more 'Big Goods' – whatever their other defects, they could at least be relied on to go! Indeed by late 1934 William Stanier's position was reputedly somewhat precarious with the prospect of dismissal being a possibility. It is interesting to record those who are the most critical of LMS practice pre-Stanier are for the most part, the same people whose stars shone brightest following his arrival.

(a) Heavy on maintenance due to poor axlebox and frame design

(b) Heavy on fuel due to the retention of short-lap valves and poor valve events

(c) Limited steam production, compounded by it being difficult to fire

Thus, as is so often the case, although there is an element of truth in Mr Cox's criticisms the real position was *far* more complicated - *as he well knew*. One does wonder at times whether his active dislike of the class, as a CME man and a *designer* affected his views, certainly his words have influenced many later enthusiasts' opinions of the class and by extension those of the Midland.

The last sentence of his quotation is a little misleading, because the valve events[5] of the Class 4 0-6-0 were to all intents *identical* to those carried by two of amongst the most spectacular classes of 4-4-0 ever to run in this realm the South Eastern & Chatham classes D1 and E1 designed by James Clayton. Later they would be applied by Mr Cox's boss to Class 5 4-6-0 N° 4767, which uniquely carried Stephenson's valve gear. As will be explained later, there would have been little to be gained from rebuilding the 'Big Goods' with large-lap valves if it was to remain primarily used for low speed goods and mineral traffic. Likewise regarding his other two criticisms. In fact being heavy on its axleboxes was symptomatic of its type – a powerful inside cylinder engine, rather than specific to the Class 4 – while obtaining a *guaranteed* crack-free plate frame performance in *any* locomotive was a problem quite beyond contemporary engineering knowledge. Nonetheless there were techniques available that would have ameliorated these and other weaknesses so the class could have been improved, certainly far more cheaply than building replacements, and given the LMS a significantly better return on its capital. Unfortunately, this approach presupposes that those in charge of locomotive design had not been so blinkered towards creating the next taper-boiler, large-lap, outside cylinder, wonder.

Background

The 'Big Goods', developed from the saturated Class 3 0-6-0 which originally carried the H round topped boiler and later the G7 Belpaire boiler, was the Midland's final goods tender engine design. The new class differed in receiving a superheated version of the Belpaire boiler coupled with larger diameter cylinders, indirect motion and piston valves in place of slide valves. The higher boiler

Fig. 1 - The first of the two earliest 'Big Goods' of 1911, N° 3835 seen here in Midland days, sometime after 1917 when the superheater damper gear and pyrometer was removed and 1922 when it changed its tender. At the time its portrait was taken N° 3835 had not been fitted with air valves or mechanical lubrication to the axleboxes. The *Wakefield* lubricator it carries was for the cylinders and valves. The small pipe leaving the frame just in front of the leading splasher conveyed steam to the left-hand by-pass valve when the regulator was shut.

pitch, necessary to clear the valves which were located above the cylinders, gave it a more massive appearance - enhanced by the shorter chimney and dome. This class was the first and only example the Midland designed with inside admission piston valves. Hitherto the company's practice with piston valves following their adoption during Mr Johnson's last years had been outside admission,

---

5 The term valve events describes where in the cycle the four main actions occurred *viz.* cut-off, release, compression and admission, although the portion of the admission that appeared in the return or compression stroke was commonly referred to as pre-admission, giving in effect a quasi fifth cardinal point.

because as Sir Henry Fowler explained, it simplified cylinder design and valve-setting while permitting a straighter more direct exhaust. Incidentally this was the reason outside admission was adopted on the Southern class Q 0-6-0 built twenty-five years later and presumably why it subsequently appeared on the Q1, although one weakness in the arrangement was that it was less easy to ensure adequate admission side volume.

The first two members of the class, N° 3835 built to O/4000 left Derby Works in October 1911 followed by N° 3836 to O/4001 in November, were not identical. Major differences being N° 3835 carried a boiler pressed to 160lbs/sq in containing 21off Schmidt superheater return bend elements with Midland-type fixing and 148 small tubes 1¾ins diameter while that fitted to N° 3836 carried a Swindon superheater housed in 14off flues and 174 tubes 1¾ins but pressed to 175lbs pressure. Other differences included the axleboxes, draughting and the cylinders, the latter were 20ins in diameter for N° 3835 but only 19ins for the 175lbs engine presumably this disparity was to give both engines approximately the same starting tractive effort. Due to Continental confusion over thermodynamic theory Dr Schmidt[6] advised the boiler pressure be reduced on superheated engines; some locomotive engineers accepted this recommendation as a means of reducing boiler maintenance.

Soon after building the two prototypes underwent a short trial period hauling goods and passenger trains while based at Saltley shed. Between 24th June and 2nd August 1912 they were tested in an extensive series of trials against two Class 3 saturated engines N° 3817 and 3818, which involved hauling coal trains between Toton and Brent via Melton Mobrey and Syston. Loaded trains comprised fifty wagons, equivalent to 600 tons, were worked south and 50 or 100 empty wagon trains hauled north with each engine making six round journeys. During the tests leakage from the joints between the superheater headers and the elements was a source of trouble on both engines. N° 3836 steamed badly on its fourth run, it also had to be provided with new piston valves and liners after its second trip.

The coal and water consumption figures recorded that N° 3835 was the most efficient performer. On its last two up trips, it consumed 0.0632lb of coal per ton-mile compared with 0.0658 for N° 3836 and 0.0756 for the saturated engines. Water consumption was 0.554lb per ton-mile compared to 0.590 and 0.691 respectively. The savings in consumption produced by N° 3835 represented 4.1 per cent over N° 3836 and 19.6 per cent over the saturated engines in terms of coal, and 6.5 per cent and 24.7 per cent respectively in water. The advantage N° 3835 shewed over N° 3836, despite its lower working pressure, was primarily due to the hotter steam its larger Schmidt superheater produced compared to the Swindon version – 620°F as opposed to 560°F according to Sir Henry. Nevertheless comparing the two superheaters on the basis of their flue free gas areas, expressed as a ratio of their respective total free gas areas, reveals the Swindon superheater, notwithstanding its fewer elements, was actually more effective at extracting heat.

In October 1913, another series of tests was conducted on Toton-Brent coal trains, only this time, with N° 3835 having proved its superiority they were restricted to a contest between it and saturated 0-6-0 N° 3815. The engines hauled trains

Table I – Coal Consumption Tests October 1913 – Time-table of Engine Working

Link : Toton to Brent		Link : Brent to Toton	
Toton	dep. 7-12am	Brent	dep. 8-10am
Brentingby Junction	arr. 8-45am dep. 9-3am	Bedford	arr. 10-31am dep. 10-41am
Wellingborough	arr. 11-7am dep. 11-22am	Wellingborough	arr. 11-30am dep. 11-53am
Brent	arr. 3-30pm	Melton	arr. 1-56pm dep. 2-8pm
		Toton	dep. 3-34pm

---

6 Wilhelm Schmidt considered superheated steam engines worked on the Carnot cycle where the highest and lowest temperatures present alone determine its efficiency. As a consequence he recommended that the boiler pressure could be reduced. The steam engine is actually better described by the Rankine cycle wherein steam pressure is also taken into account. The Midland listened to 'Hot Steam Willy' and reduced its boiler pressures, the L&YR conversely maintained the boiler pressure in its superheated engines.

south composed of forty-five loaded wagons of average weight 14 tons plus a brake van, while the down return run comprised eighty empty wagons and a brake van. The engines worked to the schedule recorded in table I while the results appear in table II. These tests recorded a saving through superheating of 14.4 per cent in coal and 20.4 per cent in water with loaded trains and 18 per cent in coal and 24.8 per cent respectively in the case of the empty return working.

Yet further tests were carried out in September 1916 again between N° 3835 and a Class 3 saturated engine running between Toton and Brent. However, as the saturated engine hauled fifty loaded wagons, but N° 3835 pulled sixty, these trials may have been to explore the additional haulage capacity of the superheated engine. Despite its heavier trains, savings of 16 per cent in coal and 22 per cent in water were obtained from the latter.

The Class 4 represents an interesting example of engine development; one in which the Midland exploited the opportunity superheating presented to obtain a more powerful locomotive for very little gain in weight. The two original examples were rated class 3, only later were they up-rated to 4, which presumably was in May 1917 when the next examples were built, and the first pair were

Table II – Coal Consumption Tests - October 1913

Date	Train	Weather	Gross weight of train	Ton-miles	Coal per ton-mile - lbs	Water per ton-mile - lbs
Engine N° 3815 - Saturated						
7 October	7-12am - up	Wet, moderate wind	698.2	88,494	0.0869	0.797
9 October	7-12am - up	Fine, light wind	720.6	91,337	0.0672	0.641
14 October	7-12am - up	Fine, moderate wind	724.5	91,837	0.0759	0.688
16 October	7-12am - up	Foggy to fine	707.9	90,791	0.0783	0.742
20 October	7-12am - up	Fine, light wind	722.5	92,661	0.0835	0.779
22 October	7-12am - up	Fine, light wind	698.7	89,608	0.0792	0.716
		Averages	712.1	90,788	0.0785	0.727
8 October	8-10am - down	Fine, light wind	579.6	73,466	0.1150	0.925
10 October	8-10am - down	Fine, strong wind	567.1	71,885	0.1245	1.024
15 October	8-10am - down	Fine, moderate wind	567.0	71,867	0.1246	0.970
17 October	8-10am - down	Foggy to fine	578.5	73,325	0.1250	0.998
21 October	8-10am - down	Fine, light wind	567.4	71,919	0.1299	0.978
23 October	8-10am - down	Fine, light wind	581.8	73,743	0.1213	0.975
		Averages	573.6	72,701	0.1234	0.978
Engine N° 3835 - Superheated						
6 October	7-12am - up	Wet, strong wind	684.6	87,796	0.0676	0.587
8 October	7-12am - up	Fine, moderate wind	708.75	90,897	0.0695	0.627
13 October	7-12am - up	Foggy to fine	702.4	90,085	0.0746	0.596
15 October	7-12am - up	Fine, light wind	723.4	92,779	0.0627	0.545
21 October	7-12am - up	Fine, light wind	706.0	89,485	0.0627	0.547
23 October	7-12am - up	Fine, light wind	679.4	86,114	0.0673	0.575
		Averages	700.7	89,526	0.0673	0.579
7 October	8-10am - down	Wet, moderate wind	555.4	70,402	0.1057	0.767
9 October	8-10am - down	Fine, light wind	588.2	74,553	0.0976	0.717
14 October	8-10am - down	Fine, light wind	568.5	72,057	0.1117	0.757
16 October	8-10am - down	Fine	574.9	72,869	0.0930	0.721
22 October	8-10am - down	Fine, light wind	580.2	73,547	0.0913	0.650
24 October	8-10am - down	Fine, light wind	571.5	72,438	0.1081	0.800
		Averages	573.1	72,644	0.1012	0.735

brought into line *viz.* 175lbs working pressure, Schmidt superheater and 20ins × 26ins cylinders.

Superheating enabled the 'Big Goods' to become Class 4, because the resulting hotter steam contained considerably more energy, which meant less was needed to produce the same horsepower. This of course was the equivalent of obtaining more power from the same quantity of coal, for the grate area of a 'Big Goods' at 21.1 square feet was identical to that of a Class 3 engine. However, we should remember that superheat temperature in a steam locomotive was *not controlled* instead its value floated, rising in accordance with the steam rate, or how hard the engine was being worked. Furthermore, there was a minimum steam rate demonstrated little real power increase over a Class 3.

Of course, when the 'Big Goods' was introduced, it pulled the Midland's most important and heaviest goods trains long distances and as we have seen in the case of the 1912 trials, the steam rates ensured a reasonably high superheat accompanied by good steaming. At that time, such an observation would have been largely academic - a situation that certainly lasted into the grouping era as this reminiscence by Bob Essery demonstrates[7]:-

"By the time I started at Saltley, the most important work for the class '4F' 0-6-0s was the Bristol express goods trains, and even so, by the early 1950s

Fig. 2 - Nº 4433 seen here pre-war heading an express goods about to pass through Elstree station on the down fast line; possibly it was such a working that Charlie Smith was referring to.

before any superheat appeared at all, while in addition it took something like ten or twenty minutes of steady steaming, depending on superheater configuration, before the steam temperature assumed a constant value. Consequently, a Class 4 0-6-0 could only demonstrate its advantage over a Class 3 engine once stable conditions had been achieved and when the engine was working reasonably hard. Conversely, whenever the class was employed on work that involved frequent starting and stopping and/or low steam rates then the engine would have they were being replaced by the Ivatt class '4MT' 2-6-0s, commonly known as 'Doodlebugs'. The majority of the class '4F' work in the Saltley area was on through mineral, empty wagon freight trains, together with many local trip jobs. However, one of my mates, Charlie Smith, used to speak of the class '4' work on the London link, pre-war, when as a fireman, he lodged in London. They ran via Wigston and so the route must have been all of 130 miles. I remember he said that he used to fill up the rear of the firebox before running under the coaling stage and bribing the coalman with a

---
7 Messers R J Essery & D Jenkinson *An Illustrated Review of Midland Locomotives Vol. 1* - Wild Swan Publications p183.

packet of Woodbine cigarettes, to 'fill up the hole'. The idea was to ensure they started with the maximum amount of coal at the front of the tender and so reduce the amount of coal which was required to be brought forward.

Charlie said that they stood in Somers' Town yard and 'as the tail lamp of the first express went by, the pegs came off and we were away – fast line to Kettering'. At this point they were booked to go onto the slow lines because, by now, hard on their heels was another express out of St. Pancras heading north. I could relate this story from my own experiences with the class '4s' – maybe not seventy miles with an express closing on my tail, but more than fifty miles before handing over our train."

However this was far from their normal work in the 1950s, by then they were being passed over on the more important workings in favour of the then new Class 4MT 2-6-0. This is an important point, for the Midland never intended it as a 'runabout' goods engine, that role was performed by others, namely its saturated 0-6-0 classes. The company instead intended it to haul heavy mineral trains at steaming rates that would ensure plenty of hot steam[8]. That later the LMS and BR sometimes chose to use the engine incorrectly, and elected not to make any modification to remedy the situation was their fault, not that of the engine! Furthermore, when those firemen who have graced us with their footplate reminiscences were doing their firing, the great majority of ex-LMS engines in power class 4 comprised the 4F 0-6-0 – the other pre-grouping designs had by then become or were rapidly becoming extinct – those coal-eating Scottish and Crewe-designed monsters. Therefore, the only class 4 engine these future authors could compare the Class 4 to, was the 'Doodlebug' and its British Railways derivative. That this latter design started off under a cloud, and then never really shone in the universal opinion of all enginemen, lends considerable support to the viewpoint, that the 4F was not so bad as some writers would have us believe[9]:-

"No other locomotive, perhaps with the exception of the LNW 0-8-0s, created so much discussion among crews of the sheds that I knew. To some a 4F was a masterly machine capable of being handled by two-year-olds, and able to pull a house down. Others, particularly LNW line men, despised the 4F and regarded it as a very poor tool."

"Almost certainly this was because the old LNWR and LYR men had no idea how to fire them. The LNWR didn't have an 0-6-0 anything like the '4F' in size or power and Midland men, who worked on ex-LYR 0-6-0s, equally didn't speak very highly of the Aspinall design, so perhaps it has something to do with the inbuilt conservatism of engine men together with a lack of knowledge in handling different types. I also believe that many writers have tended to enlarge upon the shortcomings of the '4Fs' - but whilst they were far from perfect, they were not as bad as some people would make out."

Of course, in the case of the LNWR, since George Whale's time the 'Premier Line' had traditionally employed its firemen as coal-heavers, so as soon as they were presented with a locomotive that required a little finesse, there were bound to be tears. Its firemen had after all needed special training simply to cope with the shallow firebox of the 'Experiment' class 4-6-0 – even though it retained the customary LNWR horizontal grate. Unfortunately, brute strength and stamina[10] were not the primary attributes required for firing a Class 4:-

"Two months later another unfortunate episode in passenger train operation occurred when the Springboks were playing at Leicester. A special was run from Bedford, picking up at Wellingborough, Kettering and Market Harborough, and timed to arrive at Leicester about an hour before the match. My personal *béte noire*, Class 4F 0-6-0 N° 4035, was sent specially to Bedford to work the train, but when I saw it on the Saturday afternoon passing my home about 1.30pm having difficulty making enough steam to keep the brakes off, it was evident that all was not well. It reached Leicester at half-time, causing a most serious breach of public confidence for those days, and by 5.00pm Moulang was fetched specially from his home to his office at Wellingborough and exhorted by Rudgard to find out what had happened - quickly. Moulang sent for me and at 6.00pm I was on my way to Leicester to examine the offending steed. I tested the engine in steam, but could find nothing obviously wrong. It transpired when the enginemen were interviewed that mismanagement of the

---

8 As an aside, Midland practice as stated in the Appendix to the Working Timetable (1908) required that the company's most important express goods trains (Fitted Goods N° 1) had to be worked by a passenger engine not a goods engine, with the loading of the train adjusted as necessary to suit the class of passenger engine provided to work it. Only the next tier, Fitted Goods N° 2 trains, were permitted to be worked by passenger or goods engines.

9 The first quotation is from *London Midland Fireman* Mr M F Higson - Ian Allan 1977 p28.

The second being from *An Illustrated Review of Midland Locomotives Vol. 1* Messers R J Essery & D Jenkinson - Wild Swan Publications p183.

10 Mr W G F Thorley *A Breath of Steam Vol 1* Ian Allan Ltd Shepperton 1975 pp123-4

A Defence of the Midland/LMS Class 4 0-6-0

fire had been the major cause of the fiasco. The driver had only been recently passed for driving duties and the fireman was a cleaner only recently passed for firing duties. Whilst such combinations, caused by the method in use at some sheds in covering spare jobs, often produced some first-class work, this pair did not; the over-anxiousness of both led to gross over-firing, a process heartily disliked by a Fowler 4F."

Although one or two professional engineers have written quite adversely about the 'Big Goods', with their views repeated by later authors, this criticism should be viewed against a class that was built over the unusually long period of thirty years. Over those three decades, the design was little changed except for minor details, simply because, for whatever reasons, a superior mid-power go-anywhere engine was never made available. Thus, when in 1941 the Operating Department requested more Class 4 0-6-0s, William Stanier was happy to acquiesce, for in his words[11], they were:-

"Simple, reliable, and cheap to maintain, these engines move a considerable proportion of our traffic, and beloved of the operating departments."

The cost of designing a replacement[12] was not considered economic in the face of continuing production of a standard type comprising nearly 800 examples:-

"As regards the ubiquitous 0-6-0 goods tender engine of pre-grouping times, although Stanier had evolved two designs of standard 0-6-0 locomotive, intended to become part of his standard locomotive stock, together with a design for a 2-6-0 tender engine, developed from the 2-6-4 tank engines, which was placed on the building programme diagram in 1937, in the event the Operating Department said that they did not want the 2-6-0, but with 700 odd Class 4 0-6-0s in stock all they wanted were a few more of these. He therefore arranged for the construction of a further 45 of the Class 4F "big goods" to Fowlers *(sic)* design, of which Derby built three orders, for a total of 30 locomotives in all, as follows:

Order	Locomotive Nº	Year built
O/303	4577-86	1939
O/650	4587-96	1939
O/653	4597-4606	1940-41

These engines were little altered but for the provision of the Stanier design of chimney, the use of flat as against fluted coupling rods, and the elimination of piston tail rods. With the building of these final batches, the 4Fs totalled in all 772 locomotives built over a period of 31 years of which 192 had been turned out for the Midland, 5 for the S&SJR and 575 for the LMSR."

Since Sir William was seconded to the Ministry of Production in the late summer of 1942, at the behest of the government to form one of a team of three full-time Scientific Advisers, the 'Big Goods' remained in production effectively for the whole of his time on the LMS. As O S Nock explained[13]:-

"It so happened that the most numerous of the various medium-powered 0-6-0s, the Midland Class '4F', was also the best from the viewpoint of all-round performance, reliability on the road, and low maintenance costs; and new construction of these engines continued during Stanier's time."

Following his departure, his successors were able to produce what they perceived to be the modern replacement for the 0-6-0, and we shall see quite what sort of a fist they made of it in due course.

---

11 Sir William Stanier *The Position of the Locomotive in Mechanical Engineering* - Presidential Address I Mech E 1941 p51 & p58.

12 Mr J B Radford *Derby Works and Midland Locomotives* Ian Allan Shepperton 1971 pp194-5.

13 Mr O S Nock *Sir William Stanier* Ian Allan Ltd Shepperton second edition 1975 p102.

Chapter Two

Multiplication and Modification

In 1923, apart from designing a completely new class from scratch, the *only* extant class 4 engines available to the nascent LMS for multiplication and/or development were the 'Big Goods', some LNWR eight-coupled engines, George Whale's '19ins Goods' plus a few Scottish locomotive classes the majority of which would be scrapped by 1939. These latter machines included Peter Drummond's fifteen 0-6-0s of the '279' class, built for the G&SW, which were very heavy on coal, sluggish and unpopular[1]. A second batch of eleven extended in that inimitable Scottish fashion into Moguls to support the extra weight of a true superheater, known as the '403' class were little better. The Highland's only possible contender was the 'Jones Goods' – a saturated 4-6-0 design dating back to 1894, while the Caledonian could contribute the '800' class 0-8-0 and '492' class 0-8-0T. Of the English companies only the North-Western could contribute. Its eight-coupled tender engines were old having been designed by Francis Webb and Crewe was busy rebuilding and up-rating into 'Super Ds', while of the tank engine 0-8-2 and 0-8-4 derivatives, the latter could with some justification be viewed as the drawing office version of a practical joke, which left the saturated '19ins Goods'. Many pre-grouping engines had prodigious appetites for coal but this class seems even more extravagant than most – both of the following[2] comments are from men who worked with them:-

"...but perhaps the most lucrative train of all was the one that conveyed vacuum-braked fish vans from Milford Haven to connect at Llandeilo with the 4-40 pm "Fish" from Swansea South Dock to Crewe. This train was composed entirely of vacuum braked four-wheel vans and a guard's van, and was rostered to be worked to Crewe Gresty Lane marshalling yard by a Swansea 4-6-0 4F Whale 19" Goods. Unfortunately, so voracious was the appetite of these engines, they rarely had enough coal to go beyond Shrewsbury with a heavy train - or with one of moderate loading if the wind happened to be against them..."

"When I first started firing, promotion for firemen started with the shed turner's link [shed pilot], and proceeded as for drivers, but with the advent of Whale's 'Mankillers', the drivers began to crib at having youngsters with them, as there were not even many experienced firemen who were capable of firing a '19" Goods' or an 'Experiment' in the normal way. They had to sling the coal in the middle of the firebox, let it coke and then spread it out with the long rake. A run down 'Precursor' could chew up coal faster than a normal man could shovel it in the firebox."

Given this 'gene pool', no wonder the LMS multiplied the Midland Class 4 0-6-0, a process initiated while George Hughes was at the helm, it was the only suitable design that existed in that power rating in 1923. Furthermore, the class had a proven performance and could run on the Midland, which had a particularly restricted loading gauge width combined with a severe weight limit, thereby ensuring that with only minor attention to its overall height it could go anywhere else over the newly created railway. For fifty-five years, until the last days of steam, they served as goods and mixed traffic engines for the Midland, LMS and British Railways. No doubt, had Mr Hughes been so minded, as Chief Mechanical Engineer, he could have decided that a new design be prepared, but instead he recommended building the first batches of Class 4s part way through 1923. A proposal

---

1 One of the class with 50 empty wagons took 55 minutes to negotiate the section Blackhouse Junction to Machline, 10¼ miles, some of it steeply downhill - a LMS Class 4 0-6-0 with 55 empties did it in 41 minutes.
Mr D L Smith *Locomotives of the Glasgow & South Western Railway* David & Charles Newton Abbot 1976 p119.

2 Mr H C H Burgess *Working with LMS Steam* Bradford Barton 1983 p15
Mr E Talbot *The London North Western Recalled* Oxford Publishing C° 1987 p36.
Mr K Stokes (*Both Sides of the Footplate* - Bradford Barton) records firing a '19ins Goods' from Grimesthorpe to Liverpool hauling 35 wagons of steam coal and having to transfer a couple of tons of coal from the leading wagon into the tender

---

in order to complete the journey!

accepted by the Rolling Stock Committee with the decision remaining even after the LMS was offered 300 surplus ROD 2-8-0s of Mr Robinson's Great Central design. George Hughes cautioning against purchase due to the restricted route availability of the eight-coupled engines and ironically, as it would turn out, because of concerns regarding the diameter of their coupled wheels, which he felt were too small for main-line mineral traffic. Whether the last reason was fully justifiable is a moot point given later LMS goods engine development[3], but certainly the roads that the ROD 2-8-0s could run over were very restricted compared to the 'Big Goods'. Indeed, there was probably nowhere on the company's system that did not see examples of the 0-6-0s at some time or other.

The decision taken by the LMS immediately after its formation to multiply the Class 4 can be shewn to have had a sound basis not least because of its superior route availability, reliability and all round economy in operation compared to the other extant classes – the latter had been determined initially by dynamometer tests the company conducted. Mr Cox has described they had been instigated by George Hughes, with a view to establishing the best of the pre-grouping classes to multiply. Of course, route availability is something that the Drawing Office could establish quite easily through checking the overall dimensions with the loading gauge(s), together with curve throw over, axle weights and weight per foot run of the engine, plus in the case of Derby, checking against the bridge curve etc. Indeed, it was a regular and established design exercise even if in those days obtaining the approval of the Chief Engineer to accept a new locomotive design was something of a 'black art', certainly when the likes of Ernest Trench and his successor Alexander Newlands occupied the post. Ernest Trench's obstruction towards George Hughes' proposals for a range of standard locomotives soon after the grouping, contributed to his retirement in 1925 and replacement by Sir Henry Fowler. Mr Newlands' objection as Chief Civil Engineer of the Highland Railway over the company's new 'River' class 4-6-0, had resulted in the forced resignation of Frederick Smith the Locomotive Superintendent.

It was somewhat more difficult to quantify the in-service reliability and economy of a locomotive class. However following the arrival in 1927 of Sir Josiah Stamp (later Lord Stamp), this situation altered. He came to the LMS from Nobel Industries Ltd (later a constituent of ICI Ltd), bereft of any experience of railways but with a sound background as an administrator and statistician. On arrival, he asked questions about LMS expenditure, but considered some of the replies inadequate particularly those concerning the money spent on locomotive maintenance. Against a very real need for economy[4], he instigated in the year of his arrival an Individual Costing Scheme that comprised a vast repository of data revealing the cost of running each main locomotive class. Engine sheds and works recorded the amount spent on each engine, which when combined with the annual mileages and coal statistics enabled the average expenditure in pence per mile run for coal, boiler maintenance, engine repairs and overall running costs to be compared for every principal class. Although the figures required care in interpretation, because for example the different mileages returned by locomotives employed on different services or duties, they did nevertheless present much useful data. For the first time the running costs and availability of all of the company's most important locomotive classes were quantified enabling the worth of each to be established on a sound statistical basis. This in turn became the basis for formulating future policies concerning locomotive building, scrapping or rebuilding. The LMS was the only one of the big four companies to adopt this approach, and then only from 1927 to 1937 – but this encompassed a period of relatively stable prices, so enabling reasonable comparisons to be made.

How effective Midland locomotive design was

---

3 When in the early years of the twentieth century Messers Johnson and Deeley were scheming out 0-8-0 designs for the Midland's London coal traffic, both engineers elected to adopt 4ft – 7ins diameter coupled wheels.

---

4 Some idea of the financial difficulties the railways faced from the late 1920s until the Second World War is revealed by the following statistics Mr Thorley gleaned from *The Economist*.

	1924	1929	1932
Total receipts	100	95	75
Total expenditure	100	95	80
Nett revenue	100	98	57
Nº of passengers	100	86	76
Passenger receipts	100	87	73
Tonnage of goods	100	94	74
Goods receipts	100	97	75

Mr W G F Thorley *A Breath of Steam Vol 1* Ian Allan Ltd Shepperton 1975 p95.

may be gauged from a comment[5] made by Lt-Col Harold Rudgard, by then chief officer for motive power for British Railways, but formerly LMS Midland Division Superintendent of Motive Power:-

"On the former Midland Railway, with which I was particularly associated, a tribute is due to the memory of Sir Henry Fowler. His collaboration with Cecil Padget, and their understanding of the running shed angle, helped to produce a school of design which was pre-eminent amongst all railways forming the London Midland and Scottish in 1923 for reliability and low repair costs, and which continuing under the LMS, lent itself admirably to the introduction of developments in motive power practice and organization; Sir William Stanier carried on the good work."

Indeed sample costs, quoted by David Hunt[6] for the period 1927 to 1929 shew the Standard Class 4 at 12.98d/mile was 0.8d per mile cheaper to run than the average goods tender engine, which incurred a cost of 13.78d. Since the class was averaging 27,500 miles per year, this resulted in the 727 engines generated an annual saving of approximately £67,000 compared to the same number of 'average' goods engines. As a result of Sir Josiah's statistics the older and/or less effective classes were highlighted, as the figures were intended to do, so inevitably the advantage held by the 'Big Goods' reduced with time. Consequently, between 1933 and 1935, the class recorded an overall running cost of 11.53d per mile against an average of 11.95d, which nevertheless still represented a healthy annual saving of £35,000.

Mr Cox provided in *Chronicles of Steam* details of the annual mileage, coal consumption and repair costs averaged over the ten-year they were collected – the values for the goods tender engines appear in table III. By the time these statistics started, the bulk of the Standard Class 4 0-6-0s had been built together with the first examples of the Standard Class 7 0-8-0s. Nevertheless, we may see from this table confirmation that the Standard Classes 7 and 4 were indeed less expensive to maintain and operate than the pre-grouping classes a situation admitted by E S Cox[7]:-

---

5 Lt-Col H Rudgard *The User of Locomotives for Revenue* - Presidential Address I Loco E 1948 p499.

6 Messers D Hunt, J Jennison, R Essery & F James *LMS Locomotive Profiles N° 10 The Standard Class 4 Goods 0-6-0s* Wild Swan Didcot.

7 Mr E S Cox *Chronicles of Steam* Ian Allan Shepperton 1967 p110 and
Mr E S Cox *Locomotive Panorama Vol. I* Ian Allan

"If we take first the Fowler/Anderson Standard types, some new and others derived from the former Midland Railway, it is clear that they were producing the most favourable results under all headings, and whether they achieved good, bad or indifferent performance from the train timing point of view, they thoroughly justified their selection as standard types on the basis of costs. While it is true they were given the best work to do, many of the later engines of the former companies were still employed on important duties, and in any case had the 'standards' not been intrinsically sound, their prominence on the operating scene would have increased rather than diminished their coal consumption and repair costs."

These tabulated costs of course, include the 'poor' axlebox performance, a point also conceded by Mr Cox:-

"...the class 7 0-8-0 should have been much better, but in spite of its poor axleboxes its costs ran lower than those of its ex-L&NW competitors. The same remarks are true also of the class 4 0-6-0."

"There is no doubt whatever that many aspects of Derby detail design were head and shoulders above that of any of the other constituents for reliable service. Special attention had been paid to good lubrication, and a general straightforward, accessible and robust design was demonstrably productive of lowest repair costs. Moreover, since boilers were well proportioned and had adequate steam spaces and grate areas, coal consumption was moderate in relation to the short travel valves which were universally used."

Therein lies the rub. Judged by the mileage standards achieved by later LMS outside cylinder engines the performance of the axlebox fitted to the Standard Classes 4 and 7 was weak, but when compared with that obtained from their equivalents *i.e.* other inside cylinder classes, it compared most favourably. Furthermore, this performance incidentally, was very similar to that returned by North American *outside* cylinder locomotives that used a box similar to the Churchward/Stanier design but more heavily loaded. Likewise we might point out that frame cracking was not the sole preserve of the Class 4; it also affected the taper-boiler classes but with the added observation that in this respect its taper-boilered cousins did not actually perform any better, and in some cases a good deal worse. Axlebox performance and frame cracking are two design deficiencies explored in more detail when it will be seen there were very sound reasons for the former, some of which appear to have been the result of changes

---

Shepperton 1965 pp48-9.

introduced by the LMS, although later work by the company did go some way towards rectifying it.

A more comprehensive form of table III, although restricted to the three years 1933-5 appears in *LMS Journal Nº 7*, in an article by Mr John Reeves. This latter version reveals that the overall cost per mile was inflated by a 4 per cent interest charge levied on the gross repair costs and by a 3 per cent sinking fund to finance the renewal of the locomotive at the end of its working life. In the case of the Class 4 0-6-0, the overall cost, averaged from figures collected from 459 examples of the then 727 extant examples, was 11.53d/mile, of which the coal cost 6.84d/mile based on 20/- per ton and a coal consumption of 63.8lbs per mile.

per cent respectively.

Unfortunately, although some of William Stanier's designs appeared towards the end of this ten-year period no repair details were provided. The engines were then very new and equally few in number although some coal consumption figures did appear. However, we may perhaps obtain an insight into something of the new engines if we compare the engine repair costs of the 'Horwich Mogul' with those of the 'Big Goods'. Although the 2-6-0s were returning greater annual mileages, roughly one-quarter more, its per mile repair costs had been reduced only a small amount. Furthermore, most of this reduction in repair costs achieved by this class was not in the running gear,

Table III – Ten-year Average of Annual Mileage, Coal Consumption and Repair Costs for Selected LMS Goods Engines

Power class	Locomotive class	Number in stock		Miles per annum	Coal lbs per mile	Repair and overall costs pence (d) per mile		
		1927	1936			Engine and tender	Boiler	Overall cost
7	Standard 7 0-8-0 (sup.)¶	Nil	175	22,240	72.5	3.28	0.48	13.92
	LNWR G2 0-8-0 (sup.)	60	60	23,903	74.7	4.70	0.54	15.46
	L&YR 31 Class 0-8-0 (sup.)	126	53	18,557	78.8	6.11	0.80	19.33
6	LNWR G1 0-8-0 (sup.)	401	439	21,035	72.0	4.75	0.43	15.52
	L&YR 30 Class 0-8-0 (sat.)	71	32	16,088	80.7	5.62	0.88	18.97
4P/5F	Standard 2-6-0 (Crab – sup.)	100	240	34,635	60.0	3.30	0.29	11.96
	Standard 2-6-0 Lentz (Crab – sup.)†	Nil	5	33,841	56.1	2.98	0.28	11.27
4	Standard 4 0-6-0 (sup.)	638	727	26,355	64.9	3.36	0.42	12.29
3	Midland 0-6-0 (sat.)	408	398	22,873	64.7	3.10	0.48	12.16
	L&YR 28 Class 0-6-0 (sup.)	94	53	16,784	55.1	4.11	0.35	12.68
	L&YR 27 Class 0-6-0 (sat.)	396	312	16,219	54.8	3.03	0.31	11.24
	CR various 0-6-0 (sup.)	31	32	21,953	61.9	3.34	0.42	12.71
	CR various 0-6-0 (sat.)	112	104	20,267	70.3	3.22	0.38	12.74
2	LNWR 18ins Goods 0-6-0 (sat.)	395	106	17,519	60.3	3.56	0.40	11.90
	Midland various 0-6-0 (sat.)	426	289	17,749	56.7	2.89	0.37	11.13
~	Garratt 2-6-0+0-6-2 (sup.)	3	33	22,756	118.2	6.31	1.03	25.90

¶Standard 7 0-8-0 first appeared in 1929 hence data for this class is for seven years.
†Five years' costs.
Data taken from Table 13 *Chronicles of Steam*.

Engine and tender repair costs, on the same basis as table III were 2.73d/mile with boiler repairs at 0.38d/mile. Average annual mileage was 27,590, while the mileage attained between 'general' repairs was 111,372. Total days spent under repair was 49, days available but not required for service 9 and the days in service 252, giving the class an availability of 84 per cent and a utilization of 81

but in the boiler – the shape of things to come. Piston valve and other examinations still had to be undertaken, and if conducted at similar mileages demanded likewise a similar number of days out of service, while the increased number of components, inevitable on a more complicated engine, tended to offset the savings that superior axlebox mileage was meant to realize. Admittedly this is not a true comparison since the 'Crabs' tended to be used on faster traffic than the 0-6-0s but it was, for those that had eyes to see it, a worrying trend. This effect may be seen further, when we consider engine availability. William Stanier[8] referred to some of these aspects when he compared older locomotives with their more modern counterparts:-

"Here again (as in thermal) efficiency, the older designs in certain respects fall below the standard of attainment of modern designs. In other respects, however, they show to advantage. They are cheaper in first cost and also often cheaper in repair costs per locomotive. The modern locomotive has to pay for its greatly improved performance by more expensive design and construction, but per unit of work done it would be found cheapest even although per locomotive unit it may be more expensive."

Therein lies the nub of the problem, those more modern engines, usually larger and of greater power, and precisely the sort of beast that the CME's department liked to design and produce, could only be justified if they could be given sufficient work to offset their higher initial capital and running costs. But these latter requirements did not always fit in with the Operating Department's utilization or traffic needs[9]:-

"There is only a limited demand for large locomotives – passenger and freight – the main reason being that, with the vast amount of traffic arising in small quantities in various areas, collecting it calls for small units to deal with a small number of wagons which flow into the marshalling yards. There is also the hauling of light passenger trains on cross-country routes, short runs in the neighbourhood of large stations, and regular trains between cities and large towns, which call for small or medium sized locomotives."

The result being as C R H Simpson observed[10]:-

"Despite the enormous strides made in locomotive development it is somewhat surprising that the mileages obtained per month have improved little in Britain during the last half century. In 1906 LNWR locomotives making daily round trips from Liverpool to London were covering 2,322 miles per week. Leaving 42 working days per year for examination and repair; this is equal to over 104,000 miles in 45 weeks. In 1948 the average of the 45 LMR Pacifics was 67,000 miles in the same period."

Post Second World War, the LMS pioneered the production of modern low powered engines, a practice that was perpetuated by British Railways with several of its Standard classes. However locomotive designers faced particular difficulties in producing efficient low power examples due to the requirement to include features intended to reduce maintenance, ease preparation and operation. Adopting outside cylinders and pony trucks introduced significant additional weight and effectively negated much of the benefit higher working pressures and large-lap valves were meant to bestow, resulting in compromised performance. This is another aspect that will be returned to later.

Under the LMS system the running sheds were responsible for maintaining engines between works visits in accordance with the system of periodic and mileage examinations laid down by the CME, nevertheless despite this attention they gradually accumulated wear in their main components. The boiler and firebox suffered from grooving and wastage together with broken stays, while the chemical and physical effects of residual scale on the heating surfaces after boiler washing gave rise to pitting and corrosion particularly of the boiler shell and tubes. Axleboxes developed roll and side play both of which led to rough riding, leading to further deterioration elsewhere in the engine. While knock in the axleboxes caused loose horns and horn stays, the frames were subject to alternating stresses that promoted fractures. Tyres wore on the treads and flanges, similarly cylinders and piston valves wore resulting in loss of performance coupled with increased coal consumption. In practice, water quality was often as important as design, or workmanship or the capacity of tyres, frames, boxes or running gear to resist deterioration.

Despite the work done in running sheds as engines accumulated mileage, tyre wear in some cases, but axlebox wear in the majority, determined when an engine would be called into the works for what the LMS called an intermediate repair[11], the boiler

---

8 Sir William Stanier *The Position of the Locomotive in Mechanical Engineering* - Presidential Address I Mech E 1941 p58.

9 Lt-Col H Rudgard *The User of Locomotives for Revenue* - Presidential Address I Loco E 1948 p515.

10 Mr M Rutherford *'Castles' & 'Kings' at Work* Guild Publishing London p53.

11 Up until about 1927 all locomotive repairs were classed as 'heavy' or 'light' in accordance with a government schedule drawn up originally as part of a railway accounting scheme intended to protect shareholders. There had been instances of creative accounting demonstrated by some of the old companies before the Grouping and these classifications had been introduced as a preventative measure.

These designations however created anomalies on the LMS

usually needing at that time no more attention than could be given while it remained on the frames. This being limited to such action as re-rivetting or re-nutting a limited number of firebox stays or re-expanding some tubes. By the time a second such period had been run, the boiler would be removed and replaced by another previously repaired one of the same (or similar) design from the previously repaired 'stock'. Since boiler repairs often took longer than the 'chassis' part, to reduce the time in the works there were for most classes more boilers than there were engines. In practice, since boiler defects sometimes arose that necessitated replacement 'out-of-sequence', the mileage between boiler changes seldom coincided with the miles between general repairs. Likewise, circumstances usually meant that the mileage from the previous general to the next was seldom twice that between the previous general to the first intermediate repair because for a number of reasons engines did not run an identical mileage in each period.

Table IV records the repair mileage figures obtained from some LMS locomotives for 1939, by which time the general level of performance had risen to rather more than half-way from where it

Table IV – Repair Mileages for Selected LMS Locomotive Classes – 1939

Type & power class		Locomotive class		Mileage between general repairs			Average miles general to intermediate repair	Average miles between boiler change
				Highest	Lowest	Average		
		All England		~	~	132,600	62,450	104,400
A	6P	Royal Scot	3-cyl. 4-6-0	215,657	107,902	142,546	63,513	112,992
	5XP	Rebuilt Claughton	3-cyl. 4-6-0	237,406	108,744	137,542	71,173	106,678
	4P	Compound	3-cyl. 4-4-0	200,000	110,000	133,419	65,462	106,179
	2P	Standard Class 2	4-4-0	249,613	102,000	137,989	60,599	114,317
	~	Standard Class (Garratt)	2-6-0+0-6-2	~	~	98,868	37,646	72,591
	7F	Standard Class 7	0-8-0	145,288	92,285	114,721	53,039	81,496
	4P/5F	Standard (Crab)	2-6-0	~	~	156,537	67,633	128,038
	4F	Standard Class 4	0-6-0	250,006	106,984	130,244	58,354	92,965
	4P	Standard (parallel boiler)	2-6-4 tank	249,348	117,000	131,575	67,800	119,855
	3P	Standard (parallel boiler)	2-6-2 tank	204,613	128,000	122,856	62,601	106,993
	3F	Standard (shunter)	0-6-0 tank	208,251	92,164	127,855	59,196	109,855
B	7F	LNWR G2A Class	0-8-0	177,341	92,937	132,140	56,119	90,292
	6F	LNWR G1	0-8-0	205,592	92,792	122,690	51,226	94,553
	3F	L&YR (saturated)	0-6-0	~	~	133,089	58,362	76,019
	2F	L&YR (saturated)	2-4-2 tank	~	~	122,919	53,916	83,986
		All Scotland		~	~	180,483	81,817	164,752
C	4P	Compound	3-cyl. 4-4-0	~	~	192,663	89,508	176,187
	4P	Standard (parallel boiler)	2-6-4 tank	~	~	240,774	83,744	170,269
	4P	Caledonian	4-6-0	~	~	159,081	95,421	130,871
	3P	Caledonian	4-4-0	~	~	197,559	68,682	149,148
	2P	Caledonian	0-4-4 tank	~	~	154,789	89,024	151,456
	3F	Caledonian	0-6-0	~	~	144,370	85,641	131,570
	2F	Caledonian	0-6-0	~	~	147,991	66,755	132,749

Data taken from Table 17 *Chronicles of Steam*.

---

with its split responsibilities, for example the motive power people had no idea how much life they could expect from an engine returned to them after a 'light' repair. To overcome this, the LMS introduced 'general' and 'service' or 'intermediate' repairs. General repairs were a complete overhaul following which the locomotive would have the same performance (and life to the next repair) as a new engine. Service repairs were defined as attention to tyres, axleboxes and such other details as would permit the engine to give at least another six month's service.

had been in 1923 and would go on to achieve under British Railways. Section A comprises LMS Standard classes, section B covers sample non-standard classes, while section C is a mixture of both of the above groups but for engines operated wholly in Scotland and maintained at St Rollox works. Mr Cox made a number of comments on the figures appearing in this table and these are worth considering:-

(a) The average mileage between repairs, for the English based engines, from general to intermediate and between boiler changes were quite consistent and in this respect small old locomotives were not that far behind of roughly 2 to 1 in between the highest and the lowest mileages attained between general repairs.

(c) Along with the indigenous engines, Standard classes when operating in Scotland, ran considerably further between boiler changes and in consequence between general repairs. The widespread availability of good water was the determining factor, however, it was not the reason why the 'chassis' portion ran appreciably higher mileages north of the border, although Mr Cox could offer no explanation.

(d) Mr Cox commented on the lower mileages between repairs attained by the Standard 4 and 7 classes, but there were no corresponding figures recording the former class' performance in Scotland. As will be

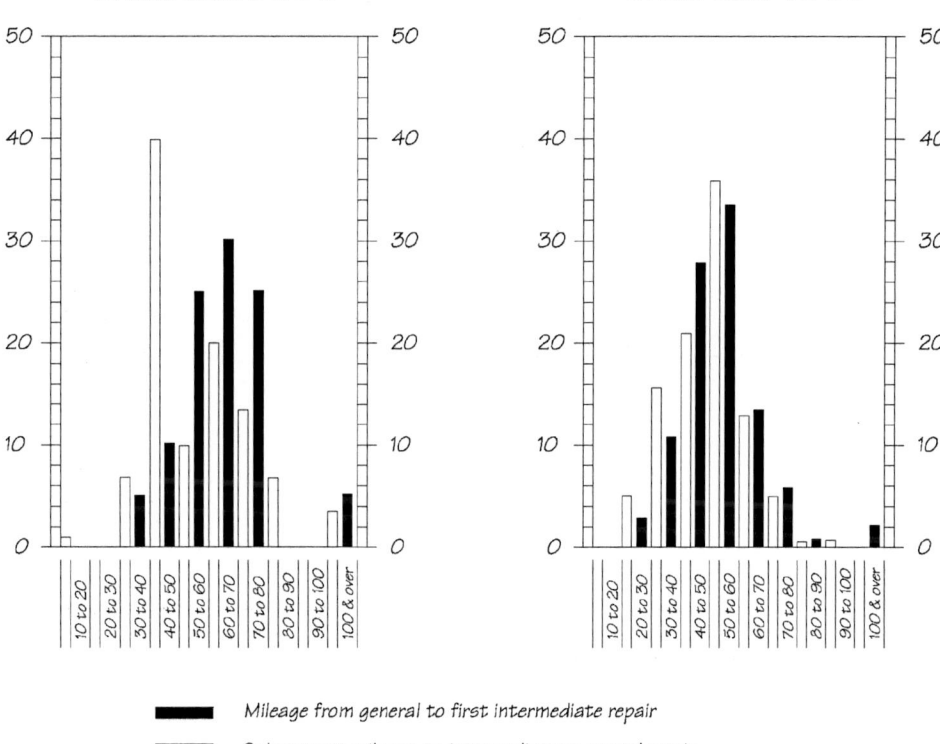

Fig. 3 – Mileages recorded by ex-LMS Class 8 2-8-0s and Class 4 0-6-0s

larger more modern engines despite the latter's improved design features. This demonstrated, as was generally the situation that provided engines undertook duties commensurate with their capacity it was the organization and quality of servicing and repairs which were the major factors determining the repair mileage. Thus, although improved design features were deemed to have contributed something to improving performance, it was of no great influence for the locomotives appearing in the table.

(b) The variation in duties between members of the same class when combined with the differences in levels of attention and skills employed resulted in a variation

demonstrated in due course these figures, certainly in the case of the 0-6-0 were not that dissimilar to those returned by more modern engines that were worked proportionately as hard, while in the case of the eight-coupled engine there were other weaknesses that demanded works attention not connected with the boxes. He also highlighted the low mileages attained by the Garratts between general to intermediate repairs and between generals, but this is in some ways an unfair comparison. Unless the running sheds were equipped with wheel drops, getting the axleboxes out for re-metalling would have been a major operation. Indeed, if the running sheds were not properly equipped to maintain the class the Operating Department had no real option but to send them to Derby for attention. This prompts another observation in that the running sheds were expected not only to deal with hot boxes, but also they often took on the re-metalling of axleboxes as a matter of course, and these figures do not record how many times this operation might have been carried out on any of the classes investigated.

In a paper[12] delivered in 1953, Roland Bond also commented on the existence of a range in the mileages run by different classes between repairs as well as the variation in the mileage run between shop repairs by individual locomotives within the same class. Figure 3 has been redrawn from information he provided and compares the mileages returned by ex-LMS Class 8 2-8-0s and Class 4 0-6-0s. These graphs make an interesting comparison between the two numerically largest former LMS goods classes. It is also very equitable since unlike the 4MT 2-6-0, then neither class was fitted with manganese steel liners to the axleboxes, although fifty 2-8-0 were to be fitted starting in 1954. These profiles include all of the improvements in workshop practices such as bearing finish the LMS was able to achieve. Inspection of figure 3 reveals that 80 per cent of the 2-8-0s could run 50,000 to 80,000 miles from

general to first intermediate repair. In contrast, under the same conditions, 73 per cent of the 0-6-0s ran 40,000 to 70,000 miles, although around 55 per cent of the class ran mileages the equal of those returned by the eight-coupled engines. We might also observe that whilst the class, doubtless due to its smaller axleboxes, ran shorter mileages between repairs, certainly by 1953 they were not that much inferior to a modern class when the latter were employed on similar low speed duties, while of course, they would have been cheaper and easier to repair.

In a perfect world, every locomotive would have been available for traffic 24 hours a day, 365 days a year, while the operators would have utilized each engine in traffic for the whole of those 8,760 hours. However, each engine due to the usage it received required maintenance, so largely but not wholly the extent to which any engine was available was a reflection of the engineering

Table V – Availability, Miles Run, Coal per Mile and Weekdays Out-of-Service for Tender Goods Engines – Western Division of the LMS Year Ending 31st December 1932

Class	N° allocated	Annual mileage	Coal lb/mile	Weekdays out-of-service			Availability
				Heavy & light repairs	Shed repairs & examinations	Total repair days	
LMS Standard Class 7 0-8-0	14	27,392	65.59	8	43	51	84
LNWR G2 superheated 0-8-0	56	23,000	76.30	18	43	61	81
LNWR G1 superheated 0-8-0	340	20,319	72.92	14	40	54	83
LNWR G1 superheated (converted)	9	16,442	69.27	18	27	45	86
LNWR 0-8-0 saturated	30	16,317	80.22	20	26	46	85
LNWR 19ins 4-6-0 saturated	138	20,978	71.30	11	31	42	87
LMS 'Crab' 2-6-0	83	36,603	58.84	17	40	57	82
LMS Standard Class 4 0-6-0	163	23,487	66.60	14	38	52	83
MR Class 3 0-6-0 saturated	16	23,278	61.17	10	24	34	89
FR class 3 0-6-0 saturated	8	13,649	65.26	12	21	33	89
LYR class 3 0-6-0 superheated	4	14,307	55.97	10	38	48	85
LNWR 4ft 3in Coal 0-6-0	117	14,896	46.69	10	25	35	89
LNWR 'Cauliflower' 0-6-0	154	15,030	59.76	7	23	30	90
MR Class 2 0-6-0	28	19,778	55.79	8	28	36	88
L&YR class 2 0-6-0	26	10,244	54.69	4	23	27	91

present in its design. The steam locomotive required routine servicing if the maximum mileage was to be obtained between repairs. This servicing, at the sheds, demanded a certain time out of service *i.e.* non-availability. Non-availability was therefore the sum of the locomotives stopped waiting to go into the works or actually in them undergoing repair together with those stopped at

---

12 Mr R C Bond *Organization and Control of Locomotive Repairs on British Railways* I Loco E Paper 520 March 1953.

sheds awaiting repair, undergoing repair or under shed examination.

Mr Cox stated in *Chronicles of Steam* that satisfactory values were 5 per cent of the total locomotive stock for the former and 10 per cent for shed based operations thereby leaving 85 per cent of the engines available to carry out whatever duties the Operating Department might require of them. Another way of expressing this availability was to say any one engine ought to be available for 310 days per year (*i.e.* 85 per cent of 365). In the same book, Mr Cox gave examples of availability calculations for thirteen 'Royal Scot' class engines allocated to the Western Division and 23 'Claughtons' running on the Midland Division for the two months December 1930 and January 1931. In these calculations, which were based on the then LMS method, the product of the total number of weekdays in both months (*i.e.* 62 less the eight Sundays) and the number of engines gave the engine-weekdays. From this total was subtracted the product of the weekdays and the number of engines that were out of service in sheds or works. Dividing this answer by the number of engine days revealed the availability. A similar exercise but with the engine-weekdays reduced further by the product of the number of weekdays and the number of engines available, but not used, gave the utilization. From this, we might conclude that the smaller the difference between the availability and the utilization figures signified the greater use made of the class. Presumably, this in turn gave an indication of the usefulness of the class in meeting the traffic requirements of the Operating Department.

Although 85 per cent availability was the target for the locomotive stock as a whole, it was difficult for high mileage engines, such as those employed on fast passenger traffic to achieve that standard. This was because availability was defined on a time basis whereas shed examinations and repairs were based on mileage accrued, so engines running high mileages in a given time required attention in the works and sheds more frequently in that time period, than one running a smaller mileage, thereby making it unavailable for more days. In view of this, any comparison between classes based on these statistics should like the case with Lord Stamp's data, be restricted to those employed on similar duties. Accordingly, in table V which originally appeared in *Breath of Steam*[13], the entries have been abridged to cover tender goods engines only, but have been extended to encompass availability as described by Mr Cox.

Mr Thorley noted that the performance of ex-Midland and L&YR types drafted onto the Western Division would have suffered somewhat from a lack of spares and because maintenance and footplate staff were relatively unfamiliar with them. Some of the conclusions to be drawn from a study of table V can only be confirmed in the light of full background information explaining the inconsistencies. For example, although the limited number of Standard Class 7 0-8-0s returned a superior coal consumption to the more numerous G1 and G2 classes this is not a vindication of the superior performance of large-lap valves – the ten-year figures appearing in table III demonstrate this was not the case. Similarly compare the consumption figures for the 'Big Goods' with the 'Austin 7' and the G1 superheated conversions.

For about twelve years following its inception, British Railways produced annual statistics demonstrating the performance of its locomotives. These figures included brief details such as the number of locomotives in each class, their average annual mileage, time spent under repair etc. Referred to as the 'Miles and Days' statistics, they were intended to demonstrate the relative effectiveness of the different classes it had inherited or created. While similar figures had been compiled by all of the 'Big Four' companies it may be seen that the British Railways procedure was very similar to that adopted by the LMS. The primary differences were in referring to utilization as productivity and acknowledging the presence of Bank Holidays. Messers Walford and Harrison[14] have described the process:-

"Productivity was defined as the number of weekdays in service out of a possible 309 days. Indications are that the figure 309 was arrived at by subtracting the number of Sundays in the year (52) from the total of 365 and also, it has been suggested, four Bank Holidays, (Good Friday, Easter Monday, Christmas Day and Boxing Day), when activity would be generally low apart from holiday excursion work at Easter. It is not clear how the incidences of leap years were dealt with; presumbably *(sic)* the figure of 310 was used for the number of days available."

---

13 Mr W G F Thorley *A Breath of Steam Vol 1* Ian Allan Ltd Shepperton 1975 pp106-7

14 Messers J Walford & P Harrison *British Railways Standard Steam Locomotives Vol IV – The 9F 2-10-0 Class* RTCS 2008 p225.

Table VI – Comparison in Availability and Productivity for a Selection of Tender Goods Engines – 1955 and 1956

Locomotive class	1955 (309 days)									1956 (310 days)								
	N° in use	Mileage	Heavy & light repairs	Shed repairs & exams	Total repair days	Availability	Days not needed	Productivity		N° in use	Mileage	Heavy & light repairs	Shed repairs & exams	Total repair days	Availability	Days not needed	Productivity
Eastern & North Eastern Regions																	
5F ex-NER J27 0-6-0	115	16,900	12	28	40	87	14	83		115	16,900	13	22	35	89	10	85
5F ex-LNER J39 0-6-0	263	17,900	17	49	66	79	19	72		262	17,500	20	46	66	79	21	72
4F ex-LMS Standard 0-6-0	13	20,400	6	35	41	87	18	81		16	20,100	13	26	39	87	8	85
London Midland Region																	
8F ex-LMS 2-8-0	316	23,200	13	33	46	85	11	82		316	21,600	12	34	46	85	5	84
8F ex-LMS 2-8-0 (ex-HMG)	22	22,800	17	35	52	83	9	80		22	22,300	13	33	46	85	4	84
8F ex-LMS 2-8-0 (ex-ORC)	275	23,000	12	33	45	85	12	82		265	23,300	12	33	45	85	4	84
8F WD 2-8-0	263	19,800	11	29	40	87	26	79		263	21,100	12	29	41	87	12	83
7F ex-S&DJR 2-8-0	11	23,200	15	70	85	72	20	66		11	23,600	19	49	68	78	21	71
7F ex-LNWR G2 0-8-0	56	17,800	18	43	61	80	18	74		55	18,700	15	42	57	82	5	80
7F ex-LNWR G2A 0-8-0	185	17,700	18	40	58	81	15	76		181	23,400	15	43	58	81	7	79
7F ex-LMS Standard 0-8-0	38	17,600	19	36	55	82	26	74		32	18,500	11	34	45	85	16	80
4F ex-LMS Standard 0-6-0	693	20,500	11	36	47	85	14	80		682	20,700	10	34	44	86	5	84
4F ex-LMS Standard 0-6-0 (ex-SDJR)	11	24,600	10	56	66	79	18	73		11	23,100	5	60	65	79	12	75
3F ex-Midland 0-6-0	292	15,200	7	29	36	88	53	71		271	14,900	4	29	33	89	51	73
3F ex-L&YR 0-6-0	136	14,000	7	27	34	89	60	70		118	14,600	9	29	38	88	45	73*
3F ex-FR 0-6-0	5	9,200	8	28	36	88	117	51		3	12,000	0	44	44	86	54	68
2F ex-Midland 0-6-0	101	13,700	7	26	33	89	52	73		88	14,600	4	29	33	89	26	81
2F ex-GCR J10 0-6-0	53	14,900	18	25	43	86	79	61		37	17,100	2	30	32	90	51	73
Beyer-Garratt 2-6-0+0-6-2	26	20,400	31	44	75	76	11	72		13	20,500	18	48	66	79	8	76
Scottish Region																	
6F ex-LNER J38 0-6-0	35	21,100	19	56	75	76	7	74		35	21,300	18	62	80	74	4	73
5F ex-NBR J37 0-6-0	104	20,200	12	46	58	81	12	77		104	19,900	14	47	61	80	6	78

*Recorded in Messers Walford & Harrison's table as 68 per cent but figures suggest 73 per cent.

Multiplication and Modification

Table VII – Comparison in Availability and Productivity for a Selection of Tender Goods Engines – 1957

Locomotive class	1957 (309 days)							
	Nº in use	Mileage	Weekdays out-of-service for			Availability	Days not needed	Productivity
			Heavy & light repairs	Shed repairs & exams	Total repair days			
London Midland Region								
8F ex-LMS 2-8-0	287	22,700	13	32	45	85	5	84
8F ex-LMS 2-8-0 (ex-HMG)	17	22,600	14	29	43	86	5	84
8F ex-LMS 2-8-0 (ex-ORC)	239	23,000	14	31	45	85	5	84
8F WD 2-8-0	144	20,700	12	30	42	86	11	83
7F ex-LNWR G2 0-8-0	55	17,600	19	44	63	80	8	77
7F ex-LNWR G2A 0-8-0	149	17,600	14	40	54	83	8	80
7F ex-LMS Standard 0-8-0	19	7,200	12	42	54	83	18	77
4F ex-LMS Standard 0-6-0	618	20,200	12	34	46	85	7	83
3F ex-Midland 0-6-0	225	14,400	4	30	34	89	49	73
3F ex-L&YR 0-6-0	70	14,200	8	27	35	89	44	74
2F ex-Midland 0-6-0	72	13,800	5	29	34	89	29	79
2F ex-GCR J10 0-6-0	31	15,700	1	39	40	87	56	69
Beyer-Garratt 2-6-0+0-6-2	1	24,100	0	41	41	87	9	84
Scottish Region								
6F ex-LNER J38 0-6-0	35	21,900	15	71	86	72	2	72
5F ex-NBR J37 0-6-0	104	20,100	17	49	66	79	7	76
4F ex-LMS Standard 0-6-0	49	19,400	11	51	62	80	14	75
3F ex-Midland 0-6-0	5	19,000	~	34	34	89	12	85

NB:- The productivity values in the original table do not tally in every case with the number of days not required, accordingly new values have been ascribed to the latter calculated by subtracting the total repair days from the total out-of-service days.

Examples of the British Railways figures for goods tender engines have been taken from Messers Walford and Harrison's book, which in abridged and modified form appear in tables VI, VII and VIII. Since the days when an engine was not required were included, it has been possible to introduce an intermediate column quantifying the availability.

These tables demonstrate annual average mileages for the 'Big Goods' for most of the 1950's was over 20,000, achieved with utilization, or productivity, values typically of around 80 per cent. The latter figures were not that dissimilar from those obtained from more modern locomotives, indeed in most years the class was one of the best, exceeding in many instances the performances of later classes. Part of this was irrespective of whatever individual improvements a class was given towards say increasing the mileage between general repairs, the piston valves, wheels and tyres, big ends and little ends, pony trucks and crank axles and the remaining other engine parts still needed regular inspection at stipulated mileage intervals, resulting in roughly similar numbers of days out of service. As an extension of this, the availability figures for the Class 4 do not suggest the class was heavier on repairs, or perhaps to be more accurate, whatever repairs/examinations it required could be accommodated in the same time demanded by other, more modern engines *e.g.* the LMS Standard Class 8 2-8-0. However Mr Wilkinson[15] has warned:-

"Beware however, that shedmasters knew how to 'play the system' - a locomotive could come on shed at 00.01 on Monday, be under repair and go off shed at 22.00 on Tuesday, having been 'in service' on both days. Hence some of the 'Black Sheep' of the flock -

---

15 Mr A Wilkinson *Stanier '8Fs' at Work* Ian Allan Shepperton 1986 p19.

Table VIII – Comparison in Availability and Productivity for a Selection of Tender Goods Engines – 1958

Locomotive class	1958 (309 days)						
	Nº in use	Mileage	Weekdays out-of-service for			Availability	Days not needed	Productivity
			Heavy & light repairs	Shed repairs & exams	Total repair days			
Western Region								
4MT ex-GWR 43xx 2-6-0	178	27,600	18	39	57	82	15	77
4F ex-LMS Standard 0-6-0	36	20,500	12	35	47	85	13	81
3MT ex-GWR 22xx 0-6-0	119	18,400	16	35	51	83	41	70
3F ex-Midland 0-6-0	23	15,900	8	36	44	86	44	72
Eastern Region								
8F ex-LMS 2-8-0	39	19,500	12	28	40	87	7	85
5F ex-LNER J39 0-6-0	127	16,600	11	48	59	81	52	64
4F ex-LMS Standard 0-6-0	63	19,200	8	35	43	86	4	85
3F ex-Midland 0-6-0	35	14,600	5	28	33	89	29	80
2F ex-Midland 0-6-0	4	14,800	5	25	30	90	51	74
North Eastern Region								
8F ex-LMS 2-8-0	55	21,800	15	40	55	82	3	81
5F ex-LNER J27 0-6-0	115	15,800	13	41	54	83	9	80
5F ex-LNER J39 0-6-0	120	15,500	15	47	62	80	32	70
4F ex-LMS Standard 0-6-0	46	18,800	9	34	43	86	3	85
3F ex-Midland 0-6-0	20	9,000	3	23	26	92	122	52
3F ex-L&YR 0-6-0	17	13,100	2	45	47	85	52	68
2F ex-Midland 0-6-0	3	14,000	0	27	27	91	56	73
London Midland Region								
8F ex-LMS 2-8-0	262	22,500	13	35	48	84	*6*	83
8F ex-LMS 2-8-0 (ex-HMG)	17	21,900	14	29	43	86	*7*	84
8F ex-LMS 2-8-0 (ex-ORC)	245	23,000	12	35	47	85	*6*	83
8F WD 2-8-0	174	20,800	11	34	45	85	11	82
7F ex-LNWR G2 0-8-0	59	15,700	8	44	52	83	*23*	75
7F ex-LNWR G2A 0-8-0	146	15,700	9	44	53	83	*22*	75
7F ex-LMS Standard 0-8-0	20	12,400	22	22	44	86	*67*	64
5F ex-LNER J39 0-6-0	31	17,900	13	55	68	78	7	76
4F ex-LMS Standard 0-6-0	554	18,800	10	37	47	85	9	78
3F ex-Midland 0-6-0	169	14,400	5	33	38	88	12	76
3F ex-L&YR 0-6-0	58	13,300	7	28	35	89	41	70
2F ex-Midland 0-6-0	62	9,900	4	24	28	91	89	62
Scottish Region								
8F ex-LMS 2-8-0	3	25,300	0	83	83	73	5	72
6F ex-LNER J38 0-6-0	35	22,100	17	62	79	74	5	73
5F ex-NBR J37 0-6-0	104	18,600	13	52	65	79	7	77

NB:- The number of days not required, shewn in italic, appear to be incorrect in the original table – productivity percentage assumed to be correct.

Garratts and 'Austin Sevens' for example - could return remarkably respectable figures."

Doubtless such 'sharp practice' did occur and not necessarily solely confined to the 'Black Sheep' classes either, but only limited remedial work could be hidden by this subterfuge. Consequently, overall it could only have had a small effect on the availability figures for the classes. Thus we can accept the figures were a pretty accurate reflection of the true situation.

Fig. 4 – LMS Standard Class 4 N° 4260 of Lot 29 to Order 6473 photographed during the summer 1926 while under construction in Derby Works

This performance, comparable with many later classes, might be taken as further evidence that superior workshop procedures and finishes in conjunction with a better performing lubricating oil, had reduced the incidences of 'hot boxes'. Indeed, further inspection of these figures suggests, as with the 1927-37 costs, the performance of other classes such as the Beyer-Garratts and the 'Austin Seven' 0-8-0 were perhaps not as dire as some might have us believe and even after allowing for some 'shedmaster tweaking' lend support as to why the Operating Department was happy to ask for more Class 4 0-6-0s as late as 1941. As Ernest Lemon one time CME of the LMS but by then one of the company's Vice-Presidents observed a few years earlier in a paper[16]. praising the Highland Railway 'Jones Goods', while the haulage feats of a class on the road might appeal to some, to a

16 Mr T Jenkins *Sir Ernest Lemon* Railway & Canal Historical Society Oxford 2011 p51.

railway company the ease and cost of maintenance and repairs could be more important than the capability of a class to haul heavy loads or maintain high speeds. Indeed some classes which gained a shinning reputation for performance on the road were costly to maintain and difficult to repair in the workshops.

Through comparing the availability and utilization figures, it is possible to appreciate the point made by Mr Cox, namely a class might have a reduced availability through it running increased mileage but its worth to the Operating Department was shewn by its utilization being close to its availability, signifying if it was available for use then it was used. It is suspected this was influencing the figures for the Somerset & Dorset Class 4 0-6-0s. They returned annual mileages between one-quarter and one-third higher than their sisters located elsewhere, due to their more extensive use on passenger trains during the summer months, which will have shortened the intervals between running repairs and examinations.

Since the percentage of the time each class was available for traffic was the basis upon which its engineering and operational worth was judged, it is interesting to see that the availability of more modern classes was not significantly greater than that of the 'Big Goods'. This was for two reasons, firstly later engines *did not* present any great *technical* advance over the older ones secondly the improvement in shop procedures introduced from the 'twenties onwards reduced the maintenance demands of the older designs, further eroding the nominal advantages of the newer classes. Hence we may appreciate why for example the Class 4MT 2-6-0s were withdrawn at approximately the same rate as the older 0-6-0s and a mere two years later. Despite Mr Cox's antithesis to inside cylinder engines, which seems to have had a somewhat

A Defence of the Midland LMS Class 4 0-6-0

spurious basis[17]:-

"... Not as yet, on the Lancashire and Yorkshire Railway, however where Cox was later to recall, putting up inside motion on new 0-8-0s on hot August afternoons, 'predisposed me against inside cylinders for the whole of my designing career'."

putting the valve gear outside and/or adopting large-lap valves did not necessarily result in a more useful engine. It must have been particularly sobering for him, when having pushed for the Class 4MT Mogul as a replacement for the Class 4 to find that its in-service performance was little better than that of the 0-6-0 and by some fundamental criteria worse. Overall, it was all a little sad especially since 36 years separated the two designs. In terms of maintenance, apart from larger axleboxes, the single biggest advantage possessed by the Class 4MT was the presence of manganese liners to the boxes and horns – an improvement later felt worthwhile to be applied to the 0-6-0 albeit only a handful. It has to be said however, that what was probably the latter class' worst defect, or at least the one of most concern to its late LMS and BR crews, namely its variable steaming was never addressed.

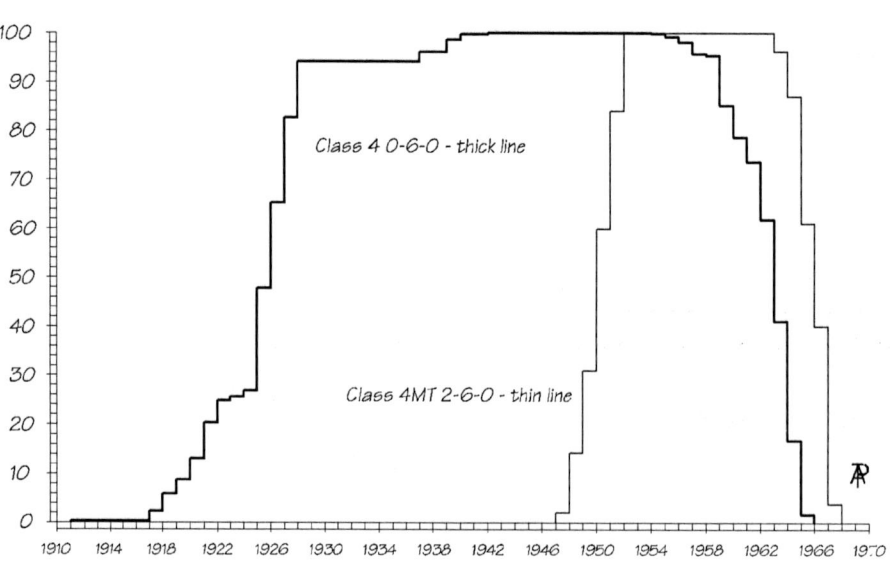

Fig. 5 - Building and withdrawal profiles for classes 4F 0-6-0 and 4MT 2-6-0

Appearing in figure 5 are the building and withdrawal of the Standard Class 4 0-6-0 and the later Class 4MT 2-6-0. The diagram records the short delay following the creation of the LMS, while George Hughes carried out his comparison tests before deciding which designs to multiply. It also suggests that although the Mogul may have been intended as the modern successor to the 'Big Goods' in practice this was not the case, in the rundown to dieselization the newer design only survived a year or two longer. Had the 2-6-0 demonstrated sufficiently large financial advantage in terms of maintenance, fuel economy and performance over the 0-6-0, one presumes the older engines would have been withdrawn at a faster rate.

Certainly there is some evidence to suggest designers did not always fully appreciate how much a larger capital or first cost could operate against the achievement of overall economy – in fuel and maintenance – of a new locomotive design over its older predecessor. As referred to earlier, in connexion with table III, locomotive economics on the LMS incurred an annual capital charge of 4 per cent and a sinking fund. These had to be liquidated by a portion of the savings from the fuel consumption, before any ultimate economy could be claimed from the introduction of a more modern locomotive class. If, the modern replacement incurred higher repair costs, or at least it did not effect a sufficiently large reduction, or its availability was no higher, then the situation becomes more difficult financially, towards justifying the introduction of a new design. Presumably, this is why Sir William was happy enough to build more Standard N° 4 Goods, rather than produce a replacement. These points are considered in figure 6, which shews how the true economy of a design was affected by the inclusion of capital charges, replacement costs, fuel consumption and repair costs. This nomogram, which has been derived from one that appeared in Mr Bond's *Presidential Address*[18], seems to include

---

17 Mr P Atkins *Britannia Birth of a Locomotive* Irwell Press Pinner 1991 p31.

18 Mr R C Bond *Years of Transition* Presidential Address I Loco E Sept 1953 figure 7.

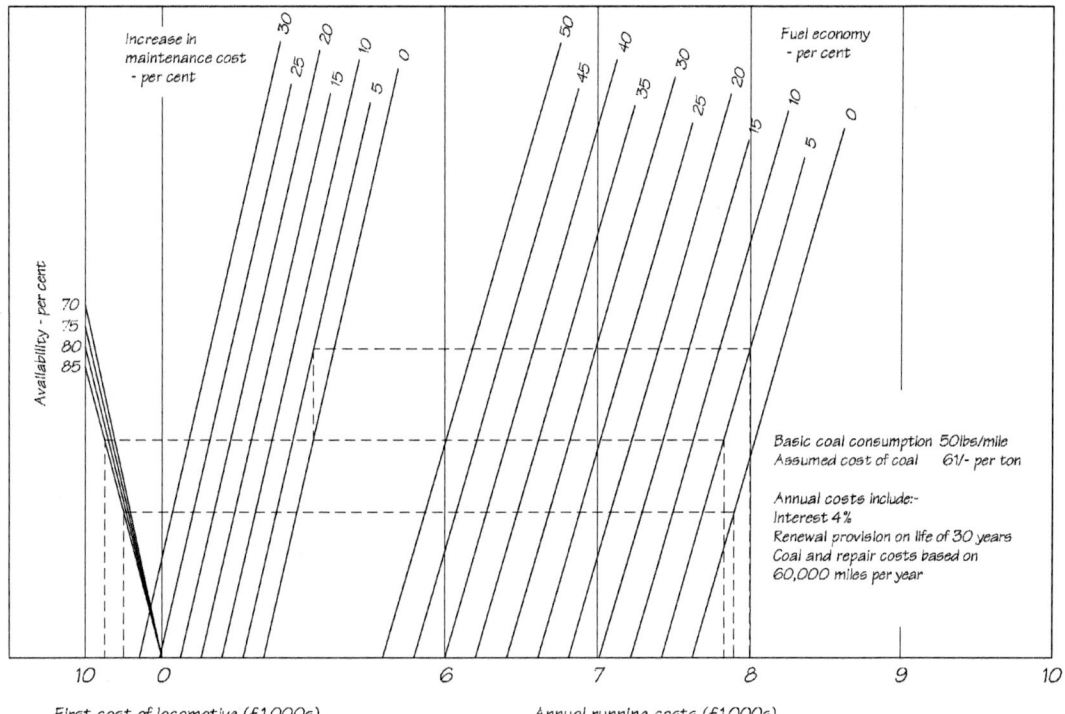

Fig. 6 - Locomotive annual running costs

a sinking fund of about 3 per cent.

David Hunt reported the last examples of 'Big Goods' delivered in 1941, cost £4,477 each, while Mr Cook reported costs for the LMS 4MT 2-6-0, built between 1947 and 1949 in the range £7,500 to £10,750 each[19]. Whilst the following comparison may not be precise because of the effects of the Second World War, we might adopt a capital cost of £5,000 for the 0-6-0 and £7,500 for the Mogul. Now as will be demonstrated later, in service, the 2-6-0 would only have returned a small saving in coal compared to the 'Big Goods' when hauling passenger or fast goods trains, while its shed maintenance requirements were probably not too dissimilar. Let us assume the fuel costs were 5 per cent less, although when the coal used in steam raising, during stand by periods or when coasting are taken into account, this might be too generous, and that the maintenance costs were the same percentage. Combined with an availability of 85 per cent for both classes, these values have been plotted by dotted lines on figure 6, wherein it we may see there was a very small saving in the annual running costs in favour of the 2-6-0. If however, the Mogul while attaining that fuel economy, it was accompanied by a 5 per cent increase in its annual maintenance cost, then it became more expensive than the 0-6-0 - these estimates again support Sir William's observation.

Modifications

The following details describe briefly some of the modifications applied to the Class 4; generally they fall into one or other of two groups the first of which was intended to improve engine reliability, while the second was to increase economy. For further information on these and other modifications applied to the class the reader is referred[20] to *LMS Locomotive Profiles Nº 10 The Standard Class 4 Goods 0-6-0s*.

Crank axles: In August 1935, William Stanier issued an instruction following an experiment conducted on an Nº 4 Goods engine crank axle wherein the original large dual-diameter fillet radii of the crankpin giving it an approximately elliptical profile had been reduced to assume a parallel section with ¾ins fillets; henceforward this

---

19 Messers D Hunt, J Jennison, R Essery & F James *LMS Locomotive Profiles Nº 10 The Standard Class 4 Goods 0-6-0s* Wild Swan Didcot.

Mr A F Cook *LMS Locomotive Design and Construction* The Railway Correspondence & Travel Society 1990 pp90 & 92.

20 Messers D Hunt, J Jennison, R Essery & F James *LMS Locomotive Profiles Nº 10 The Standard Class 4 Goods 0-6-0s* Wild Swan Didcot.

A Defence of the Midland LMS Class 4 0-6-0

was to become the standard profile. It was reported that the running of the big ends had thereby been so improved, this modification Job N° 5001 of August 1935, was applied to approximately 1,240 engines fitted with the pattern N° 23 crank axle, which included all of the 'Big Goods' and the 'Austin Sevens'.

constant diameter, and these combined to produce that aggravating 'clunk' which one heard coming from the big ends of Jinty tanks."

Notwithstanding these comments, it is not clear why the crankpins had to be modified, one feels sharpening form tools was not beyond the wit of man, after all Midland men had been able to do

N° 3976 was built by Armstrong Whitworth in January 1922 but is seen here after being fitted with a Davies & Metcalfe Class H exhaust steam injector in March 1933. The injector is located behind the cab footstep plate with its associated centrifugal grease separator positioned in front of the firebox. The lagged pipe emanating from the base of the smokebox conveyed exhaust steam to the device. On the original print the foremost and aftermost Silvertown lubricators can be seen to have been lettered 'Engine Oil' and 'Cylinder Oil' respectively.

Fig. 7 - Class 4 0-6-0 N° 3976 fitted with an exhaust steam injector

Mr Burgess who served his time at the ex-LNWR shed in Swansea during the 1930s recorded[21]:-

"On inside cylinder locomotives the big ends had to be dismantled for examination every 10-12,000 miles, which included the usual calliper check for wear. These tank engines had the M.R. type solid forged crankshaft which also had to accommodate the four eccentric sheaves for the Stephenson link valve gear. The width of the sheave bearing areas was quite generous and the feature, together with the width of the big end crank webs and axle journals, had evidently convinced the Derby Drawing Office wizards that the remaining dimensions were insufficient to provide big end bearing areas of adequate proportions. But they believed the width of the big end journal could be effectively increased if they were machined as concave hemispheres, and the big end bearings as matching convex hemispheres.

This idea seemed a reasonable solution but it failed lamentably to take into account the machining difficulties which accompanied this unusual bearing design. Specially shaped tools were provided, but how did one sharpen them, once the edge wore off? There were also difficulties in bedding the brasses by hand after machining that didn't occur with bearings of

this successfully since the days when their engines were painted dark green. It seems to represent a technology that was well understood on the originating company where it was capable of giving good results[22]. Although the pattern N° 23 crank axle dated back to 1906, the general design less the shrunk on strengthening hoops introduced by Mr Johnson, originated back in the time of Matthew Kirtley - in so far as the earliest drawings I have seen shewing the two large radii that formed the continuously curved crankpin surface date from the 1850s and 1860s. However, the skills needed to fit up this design of big end do not seem to have travelled well – or perhaps the LMS did not try to teach them – so after about eight decades of use the profile was abandoned. It is conceivable that reclaimed or otherwise high lead content white metal may also have affected the reliability of the big end bearings, possibly helping prompt the fillet radii change. Two years later, almost to the day,

---

21 Mr H C H Burgess *Working with LMS Steam* Bradford Barton 1983 p62.

22 Sir Henry Fowler referred to these radii in a report about locomotive fractures:-

"As far as design goes, all radii should be as large as possible, and certain classes (which, incidentally, never run hot) have the big end bearings practically a full semi-circle."

Sir Henry Fowler *Fractures – Locomotive* 20th January 1931.

Job Nº 5061 of August 1937 was initiated, which stipulated when pattern Nº 23 crank axles required renewing, they were to be replaced by a built-up version and the connecting rods fitted with a further design of revised big-end brasses. By 1960, all of the extant 'Big Goods' less Nº 44237 had been changed.

Narrow piston valve rings: The Midland Railway pattern of piston valve was initially fitted to the Nº 4 Goods, which was of Dr Schmidt's single wide-ring type. After LMS engineers found their examples of this design leaked excessively, Mr Cox wrote a memorandum[23] proposing that narrow ring piston valves should be substituted:-

"NARROW RINGS FOR PISTON VALVES

PRESENT POSITION.

All new engines are being fitted with narrow rings on the piston valves in place of the wide Schmidt type of ring, to reduce the amount of steam which leaks past the valve.

In addition the "Royal Scots" and "Claughtons" are being fitted as they pass through the shops. There are however a large number of engines both of the Standard, and important non-standard types to which consideration might be given as regards replacing the wide ring valve by the narrow. Of the standard types the principal are:-

162 No. 2 Class passenger.
726 No. 4 Class freight.

Of non-standard types from which a substantial reduction in coal consumption can be expected, and which are still employed on important work, there are the following:-

246 Prince of Wales 4-6-0 Passenger.
461 Crewe G1 and G2 class 0-8-0 Freight.

SAVINGS TO BE ANTICIPATED.

The last 14 "Royal Scot" engines which have six narrow rings on each piston valve head, have shown a saving of 11½% in coal compared with the original type of "Royal Scot" engine having wide rings. This saving was obtained comparing a new engine of each type. When the engines have run a considerable mileage, the narrow rings show an increased saving due to their maintaining the valves in a better state of steam tightness over long periods.

With the "Claughton" class the adoption of the narrow ring in conjunction with the suppression of the "trick" port and the use of a hollow type of valve has given coal savings of up to 30%.

A conservative estimate would place the savings to be anticipated on the types of engines proposed for fitting at 10%.

COST OF FITTING.

From estimates prepared in connection with "Royal Scot" and "Claughton" engines, the cost of fitting up a 2-cylinder engine with new valves would be about £26.

The total cost of fitting the 1595 engines would be £41,470, and the annual capital and maintenance charges on this sum would be:-

---

23 Mr E S Cox *Narrow Rings for Piston Valves* memo to Mr S J Symes 7th April 1931.

Multiplication and Modification

Interest at 5%	£2073
Depreciation on 15 years life	£2073
Maintenance 2½%	£1036
Total	£5,182

ANNUAL SAVINGS.

	Tons.	Annual cost of coal @ 17/0 per ton on tender
No. 2 Class Pass.	683	£581
No. 4 Class Freight	825	£702
Prince of Wales	783	£667
G1 Class 0-8-0	685	£582

Total annual cost of coal for 1595 engines of the above classes is:- £1,033,700
Gross saving (10%) £ 103,370
Less capital & maintenance charges £ 5,182
Net Annual saving £ 98,188

If only the 888 standard engines are fitted the cost would be £23,120 and the net annual savings £57,310.

If only the number of standard engines passing through the shops in a year are fitted in the first instance, this would mean 394 engines at a cost of £10,240.

There are also 100 2-6-0 engines and 75 Central Div. 4-6-0 engines (Class 8) which have piston valves with the old Horwich type of ring. No tests have been made to ascertain how these compare with the narrow ring, but it is possible that an investigation in this direction would disclose a further possibility of coal saving."

Approval was obtained from the Locomotive and Electrical Committee in May 1931, when it agreed to fit narrow ring piston valves to a total of 1,657 locomotives. This was initiated under Job Nº 5004 issued in August, consequently all of the 'Big Goods' (presumably the 727 then in existence not 726 as Mr Cox counted in this memo) were fitted with a new piston valve sealed with four narrow rings in each head. Although this modification took several years to complete as valves were only replaced when valve examinations required the old ones to be replaced, it will be appreciated it had been introduced *solely* to save coal.

Exhaust steam injectors: Three days later, in a second memorandum[24] Mr Cox provided details of the costs involved in fitting exhaust steam injectors to Standard classes. These, being a form of feed water heater offered a means of saving coal and water:-

---

24 Mr E S Cox *Exhaust Steam Injectors* memo to Mr S J Symes 10th April 1931.

A replacement breeches pipe was needed, provided with a 4ins diameter branch pipe to convey exhaust steam to the injector. The drawing number for this item was 10-8107, which along with the numbers of other drawings associated with the modification, suggests the Midland may originally have intended the Class 4 to be fitted with the device from new.

A Defence of the Midland LMS Class 4 0-6-0

"EXHAUST STEAM INJECTORS

Engines at present fitted.

No. 2 Class Passenger 4-4-0		73 engines
No. 3 " " 4-4-0		5 "
2-6-4 Tank Engines		75 engines
2-6-2 " "		50 "
0-6-0 No. 4 Class Freight		5 "
4-6-0 "Royal Scots"		70 "
0-8-0 No. 7 Class Freight		120 "
2-6-0 Nos. 13120 onwards		105 "
4-6-0 "Claughton"		10 "
"Garratts"		30 "
Total		543 "

Standard Engines not yet fitted.

No. 2 Class Passenger 4-4-0	162 engines
0-6-0 No. 4 Class Freight	722 "
Standard Compounds	235 "
2-6-0 Mixed Traffic	120 "
"Garratts"	3 "
Total	1,242 "

Cost of Fitting.

After making due allowance for the fittings to be removed, the average cost of fitting an engine with this apparatus is £85; capital and maintenance charges on this amount are:-

	£
Interest at 5%	4.25
Depreciation on 15 years' life	4.25
Maintenance 2½%	2.12
Total annual charges	10.62

There are three proposals as to the manner in which sanction may be asked for the work.

(1) To fit a selected number of the engines, say:-

120	2-6-0
100	No. 4 Freight
3	Garratt
3	Compound
226	

The total cost of which would be ... £19,210

(2) To fit the number of No. 2 class passenger, No. 4 class freight, and 2-6-0 engines which undergo general repairs in a year. Also 3 Compounds experimentally and the remaining Garratts. (It is desirable to fit only a small number of Compounds at first until it is seen that steaming is not affected by taking exhaust steam from the blast pipe).

This would mean –

97	No. 2 class passenger
297	No. 4 class freight
40	2-6-0
3	Garratt
3	Compound
440	

The total cost of which would be ... £37,400

(3) To fit all the remaining standard engines, 1,242 in number, the cost of which would be £105,570.

Savings.

A Dynamometer Car test with a "Royal Scot" class engine gave a saving of 8%. A saving of 7% should be realisable under average conditions.

		per mile
No. 2 class Pass. Av. yearly mileage	33,220	Av. coal 46 lbs.
No. 4 Goods. " " "	27,600	" " 67 "
2-6-0 " " "	25,400	" " 59 "
Garratt " " "	18,720	" " 120 "
Compound " " "	43,600	" " 43 "

	Annual coal burned	Annual cost of coal @ 17/- per ton on tender
by one No. 2 class Pass.	683 tons	£581
" 4 " Goods.	825 "	£702
2-6-0	668 "	£569
Garratt	1,002 "	£853
Compound	837 "	£713

The savings obtained by the three proposals outlined above would be as follows:-

Proposal No.	1	2	3
No. of engines to be fitted	226	440	1,242
Cost of fitting	£19,210	£37,400	£105,570
Total annual cost of coal	£143,178	£291,748	£839,039
Gross saving (7%)	£10,022	£20,420	£58,733
Less Capital & maint. charges	£2,400	£4,670	£13,190
(£10.62 per engine)			
Net annual saving	£7,622	£15,750	£45,543"

The Locomotive and Electrical Committee[25] approved the recommendation to fit the 1,242 Standard engines with Davies & Metcalfe Class H exhaust steam injectors, which it authorized under Job N° 5002, issued in May 1931. This, modification therefore included all 727 Class 4 0-6-0s then in existence less N° 4037-41[26] which had been fitted with Davies & Metcalfe Class F exhaust steam injectors from new in 1925. Following the arrival of William Stanier the order was rescinded long before all of the engines had been equipped. In late November 1933, the Deputy CME Hewitt Beames wrote to the Works Managers:-

"… it has now been decided to fit only a

---

25 From April 1924 the Rolling Stock Committee was separated into the Locomotive and Electrical Committee and the Carriage and Wagon Committee, only to combine in January 1932 to become the Mechanical and Electrical Engineering Committee.

26 Mr Cook identified the five pre-fitted Class 4 0-6-0s as being N° 4052-6.

Mr A F Cook *LMS Locomotive Design and Construction* The Railway Correspondence & Travel Society 1990 p120 limited number only of Standard 0-6-0 No. 4 Freight Tender engines with exhaust steam injectors... Let me know the number of this class already fitted and how many injectors are on order for this type. No more injectors for this class should be ordered."

Followed in April 1937 by a letter Sir William sent to the Works Managers:-

"Due to the introduction of larger engines for working the more important passenger and freight services, it is considered that the provision of this fitting does not afford the savings previously anticipated and it has been decided that when the present stocks of these injectors have been fitted, no more engines of the following classes will be dealt with: Class 2P 4-4-0, Class 4F 0-6-0, 2-6-0 parallel boiler."

In order for an exhaust steam injector to deliver the anticipated coal savings, the engine had to be on a service that avoided frequent starting and stopping, while more importantly, it had to be worked reasonably hard. The water saving was more or less constant across the whole working range of the engine, but the coal saving was far from constant, which is why such variable opinions were gained as to the worth of the device. With the introduction of larger locomotives not worked proportionately any harder, this saving was probably never realized with most of them either - indeed if anything, they stood even less chance than that estimated for the engines originally selected.

By-pass valves: Piston valves were normally adopted in superheated engines, as they were better able to cope with the hot steam. They had the disadvantage that unlike slide valves they could not lift from their seats should excessive compression be generated when the engine was running with steam shut off. To avoid the injurious shocks to the rods and motion that high compression would cause, Dr Schmidt arranged, as part of his superheater 'package' for a vacuum relief (snifting) valve and pressure equalizing or by-pass valve[27] to be fitted to each cylinder. His by-pass consisted of a U-shaped tube approximately 60mm/2 11/32ins bore connecting the opposite ends of the cylinder together via a manually operated shut-off cock located mid-length. The driver opened the cock immediately on closing the regulator and shut it before re-admitting steam to the cylinders.

When superheating was first adopted on the Midland a pair of 4ins vacuum relief valves, or air valves as the company termed them, with 1½ins openings into the steam chest were provided, but not Dr Schmidt's by-passes. It was soon found that serious knocking in the big and little ends of the connecting rods occurred, cylinder indicator diagram fig 8a, records the high compression that occurred when coasting without steam. Derby then fitted by-pass valves, but modified Dr Schmidt's design so that they would act automatically, thereby giving rise to Mr Anderson's by-pass valve. In this version, the cock became a piston valve having on its opposite face a connexion to the steam chest or header. Thus whenever the regulator was open the valve was held tightly shut isolating the two ends of the by-pass, conversely, when it was shut the valve fell off its seat under gravity and the compression pressure was largely destroyed. Figure 8b demonstrates the reduction - the diagram was taken with both the snifting (vacuum relief) valves and the by-pass valves in operation. Writing in 1913 Sir Henry advised a test was carried out to see whether the snifting valves were necessary, accordingly they were blanked off, with the results shewn in figure 8c. This was not quite as good as diagram 8b, but as no knocking occurred, it was decided to adopt the by-passes but omit the vacuum-relief valves.

Opposite each cylinder diagram in figure 8, is the corresponding steam chest pressure trace to the same scale. The fluctuations appearing in the lower portion of diagram 8b at one end were, according to Sir Henry because too a light spring was used in the indicator. Since N° 3835 was built with snifting valves but N° 3836 appears not to have been, it may be that these experiments were conducted on 'Big Goods', whether that is the case or not, it is known that a number of such investigations were later conducted on members of the class. These seem to have been concerned with reducing valve carbonization as well as improving their free running when coasting; Mr Summerson[28] referred to N° 3868 and 3867 being fitted with vacuum-relief valves in July 1918:-

"The report of 8 August was favourable: 'Foreman Littlewood informs me that drivers who have had the above engines are of the opinion that they run very freely and always keep the couplings tight when coasting with the train. Drivers have previously mentioned that engines of this class (not fitted with relief valves) are sluggish when coasting with the result

---

27 Some authorities refer to them as bye-pass valves; as Sir Henry spelt them without the 'e' in his superheater paper to the Institution of Civil Engineers in 1913, that convention has been followed here.

28 Mr S Summerson *Midland Railway Locomotives Vol IV* Irwell Press Ltd Clophill p91.

the train very often pushes the engine and so causes snatching on the couplings.' A hand-written note by Herbert Chambers added 'There was no sign of carbonisation inside the valve casing: mileage 2,367.' This was another problem currently causing concern. A 65% reduction in the weight of carbon removed from N° 3868 was recorded compared to the average figure from ten non fitted engines in May 1919. A comprehensive report of 30 December 1919 after 55,000 miles confirmed the benefits and it was recommended that all new superheater goods be fitted. The last five engines of O.5233, N° 3897-3901, commenced this process and the earlier engines were retrospectively equipped,"

Edgar Larkin has made brief reference[29] to some trials conducted in 1923 on engine N° 3866 investigating the effect that snifting valves had on reducing the carbonization when coasting. The temperature within the rear steam port of the left-hand cylinder was measured using a thermocouple via a pyrometer located in the cab. Readings were taken when the engine coasted a series of down gradients, between Sharnbrook and Oakley (1 in 119), Elstree and Hendon (1 in 160) and the 1 in 200 stretches between St Albans and Radlett, and between Ampthill and Bedford. Steam chest temperature before the regulator was shut was usually around 430°F, without the vacuum relief valves the temperature rose to 500°F within 30 seconds before continuing to reach 620°F by the time the regulator was opened after some 10 or 12 minutes coasting. With the air valves present and the regulator shut, the temperature quickly rose about 40°F and then gradually fell below the original steam chest temperature.

In 1934, soon after his arrival, William Stanier considered that improvements in the design of piston valves and valve gears meant that by-pass valves were no longer needed and gave instructions they were to be removed. He also disliked them because if a by-pass valve failed, it failed the locomotive. As one of his acolytes[30] later

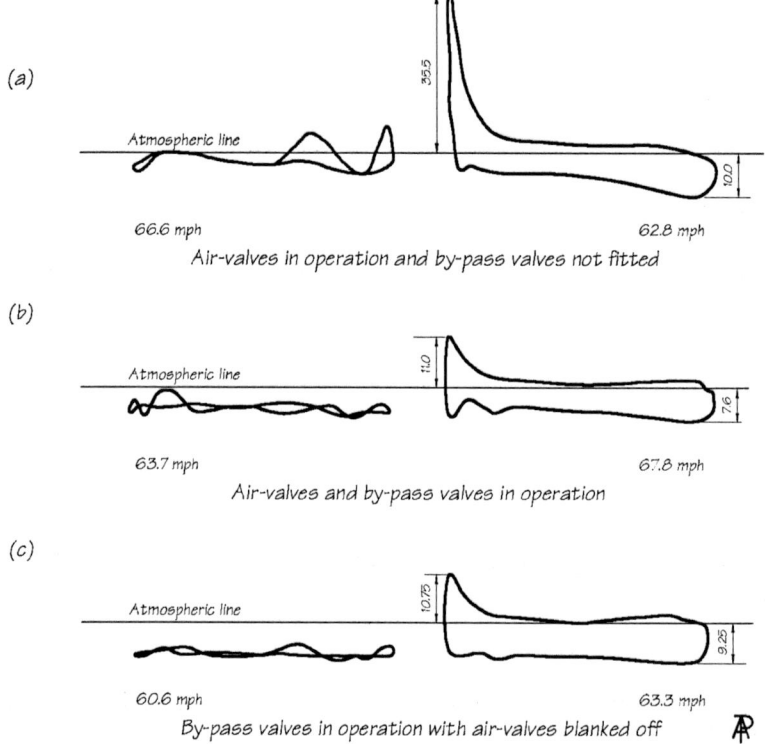

Fig. 8 - By-pass and air-valve performance indicator diagrams - Midland Railway

---

29 Mr E Larkin *Memoirs of a Railway Engineer* Mechanical Engineering Publications London 1979 p33.

30 Mr E S Cox *British Railways Standard Steam Locomotives* Ian Allan Ltd Shepperton 1966 p189.

Earlier in this book, (pp110-1) he stated the reason for applying Caprotti valve gear to some BR Standard Class 5 4-6-0s was because of the superior steam consumption obtained from the BR Class 8 4-6-2. In view of this it is interesting to see Mr Walford give another reason for adopting the gear, which was that it was anticipated to increase the mileage between piston and valve examinations - from 30,000-36,000 miles in the standard engines to 40,000-48,000 in the Caprottis. The reduced wear that permitted this extension, was attributed to the by-pass action of the valves during coasting.

Mr J Walford *British Railways Standard Steam Locomotives*

wrote:-

"... and the so-called air valves which most engines carried, intended to break the vacuum in the steam chests, were ineffective if small, and chattered themselves to pieces if they were large. Another way of reducing the pumping action was to connect the two sides of the piston while coasting by means of bye-pass valves, a feature of many early superheater engines, on which however, the connecting passage was too small to be of the slightest use except at very low speeds."

The indicator diagrams appearing in figure 8 taken at over 60 miles per hour demonstrate despite the comparative smallness of the connecting passages, by-pass valves *were* effective in reducing the resistance of the engine. Incidentally, the Germans tried by-pass valves 8 inches in diameter, which whilst undoubtedly prompted a very free engine when drifting, resulted in no compression. This could be a disadvantage especially at speed apart from the detrimental effect it had on steam economy.

The idea that 'improvements' in valves and gearing justified their removal appears to have been a somewhat spurious argument, and certainly the removal of the valves was regretted by Wellingborough drivers[31]:-

"They contended that whereas a Fowler Class 4F 0-6-0 would coast with its load of empty wagons the 14 miles from Sundon to Bedford when the by-pass valves were fitted, the application of steam was required most of the way after they were removed. I have often wondered whether any controlled tests were made to try and quantify in discrete terms the pros and cons of by-pass valves in all classes so fitted: or whether they and bogie brakes were removed by a new broom who had little experience of such fittings, looking for something to sweep clean, eagerly aided and abetted by elements in the drawing office who had not been brought up in the Midland tradition either. My view has been that it was a mistake to remove them from all classes, they were no trouble if conscientiously maintained."

Another side effect of their removal was that carbonisation once again became a problem, on certain classes at least[32]:-

"Most of the comments on the parallel boiler tank locomotives related to the carbonisation of piston valves, which had increased considerably since the removal of cylinder by-pass valves; often now valves could only be removed from liners when hot. In one case a main steam pipe had had to be removed to enable the piston rings to be broken before the valves could be withdrawn."

Removing the by-pass valves from ex-Midland and certain LMS Standard superheated engines, represented an example of LMS engineers pursuing standardization for the sake of it, even to the point where it compromised locomotive performance.

Large-lap valves: No 'Big Goods' was rebuilt with large-lap valves, although according to Mr Cox a proposal was put forward in the closing years of the Second World War[33]:-

"As has already been indicated individual costing figures and dynamometer car tests were showing up as early as the mid-thirties the coal-saving abilities of long travel valve gear, and as the operators were accumulating experience as to the greater traffic potential of engines so fitted. As one of the reports on post-war development dated 17/6/44 underlined, cylinder renewal was going on all the time, old cylinders with their barrels worn to scrapping thickness being replaced by others to identical design on engines still having a considerable life before them. To mention only two workshops, Crewe was replacing 100 cylinder castings per annum and Derby 87, and the report pointed out the advantage there would be in redesigning the replacements with larger diameter valves, better

---

Volume II: The 4-6-0 & 2-6-0 Classes RCTS 2003 p14.
31 Mr W G F Thorley *A Breath of Steam Vol 1* Ian Allan Ltd Shepperton 1975 p96.
32 Ibid p163.

33 Mr E S Cox *Chronicles of Steam* Ian Allan Shepperton 1967 pp173-4.
James Clayton had rebuilt the SE&CR classes D and E 4-4-0s in order to obtain more powerful locomotives for hauling boat trains, whilst remaining within a very strict weight limit. They performed brilliantly but the company chose not to rebuild all of the engines, although subsequently the Southern did rebuild some of the later class L. Following these examples the LNER and for largely similar reasons, also improved the performance of an inside-cylinder express class – Mr Thompson's re-building of the former GER S69/LNER B12. This improvement was carried out in two stages. Initially the valve travel of N° 8589 was increased in 1931 to 6 1/16ins in place of the original 4 3/16ins by increasing the length of the upper rocket arm at the expense of the lower, also the piston valves were modified to have a lap of 1 13/16ins, as against the original 1 1/8ins. Encouraged by this a more thorough rebuild was carried out which included a larger boiler as well as new cylinders and valves. The gear was modified the rocker arms remained their original lengths while the eccentric rods were shortened and coupled to launch-type expansion links, which were made longer than the originals. Although the eccentric throw remained unaltered at 3½ inches these changes increased valve travel so that the desired full gear travel of 6 1/16ins was again obtained. The enhanced performance of N° 8579, sufficiently impressed Sir Nigel Gresley for him to authorise another 53 examples to be rebuilt in the same way, although a side effect was an enhanced propensity for frame cracks.

ports and passages, and to introduce the unequal armed rocking shafts which would, with Stephenson's valve gear, permit an increase in travel. Such engines as the Derby standard class 2 4-4-0 and class 4 0-6-0 together totalling around 1,000 locomotives would have benefited enormously by the exchange. On the Southern Region, all students of locomotive practice will know how the old Wainwright D and E classes of 4-4-0 were galvanised by just this process, but on the L.M.S. the plea to do likewise met with no response because, unlike the present day, it was the capital expenditure itself and not the return upon capital spent which loomed largest in the eyes of accountants. Even so the additional first cost would have been relatively small if the alteration had been undertaken only when cylinders had to be renewed anyway."

not against valve gear experiments, for on 24th October 1928 the Locomotive Committee granted Sir Henry Fowler permission to rebuild five ex-LNWR 'Claughton' class 4-6-0s with Lentz rotary gear. Two years later, it was decided the 'Claughton' was not a suitable guinea pig, instead it was decided to fit the Lentz gear to *three Class 4 0-6-0s* and a pair of 2-6-4Ts. Six months or so after Sir Henry had been replaced by Ernest Lemon, it was finally decided to fit five Horwich 'Crabs' with the gear and the much delayed valve gear substitution was carried out later that year. Thus, contrary to what Mr Cox suggests, it *does* seem that if a sound case could be presented then monies

Fig. 9 - Ex-Midland 'Big Goods' Nº 3895 passing through Elstree on the up slow in early LMS days. It is seen passing under the aqueduct just before entering Elstree New Tunnel with a train it was designed to haul. Midland pattern air valves fitted to the frames near the base of the smokebox.

This seems a strange statement, for if it is taken at its face value, he is implying that the company's accountants were unwilling to accept any modification improving locomotive performance after the engine had been built – *even if it saved coal*. If these rules really applied in the manner Mr Cox suggests, then no LMS owned locomotive should have been fitted with a superheater, unless it had been *built* with one, which is plainly nonsense. For example, the last Midland built Compound was not superheated until 1928 also many of the 'Flatiron' 0-6-4Ts were not superheated until LMS days. Likewise by this reckoning, no locomotives would have been retrofitted with exhaust steam injectors, but as we have seen the Locomotive and Electrical Committee was perfectly agreeable to approving engine improvements. Furthermore, the LMS was

for an experimental rebuilding would have been made available.

Reference to table III confirms that in general goods and mineral working, as exemplified by the class 7 0-8-0s, long travel valves could effect very little improvement in coal consumption because the speed was low. Further, as Mr Holcroft demonstrated[34] and the Great Western practised, short-lap locomotives could be just as efficient as large-lap engines when employed on local and semi-fast passenger traffic, simply because the trains were not run at sufficiently high speeds for long enough for larger port openings to be of much

---

34 Mr H Holcroft *Locomotive Adventure (Vol II)* Ian Allan 1965 pp56-65.

See also to the author's book *An Introduction to Large-Lap Valves and their Use on the LMS* for a deeper exploration of this.

benefit. Although the Great Western built large numbers of locomotives fitted with large-lap valves, it was careful to ensure that by and large their presence was restricted to those engines employed on services that could exploit the benefits for a high proportion of the time[35]. Accordingly the company elected not to fit them to small engines employed on more humble duties, so as a direct consequence of this policy, it built during the '20s, '30s and '40s, as many if not more, short-lap engines than it did those fitted with large-lap valves.

In the bottom left corner is the left leading splasher, with behind it the main frame plate and the oil box serving the guides - its partner may be seen opposite on the inside of the right-hand frame plate. In the centre of the photograph are upper portions of the two rocker arms which drive the piston valves. Intermediate links provided because valve is constrained to travel in a straight line while the rocker moved in an arc. Between the nearer rocker and the frame are the two rods that drive the ratchet of the two lubricators, which in accordance with BR memo 358/16 have both been set to deliver the maximum quantity of oil. They oscillated in a fore and aft direction in unison with the short vertical link seen immediately behind the nearer piston valve rocker. This motion was derived from an upward extension provided on the nearside suspension link which supported the expansion link. Proceeding this way ensured the movement given to the lubricator was nominally the same irrespective of the cut-off although the mean angle of swing will have changed. The small bore pipes present delivered oil from the lubricators.

Fig. 10 - View of the upper portions of the rocker arms
– Class 4 N° 4027

Indeed Mr Cox had actual experience of the sense this approach when reporting some findings in a memorandum[36] he wrote to Mr Symes regarding the performance of the Standard 2-6-4 tank engines that had replaced ex-LNWR 'Precursor' tanks on Watford and Tring suburban trains:-

"Between May and August this year 12 standard 2-6-4 tank engines Nos. 2306–2309 and 2375–2382 were received at Watford Shed to replace 12 precursor Tanks nos. 6781–6794 (except Nos. 6788 and 6792) on the residential services. Of these latter, three are still in service, two are stored, and the remainder have been transferred elsewhere.

An investigation into the working of the two classes has been made, and the following are the principal points:-

Coal Consumption.

Over corresponding periods the 12 2-6-4 tanks averaged 42.8 lbs. per mile, and the 12 precursor tanks 54.1 lbs. per mile, a saving in favour of the former of 21%. The difference is accounted for by the new engines having superheated steam at 200 lbs./sq. in., piston valves, long lap valve gear and exhaust steam injectors. The old engines were saturated with slide valves and Joy's valve gear."

However, the majority of the 21 per cent reduction in coal consumption was not due to the presence of large lap valves for much of the time the engines would have been stationary, drifting, or accelerating from or slowing down for a station stops, situations when larger laps are of little benefit. Such operation will have also compromised the benefits the exhaust steam injector could bestow. In practice most of the reason for the reduced coal consumption was due to superheating allied with a boiler pressed to 40lbs/sq in higher working pressure. Of course had the short-lap 'Precursor Tanks' been superheated and provided with *grates* of identical size, then the margin of economy displayed by the 2-6-4 tanks would have been reduced yet further. After all, any number of trials conducted in the early years of the twentieth century between, otherwise identical superheated and saturated engines recorded savings in coal of around 15 to 20 per cent.

It seems highly probable, that if senior LMS locomotive engineers *had* considered rebuilding

---

35 The 28xx class 2-8-0 was perhaps a partial exception to this policy but it did use a standard cylinder casting. Interestingly, a few 28xx class members were withdrawn before the last of the Western Region's short-lap, non-standard ex-ROD 2-8-0s.
36 Mr E S Cox *Standard 2-6-4 Tank Engines and 'Precursor'*

Tank Engines on Watford and Tring Residential Services memo to Mr S J Symes 9th November 1932.

A Defence of the Midland LMS Class 4 0-6-0

the Class 4 0-6-0 with large-lap valves along the lines Mr Cox proposed was financially viable, then a case could have been made. As the examples given earlier demonstrate, Mr Cox knew precisely how to prepare a successful financial case to the Mechanical and Electrical Engineering Committee for modifying a class so that it would save coal. Perhaps the reason they were not rebuilt was not through accountant's objections *per se,* but rather the likely fuel saving was considered too small. By 1944 some of the traffic the Class 2 4-4-0 and the Class 4 0-6-0 had traditionally handled was intended to be moved by more modern classes so this would have reduced the financial benefits of such a rebuilding. Indeed, by the mid-1940s under George Ivatt thoughts were turning towards 2-6-0s; work on William Stanier's and Tom Coleman's preference for modern inside cylinder 0-6-0 replacements was stopped, outside cylinders and pony trucks were now the way forward. Although the Class 4 would still be sometimes called on to haul excursions and other passenger trains the new engines would have been expected to have creamed off most of that and the faster non-passenger traffic. Finally, as will be demonstrated later, when working low speed goods trains there was just not the saving in coal to be had from large-lap valves.

Ironically, alone of the Midland inspired LMS Standard Classes, the Class 4 0-6-0 was provided with indirect motion, and it was this arrangement of Stephenson's valve gear that Messers Clayton and Thompson exploited to lengthen the valve travel in the express engines they improved. Consequently this would have made the Standard Freight the easiest Derby design to alter. Indeed one envisages that the engine would have become even closer to its already near relative the Southern Railway class Q 0-6-0, also from the pencil of James Clayton. Of course, had this modification been proceeded with, it would all have been rather embarrassing if the rebuilt 'old-fashioned' 0-6-0 class returned a better performance than the Mogul - as I believe it had the potential to do.

Chapter Three

Frames and Cracks

Introduction

Mr Cox[1] writing in 1967 averred that the 'Big Goods' was heavy on its frames:-

> "The 0-6-0 was also an inveterate frame breaker even if not to the woeful extent of the L.N.W. engines. The extent of this defect was such that long afterwards in Fairburn's time sets of spare frames were assembled in the shops, so that they could be substituted at General Repair for badly flawed frames as they came into the works, with the object of reducing the overall time the engine was out of service."

Just how bad the situation could be, with 'an inveterate frame breaker', is demonstrated in the case of the ex-LNWR 'Prince of Wales' class[2],

---

1 Mr E S Cox *Chronicles of Steam* Ian Allan London 1967 p37.

2 Ibid pp34-5.

> "When the 'Prince of Wales' class was evolved out of the former 'Experiment' by the fitting of a superheater and larger cylinders, very little alteration had been made to the strength of the frames to take the higher stresses due to the increased piston load of the 20½" dia. as against the 19" dia. cylinders and in consequence frame fractures had reached epidemic proportions. These fractures occurred just before or just behind the left leading driving hornblocks. As soon as a crack appeared its progress was watched, and when it reached 15" or 20" in length, the frame was welded up, either at the C.M.E. shops, or, if at the shed, by welders sent down from Crewe, the shed people having prepared the fracture beforehand. For each weld the engine had to be taken out of service, the wheels dropped, horns removed and the crack vee-ed out by chipping in order to present a suitable profile. After welding, the frame had to be chipped and ground truly flat, the hornblocks rebolted in position and the wheels re-assembled. The whole process took a week to ten days, and represented very hard and disagreeable work to the staff concerned.
>
> In our investigation we found that at Crewe in 1930 for example, out of 48 engines stationed there, 24 had had their frames welded. Up to April 8th, 1931, there had been 14 further cases, six of these being on engines which had already been dealt with in 1930. One engine had had three fractures within 9 months. At Edge Hill, out of 14 stationed, 7 engines had undergone the process during the past 12 months. Of these, two were already going again, and one had fractures both in front of and behind the left leading horns simultaneously. At Preston 6 out of 12 engines stationed there were dealt with in 1930, at Patricroft 9 out of 23. But this was not all, for also during 1930, the 246 engines in the class had suffered no less than 161 hot boxes of which 117 occurred at the left leading position. These did not always happen at the moment when adjacent frame fractures were also just ready

however, Mr Cox was referring to a period about seven or eight years after the decision had been made to remove the centre bearing from those former Crewe classes fitted with Joy valve gear. Until then, a longitudinal bracket extended from the rear of the motion plate to the frame stay in front of the firebox and accommodated within it was a miniature horn and axlebox assembly that surrounded and supported the central portion of the crank axle. The presence of this bearing, reduced some of the stress that otherwise would have appeared in the frame plates around the top corners of the horn gaps. Of course, should LMS engineers[3] chose to remove them, then they have only themselves to blame for the resulting rise in frame fractures! Whatever the reasons for the cracking in the ex-LNWR classes, can we really imagine William Stanier would have tolerated

---

> for attention, and the unfortunate engines had to be taken out of service sometimes for hot boxes and at other times for fractures in a most random manner, with the opportunity of doing both jobs at once not always coinciding. The record of the right leading axleboxes, and those on the intermediate and trailing axles was much better, so that the means of lubrication and the design of the axlebox itself, although they much to be desired, were at least standing up to the loads imposed. Both the frames and the axleboxes were in fact grossly overloaded at the Left Leading position.
>
> Although all this trouble was brought to light in the manner described, the engines had been built at intervals since 1911 and there can be no question whatever that these defects must have shown themselves in progressive degree through the 20 years in between. It baffles the imagination to think of the volume of unproductive and back-breaking work which all this must have represented, and of the complacency of the then C.M.E. and design sections which had presumably looked upon it all as an act of God, and not one which called for remedy by drastic redesign. This kind of thing was one of the very worst features of so many of the old companies."

3 In private correspondence Mr Edward Talbot related to me, how during the 1930s Colonel K Cantlie, who had been a premium apprentice at Crewe during the Great War, was asked by William Stanier why so many of the former LNWR passenger classes such as the 'Princes' and 'Georges' were suffering from cracked frames. Not knowing the reason, he said he would find out - inspecting a few engines at Camden revealed the absence of the centre bearings - and the mystery was solved.

something approaching that propensity in the Class 4, which effectively remained in production for the ten years following his arrival, *if* its frame performance been as bad as this? Should it have been, then here really was incentive enough to develop the successor to the 'Big Goods' something which Sir William appears not to have taken really seriously. Fortunately, Mr Bond, who was Works Manager of Crewe during the Second World War also referred to the provision of spare frames[4]:-

"We were at this time running into a cycle of heavy frame repairs. Crewe locomotives had never had really adequate main frames, and the situation was now aggravated by increasing trouble with cracks in the high tensile frames of the standard *Class 5* 4-6-0s. A stock of spare boilers had long been regarded as indispensable for reducing the time out of traffic of locomotives undergoing repairs. If, as was now the case, heavy frame repairs were taking up to a fortnight for engines which were due out of the Erecting Shop in six to eight days, why not spare frames? It seemed to me entirely logical to apply to frames the same argument as for boilers. We obtained authority to build three sets of frames complete with cylinders, dragboxes, and all other fittings, one for *Class 5* 4-6-0s, one for L.N.W. G1 0-8-0s, and one for the standard *Class 4* 0-6-0s, these being the most numerous classes in which interchangeability could be fully exploited."

Without wishing to read too much into it, Mr Bond's account suggests the provision of a spare set of frames for the Standard Freight was primarily because the size of the class, rather than Mr Cox's suggestion that it was an awful design with a *particular* predilection to crack its frames. Indeed earlier when co-author of a major paper[5] concerning frame fractures on the LMS, he had rated the class as 'medium' in this respect; a grading it shared with the far newer Class 5 4-6-0. Indeed the *incidences* of fatigue cracking in the latter class, especially the earlier members, had become so serious Mr Ivatt commissioned a special investigation from the Research Department of the LMS. The CME's department, of which Mr Cox was by then a senior member, had in effect admitted that it was unable to solve the problem.

In an earlier short report[6], Sir Henry Fowler referred to the causes of a number of fractures in locomotives, *viz.* crank axles, straight axles (engine and tender), tyres, crank pins, coupling rods and details:-

"I have had classified the fractures and failures which have been investigated by the L.M.S. Central Materials Inspection Bureau during the five years ending December 1930, and I find that the above constitute 53.7 per cent. of the whole, the others occurring in Motion, including Valve and Reversing Gear, and miscellaneous items such as Spring Gear, Piston Details, Brake Gear, etc."

Thus, although frame cracks occurred Sir Henry made no reference to their existence, while implied in Mr Cox's opinion of the frame performance of the 'Big Goods' is the assumption that the cracking could have been easily avoided. This was not so, as the necessary analysis techniques for establishing a crack-free performance from a locomotive frame did not exist at the time the class was built. The only way such an outcome could have been achieved would have been by repeatedly testing and modification of a prototype design. This was expensive and time consuming, so because the cracks developed slowly, the desired refinement was obtained by evolution – observation of the design in service. Thus, in each of its 0-6-0 classes, and even on occasions between batches of nominally the same class, the Midland usually took the opportunity of modifying the frame in some way. In contrast, the obvious danger to life that failure of an aeroplane structure presented necessitated a different approach. The drawings and calculations, were made by highly skilled designers, stressmen and draughtmen, using the most scientific methods with every detail meticulously checked. Once these people had done their sums the strength calculations were checked independently by an entirely different team of experts. Thus the final structural predictions were about as accurate and painstaking was humanly possible. Finally, to make quite certain an actual full-scale airframe was tested to destruction, to demonstrate the structure had the strength capacity demanded plus 20 per cent. Between 1935 and 1955, roughly 100 different kinds of aeroplane were built and thoroughly tested. Given the great care taken over the design and calculations we might have expected the various test results to have appeared very close to the 120 per cent loading, but in practice nothing of the sort happened. The

---

4 Mr R C Bond *A Lifetime with Locomotives* Goose & Son Cambridge 1975 p145.

5 Mr E S Cox & Dr F C Johansen *Locomotive Frames* I Loco E Paper 473 November 1947.

6 Sir Henry Fowler *Fractures* – Locomotive 20th January 1931.

experimental strengths were randomly distributed between 50 per cent and 150 per cent of the required load. In other words, the most eminent stressmen and designers could not be relied upon to predict the strength of an aeroplane within a range of three to one – some were less than half as strong as they should have been. When we consider the resources locomotive designers had to draw on, maybe they did not do so badly with their estimates of stress intensities and their location. However, their creations were vulnerable to one specific form of failure – metal fatigue – but aeronautical designers also suffered from this as well for strength tests are not good predictors of fatigue. Fatigue is perhaps the most insidious cause of the loss of strength in a metal structure. It represents the cumulative effect of fluctuating loads, and was the overwhelming reason for cracks developing in locomotive frames. However, before we explore some of the reasons why it occurred and why designers found it so difficult to avoid its destructive powers, let us consider the loads that a frame was subjected to.

Loads Present in a Locomotive Frame

The frame was intended as the foundation to carry the boiler as well as serving as a means for attaching the cylinders and for locating and maintaining the correct positions of the wheel and axle assemblies both transversely and longitudinally. Provision had to be included to allow the engine to negotiate curves by providing sufficient transverse clearances between the flanges and the rails, the wheels and the axleboxes, and the axleboxes and the horn guides, along with whatever flexibility the designer thought the frame should possess. When in use, it experienced a complex series of forces prompted principally by the deadweight of the engine, the piston thrusts, buffing and drawbar loads plus the springing and braking loads and those incurred negotiating curves. The latter forces included those caused by the side thrust from the flanges of the wheels, though to reduce these strains the centre flanges were frequently thinned or sometimes flangeless wheels were adopted. The frame of course had to

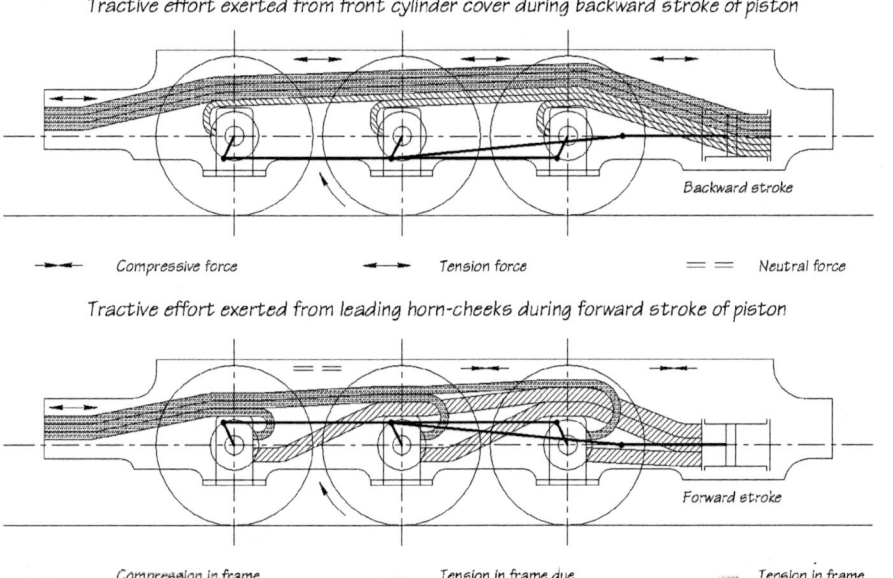

Diagram derived from a paper by Mr C W Clarke and illustrates his hypothesis regarding the distribution of stress within a frame plate. The tractive effort was exerted from the front cylinder cover for the backward stroke of the piston and from the leading faces of the coupled wheel horns during the forward stroke. The portion of the frame between the cylinders and the leading coupled axle was thus in tension for one-half of a revolution and compression for the other half. The section of frame plate behind the driving axle did not suffer compressive forces while the engine was in fore gear. For the portions of frame plate between the driving and coupled axles, the maximum tensile stress was lower than that forward of the leading coupled axle, when as here, the loads are considered to act in a horizontal plane only.

Although frame cracking patterns largely support this hypothesis, one weakness is that it assumed the tractive effort at any time was generated by all of the coupled wheels, each axle making an equal contribution. According to André Chapelon this was not the case. He averred that the coupled axles only contributed tractive effort, and then one axle at a time, once the adhesive limit of the driving axle had been exceeded. This further suggests that the axle(s) in front of the driving axle and the latter would be the most susceptible to developing cracks, with the axle(s) after the driving axle being less prone - which was broadly the case.

Fig. 11 - Traction forces in a locomotive frame

A Defence of the Midland/LMS Class 4 0-6-0

transmit without deforming, the pull produced by the engine either onto its tender drawbar or in the case of tank engines direct onto its train, while concurrently withstanding those shocks resulting from its passage over the track including points and crossings. Brian Reed estimated that the driving mechanism of a Great Northern Atlantic running from King's Cross to York experienced 95,000 reversals of stress, plus 25,000 separate uncushioned shocks on each wheel-and-axle pair through rail joints and crossings which had to be taken up by the springs to prevent transfer *in toto* to the rest of the machine. There were in addition, miscellaneous loads incurred such as the practice of lifting locomotives either bodily via attachments at the extreme ends of the frame plates or at one end only by means of shear legs. The frame structure had to be robust enough to withstand this treatment, for it was common to effect the lifting with the horn-stays removed.

In most designs, the frame plates were continuous from one end to the other, although some might incorporate joggles and offsets to provide for example additional clearances for bogie wheels, while in others, it comprised separate plates with lapped joints to serve the same purpose. In either case, the plates were held apart and parallel to one another by means of stretchers located between the front buffer beam and the drag beam. The presence of inside cylinders located under the smokebox and the drag-box assisted materially in holding the frame plates parallel to one another. In front of the firebox, there was usually a stretcher and behind the cylinders, at a distance of 2½-3½ feet was located the motion plate, which supported the slidebars as well as usually portions of the valve gear. Behind the front buffer beam, the frames were stayed by gusset supports while outside the frames some further support was provided by the platform, valance (or outside frame[7]) and the intervening stays or brackets. The drag-box,

motion plate and the stretchers could be cast, fabricated from plate and angles, or built up from pressings.

While the combination of a narrow firebox with inside cylinders and motion conspired to limit the amount of lateral stiffness that could be provided if access to the motion was not to be restricted, in practice this did not necessarily compromise frame performance. However, in the case of outside cylinder engines since designers retained the same general design, the much greater racking forces caused by the wider cylinder centres demanded more elaborate frame bracing and staying,

Fig. 12 – Another view of LMS Standard Class 4 N° 4260 of Lot 29 to Order 6473 while under construction in Derby Works.

particularly in the section extending from immediately behind the smokebox to where the outside motion brackets were attached. This was not always provided.

To allow the axleboxes vertical (and sideways) movement and for the wheel sets to be removable open slots or horn gaps were cut in the plates. These were provided with either hornblocks or horn guides which served to provide sufficient rubbing and thrust area for the driving and coupled axleboxes where they interfaced with the frames. Guides differed from hornblocks in having no connecting portion at the top. With separate guides, the vertical lug cast on their rear face was arranged to butt against the opening in the frame plate relieving the securing bolts of any shear stress. In the case of solid hornblocks, it was far more

---

[7] This was the Midland Railway's term for the valance and was presumably a hangover from Mr Kirtley's time when the outside frame really was an outside frame.

difficult to ensure the block butted up hard against the frame opening in both the fore and aft directions. Deficiencies in fitting meant that a certain degree of shear inevitably came onto the bolts securing hornblocks to the frame plate so notwithstanding the care expended during erection, the securing bolts regularly worked loose in service, no matter how well they may have been fitted initially.

Although the manner by which the reciprocating action of the piston was converted into rotary motion is well known, what is perhaps less well appreciated is the process by which the ensuing piston forces passed through the frame. For these forces, illustrated in figures 11 and 13, had a direct influence on frame performance because they inflicted an alternating stress on portions of the structure. With the engine in fore gear and the steam acting on the rear face of the piston shewn, as the crank pin moved from the back quarter (*i.e.* centre) through the top quarter to the front quarter or centre, it exerted a force that was transmitted to the front horn-cheeks via the axles and axleboxes. The force also acted on the rear of the cylinder

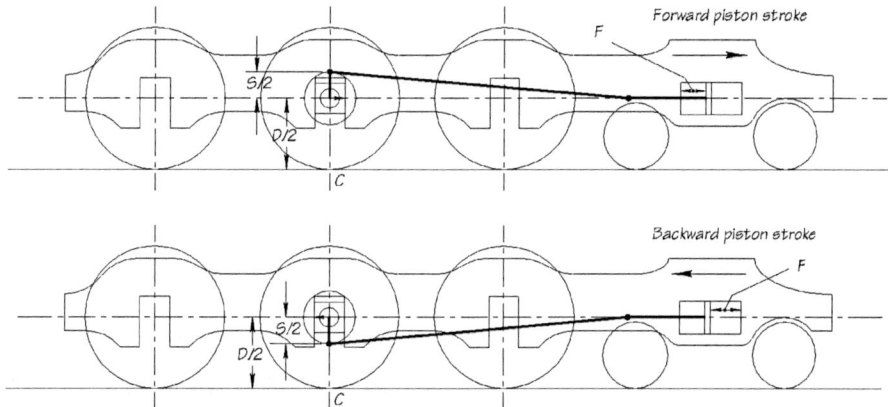

Although the diagram is of a 4-6-0, the explanation assumes it is running at speed and that the tractive effort developed is within the adhesive limit of the driving wheels with nothing transmitted through the coupling rods. The distance between the centre of the axle and the rail is equal to one-half the driving wheel diameter *(D/2)* and the throw of the crank is equal to one-half the stroke *(S/2)*.

With the engine moving forwards and the pistons moving from the rear of the cylinder to the front, the steam pressure exerts a force F lbs on the piston and via the connecting rod this force acts on the crank pin. The same force F also acts backwards on the rear cylinder cover and since the cylinder is attached to the frame, the front horn cheek is forced against the axlebox with the same force, pressing in turn the axlebox onto the axle. However, the wheel and crank pin form a lever that acts in opposition with its fulcrum formed at C the point of contact of the wheel with the rail. The force that the driving box exerts on the front horn face when there is a force of F lbs acting on the crank pin is given by:-

$$\frac{F \times (D/2 + S/2)}{D/2} \quad \text{which may be simplified to } F \times (1 + S/D)$$

So by summing the forward and backward acting forces and considering the former positive and the latter negative:-

$$[F \times (1 + S/D)] - F \quad \text{or} \quad [F + (F \times S)/D] - F$$

which simplifies to $(F \times S/D)$ *i.e.* the tractive effort exerted by the wheel

Considering the backward stroke of the piston, the action is somewhat different. The steam now exerts its force F on the front cylinder cover and this serves to pull the rear horn face onto the rear of the driving axlebox. The force F also acts on the piston but now the crank position has changed and with it the action of the lever formed by the wheel and crank. From the law of levers a force is created that pushes the driving box backwards against the rear horn face given by:-

$$\frac{-F \times (D/2 - S/2)}{D/2} \quad \text{which may be simplified to } F \times (1 - S/D)$$

Summing the forward and backward acting forces as before:-

$$F - [F \times (1 - S/D)] \quad \text{or} \quad F - [F + (F \times S)/D]$$

which simplifies to $(F \times S/D)$ the same value for tractive effort as before.

From this analysis we may see the nett pressure exerted by the driving box on the front horn face moves the engine forward on the forward piston stroke, while the nett pressure on the front cylinder cover moves it forward during the backward piston stroke. Another way of considering it, is that the piston moves through the cylinder on its forward stoke, but the cylinder moves over the piston on its backward stroke. Since the driving box is alternatively forced against the front and rear horn faces excessive wear can result in significant impacts. If the frame was cracked between the cylinder and the driving box the break would close during the forward piston stroke and open during the backward one.

Fig. 13 - How tractive effort is exerted

with the result the intervening section of frame between the driving axle and the cylinder was put into compression. During the rearward passage of the piston, when the crank pin moved from the front centre through the bottom quarter to the back centre, the engine was 'pulled' forward by the pressure on the front cylinder cover so the force on the horn-cheeks was then reversed, *i.e.* towards the rear of the engine and the intervening section of frame was put into tension.

The combination of the resultant forces arising from adding a second or more cylinders considerably complicated the position and thus the stresses in the frames, while other details, such as the position, type and strength of springs, affected the manner in which the engine rode. These were factors predominantly within the control of the designer as opposed to the enginemen, but the driver could nevertheless affect the riding of the engine through his selection of the cut-off for any given conditions of road and load. Too short a cut-off could produce rough riding and thus promote crack progression. According to André Chapelon, the first engineer to recognize that in a two-cylinder locomotive the forces set up in the frames by the cylinder thrusts were not equal on both sides was Mr Loewy of the South Western of Russia in 1893, while in the first edition of his book *La Locomotive à Vapeur*, the Frenchman gave an example demonstrating that with the cylinders at 7ft centres and the frames at 3ft 6ins centres, the stresses in the frame on the side of the leading crank were about 15 per cent higher than those in the frame plate on the opposite side.

Frame Design

Although calculations concerning the strength of discrete components were carried out in the drawing office as part of the design process, this was not necessarily a feature of every item. For as the following extract[8] confirms, obtaining an accurate assessment of the stresses in parts such as a frame stay was very difficult while stress analysing a frame plate or a complete frame was impossible:-

"The third general feature which impressed me in the drawing office was the way that many drawings were made so-to-speak by 'rule of thumb', or by the subjective criterion of whether a feature of design 'looked right'. During my technical courses I was using a slide-rule many times a day, but in just under 12 months in Doncaster Drawing Office I had occasion to use a slide-rule only twice – and that over a considerable variety of tasks. I do not wish to infer that sophisticated calculations would have produced substantially better components, but would simply state it as a fact of common occurrence that many design decisions were often arrived at by remarks such as: 'In (such-and-such) a previous design we used a plate ¾in thick, so ¾in should be all right in this application', or even: '1in diameter looks about right', or again 'The British Standard dimension is 7/16in, so we'll round it up to ½in', and 'These pins have been breaking at ½in diameter, so we had better fatten them up to 5/8in.'

The stresses could have been calculated in most parts, although many – such as frame stays – might have defied such analysis. And from these stresses the sections required could have been determined by the application of an appropriate factor of safety. But since rule-of-thumb methods saved so much bother, and since experience showed that the resultant parts did not fail in service, what was the virtue in going to the trouble of niceties of dimension? This was not, of course, so in the design of boilers, where the stresses were fairly accurately calculable, or in most of the motion components such as piston-rods. On the other hand, there were plenty of parts which were unnecessarily massive or heavy."

Nevertheless, it must be appreciated that some of these rules-of-thumb were of dubious reliability[9]:-

"The senior draughtsman under whom he had served his time in the drawing office in England had a rule of thumb based on experience. He maintained that under the best conditions, the minimum sectional area of the mild steel frame plate above the gap for ordinary conditions should be in sq. inches equal to the diameter of the cylinder. The allowance should be made 10 to 33 per cent. above it to suit the condition of service track, etc. For example, if the cylinder diameter was 20 in., he would allow 20 sq. inches as minimum, if the engine was for Brazil, he would put up, say, 27 sq. inches, if it was for England probably 22 sq. inches."

Since the magnitude of the piston load, the principal stress in a frame is the product of the cylinder diameter squared and working pressure, this empirical formula does not have a rational basis – it tends to make the frames of larger locomotives proportionately weaker.

The main reason for the absence of a full analysis of the frame stresses was simply from the shear

---

8 Mr E S Beavor *Steam Was My Calling* Ian Allan Ltd Shepperton 1974 pp51-2.

9 Mr S L Saxsena contributing to the discussion following:- Mr C W Clarke *Locomotive Hornblocks* I Loco E Paper N° 407 1939.

difficulty of estimating with sufficient accuracy the magnitude and lines of action of the various forces acting within the plates when in service. The other reason however was even if these forces could have been quantified there was no method available then, of calculating the ensuing stresses in such complicated structures. Not until during the Second World War, when the relaxation method was developed for quantifying the stresses in bridges and aeroplanes, did a method exist that could be applied to engines. Nevertheless, this method demanded large numbers of repetitive calculations – very time consuming in the days before computers – further it could not be used to design a frame from given data but rather to estimate the stresses that would appear in a frame structure that had been designed traditionally. Thus, the science of designing crack-free plate frames for steam locomotives was never solved, as the unknowns were too extensive for contemporary analytical methods. Perhaps this resulted in suspect formulae such as that used by Mr Saxsena's senior draughtsman, remaining in use.

As practically, every part of a locomotive frame plate was subject to fluctuating or alternating loads amongst the most important factors in its design were the fatigue strength of the material and of the presence of local stress raisers. Mr Beavor[10] has a pertinent comment concerning this aspect of locomotive design as well:-

"Even when locomotive parts were designed with generous factors of safety (or of ignorance) little, if any, account was taken of their dimensions in respect of resistance to fatigue. Certainly internal corners were often machined with a radius instead of being made square 'so as to avoid concentrations of stress'. But little was known about fatigue limits – thus many parts which were otherwise of satisfactory section failed after millions of reversals of stress. Whenever a component broke with the characteristic 'growth lines' of such a fracture, this was sagely described as 'metal aged' – as though it were a mysteriously unpredictable phenomenon.

To the best of my knowledge nobody ever specified a 'fatigue life' for any locomotive part, or ordered its withdrawal after so many hundreds of thousands of miles of running. Since items such as axles and connecting rods, which occasionally failed due to fatigue, were separately registered, it should have presented no special difficulty to record the mileage run by such failed parts, and to have laid down limits beyond which they would not have been permitted to run on particular engines. Some built-up crank axles were withdrawn after 250,000 miles of running, but this was due to a tendency to work loose – not due to fatigue.

The older locomotives, although often very long lived, were not much subject to this trouble since they were not intensively used, and most of them did not run at high rotational speeds which caused high reciprocating stresses. Undoubtedly many vibrating parts, particularly plate work, broke due to fatigue, and these were simply repaired by welding, or were replaced without the cause of the fracture being properly understood. Often better support could have been provided for the parts concerned, thus considerably damping the stresses by reducing the amplitude of the vibrations."

It was the practice to base the frame design of a new locomotive on previous experience with the weight of metal allowable disposed largely through tradition abiding by the need to have sufficient located to support the various components of the locomotive and their anticipated forces. In this respect, the Midland 'Big Goods' frame might be taken as typical since it represented the final development of the Midland single-framed 0-6-0 frame, which had undergone steady evolution since 1875 when the company's first examples appeared. It was not of course unique in this, for during the nineteenth century there was progress in the design and construction of all locomotive frames, facilitated initially in no small way by the introduction of single wrought iron plates long enough to suit 2-4-0s, 0-6-0s, 4-4-0s and 0-4-4Ts *etc*. The adoption of mild steel plates in the last quarter of the century allowed higher piston loads to be transmitted and weights carried without the need for any thickening of the frames over the then nearly universal one-inch thickness. The introduction of 4-4-2, 4-6-0s and 4-6-2s however marked a discernible trend by engineers in the twentieth century to adopt thicker frame plates whenever weight constraints permitted, thus 1⅛ins or even 1¼ins became not uncommon, the latter thickness being particularly favoured in Scotland. Despite this enhanced thickness, frames became a weak point, particularly in the large multi-cylinder engines then becoming popular, for they exhibited a particular propensity for cracking. Thus by 1939 not one of the 79 LNER 180lbs and 220lbs/sq in three-cylinder Pacifics of 1922-34 was still running with its original frames[11], while the

---

10 Mr E S Beavor *Steam Was My Calling* Ian Allan Ltd Shepperton 1974 pp52-3.

11 Mr B Reed *The LNER Non-Streamlined Pacifics Locomotive Profile N° 1* Profile Publications Ltd Windsor p20.

rate of frame cracks in the LMS 'Royal Scots' more than quadrupled in six years. Mr Towroe[12], a locomotive engineer trained at the Vulcan Foundry who joined the Southern Railway in 1932, commented on the impact cylinder layout could have on frame reliability in multi-cylinder locomotives. Whilst his views were directed at LSWR designs roughly contemporary with the 'Big Goods', as will be revealed they are equally applicable to some later designs and not just four-cylinder engines:-

> "The first 4-6-0s on the LSWR had been built by Drummond in 1905, the 'F13' class, with four cylinders. Two inside cylinders beneath the smokebox drove the leading pair of driving wheels, and two outside cylinders were positioned adjacent to the leading coupled wheels to drive the middle pair. The divided drive arrangement of a four-cylinder engine followed that adapted with the 4-2-2-0 type No 720 produced in 1897...
>
> ...Engine No 720 performed less well than the ordinary two-cylinder 4-4-0s but, nothing daunted, Drummond built five more 4-2-2-0s in 1901 with smaller boilers. In all his 4-2-2-0s, as with Webb's, the inside and outside cylinders were separated by a length of frame. The stresses set up by the thrusts of separate cylinders caused fatigue cracks in a portion of the frame which could not be made deeper without fouling the bogie wheels.
>
> ... Drummond was an obstinate Scot and in due time his obstinacy cost the company more money because the five 'F13' 4-6-0s cracked their frames in just the same places. Transmitting the drive in that way certainly avoided the concentration of weight and stress on one driving axle and the principle was employed by other engineers. It was the location of the cylinders which caused trouble. A better arrangement was to have the cylinder blocks in line and to divide the drive by differences in length either of the piston rods or the connecting rods, or both.
>
> Picking holes in the work of past designers, of course, can sound supercilious, so let us hasten to imagine the difficulties that they had to contend with, on the LSWR in particular. The only instrumentation that was available for test purposes was the steam engine indicator which drew a diagram of the compression and expansion within the cylinder. Alloy steels, case hardening processes, crack detectors, strain gauges, and so on, were non-existent, or in their infancy. Ultrasonic testing and industrial X-ray photography lay in the future. When parts of a locomotive broke or developed cracks the cause was often a matter of guesswork, the cure to increase the thickness of metal. Engines were allowed to run with cracked spokes, frames, hornblocks and cylinder castings, provided that the cracks were marked and regularly inspected by running shed fitters for any sign of worsening."

The first of Mr Johnson's Midland 0-6-0s comprised the 120 4ft - 10½ins class B which were built with a class B (round topped) boiler followed a few years later by the first 5ft - 2½ins examples – Dübs built class H. All of these earliest examples were provided with hornblocks, but commencing in 1880 with the next batch of 5ft - 2½ ins engines, Stephenson built class H, separate horn guides were adopted. This new arrangement was retained with only minor changes, principally concerned with the number of fixing bolts and the hornstay arrangement, for all of the Midland six-coupled engines built subsequently, including the Class 4. Furthermore, those earlier 0-6-0s given new frames in the early twentieth century, were arranged to receive separate horns. James Clayton[13], who was present in the drawing office when the replacement and Class 4 frames were designed, opined:-

> "With regard to the hornblocks, I myself have no love for the horseshoe type. I think one could not have a better example of what not to use if one wants to prevent loose axlebox guides. When the guides are coupled across the top, as in the horseshoe type, all the force is concentrated inside the frame so formed, and it is not only the pull then, but the push also, which tends to loosen the horns; and in my opinion the single slides are quite reliable. The horseshoe part of the guides does not strengthen the frame one iota, for fractures occur and develop in the frame with this as well as with any other type."

That the Midland design of separate guides was highly thought of is confirmed by Colonel Kitson who, while Chairman of the Leeds Centre of the Institution of Loco Engineers and looking back over a period of thirty years or so, singled out this particular design for praise[14]:-

> "We have made and fitted at our works all of the types of horn blocks and axleboxes which have been mentioned, viz., horseshoe and single horn blocks, with and without adjustable wedges; some without the wedges were fitted with liner plates and some not.
>
> In the case of 40 engines we supplied for the

---

12 Mr S C Towroe *'Arthurs', 'Nelsons' & 'Schools' at Work* Ian Allan Ltd Shepperton second edition 1983 p26

13 Mr J Clayton contributing to the discussion following:-
Mr A E Kyffin *Notes on Axleboxes and Axlebox Guides* I Loco E Paper 108 1921 Journal Nº 52 p46.

14 Contribution to the discussion following:-
Mr A E Kyffin *Notes on Axleboxes and Axlebox Guides* I Loco E Paper 108 1921 Journal Nº 52 pp22-3.

Midland Railway in 1891, Mr. Samuel Johnson, the locomotive superintendent at that time, used cast-iron single horn blocks, chilled on the wearing faces, and wrought iron axleboxes case hardened, which gave very satisfactory results."

What makes this statement all the more interesting, is that Kitson & C° did not build that many engines for the Midland, so these comparatively few examples class J 0-6-0s, N° 2023-2062, and later, class M 0-6-0s N° 2391-2420 and 2641-2660, had made a lasting impression. Nevertheless, this did not stop Mr Powell[15] from criticising Midland frame design:-

"Let us start at the frames. By the standards of the time they were fairly robust, though the Midland refusal to use the horse-shoe hornblock rather than separate axlebox guides left them rather prone to cracking at the top corners of the horns. Being invariably inside-cylinder, and everything behind the driving axle being occupied by firebox, there was nothing that could be done to stiffen up the frames against racking stresses. The horn clips, usually studded on to the bottom of the axlebox guides, could not be kept tight for long because of frame flexing. Another oddity was that because of limitations in the length of frame plate that Derby could machine, almost all the 4-4-0s had to have frame plates in two pieces, lapped behind the bogie at the inside motion plate."

The racking stresses, for similar piston loadings, are smaller in inside cylinder engines than outside cylinder engines, while a stiff frame was not a guarantor of a crack free life. Although later designers largely favoured hornblocks, when the 'Big Goods' was designed and for a long time afterwards, there was no evidence that hornblocks were superior at reducing frame cracking than separate horns, while a major factor determining the success or otherwise of either horn arrangement was the security of the fixing bolts. Unlike bar frames wherein the mid-length of the axlebox journal coincided with the middle of the frame thickness, in plate frames, to maximize grate area (and cylinder diameter when inside) they were spaced wider than the centres of the journals, an offset force known as a bending moment was induced on the frame. This force appeared because the lines of axlebox thrust and spring load acted a short distance from the inside face of the frame; it was also the primary reason for the hornblock/horn guide securing bolts or rivets becoming slack – the fastenings were stretched by virtue of the leverage the longitudinal loads on axlebox exerted on the frame. As engines became more powerful, trouble from loose fastening increased because of the greater bending moments acting on them prompted by the rise in piston loads coupled with the adoption of larger bearings. Longer journals could only be effected through lengthening them inwards, which increased the offset of the guides from the frame. For many designers, the solution appeared to be hornblocks, but they often performed no better. With horn guides the piston loads could only act on the bolts in one direction at a time, while some of the load was transferred directly by the abutment of the guide on the edge of the frame. In the case of hornblocks, each reversal of stress simultaneously acted on *both* sets of securing bolts, which allied with the impossibility of obtaining a good bearing of the hornblock on *both* faces of the gap, encouraged the bolts to work loose more readily. This difficulty in

---

15 Mr A J Powell *Living with London Midland Locomotives* Ian Allan Shepperton 1977 p24.

Let us put to bed this erroneous nonsense that Derby could not machine long frame plates so Midland 4-4-0s *had* to have their frame plates made in two pieces. Mr Johnson's first Midland 4-4-0 classes were provided with wrought iron frames comprising two pieces that were lapped and then fire or hammer welded together, near the motion plate so that at the cylinders they were spaced closer together than they were at the firebox. This artifice was adopted simply to provide the necessary sideways bogie wheel clearance while avoiding the need for a large cut-out in the shallow frame between the motion plate and the rear of the cylinder - the alternative solution. When steel frames were first adopted, the plates, which were a little over 28ft long, *were made* in one piece nevertheless an ogee-type joggle was introduced to serve in place of the weld. Subsequently, a bolted lapped joint was adopted instead of the joggle, and this then remained a Midland standard detail, being incorporated in due course into the '483' class 4-4-0s *et al*. That the Midland, possessed the capability to have given its 4-4-0s continuous frames located a constant distance apart, *if* it had elected to so, is demonstrated by its practice on the 0-4-4Ts. Not only were their frames longer than those of the 4-4-0s but they had precisely such a constant frame spacing combined with large cut-outs for the bogie wheel clearance. The first 0-4-4Ts comprising the '6' class were built at Derby in 1875 *prior* to the appearance of the 4-4-0s demonstrating the capacity was there from the beginning of Mr Johnson's time. A similar frame arrangement to that used on the 0-4-4Ts would in due course be fitted to the 'Flatiron' class 0-6-4T which had frames that were even longer, as of course did the 0-10-0.

Mr Atkins states in *West Coast 4-6-0s at Work* that owing to poor machine tool positioning the maximum length of main frame plate that could be slotted at Crewe was about 33 feet, the length present in the 'Bill Bailey' 4-6-0s. All of the frames of the company's other 4-6-0s had joints, as also did the 'Precursor' and 'George the Fifth' 4-4-0s, although the lap was not arranged to provide bogie wheel clearance, that was obtained by cut-outs.

One would hate to think some black engine/red engine partisanship has caused some confusion over the machining capabilities of the two Works.

A Defence of the Midland/LMS Class 4 0-6-0

Table IX – A Comparison in Maximum Bending Moments for a Selection of Locomotive Frames

Class	Distance between frames	Bearing centres	Cylinder diameter × stroke inches	Boiler pressure lbs/sq in	Driving wheel dia	Offset distance from inner face of frame to centre of bearing	Maximum load on horn guide lbs	Maximum bending moment inch-tons
MR Class 2 0-6-0	4ft - 1½ins	3ft - 11¾ins	18 × 26	160	5ft - 3ins	7/8ins	57,518	22.47
MR Class 3 0-6-0	4ft - 1½ins	3ft - 11¾ins	18½ × 26	175	5ft - 3ins	7/8ins	66,453	25.96
MR Class 4 0-6-0	4ft - 1½ins	3ft - 11¾ins	20 × 26	175	5ft - 3ins	7/8ins	77,667	30.34
LMS Class 4 2-6-4T (parallel)	4ft - 1½ins	3ft - 7ins	19 × 26	200	5ft - 9ins	3¼ins	78,073	113.28
LMS Class 5 4-6-0	4ft - 1½ins	3ft - 4¾ins	18½ × 28	225	6ft - 0ins	4 3/8ins	84,001	164.06
LMS 8 2-8-0	4ft - 1½ins	3ft - 4¾ins	18½ × 28	225	4ft - 8½ins	4 3/8ins	90,454	176.67

The vertical plate behind is the front of the dragbox. The other horn blocks were similar in design and similarly narrow. Lubrication groove provided at the top of the horn faces to aid lubrication.

Fig. 14 – View of the right-hand trailing horns of Class 4 0-6-0 Nº 3924

Consequently to exploit this effect some British engineers chose not to fit as long coupled and driving journals as they might for a little judicious frame flexing benefited bearing performance. On the other hand attempts to reduce axlebox trouble by fitting longer bearings had not been so successful. Mr Deeley, who probably knew more about bearing design and lubrication than any contemporary engineer, *including* Mr Churchward, stated why[16] short bearings were a feature of Midland, and other railways design practice:-

"To increase the size of the cylinders and boiler very much meant heavy stresses on the connecting-rod bearings and other parts. Large bearings and heavy parts are not particularly objectionable on stationary engines, but on locomotives, owing to the flexibility of frames, wheels, &c., necessary to allow the locomotive to run round curves, wide bearings are very apt to run hot owing to the cross strains set up. The use of three cylinders and cranks enabled the crank and connecting-rods to be relieved of considerable strains, whilst compounding promised to relieve the boilers very considerably."

fitting hornblocks *may* have been the reason why Samuel Johnson abandoned them in favour of horn guides even though at that time the bending moment was comparatively small, or perhaps it was to make the frame less rigid. Keeping the size of the bending moment small not only relieved the horn fastenings and improved the stability of the frame but also reduced the liability to overheating at the outer ends of the journals. In effect, the associated yielding of the frame under this offset loading, provided it was limited, equalized the load distribution along the length of the journal.

His observation, although actually referring to the Compounds, provides a reason why contemporary (not just Midland) locomotive bearings were rather shorter than later engineers would have used. The Chief Engineer of the Midland stipulated a low weight per foot run limit, which demanded a long wheelbase to spread engine weight over sufficient length, but this in turn made it more difficult for the machine to negotiate sharp curves. It may have been the desire

---
16 Mr R M Deeley *Compound Engines* **The Engineer** 17 December 1909 p623.

to enable the longer wheelbase eight-coupled class to curve with sufficient freedom that lay behind the adoption of the similarly loaded Standard Class 4 axleboxes for the Standard Class 7 0-8-0, while the Garratt 2-6-0+0-6-2 was in effect two 0-6-0s. Sure, through their smallness the bearings wore out quicker than they would otherwise have done, but it was in the belief they would be less likely to run hot. Limited evidence in the form of the ex-LNWR G1 class 0-8-0 suggests this was the case until the LMS altered the lubricating oil and the composition of the white metal.

Whether hornblocks were adopted in place of horn guides depended very much on the experience and opinion of the design draughtsman and as we have seen James Clayton was decidedly in favour of the latter. In practice it was quite common to see both arrangements used on the same locomotive, guides being present on trailing coupled axles in order to obtain sufficient depth of firebox, even though hornblocks might be present elsewhere[17]. Engineers who advocated hornblocks claimed the arrangement provided a useful reinforcement of the frame, particularly in the upper corners of the horn gaps. Conversely, the fact that cracks commonly originated in those portions of a frame 'strengthened' by the hornblock was seized on by the advocates of separate guides that they did no such thing. They argued that through omitting the bridge, the frame plate was free to 'breathe' above the axlebox and thereby avoid the liability to induce cracks[18]:-

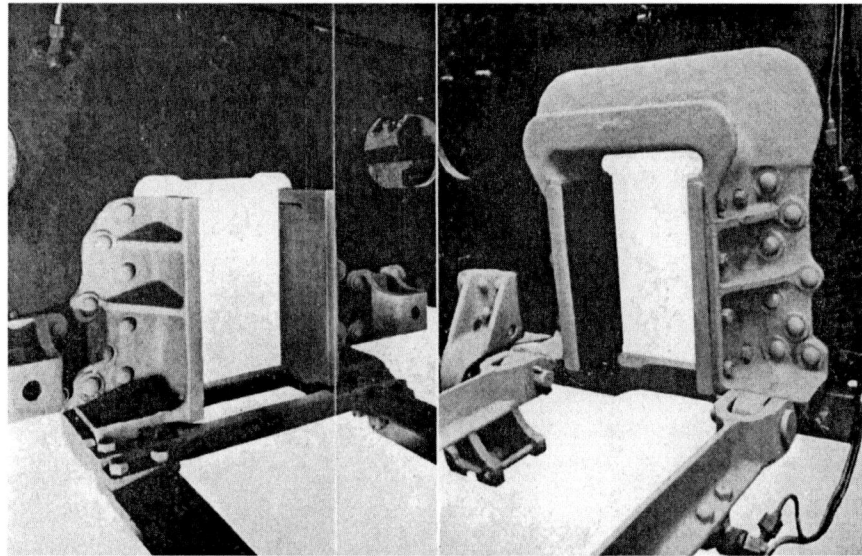

The left-hand picture shews the separate horn guides fitted to the earlier members of the class. The horn stays were secured to the underside of the guides by means of two studs at each end, while a tee section cross-stay joined the ends of the horn stay rigidly together. The cross-stays were to provide increased lateral stiffness to the bottom of the frame either side of the horn opening to prevent the frames 'breathing'. This arrangement, perhaps predictably, accelerated the fretting of the horn stay with the resulting loss of clamping pressure, markedly increasing the frame cracking experienced in the top corners of the horn gap. Appearing in the right-hand photograph is the final arrangement. A hornblock has been substituted with the tee section cross stay inverted and now pin-jointed to the hornblock. Hornstay secured to the frame via an arrangement LMS engineers called a 'Horwich stay'. Rivets securing the hornblock located away from the highly stressed region in the vicinity of the radiused corners of the horn gap opening cut in the frame. Hornblock fitted with manganese steel liners, and being double flanged around three sides is considerably stiffer.

Fig. 15 – Horn guides and hornblocks fitted to LMS Class 5 4-6-0s

"In regard to the horseshoe horn blocks which are adopted by many railways, some of our engines are running with these blocks, but we do not find them satisfactory as they are not sufficiently elastic, making the frames too rigid, and consequently when moving round sharp curves there is a tendency to break the blocks and stretch the bolts fastening the block to the frame, these bolts becoming loose. We have now gone back to the horn cheeks which are riveted to the frame at each side of the axlebox."

From the 1880s the Midland used guides almost exclusively so understandably they became accepted practice for most of the early LMS standard designs while William Stanier, who was familiar with the arrangement through Great Western practice, continued to use them on his

---

17 André Chapelon observed from stationary plant tests that the coupled wheels only contributed to the pull of the locomotive as the adhesive limit was reached for the driving wheels. Possibly the load take-up sequence, even in two-cylinder engines, was driving wheels then leading coupled wheels followed lastly by the trailing coupled wheels. For most situations with an adhesion of 600lbs/ton available, or the engine linked up, the trailing wheels would not have been required to deliver tractive force thereby relieving their horn gaps of much of the stress reversal, furthermore that axle did not experience the flange forces suffered by the leading coupled wheels.

18 Major J H Smeddle contributing to the discussion following:-

Mr A E Kyffin *Notes on Axleboxes and Axlebox Guides* I Loco E Paper N° 108 1921 Journal N° 52 p16.

taper-boiler designs. George Churchward had used guides albeit perhaps less successfully, for his frames were very prone to cracking at the top corners of the horn openings[19]:-

> "The weakest points in any plate frame are the horn gaps. Normal British practice has been to carry the top line of the frame in a generous upward curve over the horn gaps, to provide depth of metal to compensate for what has been cut away. It was also normal practice to reinforce the frames at these points by using substantial horseshoe castings for the hornblocks, riveted (or on some of the BR standard engines, welded) to the frame plates. Churchward for some strange reason did neither of these things. All his frames had straight horizontal tops, providing no extra metal over the horns where it was needed. He made things worse by always using separate horn blocks, which did not support the frame at all. Most engineers often had to use the latter for trailing coupled wheels it is true, as there was seldom room for the horseshoe type under the firebox, but it is on the driving horn gap that the worst strain usually comes, and there is no need whatever to use separate horn blocks there.
>
> I once tackled Holcroft on this matter. He seemed unable to see my point, saying that it was the business of the hornstays to provide the necessary strength and support. It is however notoriously difficult to get and maintain a perfect fit with hornstays."

Although by the appearance of *Locomotive Frames* in 1947, contemporary LMS practice had moved to favour hornblocks but as George Ivatt and his team discovered following their adoption, frames continued to crack. Consequently during the course of the discussion after the reading of their paper at Leeds, when Edward Windle Design Engineer at Doncaster asked the authors for a definite opinion on the advantages of the horseshoe type as against the single block type, Dr Johansen[20] could only offer qualified support:-

> "…the horseshoe type of horn block had been found to reduce frame fractures when properly designed and fitted, but it entailed certain fitting difficulties and was not thought to offer a complete remedy against cracking at the horn gaps when offset steam loading was possible."

The primary reason for the appearance of frame cracks in the upper corners of the horn gaps was the presence of too small fillet radii, a design fault that neither horn guides nor hornblocks of themselves could do very much to correct. The small fillet radii concentrated the stress trajectories as they passed from a horn face over the top of the horn gap prior to entering the body of the frame proper. The resulting stress concentrations increased, locally, the mean stress in the plate several-fold, while any surface defect such as a nick or notch, served to make this enhanced stress even higher at the edge of the plate. Either could prompt the creation and subsequent extension of cracks in the stressed plate although the latter as a whole, did not change metallurgically, in any obvious way.

As fatigue cracks usually developed quite slowly, they could normally be kept under observation, and to prevent failure from sudden fracture through insufficient residual cross-sectional area, were repaired once they had attained a pre-determined 'maximum' safe length. If however they were ignored or missed, then eventually there would be insufficient non-fractured cross-sectional area to carry the load whereupon the fracture would be complete, unless the crack had fortuitously stopped (or more likely delayed) itself, by running into a pre-existing rivet, bolt or lightening hole. Examination of the limited data available recording frame crack progression confirms they increased in speed as they traversed the plate.

Cracks could also start from poor workshop practices, which resulted in the initiating area now finding itself in a region of higher than intended stress. For example, in those designs of horn stay comprising a longitudinal tubular distance piece containing a bolt, as adopted by the Midland during the last few years of Mr Johnson's reign, if the tubular spacer was not a good fit, then as the bolt was tightened up the frame plate was put under additional stress. In running sheds a fitter wanting an easy life might arrange for the stay to be a loose fit, tightening up with the bolt at the risk of partially jamming the axlebox, alternatively he might leave the stay too long hammering it into position, resulting in a loose box and a stretched frame opening.

Although the cause of fatigue cracking might occasionally be obscure, we have explored by far the most common causes *viz.*, stress raisers due to too small a fillet radius, poor surface finishes and the inclusion of design features that over-estimated the engineering capability of an erector or shed fitter. These were causes that a designer might minimize through the application of intelligent

---

19 Rev J C Gibson *Great Western Locomotives* David & Charles Newton Abbot 1984 p117.
20 Mr E S Cox & Dr F C Johansen *Locomotive Frames* I Loco E Paper 473 November 1947 p196.

observation allied with reasoned performance analysis. So even though fatigue cracks could not be avoided with *absolute* certainty because the analytical techniques were not then available, designers could nevertheless progress from experience if they were minded to observe and learn, provided this *also* included a clear idea of the procedures used in the erecting shops and repair workshops not just simply improving or refining the frame profile. Accordingly the tendency for cracks to appear varied considerably, not only between different classes but also between batches of nominally the same class especially when differing levels of skill or attention had been applied during the manufacturing process.

The plate frame, as a concept, was not inherently prone to cracking *per sec*; indeed with the generally low stress levels present, the major reason for the presence or otherwise of cracks was the care the designer expended over the details *viz*. providing large radius fillet curves, specifying a good surface finish[21], avoiding awkward stress raising details and obtaining the cooperation of the shop floor in providing them. The general format of a plate frame meant repetitive stress concentrations inevitably occurred at specific points, which if they became high enough and acted for a sufficiently large number of times would initiate fatigue cracking, so despite the absence of calculations astute designers could nevertheless effect a significant improvement in frame performance. Consider the development of the LNER Pacifics[22] under Sir Nigel Gresley:-

"The main frames fitted to the last batch of 'A3's built were strengthened by the omission of all weight reducing holes behind the cylinders. The previous batch of 'A3s' *(sic)* had been given smaller holes in the frameplates and strengthened framestays as by 1929 frame fractures on the 'A1' Pacifics had reached epidemic proportions. Welding of the fractures were not always very successful and a number of engines received additional strengthening plates which partially or wholly covered the original lightening holes. During 1932 it was necessary to fit completely new frames to some engines, but it was later found that the rear section was generally sound. The practice was, therefore, adopted of renewing the front section only from ahead of the rear coupled wheel horns, by butt welding to the rear section. A patch plate was riveted to the inside of the frames over each joint. In order to speed up the repairs to the Pacifics in Doncaster Works where all overhauls had been concentrated from 1931 several sets of the displaced frames were repaired by the renewal of the front sections and assembled with frame stretchers and cylinders so that there was a float to cover locomotives coming into works requiring heavy frame repairs. The old frames were renewed and repaired as necessary and put back into the float. In the early days it had been the practice to avoid shopping Pacifics in the summer months in order to have the maximum number at work for the heavy traffic period, but this could not be achieved as more locomotives entered service. In 1932 No 2546 was fitted with new frames of Ducol steel.

In 1933 the first of the 'A3s' constructed in 1930 received new three-quarter frames and by the end of the decade 66 of the 79 'A1' and 'A3' Pacifics had been so fitted. In December 1937, 'A3' *Grand Parade* was damaged in an accident at Castlecary but by using the frame float an almost new 'A3' with the same number No 2744 was ready to leave the Plant Works within days a few days of the arrival of the wrecked locomotive.

The policy of fitting new frames continued after the war almost to the end of steam, the last to be fitted was *St Simon* by now British Railways No 60112 and nominally one of the oldest of the Pacifics dating from September 1923. It emerged from Doncaster Works in October 1962 with new three-quarter frames and an 'A4' boiler used on the 'A3s' at 220lb only to be scrapped two years later in December 1964."

"The frames of the 'A4' were slightly altered from those of the 'A3' which had given so much trouble. The portion under the cab which had given no trouble was at 3ft 2½in apart instead of the 3ft 5in in order to avoid a dish set in the frames for the wheel

---

21 Frame arrangement drawings of several LMS classes designed during the 1930s such as the Class 5 4-6-0 and Class 8 2-8-0 include three full-size part sections of the openings in the frame shewing dimensioned radiused corners. These detailed (i) section of the top edge of the frame opening for the horn guides, (ii) the radiused corner of the frame opening abutting the horn guide and (iii) the profile of all lightening holes. The draughtsmanship is such that they appear to be contemporary with the remainder of the drawing.

Notwithstanding these instructions, a stencilled note often appears on LMS frame drawings stating:-

"All corners to be rounded to a radius which where not dimensioned is to be from 1/16 to 1/8."

The Class 4 0-6-0 frame drawing appearing in *LMS Locomotive Profiles Nº 10 The Standard Class 4 Goods 0-6-0s* bears one of these instructions with the information that it was added on 14th July 1948. This drawing also carries an example of (i) above, recording that the lower edges of the horn opening were to be rounded to 3/8ins radius on both sides. It is not readily discernible from the lettering style if this was an original section contemporary with when the drawing was made or a later addition. I suspect the latter if only because the section was called X-X, which is out of sequence, and because I do not recall ever seeing it on late Midland frame drawings.

22 Mr P N Townend *East Coast Pacifics at Work* Ian Allan Shepperton 1985 - first extract pp40-41, second p76.

boss. Only one lightening hole of 1ft 0in diameter was made behind the driving wheel horns, but the most important improvement was that the design of the hornstays was changed so that instead of fastening across the horn gaps to the hornblocks only they were fitted to the frames as well. This improvement anticipated developments on the LMS which came to a similar conclusion some years later and also enabled Mr Hawkes, the Superintendent of the Crimsall Shops to say in December 1947 there had been only one fracture in an 'A4' frame up to that date."

Mr Hawkes[23] actually gave slightly more information, saying that members of the class A4, average age nine to twelve years, had suffered only one cracked engine frame; concurrently the class V2, another A3 descendant and fitted with the A4 style horn stay, of which there were 151 ranging in age from three to nine years, had had no frame fractures, notwithstanding some hard work during the War. It has to be admitted that the LMS appears to have been less successful than either the LNER or the Southern in evolving low maintenance frame designs, its profiles tended to retain overly complicated 'fiddly' details that served as stress raisers which increased the likelihood of cracks appearing.

As plate frames remained *de rigeur* in Britain, the differences between designs of comparable size and wheel arrangement were largely confined to variations in detail rather than the fundamental one of form, nonetheless, this did promote the development of two schools of frame design, particularly once outside cylinders became common. One, stressed the importance of absolute rigidity, while the other laid stress on the importance of retaining flexibility. The former supporters considered that the frame structure should be as substantial and as rigid as possible with the axleboxes/guides and the carrying wheels plus the spring suspension providing all of the flexibility needed so freeing the frame structure completely from any flexing demands when the engine was running on the road. In the other school, the diametrically opposite view was taken; the frame structure was made deliberately flexible and intended to flex when the engine negotiated curves.

The Midland undoubtedly ascribed to this latter philosophy as may be seen in the frame design for its Compound 4-4-0, just as assuredly as Mr Cox was a member of the former camp. John Smith, Chief Locomotive Draughtsman at Derby around the time of the introduction of the '2631' class, was not a supporter of stiff frames opining that flexibility was needed. Indeed, for the fifty years following the death of Matthew Kirtley, the Midland Railway had elected not to cross-brace its frames to the maximum possible extent, though one downside of the resulting greater flexibility was clearances increased more rapidly leading to somewhat faster wear in the axleboxes and rod bearings. Due to the complexity of the forces acting within an engine frame and the huge impact seemingly innocuous details could wrought, either of these approaches could result in an acceptable frame performances[24]:-

"For example, the Class 5, 2-6-0 has a most rigid, and the Class 4 Compound, one of the most flexibly designed, frames on the L.M.S. but both are "good." The Class 5X 4-6-0 is good, but the Royal Scot is bad, and yet the frame layout is very similar in the two cases. The Caledonian 4-6-0 is the best class as regards cracks on the whole L.M.S. – it doesn't have any. And yet the Highland 4-6-0, also designed in the Scottish tradition, is definitely bad."

The Compound frame was remarkably free from cracks due in part to its flexible design but also because it employed double-expansion, so the longer cut-offs employed ensured a more even turning moment on the crank axle while the drive from the three cylinders was concentrated on one axle. However this was not the complete answer, for when considering stress concentrations we must not think the effects were exclusively due to the presence of holes, notches, cracks or other deficiencies. The converse is equally true, that is, it was possible to introduce stress concentrations by *adding* material, should this result in a sudden local increase in stiffness. Thus, riveting a patch to a locomotive frame, or likewise introducing a significant but discontinuous section of greater lateral stiffness could cause problems. The reason being that the stress trajectories are diverted just as much by an area which strains too little, such as a stiff patch, as they are by an area which strains too much, such as an area weakened by a large hole.

Anything, which so to speak, is elastically out of step with the remainder of the frame structure will cause a stress concentration and so result in

---

23 Mr Hawkes contributing to the discussion at Leeds following:-
Mr E S Cox *Locomotive Frames* I Loco E Paper 473 November 1947 p192.

24 Mr E S Cox & Dr F C Johansen *Locomotive Frames* I Loco E Paper 473 November 1947 p93.

trouble. Hence of far greater importance than trying for 'absolute rigidity' or 'absolute flexibility' was ensuring the complete structure acted as a homogeneous whole. The inherent weakness of plate frames in the horizontal plane encouraged later engineers to introduce extensive and/or additional transverse bracing however, it was possible to introduce an excessive amount of rigidity, or perhaps to be more accurate too much located in inappropriate places, resulting in a frame that still suffered from cracking.

In marine circles, fatigue failures are commonly associated with discontinuities[25] being especially prevalent near 'hard spots', *i.e.* localized regions of high rigidity present in a ship's structure. The presence of a more flexible portion adjacent to a stiffer section could be predisposed to serve as a crack nursery. In effect, because the stiffness was not maintained at the same level throughout the structure, high stresses were obtained in the less restrained plate work immediately adjacent promoting fatigue cracks. There is ample evidence to demonstrate that locomotive frames behaved in an identical fashion, instances being Mr Thompson's two-cylinder rebuilds of the LNER B17 and the BR 'Britannia' classes – both of which developed cracks in the less restrained region immediately behind the cylinders. An example taken from the latter class, one of several recorded by Mr Harvey in *Bill Harvey's 60 Years in Steam*, appears in figure 40.

The Causes of Fatigue Cracks in Steel Structures

What follows is a brief introduction to a very complicated subject but hopefully it will provide enough background for us to appreciate some idea of the difficulties present in achieving a frame design free from cracks. It also, as far as practicable, makes use of techniques and knowledge contemporary with the period when the 'Big Goods' was built and ran in service. The cracking that appeared in locomotive frames, excluding accidents *etc*, was due to fatigue, but at the time, engineers did not know a great deal about the mechanism that prompted it, other than it took several years before the cracks appeared. Thus while they had plenty of experience of it, for a long time they had very little knowledge as to its causes and even less as to its prevention. Indeed the final portions of the theory were not developed until the 1950s and later - long after the last Class 4 0-6-0s had been built so Mr Cox was being a little unfair in his criticism.

Soon after the start of the Industrial Revolution engineers had noticed that parts of machinery, especially moving ones, would sometimes break at loads and stresses that would have been perfectly safe in a stationary component. Fatigue is therefore the failure of a component under a repeated or varying load, but one that never reaches a high enough level to initiate failure through a single application of load. The elementary equation for stress is given by:-

$$S = F \div A \qquad (1)$$

where:-
 S = stress in component – lbs/sq in
 F = applied force – lbs
 A = Area resisting the force – sq ins

This equation assumes that there are no discontinuities present in the cross-section of the component.

As fatigue is an insidious time-dependent type of failure, which can occur without any obvious warning some of the earliest work was prompted by the breaking of railway axles, which were sometimes accompanied by serious loss of life. In 1842-3 in a pair of papers, the Scottish polymath Professor Rankine recognized the distinctive striations of a fatigue fracture as well as the dangers of stress concentrations in machine components. Between 1852 and 1870, the German engineer August Wöhler conducted a systematic investigation into the fatigue failure in railway axles. By varying the loading on the axles and rotating them until they broke, he confirmed that the strength when subjected to cyclic loads was much lower than the monomic static strength.

Although during the first half of the twentieth

---

25 The formal inquiry into the loss of the *MV* **Derbyshire** which sank with all 44 on board when she encountered Typhoon Orchid in 1980 criticized Lloyds Register of Shipping for its approval of the design of frame 65:-

"The design approved gave rise to inadequate transfer of load from the continuous longitudinal structure forward of frame 65 into the structure aft of frame 65. The hatch side girder was substantially thicker than the longitudinal bulkhead aft of frame 65, which gave rise to an area of stress concentration and the arrangement gave rise to a risk of misalignment of major structural components of the vessel during construction. This design defect and misalignment (which in fact occurred on the starboard side), also gave rise to risks of development of fatigue cracks, propagation of such cracks into adjacent structures and, in certain conditions, initiation from such cracks of brittle fracture which was the subject of a poor repair at Sasebo."

century much effort was expended on understanding the mechanism of the fatigue process rather than simply observing its results, it remained very much within the domain of laboratory-based researchers. As Sir Henry Fowler remarked[26]:-

"Several years ago, Sir Oliver Lodge took part in a discussion between Engineers, Physicists and Mathematicians on this subject of cohesion. Speaking after an engineer, he said he supposed that what worried the previous speaker was that, when he lifted one end of his stick, the other end followed. The next speaker, also an engineer, said that was not his trouble, but the fact that, after lifting his stick, say a million times, when going to lift it the million-and-oneth time, the other end did not follow. This concisely expresses what our trouble is."

At that time, contemporary knowledge of the in-service behaviour of large steel structures subjected to alternating stresses such as ships and locomotive frames, was almost exclusively empirical, obtained from astute observation aided by, as will be seen in the example of the LMS papers, reasoned analysis of carefully collected data. As one anonymous locomotive designer recorded, not without some feeling:-

"The preceding considerations may appear to be more applicable to the framing than to design of hornblocks or slides, but since the efficiency of the running gear is so dependent upon the suitability of the framing and its adjuncts as a whole, these two factors must necessarily be considered together. As is the case with many other locomotive details, the design of hornblocks, or slides, is not a subject for rigid mathematical treatment in the drawing office, the results of past experience, however painfully acquired by trial and error process, being undoubtedly the better guide to the designer."

Unfortunately, trial and error could mislead the designer tempting him into making poor or even erroneous deductions. It was this, plus the sheer complexity of the subject, that made it so baffling for contemporary engineers. The process and theory of crack initiation and propagation was not comprehensively established until long after the Second World War had finished, although great impetus had been given through, for example the cracking and loss of several Liberty ships followed later by the de Havilland *Comet* airliner. Nevertheless, the occasional examples of fatigue failure that still occur, infer that our understanding of the subject, although deep, is not yet complete.

Figure 16 represents one of the exposed metal surfaces following a fatigue fracture, and demonstrates the three distinct stages normally present namely – crack initiation, incremental crack growth and final fracture, thus:-

Total life	=	Life to crack initiation	+	Life taken for crack to propagate to critical length	+	Life taken for crack to increase from critical length to failure

As, the final fracture stage, from critical length to complete fracture, is usually very rapid, it is not normally considered. Ignoring the final fracture stage has prompted two modern methods of fatigue analysis, the first based on local strain methods, gives component life until a crack forms. The second accepts that a crack will almost inevitably form in the structure given sufficient time, if not already present *e.g.* in weld metal, and taking a fracture mechanics approach predicts the life from initiation until a critical length is reached, at which point the crack will enter the final stage.

A complete fatigue prediction for an item would therefore use a combination of both methods.

---

26 Sir Henry Fowler *Fractures – Locomotive* 20th January 1931.
In referring to cohesion, he was alluding to the forces acting between the atoms of a material 'holding it together'. As it happens, one particularly far-sighted researcher at the time (1920) Alan Griffiths, then in the employ the Royal Aircraft Establishment who wrote a very important paper exploring why solid materials had different tensile strengths yet their molecular cohesion suggested they should be similar. Unfortunately, because this paper was concerned with 'brittle' materials (glass whiskers) rather than the 'ductile' ones engineers used it was ignored during the 1920s and 1930s and remained essentially a scientific curiosity, not starting to become of relevance until the appearance of the Liberty ships in the 1940s. These ships had an all-welded hull, as opposed to the traditional riveted hull, and this gave rise to problems through cracking. Of the roughly 2,700 Liberty ships built, approximately 400 sustained fractures of which 90 were considered serious. In 20 ships, the failure was essentially total, while of these around half had broken completely in two. This experience stimulated a great deal of research into crack behaviour and a team under G R Irwin at the US Naval Research Laboratory developed a modified form of Dr Griffith's work reformulating it in terms of stress rather than energy. Although this method was not at the time directly applicable to the ductile structural steels because of plastic deformation at the tip of the crack, when integrated with the work of others in the field it resulted in the development of 'fracture mechanics'. Yet, it was not until the 1970s engineers accepted this technique as a useful even essential design tool. As an aside Sir Henry Fowler was in charge of the Royal Aircraft Establishment for the latter half of the First World War during which time the SE5a fighter was developed.
Dr A A Griffiths *The Phenomena of Rupture and Flow in Solids* Philosophical Trans Royal Society Vol A221 pp163-98.

However, since most engineering components spend most of their working life within one or other of the two regions, it is normal only to adopt the more appropriate. If the device comprises small components, relatively stiff, formed from materials that are fairly brittle, *etc.* then its life is typically governed by time to initiation. Once a crack has formed in such a component, then it takes a relatively short time to propagate through to failure. Conversely, if the item comprises is large and fabricated from many components such as a pressure vessel, bridge, ship or aeroplane fuselage then being relatively flexible and made from normally ductile materials, any cracks propagate relatively slowly so that the fracture mechanics approach is usually more appropriate. This permits the crack to grow slowly and safely until it attains a length where it is long enough to be noticed and given remedial attention, but far shorter than its critical length so that it will never (hopefully) enter the final fracture phase. There is however an older approach third older fashioned method, known as the stress-life method. Although less accurate[27] it is easier to apply and is directly applicable to obtaining an infinite life for a component. With this caveat we may use the method to explore the desire locomotive engineers had of avoiding cracks from starting[28]:-

"The plate frame in service should last the life of the engine, and in some cases does so with very little attention. In others, however, fractures require repairs from time to time and in extreme cases call for premature renewal of the frames."

A view Mr Cox reiterated in modified form while designing the British Railway Standards[29]:-

"June 1948: The plate frame is in universal use in this country, and in locomotives of moderate power

---

27 It is still used nowadays, presumably because of its very simplicity and ease of application even though it can be very misleading and requires a degree of caution in its applications.
28 Mr E S Cox & Dr F C Johansen *Locomotive Frames* I Loco E Paper 473 November 1947 p87.
29 Mr C P Atkins *Britannia Birth of a Locomotive* Irwell Press Pinner Middlesex 1991 p15.

While some modern engines, especially those with two cylinders, had become too powerful for contemporary frame design capabilities, it does not necessarily follow that a plate frame using modern finite element analysis could not prove satisfactory. Indeed, there is contemporary evidence that it could, however a successful bar frame, especially with the wealth of design experience available in America (and to a more limited extent within say Beyer Peacock & C° or the NBL C°) could have been produced using the then available design techniques.

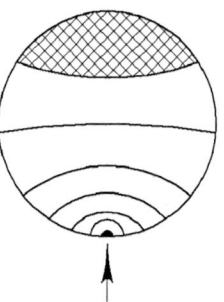

The most characteristic feature of fatigue fracture, and one which greatly worried early engineers, is that even with the most ductile materials failure occurred without revealing any plastic deformation, and generally when the part had been stressed (albeit repeatedly) below the elastic limit. Stage I is the initiation of one (or more) micro-cracks which are not normally discernible to the naked eye, but may be considered the nucleus of the crack. In stage II the micro-cracks progress to become macro-cracks, these surfaces are usually smooth and relatively bright where the two surfaces, forming the boundary of the crack, have been rubbing together. These surfaces will usually display the distinctive *beach marks* or *clamshell marks* characteristic of a fatigue failure, pointing towards the origin of the crack(s). Eventually the crack spread to such an extent (stage III) that the remaining metal could not support the combination of the applied load and the stress concentration at the head of the crack for even one more application and the crack propagated instantaneously and failure was complete. The diagram shews these three stages in the development of a fatigue fracture. The final part of the fracture, shewn hatched, displays a fractured surface which although giving the impression of revealing the grain or crystal structure, this is not actually the case. Nevertheless in the early days there arose the misnomer of a 'crystalline fracture' or crystallization implying a fundamental change in the metallurgical structure of the metal *i.e.* it had become fatigued, whereas this is not so.

Fig. 16 - Development of a fatigue crack under repeated application of load

and size can give good service. On the more powerful engines experience has been very variable, but it is a fact that many modern types experience an intolerable volume of frame fractures. There is no doubt that a frame should last the life of an engine without attention and a well designed bar frame gives promise of this."

Since locomotive engineers endeavoured to avoid cracks from starting because that was the situation present in many engine classes, we will concentrate on this, the stress-life method. Another difficulty they faced was once a crack had appeared and propagated they were unable to predict how fast it would grow, as LMS employed engineer Mr W Bradley[30] reported:-

"Generally fractures extend slowly, and the

---

30 Mr W Bradley *What a Running Shed Man Looks for in a Locomotive* I Loco E Paper 466 Nov 1945 pp249-50.

A Defence of the Midland/LMS Class 4 0-6-0

engine can be run with the fracture kept under observation at reasonable periods, but the Author recollects one instance of a 2 in. frame fracture extending to 9 in. during an outward and return run of 600 miles. This was a large passenger locomotive working over heavy gradients with a war-time loading of 20 coaches.

This case illustrates the effect of heavy loading on frame stresses."

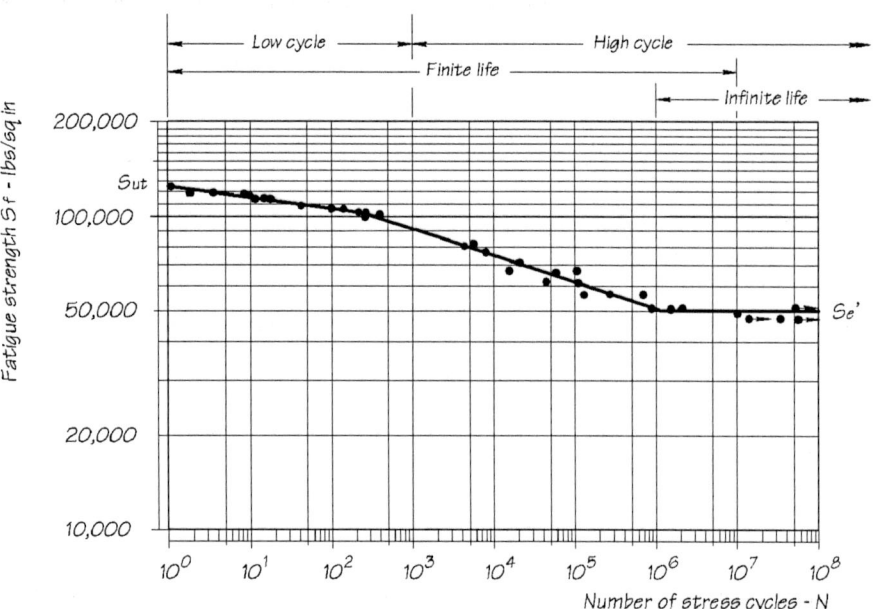

Changing the weights acting on the test-pieces before each run varied the stress amplitude, while the number of revolutions until failure is recorded on a revolutions counter.
Diagram traditionally plotted using logarithmic axes in order to emphasize the distinct junctures in each zone. Only ferrous materials demonstrate these three distinct zones.

Sut - ultimate tensile strength - 125,000 lbs/sq in in this example
Se' - endurance limit or fatigue limit - 50,000 lbs/sq in or say 40 per cent of Sut

Fig. 17 - An S-N diagram plotted from the results of completely reversed axial fatigue tests

Incidentally, although we refer to these slow developing cracks as 'fatigue cracking', the term is something of a misnomer for there was no tiredness or deterioration in the metal after repeated stressing. Test pieces taken closely adjacent to a fatigue crack invariably demonstrate the continuing soundness of the surrounding material accordingly some engineers consider a more appropriate name to be 'creeping cracks'.

Herr Wöhler's investigations into axle failures gave rise to the characterization of fatigue behaviour by means of stress amplitude-life (S-N) curves, which in turn prompted the concept of a fatigue 'endurance limit' for the material (applies to ferrous metals only). As a result, it became the norm to consider the fatigue properties of a metal in terms of a reversed stress $(\pm S)$. This reversed stress is usually plotted on a graph against the logarithm of the number N of times the stress has to be applied to a specimen to cause failure. The S-N diagram for a typical steel looks like figure 17, wherein it is seen that the 'dog-legged' curve flattens off after typically between a million and ten million reversals. The existence of a 'fatigue limit' for ferrous materials is a source of great comfort to engineers, although the actual values vary according to the precise composition of the material. However, while this diagram implies there is a value for S, which if not exceeded the material will not fail despite how many times the stress is applied and reversed, the situation is not quite as simple as this, for fatigue failures continued to occur and at stresses nominally lower than the endurance limit.

In 1901, a brand new turbine destroyer *HMS Cobra* one of the fastest ships in the world suddenly broke in two and sank in the North Sea in fairly ordinary weather with the loss of thirty-six lives. Neither the ensuing court martial nor the Admiralty Inquiry shed much light on the cause of the accident so in 1903 the Admiralty conducted experiments on a similar destroyer *HMS Wolf*. These shewed that the stresses deduced from strain measurements were less than the calculated design values. In 1913 Charles Inglis, later Professor of Engineering at Cambridge[31], shewed geometrical irregularities, such as holes, sharp corners *etc*, which had previously been ignored could raise the local stress – often over a very small area – to a very high

---

31 Mr C E Inglis *Stresses in a Plate due to the Presence of Cracks and Sharp Corners* I Naval Architects London March 1913 pp219-41.

Later still, he served on the LMS Advisory Committee on Scientific Research under the chairman Sir Harold Hartley a Vice President of the company.

Frames and Cracks

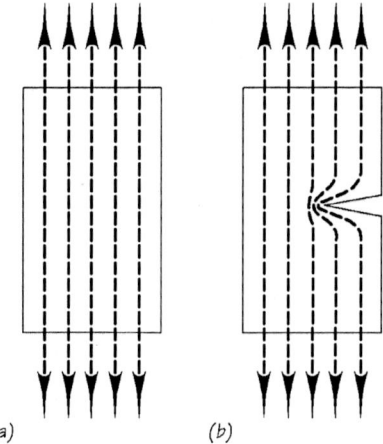

Fig. 18 - Stress trajectories in a bar uniformly loaded in tension (a) without and (b) with a crack

level. Thus holes and notches could cause the stress in the immediate vicinity to rise above the breaking stress of the material, even when, as was the case with *HMS Wolf*, the general level of stress in the surrounding material was low and general calculations suggested it was perfectly safe.

That almost any hole or corner in an otherwise continuous plate may cause a local increase in stress is demonstrated in figure 18 which shews a plate subjected to a uniform tensile stress. The dotted lines represent what are called 'stress trajectories', *i.e.* typical paths by which the stress is passed on from one molecule to the next. In the uniform plate they are straight parallel lines uniformly spaced. If the paths of some of these stress trajectories are interrupted by cutting an opening in the plate then the forces, which the trajectories represent, become modified. The forces go round the gap and in doing so are crowded together to a degree that is largely determined by the shape of the opening. Where the crowding is very close, then there was more force per square inch so the local stress would be high.

If the part shewn in figure 19 is subjected to a tensile force F, then theoretically the stress changes from the lower value in the larger left hand portion $(S_1 = F \div A_1)$ to assume a higher value in the right hand half $(S_2 = F \div A_2)$. The stress trajectories are redistributed within the region where the cross-sectional area changes. If a large fillet radius is provided between the two sections then the internal stresses have ample space to become redistributed evenly, however, if the radius is too small or non-existent then the stress trajectories do not have enough space to realign and instead crowd

together. As a result, at the base of the smaller radius fillet the actual stress becomes more than the theoretical stress $(S_2 = F \div A_2)$. This localized increase in stress caused by a sudden change of geometric shape is called a stress concentration. Holes, notches, grooves *etc* also represent sudden changes in geometric profile and likewise serve as stress concentrations in a similar manner to too small a fillet radius. In order to quantify the effect of stress concentration and to estimate the resulting stresses, stress concentration factors are used.

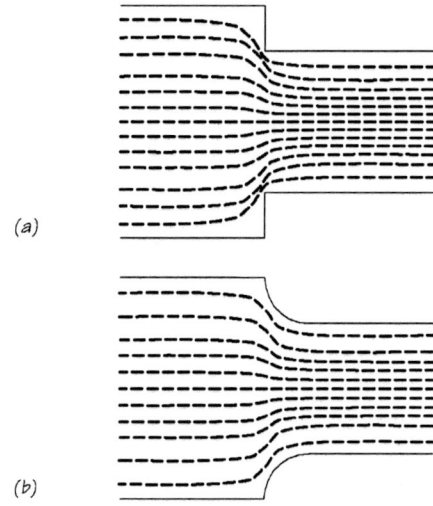

Fig. 19 - Stress concentration in a bar uniformly loaded in tension (a) without and (b) with a fillet radius

Using the theory of elasticity, Professor Inglis developed the first stress concentration factor to predict the stress at the end of an elliptical hole in a plate:-

$$Kt = [1 + 2(a \div b)] \quad (2)$$

where:-
Kt = stress concentration factor
a = half width of an ellipse perpendicular to the direction of load
b = half width of an ellipse in the direction of load

The ellipse becomes a circle when $(a = b)$ so from equation *(2)* it can be seen the theoretical stress concentration factor due to a hole in a plate subjected to tensile force is 3. Conversely, as b approaches zero the ellipse becomes sharper and sharper, effectively becoming nearer to a crack, so the stress at the end of the crack becomes ever higher - *vide* figure 20. Indeed once the width of the elliptical hole in the direction of the load approaches zero the stress concentration factor tends to infinity. Thus, using this formula we may

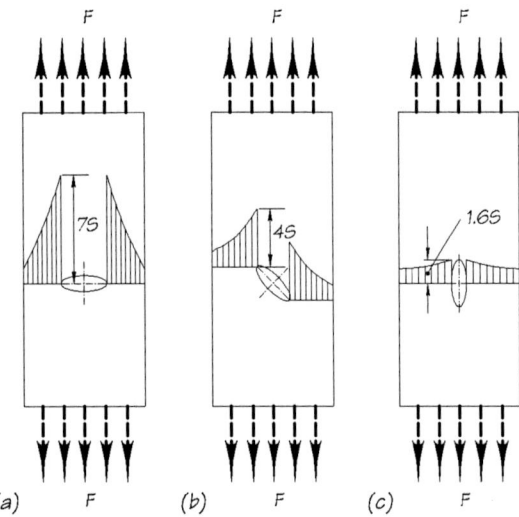

Theoretical stress concentration around an elliptical hole - major to minor axis ratio 3:1 - orientated in three different directions in an 'infinite' plate calculated from Professor Inglis' equation. Note the considerable reduction in S(max) resulting from the re-orientation of the hole major axis in the three cases (a), (b) and (c).

Fig. 20 - Stress concentration in a infinite plate with differing alignment of an elliptical hole

calculate that if we were to scratch a bridge girder hard with a dressmaker's pin the resulting stress concentration would result in the bridge collapsing. Now, not only will a bridge not fall down if it is scratched by a pin but also it will survive with all sorts of holes, notches and even cracks present, so there must be other factors at work.

Figure 21 is a calculated stress chart for a very small short crack. The contour lines appearing on it are not stress trajectories, but contours of stress concentration for stress at right angles to the plane of the crack. The number appearing by each contour represents the stress concentration factor Kt by which the mean stress remote from the crack is multiplied at each point. As the crack gets longer, assuming the tip radius remains the same, the stress concentrations increase in severity. Thus, while the contour pattern and the proportions remain similar, it results in the crack extending at a faster rate.

All of the calculations and assumptions about dangerous concentrations of stress arising assume that Hooke's law is obeyed, this is within the linear portion of the stress-strain relationship for a material. Furthermore, whilst we refer to 'concentrations of stress', but what the mathematical calculations such as Professor Inglis' formula actually supply us with, are concentrations of *strain*. Thus, if we calculate as in figure 21 that the material is strained or stretched by 201 times more than the average for the structure as a whole then we assume that the local stress is also 201 times as high and we can say that there is a stress concentration of 201. Now because metals such as mild steel and wrought iron possess good ductility, not only does this ensure their work of fracture is high, but the shape of the stress-strain curve is modified in such a way as to promote large departures from Hooke's law, if the material is strained beyond the yield point. When this occurs, the stress concentrations are usually greatly diminished - in other words ductility tends to stop cracks. This mechanism is illustrated in figure 22, when the stress in the vicinity of a discontinuity reaches the yield point, plastic deformation occurs resulting in a redistribution of the stress. This plastic deformation or yielding is highly localized being restricted to a very small area in the immediate vicinity. There is no perceptible change in the metal as a whole. Therefore, in practice, theoretical stress concentrations are normally

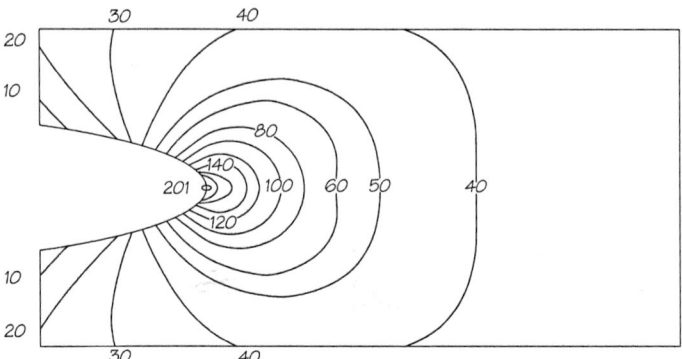

The diagram shews the stress system near to the tip of a small elliptical crack. If we assume the crack has a length a equal to 100 and a width b equal to unity (i.e. $a \div b = 100$) then using Charles Inglis' equation we find the stress concentration factor Kt attains a value of 201. The contours are lines of equi-stress concentrations for stresses at right angles to the plane of the rack i.e. parallel to the applied load. The figures indicate the number of times by which the local stress is increased as compared with the mean stress remote from the crack. The rapidity with which the stress decreases with distance from the end of the crack is very noticeable. This effect becomes more marked as the ratio $a \div b$ increases, thus if the ratio became 1000, then Kt would become 2001. The actual values of the stress concentration vary with the length of the crack, but the relative proportions remain constant.

Fig. 21 - Calculated stress concentration contours near the tip of an elliptical crack

Frames and Cracks

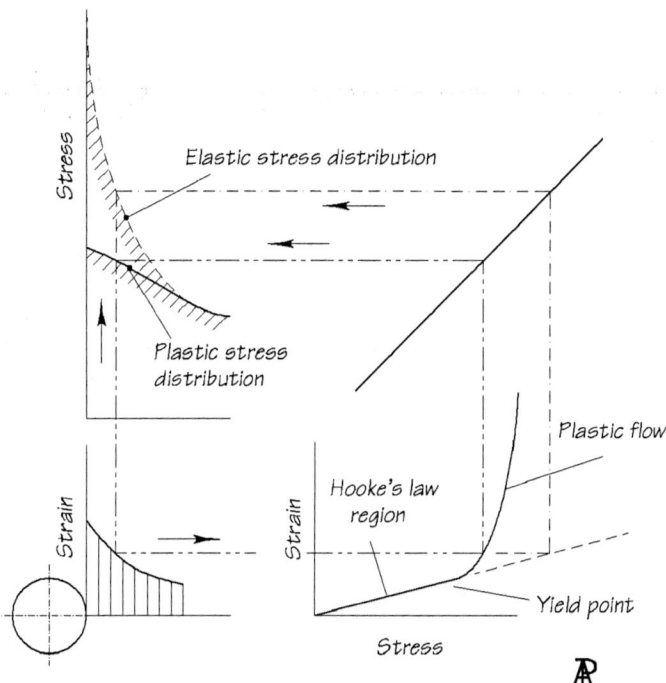

Hooke's law states that the extension is in direct proportion with the load - i.e. strain is directly proportional to stress. Most metals obey this law as long as the load does not exceed the material's elastic limit.

Fig. 22 - Practical stress distribution near a circular hole in an infinite plate.

The diagram shews how under static load, ductile materials are not affected by stress concentrations to the extent predicted in Figs. 21 and 22. When the stress in the vicinity of the discontinuity exceeds the yield point, there is time for plastic deformation to occur resulting in a redistribution of stresses. This point is demonstrated graphically, which for the sake of simplicity ignores any change in strain distribution due to plastic flow. This plastic deformation or yielding is local and restricted to a very small area in the component. There is no perceptible damage to the part as a whole, so it is common practice to ignore the theoretical stress concentration factors for components that are made from ductile materials and subjected to static load. *However, when the load is fluctuating, the stress at the discontinuities may exceed the endurance limit in which case the component may fail by fatigue.* Therefore the endurance limit of a component made from a ductile material is greatly reduced by the presence of a stress concentration. Under fatigue conditions slow changes continually take place within the crystalline structure of the metal in the immediate region of the stress concentration. Stress concentrations thus can have a devastating effect, indeed the whole secret of combating fatigue is to combat stress raisers either directly or indirectly. This very point causes some difficulty in obtaining the intrinsic fatigue strength of a metal, for any file mark, or a scratch of any kind, is a stress riser, so also, is a change of section. For this reason when conducting S-N tests the specimens must be most carefully machined and given a very high polish under controlled conditions.

ignored for components made from ductile materials and subjected to *static* load. Thus under static load conditions, ductile metals are not affected by stress concentrations to the extent this and similar formulae predict. However, when the load is fluctuating, the stress at the discontinuities may exceed the endurance limit allowing the component to fail by fatigue. Therefore, the endurance limit of components made of ductile materials has to be greatly reduced due to the stress concentration, hence the use of stress concentration factors for fatigue loadings.

Figure 23 gives the theoretical or geometric stress concentration factors K_t, for an oblong hole, of differing proportions, in an infinite plate. The subscript t indicates that the stress concentration value is a theoretical calculation based only on the geometry of the component and the nature of the discontinuity. Many of these stress factors were originally derived either mathematically as *(2)* given earlier, or from experimental methods such as photoelasticity. Nowadays, finite element analysis software would provide a latter-day locomotive engineer, as never before with the opportunity of optimizing his frame design. The graphical output readily reveals where the stress hot spots and cool spots are, so by changing plate thickness, altering fillet radii or profiles, or redesigning components it would be possible to generate a uniform stress field, theoretically making the same factor of safety throughout the structure. Theoretically, it would mean that should the frame fail, it would fail everywhere at once – although one might question whether this is sensible.

Some materials display more sensitivity than others to stress concentration factors under fluctuating loads so to allow for this difference, referred to as 'notch sensitivity', a parameter q is attributed to each material. This notch sensitivity factor is then applied to modify the theoretical stress concentration factor to become K_f – known as the fatigue stress concentration factor. When designing, the normal procedure is to find the K_t from the geometry of the component, then for the specified material obtain the notch sensitivity q, for the notch radius from a chart, thus:-

$$K_f = 1 + [q \times (K_t - 1)] \qquad (3)$$

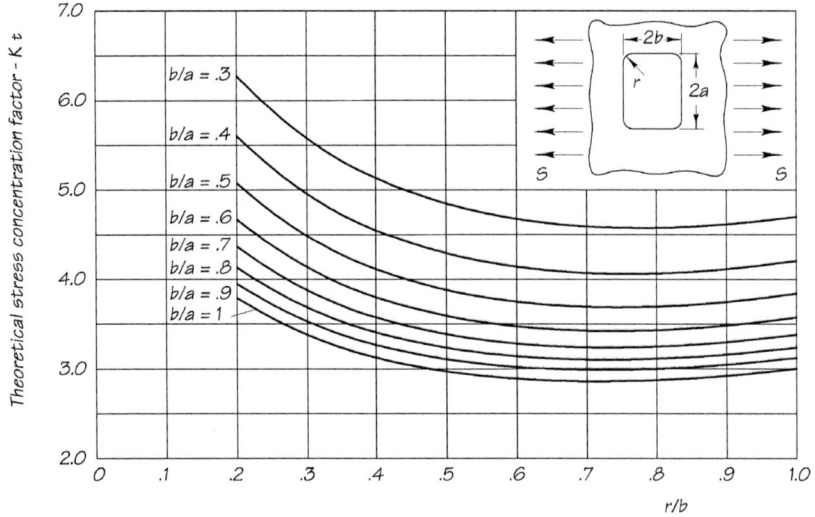

Although this diagram gives the theoretical stress concentration factor K_t for a rectangular hole, it may serve to a first approximation at least for obtaining the equivalent for a horn opening if we adopt the artifice of considering the latter as being the equivalent of a rectangular hole located in two frame plates abutting one another and assume a symmetrical stress loading.

Thus, and by way of example, taking the horn opening in a Class 4 0-6-0 frame, which was 16ins wide and 20¼ ins deep with a 1½ ins fillet radius in the top corners, $2a$ was therefore 40½ inches, $2b$ was 16 inches and r was 1½ ins. Whence $b/a = 0.395$ and $r/b = 0.1875$. Applying these values to the diagram, and extrapolating since they are slightly off the range, suggests a stress concentration factor of about 5.7.

Repeating the exercise for an early Class 5 4-6-0 - horn opening 19 ins wide and 21½ ins deep with a 1¾ ins fillet radius in the top corners, $2a$ was therefore 43 inches, $2b$ was 19 inches and r was 1¾ ins. Whence $b/a = 0.44$ and $r/b = 0.184$. Applying these values to the diagram, and extrapolating since they are again slightly out the range, suggests a stress concentration factor of about 5.3 - not much of an improvement for a locomotive designed over twenty years later.

Fig. 23 - Theoretical stress concentration factors for a rectangular hole in an infinite plate

where:-
Kf = fatigue stress concentration factor
q = notch sensitivity of the material
Kt = theoretical (or geometrical) stress concentration factor

Figure 24 records the variation in notch sensitivity q, with notch radii for an aluminium alloy and a range of steels having different ultimate tensile strengths. It will be seen for each example that beyond a certain radius the notch sensitivity tends to assume a constant value, although its magnitude differs from one metal to another. One further characteristic is that the higher the tensile strength of a steel the higher the value of q for any given radius. In other words, higher quality steels tend to be more notch sensitive and thus more liable to fail than mild steel. Furthermore, under stress, the life of a structure depends primarily on the number of cycles required before a crack can grow to such a size that it results in catastrophic failure. The fact the fatigue crack growth characteristics of steels of different strengths do not vary widely means that if a steel plate of higher tensile strength (and higher plain fatigue strength) is used in place of a mild steel one, the service life will not necessarily be increased. For, if cracks now form, they will spread just as quickly in the stronger steel as in the mild steel. Indeed, if the permissible working stress in the plate was raised in proportion to the higher tensile strength of the stronger steel, which was usually the reason for adopting it, the service life of the component can be expected to be less than if it had been made from mild steel.

The endurance limit (Se') obtained from a S-N curve (figure 17) is not an exact property of the material like ultimate tensile strength because its value is affected by factors such as component shape and size, surface finish, temperature *etc*. Furthermore, these tests although reasonably precise take a long time to produce, so sometimes the appropriate data is not available, in which case an approximate relationship linking endurance limit and ultimate tensile strength (Sut) can be used. For mild steel Se' is typically is around 55 per cent of Sut, but for alloy and higher carbon steels the percentage is lower, say 40 to 45 per cent.

The endurance limit of a component differs from the endurance limit obtained from a rotating beam specimen because while there are standard specifications and working conditions for the test pieces, those of the actual component will almost certainly differ. Accordingly, modifying factors, sometimes called de-rating factors, are introduced thereby lowering the endurance limit of the test piece. Only four commonly used factors are considered here, but there are others *e.g.* temperature, corrosion *etc*. The relationship between (Se) and (Se') thus becomes:-

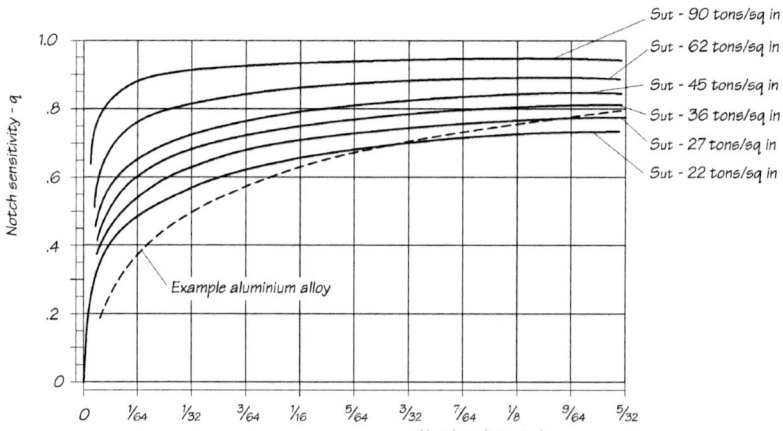

Fig. 24 - Notch sensitivity as a function of notch radius for various strength steels

The escape hatch of the *Comet I* was 19 inches wide and 21½ inches high with 4 ins fillet radius - from figure 23 we may estimate the theoretical stress concentration factor Kt was about 3.2. From this diagram, the notch sensitivity factor for an aluminium alloy is approximately 0.83, whence we may estimate Kf to have been 2.83. From figure 26, the mean stress was 12,000 lbs/sq in, allowing us to calculate the stress at the edge to have been (2.83 × 12,000) or 33,900 lbs/sq in - a reasonable estimate.

Repeating the exercise for an early Class 5 4-6-0, and adopting a notch sensitivity for a light alloy steel of say 0.8, which together with a Kt of 5.3 results in a Kf of about 4.44. From figure 41 the mean stress in the region of the rear of the leading horn gap was around 1.25 tons/sq in, which suggests a value of 5.55 tons/sq in for the stress at the edge of the horn opening - which approximately tallies with the 5.2 tons/sq in measured at strain gauge position N in figure 34 near to the corner of the horn opening.

$$Se = Ca \times Cb \times Cr \times Kd \times Se' \qquad (4)$$

where:-

Se' = Endurance limit stress of a rotating beam specimen subjected to reversed bending stress – lbs/sq in

Se = Endurance limit stress of a particular component subjected to reversed bending stress – lbs/sq in

Ca = Surface finish factor

Cb = Size factor

Cr = Reliability factor

Kd = Modifying factor to account for stress concentration

Surface finish factor: The surface of the rotating beam test piece is polished to a mirror finish ($Ca = 1$), making the specimen almost free from scratches and imperfections. It is impractical to provide such an expensive finish for the actual component. The surface finish factor takes into account the reduction in endurance limit caused by the difference in quality between the finish of the test piece and the component. Surface finish factors for steel may be calculated approximately from the following relationship:-

$$Ca = a \times Sut^b \qquad (5)$$

where:-

Sut = Ultimate tensile strength of steel – tons/sq in

a & b = Constants obtained from:-

Surface finish	Constant - a	Exponential - b
Ground	1.5	-0.085
Machined or cold drawn	2.18	-0.265
Hot rolled	8.07	-0.718
As forged	17.88	-0.995

wherein it will be seen that the ultimate tensile strength also influences the surface finish factor – as the steel strength increases the surface factor falls, hence, the reason why the finer finishing of locomotive tyres prevented fatigue fractures[32].

Size factor: With rotating beam specimens there is a size effect present because the larger the component the higher is the probability that a flaw exists somewhere in the bigger volume, thus the chances of fatigue failure originating at any one of these flaws is increased. It is normal practice therefore to use small diameter test-pieces and apply a reduction factor to the Se' endurance value. This adjustment is also required, in bending tests, when the component has a different cross-sectional shape. If however, the designer wishes to design to the absolute limit of the material, then there is no alternative to actually testing a prototype design or section – a very expensive procedure, but used in aeroplanes. For simple axial loading, Cb = unity irrespective of the shape of the component.

Reliability factor: The plotted laboratory points appearing in a *S-N* chart are usually mean values, for there is considerable dispersion of the data during a series of tests even when using the same material under nominally the same conditions. The reliability factor is unity for 50 per cent reliability *i.e.* one-half of the components will survive a given set of conditions. To ensure more than 50 per cent will survive, the stress amplitude on the component has to be lower than the endurance limit obtained from the *S-N* plot. For a reliability of 99.999%, $Cr = 0.659$.

---

32 Previously the tyre bore was coarsely machined because it was believed the roughness of the surface helped promote a better grip on the wheel centre. Fatigue tests carried out by the LMS Research Department demonstrated that the fatigue strength of coarse machined specimens was 70 per cent *lower* than that of test-pieces machined by carbide tipped tools at high speed.

A Defence of the Midland/LMS Class 4 0-6-0

Stress concentration factor: The endurance limit is reduced due to stress concentration. The stress concentration factor used for cyclic loading is less than the theoretical stress concentration factor due to the notch sensitivity of the material. The modifying factor Kd to account for the effect of stress concentration being defined as:-

$$Kd = (1 \div Kf) \qquad (6)$$

where:-

Kf = fatigue stress concentration factor

Kd = stress concentration factor

These factors are applied to the *S-N* derived endurance limit to give the maximum reversed stress that the component may be subjected to if it is to last indefinitely. In practice, a factor of safety is also normally introduced:-

Assuming the Class 4 frame was made from mild steel having an ultimate tensile strength *(Sut)* in the range 26-32 tons/sq in, or say 29 tons.

Since for mild steel Se' is typically 55 per cent of Sut, we may estimate the endurance limit at

$Se' = 0.55 \times 29$
$= 15.95$ tons/sq in

Taking a machined finish to the horn openings in the fame plates, gives $Ca = 0.89$

Assuming for simplicity pure axial loading, then $Cb = 1$

If the reliability is to be 99.999% then $Cr = 0.659$

Finally, in figure 24, the theoretical stress concentration factor for the horn opening, Kt was estimated to be around 5.7, while from figure 24, the notch sensitivity q, for a steel of around 29 tons/sq in strength is say 0.78. Putting these values into formula *(3)* gives a $Kf = 4.673$, while from formula *(6)* we establish Kd at 0.214

Whence, if the frame plate was to last the life of the engine without cracking, then the stress would have to be kept below:-

$Se = Ca \times Cb \times Cr \times Kd \times Se'$

substituting:-

$Se = 0.89 \times 1 \times 0.659 \times 0.214 \times 15.95 = 2.00$ tons/sq in
or 4,480lbs/sq in

Maximum steam load on horn opening with the crank on top quarter is 77,667lbs (table IX). Frame depth between leading coupled and driving wheels is 3 13/8ins deep by 1inch wide giving a mean stress of 2,475lbs/sq in. In practice the stress through a frame will not be uniform; as figure 41 suggests the upper portion tended to be in compression under the influence of supporting the boiler. Thus the tensile stress in the lower part will be higher than calculated above, so now we may appreciate why an engine might run 5, 7 or more years before the first cracks appeared. Of course, during that period the frames will have been subjected to millions or even perhaps tens of millions of stress

The benefit of adding the holes in the front of the frames is clearly seen. Supporting an engine at the ends of its frame will open the horn gaps unless the stays were in position, but the frequency of the operation was insufficient to initial fatigue cracks in the corners of the gaps.

Fig. 25 – View of Class 4F 0-6-0 N° 44232 slung from an overhead crane

reversals. If we repeat this calculation, this time for a Class 5 alloy steel frame plate, although Kt was slightly lower, the notch sensitivity was probably greater, so the stress value would be very similar. However, the 4-6-0 was of course a more powerful engine with larger piston thrusts, so we might predict from these calculations, that if the 'Big Goods' was an inveterate frame cracker, then the 'Black 5' will have been at least as bad and probably worse.

Finally, figures 26 and 27 give details of some stress measurements obtained at the escape hatch openings fitted to the ill-fated de Havilland *Comet*. Since these openings were were roughly similar in size and shape to locomotive horn gaps they provide an approximate insight into the stresses that would be present at the top corners of the gaps - the area of the frame most disposed to crack.

Frames and Cracks

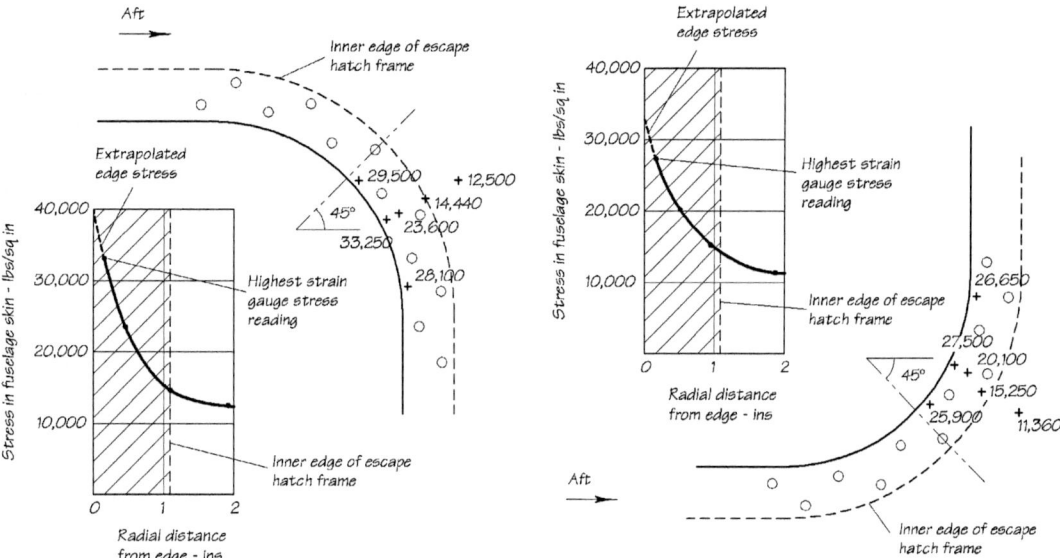

In the absence of comparable figures for a locomotive frame, we may gain an insight into the stress concentration caused by a horn cut-out by reference to the de Havilland *Comet* disaster. The crashes were due to fluctuations in the pressure difference between the inside and outside of the pressurized cabin prompting fatigue cracks which originated in rivet holes located in the highly stressed skin near the corners of the 'square' windows and escape hatches. The escape hatches were 19 ins × 21½ ins high with corner radii of 4 ins. The apertures were reinforced by a circumferential zed section bonded to the aluminium alloy skin (20 swg - 0.036 ins) with Redux adhesive and additionally riveted by 1/8ins countersunk head rivets at the corners - all somewhat reminiscent of a locomotive frame/hornblock assembly. Readings from strain gauges when the fuselage was pressurized to 8¼ lbs/sq in above atmospheric pressure illustrate the rapid in stress caused by the presence of the opening. The diagrams demonstrate how the corners of the openings acted as stress raisers, increasing the mean fuselage stress of around 12,000 lbs/sq in by a factor of 3 to 3½.

Fig. 26 - Stresses recorded in the fuselage skin at the top and bottom of the port escape hatch - *Comet I*

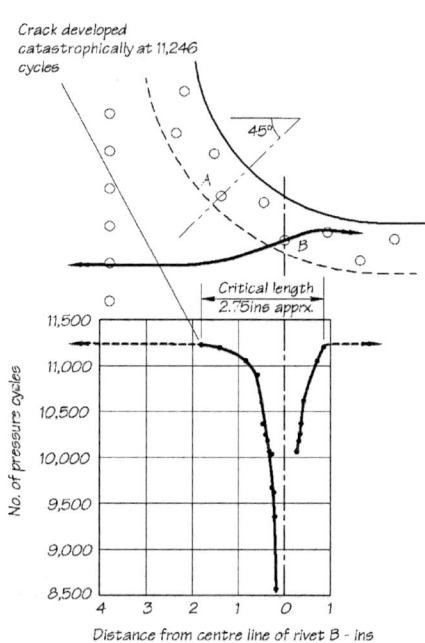

The *Comet* fuselage represents a comparatively large structure that was also highly stressed and consequently may serve as an example for demonstrating the 'fracture mechanics' approach. This technique accepts that a crack will develop in a structure given a high enough stress and a large enough number of reversals. Accordingly, the idea is that since a crack will develop the stress level should be such that the crack may safely attain a length sufficient for it to be noticed, by a bored inspector late on a Friday afternoon *i.e.* well before it reached the catastrophic final stage. This maximum safe crack extension, known as the critical length, may be simply calculated from the following formula for a crack located wholly within the bounds of a plate.

$$Lg = \frac{Gc \times E}{\pi \times S^2}$$

where:-
Lg = the critical length - inches
Gc = critical strain energy release - ins-lbs/sq in
E = Young's modulus for the material - lbs/sq in
S = the stress in the material - lbs/sq in

Assuming the stress in the fuselage skin at rivet *B* was similar to that at the diametrically opposite point on the escape hatch *i.e.* 19,000 lbs/sq in being the average of 23,600 lbs/sq in and 14,440 lbs/sq in. Gc for a low strength aluminium alloy is typically around 300 ins-lbs/sq in and E = 10,500,000 lbs/sq in.

$$Lg = \frac{300 \times 10,500,000}{\pi \times 19,000^2} = 2.78 \text{ ins}$$

Fig. 27 - Record of crack growth rate at the port forward escape hatch (bottom forward corner) - *Comet I*

- which tallies quite closely with the value appearing in the diagram - it was also far too short, consequently modern civil aeroplanes have Lg of the order of roughly ten times longer. Similarly, modern aeroplanes do not have openings in their fuselages shaped like locomotive horn gaps.

LMS Investigations into Frame Cracking

By 1939-40, a serious situation had developed on the LMS regarding locomotive availability caused by the large number of engines in which extensive frame cracking was present. Cracking was not a new phenomenon, but what was of major concern to the company was that it involved a high proportion of its most recent designs. Furthermore, it was clear the situation was getting worse for once cracks had been repaired by welding they cracked more quickly than before, usually through the weld. This was due to two causes, firstly the welding was often of poor quality containing discontinuities and slag inclusions and secondly, even when the welding was as good as it could be, the welded joint possessed a lower fatigue limit than the original plate. The company's welding engineer G Foster tackled these problems initially by improving weld quality and subsequently by moving the welds out of the highly stressed areas. This was effected by cutting out large sections of frame plate containing the cracks prior to replacing it with new plate welded onto the original by means of simple welds located in areas of much lower stress.

Despite the great deal of effort expended by Mr Foster, it soon became obvious that with the passage of time the fractures were re-occurring. With his staff unable to solve these problems, George Ivatt the CME had little option but to invite Dr F C Johansen in charge of the Engineering Section of the LMS Research Department for his section to conduct a special investigation into the causes and recommend remedial measures. A paper[33] delivered to the I Loco E and derived from this work, explained that the investigation had comprised three main sections, the first was a statistical survey wherein the frame records of every important class, standard and non-standard[34], were examined to establish location of cracks, the length of time before they appeared etc. The second part was a review of the welding repair

Table X – LMS Passenger Tender Engine Frame Cracks

Class & numbers	Building dates	Cracks	Cracks per engine per 10 years	Worst places	Frame thickness	Remarks
4-6-2 6200-6212	1933 to 1935	4 for 13 engines	0.4	(Also 26 flaws in frame behind outside cylinders)	1¼" or 1 1/8" (high tensile)	Turbomotive no flaws. Coronation & later engines have practically no flaws. General impression - good
4-6-0 Royal Scot 6100-6170	1st 50 1927. 2nd 20 1930	482 for 22 engines between 6100 & 6124	14.5	Top rivets on 2nd driving wheels & hornclips leading wheels. Many new sections of frame fitted.	1 1/8"	General impression - bad
4-6-0 5X Taper boiler 5552-5742	5552-5664 1934 & 1935. 5665-5742 1936	160 for 166 engines	1.2	Trailing axle, front top rivet hole. Also 42 cracks mostly at dragbox rivets.	11/16"	General impression - fair
4-6-0 5X Parallel boiler 5500-5551	1932-1934	29 for 48 engines	0.5	-	11/16"	General impression - good
Class 5 4-6-0 5000-5451	1934-1937	629 for 308 engines	3.0*	Leading and driving top back corners & bottoms	1" (high tensile)	General impression - bad
Compound 4-4-0 1045-1199	1924-1927	31 for 112 engines	0.2	-	1"	General impression - good
N° 2 Class Pass'r 4-4-0 563-700	1928-1932	0 for 56 engines	0	-	1"	General impression - good

* Engines N° 5000-5224 averaged 4.0 cracks per engine, engines N° 5225-5451 averaged 2.0 cracks per engine

---

33 Mr E S Cox & Dr F C Johansen *Locomotive Frames* I Loco E Paper 473 November 1947 p93.

34 Not strictly true since the ex-LNWR classes were excluded due to a lack of time. Whilst great inroads had been made into scrapping the former products of Crewe, the 0-8-0s still represented an important class.

procedures the company had devised while the final part concerned ways by which the Research Department could establish the stresses extant within a fame plate by direct measurement.

cracks occurred around the horn gaps in one of three typical positions:-

(i) In the top corners

(ii) Horizontally from the plate edge to the top axlebox

Table XI – LMS Goods Tender Engine & Tank Engine Frame Cracks

Class & numbers	Building dates	Cracks	Cracks per engine per 10 years	Worst places	Frame thickness	Remarks
2-8-0 Freight 8000-8095	1935 to 1937	96 for 87 engines	1.7	Driving horns, front & back top corners	1"	Almost all cracks at worst places. General impression - poor
0-8-0 Freight 9500-9674	1929-1932	155 for 42 engines between 9500-9549	2.6	Driving axle at front, top corner & top rivets	1"	Almost all cracks at worst place. General impression - bad
2-6-0 Taper boiler 2945-2984	1933 & 1934	(0 for 14 engines recorded at Crewe)	(0)	-	11/16"	Horwich maintained, detailed analysis not yet made, but results known to be good. General impression - good
2-6-0 Parallel boiler 2700-2944	1926 onwards	(3 for 57 engines recorded at Crewe)	(0.04)	-	11/16"	Horwich maintained, detailed analysis not yet made, but results known to be good. General impression - good
0-6-0 N° 4 Class Goods 4027-4556	1924-1928	113 for 122 Derby maintained engines	0.5	Driving axle, back top corner	1"	General impression - good
Garratt 7967-7999	1927 & 1930	162 for 25 leading units. 100 for 14 trailing units	5.0 leading units 5.5 trailing units	Top corners, outside wheels leading & trailing units	1"	General impression - bad
2-6-4T 3 cyl. Taper boiler 2500-2536	1934	25 for 31 engines	0.9	Almost all cracks at bottom of gaps	1" or 11/8" (high tensile)	General impression - good
2-6-4T 2 cyl. Taper boiler 2537-2616	1935-1937	6 for 74 engines	0.1	-	11/8"	General impression - good
2-6-4T parallel boiler 2300-2424	1927-1934	330 for 95 engines	2.7	Almost all at driving horns, top back corner	11/8"	Almost all cracks at worst place. General impression - poor
2-6-2T Taper boiler 71-144	1935	4 for 69 engines	0.07	-	1"	General impression - good
2-6-2T Parallel boiler 1-70	1930-1932	74 for 61 engines	1.1	Mostly at driving horns, top back corner	11/16"	General impression - fair

Note:- The small standard tank engines omitted from this table suffer practically no frame flaws

In fact there were two statistical based analyses produced, which were described as interim reports.

The first of these (K.50) appeared in August 1943 and concerned an analysis of the frame record cards at Crewe and Derby. It prompted some observations which in turn suggested further lines of research, some of which will be considered later. The first report revealed practically all of the guide rivet hole.

(iii) At the bottom, from the recess where the horn stay was clipped to the frame; either to the bottom guide or to the spring bracket rivets.

Occasionally cracks were observed at other locations but not being considered sufficiently numerous did not form part of the report. The different locomotive classes varied considerably in

A Defence of the Midland/LMS Class 4 0-6-0

their propensity for cracking and with regard to the places most affected. Tables X and XI record these particulars for the more important standard passenger and goods classes. To enable some sort of 'quantitative' comparison to be made between the classes, Dr Johansen introduced the concept of 'cracks per engine per 10 years' which was calculated as follows:-

that time had a only few cracks could go on to develop an increased incidence of frame cracking. The figures included cracks which appeared

Table XII – Particulars of Class 5 Frames

Engine numbers	N° in batch	Builder	Building dates	Frame thickness	Frame drawing N°	Frame plate material	Boiler throatplate	Design of axlebox guide	Type of springs
5000-5019	20	Crewe	1935	1 ins	D 13388	Ducol	Straight*	Separate	Compression link
5020-5069	50	Vulcan	1934-5	1 ins	D 13388	Ducol	Straight*	Separate	Compression link
5070-5074	5	Crewe	1935	1 ins	D 13388	LMS 4B	Straight*	Separate	Compression link
5075-5124	50	Vulcan	1935	1 ins	D 13388	Ducol	Straight*	Separate	Compression link
5125-5224	100	A-W§	1935	1 ins	D 13388	Chromador	Straight*	Separate	Compression link
5225-5451	227	A-W§	1936-7	1 ins	C 32516	LMS 4B	Sloping	Separate	Compression link
5452-5461	10	Crewe	1938	1 1/16 ins	C 33435	LMS 4A	Sloping	Separate	Compression link
5462-5471¶	10	Crewe	1938	1 1/16 ins	C 33810	LMS 4A	Sloping	Separate	Underhung
5472-5499 4800-4806	35	Derby	Building	1 1/16 ins	C 35207	LMS 4A	Sloping	Hornblocks L & D, separate T	Underhung

* Thirteen engines between N° 5002 and 5142 converted to sloping throatplate.
§Armstrong-Whitworth
¶Batch numbers mistyped 5462-6571 in original report.

through, or at the sides of old weld repairs. This investigation thus confirmed that whenever a crack had been repaired simply by welding it up there was a strong probability of it cracking again - in some cases after a very low mileage. It will be appreciated from inspection of table XI that the

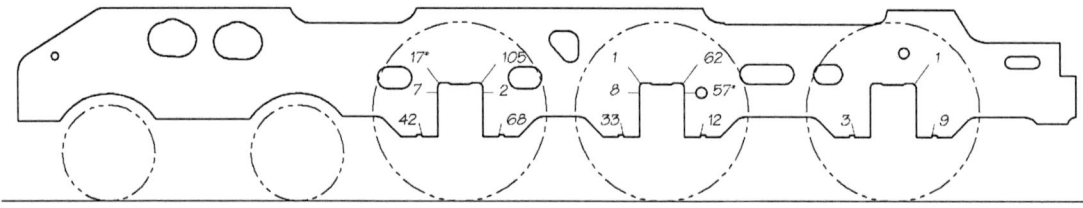

The diagram records the number of cracks recorded from new up to June 1943 for 134 engines between N° 5000-5224. The results for left and right hand frame plates have been added together, but there was a definite tendency for more cracks to appear in the left-hand plate. For engines between N° 5225 and 5451, the crack positions were generally similar although the number of cracks was roughly halved. The back corner of the leading horn gap was the most usual place for cracks, which were often very long, even on occasions extending right through to the top of the frame. The next commonest location was the equivalent position at the driving wheel gaps, where also the top rear rivet position was also prone to cracking. This was prompted by the presence of a nearby washout plug hole in the frame. There was also a large number of cracks at the leading and driving hornstays; but these were comparatively short, usually terminating in the lowest axlebox guide rivet hole. The two figures identified by an asterisk were incorrectly recorded by Mr A J Powell as 117 and 51 respectively in *Stanier 4-6-0s at Work*.

Fig. 28 - Location and number of frame cracks recorded on early LMS Class 5 4-6-0s

$$\frac{\text{Number of cracks per engine} \times 10}{\text{Engine age in years}} \qquad (7)$$

However, this was at best a very rough assessment since normally there was a period of typically 5 to 7 years after building before any cracks appeared. Furthermore the rate of cracking was not linear, there was a tendency for the rate of cracking to increase with engine age. Thus while he was attempting to establish a base rate of incidence, he did warn that certain of the newer classes which at

Class 4 0-6-0 frame was considered to be delivering a good performance.

In order to make headway, Dr Johansen concentrated his efforts on the Class 5 4-6-0 - although not the worst class the company owned for cracking, it had nevertheless been giving continual trouble almost from new, while the difference between the various batches seemingly offered a means of 'cracking' the problem.

Table XII records that three different alloy steels

Locomotives	Time in service to first crack
N° 5000-5220 Records for 148 engines Built August 1934-November 1935	Average of worst engines about 2 years About 50% of the engines had no flaws in first 5 years 11% of the engines had no flaws to June 1943
N° 5235-5330 Records for 72 engines Built August 1936-March 1937	Average of worst engines about 2 years 14% of the engines had no flaws in first 5 years 4% of the engines had no flaws to June 1943
N° 5340-5440 Records for 60 engines Built April 1937-November 1937	93% of the engines had no flaws in first 5 years 72% of the engines had no flaws to June 1943

were used in the frame plates of engines N° 5000-5224. As the 'cracks per engine per 10 years' figures for Ducol and Chromador engines were 4.3 and 3.4 respectively, Dr Johansen initially thought, erroneously as it transpired, there might have been some benefit in the latter alloy, although those engines were six months younger. LMS 4B plate material closely resembled Chromador.

From the standpoint of establishing why frames cracked and thus the remedial design measures necessary to prevent it occurring, it was considered correctly that a most important factor was the time that expired before the initial crack appeared rather than that elapsed for any subsequent cracks. Thus the statistical analysis prompted another table reproduced above which highlights the remarkable differences in the lapsed time required before the locomotives developed their first cracks. The group comprising locomotives N° 5235-5330 may be seen to have been decidedly worse than the engines N° 5000-5220, while the final group N° 5340-5440 was significantly better. The engines forming groups N° 5235-5330 and 5340-5440, corresponded closely with the first and second halves of an order for 227 locomotives made by Armstrong-Whitworth, wherein all of the engines were nominally identical and used LMS 4B steel for the frame plates. It was suggested that either some change(s) in workshop practice may have prompted this difference or that the alloy steel had differed slightly in its properties between the two batches. Perhaps prompted by the presence of metallurgists in the Research Department the latter theory was the favoured one, Analysis of the cracks found on the 2-6-4 parallel boiler tank engines built at Derby seemed to point to differences in steel properties as a cause. Engines built to O/7120 and O/7224 had suffered considerably more cracking than those built previously to O/6807 or the later ones to O/7237.

The report concluded with the observation that no clear correlation could be established between incidences of cracking and the effects of speed, route or season of the year. This is almost certainly to have been due to the relative crudeness of the analysis for the first two factors do have some considerable impact, however in mitigation, it did record there was some evidence to suggest standard locomotives working in Scotland suffered slightly higher incidences of cracking than those in England.

Late in October 1943, Roland Bond, Crewe Works Manager, commented on the findings of this first report. While accepting it generally conformed the general impressions works' staff had formed of the differences in frame performance, he argued caution to be exercised in some of the figures, particularly in those instances where the frame had been afforded a good result:-

"... 0-6-0 N° 4 Class Goods Engines are shown to be generally good, but only 122 Derby maintained engines have apparently been analysed out of a total of some 700 of the class. The general impression of these engines at Crewe is not good, and the fractures experienced with these engines appear to be on the increase. This is one of the classes for which we have spare frames, and I think it would be a good thing for closer analysis to be made of the results obtained from these engines at all centres."

He also commented on the 'Crab' 2-6-0s observing that the records of only 57 out of a total of 245 engines had been checked. While the report's findings did accurately reflect his opinion of the class he thought it important that this should be demonstrated statistically. The parallel boiler 2-6-0 was at the time the only standard class using a design of horn stay previously used at Horwich[35]

---

35 Although LMS engineers liked to refer to them as 'Horwich type' hornstays, they were identical in principle, and very similar in design, to the hornstay Matthew Kirtley had used on his locomotive frames – both inside and outside – as well as those of his tenders; the crank axles had four bearings, but the remaining coupled wheels only two. In contrast for example to Great Western double-framed engines, few of Mr Kirtley's engines suffered frame fractures – at least judging from photographs taken from the 1890s to the 1930s. In the affected examples the repair normally consisted of a narrow doubler riveted across the top of the horn gap, usually on the crank and trailing axle. The location suggests that the affected engines had experienced cracking in the corners of the gaps, presumably due in their long lives having accumulated a high enough number of stress reversal to initiate cracking

wherein stay was secured to extended legs of the frame plate in preference to the clip up design studded to the horns. If a closer analysis of the 'Crab' frame demonstrated little or no trouble with cracks at the bottom of the horn gap he suggested here was a design that could be incorporated almost immediately on new standard engines with the chance of eliminating one source of cracking in the Class 5 4-6-0. Perhaps it was a result of this comment that in due course the LMS adopted 'Horwich stays' but as Eric Langridge reported, whilst the tying-in of the horn gap opening was satisfactory, it was accompanied by the frame fracturing just above the stay's contact face to the frame - in effect the fillet radius was too small. The Works Manager directed most of his comments towards the 4-6-0:-

"The comparative immunity from fractures in the first few years is interesting, but it does rather indicate that we are about to enter upon a period of heavy frame repairs on the Class 5 and other recent standard engines.

It is, I think, a good thing that the behaviour of the Class 5, 4-6-0 has been concentrated upon in the first instance because, although they are not at the moment the worst engines we have to deal with, they are rapidly becoming so, and as a standard class still being built in considerable numbers any modifications in design shown to be desirable should be introduced at the earliest possible moment."

Commenting on table XIII he noted the engines in the first group N° 5000-5224 had been built by three different builders - two private with the other being Crewe - before expressing fears that the former did not always take as much care as the railway workshops in the way they lined up their frames.

Mr Bond referred to the practice, which he considered detrimental, whereby the private works levelled out (straightened) minor imperfections in the frame plates by peening with pneumatic hammers from the top edges of the horn gaps. He thought it induce hidden stresses of quite

Table XIII – Class 5 4-6-0 Mixed Traffic Engines

Engine numbers	N° of engines	N° of records analysed	N° of records without cracks	Built by	Frame material
5000-5019	20	5	1	Crewe	Ducol
5070-5074	5	3			LMS 4B
5020-5069	50	35	1	Vulcan	Ducol
5075-5124	50	27			
5125-5224	100	42	2	A - W	Chromador
5225-5274	50	25	0	A - W	LMS 4B
5275-5334	60	21	3	A - W	LMS 4 B
5335-5451	117	62	39	A - W	LMS 4B

considerable magnitude leading ultimately to cracking in service. Ironically it is the resulting *compressive* stresses the process generates, that are responsible for it being a method by which the

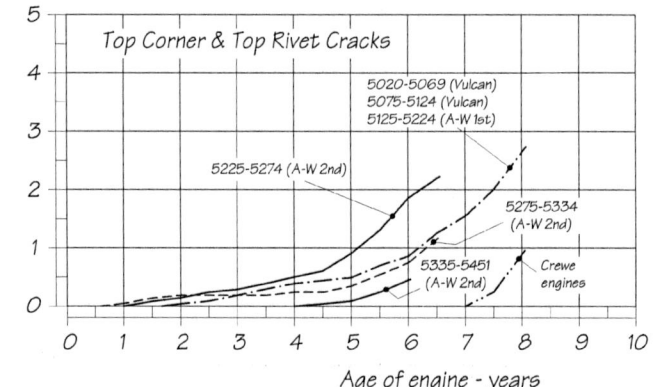

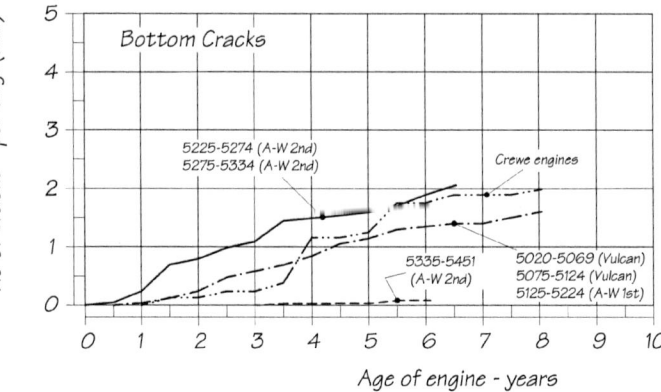

Fig. 29 – Comparison of cracks - Class 5 4-6-0

fatigue resistance of a component may be increased several-fold! Shot peening is nowadays a common way of improving the fatigue resistance of the valve springs for internal combustion engines.

Dr Johansen conducted another statistical examination of locomotive frame records which culminated in August 1944 with the appearance of

---

exacerbated perhaps in some instances by loose (or fretted and untreated) 'Horwich stays'.

a second report (K.56). Its scope was somewhat more extensive that the previous one and for our purposes is of particular interest as it gave more details concerning the performance of the Class 4. Nevertheless, in view of the great concern Class 5 frame behaviour was causing, a significant portion of its pages were devoted to the class. Some of this

Table XIV – Class 8 2-8-0 Goods Engines

Engine numbers	N° of engines	Place built	Frame material	N° of records analysed	N° of records without cracks
8000-1	2	Crewe	Ducol	5	0
8002-11	10	Crewe	Ducol	(8000-4)	
8012-26	15	Crewe	Ducol or LMS 4B	6 (8005-26	2
8027-95	69	Vulcan	Ducol or LMS 4B	31	11

has been included here because it gives further insight into frame performance as well as the difficulties engineers experienced in trying to solve it. Indeed the statistical evidence had if nothing else, implied the problem of frame cracks was one

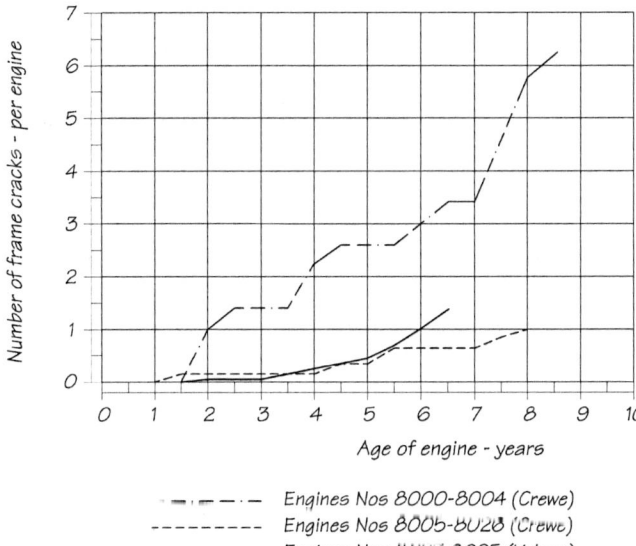

Fig. 30 – Frame cracks - Class 8 2-8-0

which did not have a simple single solution. It was appreciated that several factors gave rise to the incidences of cracking so therefore there was no single all-embracing solution.

Graphs were produced plotting the number of cracks which appeared per engine throughout its life, although to avoid confusion it was necessary to distinguish between those at the upper corners of the horns from those at the bottom. Figure 29, which represents a combined comparison between the earlier and later Class 5 engines, confirms the profile of the curve describing the incidences of cracking is similar for all engines and confirms the frequency of cracking rose with increase in engine age. However, there was a noticeable variation in the ages of the engines in the various groups before the first cracks appeared. Such wide variation in frame performance from what were nominally identical engines, in some instances from even the same maker, surprised the Research Department and was now put down to differences in workshop methods when cutting and finishing the horn gaps or fitting the cross-stays. Twelve years later the Western Region emphasized that stress raisers in the form of surface irregularities which might be produced during frame slotting should be removed by portable grinders. Dr Johansen also referred to the retro-fitting of cross-stays to the leading coupled wheels, expressing an opinion that their presence might be counterproductive in reducing the incidences of cracking. Such 'heresy' received short shrift from Mr Bond in his comments on the second report, nevertheless there is some evidence to suggest Dr Johansen was correct.

Attention was also directed to the Class 8 2-8-0 because as the report explained the class was giving considerable trouble from frame cracking with the number of cracks rapidly increasing. Figure 30 illustrates the relationship between locomotive age and the number of cracks with them grouped as per table XIV. Engines from N° 8096 and onwards, being built in or after 1938 were excluded on account of their comparatively short time in service.

The Crewe-built examples were divided for these purposes after engine N° 8004, as at that point there was a definite change in the incidences of cracking. It was suggested that four of these first five engines were patched at the driving horns early in their lives - whether it had been done badly or incorrectly is not clear - but the other Crewe-builds (N° 8005-8026) demonstrated a normal profile. Almost all of the cracks occurred at the driving horn gap top corners, distributed as follows:-

A Defence of the Midland/LMS Class 4 0-6-0

Position of cracks		N°
Driving top - right-hand side	front	22
	back	43
Driving top - left-hand side	front	16
	back	13
Other positions		2*
	Total	96

*one at the right driving back bottom and the other at the right leading back bottom

The concentration of cracks at the top of the driving gap was held to imply a local weakness prompted in part by the presence of nearby lightening holes and a washout plug opening which together acted as stress concentrations. In contrast to the Class 5, there were only two cracks at the bottom of the horns. Suggested reasons for this, were greater care had been given to the internal radius of the frame where the axlebox guide stays fitted, the lower axle loading in the 2-8-0 reduced the bending moment on its frame plate from the spring hanger bracket; there was no recess for the axlebox guide stay corresponding to that on the Class 5 nor was there a circular spigot on the bottom of the axlebox guides.

By 1944, the Standard Freight Class 4 0-6-0 was complete at 772 members, however, due to the extreme youth of the last forty-five examples compared to the others, they were not considered in the report. Table XV therefore summarizes the results for engines N° 3835 - 4556. What is immediately apparent is that the earliest Midland built examples behaved badly, but the class as a whole exhibited continuous improvement. It was thought that wartime difficulties and in the immediate aftermath had affected the manufacture of the first engines. Throughout the whole class, almost all of the cracks were at the driving axle horn gap, with the majority of these in turn appearing at the top corners. There was a preponderance for them to appear in the right hand frame plate. It will be seen there was good agreement between the frame records for the LMS-built examples maintained at Derby with those maintained at Crewe - 357 engine records inspected of which more than half (51 per cent to be precise) were free of cracks. However, a noticeably higher tendency for cracking was observed in the 47 frame records of engines maintained at St Rollox - 23 per cent free of cracks. This second report revised the number of cracks per engine per 10 years from the previous 0.5 appearing in the first report to 1.2 - thus giving some credence to Mr Bond's observation. Nevertheless, this was a significantly lower cracking rate than that present in either of the two taper-boiler classes we have considered. This result also questions the validity of comparing classes on the basis of 'cracks per engine per 10 years' - something which Dr Johansen admitted in the second report. The calculation assumes, or at least implies, a linear relationship exists between instances of crack formation and locomotive age. However, as figures 29 and 30 demonstrate, the actual relationship was not linear instead the number of cracks increased with age. Thus, when an frame was twenty years old, it would not have had twice as many cracks in it as it had when it was ten years old. It would have had more. This is very relevant to the 'Big Goods',

Table XV – N° 4 Class Goods Engines

Engine numbers	N° in batch	Built for	Builder	Building dates	N° of records analysed	N° of records without cracks	Cracks per engine per 10 years	Maintaining works
3835-3884	50	MR	Derby	1917-18	40	1	10	Derby
3885-3935	52	MR	Derby	1918-20	49	5	6.4	Derby
3937-3986*	50	MR	A-W	1921-22	48	1	6.5	Derby
3987-4026	40	MR	Derby	1921-22	38	15	2.1	Derby
4027-4556	530	LMS	Various *vide* figure 31	1924-28	404	194	1.2 / 1.1 / 1.7	Derby / Crewe / St. Rollox

*Locomotives N° 4557-4561, ex-SD&JR, also built by Armstrong-Whitworth in 1922, shew similar analysis characteristics to this group.

Table XVI – Good and Bad Orders, N° 4 Class Goods Engines

Engine numbers	Built	Characteristic	Remarks
4135-4176	Crewe	Bad	4107-34 in the same order, fair
4177-4206	St. Rollox	Bad	Northern Division engines in this batch are also known to be bad
4207-4301	Derby	Good	End of batch better than beginning
4302-4311	Crewe	Bad	
4357-4381	Barclay	Bad	
4382-4406	N British	Bad	
4407-4436	Derby	Good	

for most were built between 1924 and 1928, giving them an average age at the time of these reports of nearly twenty. Taking the reported figure of 1.2 cracks per engine per ten years and applying the formula given earlier suggests there would have been almost 2.4 cracks per engine in 1944. Comparing this figure with the curves for the Class 5 4-6-0 or the Class 8 2-8-0 and extrapolating to where these curves might reasonably have extended to once the engines were twenty years old suggests both would had suffered considerably more cracks than 2.4. Both of these more modern locomotive classes therefore had a poorer frame performance than the 0-6-0.

The LMS-built 'Big Goods' exhibited noticeable variations between the different orders from the various builders. Footplatemen have often referred to differences in performance between the different batches, but plotted in figure 31 is the frame record for each of the 357 English maintained examples inspected by the Research Department. The diagram therefore shews, whether by 1944, the engine had suffered from a frame crack. The diagram suggests for some orders there was no discernible tendency but in other cases it is clear there was a considerable number of orders in which there was a marked preponderance for either cracked or non-cracked frames. The driving factor leading to which of these two situations an engine found itself was not due to the maintaining works, but rather to the diligence and care displayed by the original building works. This situation is highlighted in table XVI.

It should be appreciated that figure 31 also shews that some of the orders built by Crewe, Derby and North British were neither conspicuously good nor bad.

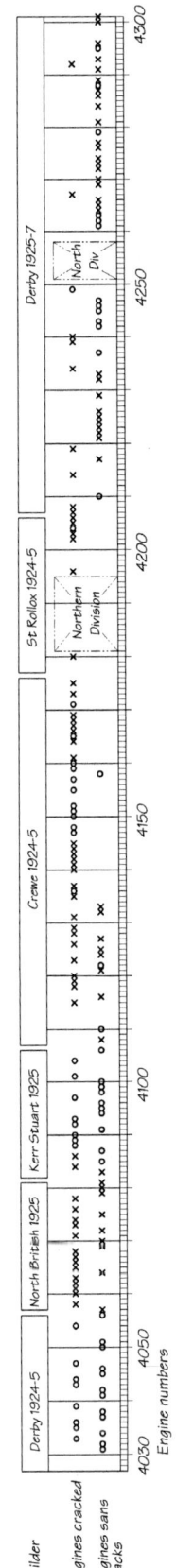
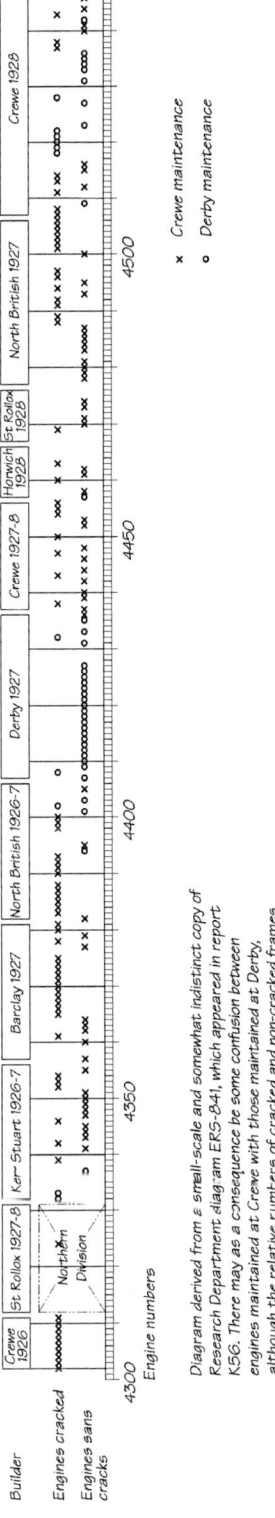

Fig. 31 - No 4 Class Goods engines - frame cracks, & works where engines built

A Defence of the Midland/LMS Class 4 0-6-0

Therefore, it seems most likely that the primary reason for these divergences in frame performance lay in differences in shop practice, particularly in respect over the care taken in the finishing of the radius at the top corners of the horns, but also of the smoothness of the horn opening generally. The smoother and more uniform the finish the higher the fatigue resistance the plate edge and the radiused corner presented towards delaying the development of a crack. This is a point that was reinforced by Mr Bond in his comments on the second interim report:-

"The importance of good workshop practice in frame building is further emphasised in the analysis of the performance of the 0-6-0 N° 4 Class Freight Engines. The summary of bad and good orders shewn in Table 11 *(reproduced as table XVI - APT)* is almost exactly what I would have expected. At the time the particular engines in question were built there is, I think, no doubt that Derby built a better frame than either Crewe or St. Rollox. And certainly the bad showing of engines built by Messers. Andrew Barclay exactly confirms my experience of this firm during the time I was inspecting those engines under construction at their Works. Their methods at that time were crude and it was difficult to convince them of the influence which workshop practice may subsequently have on performance in later years."

Of course variation in plate quality may also have played a part, but it is believed that as the twentieth century unfolded developments by steel makers in metallurgy and product consistency ensured this would have steadily reduced.

Mr Eric Riley, Locomotive Superintendent of the Midland Railway Centre, has considerable experience of working on the Standard 4, much of it gained whilst he was at Westhouses. He confirmed that those examples of the class which suffered cracking developed fractures normally from the top corners of the crank axle horn openings. These would be allowed to extend six to

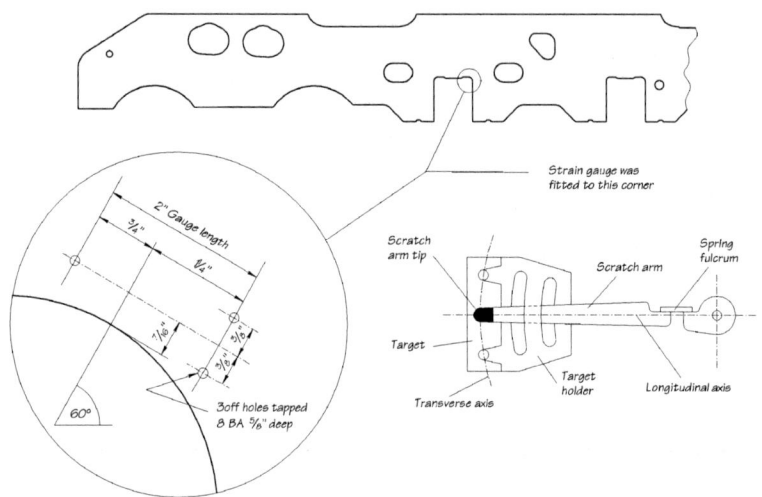

The De Forest scratch strain gauge was about the size and weight of a large grasshopper. It was attached to surfaces typically by spot welds, solder or as here by screws. The accuracy and sensitivity was a function of the microscope used to read the scratch. It comprised two parts - the arm and the target. The arm was a sheet metal finger with a gauge point at one end and at the other, a plastic patch serving as a matrix to hold a few diamond fragments that were the scratchers. Around seven fragments were usually used to ensure at least one would give a satisfactory record. The target was a chromium plated brass sheet about one inch square with two transverse slots in it. This piece served three purposes (i) it was the second gauge point; (ii) it received the scratch record; and (iii) the metal strip between the two slots served as a retainer for the arm. The retainer pressed the diamonds against the target with the correct pressure while at the same time granted lateral freedom to the arm so that it could move transversely across the target to provide a time axis in dynamic tests for plotting strain against approximate time - as was done in these tests. To obtain the lateral movement, the arm was manually displaced against a spring at the start of a test. It was held by the retainer strip in the displaced position in the static state, but when the vibratory action came on, since moving friction is less than static friction, the spring would gradually restore to arm to its original position. The time axis, although approximate, was adequate. The spring was formed by deforming the arm in a small press near to its gauge point so that a vertical fin was produced perpendicular to the normal surface of the arm. When the test piece experienced strain the two parts of the gauge moved towards or apart from one another leaving a scratch on the target of length equal to the strain experienced. As the gauge had no magnification factor to establish strains from the 2 ins gauge length the sawtooth trace was photographed at a magnification of 100 to 500 diameters, which allowed the amplitudes to be measured using a ruler. Knowing the strain values and Young's modulus for the test material enabled the stresses to be calculated.

Fig. 32 – De Forest strain gauges - Class 5 4-6-0 N° 5088

eight inches in length before they were repaired. However, he made the observation that the particular engines affected were intensively used pulling heavy coal trains. There are four preserved members of the class, N° 3924, 4027, 4123 and 4422. Referring to table XV and figure 31 suggests N° 3924 will almost certainly have experienced frame cracking by 1944. The position with N° 4027 is unclear since the frame record of this engine was not examined, conversely of the remaining pair, Crewe-built, N° 4123 featured as a cracked engine, while Derby-built N° 4422 was a crack-free example. Currently, three of these engines are in regular service hauling passenger trains on preserved lines with the fourth awaiting restoration. Accordingly, enquiries were made concerning the presence of cracks in this quartet. Whether this sample, which represents one-half of one per cent of the total number constructed can be considered as being statistically significant is left to the reader to decide, however none of the three gentlemen responsible for the maintenance and repair of these engines and who answered this enquiry, reported the presence of any cracks in the frames. Of course, since preservation the work the engines are now called on to perform, and thus the stresses experienced by their frame plates, will inevitably be considerably lighter than they experienced when they were younger and in their heyday, but interestingly no one has noticed evidence of any previous crack repairs when their charges were undergoing restoration. Presumably, had new replacement sections been welded into any of these the welds would have been ground smooth on completion. Whilst they would not be readily seen, careful inspection of the frame plates stripped of paint should reveal if they are present or not.

Inspired it seems in part at least by a hypothesis proposed by Mr C W Clarke[36] (it was referred to in the first frame report) regarding the distribution of stress between the cylinders and the leading coupled wheels, the Research Department measured strain values in the frame plates around the leading horn upper back corners in a Class 5. By fitting a pair of De Forest recoding scratch extensometers[37], fitted one to each frame plate on

Table XVII – Measured Frame Stresses in Class 5 4-6-0 N° 5088

Test N°	Conditions prevailing	Maximum stresses - tons/sq in left-hand frame	Maximum stresses - tons/sq in right-hand frame	Remarks
2	Full gear and well opened regulator, engine pulling 412-ton train 5-6mph on straight line. Coasting on 7.3 chains curve, 5 mph. Full gear and fully opened regulator, engine pulling 412-ton train 12 mph on straight line.	-7.4/+5.1 = 12.5 -2.1/0 = 2.1 -6.9/+5.6 = 12.5	-4.1/+7.4 = 11.5 +3.5/+1.4 = 2.1 -3.6/+8.9 = 12.5	See figure 33
3	Full gear and fully opened regulator, engine pulling 412-ton train 11mph on straight line. Full gear and fully opened regulator, engine pulling 412-ton train 13 mph on straight line.	-12.0/+0.4 = 12.4 -10.9/+0.8 = 11.7	-6.3/+4.3 = 10.6 -7.1/+3.8 = 10.9	
4	Full gear and fully opened regulator, light engine with steam brake on. 6mph straight line.	-5.4/+7.3 = 12.7	Instrument failed to record zero line 13.5 amplitude	
4A	Full gear and fully opened regulator, light engine running tender first. Steam brake on. 12mph 13 chains curve. Full gear and fully opened regulator, light engine running tender first. Steam brake on. 12mph 13 chains curve.	-6.4/+9.5 = 15.9 -5.5/+10.9 = 16.4	Instrument failed to record	
5	Full gear and fully opened regulator, engine tender first pulling 412-ton train 6mph on straight line. Full gear and fully opened regulator, engine tender first pulling 412-ton train 7mph on straight line. Full gear and fully opened regulator, engine tender first pulling 412-ton train 8mph on straight line.	-4.3/+11.5 = 15.8 -6.4/+8.6 = 15.0 -5.4/+11.0 = 16.4*	-5.0/+9.7 = 14.7 -5.1/+8.4 = 13.5 -4.2/+8.7 = 12.9	See figure 33
6	Full gear and fully opened regulator, engine tender first pulling 412-ton train 5mph on straight line. Full gear and fully opened regulator, engine tender first pulling 412-ton train 13mph on straight line.	-5.5/+7.8 = 13.3 -4.6/+8.8 = 13.4	-5.6/+8.6 = 14.2 -5.1/+9.6 = 14.7	

NB:- Test run N° 1 was of the nature of a preliminary run and no details were provided
*There was a range of stress of 17.9 tons/sq in during that test

---

36 Mr C W Clarke *Locomotive Hornblocks* I Loco E March 1939 p625.

Mr Clarke's stress distribution hypothesis appears in figure 11 earlier.

37 Mr T Herbert of the LMS Research Department had obtained these extensometers during a visit to the USA in 1938 where he met the scientist-inventor Professor Alfred De Forest.

A Defence of the Midland/LMS Class 4 0-6-0

their inner faces near the upper rear corner of the leading coupled axle gaps of engine N° 5088, the stresses could be estimated for various conditions of engine working and track. These early strain gauges were not suitable for a locomotive running at high speed or for any length of time, so the tests had to be conducted at low speed and were thus limited in scope. Nevertheless Dr Johansen was able to demonstrate the highest stresses recorded were caused by the steam pressure acting on the pistons. When the engine ran chimney first the change in stress from tensile to compressive and back again ranged 12-13 tons/sq in; but when N° 5088 ran tender first under similar conditions, the range of stress could rise to 15 or 16 tons/sq in. On one occasion, which was blamed on uneven track, a range of stress of 17.9 tons/sq in was measured. All of these tests, which comprised a total of 6 runs made about the time report K.50 was being complied, were conducted in the Derby environs between Etches Park Carriage Sidings, Way and Works Signal Box, Derby North Junction and Derby South Junction during the summer of 1943. Widely differing examples of track geometry were used to stress the frame - straight line, check-railed curve (7.3 chains radius at its sharpest), diamond crossings and ordinary cross-overs.

All of the results, which are summarized in table XVII, refer to the changes in stress observed in the 2-inch gauge length relative to that extant in the frame plate immediately before the test. Of course there will have been a small initial stress present in the plate before starting each run, caused by track conditions acting in association with the axlebox springs. This was held to be the reason why the stress in a frame plate differed at the end of a test from its value at the beginning - this stress

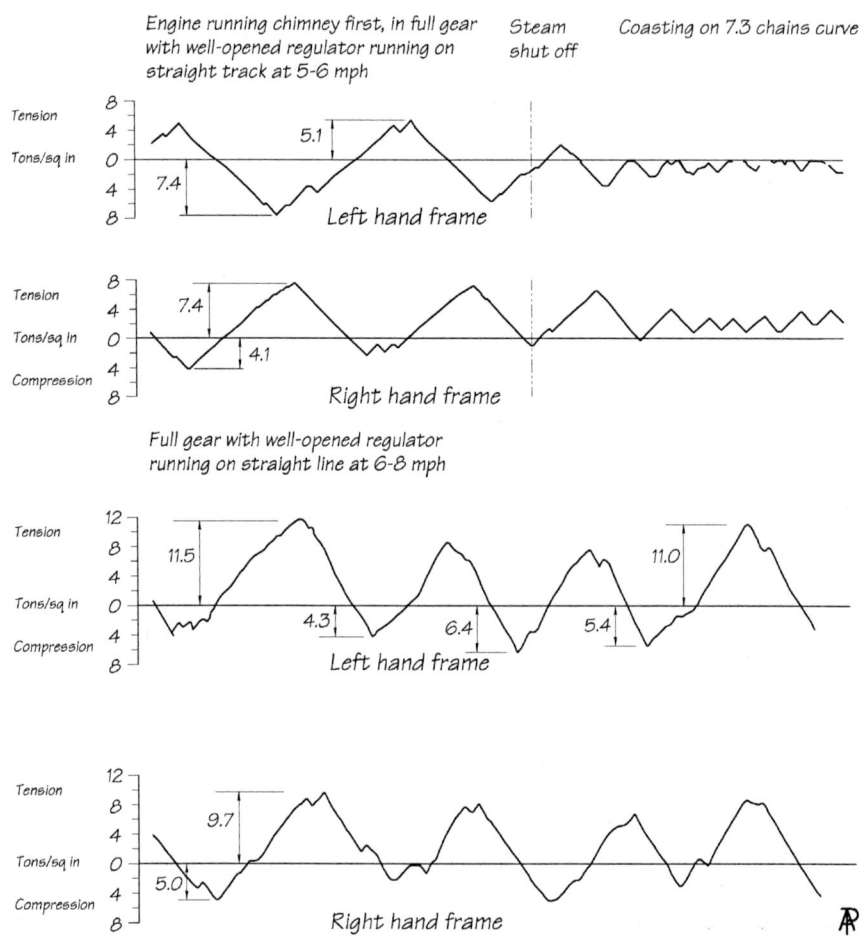

Fig. 33 - Sample frame stresses recorded on LMS Class 5 4-6-0 No. 5088

difference amounted to 4.1 tons/sq in reduction in one run. For this reason, when considering the results, Dr Johansen urged attention should be directed to the changes of stress rather than its exact tensile or compressive value above or below what could in any event be an arbitrary zero. Inspection of table XVII and figure 33 reveals steam loading dominated - the stresses generated by traversing curves or running over crossings were relatively small.

To explore these frame stresses further, which could be done more conveniently within the laboratory, the company constructed a full size section (10ft 11ins long) of the left leading horn gap of a Class 5 4-6-0 frame complete with axlebox guides and a clip up type horn stay. Stresses were measured at various positions in the plate, first with the horn stay in place and afterwards with the stay removed. Stresses were also measured in the horn stay when it was in position and the load it transmitted thereby deduced. The load, applied to the ends of the portion of frame plate, was a tensile force representing the cylinder cover load. It was applied across the axle gap acting along the centre line of the frame in the plane of the cylinder centres.

Both the frame plate and the stay were fitted with the newly developed resistance strain gauges[38] with the resulting stresses measured at various for various degrees of tightness of the horn stay nuts under a representative values of piston thrust. Two types of strain gauge were used - the single wire type where the strain direction could be predicted such as at the surface radii of the horn gap opening, and the rosette type[39] when the direction of stress was uncertain. This latter design was used on the outside face of the frame plate. From the strain measurements present in each of the three gauge wires, the two principal stresses and their directions could be calculated.

The maximum stresses were found to occur around the radii at the top corners of the horn gap. A tensile load of 40 tons across this gap produced an average stress at the radii of 5.2 tons/sq in when the horn stay was in position, rising to at least 18 tons/sq in when the stay was absent. It was also found that the stay, when tightly fitted and under the same loading, carried a tensile load of 14.3 tons. However, the stress across the *width* of the stay was very uneven. This investigation was completed by the inclusion of a

Table XVIII – Stresses Measured in Horn Gap and Horn Stay for a Steady Load of Forty Tons applied across the Gap

Position	Mean value of stress (on opposite sides of frame plate where applicable) - tons/sq in	
	With horn stay fitted	With horn stay removed
Frame plate stresses		
M & N Radii at top corners of horn gap	5.2	> 18
F Near back corner of horn gap	3.5	8.6
E Near front corner of horn gap	3.6	7.8
G Centre line above horn gap	2.2	4.6
O Front recess for horn stay clip	4.5	- 0.33
P Rear recess for horn stay clip	3.8	- 0.47
Horn stay stresses		Negative indicates compressive stress
A Bottom face, inside	- 0.92	
B Top face, inside	0.86	
C Bottom face, outside	2.45	
D Top face, outside	4.50	

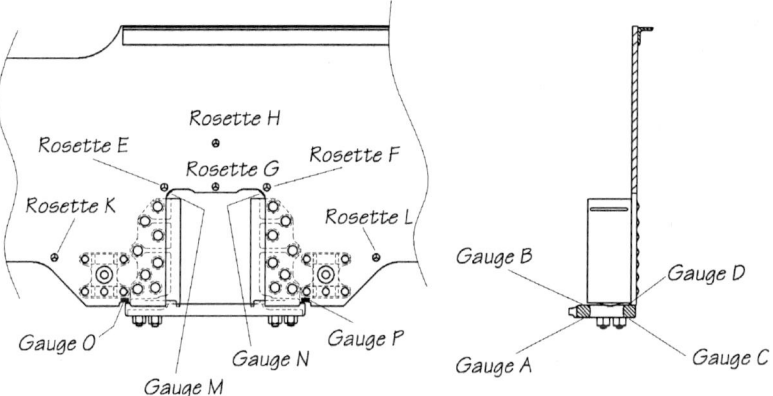

Fig. 34 - Strain gauge positions on dummy Class 5 frame

mathematical analysis estimating the stresses present in a frame plate carried out by Dr H I Andrews, employing Professor Southwell's new 'relaxation' method.

According to Dr Johansen table XVIII, which appeared in the report, summarizes the more important results obtained. They correspond to the tensile load of 40 tons - a value considered to represent the maximum longitudinal force imposed on the frame in service. Table XIX, derived from the I Loco E paper and not the original report, shews the impact that a slack horn stay had on magnitude of the stress at points *M* and *N*. Thus a stay slack to the extent of 0.035ins at each end with the nuts no more than nipped as opposed to being really tight – a situation far from unknown in service – meant the resulting slight 'working' in

---

38 This early example of the use in the UK of strain gauges was possible because of samples obtained by Mr Herbert during a second visit to the USA. Essentially, they comprise a grid of fine wire mounted on a thin paper or plastic base with two soldering tags. Early ones were about one inch long and had an electrical resistance of around 75-100 ohms. In use, the paper base was securely glued to the item to be stressed with the ends of the grid connected to and electric circuit. When the test item was stressed the resulting changes in the length of the grid could be detected as minute changes in resistance and thereby the stress quantified. Incidentally the LMS made a gift of a few to Rolls Royce at Derby.

39 Rosettes consisted of three separate gauge wires arranged either with their axes at 60° to one another to form a closed equilateral triangle, or two at 90° to one another with the third bisecting the angle.

the horn gap stressed the frame plate as much as if no stay was present[40]. In an attempt to provide greater security of the horn gap in the event of fretting or the horn stay studs slackening back, the horn stay was usually provided with upward pointing lugs whose outer edges were arranged to locate in recesses cut into the lower edge of the frame. Unfortunately, as we have seen, these recesses could be counter productive for they served as stress raisers and caused cracks to appear. However, we might suggest LMS engineers had mislead themselves into believing that to prevent cracking in the top corners of the horn gaps, the hornblocks or guides had to be rigidly attached to the frame plate. Likewise that the horn stay had to be capable of preventing the opening at the bottom of the horn gap from increasing under the influence of the fore and aft thrusts generated when the engine was hauling its train.

It was desirable for several reasons the whole assembly should be kept tight but it was really the too small radii in the horn cut out in the frame acting as a stress raiser that prompted the cracks to appear. While the frame/horn stay/horn assembly remained tight, most of the piston load was carried by the stay, which greatly reduced the stress in the top corners of the horn gaps. However, tables XIX and XX record the average stress at top corners of horn gap stress even when everything was tight was over 5 tons/sq in, which exceeds the rough estimate given earlier for the maximum stress that a Class 5 frame could endure without fatigue cracks eventually developing. This measured stress level implies that the fillet radius of the upper corners of the horn gap was too small so cracks would inevitably form there given sufficient time and reversals of stress *even if* the horn guides and horn stay had remained tight throughout. Clifford Cocks, the Chief Locomotive Draughtsman of the Southern Railway, seems to have been alert to this for he observed[41]:-

> "There must be a large number of engines actually doing useful work after the hornstay has loosened and therefore the time has surely arrived, when the foregoing should be considered in design, *i.e.* to make the frame sufficiently strong to withstand this condition."

This, at its most basic, meant ensuring that the openings cut in the frames for the horns were be given a far more generous radius, or radii since an elliptical shape was actually significantly better. Thus, when in service, if for whatever reason the horn stays could not be kept tight, then the stresses in the top corners of the horns would not have risen to a value that encouraged cracks to develop. In view of the excellent performance of the Southern 'Merchant Navy', which by 1947 still enjoyed an absence of frame cracks, it is interesting to see that Mr Cocks used a simple clip-up design secured at each end by a pair of bolts 1¼ins diameter studs and very reminiscent of the traditional design fitted to the 'Big Goods' - Mr Cox was to use a similar arrangement on his BR Class 7 4-6-2. This design approach is an example of the forward thinking displayed by the small team employed by the Southern Railway on steam locomotive design. Another is the half-elliptical profile it adopted for the profile of the top of the horn gap openings in its Q1 class 0-6-0 classes, an arrangement which it is believed, may have commenced with the earlier class Q. This same elliptical shape, albeit in the form of four quarter-ellipses, is to be found located one at each of the four corners of the hatch openings in the main decks of modern ships –

Table XIX – Stresses Measured in Horn Gap and Horn Stay for a Steady Load of Forty Tons applied across the Gap – I Loco E Results

Stay	Stay nuts	Average stress at top of corners of horn gap - tons/sq in	Load carried by stay - tons
Tight	Tight	5.5	13.2
0.005ins slack	Tight	7.0	~
0.010ins slack	Tight	8.7	~
0.020ins slack	Tight	12.5	9.4
0.035ins slack	Tight	12.9	5.3
0.035ins slack	Just nipped	17.0	1.9
No stay	~	More than 18.0	0

---

40 In service, fretting corrosion occurred at the contact or mating faces of the stay and the horns, due to tiny differences in movement between the relative parts. In effect the bolting or contact pressure was insufficient to prevent other forces, piston load was considered the most likely although it is possible there were others, causing dissimilar movement resulting in gradual wear and looseness. Thus, even if the hornstays had been fully tightened initially this ceased to be the case after the locomotive had been in service for a while, throwing increased stress onto the top corners of the horn gaps. Re-tightening the nuts by shed staff brought temporary relief before the fretting re-exerted itself.

41 Mr C S Cocks contributing to the discussion at London following:-
Mr E S Cox & Dr F C Johansen *Locomotive Frames* I Loco E Paper 473 November 1947 p129.

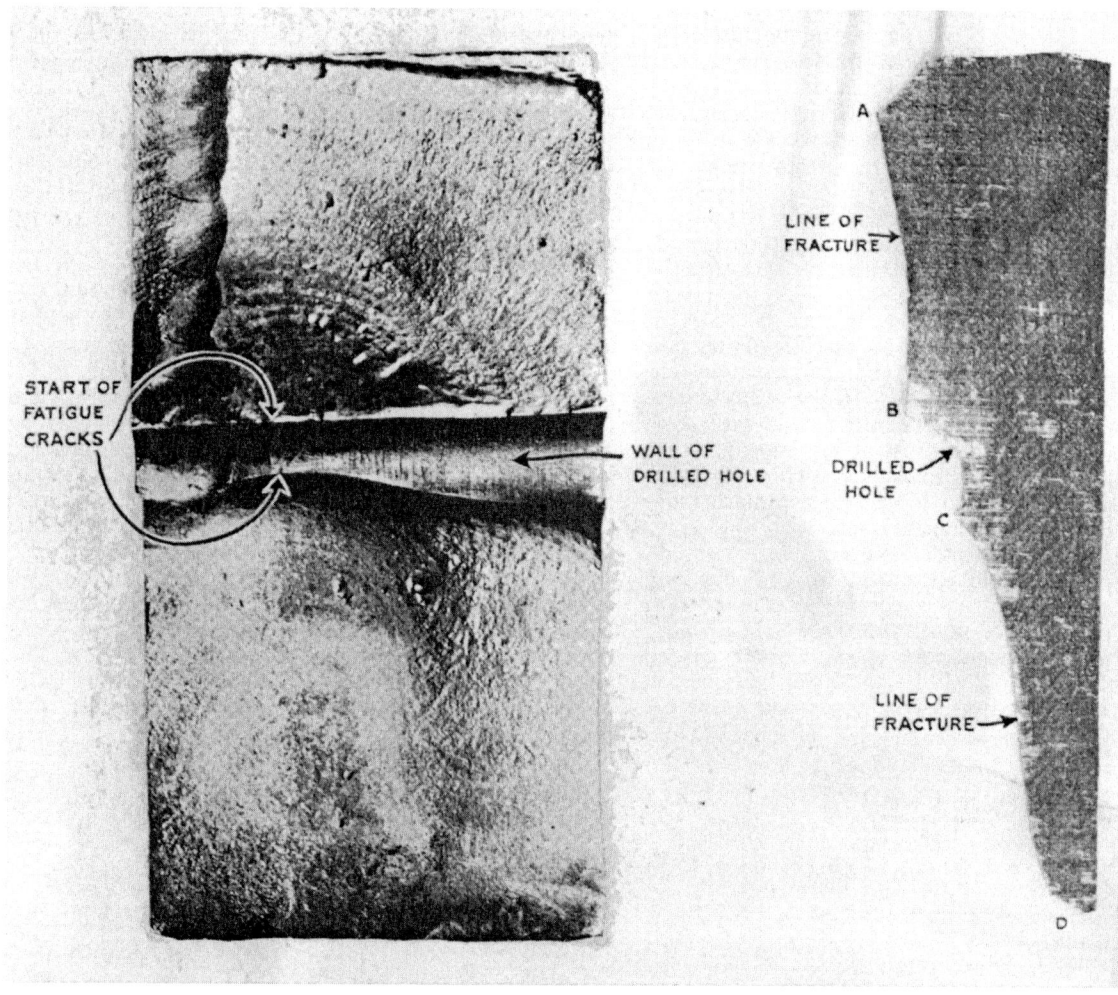

Fracture recorded in one of the rails of an American bar frame, caused by a bolt hole not having been drilled cleanly. The resulting rough and torn surface left by the drill prompted two fatigue cracks. The frame section at the break was five inches wide and nine and one-half inches deep, yet there was sufficient fluctuation in stress in the steel immediately surrounding the bolt hole to initiate the cracks, when present in conjunction with sufficiently poor surface finish.

The side view of the broken frame (right hand view) shews the paths of the cracks - almost vertically upwards in one, while in the other progressed diagonally downwards. It was concluded that the top fracture started first and was well advanced or even complete before the lower one started.

On the evidence presented by this fracture in a slab of steel five inches thick, it was perhaps somewhat naive to have expected an increase in frame plate thickness from one inch to one and one-quarter inches was going to cure anything.

Fig. 35 – Fatigue fractures in an American locomotive bar frame

another highly stressed component[42].

By contrast the approach displayed by the LMS towards solving its frame cracking was somewhat reminiscent of its scrap-and-build policy regarding locomotives. Action which also involved directing substantial resources at the problem, only in this instance it comprised statistical analysis, the construction and testing of the dummy frame section, advanced mathematical stress analysis *etc*. The other three 'Big Four' companies were not so generously funded, yet for example the LNER and the Southern were both able to effect improvements, the former for example through careful observation of its A3 class in services and the latter by adopting simpler and cheaper testing techniques particularly photoelasticity.

Photoelasticity, which developed shortly before the Great War, derives from the fact that certain transparent plastic materials such as celluloid, Perspex and some epoxy resins exhibit the

---

[42] "More recently the photo-elastic technique had revealed that a fillet shaped to the quadrant of an ellipse was better than one shaped to the quadrant of a circle".
Comment by a Dr Ward to the discussion following:-
Mr H I Andrews *Stresses in Locomotive Coupling and Connecting Rods* I Loco E Paper 517 Nov 1952.

A Defence of the Midland/LMS Class 4 0-6-0

phenomenon of 'birefringence' when viewed in polarized light while subject at the same time to stress. If therefore a two dimensional model of say a locomotive frame plate was made in Perspex sheet and loaded as it would be in service (to scale) and examined in a beam of polarized light, a pattern of coloured interference fringes will be seen, particularly in the more highly stressed areas of the model. The colours and the number of fringes are proportional to the level of stress as well as indicating its direction. Basil Byrne of the Southern Railway, who built his own polariscope, some time before the outbreak of the Second World War., used it later to demonstrate the superiority of the BFB wheel centre then being contemplated by O V S Bulleid. It was also applied, according to Mr A O Gilchrist in *A History of Engineering Research on British Railways*, with great success to the 'Merchant Navy' 4-6-2, including presumably the frame design. Whilst the latter is pure conjecture, the radii of the horn gaps were noticeably larger than those normally adopted, which suggests the change was prompted through photoelasticity.

Replying to an observation made by Mr T Robson[43] (in charge of locomotive testing on the LNER) that since calculating the stress in a locomotive frame took so long why not use photoeslasticity, Dr Johansen said the LMS had conducted some experiments on simple models made from Bakelite (BT 61893), representing a portion of a frame plate that included a horn gap. These had demonstrated the positions and relative magnitudes of stress when the horn stay was fitted and absent. However, the complete quantitative stress analysis of such a complicated

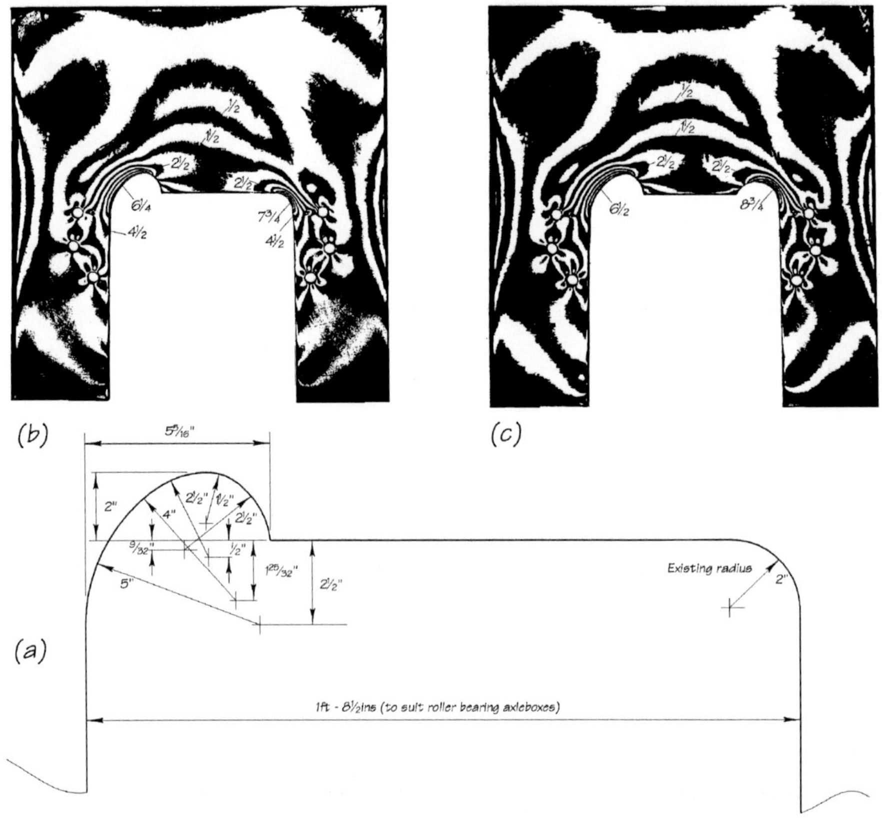

A scale model of the object of interest is made from a transparent synthetic resin such as Bakelite, Catalin, Lucite *etc*, or as here Araldite. The model is mounted in a loading frame of the photoelastic bench and strained in such a way that the conditions of loading correspond to those in practice. Certain optical effects occur which are related to the direction and magnitude of the principal stresses in the model, and which become evident by the appearance of coloured bands or alternatively bright and dark bands in the model when it is viewed through a disk of Polaroid. These coloured or light and dark fringes as shewn above can be readily interpreted to give the directions of the principal stresses and their magnitude at every point in the model. The great value of the method lies in giving a visual image of the regions where the stresses are particularly high, *i.e.* where the stress concentrations occur. Photoelasticity was a very good contemporary tool for evaluating such stress concentrations quickly and obtaining exact information on the effects changes in outline would have on the magnitude and disposition of the stress concentrations. This evaluation was often quite impossible by contemporary mathematical analysis, and even in those cases where it was possible, the amount of mathematical labour involved was prodigious. Notwithstanding the widespread use of computers in design, photoelasticity is still used today.

Fig. 36 – Photoelastic analysis of the stress concentrations in a GWR 'King' horn gap

---
43 Mr E S Cox & Dr F C Johansen *Locomotive Frames* I Loco E Paper 473 November 1947 pp180 & 183.

structure as a locomotive frame was, he thought, beyond contemporary photoelastic technique. He, therefore preferred mathematical models and full sized replicas which permitted direct measurement by strain gauges. While there is some truth in his observation regarding using photoelasticity for complicated structures, three-dimensional methods were in use, albeit in their infancy. Conversely, although calculating the stresses ought to have been the more reliable, it did rely on accurate data and the application of a large number of repetitive calculations. Incidentally the Bakelite the LMS used for its models was made in America - it was *very* expensive.

Interestingly, as a comparison between calculation and photoelasticity, Swindon was able using the latter method to design a superior horn gap profile to that used on the BR Standard locomotives, which had been developed from LMS work. In 1956, the CM&EE of the Western Region asked that a photoelastic investigation be carried on the region's locomotive frames out to locate the points of high stress concentration and to derive means of reducing them. Due to the large number of places where fractures occurred, the intention was to treat each weak point as an individual item and follow up each investigation with a report. The initial investigation was confined to the 'King' class frame but it was anticipated that some of the findings could be applied to a number of other classes. Following the inspection of a number of 'King' frames in Swindon Works, it was decided to tackle the fractures appearing at the top corners of the horn gaps first, before directing attention to the portion of frame between the cylinders.

A 1/24th scale (half inch to the foot) model of the coupled wheel portion of the frame was loaded to represent engine weight and spring reactions, under static conditions. Then additional loads were applied to represent steam load forces for two conditions - pistons in opposition (engine on dead centres) and both pistons exerting on the drawbar. In each case, similar stress concentrations were observed at the radius in the horn corners.

To examine these in greater detail, particularly the stress concentrations generated by the forces that tended to widen the horn gap opening, a pair of 1/10th full size models were made of the horn gap in Araldite. In addition to the immediate indication of high stress locations, the photoelastic model also shews regions of low stress from which material could conveniently be removed, without weakening the frame plate. Perhaps rather startling to first consideration is that *removing* material at or near a high stress concentration can effect a significant reduction in the maximum stress. By a system of repeated observations and alterations (sometimes referred to as 'file it and see') a revised top corner profile was evolved which effected a stress reduction while at the same time did not present a problem to the machine shops. Figure 36a shews details of the streamlined undercut fillet proposed, a form of transition curve possessing a continuous reduction in its radius of curvature. The advantage of this new profile is demonstrated in figure 36b wherein it is compared to the original simple 2ins radius. Not only does the revised profile represent around a 20 per cent reduction in stress but also the stress trajectory is more uniform. Perhaps rather impishly, Swindon compared its profile with the undercut radius adopted on BR Standard classes - *vide* figure 36c - and similar to late Midland and LMS practice. The latter, will be seen to have been significantly inferior, generating roughly 13 per cent increase in stress over the original 1927 design! Incidentally the impact the presence of horn guide or hornblock securing holes could have in the plate is suggested in both of the latter figures.

Taking the Western Region photoelastic test results as probably also being representative of the work conducted on the Southern, we might conclude the LMS investigation was incomplete. Whilst the statistical analysis could explain *what* had happened, it was not very good at explaining *why* it had occurred. Measuring the stresses in a frame plate was interesting, but unless it was tied in *quantitatively* to the importance of fillet profile and radii, surface finish of plate edges, *etc.* it was of limited benefit. Similarly there was no comment on the impact repetitive stress reversals effected on lowering the fatigue strength of the frame material even though the cracks were recognized as being fatigue in origin. Thus although a stress of 5 tons/sq in or so, was measured at the horn corner radius there was no mention this was sufficiently high to initiate cracking. The stress-life fatigue method was well established procedure by the 1940s, but no reference was made to it in any of the various reports Dr Johansen produced. Sure, there was not a great deal of reliable data and care had to be used in its use, particularly with large structures, but at the time it was the only approach available. It could have given guidance, particularly in details, furthermore Professor

A Defence of the Midland/LMS Class 4 0-6-0

Charles Inglis, member of the LMS Scientific Advisory Committee, through his work conducted on *HMS Wolf* looking the impact geometrical irregularities had on raising local stress values, had in effect started it all!

Tom Coleman reputedly had little time for the Research Department and on the basis of these reports it quite understandable. One feels they contained little concrete to guide a designer towards avoiding future cracking that he would not have already known or alternatively could have worked out like his colleagues on the LNER.

Briefly report K.56 concluded that the performance of a frame was largely determined at the time of building where small differences in building practice could wrought substantial differences in performance. Subsequent structural modifications could also have a significant impact. Great importance therefore should be applied (a) to careful finishing of the top corners of the horn gaps to avoid any discontinuities likely to cause stress concentration, and (b) careful fitting of the horn stay so that it could take the horizontal forces without working loose in service. There was little physical difference between a good and bad frame design while length of service had a profound effect on the cracking of nominally identical engines. Hornblocks appeared more successful that separate guides. Therefore on engines where there was a preponderance of cracks at one place, implying local weakness in an otherwise satisfactory frame, it might be worth substituting hornblocks in place of guides at that axle - a proposal that the Locomotive Drawing Office had already applied to a batch of class 5s then under construction. Adopting the former L&Y practice of attaching the stay directly to the frame was suggested, while in the case of earlier engines the stay should be re-designed to avoid the need for the small notch recess in the frame between the guide and the spring hanger bracket. More contentious however, was Dr Johansen's view that fitting cross-stays to the leading axle of the Class 5 frame was detrimental.

The derived paper *Locomotive Frames* expanded these recommendations, giving a list of ten causes for frame cracks developing and suggesting in very general terms reasons how they might be avoided. They were as per the following, however an important omission from this list was the impact of discontinuities, particularly those involving a localized region of high rigidity positioned adjacent to an area having significantly lower lateral stiffness. As we shall see this latter factor severely affected the performance of several frame designs:-

(i) Frame cracks were, almost without exception caused by fatigue originating from a localized region of stress concentration. There was nothing to suggest static loading or lifting forces was ever the cause of a fracture.

(ii) Nearly all the cracks originated at horn gaps, at one or more of the six positions indicated in figure 28. They were more common around the top corners than the bottom ones, more prevalent at the rear corners than the front and predominantly at leading or driving horn gaps the trailing ones being hardly affected.

(iii) The number of frame cracks in any batch of engines was related to frame age – illustrated by the curves appearing in figures 29, 30 and 39. Normally some years elapsed before cracks first appear, but in classes prone to cracking, the number of instances increased as the class aged.

(iv) Engine classes prone to frame cracks generally had large piston thrusts, frames not exceeding 11/8ins thickness, considerable offset between axlebox centres and frame plates, separate horn guides rather than hornblocks, and flat type horn stays.

(v) Engine classes more immune from frame cracking generally possessed some or all of the following – smaller piston thrusts and offsets, hornblocks instead of horn guides, horn stays connecting the legs of the frame and independent of the horns, frames more than 11/8ins thick.

(vi) The margin between a good design and a bad one was relatively small, so that nominally identical engines within the same class could exhibit significant differences in their propensity for cracking due to variations in building practice, frame material etc.

(vii) Workshop practices were important, particularly regarding generous fillet radii and careful finishing around the corners of horn gaps also precise fitting to help keep horn stays tight and rigid.

(viii) The reappearance of cracks in places where previous cracks had been repaired by welding suggested that such repairs, no matter how carefully carried out were not the equivalent of the original plate.

(ix) The main cause of frame fracture was piston thrust, lateral flange forces were less important while those due to vertical weight were considered secondary.

(x) Curvature of the line relative to running speed had some influence in so far cracking on some classes was higher in Scotland where the curvature tended to be more severe. Train speeds and season of the year had no significant effect.

Armed with our earlier investigation into the cause of fatigue cracks in steel structures, we could have predicted most of these findings, of which (vi) and (vii) were probably the most important, but when combating fatigue the devil is in the detail.

The profile and size of fillet radii especially relative to the proportions of the horn openings was fundamental with inevitably further significant differences in performance occurring in nominally identical engines within a given class, whenever there were variations in the fineness of the finish, or the quality of the workmanship around the horn and other openings or differences in frame material present in the various batches. Although alloy steels may be stronger, with a higher yield point and greater fatigue strength on carefully polished test pieces, unfortunately, notch sensitivity is also higher, and this alone can nullify all the other desiderata. The self-restoring tendency of mild steel – due to its appreciable yield-point stretch – is absent in many alloy steels. Moreover, high internal stresses can be present in the latter, although heat treatment can reduce them, its application cannot always be effected. Alloy steels save weight only where strength is the criterion; for equal stiffness, there is no saving, because the modulus of elasticity is unaltered. Thus, high-class steels can fail before mild steel in an actual engine. A view partially, but not wholly supported by the performance of the Class 5 members provided with low-alloy steel frames, for the situation is complicated by the different designs of cross stay used, some of which accelerated the rate of cracking in the horn gap top corners in certain of these engines.

Some Examples of Frame Performance in Practice

Possibly the fairest way to judge the frame performance of the 'Big Goods' is by comparing its frame cracking record with other locomotives. We might use as a starting point the examples which appeared in the second frame report, which also included details of former Midland, L & Y R and Scottish classes, but unfortunately not LNWR classes. Table XX compares the frame performance of LMS Standard classes on a qualitative basis. Although no attempt was made to explain in this table why cracks appeared where they did in the LMS Standard classes, the frames were tentatively classified as flexible or rigid in accordance with the amount of horizontal cross-bracing present between the smokebox saddle or cylinders to the firebox cross stay. No obvious correlation could be drawn between frame stiffness and a propensity for cracking while in any case as Dr Johansen admitted, the degree of rigidity could not be satisfactorily quantified in the absence of tests.

Regarding the positions of cracks, few it will be noticed, appeared at the trailing axle gaps, most cracking occurred at the leading or driving horns particularly the latter position. The former location was spared to a large extent the reversals of thrust in each wheel revolution that the leading and driving boxes were subjected to as demonstrated in figures 11 and 13. The tendency for cracking to appear at the rear of the leading and driving horn gaps but at the front of the trailing, was considered primarily due to the bending moment induced by the horn guides and the inclination of the cylinder centre line, coupled with local weaknesses, particularly the disposition of access holes and wash-out plug holes to the rear of the driving gap.

Dr Johansen did not find support in table XX that crank lead predisposed a frame plate to be more likely to crack. Although all of the engines were right-hand lead and therefore the right-hand frame plate would have been more heavily loaded as the next chapter will demonstrate, despite this, in some of the engines cracking was more prevalent in the left-hand plate. Possibly the impact differences in workshop techniques and procedures had in forming stress concentrations was greater than the higher stress loading induced by crank lead.

It will be seen that after two decades of use following its adoption in 1925, the LMS version of the Class 4 0-6-0 at 'fair' was not as bad a frame cracker as the Class 5, at 'bad' had achieved after less than ten years' service. In his book *Stanier 4-6-0s at Work,* Mr Powell[44] referred to the frame cracking experienced by some selected LMS classes as at June 1943. Although derived from the same source (reports K.50 and K.56) the impression he gave of some classes differed from that expressed by Mr Cox some years earlier in *Locomotive Frames*. For example, during the discussion following a reading of the paper Mr Cox was asked about the performance of the Class 8 2-8-0, replying:-

"The class 8.F. 2-8-0 occupies an intermediary

---
44 Mr A J Powell *Stanier 4-6-0s at Work* Ian Allan Ltd Shepperton 1983 p128.

Table XX – Positions Most Affected by Cracking - LMS Standard Classes

Class	N° and position of cylinders	General impression	Wheels Leading (1st driving)	Wheels Driving (2nd driving)	Wheels Trailing	Frame type	Remarks
'Princess Coronation'	4	Good	-	-	-	I	
'Princess Royal'	4	Good	-	-	-	I	Some cracking behind o/s cylinders, RHS worse
'Royal Scot'	3	Very bad	XX RHS worse	XX LHS worse	XX	R	
5XP Taper boiler	3	Fair	X RHS worse	X LHS worse	X	F	Some cracking at dragbox, RHS worse
5XP Parallel boiler	3	Good	-	-	-	F	Most cracks at trailing horn gaps
Class 5 Mixed traffic	2 outside	Bad	XX LHS worse	XX LHS worse	-	I	
Compound	3	Good		-	-	F	
N° 2 Class Passenger	2 inside	Good		-	-	F	
2-6-4 Tank 3-Cyl	3	Good	-	X	-	F	
2-6-4 Tank 2-Cyl Taper boiler	2 outside	Good	-	X	-	I	
2-6-4 Tank Parallel boiler	2 outside	Poor	X	XX	-	R	
2-6-2 Tank Taper boiler	2 outside	Good	-	-	-	F	
2-6-2 Tank Parallel boiler	2 outside	Fair	-	XX	X	R	
0-4-4 Tank	2 inside	Good		-	-	F	
2-8-0	2 outside	Poor	- leading & intermediate	XX RHS worse	-	I	
0-8-0	2 inside	Bad	X RHS worse	XX RHS worse	- Intermediate & trailing	F	
2-6-0 Taper boiler	2 outside	Good	-	-		I	
2-6-0 Parallel boiler	2 outside	Good	- RHS worse	-		R	
0-6-0 N° 4 Cl Goods	2 inside	Fair	-	XX RHS worse		F	
Garratt	2 outside each unit	Bad	XX Both units	X	X Hind unit	I	
0-6-0 Tank	2 inside	Good	-	-	-	F	
0-6-0 dock Tank	2 outside	Good	-	-	-	F	
0-4-0 Tank	2 outside	Good	-	-		F	

All engines have right hand lead
XX Large number of cracks   X Some cracks   - Few or no cracks
R Rigid frame   I Intermediate   F Flexible frame

position in the scale of frame fracture. It is neither very good nor very bad."

Not necessarily, the same 'general impression' one might derive from table XX or Mr Powell's table, but perhaps indicative of just how subjective these findings were, including one feels by extension given Mr Cox's opinion of the class, his views on the frame performance of the Standard 4 Freight. Be that as it may one thing however is certain, the Class 5 4-6-0 frame *had* to have extensive design improvement and general strengthening before it became a reliable unit, while the 'Princess Royal' class 4-6-2 not only received additional stiffening between the outside cylinders and the leading driving wheels, but also, starting in 1951 the complete front section was renewed - a piece 16ft 3ins long. Later due to rivets loosening, new first and second driving axlebox guides were fitted from 1956 having wider flanges accommodating twelve rivets in place of the former eight. No subsequent additional strengthening or design improvement was ever given to the Class 4 frame.

Table XXI, which reveals the frame performance of ex-Midland engines was derived from frame records inspected at Derby. However, these only went back approximately 13 years prior to the analysis (say 1930) although the engines were all much older. The figure for cracks per engine per 10 years was of perforce calculated on the assumption of a uniform cracking rate. Dr Johansen observed:-

(a) The LT&S engines were relatively free of cracks and were the only engines in the table fitted with hornblocks.

(b) The 2-8-0 and 0-4-0T were built in two orders and both classes exhibited a higher rate of cracking in the first batches compared to the second thereby confirming the increasing propensity for cracking with locomotive age.

(c) The N° 2 Class Passenger, N° 4 Class Goods and the 0-6-0T demonstrated a large discrepancy between the ex-Midland engines and the newer (nominally identical) Standard classes, which was held to have been caused by locomotive age.

significant changes before it became the LMS N° 2 Class Passenger,engine. For example, apart from the different cylinder design, it is believed the use of the horn stay secured by a pair of longitudinal bolts was not perpetuated. This design appears to have been more susceptible to encouraging frame cracking.

If piston thrust was the sole arbiter of frame performance then that of the Class 4 should have been worse, but this was not the case. In fact the

Table XXI – Frame Cracks in Ex-Midland Engines

Class	Engine N°	N° in class	Approx age years¶	N° of records analysed	N° of records without cracks	Cracks per engine per 10 years	Situation of majority of cracks	Remarks
N° 2 Class Passenger*	332-562	157	28	148	36	1.8	Top driving gaps, more on RHS than LHS and front than back	Corresponding LMS class:- approx age 14 years. Cracks per engine per 10 years - zero
N° 3 Class Passenger	707-775	35	39	34	3	2.6	Top driving gaps, more on RHS than LHS and front than back	Has approx same frame as Class 2, but greater cylinder power
4-4-2 Tank LTSR Class 3	2110-2160	51	20	48	36	0.6		
0-6-0 N° 2 Class Goods	22900-22984 & 2987-3764	272	57	249	76	2.6	Tops of driving gaps, more on back than front	
0-6-0 N° 3 Class Goods	3137-3774	348	45	310	144	1.7	Tops of driving gaps, more on RHS than LHS & on back than front	Effect of increase of cylinder power in nominally identical frames
	3775-3834	60	36	53	2	5.4	Tops of driving gaps, more on RHS than LHS & on back than front	
0-6-0 N° 4 Class Goods*	3835-4026	192	27	175	22	10.0 to 2.1 see detailed list table XV	Driving gaps, more on RHS than LHS	Corresponding LMS class:- approx age 18 years. Cracks per engine per 10 years - 1.2
2-8-0 S&DJR	13800-13805	6	29	6	0	3.3	Right driving top front	Effect of age on nominally identical frames
	13806-13810	5	18	4	3	0.2		
0-6-0 Tank Class 3 ex MR*	7200-7259	60	42	49	14	2.0	Tops of driving gaps, more on LHS than RHS & on back than front	Corresponding LMS class:- approx age 19 years. Cracks per engine per 10 years - 0.1
0-4-0 Shunting Tank	1528-1532	5	37	5	0	3.6		Effect of age on nominally identical frames
	1533-1537	5	25	5	4	0.2		

¶ Reckoned from date when engine was built
*These three classes are included in Standard engines, but the results for the ex-Midland engines, together with those of the ex-Midland compounds N° 1000-1044, were excluded from the analysis of Standard engines given in Report K 50.

(d) The majority of the Class 3 Goods had 18ins diameter cylinders but the last 60 were provided with 18½ins ones. The latter group exhibited approximately three times as many cracks as the former although the increased steam load was only equal to (18 ÷ 18½)² more, *i.e.* 6 per cent higher.

In contrast to the 'Big Goods' and the tank engine, the '483' Class 4-4-0 underwent a number of quite

Class 3 Goods frame did not represent a single homogeneous design with the engines differing only in cylinder diameter as Dr Johansen assumed. They also, and perhaps more importantly differed in the designs of horn guides and horn stays used. Indeed the second group refer specifically to the Class 3 0-6-0s *built* as such with Class H boilers, *i.e.* the '2736' Class, and not the later rebuilds, but with the first ten omitted (*i.e.* excluding N° 2736-40 and N° 240-4 later N° 3765-74) - put instead with the earlier engines through having 18ins cylinders. All of these engines from N° 2736 onwards were built to two frame patterns, drawing 02-5284 applied to the first ten and also for the next forty N° 245-284 (later N° 3775-814), albeit with the profile of the front of the frame above the platform cut straight instead of following a curve as per the drawing, but the final twenty N° 3815-3834 had slightly deeper frames to drawing 07-7299. All of these engines were provided with horn gaps having 1 3/8ins fillet radius, with the driving horns secured by eight bolts - 5off one-inch diameter and 3off 1 1/4ins - while the horn stay fitted between the guide faces was secured by a pair of longitudinal bolts.

When earlier Class 2 0-6-0s were *rebuilt* to become Class 3 engines through fitting H boilers (later G7) some (most?) retained their original frames, in which case the driving axle horns were secured by 7off one-inch diameter bolts with a clip up type horn stay secured by a single stud at each end. In 1915, shortly before the Belpaire G7 boiler was adopted, some H boiler rebuilds were given new frames 1 1/8ins thick. It is not certain why this change occurred but it is suspected that it was an attempt to reduce frame cracking; a hypothesis given some support by the adoption of a new horn guide design when manganese bronze axleboxes were fitted to some engines. As the boxes were wider, this necessitated the slot opening in the frame being enlarged and the opportunity was taken of providing a larger 2ins radius in the top corners. The horn guides represented a revised design in which a return was made to the clip up horn stay but this time secured by *two* studs at each end. This horn stay and horn guide arrangement was the one adopted previously for the Standard Class 4 0-6-0 save that the horn gaps in their one inch thick frame plates was 1 1/2ins radius[45].

It is believed the interim horn stay based on a pair of longitudinal horizontal bolts, which had been introduced during the last years of Mr Johnson and fitted to amongst other the '700' Class 4-4-0s and Class 3 engines N° 3765-3834, was found more susceptible to the quality of the fitting than the earlier clip up type, hence the return to that format but with enhanced clamping pressure. The additional stud fitted at each end provided more resistance to the inevitable onset of fretting as the horn guide/horn stay assembly became loose in service. For as long as the horn stays remained tight and horn guide securing bolts had not stretched then all would be well. However, the far larger bending moment present in later engines more quickly over-whelmed the fixings, so the

Table XXII – Frame Cracks in Ex-Lancashire & Yorkshire Engines

Class	Engine N°	N° in class	Approx age years§	N° of records without cracks*	Cracks per engine per 10 years	Situation of majority of cracks	Remarks
2-4-2 Tanks saturated	10621-10899	156	46	51	1.8	Front of driving horns more from bottom than at top	
2-4-2 Tanks superheated	10835-10953	29	38	2	5.0	Front of driving horns from bottom	
4-6-0 L & Y Class 8	10412-10460	10	22	4	1.1	Trailing horns at top back	Leading and driving wheels horns, trailing wheels separate guides
0-6-0 Goods L & Y Class 25	12016-12064	29	56	16	0.8	Left front top driving horns	
0-6-0 Goods L & Y Class 27	12086-12529	291	46	90	2.3¶	Front of driving horns from bottom	
0-8-0 Goods L & Y Classes 30 & 31	12710-12981	47	30	11	2.4	Driving horns from bottom	
0-6-0 Saddle tank	11307-11530	102	62	52	0.8	Trailing gaps at top	Leading and driving wheels horns, trailing wheels separate guides

* This column is approximate only
§ Reckoned from date when engine was built
¶ Amended to 1.4 as per telephone request from Mr Peacock RD 39/9/44

"All classes of L. & Y. engines have hornblocks (except at the trailing wheels on some classes). The effect of this fitting is to strengthen the tops of the axle gaps, but on L. & Y. engines it leads to the formation of peculiar, long, vertical cracks starting from the bottom edge of the frame and passing either through the bolt holes or close to the edge of the horn casting. Even including these long cracks, however, the ex L. & Y. engines appear more free from frame cracks than the ex Midland engines."

---

45 In BR days (post-1949), the bolts that formerly had secured the axlebox slides or horn guides to the Class 4 frame were in some engines replaced by 1 1/8ins diameter cold turned rivets.

assembly deteriorated sooner promoting forces within the frame plates sufficient to generate a larger number of cracks. Table XX records for the N° 4 Class Goods, Research afforded it a 'fair' rating for the frequency of its frame cracks but when the same horn guide design was used in the parallel boiler 2-6-4T, the resulting frame performance fell to 'poor'. The lower performance obtained in the tank engine frame, despite the use of a 2½ins fillet radius in the horn gap was almost certainly prompted by the larger bending moment generated by the greater distance between the centre of the bearing and the inner face of the main frame. As table IX reveals, although the maximum piston load on the horn remained approximately carried by the 'Big Goods' appears to have been the most successful, furthermore it demonstrates Derby was alert to improving frame performance. The fact the Class 4 frame was never redesigned over the life of the class lends support to the view Midland and early LMS engineers were quite right in judging its performance to be satisfactory, by contemporary standards at least. This is in contrast to many examples of the Midland's Class 2 and Class 3 0-6-0s, which *were* given new frames, normally when they were rebuilt with G6 or G7 boilers. These frames may be easily identified by their considerably deeper section between the wheels and the replacement of the former curve at the front above the platform adjacent to the

Table XXIII – Frame Cracks in Northern Division Non-Standard Engines

Class	Engine N°	N° in class	Approx age years*	N° of records analysed	N° of records without cracks	Cracks per engine per 10 years	Situation of majority of cracks	Remarks
Highland 'Clan' 4-6-0	14762-14769	8	24	8	0	5.1	Leading horns	
Caledonian (ex-Highland) 'River' 4-6-0	14758-14760	2	27	2	0	0.8	Leading horns	
Caledonian '60' Class 4-6-0	14630-14655	26	19	23	23	0		
Highland 'Castle' 4-6-0	14678-14692	8	35	9¶	4	0.9	Leading horns	
Caldonian Class 3 4-4-0	14434-14508	72	27	64	57	See remarks	Trailing horns	A few flaws in oldest of engines
Caledonian Class 3 superheated 0-6-0 18½" × 26"	17647-17691	34	26	28	25	0.1		
Caledonian Class 3 saturated 0-6-0 18½" × 26"	17550-17687	98	43	-	-	1.0	Driving horns	
Caledonian Class 2 saturated 0-6-0 18" × 26"	17230-17473	244	53	100	25 approx	1.5	Driving horns	
Caledonian Tank 0-4-4	15115-15269	124	36	110 approx	70 approx	1.1	Leading horns	
Caledonian 0-6-0 Tank Class 3	16230-16376	147	26	-	-	0.5	Driving horns	

* Reckoned from date when engine built
¶ The report did not explain why there was one more frame record than there were locomotives!

"The worst two classes are the Highland Clan and the ex-Highland River class. The C.R. 60 Class 4-6-0 (Nos.14630-14655), has a remarkably good record, and in view of its general similarity in cylinder load to that of the Class 5 4-6-0 (which has a bad record) further study of the design of the 60 Class might be desirable. Other Northern Division non-standard classes have, on the whole, few cracks considering their age."

"Almost all engines have hornblocks. It is interesting to note that, as is usual, cracks occur at the top of the horns, extending through both hornblocks and frame; but that long vertical cracks, as found on ex L. & Y. engines, are not experienced. In addition, the general number of cracks for these Northern Division engines appears to be less than for ex M.R. or ex L. & Y. engines. A critical comparison of Northern and L. & Y. designs may reveal the superior design features of the Northern Division engines."

the same, the 3¼ins offset due to the longer boxes raised the bending moment nearly four-fold. In many of the taper-boiler engines the offset increased to 4 3/8 inches, or five-times the value of the Class 4, which when combined with the higher piston loading, placed even greater stress on the horn fastenings.

Thus of these Midland designed frames, that cylinder fall plates by a straight angle. Similarly, it is quite common to see frame patches in way of the crank axle, present in late Midland/early LMS photographs of Class 2 0-6-0s, which had retained their original frames and Class B boilers. This is particularly the case with the earliest batches *e.g.* the 4ft - 10½ins engines of 1875 and the first 5ft - 2½ins examples - built with hornblocks. Although the Class 4 frame suffered from cracking it was never altered, even though by say the late 1930s some of the earliest examples had probably absorbed more cumulative stress than had the Class 2 engines when they received new frames. Thus the inference is that in the case of the 'Big Goods' the remedial work could be restricted to repair of the engine's extant frame or its replacement by a previously repaired one of the same design.

Table XXII gives details of the cracks found in the principal L&Y engines, calculated on the same basis as previously, although the Horwich records only went back approximately 7 years (say mid 1930s) but the engines were all much older. Table XXIII records details of the cracks found on the company's principal Scottish classes. The St Rollox records went back approximately 9 years, but only indicated crack position by axle.

The former Caledonian '60' Class (14630-14655) was singled out for praise, in K.56 and the paper because its 1¼ins thick frames exhibited no cracks - but was this a true assessment? Mr Atkins[46] referred to an intriguing statement that appeared in *Locomotive News and Railway Notes* for 24th May 1919:-

"... the "60" class have not been a success so far, the chief trouble being the frames, the material of which seems to have been faulty. The first to give was 61 at the end of last July."

At that time and for some time afterwards, engineers not fully appreciating the significance of poor workshop procedures and practices or even poor design details, often unfairly blamed the quality of the frame material. That frames could crack so badly and quickly as to require replacement within 2-3 years, although rare, was not unknown. Another example was the initial batch[47] of LNER B17 class 4-6-0:-

"The new engines were far from trouble-free in the early years, and were sometimes criticised for poor steaming, but minor alterations to the draughting arrangements effected a cure. More seriously, the frames were prone to fracture, and all but one of the first 10 were given new frames within two years, the problems having been traced to excessive stiffness in the original design. Whilst the trouble was being diagnosed, and a cure worked out, several of the class were out of action for a period of months."

Freedom from failure due to fatigue was the concern of the designer, but shock fractures[48] were caused by accidents or incorrect operation or poor track and were therefore the affairs of others. It is extremely improbable that any creeping crack ever had its origin in a shock load or similar mistreatment, however sometimes that is put forward as a cause. The Reverend Gibson who trained in Swindon as an engineer before taking holy orders considered lifting engines via the ends of their frames, an action which sometimes resulted in a distinct sag appearing, was the cause of the frame cracks that emanated from the corners of the horn openings. This hypothesis however is incorrect[49]:-

"Fatigue cracks were, almost exclusively of the progressive type, due to fatigue of the material at regions of local stress concentration. There is no evidence that static loading or lifting forces are ever the sole cause of fracture."

Nevertheless, the difficulty in obtaining and maintaining a perfect fit with horn stays was hardly likely to have been improved through subjecting frames to the treatment the future man of the cloth witnessed. Since *that* would then result in slack horn stays, then as table XIX indicates, the stresses in the top corners of the horn gaps would be greatly increased when the engine was running.

As Mr Cocks described earlier, an important cause of frame cracks was if the bolt or rivet holes securing the horns were positioned in areas of high stress *e.g.* adjacent the top corners of the horn gaps. Avoiding holes in such zones helped discourage cracks from starting, as did providing a good hole finish - *vide* figure 35. To prevent initial over-stressing of the frame when driving fit bolts were put in, the interference ought not be excessive nor the bolt holes too closely pitched - holes,

---

46 Mr C P Atkins *West Coast 4-6-0s at Work* Ian Allan Shepperton 1981 pp114-5.

47 Mr G Hughes *LNER 4-6-0s at Work* Ian Allan Shepperton 1988 p76.

48 Under certain circumstances *e.g.* low temperatures, normally ductile steels may fail in a brittle fashion especially if they are subjected to sudden impact loads. This does not appear to have been that common an occurrence in locomotive frames in the UK with the exception of *previous* cracks repaired by welding and has been ignored in this investigation. However it did cause problems in the early days of welded ships when several suddenly and without warning, broke in two. With no riveted joints, which can act as natural crack arresters, the crack could race from one side of the hull to the other. Whilst it would be perfectly feasible to produce an all welded aeroplane, giving a considerable saving in weight, the industry is, perhaps understandably reluctant to abandon the cushion riveted construction offers.

49 Mr E S Cox & Dr F C Johansen *Locomotive Frames* I Loco E Paper 473 November 1947 p90.

especially those containing fitted bolts, are a common cause of creeping cracks - L&YR engines were rather susceptible to this. Ideally, the hole centres followed a zigzag pattern and not a vertical line, likewise, the bolts were not to be over-tightened to avoid them becoming over-stressed and loosening in service, although it seems it was difficult preventing erectors from flogging up the nuts as hard as they could.

As we have seen, some designers adopted thicker frame plates, while latterly also making the complete structure far stiffer laterally than formerly through greater use of horizontal and racking stays. Indeed, Oliver Bulleid demonstrated in his 'Merchant Navy' and 'West Country' classes that substantial lateral bracing was even practicable when an inside cylinder, crank axle and motion were present. Yet adopting thicker scantlings and greater rigidity did not guarantee immunity from frame cracks, because the mean stresses in a frame, or at least those that could be estimated, were generally so low in the main body of the plate there was little to be gained from increasing its thickness. It was not lack of strength *per se* but rather a lack of attention and understanding of the mechanism that caused fatigue cracking to occur. Fatigue was an ever present enemy waiting to snap at the ankles of any frame designer who overlooked or ignored its presence. Thus while the Southern 'Merchant Navy' frame was successful[50]

Fig. 37 - LMS Class 4 N° 4286 under the sheerlegs with its trailing coupled wheels run out. It appears there is no horn stay present whilst the engine is left dangling.

achieved through careful attention to the whole design, a momentary minor lapse on the part of the frame draughtsman affected the 'West Country' version:-

"In 1962 some concern was expressed at the incidence of frame fractures among the 'West Country' class Pacifics, both modified and unmodified. A total of 60 engines had been modified and the remaining 50 remained unmodified. The trouble was brought to light after unmodified No 34033, *Chard*, was released to traffic following a General repair, and was found after inspection at Bournemouth Motive Power Depot to have a fractured frame behind the left trailing horn. Previously, on 14 December 1961, an unmodified engine, No 34067 *Tangmere*, had been accepted for Inter-mediate repair, and examination of the main frames disclosed a fracture behind the right trailing horn which had not been reported by the Salisbury Motive Power Depot. As a result of these failures a survey was made of the Frame Record Cards of the other 'West Country' class engines, and it was found that 14 of the modified and 27 of the unmodified had had fractured trailing end frames repaired by welding. Of the modified engines, three had had two fractures and one three. The record of the unmodified engines was worse, for eight had had two fractures, six had had three, two had had four, and one had had five. Cracks in the frames were, incidentally, difficult to see in the Sheds because they were hidden behind the BFB wheels. This state of affairs was the subject of a report issued by the Locomotive Works Manager, Eastleigh, on 7 March 1962. He was concerned at the method of repair used which he considered had been only partially successful and he attached a sketch showing a suggested improvement.

The matter was not in fact, as serious as it would appear because there is no indication that there was a risk of completely broken frames. The 110 'West Countries' were from 11 to 17 years old, had run a considerable mileage, and each of them had from four to six General repairs. The correspondence reveals, however, that the Erecting Shop had been making quick repairs of the cracks in the interests of output. The result was bad workmanship and inadequate supervision."

The importance of considering the frame as a

---

50 Col H C B Rogers Bulleid Pacifics at Work Ian Allan Shepperton 1980 pp 97-8.
"Things which never fail may be over-designed."

Oliver Bulleid's philosophical comment on being advised that some frame cracks had appeared on his 'West Country' classes.

A Defence of the Midland/LMS Class 4 0-6-0

whole, and trying to achieve equal rigidity (or flexibility) throughout the complete structure does not appear to have been fully appreciated by LMS engineers. The impact the presence of 'soft spots' adjacent to 'hard spots' certainly did not feature in their summary of the causes of fatigue cracking. This is despite a common crack nursery occurring wherever a stressed but flexible portion of frame changed to become a more rigid part of the structure - a weakness quickly revealed in the BR Class 7 4-6-2. Any dissimilarity in the stiffness possessed by adjoining sections of frame resulted in the more flexible portion suffering the majority of the flexing due to its weaker lateral strength.

The profile of a plate frame either side of the horn gaps tended to make it laterally weak at these points. The spring hangers and to a lesser extent the brake hangers being offset, resulted in a twisting force on the lower portions of the frame, while the not inconsiderable side thrusts generated when the engine negotiated curves also acted into this area. Insufficient stiffness could result in these portions of the frame plate flexing excessively – a situation witnessed by Mr Dewhurst[51]:-

"Whilst, however, it was true that a pair of plate-frames properly assembled and conn-ected across by various castings and cross-stays were theoretically a rigid box-form structure, yet anyone who had dealt with axle-boxes and horns, or closely watched engines running at speed would be aware that plate-frames did 'give' near the horns, particularly at the lower part; this was most pronounced in inside-cylindered engines, and was due to the impossibility of locating cross-stays nearer together than the motion-plate, and in the front and rear of the fire-box."

Judging from the discussions following Mr Kyffin's paper *Notes on Axleboxes and Axlebox Guides* by the 1920s locomotive engineers were in two minds over the practical benefits to be obtained from axle collars with a large majority considering them to be worthless. They considered them too small to offer any useful lateral bearing support or serve as dust guards; their sole function

Prominent in the centre of the photograph are the four cylinder relief valves required with piston valves. Cylinder drain cocks are located on branches between relief valves and mounting flanges. Originally two Anderson by-valves were fitted inboard of the relief valves, but the absence of fixing bosses suggests the cladding and/or the cylinders have been replaced. The fixing of the horn guides has been modified by BR being secured by 1in diameter cold tuned rivets, while the axleboxes are of the Midland loose brass pattern. The flanges of the axleboxes are parallel for only a few inches near their mid height so permitting the box to tilt as the wheels negotiated irregularities in the heights of the rails. Horn stay is of the clip up type secured by a pair of studs at each end - castellated nuts provided with split pins to prevent the assembly from slackening back, although some fretting movement will be inevitable. Underhung springs secured by lateral pins into mounting blocks riveted to the frames fore and aft of the axleboxes. Hangers are short, in compression and non-adjustable. Axle is waisted to improve its fatigue resistance, provide elasticity and fitted with collars. Gaps between collars and axlebox faces approximately the same on each side. A roughly similar clearance will also be present between the back of the wheel boss and the axlebox. Thus, if the left hand wheel moved to the right, as its boss made contact with its axlebox, the right hand collar would make contact with its box. When the collars are not present, then the wheel boss/box and box/guide clearances have to be completely absorbed before the side thrust can be transmitted to the other frame plate. Furthermore as this force is transmitted either side of the horn gap, via in this instance the cylinder casting and the motion plate, it generated a bend in the right hand frame plate. This bend, results in the formation of a stress in the plate (*c.f.* in *reverse*, the curved shell of a boiler resisting the internal steam pressure without the need for stays) which adds to the stress already present in the top corners of the horn gaps.

Fig. 38 - View of the underside of preserved Class 4 0-6-0 N° 44422

---

51 Mr P C Dewhurst replying to the discussion following his paper:-
Mr P C Dewhurst *British and American Locomotives – Design and Practice* I Mech E March 1922 p496.

was to act as a starting point for heating as William Rowland rather cynically expressed it. But he did admit that if an axle was required to act as a frame stay, then collars were advantageous. Interestingly two who spoke out in favour of collars both had experience of Midland practice, Alfred Whitaker of the Somerset & Dorset Joint and James Clayton. Mr Whitaker referred to some engines which had been built without collars but were subsequently provided with them after which the engines rode more steadily, while the other[52] observed:-

> "With regard to collars on axles, I have seen them taken off, and I have been there when they had to be put back again. The point about the collar is, if the engine is designed in the first instance to be without collars, then the necessary step can be taken to enable them to be dispensed with, and that is to give as good a bearing surface as possible next to the wheel."

Without collars the side thrust was absorbed initially through the frame plate immediately behind the wheel. This force could be sufficient to slightly bow the plate locally as described by Mr Dewhurst and hence increase the loading in the adjacent horn opening. The box girder-like construction of a frame could only let the force be transmitted to the opposite plate via the stretchers, which might be located some distance away, after all the clearances on the disturbing side had been taken up. When collars were present on an axle the intervening section between them acted as a strut thereby directing some of the force into the opposite axlebox and frame plate. Whilst the precise action depended on the wear/clearances present but it was possible for the designer to arrange that as the back of the wheel on the disturbing side made contact with the contact face of its adjacent axlebox the axle collar remote from that wheel could contact with the opposite axlebox thereby sharing the side thrust between the two plates and reducing the frame distortion. This action may be seen if we consider the traditional method of repairing a cracked frame. This was to rivet a horseshoe shaped patch around the horn gap on the wheel side of the frame completely covering the crack. Such however was the subtlety of frame performance that this repair, which in any case was rarely successful at arresting the continuing development of the crack, could instead cause further problems, as Mr H Fowler recounted[53]:-

> "Mr. Low had mentioned the question of stiffening up a frame on one side. He remembered a difficulty they had about 25 years ago with the old Midland No. 3 Class freight engines which on occasions broke its frame. The normal repair at the time was to fit a patch over the fracture and send it back into traffic. It was then found that the engine invariably ran hot, the box giving trouble being that directly opposite to the patch. Fitting a patch on the good frame, thus stiffening that up always proved an effective cure."

These being Midland engines, they were fitted with axle collars which shared the side thrust from the tyre flange through the wheel boss between the two frame plates, With one plate now possessing considerably greater lateral stiffness than its opposite number an imbalance was created, which combined with any slight misalignment, resulted in over heating.

Following the appearance of gas and electric-arc welding during the first decades of the twentieth century engineers[54] quickly adopted it as a means of attempting crack repairs:-

> "The FRAMES do not usually require much attention in the Shops, the chief thing to be done being to see that they are lined up properly and not cracked through the corners of the horns, the only remedy for the latter, up to recent times, being patching, the patch usually being of no greater strength than the original plates. The use of the oxy-acetylene flame for welding the frame is now practically universal, but it must always be remembered that the weld is never as strong as the original plate, and as the same forces which caused the crack in the first instance will be at work on the frame afterwards, a cover plate should be employed, although it need not be as thick as it would require to be if no welding had been done."

In practice however, until the early 1940s there was no effective repair against frame cracks, hence we may appreciate something of the anxiety experienced by LMS engineers. Hitherto the standard remedial practice had been simply to 'vee' out the crack prior to welding it up, but the weld metal contained innumerable small discontinuities and slag inclusions any of which served as an incipient crack and thus encourage a fatigue crack to reform. Laboratory tests of well executed fillet and butt welds subjected to direct stress revealed the limiting stress was reduced to one-half or perhaps two-thirds that of the original mild steel.

---

52 Mr J Clayton contributing to the discussion following:-
Mr A E Kyffin *Notes on Axleboxes and Axlebox Guides* I Loco E Paper N° 108 1921 Journal N° 52 p47.
53 Mr H Fowler contributing to the discussion at Manchester following:-
Mr E S Cox & Dr F C Johansen *Locomotive Frames* I Loco E Paper 473 November 1947 p189.
54 Mr H Fowler (later Sir) *The Maintenance and Repair of Locomotives* - Presidential Address I Loco E 1913 p13.

These low values were due to the almost inevitable blow holes, slag and other defects present in the weld metal which served as stress raisers along with 'locked in' stress concentrations caused by the welding process itself. This was the main reason why cracks would quickly reappear in the same location after the repair had been effected, hence the repetitive trouble experienced with the ex-LNWR 'Prince of Wales' class 4-6-0s described earlier. Although, in many instances the welded repair was accompanied by a horseshoe shaped patch riveted to the outside of the frame, as Mr Cox admitted this had also proved ineffective, nevertheless the practice continued. For example under Job Nº 5406 of March 1945, 145 'Jubilees', or *over three-quarters* of the class, were fitted with these patches between 1946 and 1950, yet despite the high proportion of the class having undergone such repairs, the 'Jubilee' was *not* considered an *inveterate* frame breaker! Subsequently a more extreme repair was adopted in the form of Job Nº 5598 of July 1951 which introduced welded inserts to the class. Primarily intended to enable manganese steel liners and Horwich horn stays to be fitted, the resulting surgery necessitated welding in six triangular inserts into each frame plate. Apart from the shape and specific locations of these new sections, welding in standard shaped inserts represented the final LMS practice for repairing cracked frames. Greater success had been achieved by Mr Foster with welding once he moved the welds out of regions of high stress *i.e.* hence the introduction of not insubstantial sections of plate. Although successful at combating fractures, for a while, such repairs represented a lot more work[55]:-

"Since new frames average a crack-free life of five to seven years it was considered that if large inserts were welded into the frame and were so arranged that all the defective material was removed, and the welds located in positions where cracking does not normally occur, then a further period of five to seven years could be expected before cracking recurred,"

Yet as Clifford Cocks astutely observed, despite accepting a great deal of extra work when it elected to weld in a new section or sections of plate into a frame the LMS was only carrying out half a repair, for it ignored the opportunity it had created for itself of avoiding, or at least reducing the likelihood of cracking occurring in the future in the replacement material[56]:-

" ...the LMS have had the courage to weld a completely new section into an old frame. It is surprising that as this procedure is carried out, an opportunity was not taken to improve the shape of the frame at the top corners for the axlebox guides. A further improvement could have been made by welding in the horns preparatory to inserting the new pieces of frame plate. If this had been done and the horn cheeks adequately ribbed to the new frameplates, by welding, the whole structure could then have been put in the furnace and low temperature stress relieved before it was welded to the frames. There would then have been non *(sic)* bolt holes or bolts required and in consequence, no fear of the horns becoming loose. This would have resulted in a frame in which the dangers of cracking would have been reduced to a minimum or eliminated entirely."

Yet again the Southern was demonstrating how far in advance technically it was of the 'stick-in-the-mud easy maintenance at all costs' timid mindset that assumed control of steam locomotive design during the last days of the LMS and for the remainder of its time on British Railways.

Sometimes frame reliability was reduced because of changes introduced into an existing class by later engineers. This may have been for the best of reasons but it could result in a greater propensity for cracking. The frame fitted to Mr Thompson's rebuilds of the LNER B17 class 4-6-0 represents an example of what may ensue should the structure become more heavily loaded than formerly, or at least the paths of the stress trajectories significantly altered[57]:-

---

55 Mr E S Cox & Dr F C Johansen *Locomotive Frames* I Loco E Paper 473 November 1947 p106.
Indeed one might wonder, perhaps a little impishly, if the last two sentences of the quotation regarding the 'Prince of Wales' frame cracks did not still apply!
Incidentally, as figure 21 demonstrates, the defective material (*i.e.* overstrained) was highly localized being confined to a small area immediately in front of the crack. The main reason for inserting the large sections of new plate was not therefore to remove defective material but to ensure the welds were located in positions of low stress.

56 Mr C S Cocks contributing to the discussion at London following:-
Mr E S Cox & Dr F C Johansen *Locomotive Frames* I Loco E Paper 473 November 1947 p129.
As an aside, fatigue cracks had been discovered in frame 65 of the *MV Derbyshire*, which were the subject of a poor repair at Sasebo in April 1980, or as the inquiry commented:-
"The repair carried out to the fatigue crack was by way of veeing out and re-welding. This form of repair should not have been authorised by Lloyds as it is not a solution to fatigue cracking. Local improvement of the design of the structure ought to have been required and undertaken, for without it it was inevitable that the fatigue cracking would recur."
57 Mr D W Harvey *Bill Harvey's 60 Years in Steam* David & Charles Newton Abbot 1986 p121.

"At least twice during the twelve months that I was at Cambridge, N°1671 *Royal Sovereign* was sent to Stratford Works to have short cracks that had developed in the under edge of the main frame above the trailing bogie wheels – its weakest point – repaired by electric welding; the second visit resulted from a thermal crack adjacent to the first weld. As the B17s did not suffer from this weakness it seems reasonable to suspect that the cross-bracing that replaced the centre cylinder when this was removed was not strong enough to withstand the flexing imposed on the frames by increasing the diameter of the two outside cylinders from 17½in to 20in, and the load on the pistons by raising the boiler pressure from 180 lb/sq in to 225 lb/sq in when the B1 boiler was fitted."

In attempting to overcome the weaknesses present in the Gresley-Holcroft conjugated valve gear, Mr Thompson reduced the reliability of the frame.

The LMS 'Royal Scot' class 4-6-0 presents another lesson only in this instance a misdiagnosis of the original problem, which seemingly initially solved by the remedial action, very soon resulted in the frame becoming the most unreliable one on the system. The substantial axleboxes fitted to the 'Royal Scots' had been derived from the last Midland design so comprised a manganese bronze casting fitted with brass and white metal bearing surfaces. Sized to suit journals 9ins diameter by 10½ins long and weighing 410lbs each, they were not undersized, indeed in its earliest days the class had an enviable record regarding hot boxes, yet within a very few years this situation had changed completely. Between 1930 and the end of 1932 the number of hot boxes quadrupled – rising from 25 to 102. This increase coincided with the arrival of Sir William Stanier and according to Mr Cox as no one could offer a rational reason for it, the blame was placed on the axlebox design. Accordingly, the class was fitted with a new design of cast steel box having a white metal lined pressed-in brass. The first examples of this new Great Western derived design were fitted in 1933 starting with the engine that was sent to America, this engine also uniquely received a new bogie with side bearers and no brakes. By the end of 1934, all 70 engines had been given the new axleboxes, while at the same time, the collars on the coupled axles were machined off, this also being a Great Western practice[58]. They were removed because it was considered they caused side cutting and consequential heating of the axleboxes. Alert to the reason for originally fitting them, engineers had to introduce another method for sharing the thrust with the opposite frame plate. Their solution comprised cross stays fitted low down at or near the bottom edges of the frame plates and in the case of the 'Royal Scots' they appeared between the axlebox guides at the intermediate and trailing coupled wheels. A further minor change made in 1934-5 was the substitution of laminated springs in place of the helical springs originally fitted.

Although these modifications had the desired effect of reducing the number of hot boxes, the

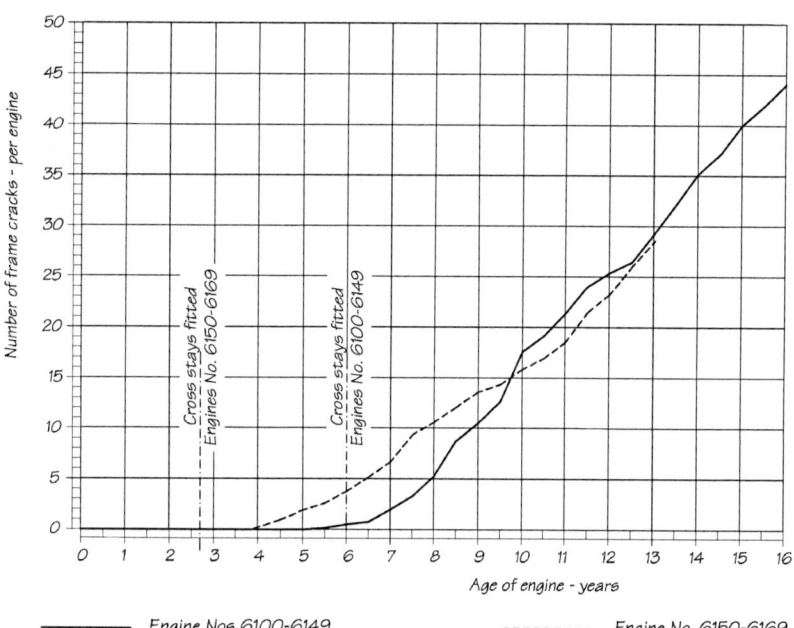

Fig. 39 - Number of frame cracks per engine from new - 'Royal Scot' class

most unwelcome side effect that they had on frame cracks is demonstrated in figure 39, which records the crack development history of the two orders of 'Royal Scots'. The curves were derived from the Crewe records of 16 engines selected as being typical of the whole class. By 1943 the 'Royal Scot' class had the worst record on the LMS with regard to frame cracks, but that was not the case

---

58 It had also been LMS practice in so far as the LMS 'Crab' parallel boiler 2-6-0 was not provided with collars nor had most of the last Lancashire & Yorkshire designs produced under the aegis of George Hughes.

earlier, despite a comparatively weak design. Although 1 1/8 inch thick, it had had to have large weight reduction holes cut into the frame plates and racking stays to remove around a ton of over-weight - it may be seen that in both batches there was a remarkable freedom from cracks (*cf* the 'Patriot' Class). Cracks then started to appear, but not at an excessive rate, and this remained the situation until the axlebox collars were removed and the cross-stays added. With the axle collars gone the side thrust from the flanges was no longer shared between the two frame plates via the axleboxes and horn guides, instead it was transmitted by means of the cross-stays directly into the opposite plate, but in a different position from formerly. This altered the stress distribution pattern and prompted the increased incidences of cracking. This cracking started, in both batches, soon after fitting the cross-stays, despite their difference in age - N° 6100-49, (1927), followed by N° 6150-69, introduced in 1930. Indeed in the case of the Derby-built engines, which had them added earlier in their lives, the resulting absence of the normal five to seven years time delay before cracking appeared, largely supports Dr Johansen's opinion it had been initiated by the addition of the cross-stays and the removal of the axle collars. The English built engines differed from the first 50 built by the North British Locomotive Company in that they had laminated springs to all coupled wheels from new. N° 6100-49 had been built with coil springs to the first and second driving wheels, but they were altered to laminated springs about the same time that the cross-stays were added. Figure 39 suggests that, following the fitting of the stays, the second order had a slightly lower propensity to crack, possibly due to better workmanship in building, but by 1943 the tendency was about the same since by then both batches were old enough to develop fatigue cracks.

The unintended deleterious impact removing axle collars could have on frame performance had been referred to previously by John Smith[59]:-

"In connection with the omitting of collars on the journals, he remarked that years ago they had some trouble with tender axles and the outer collars were turned off. The result was that the frames bulged outwards. If one takes the collars off one is taking stiffness from the frames. If one omits collars on the inside the frame goes in and one gets the weight on the wheel boss. That is one point in locomotive design – when curing one fault one has to be sure it does not create a worse."

When the 'Royal Scot' class was built the initial side control given to the bogie was ¾ ton[60], the same amount that had been given to earlier, and smaller 4-4-0s. This was insufficient for such a large engine which yawed or 'rotated laterally' about a vertical centre line that passed through its centre of gravity. This resulted in the axleboxes in the rear half of the engine being slammed alternately against the wheel boss faces and the axle collars, action which further increased with wear[61] thereby exacerbating the side 'slogger' and rough riding. Worst still, these violent crashes understandably disturbed the fit of the brass dovetail strips and with it the security of the white metal in the Midland pattern axlebox. Once this had occurred, it was only a matter of a short time

---

59 Mr J W Smith contribution to the discussion at Manchester following:-
Mr W A Lelean *Presidential Address* I Loco E Paper September 1932 p669.

60 Mr E S Cox *Chronicles of Steam* Ian Allan London 1967 p35.
On 14th January 1930 'Royal Scot' N° 6131 **Planet** suffered a partial derailment while negotiating at approximately 70mph a facing point forming part of Weaver Junction which had a *maximum* speed limit of 55mph. Nine days later on the 23rd, 'Lord Nelson' N° E853 **Sir Richard Grenville** experienced a partial derailment near Kent House, also while negotiating a set of facing points. Due to the similarity of these two incidents it was suspected there might have been a common cause, accordingly the Ministry of Transport inspecting officer Lt. Col. Anderson took the unusual step of investigating the derailments together. In both reports, dated 9th July 1930, he made the recommendation that increasing the guiding effect of the bogie should be considered. Since the two classes of 4-6-0 were similar in size, it is interesting to compare the bogie side control spring values extant at the time of the accidents:-

	Initial value tons	Max. compression tons	Max. lateral ins each side
'Royal Scot'	0.596	2.34	2.375
'Lord Nelson'	1.12	3.0	3.25

Starting in 1931, Mr Cox stated the original bogie side control springs on the 'Royal Scots' were replaced with ones having an initial compression of 2 tons. According to him this was to increase spring life rather than to improve engine riding although Mr Cox reported that in a November (1930/31?) he had been instructed to visit the Southern Railway. He rode 'Lord Nelsons' and found these 4-6-0s behaved much better than the 'Royal Scots'. LMS engineers considered the 2 tons initial compression was still insufficient for the 'Royal Scots' and this may have suggested the substitution of the side bearer bogie with its potential for friction damping for the North American trip, while following the Indian Pacific inquiry the side control was increased even further.

61 The clearances of N° 6131 **Planet** were measured for the report following its partial derailment at Weaver Junction. The actual side play values of the wheels relative to the frames, extreme left to extreme right, were: leading coupled axle 3/32ins, intermediate coupled 5/16ins, trailing coupled 13/32ins, compared to the normal total of ¼ins for each axle.

before a hot box resulted. Unfortunately the contemporary lack of understanding amongst the LMS engineers regarding how a locomotive moved along track meant insufficient bogie side control was not fully appreciated. Hence, once William Stanier applied his Great Western axlebox and other features, although seemingly curing the hotbox problem, gave rise eventually to a more serious problem in another area – altogether a classic example of misdiagnosis – in effect, they treated the symptoms and not the disease. When it was subsequently decided to 'convert' the 'Royal Scots' along with a 2A taper boiler and double chimney *etc*, they were given new frames, replacement side-bearer bogies and a revised suspension[62] to the driving wheels. The extant frame stretchers were reused, half inch thick doubler plates were riveted to the outside of the frame plates in way of the horn gaps and the original arrangement of separate horn guides with clip up horn stays was retained although the last forty engines to be modified received Horwich horn stays. Whether the rebuilt 'Royal Scots' continued to suffer from frame cracking as they had previously is not clear. Certainly the Horwich stay kept the assembly tighter for longer, which should have helped delay their appearance, as would careful attention to the finish of the frame edges in the higher stressed areas, while the technique of welding in replacement frame sections which the LMS had perfected offered a means of combating the problem. Being essentially new engines dating from 1943 to 1955 they lasted reasonably well into the diesel era. Withdrawal did not commence until 1962, but apart from four which went in 1965, was complete by the end of 1964. The oldest of the rebuilt engines lasted around 19-20 years, for many their lives were 11-12 years, but as the final ones to be converted lasted typically only 7-10 years this suggests frame cracking *may* have been a factor influencing the decision to withdraw.

Another factor influencing frame cracking which neither the LMS engineers nor we have so far considered, concerns observation (x), train speeds and time of year. Mr Harvey[63] might disagree with the observation that train speed had no influence on the rate of crack propagation:-

"Cracks in frames and the rate at which they developed provided a particularly interesting study. While on express work these extended with increasing rapidity but when the locomotive was confined to slow freight work pending its departure to shops, no further

---

[62] In place of the previous Midland arrangement of non-adjustable hangers used in compression, adjustable hangers arranged in tension were adopted. The latter was considered by the likes of Messers Cox and Powell to have been 'more correct' mechanically, however it was the major factor along with uncontrolled excessive sideplay which resulted in the poorer riding of the rebuilt engines. John Powell criticised the Midland arrangement in *Living with London Midland Locomotives*:-

"The Midland's ideas on springing were rudimentary in the extreme. No such things as J-hangers on the frames with adjustable spring links in tension as most lines used, but just crude, non-adjustable links in compression, an inherently unstable arrangement dependent on the integrity of the spring buckle securing device."

We can ignore the red herring concerning the integrity of the spring buckle since the J-hanger type is equally dependant on it and instead consider what he meant by it being an unstable arrangement. When the centre of gravity of a body lies above the point of support or suspension, the body is said to be in unstable equilibrium; thus, if the body is slightly disturbed from its current position it will not return to its original position *by itself*. Conversely, when the centre of gravity of a body lies below the point of suspension or support, the body is in stable equilibrium. If the body is slightly displaced from its current position it will automatically return to that position. The original 'Royal Scots' had a large high pitched boiler and while at times they could be rough at the trailing end they did not exhibit the same rolling characteristic as the rebuilds. The compression hanger, being in unstable equilibrium ensured that after the back end of the engine had crashed over to one side the tendency was for it to remain there until a flange blow of sufficient intensity in the opposite direction would flop it back to the other side. With tension hangers the locomotive was suspended in stable equilibrium, which meant following a sideways displacement the system tried automatically to return to its pre-displacement position but in doing so it acted something akin to a pendulum. Once a certain degree of sideplay was present it meant the mass of the frame and boiler could be thrown from side to side approximately through this distance, estimated by E S Cox to amount to a possible total of 1 7/8ins, at a frequency of about once per second. Since the centre of gravity of the suspended mass was above the axle, at each contact of flange with rail and axlebox with wheel boss, there was a rolling action set up which momentarily depressed the springs on that side. The 'Royal Scots' had insufficient damping so once the phenomenon started, it built up and became self perpetuating unless the driver broke the cycle by shutting off steam and braking.

The Midland springing design was one of the features Samuel Johnson brought with him from his previous practice used on the Great Eastern and possibly even prior to that. In its earliest applications the hangers were threaded and adjustable however the Midland quickly elected to make them solid and non-adjustable and that is the way they remained for half a century. During that period it had been applied to several thousand individual engines including of course all of the 'Big Goods', so despite Mr Powell's concerns the design had a proven and successful track record!

A very similar arrangement was used on several other pre-Grouping companies including the L&YR.

[63] Mr D W Harvey *Bill Harvey's 60 Years in Steam* David & Charles Newton Abbot 1986 p191.

extension took place; to use an equine analogy it is the pace that kills!"

Since the cracks he recorded in the BR Class 7 4-6-2s appear not to have propagated when these engines were employed on goods trains we can only surmise that reduced stresses accompanied perhaps by a later cut-off coupled with the lower frequency provided insufficient energy for them to grow. Since the LMS reports were based on frame records, they presumably contained very little or no information regarding the relative *rate* of crack propagation on specific locomotives when they were used on different duties. This seems the likely explanation for the discrepancy between the LMS conclusion and Bill Harvey's correct observation.

Having started this chapter with Mr Cox's opinion of the frame performance of the Class 4 0-6-0, and then seen something of the difficulties inherent in frame design, it is perhaps now germane to see how successful was one of the frame designs *he* was involved in. Several of the conclusions from his frame paper - plates 11/8in or more in thickness, smaller axlebox/frame offsets and stiffer frame structures - were incorporated into his BR 'Britannia' class 4-6-2. So it must have been somewhat galling for him to have learnt of its subsequent in-service performance[64]:-

> "Great care was taken to avoid past error as far as humanly possible, and besides using the greatest thickness of plate which the permissible weight would allow, the hornstays which close the frame gap below the axleboxes received particular attention both in design and manufacture to ensure, once again, that the effects of strain did not undermine the tightness of the assembly. While it is hardly correct to think of locomotive main frames as a quivering mass, nevertheless when the engine is in motion every plate, casting, rivet and bolt is subject to reversals of strain in a manner which has only partially been charted either by theory or by strain gauging, so that the placing of the different members and their connections one to the other in the course of design has been as much a matter of art as of science. It is for this reason that the all-welded frame gained little acceptance in steam practice, even though at first sight it seemed an obvious development. But weld metal is more akin to cast than to wrought material, and as such is not very ductile. In the frame layout which the traditional form of the steam engine made obligatory, the breathing capacity of the riveted or bolted joint gave much more margin for design error, where the strains and forces involved were still only imperfectly mapped out. This is a piece of unfinished business to which more attention would have had to be given, had steam traction continued."

The 1¼ins thick frame plates adopted on the BR Standard Pacifics – firmly in the north British solid build tradition, as befitted the Scot E S Cox – were adopted with the intention they would last the life of the locomotive without attention - all in line with the findings of his 1947 paper. The frame was notable for the extensive horizontal or rack staying present, perhaps the most abundant provided on any British locomotive until then. In this respect, Mr Cox was trying to emulate the performance of the LMS 'Crab' parallel boiler 2-6-0, whose frame structure returned a very good performance, which it was held was due to the presence of extensive staying. However, significant cracking appeared within sixteen months of the first 'Britannia' class 4-6-2s arriving, close to the bottom of coupled wheel horns adjacent to the spring hanger brackets. Despite its greater than normal thickness, flexing of the frame along its bottom edge enabled cracks to develop in the region where the plate was unsupported by either the horn/hornclip assembly or the adjacent spring hanger bracket. Another disadvantage of the J-bracket suspension is that it set up a bending and twisting action on the bracket itself tending to loosen the fixings or induce cracks in the frame. To overcome this problem, a *redesigned* and more substantial spring hanger was substituted which through an longitudinal extension eliminated the previous unsupported length of frame. Not long after this problem had arisen, fracturing of the frame stay rivets also occurred, being the inevitable outcome of attempting to flex a very rigid structure. Mr Atkins quoted[65] from the Standard Locomotive Committee minutes:-

> "...3rd September 1957: Trouble has been experienced on the Western Region with loosening of (smokebox) saddle bolts and fracturing of frame stay rivets. Although cases of similar trouble have been found on other regions, they have so far been of an isolated nature."

Perhaps it was a final vindication of Derby's previous wisdom in providing flexible frames – since it is rather amusing to relate the trouble also appeared on engines running on former Midland lines[66]:-

---

64 Mr E S Cox *British Railways Standard Steam Locomotives* Ian Allan Shepperton 1966 pp87-8.

65 Mr C P Atkins *Britannia Birth of a Locomotive* Irwell Press Pinner 1991 p15.

66 Dr P T Gilbert & Mr P J Chancellor *A Detailed History of British Railways Standard Steam Locomotives – Vol I* RCTS 1994 p77.

Frames and Cracks

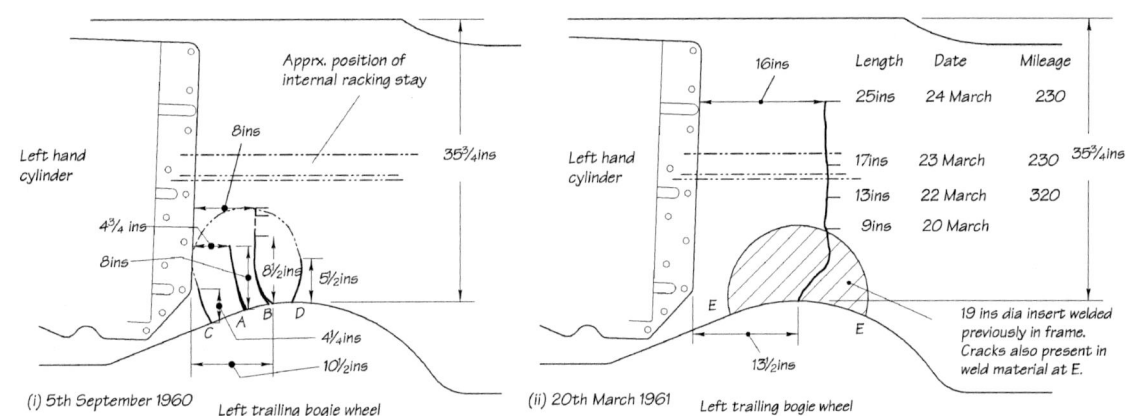

BR 7 Class Nº 70007 *Coeur de Lion* built April 1951

25th October 1960 returned from Doncaster having had crack *A* welded up.

14th December 1960 second crack appeared *B* - appears crack was 8½ins long when noticed.

17th December 1960 extended to 11ins after 460 miles.

18th December 1960 crack had grown to 12½ins after 230 miles, also opened up at bottom.

30th December 1960 there had been no growth in the crack length (12½ ins) although the engine had run 1,230 miles on parcels, local passenger and Class D goods trains.

31st December 1960 sent to Doncaster for repair.

19th January 1961 returned from Doncaster, frame repaired by welding in an insert 19ins deep by 10ins wide at bottom.

18th February 1961 cracks *C* (4½ins long) and *D* (5½ins long) found at junction of insert with original frame material.

Appears engine in Doncaster 18th February to 13th March 1961 when new insert - 19 ins diameter - welded in.

20th March 1961 frame fractured through new insert, crack 9 ins long.

22nd March 1961 crack extended to 13 ins.

23rd March 1961 it had grown to 17 ins long.

25th March 1961 crack extended to 25 ins long. Record finished on 25th March 1961 with the engine out of service.

Record of periods out of service due to recurrent frame fractures:-
6th September 1960 to 25th October 1960   42 working days
31st December 1960 to 19th January 1961   16   - do -
18th February 1961 to 13th March 1961   19   - do -
25th March 1961 - presumably sent to Doncaster for repair
Nº 70007 was the first 'Britannia' to be withdrawn in June 1965.

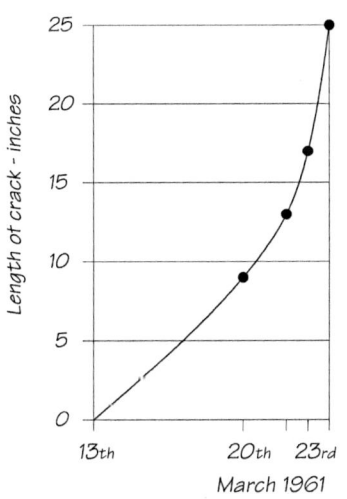

Figures 26 and 27 illustrate a simplified example of the fracture mechanics approach, based on figures derived from the de Havilland *Comet* disaster. Incidentally this analysis was not carried out until 1956, two years after the crashes. We can apply the technique to a 'Britannia' frame using Research Department figures, which referred to a maximum tensile stress of 7.1tons/sq in at the rear bogie wheel cut-out - equivalent to 15,900 lbs/sq in. A reasonable value for Gc for mild steel might be 570 ins-lbs/sq in while $E = 30,000,000$ lbs/sq in. Hence the estimate for the critical length becomes:-

$$Lg = \frac{Gc \times E}{\pi \times S^2}$$

where:-
Lg = the critical length - inches
Gc = critical strain energy release - ins-lbs/sq in
E = Young's modulus for the material - lbs/sq in
S = the stress in the material - lbs/sq in

$$Lg = \frac{570 \times 30,000,000}{\pi \times 15,900^2} \approx 21.5 \text{ ins}$$

- a critical length of 21.5 ins is shorter than the observed crack length, suggesting the stress was not so high or the steel had a different value for Gc. Unlike E which is a well-defined property of a material, Gc exhibits considerable sensitivity to the micro-structure of the steel, which in turn is affected by the manufacturing procedures, surface finish and the testing method used to determine it. The accompanying graph records the rate of growth of the crack against time for the one appearing in the top right-hand diagram. From the profile of the curve we may opine that the engine was taken out of service only just in time. The gradient of the curve was rapidly steepening and possibly in one more day it would have become infinite and the plate instantaneously fractured.

The stresses experienced by a locomotive frame constantly changed, predominant was the steam loading but this was highly variable - changing throughout the stroke with cut-off and speed - to which has to be added the influences of the other loads *e.g.* boiler weight, axleboxes *etc*. Once a crack formed, it would slowly extend, albeit at increasing rate, until the frame plate was completely fractured - a situation which is known to have occurred in 'Britannia' frames. However should the duties of the engine alter once the crack had formed, then its progression would reflect the change in stress levels. When they were high enough the crack would propagate but at other times should they be reduced then there might be a slow down or even no growth.

Fig. 40 - Cracks recorded in BR 'Britannia' Class 4-6-2 No. 70007 *Coeur de Lion* in six months

A Defence of the Midland/LMS Class 4 0-6-0

"It was reported in *Trains Illustrated* however, that the engines working the Manchester-Derby section suffered from failures of the smokebox saddle and loosening of the main frame cross stretchers due to the sharp curvature on the line."

Worst was to come, for by 1958-61 quite severe cracking was present in some frames, mostly locomotives built in 1951. These cracks appeared particularly behind the cylinders or emanated from the top corners of the horns – classic locations and age for fatigue cracking. The former, if not caused by the greater than normal offset of the cylinders from the outside surface of the frame plates were certainly exacerbated by it, coupled with the absence of an inside cylinder which reduced the stiffness. Indeed Mr Harvey[67] provided extensive details of the frame cracking he witnessed on the BR Class 7 4-6-2s in his charge at Norwich including one, Nº 70035 **Rudyard Kipling**, which when eight years old experienced the complete fracture of its right-hand frame plate with only the horn stay and the cross stays, keeping the two portions together. A feat that was not was achieved by a Class 4 0-6-0 as far as the author knows! Incidentally, this crack, originated in the rear corner of the leading horn gap extended vertically 23½ inches in extent. In view of this performance, we should be aware that the thinner 11/8in thick frame, fitted to the three-cylinder 'Merchant Navy' class Pacific of the Southern Railway, which was similar in design and effectively the prototype for the 'Britannia' frame, was far more successful. Mr Cocks was able to report in 1948, when the Southern engines were around seven years old, that no cracks had yet appeared. As we have seen, this, was primarily the result of careful attention to detail, for example providing the contour of the horn guides and frame at the top corners where fractures commonly occurred with a 4in radius to reduce stress concentration – the corresponding dimension on the 'Britannia' was smaller.

Although, as E S Cox stated, a great deal of effort was directed towards producing an effective frame design for the 'Britannia', unfortunately as has been related it was *very* susceptible to cracking. This was despite Eric Langridge[68] having supplied the Research Department with frame drawings (DE 5/708 and DRS 5889) before the class was built, which in turn prompted the appearance of a six-page report, K.113A, in November 1949.

The report was concerned with the stress distribution in the frame and commented on the design of the horns. The estimates of the stresses at various parts of the frame were extrapolated from an earlier Research Department report, K.89, which contained calculated values for the corresponding stresses in the Class 5 frame derived from *its* steam load. The figures in K.89 had been obtained by the relaxation technique - at the time the only approach possible for estimating the stresses in complicated structures. It was adopted as it offered a way of quantifying to a reasonable degree of accuracy the stresses in portions of the frame where experience suggested it reached critical values. However, it entailed laborious calculations, and by the appearance of the frame paper the LMS had only one example, that of a Class 5 and then only at a single steam loading. It is not certain how many more examples it produced, probably very few, if any. According to the paper *Locomotive Frames* this one example represented about 6 months' work for an individual even using a calculating machine. The work culminated in a set of diagrams giving stress contours over the face of the frame - *vide* figure 41 for an example.

In investigating the stresses in the proposed BR 7 frame, several sections were considered, including those at the bogie trailing wheels and at the horn gaps. In order to obtain reasonable estimates for the BR 7 stresses, from those appearing in K.89, the 4-6-0 steam load values were increased by nearly one-quarter to allow for the larger cylinder diameter and higher working pressure of the Pacific. Allowances were also made for the heavier scantling of its frame and the plates being located on the centre line of the axleboxes.

The highest estimated tensile and compressive stress values in way of the trailing bogie wheel cut-away for the Pacific, were 7.1tons/sq in and -5.8tons/sq in respectively. These compare with 9.00tons/sq in and -7.05tons/sq in which were quoted for the equivalent positions in the 1inch thick frame of the Class 5. A similar sized tensile stress, but lower compressive value appear in figure 41. The discrepancy between the stresses in the report and those appearing in figure 41, may indicate another set of calculations having been carried out at a similar frame loading. Or, possibly the stress values quoted above for the Class 5 represent measured principal stress values obtained

---

67 Mr D W Harvey *Bill Harvey's 60 Years in Steam* David & Charles Newton Abbot 1986 p192.

68 Mr E Langridge *Under 10 CMEs Volume Two: C E Fairburn to J F Harrison* Oakwood Press Usk 2011 p115.

from strain gauge readings as opposed to the calculated horizontal only stresses that appear in figure 41. Either way, what is revealing is that the report observed since at least one failure was known to have occurred in a Class 5 frame in this region, it recommended reducing the stress in the BR 7 frame at this point.

It suggested either the three rivets in the stretcher plate flange located directly above the cut-out were omitted or the stretcher plate was raised until its web was in the plane of the cylinder centre lines. Figure 41 suggests the maximum tensile stress occurred where one would expect it, at the frame edge, so it is not clear how raising the stretcher would effect a remedy, while the edge stress was really too high. So perhaps it is not surprising to observe the catalogue of frame cracks which appeared above the bogie cut-out in service.

Turning to the leading coupled gap, the loading was identified as a large direct stress load over the frame section plus a smaller axlebox force. Since the stress in the frame plate was known to be far from uniform, this time recourse was made to the tests conducted on the dummy Class 5 frame referred to earlier - report S.10. Upper and lower stress range values for the horn gap top corners of about 9.8tons/sq in and -7.9tons/sq in were estimated - assuming the horn stay was tightly fitted - the corresponding values for the 4-6-0 were quoted as 8.35 and -6.5tons/sq in, which incidentally differ from the values appearing in either of tables XVIII or XIX.

In estimating the stress in the BR Class 7 horn gap the Research Department proposed ignoring any strengthening effect the welded-in horn guide could provide. Whilst its tee-section face might be thought to

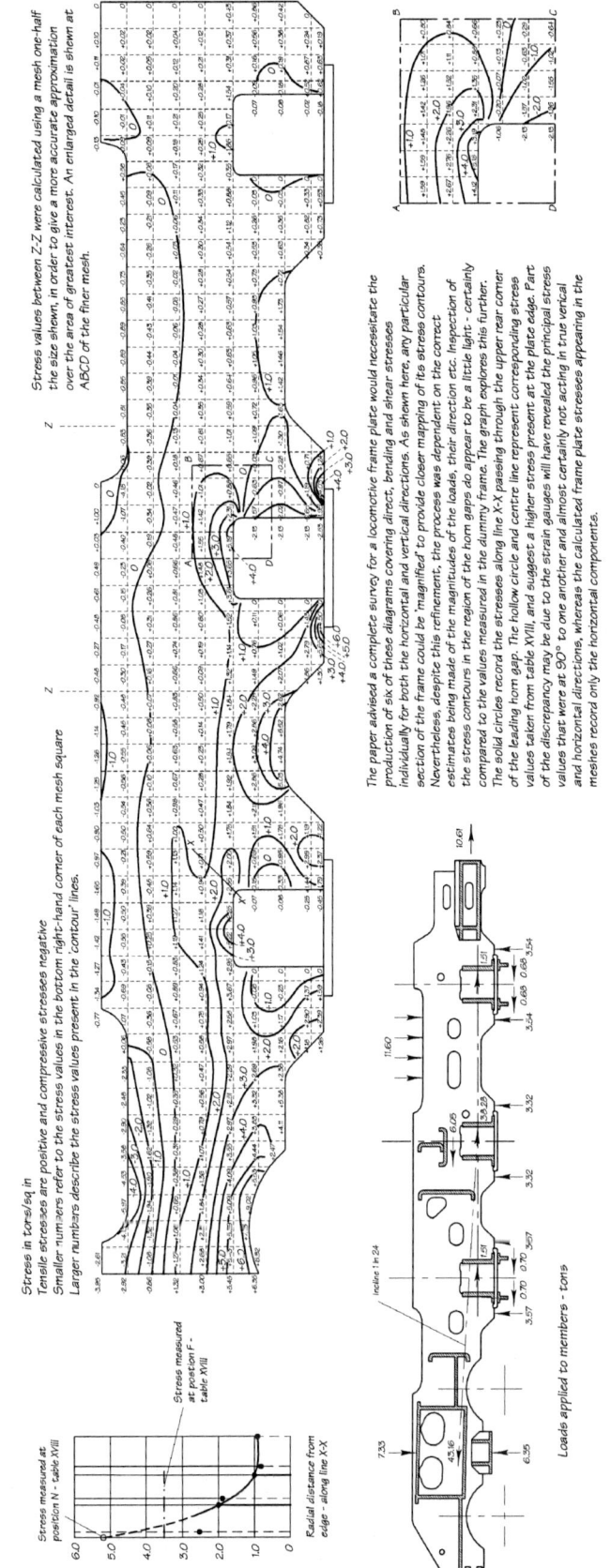

Fig. 41 - Diagram of horizontal stresses in a Class 5 frame plate obtained by relaxation

have given some benefit in acting akin to the integral bulb edge occasionally seen on some rolled steel sections used as longitudinal stiffeners, the report discarded any such contribution:-

"(a) The inner and outer edges of the guide are free to distort, and in consequence will take very little stress. A simple test with a curved piece of paper thus:- (*vide* figure 42b - APT) pulling as shown by the arrows on the centre line, will demonstrate the lack of stress in the outer edges at *X* and *Y*.

(b) The weld between the main frame plate and the rolled guide plate is in a region of fairly high stress (see Report S.10) and any bulb effect mentioned above would tend to increase the stress in the corner welds, and might lead to stresses dangerously close to the low fatigue strength of the weld metal.

Experience on the Southern Region suggests

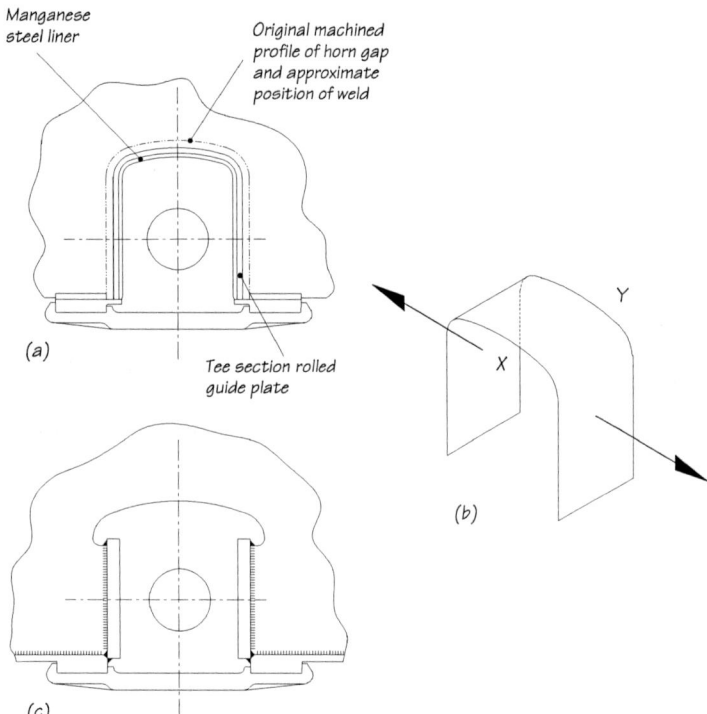

Fig. 42 - BR Class 7 horn designs

that this horn design is good, but it should be pointed out that the locomotives concerned have hardly been running long enough for defects to manifest themselves, LMR experience indicating that a minimum of five to six years elapses before trouble with frames may be expected.

The proposed frame design therefore appears to possess very little factor of safety in the neighbourhood of the top corners, since the stresses there, calculated under extreme conditions are higher than the comparable stresses on a Class 5, on which trouble at the top horn gaps are known to occur."

The Research Department suggested modifying the original design so the stress concentration represented by the horn corner was cut away, somewhat in the manner shewn in figure 42c. A photoelastic test was also proposed presumably to help refine the exact profile. The idea of cutting away the highly stressed area in this manner to avoid stress concentrations bears some affinity to the Frèmont slot sometimes seen in crank webs, but more interestingly it represented a revision of the Research Department's previous endorsement of the hornblock concept - *vide* Dr Johansen's reply to Edward Windle[69]. For this modified design, was nothing less than a return to the long-standing Midland practice of separate horn guides allied with a clip up horn stay, albeit modified to exploit welding rather than bolting or riveting of the guide faces and with the shape of the opening in the frame plate carefully profiled to avoid stress concentrations. Tacit admission the original Derby arrangement as used by Messers Johnson, Deeley, Clayton *et al* was not that erroneous!

In the event, the original horn guide design (figure 42a) was retained. While the author of the report was somewhat pessimistic in respect of the 'Merchant Navy' frame, he was absolutely correct in his prediction the 'Britannia' frame would prove susceptible to developing cracks in the rear bogie cut-out and from the welds in the upper corners of the horn gaps - as Bill Harvey confirmed.

Sir William Stanier[70], another believer in separate guides while answering a question on frame design posed by the Rev. Gibson, appeared not to be wholly enamoured of the BR Class 7 horn design. Incidentally it will be

---

69 Dr F C Johansen had been recruited to the LMS from the National Physical Laboratory in 1932 where he had conducted research into the resistance of passenger trains for the LNER and the LMS. In 1935 he moved to Derby from Euston as Senior Research Engineer to head up the Engineering Section of the Research Department. After fourteen years in the post he resigned in late 1949 to become Director of Research for the W & T Avery group. It seems likely that he was aware of the report's content and recommendations.

70 Sir W A Stanier *George Jackson Churchward, CME, GWR* Newcomen Society October 1955, pp9-10.

seen he did not favour a completely rigid structure:-

> "Locomotive engineers had been trying for generations to find a way of preventing frames cracking. When locomotives had boilers with the fire box *(sic)* fitting between the frames, to ensure the maximum width of fire box, the frames have to be as wide apart as possible, so they come just inside the driving wheels. This means offset horns and springs, and this puts a bending stress in the frames at each of the horns.
>
> When the boiler has a wide fire box which passes over the frames, the frames can pass through the centre line of the axle box *(sic)* and the spring is under or over the centre. This has been arranged on the Merchant Navy and Britannia classes. It makes a much better arrangement of frames, and these frames should be freer from cracks at the horn gaps. He did not think however that the question of frame cracking was solved. The Indian Railways put stiffeners all along the frames and made a very stiff frame. His own feeling was that it was much better to have a frame rigid between the cylinders and the motion plate and something that would give laterally behind that."

We started this investigation into frame cracking because of Mr Cox's opinion of the Class 4 0-6-0 being an inveterate frame breaker. So before finishing this chapter and armed with our insight into frame performance let us revisit his statement in *Chronicles of Steam*. A few lines previously[71] he had referred to the frame performance of four further early LMS Standard locomotive classes:-

> "The Compound 4-4-0's *(sic)* and the class 4 2-6-4 Tanks were excellent performers and the class 2 4-4-0's *(sic)* and the class 3 2-6-2 Tanks were feeble performers, but all of these classes had in common a pleasing freedom from major ills. It is true that the Derby design of manganese bronze axlebox was rather sensitive, giving a liability to every engine of a hot box every two years or so, but the frames were excellent, being rarely prone to fracture, and most of the detail work was robust and trouble free."

The Compound frame is confirmed by table X to have returned an excellent performance and this was also the situation with the Class 2 4-4-0, but it was arguably not the case with the Class 3 2-6-2T, which was similar to the 'Big Goods', while it was most definitely *not* the case with the Class 4 2-6-4T. Reference to the table appearing in *Locomotive Frames* reveals that precisely twenty years before, Mr Cox considered the 2-6-4T frame to have been *bad*, a category worse than that of the 'Big Goods' *and* the Class 5 4-6-0s. Conversely, Mr Powell in *Stanier 4-6-0s at Work*, described it as *poor* with an average figure of 2.7 cracks per engine after 10 years, considered it *better* than the Class 5. This is perhaps reasonable since a crack frequency of 2.7 is slightly less than the mean figure of 3.0 recorded for Class 5 4-6-0s Nº 5000-5451 - a value which had prompted so much of the anguish experienced by LMS engineers. It is also in keeping with the LMS classification recorded in table XX, yet in his earlier book *Living with London Midland Locomotives*[72] John Powell only briefly referred to the frame cracking experienced with the Class 4 2-6-4 tanks, airily dismissing the problem thus:-

> "There was a certain amount of frame fracture trouble at the coupled axlebox horns, for which the clip-up hornstays were partly responsible."

Such inconsistency perhaps justifies directing a degree of scepticism towards Mr Cox's statement the 'Big Goods' was an inveterate frame breaker being either a true reflection its frame performance or by implication that it was one of the worst performing classes the company possessed.

---

71 Mr E S Cox *Chronicles of Steam* Ian Allan London 1967 p37.

72 Mr A J Powell *Living with London Midland Locomotives* Ian Allan Shepperton 1977 p88.

Appendix 3.1

Some Notes Concerning Crack Development

Alan Griffith's starting point in 1920 was to consider cracking to be the result of an energy balance. He was aware of Professor Inglis' work in calculating stress concentrations around an elliptical hole, but his enlightened approach was to consider a stress concentration as an amplifier by which strain energy could be locally magnified in value to the point where it could destroy the atomic bonds of a material *i.e.* to enable a crack to propagate. The stress concentration serves this purpose whenever it is provided with sufficient strain energy. Should the supply of strain energy be insufficient, or cease, then the fracture process will stop.

When a piece of material is subjected to stress, it will increase in length - this increase being referred to as the strain and it represents a stored energy exactly like a stretched piece of rubber or the wound-up main spring of a watch. Since the mean stress in a locomotive frame was low it remained within the linear portion of the stress/strain curve for the material *i.e.* Hooke's law was being obeyed - *vide* figure 22:-

$$E = \frac{\text{Stress}}{\text{Strain}} = \frac{S}{e}$$

where:-
- E = Young's modulus - lbs/sq in
- S = stress - lbs/sq in
- e = strain - the ratio of the increase in length divided by the original length

From this it can be shewn the strain energy U per unit volume of plate is given by:-

$$U = \frac{E \times e}{2} = \frac{S^2}{2 \times E} \qquad (i)$$

For a crack to grow through a stretched frame plate, the energy required to destroy the atomic bonds has to be paid for by a relaxation of some of the strain energy within the frame *i.e.* the stress is relaxed on either side of the crack. If we take figure 18 and look at it in terms of strain energy, the two shaded areas (figure 43), which are roughly triangular, give up strain energy.

Whatever the length of the crack L these triangles retain roughly the same proportions, so their areas increase as the square of the crack length. For

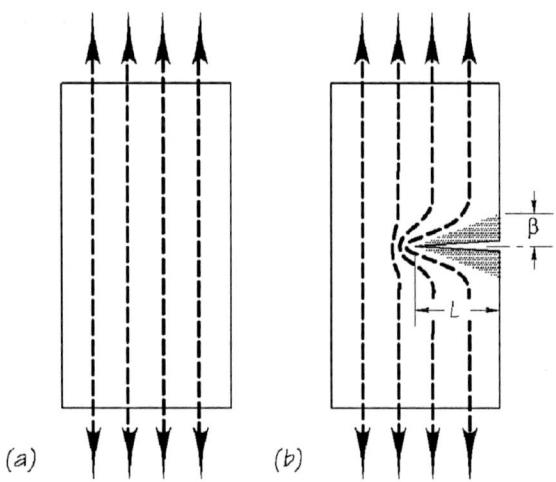

Fig. 43 - The unloaded regions adjoining the crack flanks

plane stress loading it can be demonstrated that the value β is equal to π. Thus the total strain energy *released* is the product of the strain energy per unit volume and the volume contained in the two shaded triangles:-

$$U = \frac{S^2 \times \pi \times L^2}{2 \times E} \qquad (ii)$$

However, the energy W to break the atomic bonds, which in effect is absorbed by the material, assuming a crack L long in a plate of unit thickness is given by:-

$$W = 2 \times \gamma s \times L \qquad (iii)$$

where:-
- γs = the surface energy - inch-lbs/sq in
- L = length - inches

The constant 2 is needed because two free surfaces are formed

These two relationships can then be plotted on a graph thereby revealing the resultant nett energy required for the crack to propagate.

Curve *I* represents the internal energy absorbed as the crack extends and is a straight line. Curve *II* describes the energy released as the crack propagates and follows a square law. The nett energy balance for any length of crack - represented by curve *III* - is the arithmetical difference between the energy absorbed to create the surfaces and the energy released when the regions near the crack flanks become unloaded.

Frames and Cracks

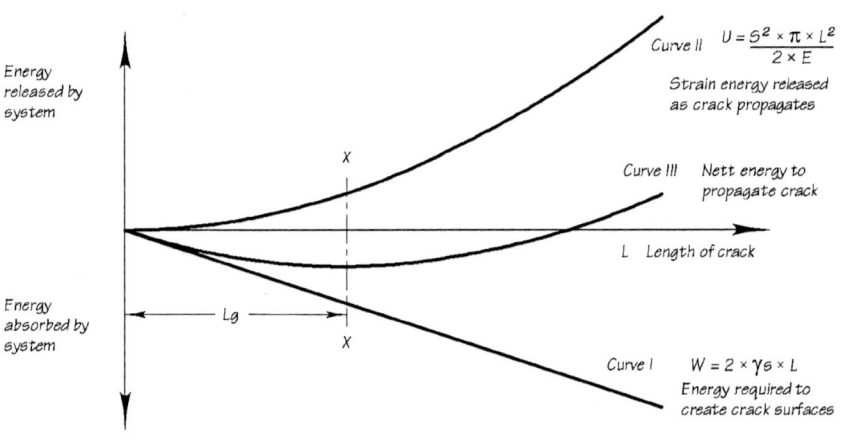

Fig. 44 - The Griffith fracture energy balance

Up to the point *X-X* the system is consuming energy, but beyond point *X-X* energy is instead released by the system *i.e.* if the crack grows longer, the quadratic relationship describing the strain energy release eventually dominates over the surface energy so beyond a critical crack length *Lg* the plate will lower its energy by letting the crack grow longer still. Up to the point *Lg* the crack will only grow if the stress is increased or fluctuates, beyond *Lg*, crack growth is spontaneous and catastrophic. The value of *Lg* can be found by differentiation of the total energy *(U + W)* and equating the derivative to zero:-

$$(U + W) = \frac{S^2 \times \pi \times L^2}{2 \times E} - 2 \times \gamma s \times L$$

whence:-

$$= \frac{S^2 \times \pi \times L}{E} - 2 \times \gamma s = 0$$

rearranging:-

$$S = \frac{(2 \times \gamma s \times E)^{1/2}}{(\pi \times L)^{1/2}} \quad (iv)$$

Dr Griffith's work involved glass rods and when applied to materials possessing greater ductility simply considering the surface energy alone results in errors, which discouraged engineers from considering this approach. Also it does not provide the full answer to the conundrum represented by the dressmaker's pin - Professor Inglis' analysis highlighted the mathematical difficulty that in a perfectly sharp crack the stress at the tip would become infinitely large so any material would be vulnerable to the tiniest loads since the resulting stress would become sufficiently high to fracture the atomic bonds.

Professor George Irwin, who had investigated the weld fractures in the Liberty ships, suggested in 1948, that in a ductile material the overwhelming portion of the released strain energy was not absorbed in creating new surfaces but rather it was dissipated due to plastic flow within the material immediately adjacent to the crack tip. Stress analysis such as that appearing in figure 21 demonstrates that the local stress quickly reduces with distance from the crack.

In a ductile material, there is plastic deformation of the material in the region where the local stress exceeds the yield stress, which may be some distance in advance of the crack tip. Thus, Professor Irwin modified formula *(iv)* by incorporating a plastic work of fracture γp in addition to the surface energy of crack formation, which he did by defining the total energy consumed when a unit area of new crack is formed as the toughness *Gc* of the material:-

i.e. $Gc = (\gamma s + \gamma p)$

Gc is a material property with units of inch-lbs/sq in thereby enabling the Griffith equation to be rewritten:-

$$S = \frac{(Gc \times E)^{1/2}}{(\pi \times Lg)^{1/2}} \quad (v)$$

This formula describes the interrelationships of three important aspects of the fracture process - the material, as described by the critical strain energy release rate *Gc* and its stiffness *E*, the stress level *S* and the size of the flaw or crack *L*. In brittle materials such as glass, the surface energy represents a significant portion of the total energy, *Gc* is low and crack propagation occurs readily at low strains. Conversely, in ductile materials such as mild steel, the opposite is the case, the energy consumed in plastic deformation as the crack propagates is many orders of magnitude greater than the new surface energy, consequently *Gc* is high and fracture demands much higher strains. Engineers take great care to avoid fast fractures and one way of doing so is by using materials having high *Gc* values, hence the popularity of mild steel for structures. However obtaining consistent figures for values of *Gc* is not easy, not least because they are affected by the way in which the tests are done, incidentally as a general rule the toughness of most metals reduces quite considerably as the tensile strength increases.

If a material is strained beyond its yield point *i.e.* plastically, then once the stress is released it no longer returns back to its original dimensions in other words Hook's law is no longer obeyed precisely. Instead it exhibits a set, signifying a small portion of the ductility has been lost, so the next time it is stressed plastically it does not behave exactly as it did previously *i.e.* some hysteresis has been introduced and the set increases. In effect, the fluctuating stress destroys the ductility through weakening the atomic structure of the metal within the plastic zone *immediately* adjacent to the crack tip reducing its resistance to the applied load. The crack is thus able to advance a tiny amount before encountering metal that has not been strained so highly and thus able to withstand the loading - that is until the next application of sufficiently high tensile loading when the process repeats. Hence the development of a creeping or fatigue crack whose speed of advance, until the critical length is obtained, is largely determined by the frequency with which its plate is strained beyond the yield point. At other times if the loadings are lower then the crack will pause in its propagation. We can now gain some appreciation of the variation in crack growth rates when for example Mr Bradley reported an existing frame crack increasing seven inches in a round trip of 1,200 miles, conversely 'Britannia' class 4-6-2 N° 70007 at the time possessing a frame crack 12½ inches long, ran an almost identical mileage on lighter/slower duties, but because of the lower stresses the crack did not progress.

Although the energy-balance approach, as described here, provides a useful insight into the fracture process, engineers nowadays favour newer methods which consider directly the stress state near the crack tip. This involves the use of stress intensity factors but does enable complex fatigue problems to be solved such as those involving specific geometries that in turn are subjected to various degrees and types of loading. However application of this demands either accurate knowledge of the dynamic loadings and stresses present in the structure or the substitution of an equivalent model - all of which was *quite* beyond the engineers of the 1940s designing locomotive frames let alone their predecessors of 1911.

Chapter Four

Axleboxes, Bearing Metals and Lubricants

Introduction

The Standard Class 4 0-6-0 has long had a reputation for having been heavy on its axleboxes, but as Mr Cox admitted, it was by no means the worst offender on the LMS. Thus, another way of describing the situation might be to say that it was a standard class, comprising a large number of engines, which returned a bearing performance poorer than the best, as typified by that obtained from the later taper-boiler outside-cylinder classes. In practice most locomotive engineers were plagued by poor axlebox life from their creations as the former Alco designer Alfred Bruce writing during the twilight of American steam locomotives explained[1]:-

> "Probably no machinery detail of the steam engine has given more trouble than the driving box, owing to overloading and improper lubrication."

However, it should be appreciated the performance Mr Bruce was expecting from a box was a world away from what others were proudly touting as triumphs of locomotive bearing design on this side of the Atlantic. Indeed the Churchward/Stanier design of axlebox had long been superseded in America, the land of its birth, simply because it could no longer deliver the performance required. That LMS engineers were able to obtain high mileages, in certain classes fitted with this design, *was not* due to any special features it possessed, but rather because the locomotives that carried them delivered a low specific power output – horsepower per ton of engine weight - the bearings were not heavily stressed.

Until the adoption of roller bearings, overloaded axleboxes were almost inevitable in any steam locomotive design, *whenever* the machine was worked to its full potential, due primarily to lack of sufficient space, or to be more precise the competing demands of other components for the limited space available. Thus, bearing area was commonly and knowingly sacrificed to avoid compromising the performance of items considered more important. Shortage of space was particularly acute in *all* engines fitted with large diameter inside cylinders, for the fixed distance between the driving wheels made it difficult to accommodate conventional axleboxes *and* crank webs wide enough to withstand the combined effects of the connecting rod and piston rod thrusts. Consequently, since crank axle strength understandably was held to be more important, of perforce inside cylinder engines were fitted with axleboxes that had a smaller bearing area for the loads imposed on them, so they simply wore out at lower mileages. Strictly speaking, this comment should be confined to standard gauge engines only, but it appears many broad gauge inside cylinder engines were not really given as large a bearings as they could have been.

Although size was the fundamental influence, there were other factors affecting bearing life and it is clear that they could have a significant impact, as is hinted in the following table wherein it will be seen the bearing load on the 'Big Goods' was far from the highest. If unit loading alone determined bearing performance then one might wonder how the Great Northern examples appearing in table XXIV left their sheds without encountering hot boxes! That these two classes, ran successfully for a large number of years, twenty-five in the case of the 0-8-0, and thirty-five for the 0-6-2T on intensive suburban services, confirms that size was far from the only criteria determining axlebox performance. The J27 and the LMS Standard 7 0-

---

[1] Mr A W Bruce *The Steam Locomotive in America* Bonanza Books New York 1952 p224.

This weakness was present in other schools of steam reciprocating machinery, thus the classic marine triple expansion engine, which employed bearing technologies identical with the steam locomotive, was not very reliable when pressed hard as in naval ships. With the noise, vibration, steam leaks and hose pipes continuously played on hot bearings to keep them cool, perhaps understandably, Admiral Lord Jacky Fisher once likened working in a warship's engine room at full speed to living in a snipe marsh.

A Defence of the Midland/LMS Class 4 0-6-0

Table XXIV - Piston and Bearing Loads for a Selection of Inside Cylinder Locomotives

Locomotive	Cylinder diameter - inches	Boiler pressure - lbs/sq in	Crank axle journals Diameter × length - inches	Projected area - sq in	Maximum piston load - lbs	Bearing load - lbs/sq in
LNWR Class G2 0-8-0†	20½	175	7½ × 9*	67.5*	57,761	856
LMS Class 7 0-8-0	19	200	8½ × 8¼	70.125	56,705	809
Midland/LMS Class 4 0-6-0	20	175	8½ × 8¼	70.125	54,978	796
Midland 999 Class 4-4-0 (sat.)¶	19	220	8¼ × 9	74.25	62,376	840
GER 'Claud Hamilton' 4-4-0	19	180	7⅝ × 8 1/16	61.477	51,035	830
GER S69/LNER B12 4-6-0	20	180	8½ × 8¾	74.375	56,549	760
GER (LNER J20) 0-6-0	20	180	8½ × 8	68.0	56,549	832
NER P3 (LNER J27) 0-6-0¤	18½	180	7½ × 8	60.0	48,384	806
LNER J38 & J39 0-6-0¤	20	180	8 × 9	72.0	56,549	785
GNR/LNER N2 0-6-2T	19	170	7½ × 7	52.5	48,200	918
GNR K1/LNER Q1 0-8-0 (sat.)	19¾	175	8½ × 6½#	55.25	53,612	970
GNR K1/LNER Q2 0-8-0 (sup.)	21	170	8½ × 6½#	55.25	58,881	1,066
CR 721 Class 4-4-0 - Dunalastair I	18¼	160	8 × 7½	60.0	41,854	698
CR 766 Class 4-4-0 - Dunalastair II & III	19	175	8½ × 7½	63.75	49,618	778
CR 140 Class 4-4-0 - Dunalastair IV	19	180	9¼ × 7½§	69.375	51,035	736
CR 903 Class 4-6-0 - Cardean	20	200	9½ × 10½	99.75	62,832	630
SE&CR E1 4-4-0	19	180	8½ × 7¾	65.875	51,035	775
Southern Q1 0-6-0	19	230	8¾ × 8 13/16	77.11	65,212	846
LMS Standard Class 5 4-6-0/Class 8 2-8-0	18½	225	8½ × 10⅞	92.4375	60,481	654
Canadian Pacific 'Selkirk' 2-10-4	25½	275	12 × 14	168	140,444	836

NB:- These bearing pressures are based on journal size not box size, likewise the effects of fillet radii in reducing bearing area have been omitted in this table, as in most cases their dimensions were not available. The calculation method is the one used by Mr E C Poultney in *Locomotive Axleboxes*.

†Classes G2 and G1 very similar, principal difference was a working pressure of 175lbs/sq in for the former and 160lbs/sq in for the latter, reducing its piston load to 52,810lbs, giving a bearing load of 783lbs/sq in.

*Bearing area ignores any contribution made from the centre bearing – 7¼" × 5" scaled from a GA drawing – originally present, if this is included, pressure drops to 675lbs/sq in. Centre bearings had been a feature of Crewe engines fitted with Joy valve gear although the LMS hardly improved LNWR bearing performance when it removed them from some classes (*all? – APT*) including the 'Super Ds'. Certainly, the 0-8-0 class was considered by the LMS to have had a poor bearing performance – it too received special lubricating oil.

¶The earliest superheated examples were provided with 20½ins diameter cylinders while retaining 220lbs boilers giving a bearing pressure of 978lbs/sq in later reduced to 800lbs/sq in when the boilers were set to 180lbs/sq in.

¤Dimensions obtained from *LNER Encyclopedia* website.

#Dimensions for the saturated engines taken from *Great Northern Locomotive History Vol 3A - Ivatt Era* by N Groves, scaling from a very small scale drawing of a superheated example - *British Locomotives of 20th Century Vol 1* by O S Nock suggests the bearings were longer approx 9ins, giving significantly lower pressures *viz* 701lbs/sq in & 770lbs.

§*Scottish Locomotive History 1831-1923* by Campbell Highet gives 7½ins for the length, interpretation of a small-scale reproduction of a General Arrangement drawing in *Caledonian Dunalastairs* by O S Nock suggest 8ins whence the pressure reduces to 690lbs/sq ins.

The two shaded entries are outside cylinder locomotives, with the second being an example of a North American engine and demonstrates why the 'American' style of axlebox was superseded on that continent.

8-0 had similar bearing pressures yet one lasted until the end of steam in the North East while the other was withdrawn prematurely. In fact the problems experienced with the 'Big Goods' and the 'Austin Seven' were not simply due to the 'presence of Midland under-sized axleboxes' as some would have us believe, but rather they encompassed a number of seemingly unrelated other factors, such as poor and/or imperfect re-metalling techniques, a less than optimum choice of white metal combined with a poorly performing lubricant. Or as locomotive designer Eric Langridge[2] commented on the situation:-

> "The bearings that were sufficient for MR days were not equal to the rough and tumble of LMS handling. Quality of materials went down with economic pressure from commercially-minded managers and oil became poor. All this can be false economy from an engineering point of view; cheapness does not really pay. However, I sometimes wonder if critics of bearing sizes ever had a go at designing themselves!"

From this we may infer, if size *alone* had indeed been the *sole* reason, then *all* engines fitted with small bearings would *always* have run hot. Furthermore, it suggests that such behaviour should have been readily anticipated while the engine was on the drawing board and ought never have occurred save by those fools in Derby Locomotive Drawing Office, who insisted in fitting under-sized boxes. Unfortunately, in practice hot boxes came and went, furthermore they could be caused by such a diverse variety of factors, that this alone made their accurate diagnosis when they did occur, all the more difficult and *time* consuming to pin-point, a point touched on by Mr Bell[3]:-

> "An ailment which affects all locomotives at times is the 'hot box', and a frequent cause for anxiety on the part of the running-shed foreman. The chief causes of trouble are insufficient lubrication, wrong brand of oil, badly made trimmings, and dust or sand working in between brass and journal; cases have been known, however, where boxes ran hot owing to the incorrect alignment of the frame."

Thus, what the provision of 'under-sized' bearings *really* meant was that locomotives so shod were more sensitive to the factors highlighted above than were ones given more generously sized bearings. Apart from this, as will be demonstrated, there was very little difference in the performance of the Churchward/Stanier design of axlebox over that of its Midland predecessor. The major reason for the short bearing life returned by the Class 4 was simply the presence of inside cylinders which limited axlebox size, while changes made by the LMS initially worsened the situation. Although LMS engineers were later able to obtain significantly better axlebox performance from this and other inside cylinder classes, the evidence suggests they were never so minded to go as far as was possible – probably by then they did not consider it a high enough priority. Certainly, there are instances of contemporary engineers in the employ of other companies obtaining significant

Table XXV - Hot Box Performance Record of the ex-LNWR G1 and G2 0-8-0 Classes During the Period 1942-1946

Year	G1 Class			G2 Class		
	N° of hot boxes	N° of engines	Equivalent to one hot box per engine in months	N° of hot boxes	N° of engines	Equivalent to one hot box per engine in months
1942	272	200	8.8	433	308	8.5
1943	197	191	11.6	313	318	12.2
1944	132	180	16.4	252	329	15.7
1945	70	172	29.5	141	337	28.7
1946	62	152	29.4	120	357	35.7

improvement in box performance, in many cases simply through careful observation but allied in others by the active modification of the existing designs. By way of example, let us refer to a memorandum[4] dated 9th June 1931 to Mr S J Symes in which E S Cox reported that in 1930 the Standard Class 7 0-8-0 suffered 53 hotboxes out of 120 engines, which is the equivalent of one hot box per engine in 27.2 months. He considered some of this heating caused by excessive side thrust in the right driving boxes arising from inaccurate box machining and referred to the adoption of a revised axlebox with end thrust pads as fitted to the N° 4 Class Goods effecting some improvement. The ex-LNWR G1 and G2 0-8-0 classes were also mentioned in the memo with corresponding hot box figures provided for them, again for 1930. The G1 class suffered 40 hotboxes out of 401 engines

---

2 Mr E Langridge *Under 10 CMEs Volume One: Dugald Drummond to W A Stanier* Oakwood Press Usk 2011 p119.

3 Mr A M Bell *Locomotives – their Construction, Maintenance and Operation Vol II* Virtue & C° Ltd London sixth edition 1948 p239.

4 Mr E S Cox *8-wheeled Coupled Freight Engines* memo to Mr S J Symes 9th June 1931.

while the G2 (60 engines) had 22 hot boxes. This is the equivalent for the G1 of one hot box per engine in just over ten years, which puts them on a par with the 1939 figures Mr Cox proudly quoted[5] as the average performance of all the new taper-boiler classes plus the 'Royal Scots' which by then had all been fitted with Stanier boxes. In contrast the corresponding figure for the G2 0-8-0 was one hot box per engine in 32.7 months – little better than the Standard Class 7. Later, Lt. Col. Harold Rudgard provided further figures[6] for the two ex-LNWR classes, which are summarized in table XXV. In the original data, although there were figures given for the numbers of hot boxes that occurred in 1946, there were none for the number of engines but Mr Talbot kindly provided these so the table has been completed by the shaded entries.

In 1943, the LMS adopted a lubricating oil that had been specifically developed for highly loaded boxes, which it used on its 'difficult' classes *viz.*:- G1, G2, 'Austin 7' and 'Big Goods'. Inspection of this table reveals a drop in the incidences of hot boxes following its adoption. However, what is not explained by these figures is the astronomical rise that had occurred in the incidences of hot boxes in the G1 class between 1930 and 1942. It is known that sometime prior to the Second World War the LMS adopted a white metal containing a high percentage of lead for its axleboxes – the Midland for example by contrast had used a white metal containing no lead for that same purpose. Mr Cox admitted that white metal containing a high proportion of lead had caused problems with big ends overheating which disappeared when white metal containing no lead was re-adopted.

At some stage, the centre bearings were removed from ex-LNWR engines fitted with Joy valve gear. This was certainly LMS policy in the 1930s although the Reverend H G Neale who served his time at Crewe in the mid-1920s suggests the practice may have started earlier - correspondence from Mr Talbot suggests possibly 1923. Finally, it is known that the LMS used inferior blends of oil, utilizing inappropriate mineral oil bases or additives, for axlebox lubrication, which will have adversely affected these four classes prior to the introduction of the new oil.

While the new outside cylinder LMS engines which were given more generously proportioned axleboxes could cope with these changes (although that of itself brought significant other disadvantages) it does seen that LMS engineers have only themselves to blame for not a small proportion of the hot boxes suffered by two Standard and two important non-standard classes. In short, saving a few shillings' worth of more expensive oil and white metal wasted hours of fitters' time in re-metalling and machining axleboxes. Each hotbox repair was estimated in 1947 to cost £40 to remedy. Thus, had the casualty rates recorded in 1930 with the two ex-LNWR classes been maintained in 1942 in place of those that actually occurred, there would have been a reduction of 252 hot G1 boxes and 320 hot G2 boxes giving a total saving of £22,880. Whilst, wartime conditions doubtless inflated the casualty figures nevertheless one does at times wonder how much the criticism directed by some at the box performance of inside cylinder engines was a smokescreen to deflect attention from inappropriate decisions made by senior LMS officers.

We should never overlook the human factor, when considering the relative performance of different axleboxes – an example is furnished by the Caledonian 'Dunalastairs'. Table XXIV shews that as successive batches of this famous series of 4-4-0s were increased in size, the bearing area was likewise enlarged so that the later engines carried bearing pressures little or no higher than the earlier examples. Yet two Scottish locomotive engineers, albeit both trained in England, could give divergent opinions of Caledonian box performance; starting with Mr Highet[7]:-

"Ample bearing surface was provided on the axle journal thereby contributing to the freedom from heated axle bearings enjoyed by the whole of the genus 'Dunalastair'."

According to Mr Cox[8] however:-

"....Solid bronze - LMS experience with this type has been indeterminate, since the size and design of the boxes on the old L&Y and Caledonian engines were inadequate and gave a poor record in wear and heating."

---

5 Mr E S Cox *Locomotive Axleboxes* I Loco E Paper N° 447 April 1944 p302.

6 Lt-Col H Rudgard *Organisation and Carrying-Out of Examinations and Repairs of Locomotives at Running Sheds in Relationship to Locomotive Performance and Availability* I Loco E Paper 464 January 1947 pp88 & 133.

7 Mr C Highet *Scottish Locomotive History 1831-1923* George Allen & Unwin London 1970 p192.

8 Mr E S Cox *Locomotive Axleboxes* I Loco E Paper N° 447 April 1944 p289.

Mr Nock[9] also touched on the subject of 'Dunalastair' box performance, agreeing with Campbell Highet:-

"They were designed for hard slogging work, and a most significant change from the original engines was a marked increase in the dimensions of the coupled wheel bearings. The Caledonian freedom from trouble with hot boxes can no doubt be attributed to the generous size of the journals."

Given these divergent opinions by two professional locomotive engineers it is difficult at face value to decide quite where the truth lay. We know as a general rule that in Britain at least, the axleboxes on inside cylinder engines did not last as long as those on their outside cousins but keep it *sotto voce*, one does wonder if at times the known personal dislikes of high-placed LMS engineers towards the former were not sometimes at work. Be that as it may, let us start with a brief look at axlebox development before considering bearing performance and how this is applicable to the experiences recorded with the 'Big Goods' axleboxes and those of contemporary classes.

Some Notes on Axlebox Development

Solid bronze or hard brass axleboxes had been very popular throughout the nineteenth century on both sides of the Atlantic, but by 1900, most American designers had stopped using them. Such axleboxes could give excellent service provided their dimensions were large enough, but they were expensive albeit retaining a high residual scrap value. Due to their lower tensile strength, they were usually larger than their ferrous equivalents, but they had the advantage that a separate fitted bearing brass was not needed, while any white metal inserts could be poured directly in. Another advantage was their higher thermal conductivity promoted cooler running temperatures. LMS experience of solid bronze axleboxes according to Mr Cox was poor because those examples the company inherited *e.g.* L&YR and Caledonian were restricted in size. Notwithstanding these observations, the type remained in favour in Britain and elsewhere, for a long time, indeed even during the Second World War Oliver Bulleid determined to fit them to his designs.

Although the manganese bronze axlebox used by the Midland Railway and illustrated in figure 45 embodied for a non-ferrous box certain novel features, its design represented a logical progression arising from a sound understanding of the forces acting within the driving axleboxes of inside-cylinder engines and the resulting wear patterns. A hypothesis given considerable support by the following statement made by James Clayton[10], a one-time senior member of Derby Locomotive Drawing Office familiar with and involved in Midland axlebox design:-

"The bronze axlebox has a great many advocates. There are not many engineers who would go to the trouble of putting in bronze axleboxes unless they were very sure of their ground, as the money lying idle there is very obvious; but the bronze box has one very good point – if it is well cared for and fairly well maintained, it is not so subject to heating as other types, at any rate in my experience, extending over some 35 years of observation. The cast steel axlebox with a good brass runs it very close, but on the whole I think it may be said that the bronze box is rather better. The point with the bronze box is that when one is committed to it one cannot afford to scrap it. The thing is, if they have done so well, to keep them going. Don't let the box run too far, but before it has got to the scrapping thickness dovetail a crown across the top of the box and a side fillet on either side to take the thrust, and the brass box, together with its liners and horn-cheek guides, is practically as everlasting as the cast steel box. With the manganese bronze which it is possible to get nowadays for this purpose, with 32 to 37 tons tensile, it is practically as good as the best cast steel and not so prone to heating."

In the Midland manganese bronze box, from new, the actual bearing for the axle was formed by a combination of white metal and three gunmetal (bronze) strips, as manganese bronze[11] reputedly

---

9 Mr O S Nock *The Caledonian Dunalastairs* David & Charles Newton Abbot 1968 p40.

10 Mr J Clayton contributing to the discussion following the London reading of the paper:-

Mr A E Kyffin Notes on Axleboxes and Axlebox Guides I Loco E Paper Nº 108 Journal Nº 52 1921 p45-46.

11 To be strictly correct it was not manganese bronze, but rather a manganese *brass* having the following analysis copper 60%, zinc 37%, aluminium 1.5%, iron 1.0% and manganese .5%; tin and nickel were sometimes present as impurities. This high tensile brass had yield strength of 17.2 tons/sq in, an ultimate strength of 37 tons/sq in and an elongation of 30%. Mr Summerson referred to some experiments made in April 1918 wherein manganese bronze axleboxes were fitted but provided, it appears with different antifriction metals – Nº 3858, 3863 and 3865 had Parson's mixture (tin 58½%, zinc 39½% antimony 2%) while Nº 3868 had Woolwich mixture. Concurrently Nº 3867 and 3869 were given steel boxes with manganese bearings presumably either cast or pressed in. Interestingly, the pressed in brasses fitted to the cast steel axleboxes of the Southern 'Schools' class 4-4-0, were of manganese bronze, white metal lined apart from the lower

was not considered suitable as a bearing material for the journal being very tough and far too hard. However, it did serve as the wearing surface against the horn faces and for rubbing against the wheel boss and crank webs. The two lowest bronze strips were there to resist the horizontal thrust and pull of the piston as well as to act as stops for the white metal. The third strip was located at the crown thereby forming a non-fusible entry for the two oil holes that fed an oval oil groove cut into the upper portion of the bearing. They were also intended to permit the engine to be worked home in the event of the white metal having been seriously damaged by overheating or abrasion. All three gunmetal strips were dovetailed into the manganese bronze body but the crown strip was additionally secured by means of three gunmetal countersunk screws. The white metal was continuous over the full length of the bearing, thereby facilitating the machining while encouraging a good union between it and the bronze strips. Normally no lubricating pad was used with this design.

In Britain and elsewhere the case-hardened wrought iron or steel box had been widely used during Queen Victoria's reign but as neither ferrous material was suitable as a bearing metal a separate brass, usually with a significant area of white metal was provided as the rubbing surface on the journal. There were two methods of locating the brass, latterly under American influence it was forced it into the body of the box but a far older and more common method was to locate it as a 'loose' brass or 'step', but in either arrangement, it was retained within a machined recess. The loose brass was a machined casting, arranged to have either a five-sided contour, or a simpler rectangular profile. The former shape was lighter and considered superior because a good close fit could be more easily obtained in the ferrous box body. The loose brass not only had to be a very tight fit within the box but also provision had to be included to prevent subsequent sideways or longitudinal movement in service. Collars were sometimes present on the brass to prevent lateral movement, but a more common arrangement was a recess cut in the crown of the box, which received a matching machined circular projection cast onto the top of the brass. James Clayton[12] opined:-

"The wrought steel box has the disadvantage of the loose brass which requires to be extremely well fitted, and the box generally is rather expensive to make. At the same time, there are engineers in this country who swear by it, and a long experience on the Midland proved that it was a good form of box. Provided that brasses are well fitted with bronze wearing faces on the box, both to the wheel face and the axlebox guides, and made renewable, the body of the box is practically everlasting."

However well the loose brasses were fitted up initially, the number of fitted faces did offer an opportunity for fretting and consequential wear, nevertheless contrary to what the following extract might have us believe, they were a very successful long-lived design whose use was *far* from confined to the Midland Railway:-

"Then the axleboxes: they were really rather prehistoric. They consisted of a steel horse-shoe body, with parallel sides and square crown into which fitted (loose) the 'brass'. This located by a circular machined boss which engaged in a matching recess in the crown of the steel body. A straightforward keep containing an oil pad, held in place by the pin of the spring D-link, completed the assembly. You could only get at the pad by dropping the wheels, of course! Lubrication, from oil box or mechanical lubricator, was taken to the crown of the steel box and thence to the top boss of the brass and the crown of the bearing. The bearing area was very inadequate - the use of inside crank axles with two pairs of eccentric sheaves leaves no room for journals more than about 8½in long - and so hot boxes were all too frequent. These occurred because of various deficiencies in the oil supply, inadequately backed up by the underpad, and also due to the fore-and-aft 'roll' which developed on the bearing when, for instance, Class 4Fs were involved in heavy, slow-speed pulling; all these could prevent the maintenance of a proper oil film."

While the above criticism of Midland axlebox design by Mr A J Powell[13] is pretty damning, this was not a view shared by James Clayton or by others who had rather more experience of the design. The loose brass axleboxes had been widely used in Britain, while some companies were later converts. An example of the latter being the North Eastern Railway which adopted the design because they found them to be more reliable than the solid

---

2ins at the ends.
Mr S Summerson *Midland Railway Locomotives Vol IV* Irwell Press Ltd Clophill pp91-2.

12 Mr J Clayton contributing to the discussion following the London reading of the paper:-
Mr A E Kyffin Notes on Axleboxes and Axlebox Guides I Loco E Paper N° 108 Journal N° 52 1921 p45.
13 Mr A J Powell *Living with London Midland Locomotives* Ian Allan Shepperton 1977 p25.

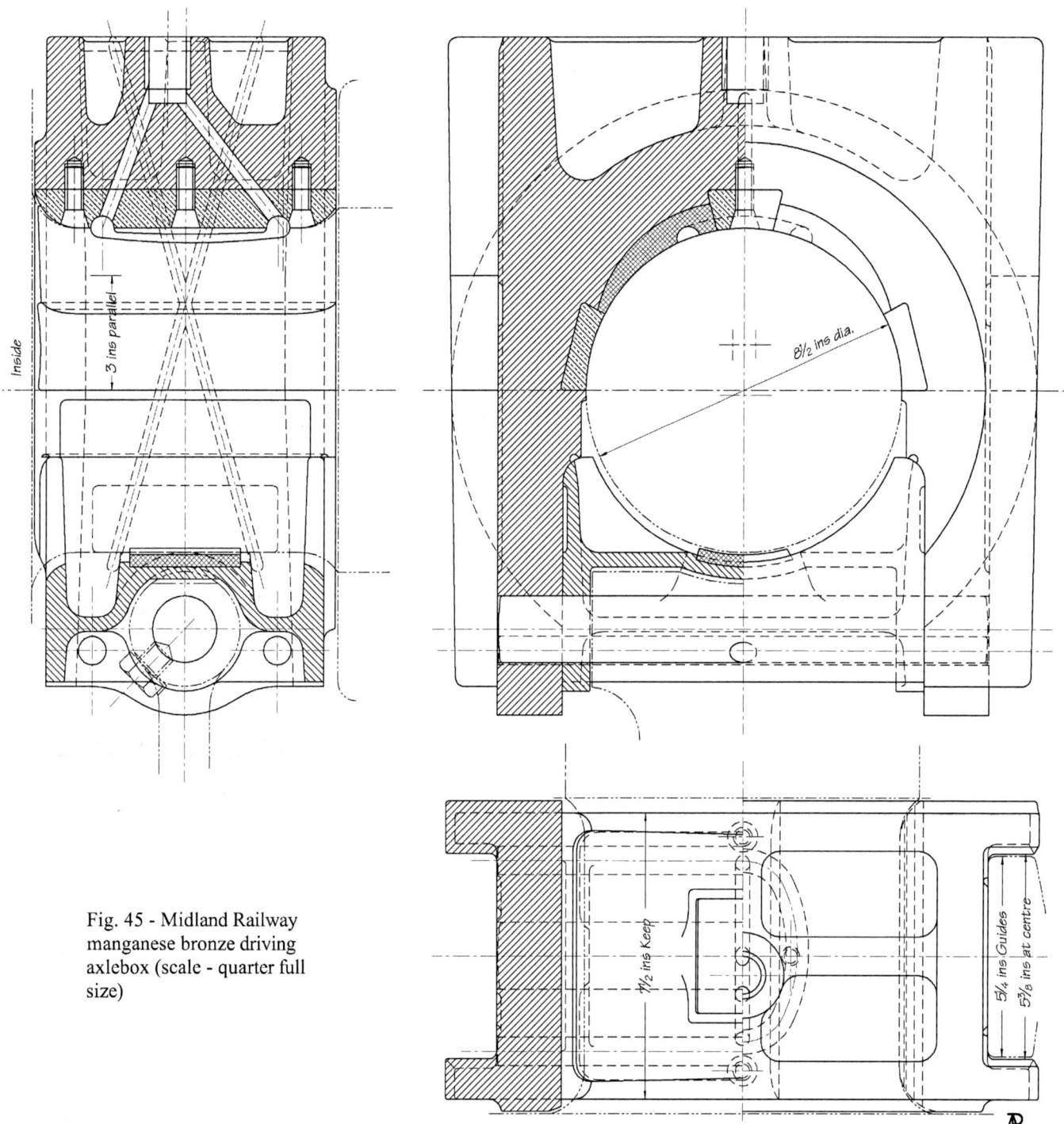

Fig. 45 - Midland Railway manganese bronze driving axlebox (scale - quarter full size)

Bearing for journal provided by white metal and gunmetal, with wearing surfaces of manganese bronze for the horn faces, wheel boss and crank web. Two gunmetal strips were provided for resisting the horizontal thrust and pull of the piston, a third strip located in the crown served as a non-fusible lead for two oil holes, and to permit the engine to be worked home in the event of the white metal being seriously damaged by overheating or abrasion. These bearing strips were dovetailed into the manganese bronze body of the axlebox, while the crown strip was further secured by three gunmetal countersunk screws. The white metal was continuous over the full length of the bearing, so permitting ready machining of a suitable bed in the box thereby facilitating a good bond of the white metal on a clean surface.

End fillets given a radius of 13/16ins and were clear of the axle in the normal running position, actual bearing contact only made when the wheel boss, or crank web had taken up lateral clearance of 1/16in. The recesses in the axlebox crown were to reduce weight, not oil receptacles. Lubrication was solely via the oil holes in the crown. Lubricant was supplied from an external oil box or lubricator through a sliding connexion into an oil feed pipe screwed into the top of the box.

The keep was of cast iron and although it had no load to bear when the engine was working was of strong design. As was common Midland practice, no lubricating pad was used, but instead a white metal pad was provided, albeit it was clear of the journal under normal running conditions. This pad served to support the axle when the engine was lifted and could act as a bearing when the axlebox was packed up and the crank axle rotated during valve setting or similar operations. The ends of the keep were quite clear of the journal fillets.

Ample allowance was provided for the rolling movements of the engine or irregularities in the height of the two rails, by making the flanges parallel for a length of 3ins only, above the centre line of the axle, the width between the flanges at the latter point being 53/8ins, or 1/8in more than the width of the hornblock face. Thus the axle could have an inclination of 1 in 24 with its normal level, representing a difference in the journal levels of about 17/8ins. Above and below the parallel middle portion of the axlebox, the flanges were tapered off at an incline of 1 in 33 1/3 above, and 1 in 31 below, permitting approximately, a difference of 13/8ins between the axlebox levels, without any tendency for the journal to bear on one end of the brass only.

A Defence of the Midland/LMS Class 4 0-6-0

Early version of the 'Stanier' axlebox as used on the 2-6-4T introduced in 1934. This Great Western inspired design comprised a steel body with a pressed-in circular brass, large keep containing an auxiliary spring-loaded oil pad. This was intended as a back up to the main feed from the mechanical lubricator thereby ensuring continuity of supply. The slide-out keep could be removed for inspection. The white metal was only shrouded at ends but the brass was provided with serrations to improve bonding.

Oil from the mechanical lubricator entered through the top of the axlebox, whence it reached the journal via two internal passages and two oil grooves located at 40° to the vertical centre line. Later practice was to reduce the thickness of the white metal and to groove the back of the brass so permitting oil delivery on the horizontal centre line. However, this arrangement although providing a bearing surface undisrupted by oil grooves, was not successful in boxes having high bearing loads in the region of oil delivery. For them a reversion was made to the arrangement shewn here.

Fig. 46 - LMS 'Stanier' steel axlebox with pressed in brass (scale - quarter full size)

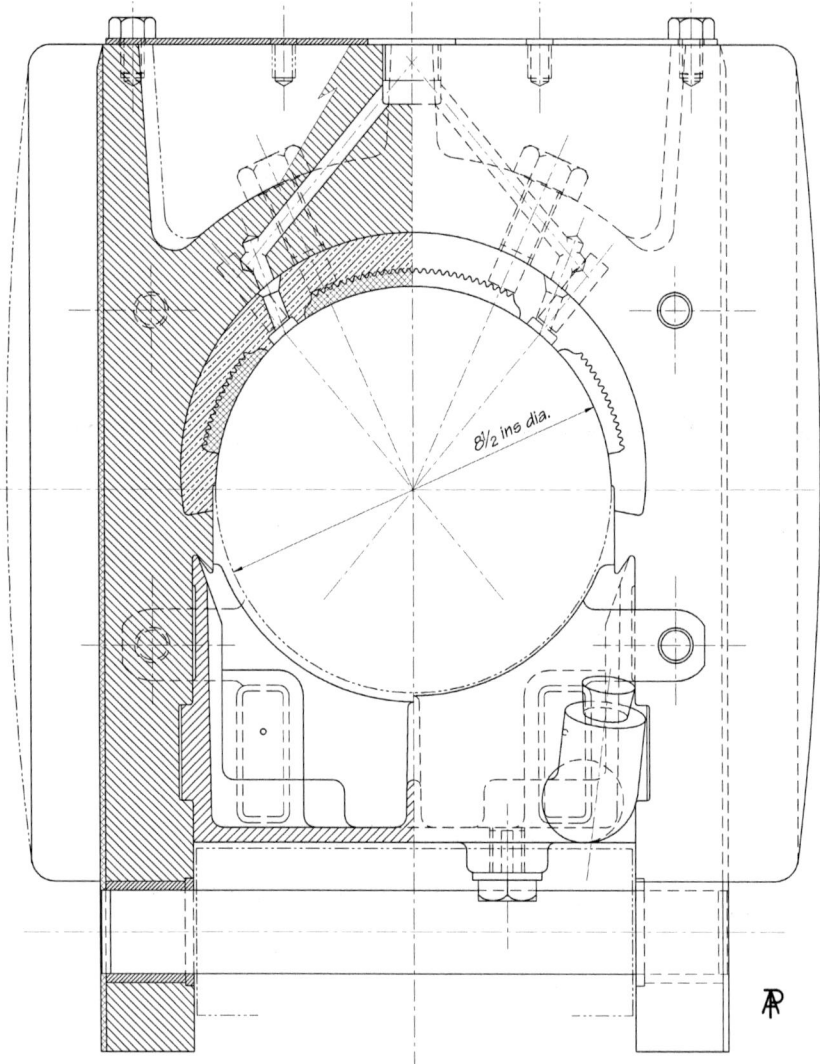

bronze version[14], while Germany and many Eastern European countries post-1945 continued to use large numbers of such boxes in their most modern locomotives. One advantage for the loose brass box was that in some designs at least, it was possible to inspect the bearing surface without removing the wheels.

According to Mr Bond[15], the Class 4 superheater goods engines originally had steel axleboxes with loose brasses, but the later examples, presumably starting in 1918, were provided with manganese bronze boxes for the driving wheels only, in an effort to obtain cooler running. In the loose brass design heat in the brass had to pass across the interstice between the brass and the steel body of the box, which introduced a thermal resistance while the steel possessed lower thermal conductivity. The earlier members of the class had their steel driving boxes replaced by manganese bronze boxes as they came into shops for renewal. Mr Cox[16] confirmed later the use of loose brass axleboxes[17] in Sir Henry Fowler's LMS engines

---

14 The following is a contribution made by Major J H Smeddle to the discussion following:-

"We have on the N.E.R. tried many kinds of axleboxes, including the solid brass, which we have practically discarded, and we have now adopted a wrought iron axlebox with loose brass which we have found very successful."

Mr A E Kyffin *Notes on Axleboxes and Axlebox Guides* I Loco E Paper 108 1921 Journal N° 52 p16. Two other NER employees present, Messers J Weatherburn and H J Stephenson also praised the loose brass box.

15 Mr R C Bond *The Design of a Locomotive Axlebox* paper delivered to Associate Section, Midland Railway Engineering Club 8th February 1923.

16 Mr E S Cox *Locomotive Axleboxes* I Loco E Paper N° 447 April 1944 p305.

17 This gunmetal alloy, referred to as A.1. by the Midland, was composed of 87 per cent copper, 9 per cent tin, 2 per cent

was restricted to the coupled wheels and never the more heavily loaded driving boxes. Since for standardization the existing width between the horn faces was retained in the later class members, this prevented an ordinary solid gunmetal box being fitted due to the risk of this weak alloy fracturing through insufficient cross-sectional area, hence the development of the higher strength manganese bronze box. Finally a six-feed mechanical lubricator was substituted for the previous syphon trimmings but these were retained for lubricating the horn faces.

During the last decade or two of the nineteenth century when for cheapness and to save weight, the Americans stopped using solid bronze boxes, they substituted a steel axlebox having a pressed in brass. The brass was segmental in cross-section and forced into position, while its ends were dovetailed into the box to prevent a tendency for the extremities of the brass to close in and pinch the journal causing it to run hot. In order further to safeguard the retention of the brass, it was normally additionally secured by means of two angled bolts[18] that entered from the top of the box one on either side and were screwed into the brass. One weakness, albeit this was potentially more likely with grease lubrication due to its higher operating temperature were the effects of differential expansion. The bronze bearing expanded more than its steel housing, and ultimately yielded in compression. On cooling, the brass became loose in the box or in worse cases shrank on to the journal. Another reason for fitting the bolts, was that their presence prevented a brass that had become loose from falling out of the axlebox should no collars be present on the axle – a logical development with bar frames. This design, commonly known as the 'American box' was destined to spread throughout the world and as is well known, an early devotee was George Churchward of the Great Western. Although reputedly, one of the features William Stanier introduced to the LMS - figure 46 - the later standard LNWR axlebox was precisely of this form, albeit of smaller dimensions[19] to suit crank axles.

It is perhaps germane to remain with American axlebox development for it was possibly in the USA that the greatest progress was made towards obtaining a reasonable axlebox life while subjecting it to very high loadings. Since outside cylinders were almost *de rigour* in America this, initially, enabled more generous axleboxes to be used, reducing bearing pressures, which combined with the nominally lower loadings inherent in outside cylinder engines resulted, by and large in superior performance than contemporary British boxes. A further benefit followed from the almost universal use in America of bar frames and overhung springs. The former ensured the box was centrally located and thus largely symmetrically loaded, while the latter afforded American engineers the opportunity of fitting a generous sized underkeep that could be slid out for inspection without dismantling anything else. It was usually arranged to contain a spring loaded oil soaked pad or increasingly from 1900, a generous sized block of hard grease that was drawn up against the underside of the journal. Replying to a question asked by Sir Nigel Gresley at the 1925 International Railway Congress, held in London, Mr Wallis of the Pennsylvania Railroad said that 98 per cent of contemporary American locomotives had grease lubrication.

Provided the 'American box' was neither overloaded nor inadequately lubricated, it gave good service, but with the rise in locomotive size and power during the twentieth century its performance proportionately reduced so of perforce new designs were developed. During the

---

zinc and 2 per cent lead – the zinc made the metal flow more freely by combining with any free or combined oxygen, while the lead improved machining. Sir William Stanier's brasses on the LMS comprised 86 per cent copper, 7 per cent tin, 4 per cent zinc and 3 per cent lead.

18 "Even when these brasses are accurately fitted and pressed in the box very tightly, they will in time become loose and will have to be replaced. In order to make these brasses remain tight in the box for a greater period of time, some master-mechanics will drive two brass pins ¾ inch in diameter, through each side of the box and brass."
Mr J G A Meyer *Modern Locomotive Construction* - John Wiley & Son New York 1892 p205.

19 "Steel with pressed in brass - this was standard on the old L&NW, but bearing performance on these engines was and is below standard due to insufficient size, excessive loads and inadequate oiling arrangement...."
Mr E S Cox *Locomotive Axleboxes* I Loco E Paper N° 447 April 1944 p285.

It seems reasonable to assume that the Midland along with the Great Northern and the Great Central also had some experience of the 'American' type of axlebox with a pressed in brass by virtue of their purchase of Baldwin and Schenectady built 2-6-0s. A General Arrangement drawing of a Baldwin built example for the Midland suggests a steel box with a pressed in brass fitting a journal 7ins diameter and 8ins long, but being shewn in cross-section, it is not clear if the brass was of the later circular type or the short-lived rectangular version.

First World War and afterwards, big ten-coupled engines were introduced in the USA and to carry the larger bearing loads, the journals were increased in length by about one-half. Despite this greater width, the box was arranged to remain symmetrical in the 'horns' and the vertical spring load was also arranged to act on the centre of each journal by means of a bridge-type spring saddle. While the enhanced journal size ensured the nominal bearing loading pressure was no higher, the piston thrusts were concentrated more on the wheel half (or outboard) side of the bearings because of the greater offset between the centres of the axleboxes and those of the cylinders. This resulted in the journals wearing taper[20] in service with the smallest diameter appearing next to the hub prompting engineers to search for a better solution.

Continuous axleboxes were tried and discarded but when the opposite action was taken, namely the box length reduced and the bearing changed to include a grease-lubricated floating bush, greater success was obtained. The floating bush, which comprised usually two, sometimes three, arc-shaped sections split to form when assembled a continuous surface around the journal, enabled the wear to be taken on both its inside and outside faces. This simple sturdy design also permitted the use of full bearing circular hub liners to rub against the wheels. Appearing in the late twenties it was technically superseded very soon afterwards by the general adoption in America of roller bearings. In Britain Mr O Bulleid tested an axlebox incorporating a floating bush, presumably something along the lines used in America, but apparently without success.

The 'Grisco' axlebox was another attempt to overcome high piston thrusts while avoiding a significant increase bearing width. In this design the box was given two supplementary adjustable bearing surfaces located fore and aft of the journal symmetrically above and below the horizontal centre line. These surfaces extended the bearing beyond 180° and being adjustable sliding on laterally located 1 in 12 tapered wedges, were able to take up the wear emanating from the steam loads. The Deutsche Reichsbahn standard Bauart Mangold axlebox, was provided with two similar side wedges thereby extending the total bearing surface to approximately 270° in place of the more normal shade under 180°. Lubrication was completely derived from the underkeep with no oil grooves cut into the white metal. Providing additional bearing area below the horizontal centre line was tried elsewhere in the world e.g. India, although in some like the German Bauart Obergethmann box, it was not adjustable.

Roller bearings represented the final development of the steam locomotive axlebox. They provided full encirclement of the axle journal combined with excellent lubrication and minimal friction, while their load carrying capacity was far above that of a similar sized plain bearing. Further, being capable of absorbing side thrusts internally enabled the wear at the wheel boss/axlebox interface to be eliminated. Several designs of roller bearing were developed but usually they incorporated taper, barrel, or occasionally special patent shaped rollers disposed in one, two or more rows to absorb the side thrusts. The principal reason the Americans adopted roller bearings on the driving wheels was a reduction in the cost of maintenance. On heavy work, new crown brasses and hub liners were required about every three months; much longer service could be obtained from roller bearings so the time required for maintenance and lubrication was reduced. André Chapelon reported that substituting roller bearings, effected lifetime savings of around one-half over the cost of bronze brasses and grease lubrication, despite their significantly greater capital cost. In the case of the Norfolk and Western Railroad, the intervals between lifting for axlebox attention increased from 50,000 to 250,000 miles on the class A high speed 2-6-6-4 simple Mallet goods engines.

Some Fundamental Journal Bearing Characteristics

A conventional locomotive axlebox is an example of a plain bearing, albeit of somewhat specialized form and referred to as a partial bearing – a format incidentally shared with rolling mills. When two surfaces e.g. an axle and its bearing that are in contact move relative to one another a resistance known as friction appears, which tries to prevent

---

[20] Wearing taper on long bearings also occurred in Britain; referring to the LNER Class A3 4-6-2 Brian Reed wrote:-

"An additional trouble was heating of the right-hand driving axlebox, which tended to wear taper. This developed after some time in service, and in the last decade of life the Eastern Region practice was to change the driving boxes (not the coupled boxes) after 36,000 to 40,000 miles."

Mr B Reed *The LNER Non-Streamlined Pacifics Locomotive Profile N° 1* Profile Publications Ltd Windsor p21.

this movement. The size of the friction resistance was determined of course by the magnitude of the load, but it was also influenced by amongst other factors, the choice of bearing materials, their surface finish, the lubricant and the quantity provided.

How and why bearings worked, and why introducing lubricant reduced the friction remained much of a mystery until late in the

Table XXVI – Sample Friction Values Obtained by Beauchamp Tower – Lubricant Rape Oil, Journal Speed 150 rpm

Type of lubrication	Average load lbs/sq in	Coefficient of friction	Comparative value
Oil pad	252	0.00900	6.5
Syphon	272	0.00980	7.0
Oil bath	263	0.00139	1.0

The comparative values represents how much higher were the friction values obtained when the journal was lubricated by either an oil pad or a syphon than when the shaft dipped into the oil reservoir.

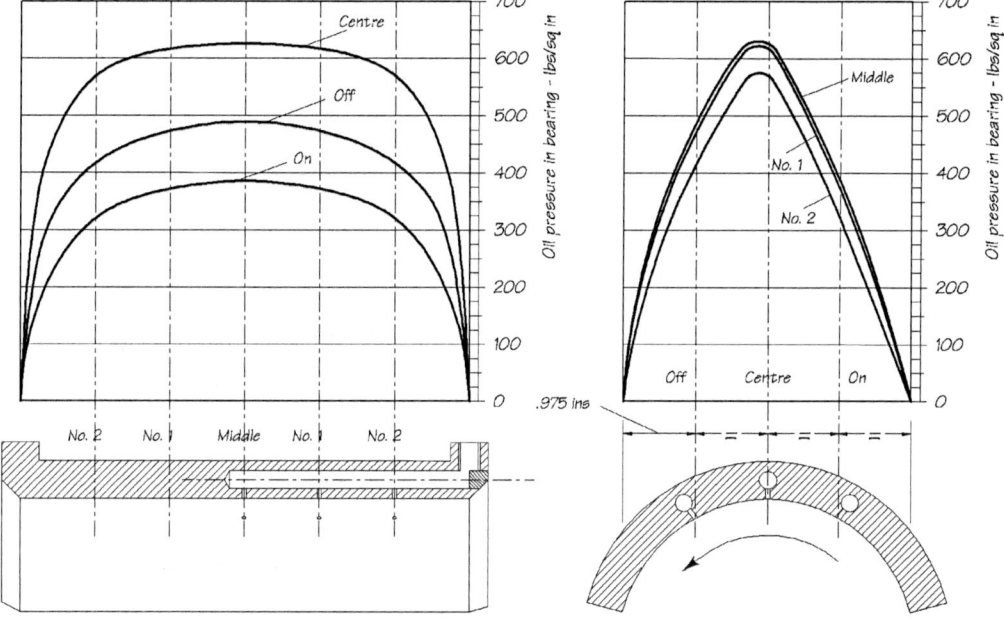

Mr Tower's *'Second Report on Friction Experiments'* (1885) was devoted to the question of pressure distribution in a partial journal bearing embracing slightly less than 180° of arc. The diameter and length were once again 4ins and 6ins respectively, the lubricant was a heavy mineral oil, with the journal bearing half immersed in an oil-bath and the speed of rotation was 150rpm.

Pressure was measured by connecting a Bourdon pressure gauge to one of three ¼ins axial holes drilled in the brass spaced to divide the area of contact into four equal regions. A 1/16ins diameter hole was drilled from the bearing surface into the longitudinal holes and once the pressure had been ascertained the hole was stopped up and another hole drilled until readings had been recorded at nine points.

This study yielded the illuminating axial and circumferential pressure distribution shewn above. the sides of the bearing on which the rotating shaft entered and left he called the 'on' and 'off' sides - a designation that has been retained to the present day. Mr Tower's comment on the recorded pressures was that, "... Their most clearly marked feature is seen to be that the place of greatest pressure is on the 'off' side of the centre, the pressure at the holes in the 'on' side being in every case considerably less than that at the corresponding holes on the 'off' side."

A testimony to the skill displayed by Beachamp Tower and the accuracy of the experiments is revealed by comparing the integrated pressures yielding a load-carrying capacity of 7,988lbs compared with the actual applied load of 8,008lbs - a difference of 20lbs, which he ascribed to "... errors of observations."

Fig. 47 - Beachamp Tower's experiments on the pressure distribution in a partial bearing

nineteenth century, yet most of the research had been spurred by the need to solve the axlebox problems then plaguing the railways. Railway engineers worldwide sought to increase the load and speed capacity of their locomotives and rolling stock, but a major curb on their efforts was the problem they encountered with axlebox performance. Matters were not helped by the presence of much seemingly contradictory evidence and by the introduction of cheap, but somewhat deficient mineral oils, in place of the straight vegetable and animal oils and fats that had previously been used. Although many careful experiments were conducted from the 1840s onwards, almost exclusively concerned with railway axleboxes either directly on the road or indirectly in laboratories, the resulting performance data was confusing, some experimenters found friction fell with rise in speed, others reported that it rose.

In response to this lack of understanding, the recently created Research Committee of the Institution of Mechanical Engineers engaged Mr Beauchamp Tower from 1882 to 1891 to study the friction in railway axleboxes. The tests were carried out near Edgware Road Station in the Chapel Street Works of the Metropolitan Railway. The journal was 6 inches long and 4 inches diameter with its axis horizontal. A partial gunmetal bearing rested on the shaft thereby simulating a rolling stock axlebox. The angle of wrap was about 157° in most experiments, but in others, it reduced to 68°. A selection of lubricants was used and the speed ranged from 100 to 450rpm while the unit load based on projected area ranged from 100 to 625lbs per sq in. Some typical results obtained by Mr Tower appear in table XXVI. With the ordinary methods of lubrication then in use *i.e.* a syphon or oil pad, he could not obtain consistent or reliable results because they were unable to deliver sufficient oil. Only after he had taken the unorthodox approach of completely flooding the bearing surface with oil did he find that not only was the reliability of the observations distinctly increased, but also the frictional resistance was greatly reduced.

Later he found that essentially the same results were obtained if the exposed lower portion of the journal just dipped into the oil contained in an open reservoir or bath, which then 'picked up' a thin coating of oil that it conveyed into the bearing. The most important albeit accidental effect found through introducing the oil bath was the discovery of oil film pressure:-

"A very interesting discovery was made when the oil-bath experiments were on the point of completion. The experiments being carried on were those on mineral oil; and the bearing having seized with 625 lbs. per sq. in., the brass was taken out and examined, and the experiment repeated. While the brass was out, the opportunity was taken to drill a ½-in. hole for an ordinary lubricator through the cast-iron cap and the brass. On the machine being put together again and started with oil in the bath, oil was observed to rise in the hole which had been drilled for the lubricator. The oil flowing over the top of the cap made a mess, and an attempt was made to plug up the hole, first with a cork and then with a wooden plug. When the machine was started the plug was slowly forced out by the oil in a way which showed that it was acted on by a considerable pressure. A pressure-gauge was screwed into the hole, and on the machine being started the pressure, as indicated by the gauge, gradually rose to above 200 lbs. per sq. in. The gauge was only graduated up to 200 lbs., and the pointer went beyond the highest graduation. The mean load on the horizontal section of the journal was only 100 lbs. per sq. in. This experiment showed conclusively that the brass was actually floating on a film of oil, subject to a pressure due to the load. The pressure in the middle of the brass was thus more than double the mean pressure. No doubt if there had been a number of pressure-gauges connected to various parts of the brass, they would have shown that the

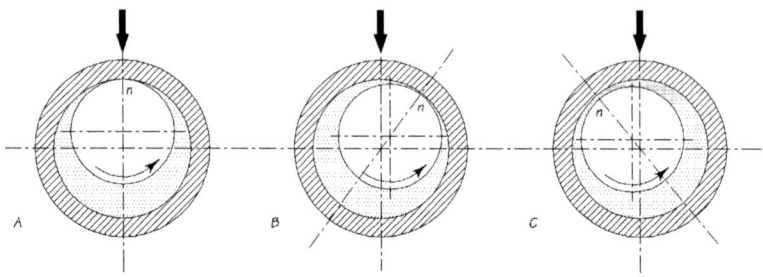

The load is considered to act downwards and the clearance, exaggerated for simplicity, is assumed to be flooded with oil at all times. When the journal is at rest, the oil film is squeezed out beneath the load and there is contact between the journal and the bearing at point *n* in *A*. As the shaft begins to rotate counter clockwise, the boundary or greasy friction at the point of contact causes it to roll or climb to the right as indicated in *B*. However as a thin film of oil is now present at the point of nearest approach the rotation of the shaft drags more oil into this region. The friction decreases as the film is formed and thickens, while the pressure caused by the wedge shape of the converging oil film lifts or 'floats' the bearing. Finally, *C*, the shaft attains a steady position and the point *n* of minimum film thickness will be a few degrees beyond the load line in the direction of rotation. The shaft movement can be considered as comprising two components a horizontal shift and a vertical rise which together form the diagonal displacement. The pressure profile generated in the clearance space is equal to and opposes the bearing load. To create hydrodynamically lubricated bearings it is not necessary to supply the oil under pressure, although it is in steam turbines and internal combustion engines, simple oil rings will suffice. The main requirements are sufficient and continuous supply of lubricant *circulating* through the bearing to make good the leakage from the sides of 'pressurized wedge' back into the sump, also the brass should not suddenly detach from the journal. If this occurs, which is possible in partial bearings, rupture of the film occurs with most of the oil escaping before the brass returns to its bed on the journal.

Fig. 48 - Formation of the hydrodynamic oil film in a clearance bearing

pressure was highest in the middle, and diminished to nothing towards the edges of the brass."

This fundamental study in journal/bearing friction by was crucial in dispelling the confusion that had arisen over the preceding decades, which had primarily been concerned with friction with little attention given to the mechanism of lubrication. In a subsequent report delivered in 1885, figure 47, he was able to determine the profile of the pressure distribution in a partial journal bearing embracing slightly less than 180° of arc.

Once a journal, generously supplied with oil, revolves at a suitable speed, an oil film forms between the journal and the bearing. The oil by virtue of its viscosity is dragged into the bearing by the rotation, thereby building up a film, generally a few thousandths of an inch thick. The wedge action results in the film possessing a mean pressure equal to the mean load (in terms of pressure) acting on the bearing, thereby exactly balancing it while supporting the load clear of the journal. However under the influence of the load, oil continuously escapes from the edges of the bearing; the loss being made good by fresh oil delivered to the bearing. Figure 48 shews the running position, for what nowadays is called a hydrodynamically lubricated journal, wherein it will be seen that the lubricant film is 'tapered', it is this 'taper' that is responsible for creating the pressure build up within the bearing film. Equally important to note is that the journal assumes an eccentric position within its bearing and the maximum pressure attained in the profile of the pressure film is not in alignment with the applied load. Once a journal is running hydrodynamically, the friction reduces becoming simply a direct function of the viscosity of the lubricant because metal-to-metal contact has ceased, or as Beauchamp Tower expressed it

"The wear should be on the oil and not on the metal."

Beauchamp Tower reported his findings in several reports delivered to the Institution but crucially the 1885 results were analysed by Professor Osborne Reynolds, who in 1886 presented his hydrodynamic theory of lubrication in a three-section paper[21]. The first part described experiments concerning the relationship between the viscosity of lubricating oil (olive oil) with temperature. This was based on the understanding that knowing the viscosity of the oil within a bearing was essential if a quantitative evaluation was to be attempted. The second section explained the hydrodynamic mechanism mathematically, while the final part gave a comparison between the theoretical pressure distribution and that experienced in the only set of results then in existence. On only very few occasions subsequently have theory and experiment agreed so well; even today it remains the basis of all successful bearing design. Later researchers demonstrated hydrodynamic lubrication, is a function of oil viscosity Z, the speed of rotation N and the pressure P, also that the oil film thickness increased with rise in oil viscosity and journal speed, but decreased with bearing load. It

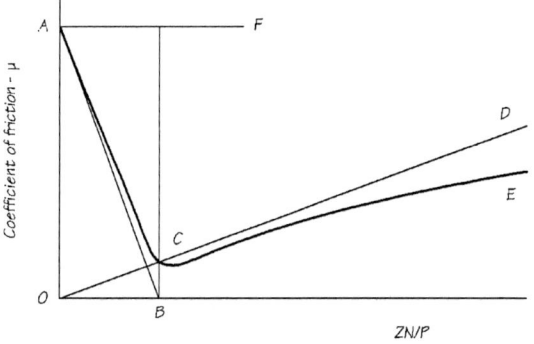

Fig. 49 - Theoretical consideration of journal bearing performance

quickly became the practice to explain this hydrodynamic behaviour by means of a group factor describing the friction:-

$$\mu \ \alpha \ \frac{Z \times N}{P} \qquad (8)$$

where:-

μ = the friction – unitless
Z = dynamic viscosity – lb sec/sq in (or centipoises)[22]

---

[21] Professor O Reynolds *On the Theory of Lubrication and its Application to Mr Beachamp Tower's Experiments Including an Experimental Determination of the Viscosity of Olive Oil* Phil Trans Royal Society 1886 Vol 177 (i) pp157-234.

[22] With consistent units, this relationship becomes a dimensionless number, sometimes denoted the bearing characteristic number, but very often Z was quoted in centipoises, while the remaining values were Imperial. Sometimes this variable was referred to as the Hersey number but nowadays it is more common to use the Sommerfeld number (S) in honour of the work done by the German Arnold Sommerfeld in finding a closed form solution to Osborne Reynolds' formula. The use of Imperial and metric units is not logical but the quantity ZN/P is of long standing and in any case curves plotted against ZN/P are very similar to those plotted against the more correct Sommerfeld number. Incidentally, the adoption of the term poise as a unit for viscosity followed a proposal by Messers R M Deeley and P H Parr in 1913 in honour of Jean Poiseuille a French physician who first established experimentally the law governing viscous flow in pipes.

N = revolutions per minute
P = bearing load – lbs/sq in

Unfortunately, whilst Mr Tower's experiments formed an invaluable starting point for modern bearing design, they are a bit of a red herring in respect of most axleboxes. This is because they were subjected to high loads, low journal speed, an inadequate supply of lubricant in terms of the quantity needed to generate a full hydrodynamic effect, often combined with a less than optimum method of introduction, roughness of the bearing surfaces and poor geometric shape. The last included features such as sharp edges on the brasses, which could act as scrapers partially removing the already meagre quantity of oil from the journal as could oil grooves injudiciously located or profiled.

In order to obtain a better appreciation of the situation pertaining in an axlebox we might refer to an experimental curve developed by the American brothers S A McKee and T R McKee in 1920s - figure 50 derived from the data appearing in table XXVII. The profile of this curve, which was based on a bearing subjected to a constant load P has been considered theoretically in figure 49. At the instant rotation begins there is solid friction between the journal and bearing surfaces with the result the coefficient of friction μ assumes a high value, its precise value depending on the oiliness[23], a property of the lubricant used. If there were no lubricant other than the greasy film on the journal and bearing surfaces, then μ would remain approximately constant for all values of ZN/P, as indicated by line AF.

Curve OD has been based a contemporary theory for calculating μ derived from Osborne Reynold's work. It assumed the two surfaces were separated by an oil film of constant thickness and viscosity, with the result μ varied directly with ZN/P. Comparing the two curves reveals reasonable correlation between theory and practice for values of

Table XXVII – Record of a Journal Bearing Test - 1929

Average speed of shaft - N rpm	Bearing temperature - °F	Viscosity of lubricant Z - centipoise	Coefficient of friction - μ	ZN/P	P Lbs/sq in
193.0	78.1	40.5	0.0062	121.0	*64.6*
156.0	78.0	40.7	0.0053	98.5	*64.5*
110.5	77.9	40.8	0.0041	70.0	*64.4*
85.5	76.9	41.9	0.0036	55.8	*64.2*
62.5	77.0	41.8	0.0029	40.7	*64.2*
46.0	77.1	41.7	0.0026	30.0	*63.9*
36.0	77.0	41.8	0.0026	23.6	*63.8*
28.0	77.0	41.8	0.0029	18.3	*64.0*
20.5	76.9	41.9	0.0058	13.4	*64.1*
17.5	76.9	41.9	0.0089	11.5	*63.8*
15.0	76.9	41.9	0.0128	9.7	*64.8*

The last column revealing the value of the load on the bearing P has been calculated from the results.

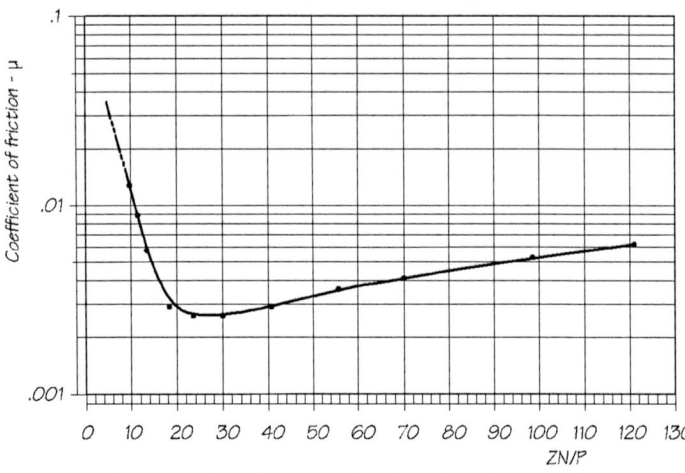

The continuous line is a plot of the data appearing in table XXVII, obtained experimentally by the McKee brothers, but adopting a logarithmic scale for the friction axis. The chain dotted line extended back towards the ordinate axis whilst not forming part of the original data gives approximate extrapolated values for the coefficient of friction for lower values of ZN/P.

Fig 50 - Record of a journal bearing test - 1929

---

23 The term oiliness was invented by Messers R M Deeley and L Archbutt and appeared in the first edition of their lubrication book in 1899. Later Mountford Deeley designed a machine for determining its value.

ZN/P to the right of the minimum point on the experimentally derived curve. The theoretical line *OD* departs from the empirical curve *CE* for two reasons. Firstly, the thickness of the hydrodynamic film is not constant, but tends to thicken with rise in speed *N* and secondly, the viscosity *Z* of the lubricant reduces as the speed increases because of the larger quantity of heat generated in the hydrodynamic film and the consequential rise in temperature of the bearing and lubricant.

From inspection of the empirical curve, we might reasonably conclude that a phenomenon differing from either full hydrodynamic action (*i.e.* thick film) or solid friction (*i.e. AF*), was taking place to the left of the point *C*, where μ assumed a minimum value. In this zone, the effect an increase in speed made in a bearing with a slowly increasing supply of lubricant is that more and more of the load is carried by the embryonic convergent film and less and less supported by the small surface of the bearing that is actually in contact with the journal. Hence that part of the friction that was due to solid friction diminished continuously as shewn by the line *AB*, becoming zero for that value of *ZN/P i.e.* speed at which the film broke through and separated the journal and bearing surfaces. The variation in the value of μ in this zone, known as the thin-film or mixed-film region, is seen not only to be close to experimentally derived curve, but also its magnitude changes quite dramatically.

Since we are no longer dealing with hydrodynamic lubrication in this region, it may also be expected that the parameters derived from the *ZN/P* relationship will no longer suffice. That this hypothesis is also true, is demonstrated in figure 51 wherein the coefficient of friction of a test bearing, has been plotted for two oils – a mineral oil and a lard oil. For high values of *ZN/P* the difference between the two oils is slight, but in this instance, for values less than 35, the coefficient of friction is no longer determined solely by *ZN/P*. The difference in the value of the friction coefficient for the same *ZN/P* was due to the different oiliness possessed by the two oils. If two lubricants possessing identical viscosities are lightly smeared on two surfaces and the friction between these

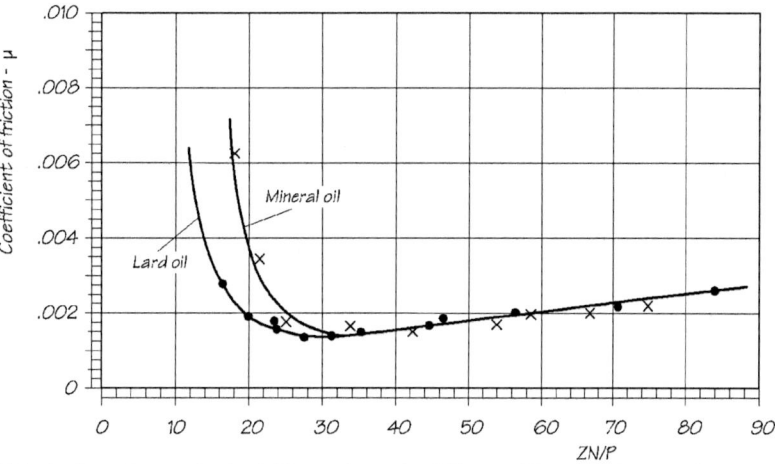

Within the boundary and mixed-film regions, the different oiliness of the two oils results in different coefficients of friction for the same *ZN/P* values. Thus, in this instance, for a *ZN/P* of 20 the friction when the bearing was lubricated by a straight mineral oil was about twice the value it assumed when lard oil was used. Accordingly the straight mineral oil lubricated bearing would have had to dissipate twice the heat when lard oil was used, hence it would have run at a higher temperature under the same conditions.

Fig. 51. - Effect of oiliness on the coefficient of friction

surfaces measured under otherwise identical conditions *e.g.* temperature, metals, surface finishes *etc.*, the friction force will be lower with the lubricant possessing the higher oiliness. Viscosity and oiliness are entirely independent properties, but which of the two properties exercises the controlling influence on the friction between two surfaces depends on the thickness of the layer of lubricant. If the layer is of such a thickness that no actual contact takes place between the surfaces, *i.e.* bearing operation is near to or to the right of point *C* then the friction is determined by the viscosity of the lubricant. If the layer is only a few molecules thick, the friction is determined by the oiliness of the lubricant.

An important aspect of oiliness but one commonly overlooked is that it is a joint property of the lubricant *and* the metals forming the bearing surfaces. This difference in friction coefficient thus serves as evidence for the existence of a distinct lubrication regime referred to originally as thin-film lubrication, nowadays however, it is normal to sub-divide this area into two zones known as boundary lubrication and mixed-film lubrication.

As a comparison, figure 52 records the friction–*ZN/P* curve for a ball (or roller) bearing which can

A Defence of the Midland/LMS Class 4 0-6-0

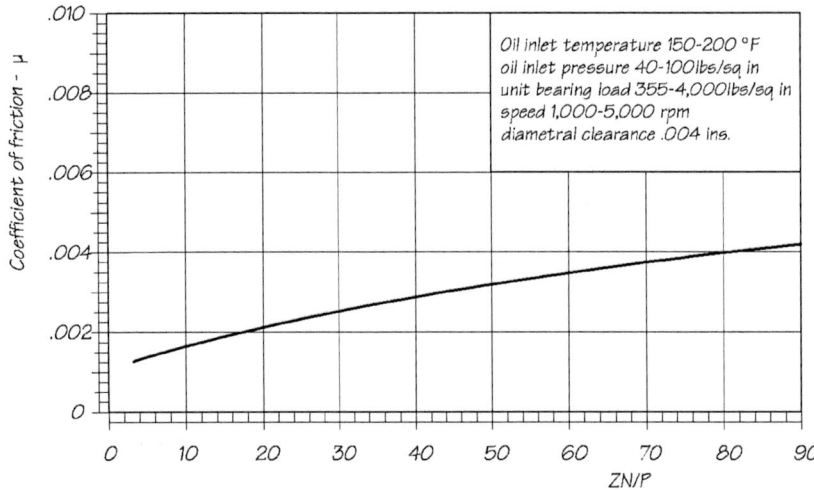

Although the lubrication of rolling objects operates on a considerably different principle from that of sliding (*i.e.* plain) bearings, the principles of hydrodynamic lubrication can be applied, within limits, to explain the lubrication of roller bearings - sometimes referred to as 'elastohydrodynamic' lubrication. An oil wedge, similar to that which occurs in hydrodynamic lubrication exists at the leading edge of loaded rollers. Adhesion of lubricant to the sliding element increases the pressure and creates a film between the rollers and the race. Due to the very small contact area, the force per unit area exerted by the rollers is very high - typically 5,000lbs/sq in or more - sufficient to cause significant, albeit microscopic, elastic deformation of the races and the rollers. This deformation increases the area of contact between the loaded rollers and the races on the 'on' side causing a 'piling up' of material, while behind them there is a decrease in contact area. Under these pressures one might assume that the lubricant would be squeezed out completely from between the roller and the race. In practice the viscosity of the lubricant increases under the extremely high pressure and this serves to prevent it from being entirely squeezed out, so a thin film is maintained.

Along with the friction created by roller/race deformation, the lubricant also generates friction from the churning it experiences when the bearing is in use, consequently the friction in a roller bearing is not necessarily any lower than that of a well designed plain bearing operating in the hydrodynamic region, assuming forced oil circulation in both cases. However, the friction when starting from rest is far lower, perhaps only 10 or 20 per cent of that present in the equivalent plain axlebox bearing.

Incidentally it is the deformation suffered by the rollers and their races in operation which results in these anti-friction bearings, as they are sometimes called, having a finite life due to fatigue. The life of a roller (or ball) bearing is therefore a function of the applied load and the number of revolutions.

Fig. 52 - Characteristic curve for a forced oil-circulation ball bearing

be seen to exhibit a completely different profile. The friction in this case simply rises from a comparatively low value at low or even zero values of ZN/P, thus demonstrating the very great advantage of this type of bearing possessed for dealing with high piston thrusts accompanied by low speeds – making it ideal for goods engines.

Figure 53, serves as a useful starting point for investigating a conventional axlebox bearing for apart from shewing the three fundamental lubrication zones, also appearing are the three main operating factors that affected bearing performance and which in turn were determined by the lubrication zones, these being:-

Friction coefficient: a measure of the effort needed to move the surfaces relative to each other.

Wear coefficient: a measure of the amount of material loss during the sliding and a determining factor in bearing durability or life.

Bearing temperature: a measure of the likelihood that sudden failure may be experienced.

The magnitude of the ZN/P value gives a feel for how the load will be supported in the bearing. A high value usually means a relatively thick lubrication film which occurs at high speeds, high viscosities and/or low loads. Here lubricant properties alone determine the friction as the metallic surfaces are completely separated by the presence of the lubricant with the load carried by the self-generated fluid pressure alone. Wear in this regime is very low to non-existent, while bearing temperature is also low being essentially a function of fluid *i.e.* lubricant friction. Within the mixed-film regime, the lower ZN/P signifies thinner film thickness and the bearing is now subject to a combination of increasing surface interactions combined with reducing fluid film effect. Wear is moderate to high, depending on the chemical activity of the lubricant, the bearing materials and on the nature of the bearing and journal surfaces. Bearing temperature would be higher due to the increased friction with the value attained also affected by the latter factors. Finally, at the very lowest ZN/P values, the boundary lubrication regime is entered, wherein the load is carried solely by asperities and wear is high to heavy because surface interactions are the principal factors determining friction coefficient, bearing temperature and wear rate. There is no longer any fluid film effect present at all.

Axleboxes, Bearing Metals and Lubricants

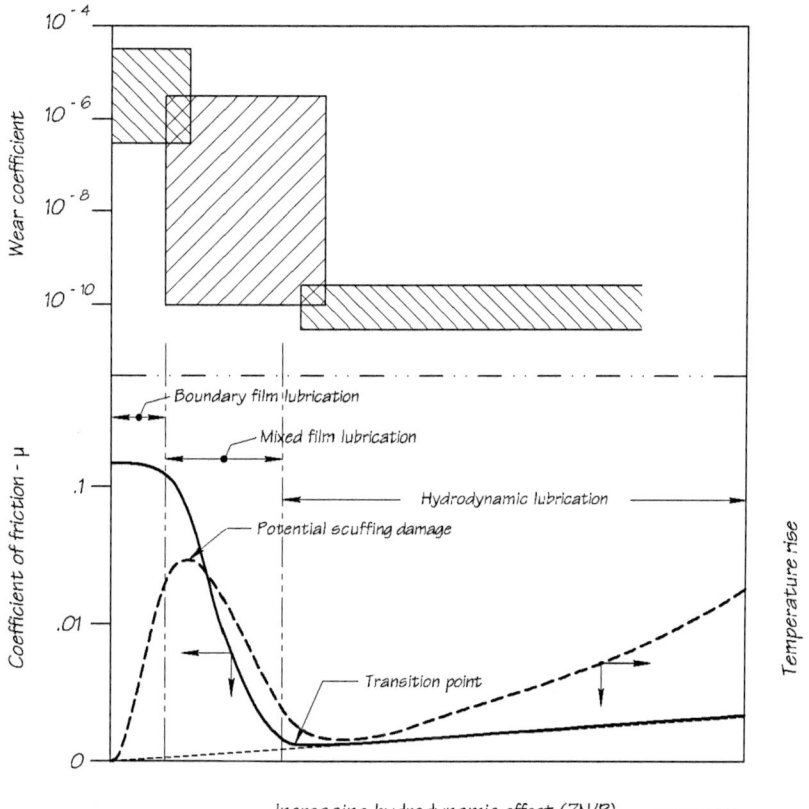

Bearing Friction (thick solid line) - initially remains almost constant within the boundary lubrication region before experiencing a rather sudden drop in the mixed-film lubrication region. The lowest friction appears at the transition point after which the friction rises slowly within the hydrodynamic zone. The explanation for this characteristic is that the friction within the former two regions is almost completely determined by surface interaction, but within the hydrodynamic region it is almost exclusively fluid friction (thin dashed line).

Asperity friction may be due to adhesive or abrasive contact. The friction level depends on the bearing materials and their chemical interaction with the lubricant. Friction level in the boundary zone is nearly velocity independent, so to achieve low friction in this region is thus a materials selection issue. In the hydrodynamic region the nature of the bearing surfaces are irrelevant because there is no asperity contact due to the thicker oil film present. The rise in friction in this zone is caused by increased redundant work in the lubricant. Conversely, in the mixed-film region the friction represents a combination of these two influences, a reducing asperity contact consequential upon a slowly increasing film thickness.

The plateau value for friction in the boundary regime may not occur if the lubricant does not possess the proper chemistry, consequently the friction may continue increasing with decreasing film thickness.

Bearing Wear (upper half of diagram) - decreases drastically as operation moves from boundary operation into the hydrodynamic region, shewing a rather sudden reduction in the mixed-film zone. This sudden drop occures for the same reason that the friction drops, namely the reduction in asperity interaction consequent upon the increased load support given by the lubricant film.

Wear life is least for bearings operating in the boundary lubricated regime and longest for those operating in the hydrodynamic zone. In the mixed-film region intermediate lives are obtained, determined by the thickness of the oil film while the latter is determined by the ZN/P factor. Thus, all other things being equal, a more heavily loaded bearing (*i.e.* smaller ZN/P) will have a shorter life than a less heavily loaded one.

Bearing Temperature (thick dotted line) - results from the product of friction and sliding velocity and is low at low sliding speed before attaining a peak following which it reduces due to a drop in friction. Further increase in speed produces a minimum temperature before it commences to rise again. The initial temperature rise is almost exclusively the result of solid friction, while in the hydrodynamic region it is almost completely due to fluid friction (*i.e.* viscosity).

The initial rapid rise is the result of high friction coupled with the velocity difference between the two surfaces. Since this is the boundary lubrication zone almost all of the bearing load is carried by direct asperity contact, so the friction is due to adhesion and abrasive asperity contact. Depending on the materials and lubricant a sufficiently high temperature may be reached to cause scuffing damage. Scuffing may lead to a 'hot box' and if sufficiently severe may lead to catastrophic bearing failure from galling or even the white metal melting and running out. Key factors that reduce peak bearing temperatures are low friction (optimum bearing materials and good surface finish), high oiliness in the lubricant, good heat conduction through the bearing and lower bearing loads.

Fig. 53 - Modified Stribeck curve for a plain journal

The extent of the mixed-film region may be inferred from the friction behaviour of a bearing system. Thus a superior finish of the bearing and journal, obtained either following incipient 'bedding in' or by means of lapping before final assembly, not only gave a lower mixed-film friction for a given *ZN/P* but also displaced the minimum part of the friction – *ZN/P* diagram to the left. In addition, when the finish is good the transition point became more clearly defined as the fall in friction within the mixed-film zone was steeper. Conversely, with increased roughness the minimum point shifted to higher values of ZN/P accompanied by higher values for the coefficient of friction, furthermore it was less clearly defined also resulting in higher friction in the boundary region. Figure 54 attempts to demonstrate these effects.

In the mixed-film region, a decrease in oil viscosity raises the friction and hence the heat generated, which in turn tends to still further reduce the viscosity. This situation is made worse since all the heat generated had to be dissipated through the bearing, as very little lubricant passed through. A bearing equilibrium temperature therefore appeared for each condition determined by on one hand the rate of heat gain and on the other by the rate of heat dissipation.

In summary, satisfactory operation of locomotive axleboxes was best obtained by using lubricants possessing an appropriate viscosity combined with a high oiliness in association with the bearing metals present, employing good surface finishes, arranging for the heat to be readily dissipated through the box, and through care in keeping the lubricant clean.

Why Locomotive and other Axleboxes Operated in the Mixed-film Region

Seeing how much the railways were instrumental for the initial investigations into bearing behaviour, it is rather ironic to report how little of the vast bearing research subsequently conducted was applicable to steam locomotives. Unfortunately, the research for several decades was directed almost exclusively at understanding and exploring the hydrodynamic region discovered by Beauchamp Tower and explained by Osborne Reynolds. Whilst this work was of crucial importance towards expanding knowledge about bearing behaviour as a whole, little was *directly* applicable to railway axleboxes because as we have seen they operated within the boundary and mixed-film lubrication zones, *notwithstanding the provision or otherwise of underfeed pads*.

Anthony George Michell, inventor of the tilting pad thrust bearing[24], demonstrated the quantity of

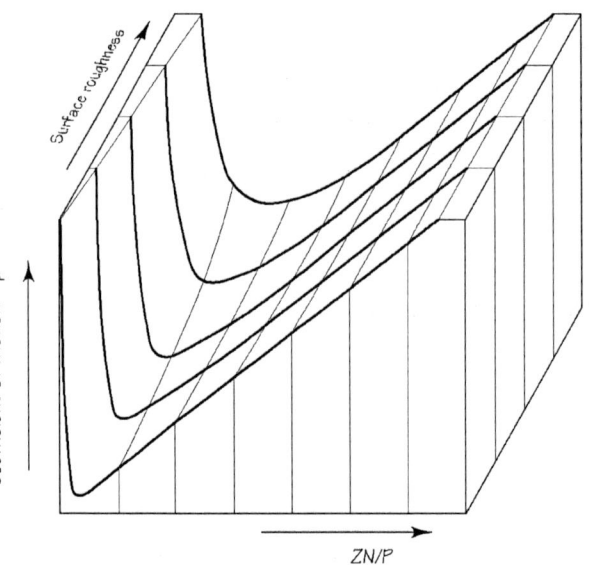

Fig. 54 - Effect of surface finish on the coefficient of friction

lubricant that could be supplied by an oil-filled underpad, was always insufficient for fully effective hydrodynamic lubrication. By extension, this same observation may also be made regarding the delivery from trimming boxes and mechanical lubricators. An example of his calculation appears in the Appendix at the end of the chapter. This reveals the flow rate needed to obtain hydrodynamic lubrication, which he estimated at about 6 1/3 pints per hour to overcome the leakage from a small axlebox such as one fitted to a carriage or wagon, exceeded the delivery possible from a porous capillary pad or similar, compact

---

24 The great merits of the tilting pad thrust bearing - the means by which the 'push' generated by the propeller was transmitted to the hull - were very quickly recognized in marine circles with the first British application being to the LB&SCR cross-Channel steamer *Paris* in 1913, followed by many naval vessels during the Great War. The practical results were significant, coefficients of friction reduced twenty-fold from around 0.03 to 0.0015. Mr Archbutt stated the design saved the Royal Navy £600,000 worth of coal during the conflict. It had been patented in January 1905, while the following month Mountford Deeley fitted a bearing of this type, but of his own design, to a Midland Railway owned 'hydro-extractor'.

enough to be contained within a box. Indeed, the pad could barely deliver rape oil to the journal at one-eleventh of the necessary rate. As an extension of this, it may likewise be shewn that the capacity of the oil reservoirs fitted to the likes of big-ends, coupling rods as well as mechanical lubricators was insufficient to hold, let alone deliver, the quantity of oil required for hydrodynamic lubrication and not be depleted during the course of a run[25]. The lubricant was therefore meant to be retained within in the bearing for as long as possible before it inevitably escaped via the ends and the side clearance and was lost. That there could be a small 'build up' of oil with time is demonstrated in figure 84, but it was still insufficient. Conversely, with conventional hydrodynamic lubrication, the oil passes quickly through the bearing, escapes from the edges, is captured and drained back to the sump (or the oil bath as in Mr Tower's experiments). The oil is not lost, instead it is continuously *circulated* through the bearing and lubrication system. The Great Western had an experimental testing rig composed of a full-sized axle and axlebox, spring loaded to give full working weights located in AM Shop. Mr Cook[26] referred to a test in which the oil reservoir of a coupled wheel axlebox was filled up and run the bearing run to destruction while capturing from various points all of the oil that escaped from the bearing. The reservoir held 5.81 pints of oil and *after ten days*, the bearing seized, but by then 5.55 pints of oil (*i.e.* 95½ per cent) had escaped from the bearing to be captured and measured. Thus, we are forced to conclude that conventional axleboxes worked *exclusively* within the boundary and mixed-film regions. We find further evidence supporting this conclusion when we compare the different values engineers recorded for the coefficients of friction. Mr Phillipson[27] stated a typical value for the friction of a coupled wheel axlebox was 0.05, which from figure 53 puts it roughly in the upper half of the thin-film regime, while Beachamp Tower had obtained with a pad under the journal 0.009, a syphon lubricator 0.0098 and an oil bath 0.00139 respectively. Notice the similarity in the friction values when the oil was supplied to the journal by means of an oil pad or a syphon. By contrast, the *oil bath* was gave a much lower coefficient of friction *simply because a far greater quantity of oil was conveyed into the bearing* so enabling it to operate in full hydrodynamic mode.

Full hydrodynamic lubrication of railway journals is possible but only if a form of 'pump' was introduced within the box and the oil was prevented from escaping from the bearing. The French Isothermos box, which of the outside bearing type carried a disk or 'palette' bolted to the end of the axle. This dipped into the oil sitting in the reservoir in the bottom of the box, entrained some before carrying and delivering it to the upper part of the axlebox above the journal through a combination of centrifugal force and drip. Where the axle passed out through the rear of the box, it was provided with an 'oil thrower' or obturating ring that prevented oil from escaping via the dust-shield. Instead, oil that crept along the shaft was picked up and thrown back into the box where it drained down via a filter into the reservoir. At only 25 miles per hour, the revolving palette delivered from 3 to 4 gallons per hour or 4 to 6 times as much as Mr Michell estimated was needed to establish hydrodymamic lubrication. Another example of fluid friction outside bearing axlebox that worked on similar principles was the Peyinghaus[28]. In both of these designs, although the seal provided around the journal at its exit from the box could prevent the escape of the oil splashing around inside under normal operation, it was incapable of retaining oil under the slight pressure generated by a fluid static head should the box be over-filled.

Railway axleboxes therefore presented several peculiarities compared to other journal bearings and these served to compromise the formation of

---

25 The oil reservoir of a big-end bearing suitable for a 300-mile run was, according to E A Phillipson, 20 cubic inches or say 0.57 pint. Assuming the big-end diameter was the same size as Mr Michell's rolling stock journal then if hydrodynamic lubrication was attempted, the reservoir would be exhausted in about five minutes.

The approximate usable volume of the keep of a large modern-style locomotive axlebox was 250-300 cubic inches. Since the axle would be more than twice the diameter, we might expect double the leakage rate, thus a keep if full only of oil, would have emptied in 30-40 minutes. In the case of mechanical lubrication, one lubricator set on maximum output would have been need *per* axlebox.

26 Mr K J Cook *Swindon Steam 1921-1951* Ian Allan Ltd Shepperton 1974 p121.

27 Mr E A Phillipson *Steam Locomotive Design: Data and Formulae* The Locomotive Publishing C° Ltd London 1936 p278.

28 In the 1950s Dennis Monk worked on an axlebox scheme which appears to have comprised a circulation system. Oil was pumped to the top of the axlebox by utilizing the side-to-side movement of the axle to act as a swash plate. It is believed no engines were ever fitted with the design.

hydrodynamic lubrication. The most obvious of these was the need for the box to be penetrated on at least one and in the case of locomotives two sides, in order to receive the axle. Consequently, unless these openings could be effectively sealed against loss of oil standing higher in the box than the lowest surface of the journal – and sealing to this standard was almost impracticable under the usual conditions of operation – special means had to be employed to deliver the lubricant to the journal. A second peculiarity was the limited quantity of lubricant available, which in the case of most locomotives was a total loss system.

As a consequence, the reservoir forming the base of the axlebox or the body of a mechanical lubricator or a trimming box had to contain the whole of the lubricant needed for at least one journey. Axleboxes presented another unusual feature, which whilst not peculiar to them is not commonly met with in other bearings, namely the journal was required to run with equal alacrity and frequency in either direction. Another circumstance that served to increase the practical problems of a solution was that an axlebox had to do more than simply support a spring-borne vertical load. It also had to accommodate the forces caused by acceleration and retardation of the vehicle that acted in a horizontal direction, although the latter line of action was modified if automatic brakes were present. Irregularities in the track such as rail joints and crossings produced shock-loads that acted at various angular directions between the vertical and the horizontal. In the case of engines these considerations were further complicated in the driving and coupled axleboxes by the very large near horizontal loadings caused by the action of the connecting and coupling rods.

Accepting a combination of boundary and mixed-film lubrication zones represented the operating region for conventional railway axleboxes enables us to appreciate the difficulties experienced by locomotive engineers as well as seeing how improvements could be effected. For at the limits of the boundary region the fraction of the load carried by the lubricant film varied from nil to very little. However, in the mixed-film zone this fraction changed from to very little to 100 per cent at the transition point, so as figure 53 reveals, the friction, wear rate and temperature could alter substantially and rapidly for very small changes in ZN/P factor. Consequently, seemingly very minor alterations in axlebox design, machining details, bearing metals, lubricant, alignment, operation *etc.* resulted in significant differences in the value of the coefficient of friction and thence bearing performance and life. Some of these influences are considered in the ensuing sections.

Bearing Materials

Probably the correct choice of the bearing metals was only equalled in importance by the selection of an appropriate lubricant – the latter a matter also to be explored in more detail later.

For successful *long-term* operation within the boundary and mixed-film regions, the designer had to select materials that possessed a low coefficient of friction and would work together when the lubrication might be imperfect. Furthermore, the combination ought to tolerate errors in adjustment and alignment – ensured by the alloy possessing sufficient plasticity combined with enough compressive strength to carry the load. Since the life of a bearing, not operating in the hydrodynamic zone is largely determined by the friction - responsible for the heating and wear - it later became common practice, in *non-locomotive* bearings, to include the combined effect of the load and journal speed in the selection. This is referred to as complying with a bearing material's PV limit, (where P is the specific load lbs/sq in and V the journal velocity ft/min). The PV value represents therefore a simple method of quantifying the capacity of the bearing material operating in the boundary and mixed-film regimes, to accommodate the frictional energy generated between the brass and the journal. Careful choice of lubricant could raise the PV value for the same alloy, while different alloys had markedly different recommended PV values, under similar conditions, those for the leaded bronzes being roughly three times larger than high-tin white metals. Nevertheless, if the PV value demanded of a bearing exceeds the PV value for the material, then a shortened bearing life will result while in extreme cases, the bearing would not achieve a stable temperature prompting a rapid failure, if constantly loaded:-

$$PV = \frac{W}{L \times D} \times \frac{\pi \times D \times N}{12}$$

Simplifying and rearranging:-

$$PV = \frac{W \times N}{3.82 \times L} \qquad (9)$$

where:-
W = load on bearing – lbs
D = diameter of journal – ins
N = journal speed – rpm
P = nominal bearing load – lbs/sq in
L = length of journal – ins
V = journal surface velocity – ft/min

At 15mph, a 'Big Goods' was running at 80 rpm, while journal length was 6¼ inches with the fillets omitted. Introducing typical (non-railway) values for a tin-based white metal lubricated with a mineral oil of P up to 1,500lbs/sq in, and PV of 40,000 reveals an allowable bearing load W of 11,938lbs. – the spring borne load *alone* on a 'Big Goods' axlebox was around 6.75 tons or 15,120 lbs, and of course in service the engine could be called upon to run considerably faster than 15 mph. In practice, PV values were of little use to the locomotive engineer since the loadings on his axleboxes in normal running grossly exceeded the limits for the material, however, they do give us an insight into just how little was the margin of reserve. Overloading the bearing in this way ensured a hot box could easily result from periods of sustained high power output, running at high speeds continuously, interruptions in the oil supply or an inferior lubricant.

Since British locomotive axles were manufactured largely from unhardened low carbon steels[29], to prevent premature wear their ideal bearing metal partners were the relatively soft bearing alloys known collectively[30] as 'white metals', or Babbit metals, after Isaac Babbit who in 1839 patented the bonding of such an alloy to a strong backing material. However, in many British coupled axlebox designs of the nineteenth century the white metal was quite restricted in area and located in deep recesses[31] cast into the brass, so the latter served as a significant portion of the bearing surface.

Only latterly, did designers increase the area of white metal at the expense of the bronze until it extended over the entire, or nearly entire, surface

---

29 According to Sir Henry Fowler, a typical analysis of Midland crank axle steel was carbon 0.28%, silicon 0.16%, manganese 0.70%, sulphur and phosphorus under 0.04%.

30 The term white metal strictly only applies to bearing metals containing 50 per cent or more tin, however it was commonly used to describe all tin/lead alloys – *c.f.* a whitesmith is another name for a tinsmith.

31 The recesses were deep to allow for re-machining of the box after wear, whereupon the bore was displaced vertically upwards.

of the bearing[32]. The enhanced white metal surface, due to its plasticity, ensured high load points caused by misalignment were instead compressed or flattened, rather than heating or breaking off which occurred with harder alloys. Contemporary engineers believed that a good bearing alloy comprised a soft plastic matrix, into which one or more, much harder constituents were uniformly embedded. The soft matrix was to permit plastic yield sufficient to ensure conformity with the journal while serving to accommodate foreign matter by virtue of its embeddability. A small degree of self-alignment, highly desirable in what were often less than perfectly aligned plate frames, was obtained because white metal alloys are self-annealing at the normal temperatures. This

---

32 Contemporary US engineers went in the opposite direction largely eschewing the use of any white metal in their bearings. Thus a commonly used American bearing metal of the '80s and '90s was a pure bronze (copper-tin) composed of 87½ per cent copper and 12½ per cent tin. Such hard bronzes having high compressive strength were adopted in an attempt to counter heavy bearing pressures. A common fallacy is that harder metals will give better resistance to wear, but this was not often realized in practice. Copper-based bearing metals might give the desired low coefficient of friction due to their comparative hardness, but this in turn made them more liable to heat under abnormal conditions. This was because they lacked any means of accommodating bearing misalignment or foreign particles that lodged between the journal and the bearing surface so they would heat upon the least provocation accompanied by high wear rates. The high wear rates arose because misalignment *etc.* created concentrated point loadings on the bearing surface, such 'edge-loading' then resulting in the contact points rapidly wearing or even splitting off.

If bearings could have been kept in perfect adjustment and alignment, then hard alloys would have given the better service, however it was found preferable to sacrifice some of the load carrying capacity, by introducing some plasticity into bearing alloy; an artifice that improved wear resistance. In America, this was achieved by changing the composition of the bronze, for example, by 1892 the Pennsylvania Railroad had adopted a leaded bronze – 77 per cent copper, 8 per cent tin and 15 per cent lead – which it referred to as 'Ex. B. metal'. This alloy was still in use in the 'twenties and beyond, while with slightly different proportions it was used quite extensively elsewhere in the world. Being softer, these alloys had a slower rate of wear than a pure bronze as well as being less liable to heat in service. Indeed, increasing the lead content at the expense of the copper, while keeping the tin at around 5 per cent, further improved the performance of leaded bronzes as bearing metals, but in doing so made them progressively more difficult to cast because the lead being so much heavier than the other constituents sank to the bottom of the casting. However, such were the benefits several patent techniques were developed solely to obtain good, uniform high leaded bronze castings; unfortunately, this tended to make the alloys expensive. These leaded bronzes were used for many years very successfully in conjunction with grease lubrication of coupled and driving boxes.

obviated the embrittlement normally associated with such severe cold-working as the matrix yielded to absorb small degrees of misalignment. Although later bearing research resulted in the successful use of bearing metals that do not conform to this theory it did apply to white metal and other soft alloys. Another commonly held contemporary theory[33] about how bearing metals performed has long been proved erroneous following greater understanding of boundary lubrication.

Steam locomotives engineers considered their white metal alloys as belonging to one or other of two groups – tin/antimony/copper and lead/tin/antimony. As the tin/antimony/copper group was more expensive[34] some engineers reduced their white metal costs by introducing lead into the mixture – George Hughes[35] writing in the 1890s:-

> "White and antifriction metals are almost without number, and until recently their base was tin – in some cases to the extent of 78 to 86 per cent. Now, generally speaking, lead has taken the place of tin as a base, with from 10 to 20 per cent. of antimony as a hardener, and sometimes arsenic. Copper is in most cases added to the extent of 2 to 10 per cent. It will be found, as in the case of brass and bronze, that every shop has its own mixing, which is quite as good as any floated upon the market, and mostly having the same ingredients, and nearly equal percentages. The chief object in a good metal is to have a low melting point, especially where there is a lot of work, so that it can be used over a pot fire, that is, without the aid of crucibles. It should be thin when melted, but slow to set, having a lengthy plastic stage, so that the workmen can follow it up in a similar manner to wiping a plumbing joint when soldering two lead pipes."

---

33 I remember the following explanation being given to me very early in my apprenticeship – *viz.* the hard constituents in the alloy were to resist wear and give the strength necessary to support the load, while the softer matrix quickly wore down in service leaving the harder alloy constituents slightly proud, so forming spaces that ensured the retention of an adequate surface lubricant film.

34 In *A Manual of Marine Engineering* (1903) Mr A E Seaton lists the following prices for the constituents of white metals - tin ingots £124–0–0 per ton, lead pigs £11–5–0 per ton, copper ingots £533–10–0 per ton and antimony cakes £30–0–0 per ton.
Mr C W Clarke observed, due to the low power to weight ratio of the steam locomotives the cost of the bearing metals could be doubled without affecting the cost of locomotive power by more than ¼ per cent, so there was comparatively little saving in attempts to reduce the cost of locomotive bearing metals.

35 Mr G Hughes *The Construction of the Modern Locomotive* E & F Spon London 1894 p101.

The alloys differed in their physical characteristics, but as a general observation, the unadulterated tin/antimony/copper based alloys possessed better wear resistance, withstood higher loads, were not as brittle, had somewhat higher fatigue strength and more corrosion resistance.

In 1928, E Gilson reported of a series of tests he had conducted on a journal loaded at 10lbs/sq in running at 2,000rpm and intended to be operating hydrodynamically (but it is not clear if it was achieved). All of the variables were kept constant, with the exception of the composition of the alloys used, yet a variation of 53 per cent occurred in the coefficient of friction. The frictional properties of white metals containing lead could be slightly better than those where it was absent, but they tended to be somewhat softer, nevertheless, apart from when the mechanical properties of the bearing metal played a vital role in the behaviour of the bearing, the lead-containing alloys could perform as well as those where it was absent. Thus, for bearings operating within or near to the hydrodynamic zone, or not subjected to excessive unit loading, they could serve as successful bearing metals, but under boundary and mixed-film conditions and in bearings subjected to high loading, a lead-containing alloy could suffer from *much* higher wear. Lead also reduced the shock loading capacity of a bearing, so white metals containing much lead need more lateral support against spreading and squeezing out should the load be intermittent and in the nature of blows as in the connecting rod big-ends and driving axleboxes. In these situations the white metal would roll out or be pounded out with the added risk of it obstructing any oil delivery holes. It would also probably hug the journal squeezing out the oil film becoming heated in the process and eventually be destroyed. The Association of Railway Locomotive Engineers (ARLE) promoted three distinct white metal mixtures:-

Constituents	ARLE Nº 1*	ARLE Nº 2†	ARLE Nº 3*
Tin	85	60	12
Copper	5	2	~
Antimony	10	10	13
Lead	~	28	75

*Proportions taken from Mr Phillipson's *Locomotive Design Data & Formulae* - Nº 1 Mixture was for coupled axleboxes and Nº 3 Mixture for other boxes.
†Proportions of the Nº 2 Mixture taken from Mr R C Bond's paper on axlebox design, the proportions for this alloy quoted in Mr Cox's paper *Locomotive Axleboxes*, but by then the LMS referred to it as NF6K, were tin 58-60%, lead 24-31%, antimony 9-10% and copper 2-6%.

Since axleboxes differed widely in size and loading, the characteristics of a white metal alloy suitable for the boxes of one class was not necessarily appropriate for another should its box loading or size, differ significantly. From these considerations, we may appreciate that the choice of white metal alloy used in the boxes could have a major influence on the ensuing performance of a locomotive. During the period 1875 to 1901, the Midland consistently specified for all of its 0-6-0s built by outside contractors that their white metal should be tin-based and contain no lead. The actual composition being 16 parts tin, 1½ parts copper and 2 parts antimony, or expressed as percentages, 82 per cent, 7.7 per cent and 10.3 per cent respectively, similar to the ARLE N° 1 mixture. No six-coupled engines were built outside Derby during Mr Deeley's tenure, while only a single batch of 'Big Goods' was built by a contractor *viz*. Armstrong Whitworth in 1920-21. Currently their white metal mixture is not confirmed – the NRM is unable to provide a copy of the specification – however Roland Bond[36], who served his pupillage at Derby from 1920-25 states that a high quality tin-based white metal was still used for locomotive axleboxes and big-ends in 1923:-

"David Rushton, with bushy eyebrows and a battered bowler hat, the white metalling chargehand, taught me about the procedures for segregating and renovating to the standard analysis the metal melted out from the parts sent in for repairs. Two alloys predominated – No. 1 for bearings subjected to heavy alternating loads such as coupled axlebox brasses (Tin 85 per cent, Antimony 10 per cent, Copper 5 per cent) and No. 3 for bogie and tender axlebox bearings, of quite a different composition (Lead 75 per cent, Antimony 13 per cent, Tin 12 per cent).

The very different composition and high cost of these alloys clearly emphasised the importance of careful segregation to ensure that expenditure on new metals for restoring secondhand melts to the standard analysis was kept within reasonable bounds. Rushton kept a firm hand on this work in the Shop. But it was a constant battle with the machine shop and outstation depots who were not always as careful as they should have been in segregating the various grades of mixed bronze and white metal cuttings from machining operations returned to the shop for renovation."

Mountford Deeley seemingly implied in his table *'White Metals used on Railways in the British Empire'*, compiled[37] from information provided by Sir Henry Fowler, that the use of a high lead containing alloy had become standard Horwich practice:-

Constituents	N° 1	N° 2	N° 3	N° 4
Tin	85	60	12	40
Antimony	10	10	13	10
Lead	~	28	75	48
Copper	5	2	~	2

"N° 1, 2 & 3 were adopted by the Association of Railway Locomotive Engineers as a group of standard alloys capable of meeting all requirements. N° 1 is used by nearly all the English, Scotch, and Irish railways where the bearings are subjected to hammering stresses. N° 3 alloy is used chiefly for tender and wagon axle bearings. N° 2 alloy is used by one English railway for all bearings."

Although this table was taken from the 1927 edition, the accompanying note might suggest it refers to pre-1923 practice, with the "English railway using N° 2 metal for all bearings" being the L&YR, but because in an accompanying analysis "The Scottish section of one railway is exceptional in using a zinc base alloy ..." is known to pertain to the Caledonian Railway[38] it implies it is post-Grouping and thus refers to the LMS. Nevertheless, although the date may be uncertain, writing in 1943 Mr Cox stated in his paper *Locomotive Axleboxes* that *pre-war* an alloy designated NF6K by the LMS but equivalent to ARLE N° 2, was used *for all* locomotive axleboxes. A statement given further support by Mr Burgess[39] in the following extract while his description of the 'pasting on' process used to apply metal and the absence of moulds is indicative of a lead containing white metal:-

"White bearing metal came in 14lb ingots, identified by the cryptic symbols WM1, WM2, & WM3, denoting the surfaces on which it should be used. It was an alloy of tin, antimony, copper and lead, and resistance to wear increased proportionately to its tin content. Unfortunately, so did the price, and for that reason WM1, containing the greatest tin content, was restricted to use on the highest load-bearing surfaces such as big end bearings. WM2 and WM3 were intended for use on surfaces of progressively lighter loadings, and contained less tin."

---

36 Mr R C Bond *A Lifetime with Locomotives* Goose & Son 1975 p30, also *The Design of a Locomotive Axlebox* February 1923.

37 Messers R M Deeley & L H Archbutt *Lubrication and Lubricants* Charles Griffin & C° London Fifth Edition 1927 p507.

38 It comprised – zinc 78%, tin 13.8%, copper 6.0%, iron 1.0%, lead 0.8% and antimony 0.3%.

39 Mr H C H Burgess *Working With LMS Steam* Bradford Barton Truro 1983 p22

While the evidence is perhaps circumstantial it appears not long after its formation the LMS adopted ARLE Nº 2, a high lead containing tin-based alloy, in place of the higher quality lead-free metal the Midland had used for the same duty. Presumably this was on the orders of George Hughes to reduce costs, who earlier whilst in the employ of the Lancashire & Yorkshire had promoted high lead content white metals. This is hypothesis is supported by the difference in hot box performance between the LNWR G1 and G2 classes recorded at the beginning of this chapter[40]. However, it has to be admitted that it is a puzzle, because in *The Metallurgy of a High-Speed Locomotive*[41], written with the support of the LMS, the white metal for the axleboxes of the 'Princess Coronation' class 4-6-2 featured, was referred to in some detail:-

"It is essential that bearing metals for locomotives of this kind should have good fatigue resistance, and consequently they are of the high-tin base type. The analysis of the metal used on the big and little ends of the connecting rods and the axlebox bearings, is as follows:-

Tin	85 per cent
Copper	5 per cent
Antimony	10 per cent

The lining of details is a carefully controlled operation, all white-metal pots being fitted with thermocouples and recorders, and in some cases thermostatic control. The bath used for the tinning of smaller details such as coupling-rod bushes, is also controlled by a thermocouple. This is in accordance with the general methods employed on L.M.S.R. locomotives, and was followed in the case of the *Princess Coronation* engines. The tinning medium used is an alloy of the following composition:-

Tin	59.0 per cent
Antimony	9.5 per cent
Copper	3.0 per cent
Lead	28.5 per cent

This was arrived at after considerable investigatory work. An interesting test has been developed in connection with the adhesion of the white metal to the brass shells. This test is made by removing a strip of the actual detail, and subjecting it to blows on the Izod testing machine. Periodic checks are made in order to see if the standard of tinning and melting is being maintained."

The alloy used in the axleboxes of these 4-6-2 engines was clearly ARLE Nº 1, so while this article recognized the benefits of high tin white metal for high-speed engines, did it mean the use of this alloy was restricted to locomotives employed on those duties, or did it represent a rethink by the company over the use of NF6K? Either way, for a period, the LMS adopted an inferior grade of white metal, which despite its less appropriate properties, it proceeded to use on its most highly loaded axlebox bearings – at least those in engines employed on humbler duties. This change will have reduced the performance of the affected axleboxes, whose capacity in many instances had little or no reserve, and were in any case sensitive to the reaction between the bearing metal and the lubricant, so in this respect the LMS scored a bit of an own goal.

Due to the retention of poor out-dated workshop practices, the success or otherwise of an anti-friction alloy for a long time depended more on the resulting internal crystal structure than upon its absolute composition. The crystals in turn being affected by the temperature at which the alloy was poured into the bearing and even the rate at which it was allowed to cool. In effect, the complete absence of guidance or 'quality control' over tinning temperature, pouring temperature and cooling rate for a long time had as great an impact, if not more on the success of a bearing than did the precise composition of its alloy, hence the proliferation of white metal mixtures.

Since fitters traditionally ascertained the temperature of the molten metal in its pot by stroking it with strips of paper to see whether they yellowed, scorched or caught fire, superior alloys could have their structures ruined through overheating. Mr Burgess[42] has described just how crude the re-metalling process could be in a pre-war locomotive running shed, while Lieut-Colonel L F R Fell, then of the Directorate of Research at the Air Ministry later the designer of the 'Fell' diesel mechanical locomotive Nº 10100, commented in a discussion on contemporary locomotive practices[43]:-

---

40 Most of the G2s were created during LMS period by giving G1s boilers pressed to 175lbs/sq in, presumably in works when their axleboxes were re-metalled with NF6K alloy. In 1930, the majority of the G1s might still have been shod with boxes containing LNWR composition antifriction metal – the NF6K alloy only starting to come into use.

41 *The Metallurgy of a High-Speed Locomotive* **Railway Gazette** February 18 & 25 1938.

42 Mr H C H Burgess *Working With LMS Steam* Bradford Barton Truro 1983.

43 Mr P C Dewhurst *British and American Locomotives – Design and Practice* I Mech E March 1922 pp490-1.

"An aero-engine big-end remetalled on the lines he was accustomed to see before leaving the railway would not last half an hour. It was considered that the majority of failures of axle-box white metalling was due to composition of the metal having been destroyed before pouring by overheating. In white metalling the big-ends of aeroplane engines – which, though not very much more heavily loaded than locomotive bearings, ran at a higher temperature and without the benefit of the air-cooling which all locomotive bearings got – it had been found that the temperature at which the tinning was done before running in the white metal, and the temperature at which the white metal was maintained before pouring, must be within a few degrees of the correct one, generally 320°C., in order to get any life from the bearing. It had also been found that there was no necessity to have a great thickness of white metal, as was so frequently the case with locomotive axle-boxes."

Adding antimony to the tin made the alloy harder and stronger in compression through dissolving in the tin, but inspection of table XXVIII suggests once the antimony content exceeded 8 per cent the gain in hardness reduced. This is because there is a limit to the amount of antimony the tin can dissolve so in alloys containing above 8 per cent, the excess antimony instead forms hard cuboid particles of tin-antimony (SnSb). These however are lighter than the matrix so tend to float - assuming the time for cooling is sufficiently prolonged to permit it. This effect can be reduced however by the addition of a small quantity of a third metal to the alloy, thus a modest amount of copper is introduced. Tin-copper crystals, which usually produce feathery needles are the first to solidify in the cooling alloy; exhibiting little tendency to segregation they form a net or sponge in which the remainder of the melt is held. As this continues to cool, the cuboid crystals of tin-antimony form, but becoming enmeshed in the felt of tin-copper needles are prevented from floating to the top of the cooling liquid, so remaining instead largely in the positions where they were formed.

Table XXVIII reveals the effect the presence of copper had on hardness in alloys containing 8-10 per cent of antimony - the usual proportions - was quite small until the cuprous content had reached about 4 per cent. This is because a minimum quantity of copper has to be present in the tin - approximately 1 per cent - before any tin-copper

The white squares appearing in the photograph are the hard constituent comprising cuboids of antimony in solid solution with the tin. The distribution of these hard blocks throughout the mass in the tin base alloy is helped by the formation of hard copper-tin needles, often accompanied as in this example by stars. These needles and stars prevented the tendency of the cuboids to rise to the surface, instead enmeshing them in the network. Both compounds can be seen on a polished surface of the alloy, but etching it with hydrochloric acid makes them more apparent.

Fig. 55 - Micrograph of ARLE N° 1 tin-antimony-copper white metal - magnification × 75 approx.

needles could separate out. It was considered the proportion of copper present influenced the size of the tin-antimony cuboids making them larger when the copper content was higher. Contemporary opinion was also that the copper content should not exceed about 7 per cent in bearings that were likely to exceed 165°F because it tended to embrittle the matrix. The hardness of the white metal used by the Midland Railway will have been close to the

---

Incidentally, the main and big end bearings of early internal combustion engines were simply lined with white metal in a similar manner to locomotive axleboxes. As bearing pressures increased to improve engine performance it was found necessary to make this layer ever thinner so that the fatigue strength of the lining remained adequate to carry the loads required. The modern thin wall shell bearing is a development of that requirement, comprising a thin steel backing, onto which is bonded the bearing metal.

last column of the final row.

During the final years of the nineteenth century Frenchman G Charpy conducted compressive tests on twenty mixtures of tin, antimony and copper alloyed in differing proportions. The test samples were 15mm high with a cross sectional area of 10 sq mm. The results appear in table XXIX and in figure 56 plotted in the form of a triangular diagram. The curved lines represent contours of loads that resulted in a compression of 0.008in or 0.2mm. Alloys 1, 2, 3, 6, 8, 9 and 16 broke at the beginning of the compression while N° 4, 10, 13 and 17 developed internal cracks before a compression of 7.5mm was obtained. It follows therefore that all of these alloys are too hard, so line $A - A$ may be regarded as the limit of the useful alloys, and within this limit the alloy N° 14 of the series had the highest compressive strength. The white metal used by the Midland Railway would appear to have had a slightly superior compressive strength while remaining the correct side of $A - A$, Subsequently in 1901, M Charpy proposed that the best alloy in the tin/antimony/copper series comprised 83 per cent tin, 11 per cent antimony and 6 per cent copper, which once again represents a composition close to Derby's mixture.

The Germans Professor Behrens and Mr Baucke demonstrated in the late 1890s the hardness of the matrix in a white metal (tin 82 per cent, antimony

Table XXVIII – Record of Brinell Hardness Tests on Tin, Antimony & Copper Alloys

Copper - per cent	Temp - °F	Brinell hardness Antimony - per cent				
		2	4	6	8	10
.5	71	9.5	12.1	14.6	18.6	18.7
	122	~	9.3	11.2	14.4	15.2
	167	5.9*	8.3*	8.3	10.6	11.9
	212	5.0*	5.9*	8.3*	7.4	8.1
1.0	71	11.3	14.7	17.0	19.9	20.8
	122	7.1	11.7	13.3	16.6	16.7
	167	7.3*	9.0	10.0	10.9	11.5
	212	5.2*	~	7.8	9.9	10.2
2.0	71	12.3	15.0	19.2	21.7	20.8
	122	8.5	10.7	14.5	16.2	15.8
	167	7.5*	8.1	11.1	13.2	13.8
	212	5.7*	5.9	8.6	10.2	9.0
4.0	71	13.0	16.7	19.5	21.9	22.6
	122	9.5	12.6	14.9	17.2	18.8
	167	8.6*	9.9	11.7	14.5	14.6
	212	6.5*	8.1	7.6	9.8	11.1
8.0	71	15.3	20.8	26.6	26.1	30.4
	122	12.9	17.0	19.1	21.4	23.4
	167	11.5	12.3	14.6	15.8	17.4
	212	8.7*	8.7	13.7	13.0	13.5

*Obtained with 350kg/770lbs load in place of the 500kg/1100lbs of the remainder
Data taken from *Bearing Metals and Alloys* H N Bassett Edward Arnold & C° Ltd London 1937.

Table XXIX – Record of Compressive Tests on Tin, Antimony & Copper Alloys - 1899

N° of alloy	Composition			Load corresponding to a compression of 0.2mm - kgs	Load corresponding to a compression of 7.5mm - kgs
	Tin	Antimony	Copper		
1	50	~	50	broke*	broke
2	66	~	34	2810	broke
3	75	~	25	2000	2000
4	83	~	17	1325	*1550*
5	88	~	12	550	broke
6	75	8	17	2075	2258
7	88	4	8	875	broke
8	50	25	25	3760	broke
9	66	17	17	2780	broke
10	75	12.5	12.5	1730	*2550*
11	83	8.5	8.5	1200	2550
12	88	6	6	980	2550
13	75	17	8	1780	*2750*
14	83	11.5	5.5	1330	2475
15	88	8	4	1000	broke
16	50	50	~	2220	broke
17	66	34	~	1790	broke
18	75	25	~	1500	2600
19	83	17	~	1000	2650
20	88	12	~	600	2150

*Broke without deformation
Entries in italic developed internal cracks before full compression load could be applied
NB:- Certain of the alloy proportions in the original table did not match the diagram - the copper and antimony values being transposed. Data taken from *Alloys and their Industrial Applications* Mr E F Law Charles Griffin & C° Ltd London 1919.

9 per cent and copper 9 per cent) varied with the rate of cooling. The size and number of the tin-antimony cuboids, the component responsible for most of the hardness, is also influenced by the rate of cooling. In slowly cooled examples - cast around a red hot core - the cuboids measured as much as 0.020in (0.5mm) and the tin-copper crystals 0.008in (0.2mm), but in chilled samples - cast around chills cooled by running water - the crystals were small imperfectly formed, confused and hardly detectable. Instances of both of these structures were seen in hot boxes *i.e.* the white metal had been ruined during the casting process. Conversely, the structure in satisfactory bearings was intermediate between the two. Casting around cores maintained at the boiling point of water resulted in cuboid crystals that were well formed, numerous and not exceeding 0.010 in (0.25mm). Bearings formed from metal samples subjected to the three cooling rates were then turned to fit a polished steel shaft 16mm diameter, which was rotated at 1600rpm. The pressure on the bearings was varied with the rise in temperature determined via thermometers secured in holes in the bearing blocks by soft amalgam. The increase in temperature (°C) after running for one minute with pressures up to 3kg/sq cm was as follows:-

	0.3kg/sq cm	0.4kg/sq cm	0.6kg/sq cm	1.2kg/sq cm	3.0kg/sq cm
Red hot core	0.65	1.6	1.72	2.62	4.64
Cold core	0.50	0.82	1.12	1.50	3.80
Core held at 212°F/100°C	0.64	0.64	0.74	0.75	1.64

Sir Henry Fowler confirmed in 1922 if the cuboids in a tin/antimony/copper white metal were too large, through say faulty foundry practice, there was a tendency for the bearing to run hot. Under the high loadings present in axleboxes and big ends the large crystals would be torn out of the matrix and combining with the lubricant present formed an abrasive something akin to emery powder.

Later workers reported that the temperature of the moulds and mandrels had little effect on the sizes of the tin-antimony cuboids and essentially it was the casting temperature that was crucial. Hence the introduction of temperature controlled melting pots and crucibles. It was found there is a critical temperature for each alloy whose value varied with the composition of the alloy. As a rough

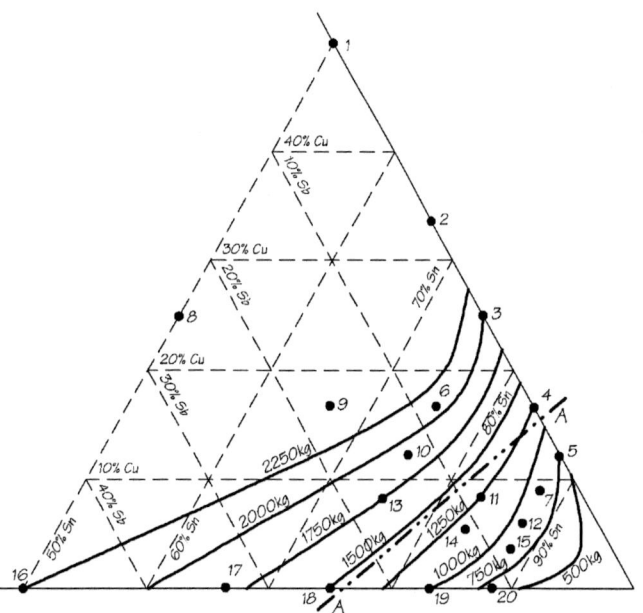

Fig. 56 - Compressive strengths of the alloys of tin, antimony and copper

generalization it is around 50°C/90°F above the temperature at which the white metal begins to solidify. Provided the temperature of the metal when it was poured was within its critical range, the kind of crystals formed was not affected by mould temperature which had only a small impact on the size of the tin-antimony cuboids. It was the rate of cooling that most directly influenced crystal size, especially the cuboids, while a protracted cooling period could lead to a certain amount of segregation. The optimum temperature ensured the shortest cooling time possible to give the required crystal size and maintain alloy consistency. The chilling effect of a cold mandrel does result in a fine structure appearing in the white metal immediately in contact with it. However, such a chill effect does not normally extend far into the metal, and as this portion of the bearing surface is usually removed during the subsequent machining operations it is not a problem. So from a practical point of view bearings cast against a mandrel will have substantially the same structure whether the mould was initially at ambient temperature or has been heated by successive castings.

These later findings to some extent contradict the two German experimenters, however there are two further considerations. Firstly, the relative masses

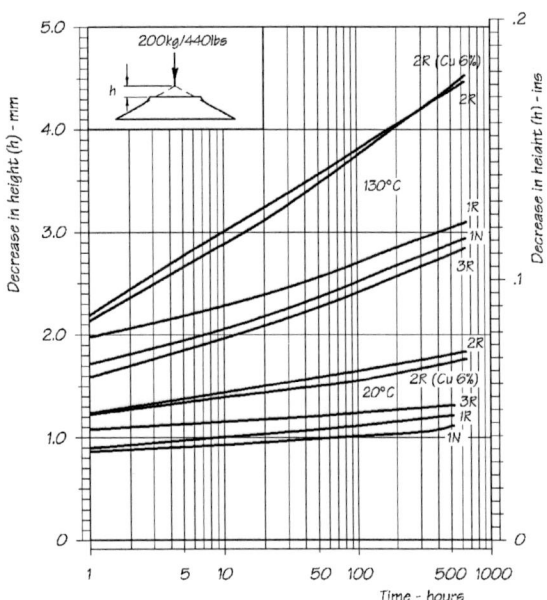

Fig. 57 - Creep tests on LMS standard bearing metals

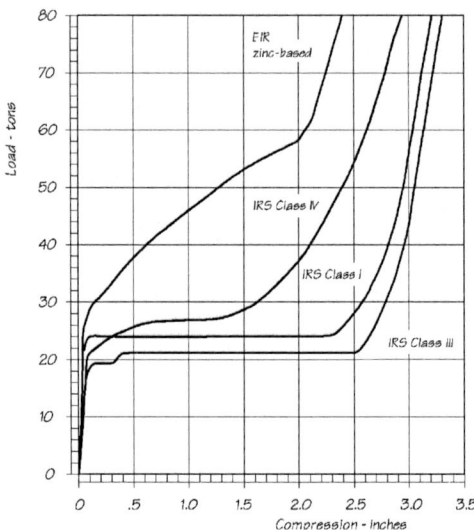

Bearing Metal Mixtures - India
EIR — Zinc 65.0%, tin 29.5%, copper 5.5%, lead 0.12%
IRS Class I — Tin 60.0%, lead 21.0%, antimony 12.0%, copper 6.0%, impurities ≤ 1%
IRS Class III — Lead 79.0%, antimony 13.0%, tin 6.0%, copper 1.0%, impurities ≤ 1%
IRS Class IV — Tin 81.0%, antimony 10.5%, copper 5.5%, lead 2.5%, impurities ≤ 0.5%

Compressive tests at 94°F on white metal blocks 4ins × 2ins × 2ins. IRS Classes I and III alloys collapsed suddenly after initial failure. Class IV retained a slight residual resistance. EIR zinc-base demonstrates higher resistance but the alloy was held to possess certain disadvantages, although high zinc alloys were used by others *e.g.* the pre-War Reichsbahn standard white metal, which had been tin 80%, antimony 12%, copper 6%, zinc 2% become zinc-based during the Second World War, thus the Class 52 2-10-0 Kriegslokomotive had the following alloy in its axleboxes, zinc 73.5%, antimony 15.5%, tin 10%, copper 1%.

Fig. 58 - Compression tests - IRS bearing metals

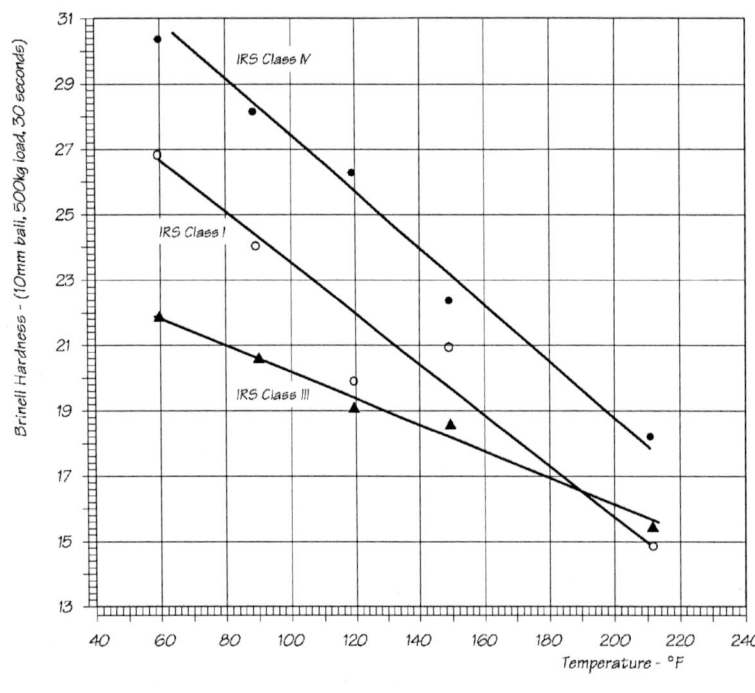

Hardness is a measure of the resistance of the alloy to wear. Curves suggest ARLE No. 1 mixture, which in composition resembled approximately the IRS Class IV mix, probably returned a roughly similar advantage. IRS Class I alloy approximates to ARLE No. 2 mixture.

Fig. 59 - Hardness - temperature curves for a selection of IRS white metals

of the hot white metal compared to the relatively cold axlebox and mould can result in severe chilling of the former from two directions. Secondly, if the antimony content of the white metal is in the range 8-9 per cent, then it is only just sufficient to promote the appearance of the tin-antimony cuboids. With these alloys the temperature of the mould becomes of greater importance. A cold or chilled mandrel *can* then

content in the IRS Class I alloy (similar in composition to ARLE N° 2) tended to fail completely if their oil supply was insufficient or intermittent through say a temporary obstruction. Prompted partly through the bearing troubles it was experiencing about the same time, and because white metals lost a considerable portion of their ability to carry high bearing pressures at comparatively low temperatures, the LMS

Table XXX – Composition and Mechanical Properties of LMS Bearing Alloys

Alloy		ARLE N° 1N LMS N° 6H	ARLE N° 1R LMS N° 6J	ARLE N° 2R LMS N° 6K		ARLE N° 3R ~
Specification	- limits (per cent)					
	Tin	84-86	80-85	58-60		11-13
	Copper	4-6	4-6	2-6		1.0 max
	Antimony	9-12	8-10	9-10		12-14
	Lead	0.2 max	5.0 max	Difference		Difference
Specification	- typical examples (per cent)					
	Tin	85.0	81.2	58.9	59.1	11.0
	Copper	5.0	4.3	2.4	6.2	.4
	Antimony	9.73	9.8	9.3	9.8	13.0
	Lead	.26	4.7	24.9	24.9	75.6
Brinell hardness at 20°C/68°F		28.0	32.3	23.9	30	22.8
Mallock hardness after 21 days						
	@ 20°C/68°F	10.9	9.68	3.58	4.53	8.63
	@ 130°C/266°F	2.02	1.72	0.65	0.66	2.09
Limit of proportionality*	lbs/sq in	1500	1061	Low	~	1132
Young's modulus (E)	× 1,000,000 lbs/sq in					
	@ 20°C/68°F	7.7	7.5	4.8	~	4.3
	@ 60°C/140°F	7.0	6.7	4.3	~	4.2
	@ 130°C/266°F	4.6	3.4	1.0	~	2.9

It is suspected, but not proved, the N and R designations appearing in the ARLE identities refer to 'new' and 'reclaimed' respectively. The Mallock hardness numbers were obtained after 21 days when flow had practically ceased.
*The properties indicated by an asterisk were selected from results derived by the LMS from similar alloys.

modify the crystalline structure quite considerably and to a greater depth again with detrimental effect on the anti-frictional properties of the bearing.

By the 1930s, assisted by the introduction of superior temperature control while tinning the bearing brasses and when casting the white metal, meant engineers obtained a far clearer appreciation of the in-service performance of bearing alloys having different compositions together with the further contribution made by the lubricant. Figures 58 and 59 compare the compression and hardness values for some white metals used in the sub-continent, but similar in composition to the ARLE mixtures used in Britain. It was reported in India that locomotive bearings lined with the high lead

conducted an investigation[44] into the performance of four different bearing alloys. One was composed of virgin metal, and corresponded to ARLE N° 1, the others were reclaimed samples representing examples of all three ARLE mixtures and thus were formed from alloyed particles, which had already been used at least once previously. Reclaiming white metal was in theory a sound practice, but as Roland Bond reported it was not

---

44 Mr J N Bradley & Dr H O'Neill *Railway Bearing Metals: Their Control & Recovery* Institute of Metals September 1942 reprinted in abridged form in I Loco E Journal N° 169.

Dr O'Neill, Chief Metallurgist of the LMS was recruited from Manchester University, where he had previously earned a considerable reputation for work with complex ternary and quaternary non-ferrous alloys *i.e.* white metals *etc.*

always possible to keep the turnings and swarf properly segregated. The presence of even quite small quantities of lead could be very detrimental.

The test samples were 'as cast' cones having an included angle of 120° and stood about 0.66 inches high. They were tested at two temperatures 20°C/68°F and 130°C/266°F by immersion in an oil bath maintained at one or other temperature. A constant force of 440lbs/200kgs was applied onto the apex of each specimen and the resulting decrease in height due to creep – a characteristic of a metal subjected to steady load – is recorded in figure 57, while details of the alloys appear in table XXX. Figure 57 demonstrates that alloys 1R, 2R and a version of 2R wherein the copper content was increased to 6 per cent, all had their strength reduced through the lead creating a low melting point lead-tin eutectic[45]; they also suffered worst from creep. The lead-based alloy N° 3R will be seen to be superior in this respect compared to the 60 per cent tin alloy N° 2R used in locomotive boxes. LMS scientists claimed that N° 3R alloy offered a superior resistance to pounding or repeated impact than N° 2R, although other authorities considered there was very little difference.

High tin-based white metals, such as ARLE N° 1, had their suitability for service in heavy-duty bearings destroyed if the lead content exceeded about 0.25 per cent as the latter metal acted as a contaminant forming a lead-tin eutectic. If such a bearing ran hot attaining the eutectic temperature, the molten portion was squeezed out of the felted mass of higher melting constituents by the pressure on the journal and appeared on the surface in the form of small droplets, which as the journal rotated were smeared over the bearing surface. The results of a bearing that has been 'wiped' in this way shewed (a) numerous very thin, roughly elliptical, 'smears' of relatively soft metal, which were only loosely adherent to the surface on account of the oil-film underneath them, and (b) areas with an uneven (depressed) surface, which were produced by the removal of the eutectic constituent. The remedy for this exfoliation was to use an anti-friction metal containing no lead (*i.e.* less than 0.25 per cent). In such an alloy the *solidus* temperature is about 450°F (the temperature of solidification of the tin-rich matrix), which meant, if the bearing ran hot, wiping would not occur until a temperature of over 85 degrees higher was reached. It should be understood, the raising of the *solidus* by cutting out lead did not mean that it was safe to run the bearing at temperatures of 390-400°F. At such a temperature the resistance to compression of the white metal will have reduced to a very low figure, about one-fifth of its compressive strength at ordinary temperatures, so it was likely the bearing would fail by squeezing out, but it could avoid serious damage if the heating was only momentary.

The LMS experienced extreme trouble with some big-end bearings during 1933 through exfoliation when alloy N° 1R (5 per cent lead) was used, but which disappeared when the low lead alloy N° 1N was substituted. Comparing the properties of the N° 1R alloy with those of the N° 1N reveals the latter was significantly superior, apart from any considerations regarding the eutectic temperature. In his report[46] into the Gresley/Holcroft conjugated valve gear, instigated at the behest of Edward Thompson, Mr Cox included the following observation on the design of Sir Nigel's inside big end, which at that time had a predilection for running hot:-

"A brass strip, 1½" wide, is allowed to bear on the crank pin on the horizontal centre line instead of containing the white metal all round each half of the bearing. L.M.S. experience has shewn this to be undesirable since, if the adjacent white metal is heated sufficiently it can flow over the brass strip, reducing the clearance, and eventually cause a hot big end.

The white metal used contains 5% of lead. Investigations by the L.M.S. Research Department has

---

45 The melting point of an alloy or mixture of two substances depends on the proportions in which they are mixed and may be lower than the melting point of either of the constituents. The mixture whose proportions give the lowest melting point is called the eutectic mixture and the corresponding melting point is the eutectic temperature. For all other proportions, there is a range of temperatures between the eutectic temperature or '*solidus*', and the temperature at which the whole mixture melts, or '*liquidus*', within which there is a molten eutectic mixture and a solid excess of one or other constituent. With tin-lead solders, *i.e.* white metals without the copper or antimony, which in any case have very little effect, the eutectic mixture is 63 per cent tin 37 per cent lead. The eutectic temperature is about 365°F while the melting point of pure tin is 450°F, and for lead 620°F. All lead-tin mixtures, irrespective of the proportions of the two constituents commence to melt (soften) at 365°F, where they differ is that the eutectic mixture becomes a liquid at that temperature while all of the others go through a softening or 'pasty' stage, not becoming wholly liquid until a higher temperature is reached. It was the presence of this pasty stage, which enabled an old-style plumber to produce the traditional bulbous wiped joint at the ends of his lead water pipe connexions.

46 Report entitled *2 to 1 valve Gear L.N.E.R. 3-Cylinder Locomotives* June 1942.

shewn that the matrix of such a metal will contain a constituent which becomes completely molten at about 185°C. If the working temperature of the big end reaches 100°C., as is possible when the loading bears heavily on the brass strip, this fusible constituent which honeycombs the alloy will begin to flow and smear. The L.M.S. use a white metal in which the lead is limited to 0.2% maximum. In this metal the easily fusible constituent is not formed, and no melting occurs until a temperature of 239°C. has been reached. Mechanical tests shew that this alloy has greater rigidity and resistance to creep at working temperatures than the somewhat similar alloy containing 5% lead. Some years ago the L.M.S. had several big end bearing failures where exfoliation of the white metal occurred at which time the alloy in use was similar to the L.N.E. metal."

The horizontal brass strips fitted in this LNER bearing were similar in purpose and principle to those present in the Midland manganese bronze axlebox. Therefore, it seems reasonable that this weaknesses described by Mr Cox in the big end design, will have become more pronounced in the Midland box *after* the LMS had substituted N° NF6K white metal containing 28 per cent lead. While the taper boiler engines provided with the more generously proportioned bearings (*i.e.* less highly loaded) introduced by William Stanier could seemingly cope with a high lead white metal, in fact their performance *pro rata* was no better, it was simply their larger size meant they just took longer to wear out. Certainly, white metals containing between 75 and 12 per cent tin *i.e.* equivalent to ARLE mixtures N° 2 and 3 in due course were found to possess inferior mechanical properties and nowadays are no longer used in heavily loaded bearings.

A further consideration influencing the choice, or at least should have been present, in the case of bearings subjected to dynamic loads, such as axleboxes was fatigue[47]. The low fatigue strength possessed by the white metals was their major weakness, although once again tin-based alloys containing no lead were somewhat better. Operation beyond the fatigue capacity of an alloy resulted in cracks developing which loosened small areas of metal. These areas or 'tiles' increased in number until insufficient surface remained to carry the load and a hot bearing resulted. White metal fatigue strength, in common with its compressive strength, was also extremely sensitive to temperature – a 40°F rise can halve the fatigue life of some alloys. The superior fatigue life and compressive strength of *thin* layer white metal bearings is demonstrated by the reliable performance of the 'thin shell' type bearing used in the big end and the main bearings of modern internal combustion engines. The loads and speeds carried successfully by such *hydrodynamically* lubricated bearings have fatigue lives far in excess of anything obtained in a steam railway locomotive, whose big-ends and axleboxes were also subject to considerable wear.

In consideration of this latter point and to obtain a reasonable life, many designers were tempted into applying thick layers of white metal, but to prevent the soft alloy from spreading under alternating loads, mechanical anchoring was used. Usually this was by deep pockets, dovetails, serrations *etc.* that could contain the white metal should it soften with heat or even retain pieces of it in the event of cracking. Later it was appreciated the presence of these retaining features was counter-productive, for the white metal was differentially compressed under load with the metal located in the deeper portions of variable depth pockets or between the serrations becoming more compressed than that in the shallower portions. Hence these features instead promoted bearing failure through fatigue, furthermore, it was not easy to obtain a good bond between the white metal and brass with deep cast-in pockets as it was very difficult to obtain a chemically clean surface.

It was found that bonding the white metal carefully to a smooth uniformly curved step or bearing that could be chemically cleaned or machined immediately prior to being tinned encouraged a superior 'bimetallic' composition at the interface, which promoted much better load distribution and heat dissipation between the white metal and the bearing. The overall result of these design and workshop changes was a gradual improvement in

---

47 In every respect, bar one, babbit metals probably represented the best all round bearing alloys, their one limitation being their comparatively *low fatigue strength*. Due to this limitation, present in even the best, there was a demand for bearing materials having significantly higher fatigue strength, so the simple tin/antimony/copper alloys familiar to locomotive engineers, were superseded by new higher-strength materials, particularly in internal combustion engines for the aeroplane and motor vehicle industries. In developing these new high-strength alloys, the traditional hypothesis of a duplex structure being a necessary pre-requisite if a bearing was to function correctly no longer held. For good results were obtained from high duty bearings that wore quite uniformly and had no soft plastic matrix, consequently nowadays the advantage of the traditional white metals is believed to lie chiefly in their greater tolerance towards misalignment

(conformability) and dirt (embedability).

physical strength and fatigue life of the bearings. Hence, Mr Cox could report in his axlebox paper that improvements in methods and quality control had demonstrated the serrations could be omitted[48] while the thickness of the white metal lining was reduced to become 1/8 inch thick bonded to a plain, machined surface. This reduced white metal layer still remained thicker than desirable, but such a thickness was considered necessary by LMS engineers in order that re-metalling and subsequent re-boring could be more readily accommodated. Nevertheless, we may observe Oliver Bulleid was able to arrange for the big end brasses fitted to his Southern class Q1 to carry only 1/32ins of white metal.

Fitting and Wear

The 'full' journal bearing *i.e.* one which completely surrounds the axle, was not much used for locomotive axleboxes although from time to time designers were tempted to try it, for example Samuel Johnson during the 1880s, Oliver Bulleid some sixty years later and between times (and rather more successfully), by North American engineers with their floating bush boxes. Instead, most engines and rolling stock axleboxes were partial bearings. These extended only part way round the upper half of the journal so they could only accept load from a limited range of directions, but they have the advantage of being:-

(i) simple in construction
(ii) it is usually easier to supply lubricant to them
(iii) the frictional loss is less, so the temperature rise tends to be lower
(iv) they permit the use of 'fitted' or 'bedded' bearings.

Most bearings in other engineering applications are full and because they totally enclose the journal they are bored out slightly larger than the journal to provide enough clearance to accommodate the hydrodynamic oil film. Partial bearings can be treated similarly but traditionally, axleboxes were 'fitted' or 'bedded', being provided with zero clearance *i.e.* the radius of the journal and the bearing were nominally the same. A fitted box presented a very real manufacturing advantage, since verification of the correctness of the radius of the brass did not rely on the accuracy of ascertaining the very small difference between the radii of the journal and the bearing. Instead, it was readily checked by the direct application of the brass to the journal. Mr Cox has described[49] the process:-

"Among the heaviest jobs was the bedding in of axleboxes. In later days of steam, machining of both axle journal and boxes became sufficiently accurate for the one to be assembled to the other without any fitting. Then, however, each box had to be manoeuvred up and down an inclined plank while the white metal bearing was successively scraped and tried on the journal. This process was repeated several times before the tell-tale red lead indicated that contact between the two was established over a sufficient area. This crude mating process was far from finished when the engine went out. Trial trips near the works, and light duties for a few days at the home shed completed the procedure. It is small wonder that hot bearings were an epidemic disease of most pre-World War I railways, especially when, as was too often the case excessive bearing loads and poor facilities for lubrication were combined with so inconsistent a means of winning the required bearing surface."

It is difficult to measure the radius of any brass if its bearing surface forms less than half a cylinder as the usual methods *e.g.*, inside callipers or internal micrometer are impractical. To overcome this, many turners bored to radius gauges they made themselves from thin sheet metal, typically in steps of 1/32 inch. After boring as close as possible to journal size, using the appropriate gauge, the axlebox was hand bedded to its journal and the ends relieved using files and scrapers. The

---

48 Bob Meanley believes this omission applied only to later Class 5 4-6-0s, the earlier members of the class kept their serrations *i.e.* the improvement was not applied retrospectively to older batches or classes, however David Reed stated the serrations were omitted from the 'Royal Scots'. Perhaps when they were rebuilt they received new axleboxes.

49 Mr E S Cox *Locomotive Panorama Vol. I* Ian Allan Shepperton 1965 pp66-7.

Quite how crude the mating process was, depended very much on the skill and aptitude of the fitter. Professor Robert Thurston held a consultancy with the Pennsylvania Railroad and one of his responsibilities was testing new shipments of babbit for rolling stock bearings. This was achieved by scraping a bearing metalled with the sample babbit to fit the journal of one of his testing machines and thereby determine the coefficient of friction. His assistant Albert Kingsbury, who was skilled in workshop practice did such a professional scraping job that the bearings he fitted were able to act hydrodynamically returning coefficients of friction lower than anything Professor Thurston had ever witnessed before. Since this pre-dated Beauchamp Tower's work by a few years neither was able to explain why! Following this introduction to tribology Mr Kingsbury subsequently invented a tilting pad bearing similar in principle, and concurrently with, but independently of, Mr Michell.

aim was to achieve through careful scraping a continuous bedded area extending say 60° either side of the crown and across the complete length of the brass. When in-service the journal rotated it tried to assume an eccentric position within the bearing *i.e.* the vertical centre-lines of the brass and the axle no longer coincided, as they did at rest, but it was largely thwarted in this endeavour due to the geometry of the bearing and the limited lubrication provided. As the clearance of a bedded bearing is practically nil, the horizontal shift of the journal is extremely small. Professor Goodman demonstrated[50] with pad lubrication, the vertical lift of a fitted bearing was also to all intents non-existent, though his underpad did not appear to be very efficient at delivering oil, so this might be considered as representing the boundary regime end of the mixed-film region.

Afterwards this same bearing, which was semi-circular in section having a wrap of 146° with the ends relieved to provide a chamfered approach and recess on the 'on' and 'off' sides, was run with the underside of its journal dipping into an oil bath. Due to the greater lubricant supply he observed the bearing lift vertically; he also obtained pressure profiles - an example appears in figure 79. They differ considerably from Mr Tower's profiles also derived from a fitted bearing. Unfortunately,

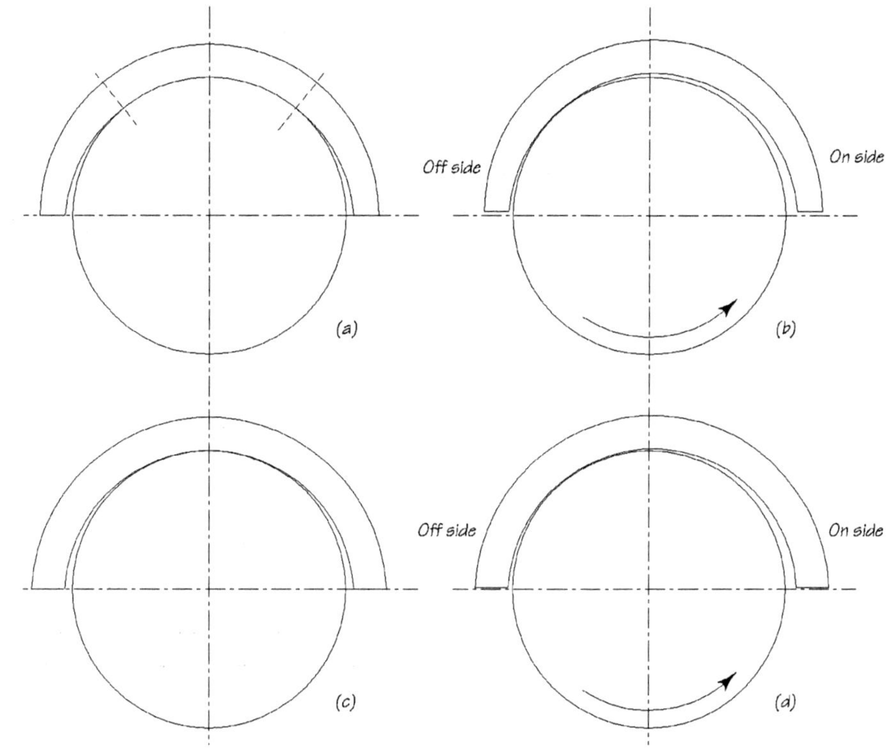

Upper pair of diagrams shew at *(a)* a fitted partial bearing at rest. The bedded area extends between the two dotted lines over the crown while the ends of the brass have been relieved. At *(b)* the journal is rotating with the shaft and bearing assuming eccentric positions relative to one another. The relief at the ends of the bearing ensures the off side does not 'drag' or otherwise make contact with the journal.

The lower pair shew at *(c)* a clearance partial bearing at rest. The concentrically bored bearing ensures the contact area becomes a line at the crown of the brass with an increasing clearance towards the ends. At *(d)* the journal is rotating and again the centres of the journal and bearing no longer coincide. As in *(b)* above, the relief at the ends of the brass ensure the off side is not in contact with the journal.

Fig. 60 - Partial bearings

information on partial *fitted* bearings is scanty, so while modern practice accepts Beauchamp Tower's profiles as correct, identical results would also be obtained from an oil bath lubricated partial bearing possessing some clearance. Nevertheless we can conclude even a very slight change in the relative positions of the journal and its bearing helped draw the limited lubricant available into the converging gap, their action created, promoting some mixed-film action.

This small relative movement was normally of little consequence in the case of carrying axles since their arcs of contact seldom exceeded 90° and frequently were less, furthermore the load they supported was largely constant and acted vertically downwards. Thus, providing the longitudinal edges of the step were rounded or otherwise relieved to prevent them scraping the oil off the journal in either direction of travel, fitted bearings functioned very well, but in the case of driving and coupled axleboxes, the situation was somewhat different.

---

50 Professor J Goodman *An Experimental Determination of the Distribution and Thickness of the Oil-Film in a Flooded Cylindrical Bearing (Part II)* Paper N° 4826 Inst Civil Engineers 1932

Fig. 61 - Bedding the axleboxes of 'Big Goods' 0-6-0s in N° 2 Bay of Derby Erecting Shop in 1929

The man on the left is scraping the loose brass of a Midland pattern, case-hardened steel or wrought iron axlebox, to mate with the journal of a coupled axle. Possibly one of the pair in front of him, however as the same box was also fitted to the driving axles of some Midland classes, it could equally be destined for one of the crank axle journals of the passenger engine wheel set behind him. A loose brass axlebox is also being fitted to the journals of the next two pairs of wheels. Suspended from the air hoist on the extreme right however, is a manganese axlebox destined for a crank or driving axle although its recipient is not visible.

Firstly, the brass extended over a longer arc and secondly the load, as will be demonstrated in a subsequent section, was highly variable in terms of magnitude and direction, so the relative degree of eccentricity of the journal within the bearing continuously changed. Accordingly, as in Professor Goodman's brass, the 'on' and 'off' sides were given matching scraped profiles to ensure they were clear of the journal *i.e.* they were relieved. However, being essentially a manual procedure relying very much on the skill of the artisan, it resulted in a highly variable standard of fitting and in turn bearing performance. Should for example the relief at the ends be insufficient, then there was a strong likelihood of the box running hot with the lowest portions of the bearing acting instead somewhat akin to an oil scraper rather than as an oil lead-in. Furthermore, for contact areas greater than 150° or so, there was the further risk that the journal might be nipped by the bearing should it overheat. The horn faces could restrict the outward expansion of the box, so instead it was forced to move inwards. Later improvements made possible by better machine tools enabled this manual exercise to be omitted, thus following William Stanier's arrival and the introduction of new standards of accuracy and finish in the machining of the bearing finishes, the LMS abandoned scraping and fitting for most of its classes[51]:-

---

51 Sir William Stanier *Lubrication Applied to Locomotive Journals* I Mech E 1937.

In a conference on super finishes hosted by the I Mech E in March 1945, Dr Johansen gave more details of the procedures employed:-

"…. Thus, journals of coupled wheel axles have shown, over a number of years, that progressive improvement of surface finish diminishes the occurrence of overheated bearings, especially in the early stages of use. The present tendency, therefore, is for all engine and tender journals to be fine-turned, fine-ground, and finally lapped. The machine by which this lapping is done in the London, Midland, and Scottish Railway workshops is illustrated in Fig. 36, Plate 6 (omitted APT). Shrouded leather split collars, enclosing felt pads loaded with oil and emery powder, are strapped around the journals, and are belt-driven by electric motors. Simultaneously the motors are oscillated axially, and the wheel-axle assembly is slowly revolved. Crankpins are usually hand polished after being ground, but crank journals can be machine-lapped, the driving motors for this purpose being adapted to run up and down inclined rails. As an alternative to the lapping machine, the cylindrical parts of journals and the radiused fillets at their ends are polished (after the fine-turning operation) by felt pad and emery, applied while the assembly is mounted in a lathe.

Although statistics or comparative test results are not available, it is established that the polished surface diminishes bearing troubles, both immediately and throughout the life of the journal. Early scoring, which would persist until the journal came in for repreparation, is avoided and the journal surface is commonly more highly polished after service than when newly

"The journals are turned, ground, and finally lapped with a mixture of emery powder and oil, the latter operation, being preferred to rolling.

After boring the boxes, the latest practice is to burnish, an operation which removes the need for bedding-on; when completed, an express engine is given two running trips, light, each of 60 to 100 miles at a commencing speed of 25-30 m.p.h. and reaching a final speed of 70 m.p.h., before being put to work."

The new procedure, termed counter boring, was simply to bore the axlebox out to the appropriate clearance size *C* which was a few thousandths of an inch larger in diameter than the journal and then burnish it – *vide* figure 62. This method however resulted in the bearing assuming a line contact at rest and a built-in roll each way equal to one-half the clearance. According to Mr H A Bulleid[52] William Stanier:-

"... also succeeded, though with difficulty, in getting them to machine axleboxes to running size: the size stemming from his 1903-11 experience when a

---

lapped. It is found adequate for the associated whitemetal bearings to be bored and machine-burnished. Inside big-end bushes and eccentric liners are bored and, if necessary, hand-scraped, but outside connecting-rod bushes are not hand-scraped in L.M.S.R. practice. The wheel boss faces, which take axial thrust, receive no more than a smooth turned finish."

Sir William Stanier contributed to the discussion, which included an incorrect reference to the use of caborundum:-

"With regard to the lapping machine on the London, Midland, and Scottish Railway, to which Mr. Johansen referred in his paper, that machine had been devised about twenty years ago by Sam Holborough, foreman of the wheel shop in the Great Western Railway works at Swindon. It was thought important that locomotive journals should be parallel and round, so grinding machines were installed, which resulted in a considerable increase in the number of hot boxes. It was realized at once, of course, that the grinding finish, if done commercially, *i.e.* reasonably quickly, gave a rather matt surface, and so the experienced chargeman in the erecting shop took some emery paper and went over the journal with a circular motion, and then it was all right. Sam Holborough thought that was an old-fashioned way of doing things, so he made the lapping machine.

When he went to the London, Midland, and Scottish Railway he had a similar machine installed in that company's shops. Mr. Johansen said in his paper that oil and emery powder were used, but he thought it was more correct to say oil and carborundum powder. The great advantage was that not only was the journal parallel and round but it had a finish that was otherwise acquired only after a certain number of trial trips. The axleboxes were bored and afterwards burnished, and could be put straight on the journal without any hand scraping at all, and with greatly improved results."

52 Mr H A V Bullied *Master Builders of Steam* Ian Allan Ltd London 2nd Edition 1983 p142.

Bob Meanley quotes William Stanier's retort made during a visit to Crewe in 1932/3. On having observed bearings being scraped and told it created valleys to hold the oil, he replied:-

"Yes but it leaves hills to remove it!"

rule-of-thumb clearance of 14 thousandths on an 8 in. journal was found to promote the necessary oil film. Simultaneously he imported the process evolved by the Swindon wheel shop foreman in 1929 for finishing journals and crank-pins."

Had sufficient oil been delivered then potentially counter bored boxes would have operated in full hydrodynamic mode and thus experienced no wear. Since wear occurred - *vide* table XXXI - and as fitted bearings were equally capable of generating the desired oil film it seems the main advantage of

Diameter of journal - inches	Dimension A - inches	Dimension B - inches
9 to 10	0.01	3½
8 to 9	0.0078	2¾
7 to 8	0.0058	2
Below 7	0.0043	1½

Data from Sir William's paper *Lubrication as Applied Applied to Locomotive Journals* - I Mech E Oct. 1937.

It is believed these dimensions were identical to those used by the Great Western.

NB:- No machining details were provided

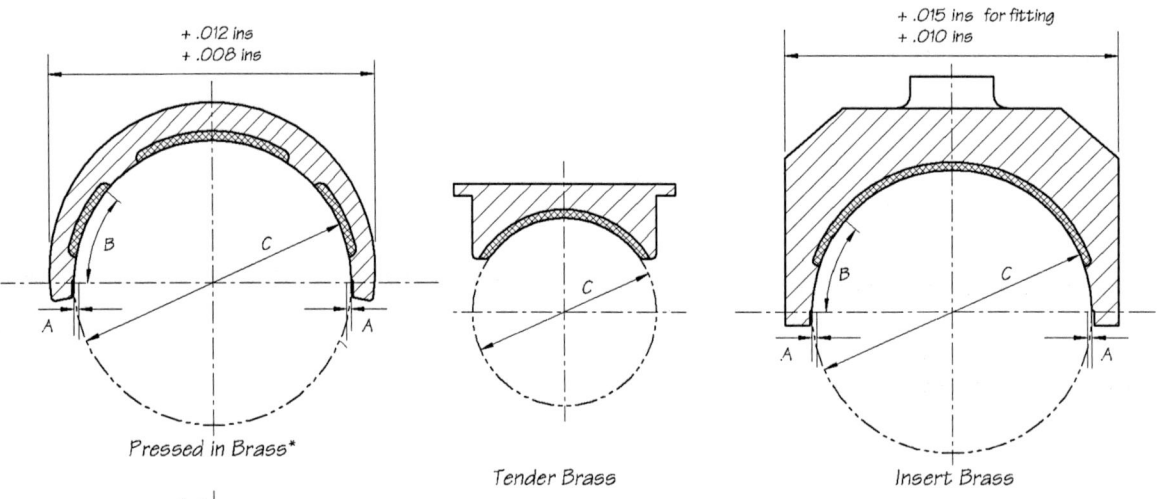

Pressed in Brass* Tender Brass Insert Brass

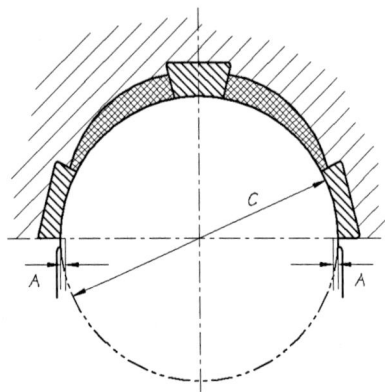

Brass Inserts for Manganese Boxes

No reason was given for presence of dimension *B*, but it appears it is the point where the clearance between the journal and the bearing surface has reduced to 0.003ins. Possibly the correct boring size was confirmed by *B* being the desired depth of penetration of a .003ins feeler gauge.

Diameter of journal - ins	Dimension A - inches	Dimension B - inches	Boring size C - ins	
			High	Low
9 to 10	0.010	3.5	+ 0.020	+ 0.018
8 to below 9	0.0078	2.75	+ 0.016	+ 0.014
7 to below 8	0.0058	2.0	+ 0.013	+ 0.011
Below 7	0.0043	1.5	+ 0.010	+ 0.008

Data obtained from LMS 1945 edition of *Limits & Fits - Axleboxes*

Machining details were provided:-

For all coupled axleboxes the exact size of the journal is taken as nominal, and when the brass is bored to *C* limits, it gives the clearance as shewn at *A* and *B* and no fitting of brass is required.

*Bottom lips of brass fitted to give pressing in allowance of 15 to 17 tons.

Machined surfaces and lengths for which no limits are given on the drawing are to be within ± 0.010ins.

Fig. 62 - Clearances of brasses for LMS locomotive axleboxes

the system was that it eliminated hand work thereby giving consistent fore and aft clearances at the ends of the brass combined with a finer finish to the bearing surface. However, it was not the only way of eliminating hand fitting, it could also be done with bedded bearings. Southern practice[53] was to bore the axlebox in two stages, known as double boring; possibly also the LNER since D W Harvey sort of describes the method in *Steam Locomotive Restoration & Preservation*. The axlebox was first bored typically 1/64 of an inch larger in diameter than the journal then the box was moved while still in the chuck by roughly a similar amount towards the lathe centre, before being bored out this time to journal diameter. The displacement was carefully calculated using the sine rule so the circumferences of the two bores intersected at a desired point a couple of inches or so above the axle horizontal centre line, thereby providing the necessary backing off and typically 100° to 160° of coincidental surface at the crown. A fitted axlebox possessed the valuable

improve initial surface condition as the asperities wore down with either machining method, but the larger extent of coincidental area in a bedded bearing should have been of advantage. The LMS presumably took the view if the surfaces were made smoother to start with then that should make the bearing last long enough before it needed re-metalling while the *consistency* of fit obtained by eliminating hand work improved reliability and helped promote cooler running.

Figure 63 illustrates at (a) and (b) two typical turned surfaces and at (c) a typical ground surface of similar roughness. We may see that although the crests in (a) are much sharper than (b) both exhibit a repeating pattern or periodicity. The ground surface (c) is typically random but with quite sharp peaks and valleys. A similar amount of wear W in these examples through truncating the peaks produces a totally different surface pattern, the resulting plateaux occupying a greater proportion of the surface in the case of (b) and (c) than (a). At

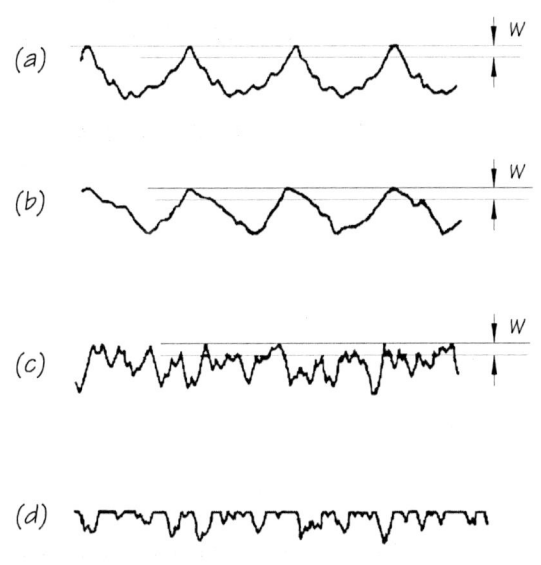

Diagram shews at *(a)* and *(b)* two typical turned surfaces and at *(c)* a typical ground surface of similar roughness. It will be seen that the asperities in *(a)* are much sharper than *(b)* although both exhibit a similar pattern of periodicity. The ground surface *(c)* is characteristically random but with quite sharp peaks and valleys. A similar amount of wear, shewn as W by truncating the peaks will produce a totally different surface pattern, the resulting plateaux occupying a greater proportion of the surface in the case of *(b)* and *(c)* than *(a)*.

The effect of running-in is to truncate the peaks by the wear process, abrasion and minute seizures paring away the crests and the resulting debris being washed out with the lubricant. The mechanism occurs at its highest rate during the boundary regime when there is no true oil film to separate the surfaces and during the initial stages of the mixed film zone when the oil film is very thin. If the peaks are disproportionately high, then the wear process cannot occur gradually enough to avoid disaster and a hot box is likely to occur. It follows then that the surface finishes of the journal and the bearing must be arranged to suit the operating conditions, particularly the starting and stopping cycles. At *(d)* is shewn a typical run-in surface. This can be produced artificially by the machining method adopted *i.e.* by lapping, honing or super-finishing, usually after a fine grinding operation.

Fig. 63 - Surface profiles

(d) is shewn a typical bedded-in surface – a condition that could be replicated artificially by a variety of machining methods *e.g.* by lapping, honing or super finishing, usually carried out after a fine grinding operation.

characteristic of a mutual contact *area* between the journal and the bearing not being reduced as in counter bored boxes to a *line*, thereby reducing the risk of damage to the surfaces. Under brief periods of running with deficient lubrication such as when starting and stopping (provided correct choice was made of materials) a fitted box was considered to suffer less injury. In practice such action tended to

Because full hydrodynamic lubrication was not present in axleboxes, it meant they were subject to wear continuously from the moment the engine entered service. A finite bearing life was the price locomotive engineers paid for remaining with simple total loss lubrication systems. Had they

---

53 Mr E A Phillipson *Steam Locomotive Design: Data and Formulae* The Locomotive Publishing C° Ltd London 1936 Plate N° 19 facing p272.

instead chosen to adopt continuous oil-circulation systems, then the resulting higher flow rates would have moved bearing performance into the hydrodynamic zone – a region of little to no wear. Nevertheless reference to figure 53 reveals the *rate* of bearing wear, which may be caused by adhesion or abrasion, altered significantly within the mixed-film lubrication region. The rapid fall occurred for the same reason that the friction dropped, namely the reduced asperity interaction due to the greater, albeit incomplete, load support given by the increasing lubricant film thickness. This asperity action could assume two forms. In adhesive wear the asperities, subjected to localized high pressure from the bearing load formed solid bonds at their points of contact. Welding of these asperities could occur on contact but occurred more readily if relative motion took place. The subsequent sliding of the bearing and the journal surfaces relative to one another made and sheared these bonds, which prompted the breaking off and removal of surface material creating wear particles. When adhesive wear is severe, it is referred to as scuffing. Frictional heating, if the temperature became high enough (typically 220-230°F), decomposed the protective film formed by the lubricant on the bearing surfaces – a situation that could prompt the quite rapid destruction of the bearing. Abrasion occurred when the metal surfaces made direct contact and asperities from the harder surface penetrated into the softer material. It may be visualised as being akin to ploughing, with material removed from the softer surface. Adhesive and abrasive wear took place when the surface separation was less than the mean operating roughness. Adhesion can be reduced by selecting bearing materials such as tin or lead, which have a low solubility in steel, while abrasion may be minimized by selecting harder bearing materials or by reducing the surface roughness of the two surfaces, especially that of the harder one. However, increasing the hardness of the bearing material too far can be detrimental.

Abrasion may also be due to hard particles entering the bearing directly or via the lubricant, such as dust and sand, or they could originate within it *e.g.* wear particles. Keeping the oil clean and seals in good condition helped reduce abrasion, but when it was caused by self-generating wear particles, the restricted oil flow prevented them from being readily flushed out of the bearing – a solution possible in fluid-film bearings – hence another reason for using softer materials *e.g.* white metals.

The white metal served to reduce damage from large, hard abrasive particles because it acted as an accommodation mechanism. However, too thick a layer of such soft material amongst other disadvantages could lead to abrasive wear being resumed should the embedded particles act as a lap. Perhaps the classic example of wear prompted by the presence of hard foreign particles was demonstrated by the Great Western, which during the late nineteenth century in common with a number of other companies, but *not* the Midland, suffered from quite frequent hot carriage boxes[54]. The company's inspectors usually blamed dirty oil but Mr Churchward though otherwise believing instead that failure of the lubrication film allowed direct contact between the journal and the step. In an experiment related by William Stanier[55], he took a carriage brake van out of service and arranged for holes to be drilled in the floor of the van and a corner of an axlebox. Through these, he threaded a copper pipe, which terminated at its upper end in a tundish. This allowed him to introduce very fine 'dirt' in the form of emery flour directly into the bearing. At the end of a journey from Swindon to Paddington the axlebox was found to be cool, although the emery had resulted in the journal

---

54 "Then there was a sudden and serious upsurge in cases of hot axle bearings. This became alarming and culminated in terse comments and a demand for monthly statistics, when the Chairman had to change carriages twice between Leeds and King's Cross on account of hot boxes. The Midland had an enviable reputation for freedom from this trouble and, accordingly, Ivatt arranged with S. W. Johnson to obtain not only the standard white metal used by the Midland but also their special lubricating oil mixture: and right into the 1920s G.N.R. and L.N.E.R. carriage axle boxes were marked M.M. – Midland Mixture."

Mr H A V Bullied *Master Builders of Steam* Ian Allan Ltd London 2nd Edition 1983 p59, while Mr J I Hill wrote in 1934:-

"For the lubrication of carriage axles, mineral oils are in common use, but for long runs such as that of the 'Flying Scotsman', a special lubricant containing olive oil is used."

55 According to Mr H Webster *Locomotive Running Shed Practice* Oxford University Press 1947 p83, Sir William Stanier first mentioned this experiment in his presidential address to the City and Guilds College Engineering Society March 1943; he also referred to it in his Newcomen Society paper *George Jackson Churchward* of twelve years later. Sir William explained therein that the experiment had been conducted during the development of the O.K. axlebox.

"He had studied the theory of lubrication of Osborne Reynolds and in the design of the box he not only saw that oil could get between the surfaces of the journal and bearing, but that there was a good pad below the journal to feed and maintain the oil film. He also designed the box so that there was proper metallic contact between the brass and the box to conduct the heat away; for he knew that provided the work was done properly, dirt should not heat the box although it might cut the journal."

having a pronounced hourglass profile. Hindsight suggests it was probably the fineness of the 'dirt' he used, that enabled this experiment to have been carried out without the journal overheating. Certainly when the dust and grit contamination was more extensive, or comprised larger particles, as in the hot dusty plains of India during the dry season, it could result in extensive bearing trouble. For example in North America during the dust storms of 1935, the number of hot boxes tripled. Nearer to home, Mr Burgess[56] has referred to the effects of sand:-

"It was the two-mile stretch between Swansea Bay and Mumbles Road stations which provided the unique environment so conducive to hot bearings and excessive wear in other moving parts. Nowhere in the British Isles has a length of track been regarded with such grateful reverence by loco maintenance staff as was this one. It was our benefactor, not inconsiderable amounts of overtime and work for at least one more fitter than would have normally been required. Between these two stations the tracks were laid over sand dunes – sleepers and ballast must have been there yet nobody but the platelayers ever saw them, for they were buried in soft, fine sand which rose in all-pervading clouds to find its way into bearing surfaces each time a train passed over."

The main problem with wear is that it altered the relative shapes of the bearing members so that after a certain mileage their correct operation ceased. A situation that was clearly cumulative and once the clearance became too large in effect, the axle could move in an uncontrolled manner within the box, resulting in hammering, pounding and possible fatigue cracking of the white metal. The following table from *Locomotive Axleboxes*, gives particulars of the clearances present on LMS stock when the locomotive was new or newly shopped and the average sizes of those clearances once it was due for shopping.

In practice, the factor determining shopping was 'knock' *i.e.* the total effect of the longitudinal wear in the direction of the main frames, although on high speed locomotives side play also had to be considered, for once excessive it affected lateral stability. That not all railway companies worked to these initial clearances or considered them appropriate is demonstrated by the following comments[57]:-

"As for the axleboxes – 'Bronze of course,' Bulleid said, 'they are the best and can be re-cycled.' Moreover individual push-fits were used and often there was still no axlebox knock after 70,000 miles, compared with what rude Southern Railway engineers described as the 'initial built-in knock' of the small tolerances specified by the LMS."

The following refers to the rebuilding of his Pacifics in the 1950s:-

Table XXXI – LMS Locomotive Axlebox Clearances

Clearance	New	Approx shopping condition
Lateral play of the axlebox on journal	Varies with class of engine, usually 1/16in leading and driving 3/16in trailing between axlebox and wheel boss on each side	1/16in to 1/8in increase over new clearance on each side
Lateral play of the axlebox in the horns	1/16in each way	1/16in increase of clearance on each side
Longitudinal play of axle in bearing on horizontal centre line (roll)	0.0075 in on each side*	1/8in roll on each side of centre line
Longitudinal play of axlebox in horn gap	0.005in (.010in total)	3/16in total play each side

*This distance suggests a journal 8 ins to 9 ins in diameter.

"Bulleid took a strong dislike only to two details – the change to manganese steel axleboxes and horn guides; and the elimination of the 'hexagon-pentagon' securing cap for the coupling rods. The steel axleboxes certainly landed the engines with a new and unnecessary 'play' of 0.03in before any wear increased it."

Figure 64 illustrates the distribution of wear in a locomotive axlebox; although the patterns were similar in all, it tended to be greater in the driving as opposed to the coupled boxes. The upper portion *A* of the brass was subject to wear arising from the weight acting on the box; the portions *B*

---

56 Mr H C H Burgess *Working With LMS Steam* Bradford Barton Truro 1983 p9.

57 Mr H A V Bulleid *Bulleid of the Southern* Ian Allan Ltd Shepperton 1977 pp 58 & 119.

particularly near the ends were subject to wear generated by the alternating thrust of the piston acting on the journal. This thrust typically exceeded the weight acting on the box by a factor of three or four. Hence, the greater wear at the lower ends of the brass eventually caused the journal to pound in the brass prompting in turn wear in the rods and tyres. In order to help reduce the wear at B, it was quite common in America and elsewhere, in the world to extend the brass below the axle centre line by means of separate extension pieces curved to match the journal located in front and behind. Known in America as quarter bearings they usually incorporated a facility for taking up the wear by means of traverse adjusting wedges which moved the bearing sections longitudinally against the journals.

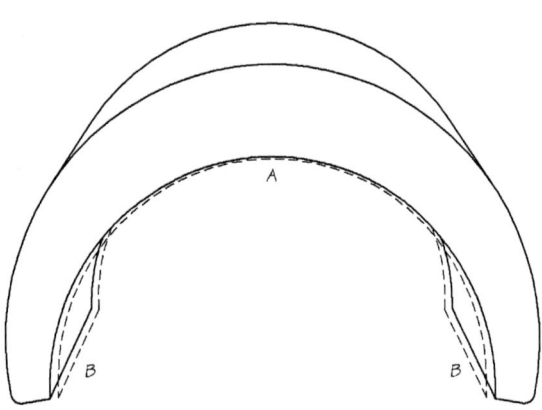

The dotted lines indicate the original profile. the top portion A at the crown of the brass is subject to wear owing to the axle load on the box; the portion B particularly near the ends are subject to the thrust of the piston on the journals. This thrust typically exceeds the weight on the box by three or four, hence the greater wear. This wear once it becomes too large allows the journal to pound in the brass thereby promoting wear and tear in the rods together with greater tyre wear.

Fig. 64 - Wear pattern in an axlebox brass

During its last years, the Midland Railway maintained its locomotives strictly in accordance with a system[58] introduced by that very gifted engineer Cecil Padget. This provided for the complete or partial dismantling of boilers, boiler fittings and other 'stationary' equipment such as brake gear, carriage warming apparatus *etc.* on a time basis *e.g.* 3-5 weeks, 7-9 weeks *etc.*, these intervals being a reflection of time in steam. By contrast, the moving parts such as pistons, valves, motion, connecting and coupling rods were examined on a mileage basis of 5,000-6,000 miles and multiples thereof. As practised by the Midland at the time of the Grouping, a light repair was given to an engine at 40,000 to 48,000 miles in order to extend the period from one shopping to the next. A typical light repair consisted of lifting the engine, the wheels taken out and turned up, and re-metalling of the axleboxes. At the same time, any necessary attention would be given to the motion, the blast-pipe would be removed for cleaning, a number of tubes taken out of the boiler so that all dirt might be removed, and any firebox repairs of a light nature carried out.

Since the 'Big Goods' appeared in 1911 it is reasonable to conclude the engine was designed either consciously or sub-consciously to comply with this maintenance regime, thus in those halcyon days pertaining before 1914, provided its bearings would run 40,000-48,000 miles then its performance would be acceptable. Furthermore, when the next batch appeared in 1917, there was no reason to doubt that pre-war conditions would not return. How the Midland might have modified its operating procedures post-Great War had the Grouping never taken place is impossible to predict, but what is certain is the most vociferous criticism concerning its axlebox performance has emanated from engineers who either, were not Derby trained, or else are writing from the skewed perspective of the Depression and post-Stanier experience. Quite what axlebox mileages were achieved by the class in Midland days is not clear although it is believed they exceeded those achieved by the LMS after the latter company changed the white metal. By the time of his axlebox paper, Mr Cox averred Class 4 0-6-0s were averaging 60,700 miles from general to first service repair in an average period of 24½ months. In some trials to be referred to shortly, the wear had become sufficient at 35-40,000 miles to warrant repairing the bearings. However, since on average at that time each engine ran a hot box once in 20 months, usually one of the more heavily loaded driving boxes and since both boxes on the same axle were usually re-metalled at the same time, the result was the engine would then ran on

---

58 The Railway Operating Division of the Royal Engineers adopted the system around 1920. In a modified form, the LMS applied it to all of its engines, followed by the LNER and later still by British Railways.

to its first service repair.

In contrast, the pressed brass/steel axleboxes fitted to the outside cylinder locomotives introduced by William Stanier only suffered a hot box on average per engine once every 120 months or ten years. This superior performance prompted the application of this axlebox technology to the Class 4, differing only in the smaller dimensions needed to suit its smaller journals, an action that commenced in March 1934 under retrospectively identified Job N° 4916. By 1939, a large number had been fitted with steel driving boxes, but there was no improvement in wear or reduction in the incidence of hot boxes, in other words, the much-lauded Churchward/Stanier axlebox performed *no better* than the Midland version. Thereby implying the fundamental reason for the lack of performance returned by the latter was not due to its axlebox design *per se*, but simply the limited bearing size that could be fitted to an inside cylinder engine.

This finding is given further support if we compare the mean axlebox performance of the taper boiler LMS Standard Class 5 4-6-0 with the equivalent Class 8 2-8-0. Both of these classes were fitted with the same size cylinders and axleboxes, and carried identical boiler pressure, yet the mileages Mr Cox quoted[59] for axlebox performance were 74,303 for the six-coupled engine, but only 62,174 miles for the 2-8-0. The shorter bearing life in the eight-coupled engine was because a higher proportion of its work was carried out at low speed 'slogging' goods trains. The 'Jubilee', which carried similar sized axleboxes, was able to run 95,490 miles – a reflection of its three-cylinder propulsion which reduced the maximum piston thrusts and of the longer periods being an express engine when the lubrication conditions were nearer the transition point[60]. As the Class 8 2-8-0 and the Class 4 0-6-0 were both engaged on similar work, and their journals were the same diameter, it is more appropriate and equitable to compare the box performance of these classes.

---

59 Mr E S Cox *Locomotive Axleboxes* I Loco E Paper N° 447 April 1944 p296.

60 Due to the presence of the crank webs and eccentric the slide out keep of the standard axlebox could not be applied to the leading coupled axle, consequently the lubrication of these boxes was wholly by means of a mechanical lubricator. Messers J W P Rowledge and B Reed *The Stanier 4-6-0s of the LMS* David and Charles Newton Abbot 1977 p22.

Similarly, the feeder and tray was omitted on the crank axle of Great Western four-cylinder locomotives.

Axleboxes, Bearing Metals and Lubricants

If we assume the engines were loaded in proportion to their tractive efforts, and table LVII suggests this is reasonable, then, their piston thrusts would be roughly in proportion. If we also assume initially, the axleboxes were the same length in both classes then because the driving wheels of the eight-coupled engine were about 10 per cent smaller in diameter but its piston thrust was about 10 per cent larger so the ZN/P values would be similar. Under these circumstances, from diagram 53, as wear rate is determined by the ZN/P value we would expect similar axlebox life for the two classes. Of course, the bearings were not the same length, so we might at first have anticipated a higher ZN/P value for the 2-8-0 since N would be greater and P lower, and therefore a very much lower wear rate. However, some GIPR tests infer the operating temperatures of wide and narrow bearings were the same, suggesting similar values for the coefficient of friction and therefore ZN/P. Presumably the lubricant supply to the wider bearing was not increased proportionately for it to reduce the friction. The bearing surfaces, of the axlebox fitted to the 2-8-0, were 8½ins diameter by 107/8ins long reducing to 109/32ins ignoring the fillet radii at the ends. The corresponding dimensions for the 0-6-0 were 8½ins diameter by 81/8ins long, and with the end radii omitted the bearing length shortens approximately one inch at each end becoming 61/8ins. Thus, the length of axlebox on the 0-6-0 was 60 per cent that of the 2-8-0, so presenting only 60 per cent of the metal to be removed for the same final diametrical clearance, whence we might anticipate the 0-6-0's axlebox would last only 60 per cent of the mileage of the eight-coupled engine. Indeed 60 per cent of 62,174 miles is 37,300, more or less the middle of the mileage range Mr Cox quoted for the Class 4 mileage thereby supporting the evidence presented in the paper that the Stanier axlebox, did not *of itself*, represent any real improvement if the operating conditions were similar. Indeed, Mr Powell confirmed the Stanier axlebox would return a poor performance if it was too small for the loads demanded of it[61]:-

'The 2-6-2s were the only Stanier design which was not generously proportioned in the coupled axleboxes and spring gear. Presumably this arose in building down to a severe weight limit. But hot boxes resulted on engines doing more than a bit of branch line pottering, coupled spring life was comparatively short,

---

61 Mr A J Powell *Living with London Midland Locomotives* Ian Allan Shepperton 1977 p96.

and the engine tended to settle down quickly, coming more heavily on to the two bissel trucks and thereby relieving the adhesion weight.'

The mileages for the Class 5 and 'Jubilee' 4-6-0s given earlier, suggest the axleboxes of these and later British engines were not stressed to the same extent as was common in the USA or elsewhere in the world. Had they been, then they would *also* have suffered from reduced bearing performance. An observation supported by the more heavily worked 'Royal Scots', like the '5XP' three-cylinder, which averaged 63,500 miles and also North American experience, which was such that driving boxes usually needed reconditioning several times between shoppings - in the case of high power output engines every 30,000 or 40,000 miles.

Nowadays predictions of the amount of diametrical wear suffered in a bearing operating within the boundary and mixed-film regimes over time are estimated from formulae such as the following:-

$$w = K \times P \times V \times T_s \qquad (10)$$

where:-

w = diametrical wear – ins
K = wear coefficient
  – ins min/ft lb hr
P = nominal bearing load
  – lbs/sq in
T_s = total sliding time – hours
V = journal surface velocity
  – ft/min

To account for the higher wear rate present during the 'running in' period two different wear coefficients are sometimes used. The rate of bearing wear especially initially, until the bearing had bedded-in is particularly influenced by the quality of the surface finishes of the matching surfaces.

Unfortunately, this formula is not readily applicable to a steam locomotive because the speed and load were both highly variable. Despite this, we can obtain an approximation insight using some sample big end wear figures provided by Mr K Cook[62]. These were for engines that had enjoyed the improvements in accuracy of frame alignment and bearing super finishing he had introduced. Wear in WD 2-8-0 big ends averaged 0.005-0.010ins in 39,000 miles and

---

62 Mr K J Cook *The Steam Locomotive: A Machine of Precision* Presidential Address L Loco E 1955.

0.004ins in 50,000 miles for Gresley inside big ends.

If we allow say 15mph as the average speed for the goods engine, this gives therefore 2,600 hours for a mean wear of 0.0075ins or 2.9×10^{-6}ins/hr,

Photograph of the left trailing axlebox from LMS built Class 2 4-4-0 Nº 59? (there appears to be a third digit visible in the original photograph). In service, the journal has worn through the loose brass before finally bearing on the case hardened ferrous body of the axlebox, to the extent of partly obliterating the recess that located the brass. That the assembly could survive for sufficient length of time for this degree of damage to occur supports M Chapelon's hypothesis that the coupled wheels contributed tractive effort only when the adhesive limit of the driving axle was exceeded, for the remainder of the time they acted as carrying wheels, bearing essentially the vertical spring load.

Fig. 65 – Wear observed in a Midland loose brass axlebox

adopting an average speed of perhaps 40mph for the other bearing or 1,250 hours reveals a wear rate of 3.2×10^{-6}ins/hr.

In his axlebox paper, Mr Cox referred to a trial conducted on a number of specially selected 'Big Goods' wherein axlebox wear was closely monitored at 5,000-mile intervals. These examinations revealed certain common wear patterns:-

Axleboxes, Bearing Metals and Lubricants

Fig. 66a – In-service wear observed in a Stanier pattern driving axlebox fitted to a Standard Class 4 0-6-0.

Single straight oil groove located in the crown, possibly cut in a non-white metal section. Appears to be signs of pitting over the surface of the white metal with heavy wear noticeable on the fillet radius.

Fig. 66b – In-service wear observed in a Stanier pattern driving axlebox fitted to a Standard Class 4 0-6-0.

Elliptical oil groove located in the crown. Groove appears to have lost more depth on one side than the other, also at its ends where it abuts the brass near the centre line, the white metal lining has worn thin enough to have started flaking and breaking away.

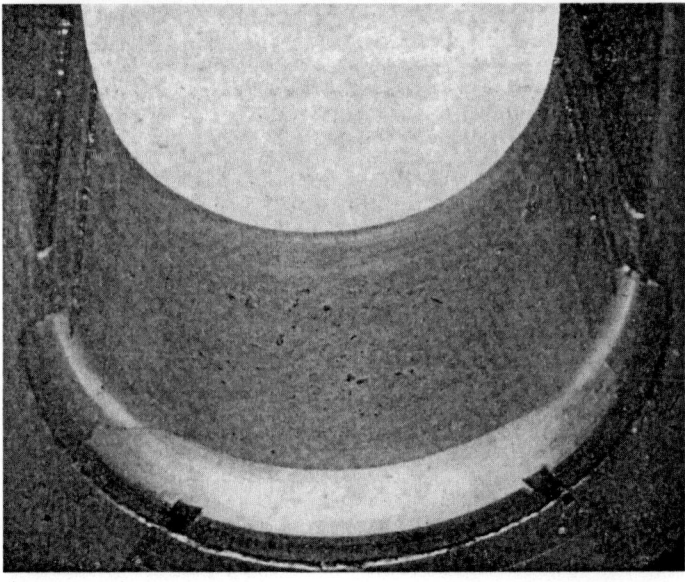

Fig. 66c – In-service wear observed in a Stanier pattern driving axlebox fitted to a Standard Class 4 0-6-0.

Oil delivery by means of two rows of holes located within the brass - one row on each side - near the horizontal centre line of the bearing. Holes trying to deliver oil near a region of maximum bearing load. When used with a continuous white metal surface the oils were blocked by smeared white metal. Pitting present on the white metal surface particularly near the crown, possibly suggesting reduced lubrication delivery with the bearing surviving on the 'squeeze-film' properties of the lubricant.

"(a) Signs of very heavy pressure below 30° from horizontal centre line.
(b) In a number of cases commencement of disintegration of white metal in the high pressure area.
(c) Most of the bearings showed pock marks over the whole surface. This feature was rather puzzling because it occurred with white metal, oil, type of oil feed and design of brass identical with that on other lower loaded bearings which present a highly polished smooth bearing surface on examination. It can only be assumed that the pock marks are due to small shreds of white metal squeezed off the surface subject to high pressure and embedded temporarily and irregularly as they passed round the bearing.
(d) In most cases sufficient wear and roll had developed in the brass by 35-40,000 miles to warrant changing.
(e) Wear was worst with steel boxes having centre line lubrication. There was little to choose between the other steel types and the manganese bronze. The failure of the centre line lubrication here is probably due to the oil being introduced very near the point of maximum bearing pressure when the engine is working hard."

High loads ensured a short life for white metal bearings through more rapid wear, aggravated whenever they were of an alternating nature, by fatigue and/or cavitation damage. The latter observation is suggested as possible causes for the pock marks reported by Mr Cox. When the load continuously changed its line of action, as in the case of the driving wheel axleboxes, but to a lesser extent on the coupled wheel boxes, the effect on the oil film could be considerable.

Figure 67 shews the hypothetical case where the journal rotating in one direction at a speed of N revolutions per minute, the load is in a downward direction, but the outside of the bearing shell, is rotating in the opposite direction to the journal at N revolutions per minute. Clearly under these conditions, a film of oil of any thickness cannot possibly build up as the shell will drag oil out just as quickly as the journal tries to drag it in. This condition is the same as that pertaining in a bearing where the shell was stationary but the load was changing its position at half the speed of rotation of the journal.

Since the steam thrust loading on the driving axleboxes was highly variable, such conditions could be approached or even obtained over a number of degrees of crank-axle rotation for unfortunate combinations of regulator opening, steam pressure, cut-off, speed, and the balance weight position, thereby leading to momentary complete failures of the oil film.

Under these circumstances, the bearings were functioning (and surviving) simply because of the response of the lubricating film when subjected to such dynamic loads, which acted in two ways.

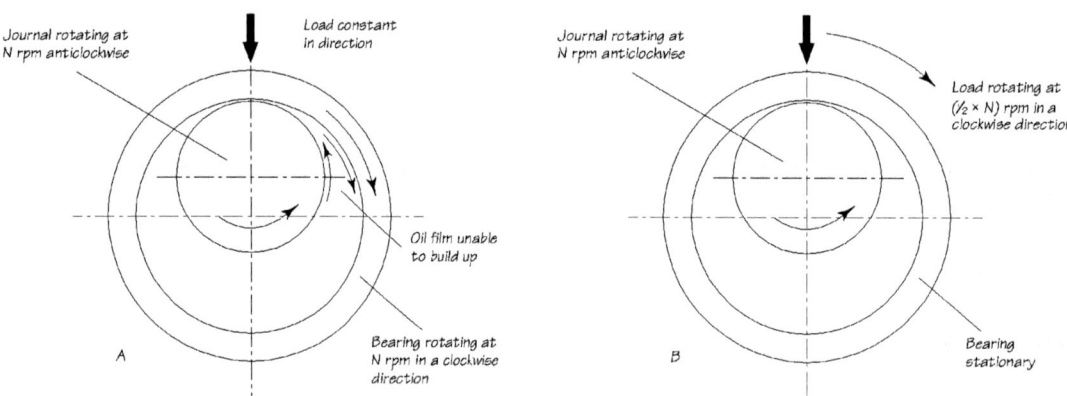

In a steadily loaded bearing, the journal takes up an eccentric position within the bearing and maintains a wedge of oil and a constant film thickness. When the load changes direction, the effect it has on the oil film thickness can be considerable. Consider diagram *A* above, where we have the journal rotating in one direction at a speed of N rpm, the load steadily applied in a downward direction and the bearing itself rotating in the opposite direction to the journal at exactly the same speed. Clearly under these conditions, an oil film cannot possibly build-up as the bearing drags the oil out just as fast as the journal tries to drag it in. This condition is exactly the same as would pertain in a bearing where the brass was stationary and the load was changing its position at one-half the speed of rotation of the journal - diagram *B*. During the cycle of loading of the driving boxes, under steam or piston loading, such a condition could be approached or may even been obtained for a number of degrees of crank rotation and thereby lead to complete failure of the oil film. Under these conditions, the bearing relies on the film strength of the lubricant for survival, *i.e.* the ability of the lubricant to avoid being 'squeezed out' under extreme loading and thereby preventing metal-to-metal contact.

Fig. 67 - Effects of rotating load and half-speed load vector

When the load tried to force the bearing surfaces towards each other squeeze pressure developed in the oil layer as the oil tried to flow away from the area. However, the increase in pressure also raised the viscosity of the oil so it exhibited a greater resistance to being squeezed out of the bearing, which delayed its escape. This temporary viscosity increase permitted a heavy load to be supported momentarily. Sooner or later however, should the load continue to be applied, all of the oil would be forced out from between the surfaces resulting in metal-to-metal contact, but for short periods an oil having a suitable squeeze film strength can support heavy loads. The tenacity of some squeeze-films is remarkable despite their extreme thinness, and the survival of many locomotive axleboxes and big-ends stands as testimony to their capacity.

The subsequent load removal permitted the entry of oil thereby 'restoring' the film but the second important action was associated with the metallic surfaces as they separated. The very small, relative, velocities of separation could create extremely low pressures within the lubricant film that might cause cavitation damage triggered by gas release or boiling. These sub-atmospheric pressures extant within the 'separating' lubricant resulted in bubbles or vapour cavities forming whose subsequent collapse at great velocity resulted in impact pressures (tens or even hundreds of tons per sq in) that exceed the fatigue strength of the bearing metal forming a tiny pit that enlarged with time. Cavitation damage also sometimes appeared elsewhere on the white metal surface *e.g.* around oil entry grooves and holes should the load changes momentarily disrupt the lubricant flow into the bearing.

Furthermore reciprocating load plain bearings are subject to another disease, which is theirs alone, namely fatigue of the bearing-surface metal caused by the repeated loading and unloading under the continually changing load pattern. Thus, reciprocating load bearings have a life limited in a manner reminiscent of roller bearings, whose life is also limited by fatigue - *vide* figure 52. After making a large number of cycles, the white metal would exhibit surface fatigue evidenced by localized pitting or flaking. The time to onset of this form of failure was highly dependent on stress aggravated by the thin-film conditions and design features such as thick white metal layers, which reduced the fatigue limit of the alloy. The fatigue life of a white metal lining, even after nominally the same amount of wear had occurred in otherwise identical bearings was highly variable because it was greatly affected by several diverse factors – *viz.* white metal composition, thickness and pouring temperature, bearing loads, axle alignment and lubricant, *etc.* Under pounding loads, the resulting cracks at first propagated radially, but before they reached the full depth of the white metal, they would normally alter direction to follow a circumferential or longitudinal path giving the surface of the white metal a tessellated appearance. This broke up the bearing surface into loose pieces that eventually became dislodged before passing around the bearing and possibly causing a wipe. Sometimes, before this latter stage was reached, the numerous cracks precipitated bearing failure through the penetration of lubricant, under pressure into these cracks. Another important factor was the influence that drivers, or more correctly their individual driving techniques could wrought on bearing performance, particularly when the engine was drifting.

Thus LMS locomotive big-end brasses, inside and outside were inspected and frequently refitted at intervals as short as 10-12,000 miles, any remedial work needed ranging from filing the butts in the case of goods engines to re-metalling and machining in passenger engines. It is interesting to report that after Ken Cook had transferred to Doncaster and improved the LNER inside big ends of Sir Nigel's Pacifics along Great Western lines, this class on average required re-metalling every 25,000 miles or so in order to maintain reliability.

Bearing Temperature

The temperatures obtained in the boundary region are almost exclusively the result of the high friction extant between the two surfaces coupled with the velocity difference between them, as the bearing load is carried by direct asperity contact. The friction in this zone is caused by adhesive and abrasive asperity contact while any rise in temperature increased the adhesion between materials and thus the propensity for the asperities to weld together with the risk of accelerated damage if the operating conditions are maintained. Within this region, whatever beneficial effects the lubricant might bestow became crucial. A similar situation pertains in the mixed-film region, albeit conditions are mitigated by the slowly increasing film thickness, nevertheless, depending on the

A Defence of the Midland/LMS Class 4 0-6-0

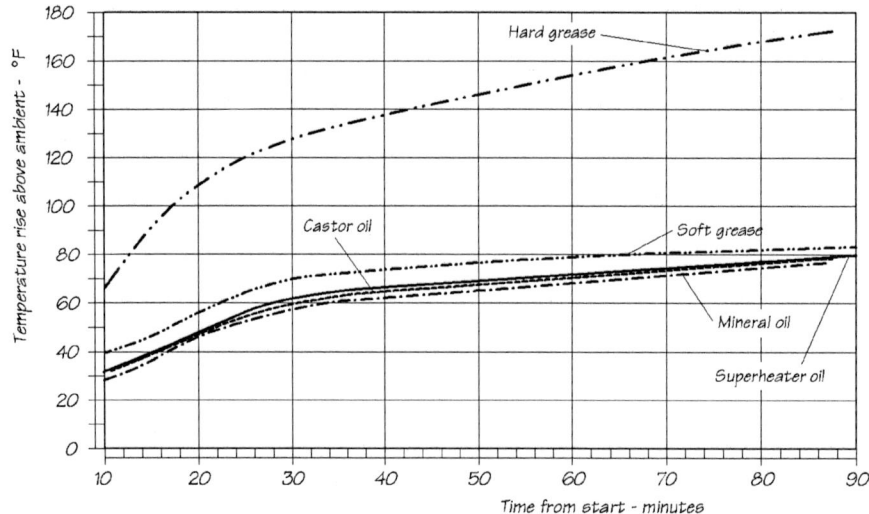

Diagram relates to tests conducted on BESA 4-6-0 engines hauling trains at 45-55 mph - GIP dynamometer car reports No. 19, 1934 and No. 19B, 1938. Thermocouples were located into holes drilled in the locomotive axleboxes, with the running temperature recorded in the dynamometer car. Tests involved different lubricants and methods of application. For a given box, its temperature rise was mainly dependent upon speed while viscosity (within limits) had relatively little influence. Drawbar horsepower curves were present on the dynamometer record charts along with the bearing temperature and train speed traces but no attempt appears to have been made to obtain ZN/P values.

For long periods day temperatures in India are in the range 90-115°F, which resulted in beaing temperatures in the region of 180°F. Reference to figure 59 - Hardness-Temperature reveals that at 180°F only the best quality white metals could be expected to give good service but even then the margin was slim. This diagram also suggests why thick unshrouded white metal linings were unlikely to be successful.

The bearing temperature rise over ambient corresponded to the order of viscosity of the different lubricants. It is suspected that in the case of the hard grease the lubrication was closer to the boundary zone, while the other lubricants permitted operation further into the mixed-film regime.

Fig. 68 - Axlebox temperature-time relationship - GIP Railway, India

materials and loads, a sufficiently high temperature might be reached to initiate scuffing damage, which if allowed to continue uninterrupted will result in catastrophic failure of the bearing through galling, seizure and melting of the bearing material. During the 1930s, the GIPR conducted a series of tests[63] exploring the temperatures of locomotive axleboxes. Some of the findings, which appear as figures 68 and 69, support similar work conducted on the LMS. From the first diagram, which records axlebox temperatures against time for a selection of different lubricants, Mr Renwick was able to opine for axleboxes of the same size and type:-

(a) Assuming the same initial ambient temperature, the steady operating (or equilibrium) temperature attained by an axlebox was a function of the characteristics of the oil.

(b) Axlebox temperature was greatly influenced by the journal speed.

(c) No relationship was found between drawbar horsepower output and axlebox temperature.

(d) The steady temperature attained by an axlebox was influenced by the viscosity of the oil.

His confirmed a lower running or equilibrium temperature would be obtained if an axlebox could dissipate the generated heat more effectively. However, conversely it may also be shewn that a warm running temperature did not of itself, indicate the reliability or otherwise of an axlebox, or even its freedom from over-heating.

Figure 69 shews the findings of an investigation into whether a relationship could be established between bearing area, and thereby its specific load (lbs/sq in), and running temperature. Two BESA locomotive classes were used comprising, a 4-6-0 express engine and a 2-8-0 goods engine. The standard bearings on these classes were 8ins diameter and 9ins long, but an example of each type was given solid bronze boxes, 13½ long *i.e.* 50 per cent longer. Trials were then run with the examples fitted with these longer bearings as against other representatives of the two classes fitted with bronze boxes 9ins long and steel boxes fitted with loose or 'slip in' brasses. Inspection of figure 69 together with the observations made by Mr Renwick demonstrate that the equilibrium temperature attained after running at constant speed is determined primarily by journal speed, so any reduction in speed would result in a reduced axlebox temperature and *visa versa*. In the LMS tests, the temperatures of four coupled axleboxes were measured and at 60 miles per hour, all of the boxes varied between 122°F and 143½°F, but an increase in speed to 70 miles per hour added 3½°F

---
63 Mr H P Renwick *Some Practical Reflections on Locomotive Axlebox Design* I Loco E Paper N° 423 1939.

to 5½°F rise in their temperature. Bearing temperature was also influenced by the different conditions each axlebox experienced in service *e.g.* heat radiated from the ashpan, the larger flange forces absorbed by the leading coupled wheels *etc*.

The conclusion appearing in the official report on the normal and extended journal axleboxes shewed that the steady running temperatures were identical in spite of the large differences in unit loading, but with the lower intensity of pressure the extended journal increased the reliability of the bearing *i.e.* the limiting pressure at which the oil film was broken. This suggests that the equilibrium temperature, was primarily determined by journal bearing ran 10-15°F warmer than one that had 'bedded in' – a difference larger than those measured between the long and the short axleboxes. With newly fitted counter bored boxes the LMS recorded temperatures as high as 176°F but these fell to around 130°F once they bedded themselves, while according to Mr K Cook, tests conducted by the Great Western demonstrated that axleboxes finished by its lapping methods ran 10°F cooler, than did those finished by other techniques.

Mr Renwick's paper considered the reliability of an axlebox depended on three factors:-

(a) The use of a suitable bearing material

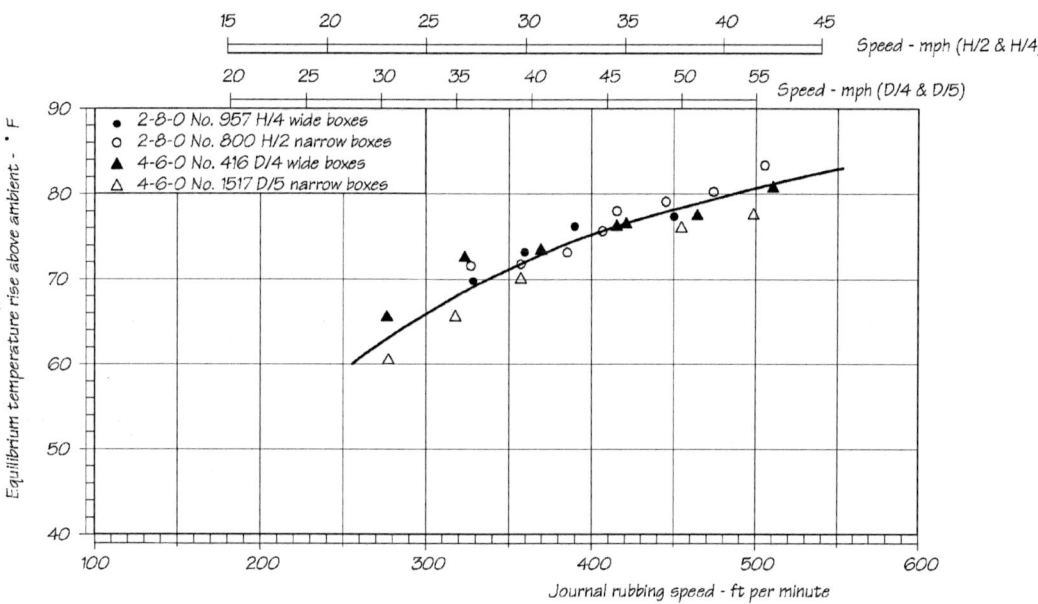

Diagram exploring the relationship between bearing area and thus *P* lbs/sq in and running temperature - GIP dynamometer car report No. 19A, 1936. Engines used BESA 4-6-0 passenger and 2-8-0 goods with mineral oil lubricated axleboxes - 8 ins dia journals but with solid bronze bearings 13½ ins in length in place of the standard 9 ins. These trials suggest that increasing the bearing length had no discernible effect on running temperature. With the particular oil used, the equilibrium temperatures varied from 65°F above ambient at journal rubbing speed of 300ft/min *i.e.* equivalent to 25 and 33 mph for the goods and passenger engines respectively, to about 85°F at the highest rubbing speed of 600ft/min *i.e.* 50 mph for the 2-8-0 and 66 mph for the 4-6-0.
Loose brass axleboxes ran approx 10°F hotter than solid bearings presumably a reflection of their inferior conduction. Mechanical lubrication reduced the running temperature by some 10°F. Consideration of the *ZN/P* relationship suggests the coefficient of friction, and thus the bearing temperature, should have reduced due to the enhanced bearing area. If however the oil supply was not increased commensurately in the larger bearings the relative oil film thickness would have reduced so the anticipated reduction in the coefficient of friction will not have taken place so maintaining a similar heat generation. This hypothesis appears to be borne out by the mechanically lubricated boxes running cooler.
Fig. 69 - Influence of speed on axlebox equilibrium temperature - GIP Railway, India

velocity and the lubricant, with bearing pressure having less impact, or perhaps its influence was being masked by the other factors. Incidentally, loose brass boxes were reported as running some 10°F warmer than solid axleboxes.

The effect of reducing the height of the asperities was also demonstrated, thus, a newly metalled correctly applied.

(b) The use of a suitable grade of lubricant.

(c) The maintenance of an adequate film of lubricant of sufficient 'strength' between the bearing and the journal.

Reducing the rate of wear in an axlebox *i.e.* extending its effective life was influenced by the following:-

(a) The provision of adequate bearing surface area to reduce bearing load.

(b) The exclusion of all dirt and extraneous matter likely to cause abrasion of the bearing surfaces.

(c) The maintenance of an adequate film of lubricant of sufficient 'strength' between the bearing and the journal.

The energy loss Q in the bearing may be calculated from the product of the frictional force and the sliding velocity:-

$$Q = \frac{W \times \mu \times V}{778} \qquad (11)$$

where:-
Q = heat generated – BTU/min
W = load on the journal – lbs
μ = coefficient of friction
V = journal surface velocity – ft/min

This energy will result in a rise in bearing temperature, whose value is dependant upon how effectively the heat may be dissipated. The primary mechanism for a locomotive axlebox was forced convection accompanied by conduction, although when the engine was stationary the former reduced to the less effective natural convection. Both are complex mechanisms that traditionally were solved by applying dimensionless numbers to models, but any attempt was complicated by the coefficient of friction being so highly variable[64]. We may however adopt a simplified approach hence:-

$$Q = U \times A \times (\theta b - \theta a) \qquad (12)$$

where:-
Q = heat dissipated – BTU/min
U = overall heat transfer coefficient
– BTU/sq ft/hr per °F
A = outer surface area of axlebox
– sq ft
θb = bearing temperature – °F
θa = ambient temperature – °F

For a stable temperature to be obtained, the heat generated must equal that convected away:-

$$Q = \frac{W \times \mu \times V}{778} = \frac{U \times A \times (\theta b - \theta a)}{60} \qquad (13)$$

Simplifying and rearranging:-

$$\theta b = \frac{W \times \mu \times V}{12.97 \times U \times A} + \theta a \qquad (14)$$

Examination of the wear equation and the bearing temperature relationship *(10)* and *(11)*, reveals that the product of pressure and velocity appear in both – or would if bearing load was expressed as the product of pressure and bearing area. It was this observation that prompted the *PV* factor referred to earlier in connexion with bearing materials.

Bearing Loads

In the case of carrying wheels, the bearing load (lbs/sq in) was usually obtained by simply dividing one-half the axle load by the projected area of the bearing (length × width). Although to be strictly correct, an allowance ought to be made for the width of the bearing being normally only around two-thirds the diameter of the journal. Similarly an allowance should also be made for the presence of the fillet radii at the ends of the bearing, but neither of these corrections was normally carried out.

However, such simple calculations could not be applied to the driving and coupled axleboxes, as the maximum pressure was not only greater but also its line of action no longer acted vertically downwards for it was modified by the magnitude and lines of action of the other forces acting on the box – of which there were at least five:-

(a) the unidirectional vertical spring load

(b) the horizontal or nearly horizontal fore and aft braking force

(c) the horizontal force arising from the generation of tractive effort at the wheel tread

(d) the horizontal or nearly horizontal force due to piston load acting on the connecting rod, or in the case of coupled axles the resultant of the coupling and connecting rod forces

(e) the lateral horizontal forces due to flange pressure or frictional resistance at the tread of wheel to movement across the rail.

---

[64] In bearings provided with forced circulation of the oil, such as those fitted to steam turbines, it was possible to ensure that bearing temperatures did not exceed the safe operating temperature of the white metal by providing a high enough flow of oil through the bearing, which then served as a coolant as well as a lubricant. Indeed in such applications, the heat generated by the friction in the bearing was tiny compared to the heat that the oil removed from the journal through conduction, occasioned by the highly superheated steam passing through the turbine thereby heating the rotor.

Axleboxes, Bearing Metals and Lubricants

Example of the calculated component curves resulting in the combined horizontal forces acting on a locomotive axlebox - right hand box engine running at 15mph, two inside cylinders, coupling rod cranks at 180° to adjacent connecting rod, right-hand crank lead

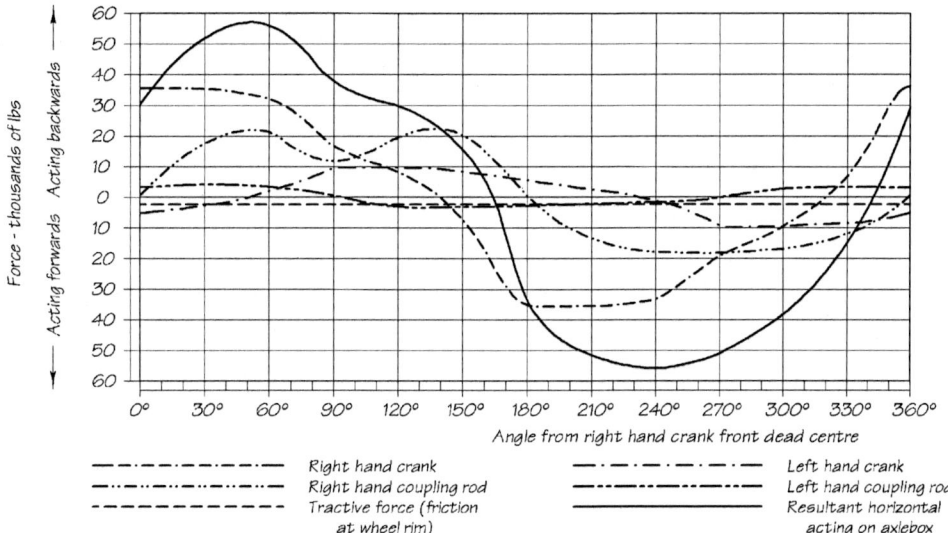

— — — — — Right hand crank
— ·· — ·· — Right hand coupling rod
— — — — — Tractive force (friction at wheel rim)

— · — · — · — Left hand crank
— ··· — ··· — Left hand coupling rod
———————— Resultant horizontal acting on axlebox

Fig. 70 - Calculated individual component forces acting on a locomotive axlebox

Calculated horizontal forces acting on the right hand axlebox cut-off 30% and engine running at 15 mph - right hand crank leads

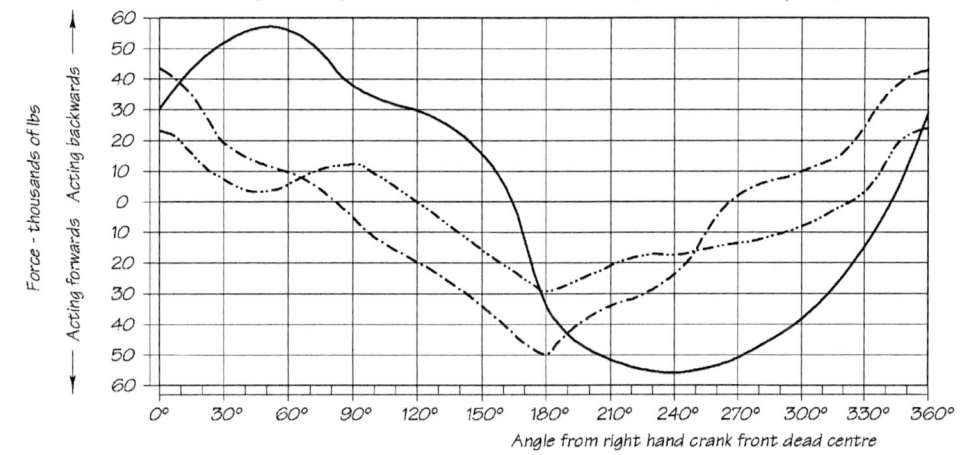

Calculated horizontal forces acting on the left hand axlebox cut-off 30% and engine running at 15 mph - right hand crank leads

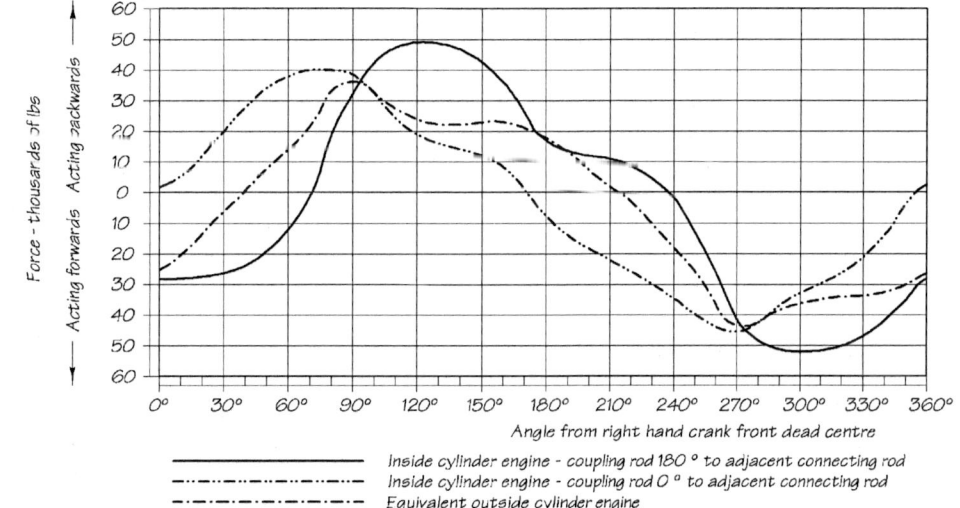

———————— Inside cylinder engine - coupling rod 180° to adjacent connecting rod
— ·· — ·· — Inside cylinder engine - coupling rod 0° to adjacent connecting rod
— · — · — · — Equivalent outside cylinder engine

Fig. 71 - Calculated resultant horizontal forces acting on locomotive axleboxes

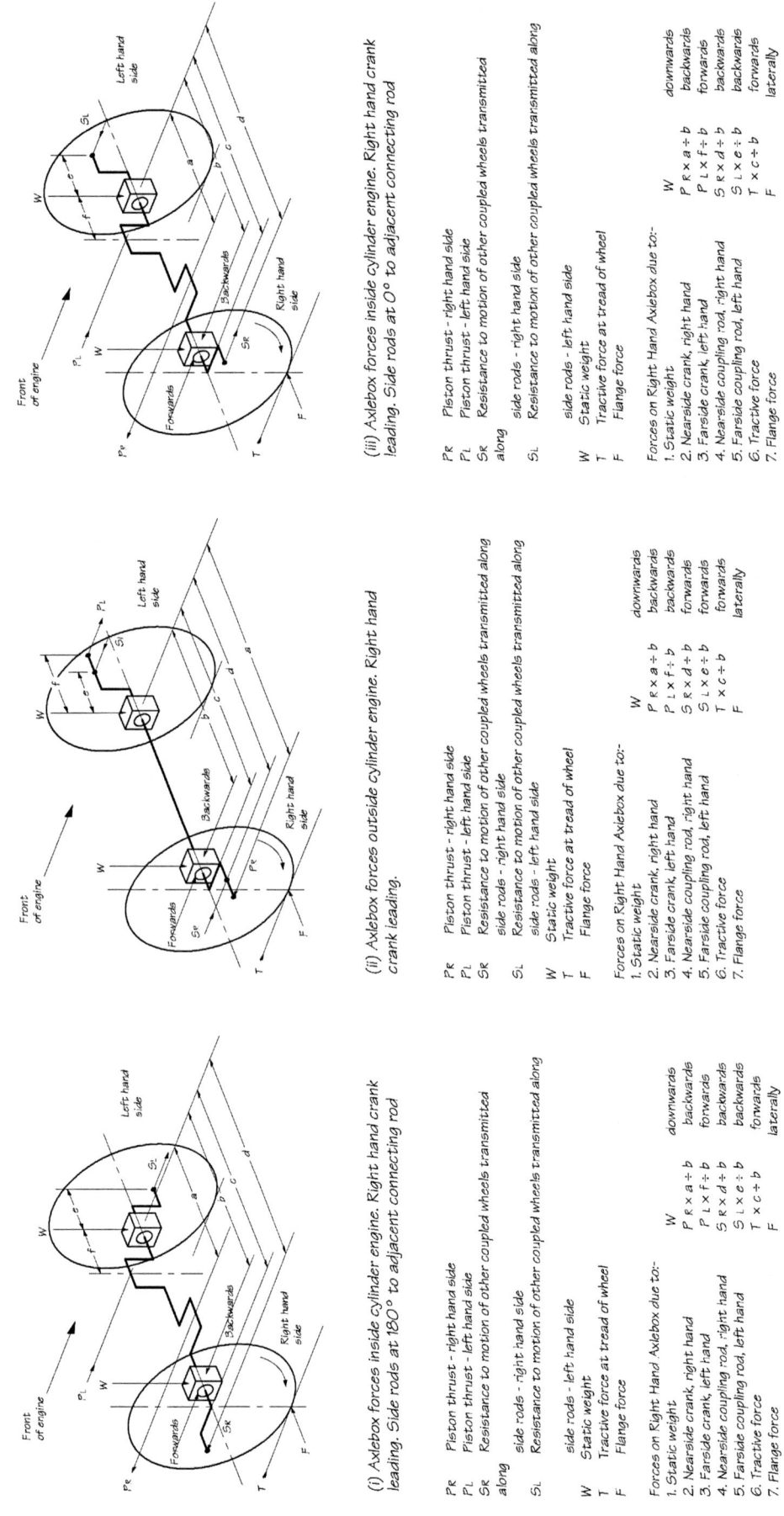

Fig. 64 - Calculation of individual forces acting on an axlebox

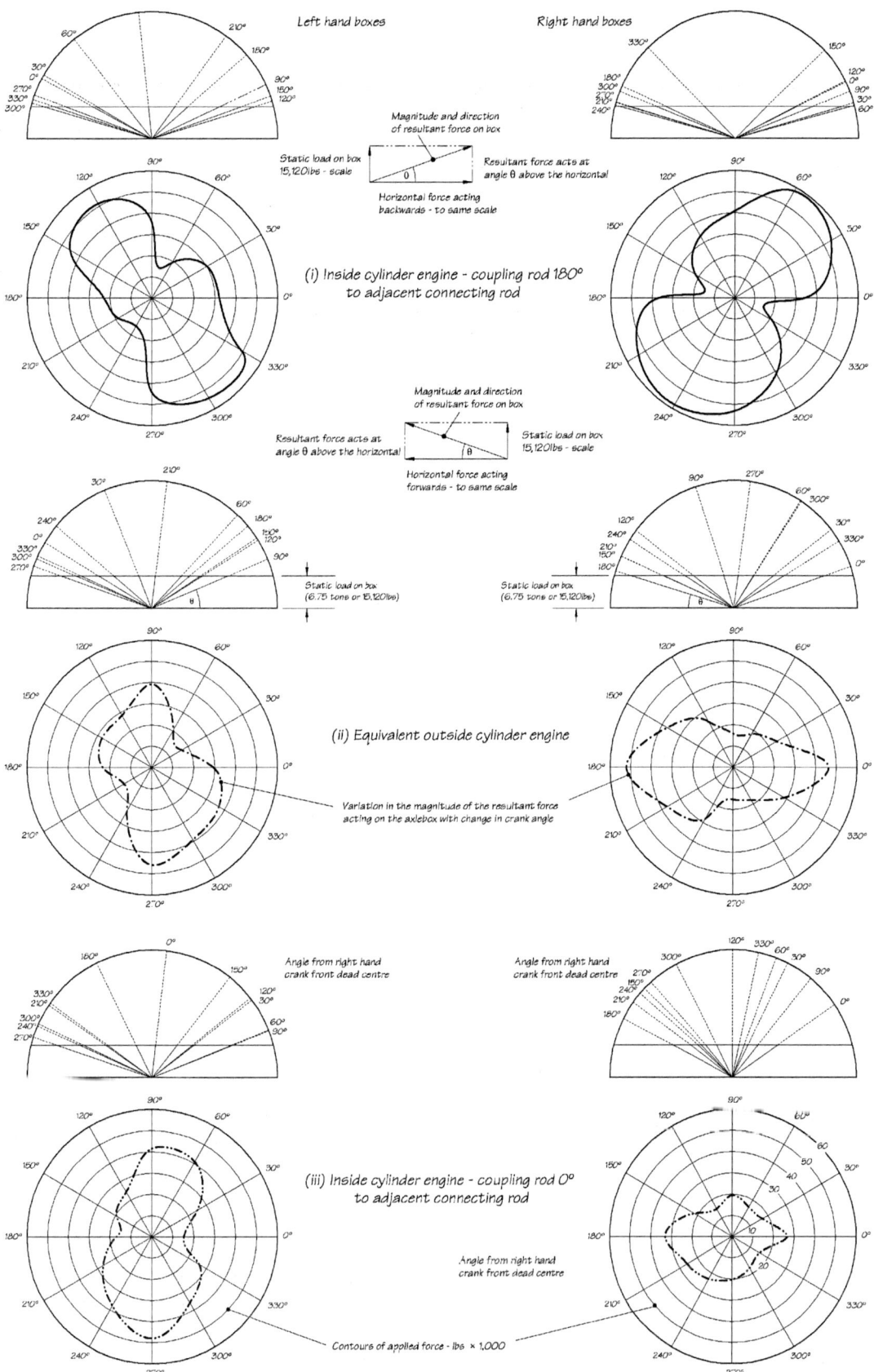

Fig. 73 - Vector and polar diagrams of the forces acting on axleboxes at 15 mph

Braking forces (b) will not be considered any further as their magnitude was less than the piston thrust while it was not normally present when steam was on. Flange forces (e) appeared whenever a locomotive negotiated a curve, or as it oscillated when running along straight track and were transferred indirectly via the wheel boss onto the face of the axlebox, subject to any minor flexing of the wheel centre relative to its rim. Theoretical calculation of flange forces was very much in its infancy during the time of the Big Four, although direct measurements had been made in India, France and elsewhere. These had recorded lateral forces of 15 tons acting on the leading coupled boxes of engines not provided with guiding wheels, or as with the 'Royal Scots' on classes provided with insufficient bogie side control. Conversely, on well-designed locomotives having guiding wheels fore and aft of the coupled wheels and adequate side control, the flange forces were more normally around 5 tons. Of these identified forces, (d) was normally by far the biggest, and had the greatest individual effect although it appears that designers, when scheming their axleboxes (and big-ends for that matter) did not always fully appreciate either its magnitude or line of action. In fact, the steam load was neither steady nor constant in its line of action, instead, it followed a more or less repetitive albeit highly variable cycle. Subsequently analysis techniques were developed for internal combustion engines which converted the variable magnitude and direction loads into an equivalent stationary bearing load, although this was all too late for steam locomotives.

Piston thrusts cannot be readily quantified without a considerable amount of repetitive calculation, because their effect varied with the instantaneous steam pressure in the cylinder. They were further modified by cut-off, engine speed and inertia effects, but as the driving axleboxes were the most heavily loaded Mr Cox had them analysed, in a simplified form by Mr R G Jarvis[65], for his axlebox paper.

A 'Big Goods' 0-6-0 served as the example – cylinders 20ins diameter by 26ins stroke, boiler pressure 175lbs/sq in, coupled wheels 5ft – 3ins, axleboxes 8½ins diameter by 8 1/8ins long, right hand crank leading with the engine running at 15 miles per hour cutting-off at 30 per cent. Three sets of calculations were performed, the first being for the engine as it existed, the second set was a hypothetical equivalent, identical in all dimensions save that it was provided with outside-cylinders, while the third was as if the Class 4 had had its cranks repositioned *à le Stroudley*. For speed and simplicity, this analysis made a number of assumptions so these findings should be considered as being indicative rather than definitive:-

(i) the piston thrusts acted horizontally through the centre line of the axlebox

(ii) the driving wheels could absorb torque at the maximum value of their adhesion

(iii) when calculating the effect of coupling and connecting rod forces on the selected axlebox, the box on the opposite side of the engine was considered as the fulcrum about which they acted

(iv) any effects due to working clearances and those due to wear which could cause impact forces were disregarded

(v) no reference was made to the inertia forces present in the rods and crank axle - their effects were ignored as the speed was low

Figure 70 records, for one complete revolution of the crank, the magnitude and direction of the different individual horizontal forces acting, on the right hand driving axlebox of the notional Class 4 0-6-0. The thick line is the nett horizontal force after all the individual components have been combined together. The corresponding nett horizontal forces for the left-hand and right-hand boxes for this engine, the hypothetical outside cylinder equivalent and a 'Big Goods' reset with zero angle between the adjacent inside and outside cranks are compared in figure 71.

Figure 72 summarizes the lines of action for the three cases and something of how the original I Loco E traces were obtained, through taking moments. Appearing in figure 73 are vector and polar diagrams illustrating the lines of action of the

---

[65] Mr J E Chacksfield *Ron Jarvis from Midland Compound to the HST* Oakwood Press Usk 2004 p67.

"Despite the urgency of the war, there were occasional times of slackness, and Ron filled in his time by embarking on an analysis of the forces acting on the driving axle-boxes of locomotives having two inside cylinders. This showed that, on one side of the engine, a very large horizontal force was created on the bearing, leaving the bearing prone to running hot.

...Further analysis showed that with locomotives having their adjacent inside cranks and outside coupling rod pins in phase, rather than the usual 180 degrees, the force on the axleboxes were much reduced."

In the acknowledgements, Mr Cox thanked Ron Jones for his "preparation of the diagrams and tables in the section on bearing pressures".

resultant force – the horizontal force acting on each box combined with the constant vertical spring load – for one revolution of the crank. Both forms of diagram are conveying the same information, but the vector diagram perhaps is better at shewing the narrow range of angles through which the resultant forces acted on the box, while the polar diagram enables their magnitude to be appreciated at each angle. In all of these figures, the crank angles (left and right) are measured taking the right hand crank front dead centre as 0°.

Comparing these diagrams reveals that with the conventional 180° crank disposition between adjacent inside and outside cranks used on inside cylinder engines, there is a noticeably greater loading on its driving boxes than with either of the other two arrangements. Figures 73 demonstrates the angle at which the resultant force (or load line) acted not only varied throughout each revolution, but also its intensity. In the case of inside cylinders, the resultant remained for nearly one-half of a revolution within 30° above a horizontal centre line drawn through the axlebox, before it rapidly reversed to produce a similar loading pattern within a similarly restricted angle on the opposite side of the box. Thus, under the selected conditions, which represented heavy 'slogging', the axlebox was almost continuously loaded near the ends of the bearing surface, a portion of its anatomy not well disposed to receive it, only momentarily in each revolution was it loaded on its vertical centre line.

Incidentally, the inequality in the loading between left hand and right hand axleboxes in all three cases was inevitable because the cranks in a two-cylinder engine were set at 90° to one another; while the crank lead – right-hand in this instance – determined on which side the boxes would be more heavily loaded. Only through setting the cranks at 180°, an impractical arrangement in a two-cylinder locomotive, could this inequality be avoided.

These diagrams demonstrate that the axlebox loadings were not only very variable but also they could attain high values. Furthermore they also demonstrate that it is inherent in the nature of a conventionally arranged inside cylinder engine for it to be heavier on its axleboxes than the equivalent outside cylinder one. In an inside cylinder engine, with a conventional 180° adjacent crank setting, nearly all of the piston load, is transmitted through the crank-axle boxes no matter how many coupled wheels are present. By contrast in the case of the outside cylinder engine, a portion of the piston load is distributed directly along the coupling rods to the coupled wheels relieving the driving axleboxes of that fraction, while making the bearing loads somewhat more equitable[66]. In addition, this advantage favouring the outside cylinder engine was further increased if the opportunity was taken in the absence of a crank-axle to fit longer bearings. However, shewn in the diagrams is another way of avoiding heavy loading on the driving axleboxes of an inside cylinder engine and that was by placing the coupling rod crank pins on the same centres as the adjacent inside cranks[67]:-

"There has been, from the earliest history of the locomotive, a diversity of opinion as to the relative merits of outside- as compared with inside-cylinder engines, many advantages being peculiar to each system. The Author has endeavoured to combine the best points of the two, having had a long experience with both. He observed that the axle-boxes, brasses, horn-blocks, and side-rods of the outside-cylinder engine would endure at least twice as long as those of an equally well made inside-cylinder engine; this he accounted for by the fact that, whereas in the former all the rods and strains were in account, those of the latter were in opposition. He therefore placed the outside crank-pin on the same side of the axle as the inside crank; the result as to durability being superior to that obtained in an outside-cylinder engine, by reason that the strain is divided between the frames, whilst the latter has a considerable overhang, which increases the load upon the axle-box above that given by the piston."

In effect, William Stroudley introduced into an inside-cylinder engine, the same relative disposition of cranks and coupling rods inherent in an outside-cylinder machine. Or, as he explained[68]

---

66 These calculations assume each coupled wheel contributed equally towards the total tractive effort exerted by the engine. André Chapelon thought this was not so, in which case the load on the driving boxes of an outside cylinder engine will have been higher than these sums suggest. His opinion is supported by stress readings taken in coupling rods and the wear comparison made earlier between the Standard Class 4 and the Standard Class 8.

67 Mr W Stroudley *The Construction of Locomotive Engines, with some Results of the Working of those on the London, Brighton, and South Coast Railway* ICE Paper N° 2027 p77.
Incidentally Mr D K Clark quoted Mr Stroudley:-

" ...and when the stress of the steam is applied to the inner crank-pin, the outer crank-pin takes its share of the reaction, leaving but little for the axle-boxes to carry except the first thrust when on the centre. The axle-boxes and brasses of these engines run for many years without being adjusted, and a broken inside or outside rod is unknown."

68 Ibid pp94-5.

A Defence of the Midland/LMS Class 4 0-6-0

it when comparing his arrangement with the normal one of the inner and outer cranks disposed at 180° to one another:-

"When the thrust of the connecting-rod is driving the crank-shaft in a backward direction the axle is forced to the back side of the axle-box, and the axle-box to the back face of the horn-block; but, before assistance can be obtained from the outside rod on that side of the engine in propelling the train, the latter must be put in tension; and before this can take place the whole of the distance which the crank-shaft is moved backwards, and the whole of the play of the side-rod, brasses, &c., must be taken up by the slipping of the wheels. This causes great wear and tear of the crank-pins, and heavy strain on the connecting-rods, which do their work by a series of blows instead of taking it up smoothly, as when the cranks are placed both on the same side of the axle, which has been the author's practice since 1866."

Although adopting zero angle between the inside and outside crank ensured the axlebox loadings become more reminiscent of those pertaining to an outside cylinder engine, there were several objections, which most engineers appear to have considered reason enough for not adopting the practice. There was a significant increase in the inequality of loading of the axleboxes on the opposite sides of the engine, a situation, which is clearly shewn in figure 73. The bending moment in the crank axle was thereby increased, and this in turn increased the stress in that item, perhaps by as much as one-half. By the nineteen twenties and 'thirties, crank axles were normally built-up so this objection possibly had less standing, but in the days of solid crank axles, which until comparatively recently had commonly run quite limited mileage before fatigue cracks appeared, this was a very real objection. Re-metalling boxes was a lot cheaper than supplying replacement crank axles. The biggest objection however was the system demanded significantly larger balance weights in the driving wheels as with the normal arrangement the big-end portion of the connecting rod partially balanced the weight of the coupling rod. Mr Cox stated this increase might be 800lbs in a large 0-6-0, while all of it

Fig. 74 - Nº 44578 built at Derby in 1939 demonstrates that it has its cranks positioned *à le Stroudley*, and it is believed to be left-hand crank lead. It also exhibits changes instigated by William Stanier such as plain coupling rods, triangular section wheel rims, no tail rods and his version of a flat-sided 3,500 gallons tender.

represented unsprung[69] weight – a figure that was

Interestingly, Robert Billington, who for four years previously was Assistant to Mr Stroudley in charge of design and construction of locomotives and rolling stock and presumably familiar with this crank disposition, was unable (or maybe never tried) to influence Mr Johnson into adopting it when he joined the Midland as Chief Draughtsman in 1874. Certainly however, when he returned south after fifteen years to succeed his former boss, he did not adopt Bill Stroudley's crank setting on *his* engines.

[69] In isolated cases, such large weights could lead to another problem because a two-cylinder engine cannot be perfectly balanced. Thus, when a two-cylinder engine moved, it promoted a fore-and-aft fluctuating force, whose magnitude was a function of engine weight and the residual unbalanced reciprocating weight. Normally, disregarding any impact it might have on the locomotive this force had little other effect, however on occasions it could under certain conditions set up resonance within the drawhook springs, when it then subjected the passengers to an unpleasant forwards and backwards rapid jerking action. The effect was experienced by the Southern Railway when it rebuilt eleven ex-LB&SC class E1 0-6-0 tanks into 0-6-2Ts by giving them spare class N 2-6-0 pony trucks before it transferred them to the West Country. One of their duties was to haul a sharply timed train, which included through coaches of the Atlantic Coast Express, and it was found that a certain speed an unpleasant longitudinal movement was established. It was cured by setting the cranks the conventional 180° and reducing the size of the balance weights. The re-balanced Great Western 56xx 0-6-2Ts, when used on passenger trains, seem to have suffered from this

perhaps rather more than an estimate. The late Dennis Monk advised that it was Ron Jarvis who suggested that the LMS Standard Classes 4 and 7 might be improved if they had their cranks repositioned. In due course at least four engines (probably more judging from photographs) from the last batches of 'Big Goods' built between 1937 and 1940 were given left-hand crank lead and fitted with their inside and outside cranks positioned *á le Stroudley*. The last of these engines had appeared four years *before* Mr Cox's axlebox paper, yet he made no reference to their existence. No report seems to have survived regarding the success or otherwise of this modification. Presumably, this crank resetting had been made with the knowledge and agreement of Tom Coleman the Chief Locomotive Draughtsman. Certainly, he was very much in favour of the traditional inside cylinder six-coupled engine, which was in direct contrast to the prejudice towards such engines that undoubtedly existed amongst *some* members of Sir William's team. Perhaps equally interestingly is that this crank modification was extensively and retrospectively applied by Swindon to encompass most of the 200 examples of the 56xx class 0-6-2Ts built by Charles Collet between 1924 and 1928 – the converted engines may be readily identified by the very large balance weights in the driving wheels. This class had cylinders 18ins diameter, 8ins diameter short lap piston valves (1 1/8in) and a working pressure of 200lbs/sq in, delivered a maximum piston thrust of 50,894lbs. The crank repositioning was simply to reduce the loading and resulting wear[70] on the axleboxes despite the latter having been designed by the Great Western!

"With their modern ports and valve gear *(sic)*, they had a good turn of speed for 4ft 7in driving wheels, and they were powerful, with a tractive effort of nearly 26,000lb. This last was a source of trouble. As so often happened with high powered inside-cylinder engines (the LNER J39 0-6-0s and the LMS Class 7F 0-8-0s were other examples), the driving axleboxes wore very rapidly. There were two reasons why this was inevitable. The bearings of the outside-cylinder GWR engines were 10in long. On the 56xx class there was only room for 7in between the wheel and the crank web. Not only were the bearings little more than half the area, but with inside and outside cranks set at 180° the fore-and-aft thrust on the axleboxes is greatly increased.

(*vide Swindon Apprentice* Mr A E Durrant Runpast Publishing Cheltenham 1989 p125).

70 Rev J C Gibson *Great Western Locomotive Design* David & Charles Newton Abbot 1984 pp136-7.

Connecting and coupling rods are pulling in opposite directions, and all the force of this reversal has to be taken by the driving axleboxes, which are well suited to cope with vertical loads, but very ill-adapted to near-horizontal thrusts.

In an attempt to reduce this heavy wear, which greatly reduced the mileage run between shoppings and so was very costly, a number of the class were after a time altered to have the Stroudley arrangement of cranks. In this the inside and outside cranks are in phase instead of opposite each other. It reduces the thrust by about half and so lessens wear, but since both cranks, big-end and connecting rod are on the same side, instead of largely balancing out, the balance weights have to be so large that they are difficult to accommodate in small wheels. They add very considerably to an already heavy axle load, and this is made more serious by the fact that this extra weight is unsprung."

The Great Western had adopted that crank arrangement briefly some years earlier in a few classes built during the tenure of Mr Dean with the intention of extending axlebox life. It was also present on all bar the first examples of Stephen Holden's GER class S69 4-6-0, perhaps better known as the class B12 – Holden *père* had been William Dean's Works Manager at Swindon before his move to Stratford.

Lubricating Oils

Axlebox performance was *very* dependant on the correct choice of lubricant, for the latter had to possess special properties, if the bearings were to enjoy a reasonable life or freedom from heating under the boundary and mixed-film regimes in which they operated. Consequently, perhaps the three most important properties that had to be correct in an axlebox lubricant were oiliness, film strength and viscosity.

Within the boundary region, where the thickness of the oil film extant between the bearing surfaces assumed molecular dimensions oiliness was the pre-eminent property, far more so than viscosity, which under pure boundary conditions has little or no benefit on bearing performance. As operation entered the mixed-film region, oiliness slowly reduced in importance with the rise in ZN/P so that by the transition point it had little or no effect. In contrast, the importance of viscosity increased so by the transition point it had become the dominant property since the work of shearing a hydrodynamically lubricated oil film was a function of the viscosity. Thus, depending on towards which end of the mixed-film zone the locomotive habitually spent the majority of its operating time determined on whether oiliness was simply important or absolutely vital.

Prior to the appearance of mineral oils during the second half of the nineteenth century, vegetable oils such as olive, rape, coconut and castor oils, and animal oils which included tallow, lard, neat's-foot, sperm and other cetacean-based oils had all been extensively used as lubricants. These excellent albeit expensive lubricants are known as fixed oils or fatty oils, because they needed no distillation to create them, indeed if subjected to too much heat they decompose. A common characteristic is that they contain a free fatty acid, which incidentally could cause corrosion especially if exposed to heat and water *viz.* tallow and cast iron cylinders. They also suffer from the disadvantage of readily oxidizing, which when combined with the effects of the fatty acids they contain, results in substantial increase in viscosity and the formation of gums and further acids. This makes them unsuitable for circulated or closed lubrication systems. However, one great advantage of these animal and vegetable derived lubricants is that their fatty acids react with metal surfaces, in the presence of atmospheric air and moisture, to form 'soap' layers that tenaciously adhere to clean metal surfaces. Amongst these fatty acids are polar molecules, of which the carboxyl groups are perhaps the most important, which orientate themselves into an upright position in a manner similar to the pile of a carpet as illustrated in figure 75. This way they offer solid films of low shear strength resistance as the surface asperities pass over them, while also serving to retain the oil so preventing a large proportion of the metal-to-metal contact and wear. The load applied to the bearing tends to squeeze out all the lubricant save that held by adsorption onto the metal surfaces. This microscopic layer of lubricant thus serves as the only source of lubrication until time and speed enabled some limited hydrodynamic action to develop within the mixed-film region.

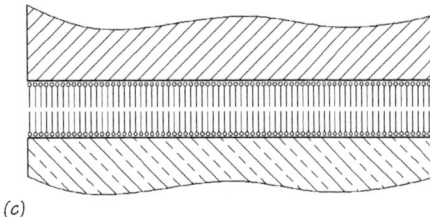

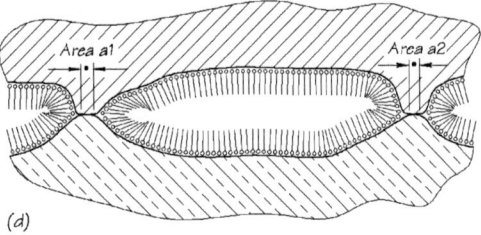

The molecules of mineral oils are chiefly composed of long chain compounds of saturated hydrocarbons such as the paraffin series, which is depicted in a simplified form as the top diagram *(a)*.

Conversely, although the molecules of fatty acids are also long chain compounds, they possess a carboxyl group giving them a polar head *(b)*. The polar head represents the 'active end' of the molecule and adheres to the metal surfaces with sufficient strength to avoid being torn off during the rubbing contact. This chemical reaction produces a metallic soap film which chemically bonds to the metal and incidentally possesses a higher melting point than the corresponding fatty acid. The metals that fatty acids react with in this way include many of those commonly used in locomotive axleboxes *e.g.* copper, tin, lead, zinc *etc.*

Diagram *(c)* is an idealized representation of boundary lubrication with the polar molecules aligned at 90° to the surfaces of the bearing and journal thereby forming a low resistance shear film when sliding or rotation occurs.

The lowest diagram *(d)* attempts to give a more realistic situation where the surfaces are not perfect over the projected bearing area A (*i.e.* length × width). The lubricant film supports most of the load, but over a small fraction of A metallic junctions are formed where the lubricant film is punctured. In total these equal the sum of all the individual contact areas *i.e.* $\sum(a1 + a2 + ...)$, which in turn can be expressed as xA, where x is the fraction of area A over which metallic junctions are formed.

The total frictional force F of the bearing may therefore be expressed as comprising the sum of two terms:-

(i) the force $SmxA$ required to shear the metal junctions where and Sm is the shear strength of the metal

(ii) the force to shear the lubrication film $Sl(1 - x)A$ where Sl is the shear strength of the lubricant. Thus the friction is given by:-

$$F = A[Smx + (1 - x)Sl]$$

In good boundary lubricants xA is very small keeping the friction low; the metallic junctions therefore contribute little to the friction but are responsible for the wear.

Fig. 75 - The mechanism of boundary lubrication

In due course mineral lubricating oils, distilled from petroleum feedstock became the preferred lubricant, not least because they were cheaper, more resistant to oxidation at normal and elevated temperatures and readily available in a wide range of viscosities; they were not however ideal axlebox lubricants. Straight mineral oils do not usually possess the polar molecules necessary for successful boundary lubricants, so they were very poor at preventing scuffing and seizure, but if a quantity of fixed oil was added, then the necessary oiliness might be imbued into the mineral base forming what are known as compounded oils. Given an *appropriate* mineral oil base compounded oils, could make *very* successful axlebox lubricants, for in forming the tangible adsorbed soap layer, the fatty acid of the fixed oil gave the mineral oil extra 'oiliness' thereby giving the oil a lower coefficient of friction compared to a straight mineral oil of the same viscosity. The oiliness of a lubricating oil, may be defined numerically as the reciprocal of the coefficient of friction, under boundary lubrication conditions, for a particular combination of bearing metals and lubricant. The coefficient of friction of an oil in contact with metallic surfaces was determined in a test instrument[71] by measuring the force in pounds that would just cause a heavy block of metal to slide over a metallic horizontal plane when lubricated with a film of the test oil. The coefficient of friction, μ is the ratio of the force in pounds to the weight of the block in pounds; thus if the block weighed 10lb and a force equal to a weight of 2lb will just cause the block to slide horizontally, then:-

$$\mu = 2 \div 10 = 0.2$$

Compounded oils possess a higher degree of oiliness than mineral oils, as may be seen in the following table comparing the coefficients of static friction in a test instrument lubricated by a mineral oil before and after the addition of a fatty acid.

Oil	Coefficient of friction - μ	Oiliness - $(1 \div \mu)$
Straight mineral oil	0.17	5.9
Mineral oil plus 1% oleic acid	0.10	10.0

In this example, a very small quantity of fatty acid has been introduced rather than a larger quantity of a fixed oil to effect a similar improvement in oiliness. This was because shortly after the Kaiser's War it was found that a small amount of a free fatty acid, sufficient to provide 1-2 per cent fatty acid content in the mineral oil could be substituted for a larger quantity of a fixed oil. Just prior to the Grouping, the Midland Railway's Chief Chemist Mr Archbutt, reported[72] that some experiments had been conducted using such a compounded oil for trial in the company's locomotive and carriage axleboxes, with 'quite successful' results. As events were to prove, this qualified endorsement was significant, as superior oiliness is not the only desirable property needed in an axlebox lubricant. Incidentally, as well as being crucial at reducing friction and wear under boundary conditions, compounded oils also exhibited superior resistance from being displaced by water or steam.

For a long time it was though the slight tool marking in the final finish of the bearing left for example by hand scraping were beneficial acting as 'reservoirs' thereby retaining the oil. The realization that in boundary lubrication the adsorbed layer of lubricant existed as a *continuous film* over each metal surface subsequently disproved this theory. Since this film separating the sliding surfaces of journal and bearing, was perhaps only one or two molecules thick, occasional contact would occur whenever the film was penetrated by asperities, hence the finish of journals and bearings is extremely important under boundary conditions. This penetration also being that much more likely if the bearing had not 'bedded down' or if the load was too much for the carrying capacity of the lubricant. Thus, while the

---

71 Mountford Deeley invented an adsorbed film testing machine which was later made available commercially, prior to his becoming a member of the Lubricants and Lubrication Inquiry Committee in 1917, having been appointed by the department of Scientific and Industrial Research. This hand-driven machine measured the friction of lubricated surfaces under conditions when the 'oiliness' of the lubricant was its most important property. In the machine, three flat-ended metal studs or pegs, 5/32ins diameter fitted symmetrically as feet to a metal disk approximately 3ins in diameter, rested upon another metal disk of the same diameter, which was slowly rotated. The upper disk was weighted to represent different loads and via suitable gearing and linkage, a reading was presented on a scale from which the friction coefficient could be calculated. Using this instrument, he made a number of experiments to establish the forces required to cause lubricated surfaces to slip, discovering that the force varied not only with the lubricant, but also with the metals in use, concluding that oiliness is strictly an effect produced by the lubricant upon the surfaces, than a property of the lubricant as a liquid. Such was his understanding of the subject, this very clever man was also one of the first to appreciate that the lubricant formed a chemical layer as it bonded with the surface of the bearing surface.

72 Mr L Archbutt *Lubrication and Lubricants* I Loco E Paper 101 March 1921 p431.

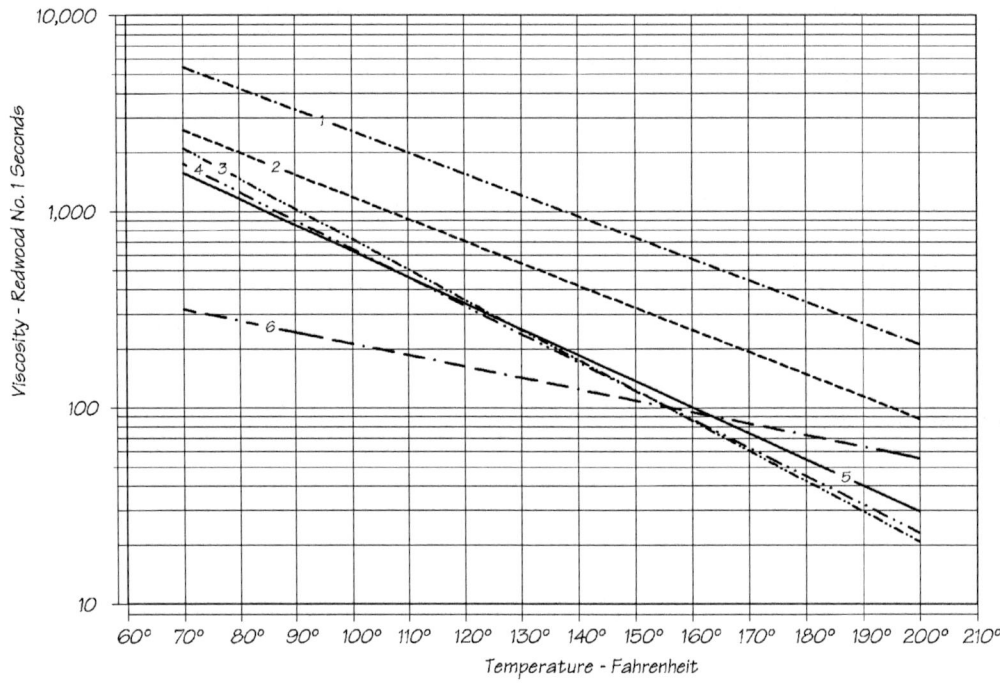

1 - BR specification superheater oil (97% mineral oil & 3% acidless tallow oil)
2 - Castor oil
3 - LMS specification T general axlebox oil (90% dark mineral oil & 10% rape oil)
4 - LMS specification T general axlebox oil (98½% dark mineral oil & 1½% FFA)
5 - LNER specification W axlebox oil (85% dark mineral oil & 15% rape oil)
6 - Rape oil

The effect of compounding a mineral oil with rape was also to improve the viscosity - temperature relationship. For oils having the same base, the film strength rises with increases in viscosity.

Fig. 76 - Temperature - viscosity relationship

methods used for finishing the bearing surfaces varied from company to company, hand scraping was largely abandoned by the Big Four being replaced by the adoption of superior finishes obtained by more accurate machining techniques.

These improvements in finishing techniques were important for they greatly reduced the asperity contact and thus the operating temperature of the bearing, particularly during the vulnerable bedding-in period. The adsorbed layer formed by the fatty acids was sensitive to surface temperature with the beneficial effect being destroyed should the bearing surfaces exceed 250-300°F. With some fatty acids the adverse effect commenced at transition temperatures as low as 220-230°F when the layers began to become desorbed resulting in a loss of oiliness accompanied by a rise in the coefficient of friction and wear. The effect was reversible, and on cooling the surfaces, the friction fell to its original low value and the surface damage could be slight. If however too high a temperature was attained, or if it was prolonged then irreversible effects could result largely through oxidation. One of the reasons for the popularity of rape oil as a compounding agent was that it withstood a higher temperature before breakdown than other fixed oils so it became the preferred additive. Adding this vegetable oil, sometimes known as colza oil, also had the effect of reducing the viscosity of the mineral oil base at ambient temperatures while helping the oil to retain its viscosity at higher ones. It also improved the syphoning capability of worsted trimmings.

The viscosity of most lubricants falls with increasing temperature, which directly affects the load capacity of the axlebox, as may be seen from considering the *ZN/P* relationship within the mixed-film zone. A fall in viscosity demands a reduced load to maintain the same *ZN/P* value or else a reduced *ZN/P* for the same load. However, the heat generated in a bearing was a function of the load as well as the journal speed with the resulting temperature being acquired by the whole mass of the box. On reducing speed or stopping after a period of running, the oil could not immediately regain its earlier viscosity because of the heat retained in the axlebox. Under these circumstances, the axlebox had to rely to an even greater extent on its lubricant's boundary lubrication properties, although this situation could be eased by adopting a thicker oil, or at least one whose viscosity was less affected by temperature, since this ought to ensure a higher viscosity following a slackening in speed. However, an objection, should this velocity gain have been obtained through simply substituting a thicker oil, was that it increased the wastage of energy occurred in shearing the oil film. Since the whole of the energy loss in a bearing appeared as heat,

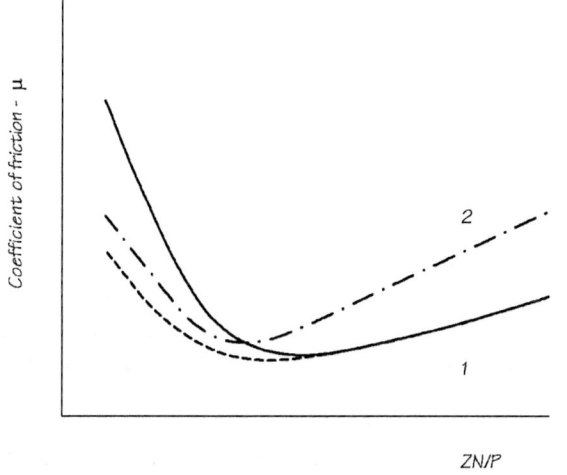

Fig. 77 - Influence of viscosity on bearing performance

axlebox temperature represented an indication of its magnitude. Conversely, if an oil of say twice the viscosity under identical conditions of speed and load, gave the same bearing temperature as a thinner oil, then for equality in the energy release, a higher coefficient of friction was present with the latter oil, which meant it was not viscous enough or deficient in oiliness. These relationships between friction and viscosity, are explored in figure 77, wherein curve *1* shews the conditions pertaining when a thin oil is used, while for curve *2* a thicker oil has been substituted. The broken line of curve *1* represents the conditions, if say a superior compounded oil having the same viscosity but possessing better adsorbent properties, is substituted. That the sustaining power of a bearing could be increased by using a more viscous lubricant, was referred to by Mr Cox[73] as for a while, the LMS used superheater oil as an axlebox lubricant:-

---

73 Mr E S Cox *Locomotive Axleboxes* I Loco E Paper N° 447 April 1944 p293.

"The use of superheater cylinder oil may seem an unusual approach. Although open to criticism as a bearing oil it was introduced on the Cl. 4 freight engine at a time *when heated bearings were becoming especially troublesome arising from a variety of factors* (my italics – APT). It was in fact successful in arresting the upward trend, although it produced no actual improvement. It could of course, only be used with a mechanical lubricator, and has now been superseded."

Would that Mr Cox had elaborated on the variety of factors - nevertheless here is confirmation from the arch-critic of the 'Big Goods' that bearing size was not the only cause of hot boxes!

The introduction of extreme pressure (EP) additives into lubricating oils in the early 1930s to combat the noticeable increases in horsepower and speed demanded of contemporary *internal* combustion engines stimulated interest in the film strength of lubricants. At the time, it was generally believed that the value obtained from a Timken[74] machine and the film strength of the lubricant were directly related, although this is not strictly true it will serve our purposes if we assume that it still is the case. Table XXXII lists Timken test results for some axlebox lubricants.

The breakdown loading can be related (approximately only) to the lever loading as the real grading was a calculation involving the width of the score on the test piece as well as the applied load. The entry identified by an asterisk was obtained using a different Timken machine operated under different conditions of speed *etc.* – this classified castor oil and blown rape oil as equivalent at 18.6lbs lever load, while mineral oils ranged from 9.6 to 11.6 according to viscosity. We may disregard this certain lack of quantitative agreement between the two machines by considering them qualitatively. Thus, the important thing to appreciate is that the vegetable oils

---

74 Between 1935 and 1972, the Timken Company produced a lubricant test machine that was used to determine the extreme pressure characteristics of lubricants, by establishing the film strength of an oil sample. It became, and remains an industry standard test, although its use has tended to decline. A ball race was mounted on a stub shaft that was rotated at a high speed. A small square steel test block mounted on a loaded lever arm was pressed against the contact area flooded with the lubricant under test. The lever arm was loaded up with individual 2lbs weights, until the oil film, was broken and the rotating race produced a score mark on the test block. The load bearing capacity of the lubricant in lbs/sq in was a function of the loading weight and the width of the score.

performed significantly better than the pure mineral oil, but the latter were much improved following their blending with rape oil. Test results for superheater cylinder oils obtained from the second Timken machine gave around 12lbs lever load. Possibly the most surprising result is that

Table XXXII – Timken Machine Oil Film Strength Results

Lubricant	Lever load (lbs)	Film rupture strength (lbs/sq in)
Castor oil	21	10,600
Rape oil (base)	20	10,000
Rape oil (blown)	25	10,000
Mineral oil (light)	~	~
Mineral oil (medium)	~	~
Mineral oil (heavy)	~	~
Mineral oil (heavy) and 10% rape oil (raw)	9	6,300
Mineral oil (heavy) and 20% rape oil (raw)	12	8,400
Mineral oil (heavy) and 10% rape oil (blown)	16	8,200
Mineral oil (heavy) and 20% rape oil (blown)	19	7,800
Mineral oil (medium) and 0.5% free fatty acid*	10.6	4,500

adding a small quantity of free fatty acid to mineral oils had little or no effect on raising the squeeze film strength over the straight mineral oil.

From these results we may see that adding a fixed oil such as rape *or* a free fatty acid to a mineral oil improved the oiliness of the lubricant and both lubricants were likely to give similar performances within the boundary region. Likewise, when the bearing was operating in the mixed-film region, if their viscosities and syphoning characteristics were similar, then the two oils would again return a similar performance. However, whenever the bearing operated under squeeze-film conditions, a situation experienced by driving wheel axleboxes the performance of the oil containing rape would be significantly better due to its higher film strength – hence we may appreciate Leonard Archbutt's caution. Superheater oil, having a higher viscosity, might have returned a useful gain in film strength over the normal mineral based lubricating oil and could function well enough in the mixed-film zone. However, being commonly only a lightly compounded oil[75], it will have been less effective under boundary conditions than a more appropriate mineral oil base containing say 10 per cent of rape oil. That the proportion of rape oil to mineral oil could have a significant impact on bearing performance is confirmed by Oliver Bulleid[76] when he referred to the effectiveness of vegetable oils in mitigating trouble from hot boxes:-

"The older members in particular would remember that they used to use oils containing up to 75 per cent. of rape, and the lucky ones had 75 per cent. for the best engines, 25 per cent. for the others and none for the shunting engines. It was common knowledge in the old days that there were certain engines which would never run on the mineral oil, and some of the "bad ones" would have to be given what was called "express engine oil," with up to 75 per cent. of rape, if they were to run without overheating.

Later, the proportion of rape became reduced and reduced and reduced, until the chemists assured them that 10 per cent. – and he had even heard it said 5 per cent. – was the total quantity of rape in a good mineral oil which was any use. One of the companies recently reduced the percentage below 15, but were very glad to bring it back to 15 again."

Using this brief introduction into lubricating oil properties, we may now explore some of the oils used by the LMS. For convenience in operation, with the exception of cylinder lubrication, it was normal to use the same lubricating oil for the journals, motion and elsewhere. Mr Thorley reported in *Breath of Steam* that in 1930 for the locomotives at Wellingborough, principally goods and local passenger, the LMS provided two blends of lubricating oil for trimming fed bearings – 'Texas' and 'G' but he provided no other details as to their make up. Normal locomotive practice was to use different grades of oil for different classes of engine work, with the oil for express engines being of the highest quality containing a large proportion of fatty oil because their working conditions were considered stiffest. For ordinary engine use, less fatty oil was deemed sufficient whilst shunting engines received straight mineral oil. William Stanier reported the oils used by the 'Big Four'

---

75 Although black and opaque, superheater oils were very pure and chemically inert – LNER practice was to compound it with lard oil.

76 Mr O V S Bulleid contributing to the discussion following:-
Mr E S Cox *Locomotive Axleboxes* I Loco E Paper 447 April 1944 pp325-6.

companies differed in detail but all comprised a mineral oil selected on the basis of specific gravity, viscosity, pour point, asphaltic matter content and purity, blended with a quantity of refined rape oil. The fraction of fixed oil provided however differed considerably being influenced not only on the work demanded of the engine but also the preferences and experiences of the owning company.

Table XXXIII was included in a paper delivered by Sir William in 1937, and while it describes the practices of the Grouping companies, it is unfortunate that he elected not to identify them. Due to the trouble the LMS had experienced from hot boxes, it instigated an enquiry into their causes. This took the form of a statistical analysis – one of Mr Cox's favourite *modus operandi* for investigating the company's locomotive problems. It also featured to a large extent in the frame paper but it was not by any means a foolproof method. Nonetheless, from the former exercise, Sir William reported[77] in 1937, that the axlebox failures were caused by:-

    (i) defects in bearing

    (ii) other defects in locomotive causing abnormal conditions in bearing

    (iii) defects in lubricating arrangements

    (iv) presence of grit, water and inferior oil

From this analysis, the LMS further concluded that there was no evidence, despite (iv) above, that adopting a higher quality oil would effect any improvement. It is unclear for how long this view was current, but it was contrary to the general experience of engineers on other railways.

According to Mr Cox, the LMS had had a great deal of experience in the performance of the oils detailed in table XXXIV. The first of these was the general standard lubricating oil and had proved satisfactory with the outside cylinder classes and presumably those inside cylinder engines whose bearings were not too heavily loaded. This may have been the 'Texas' oil referred to by William Thorley; interestingly Mr Cox made no reference to the express engine oil (table XXXIII) containing the larger percentage of rape oil mentioned by William Stanier. The second version of the 'T' oil was introduced as a precautionary measure in case the supply of rape oil was interrupted during the Second World War. In it, the compounding medium was free fatty acid rather than rape oil. The main active chemical present in rape oil improving its oiliness was oleic acid, which could be derived from olein thereby making it a potential additive in its own right – and this may have been the free fatty acid used in the 'T' oil. During the Second World War, it was difficult to obtain sufficient rape oil – according to Mr Deeley the main growing areas were Belgium, France, India and China, all bar one in the Axis zone – so while this might have appeared a sensible precaution by the LMS, it was not that effective a substitute[78]:-

Table XXXIII – Percentage of Rape Oil Used in Railway Lubricating Oils

Class of work		Company			
		A	B	C	D
Express engines	per cent	25	20	15	5
Local passenger & goods engines	per cent	10	10	15	5
Shunting engines	per cent	~	~	15	5

Data taken from *Lubrication as Applied to Locomotive Journals* I Mech E October 1937.

"With mechanical lubrication it can be said to have given fairly satisfactory results but with trimming feed some adjustment in the number of trimmings was found desirable since this compound has not in general such good syphoning properties."

which again confirms the choice of the mineral oil base was equally important. In this instance once the beneficial influence 10 per cent rape oil made was removed, the original mineral oil base was not necessarily suitable. The next two entries were attempts by the LMS to improve the performance of the highest loaded boxes, where as Mr Cox stated, a greater film strength and oiliness were needed to withstand the pulsating and heavy loads on large inside cylinder engines. Comment has already been made to the use of superheater cylinder oil as a lubricant in the boxes of the Class 4 0-6-0 but it was superseded by the 'W' oil.

Under Mr J Hill, District Chemist of the LNER laboratory at Stratford, which specialized in

---

77 Sir William Stanier *Lubrication as Applied to Locomotive Journals* I Mech E 1937 p308.

78 Ibid p293.

lubrication, the company developed the 'W' oil at the request of Sir Nigel Gresley as the incidences of hot boxes under wartime conditions had risen to a disturbing figure. Mr Hill considered that hitherto the results of lubricating oil tests[79] had failed to establish a direct connexion between oiliness and the fixed oil content. Furthermore, when engineers had specified oils previously, they had not necessarily given enough attention to the importance of viscosity and oiliness.

new requirement based on practical experience that the mineral base should contain a minimum proportion of clear residual oil, known as bright stock – a refined high viscosity base oil. Figure 76 reveals 'W' oil retained its viscosity better than either version of 'T' lubricating oil. This lower sensitivity to temperature being particularly noticeable when it is compared to the 'T' oil compounded with 1½ per cent free fatty acid.

Table XXXIV – Details of Lubricating Oils Used on the LMS – 1944

Oil designation	Purpose	Composition	per cent	Specific gravity at 60°F – not above	Redwood viscosity 140°F – not below	Redwood viscosity 70°F – not above	*Viscosity ratio – maximum*
T	General & axlebox lubrication	Dark mineral	90	0.930	170	1750	*70–140°F 10.3*
T	General & axlebox lubrication	Rape	10	0.930	170	1750	*70–140°F 10.3*
T (1½ % FFA)	General & axlebox lubrication	Dark mineral	98.5	0.930	175	2100	*70–140°F 12.0*
T (1½ % FFA)	General & axlebox lubrication	Free fatty acid	1.5	0.930	175	2100	*70–140°F 12.0*
Superheater cylinder oil	Axleboxes on:- Standard Class 4	Dark mineral	95	0.915	Not above 920	~	~
Superheater cylinder oil	Axleboxes on:- Standard Class 4	Saponifiable	5	0.915	Not above 920	~	~
W	Axleboxes on:- Standard Class 4 0-6-0 Standard Class 7 0-8-0 Ex-LNWR G1 & G2 0-8-0	Dark mineral	85	0.915	180-190	1530-1615	*70–140°F 9.0*
W	Axleboxes on:- Standard Class 4 0-6-0 Standard Class 7 0-8-0 Ex-LNWR G1 & G2 0-8-0	Rape	15	0.915	180-190	1530-1615	*70–140°F 9.0*
Straight mineral oil	Axleboxes on shunting engines	Dark mineral	100	0.935	180-200	2200	*70–140°F 12.2*

Data taken from Mr E S Cox *Locomotive Axleboxes*. The last column did not appear in the original table but has been added to form a contrast with the tabulated British Railways lubrication specifications.

The viscosity characteristics of the 'W' oil were designed to make it suitable for use in all supply systems, to retain a high viscosity at maximum bearing temperatures while retaining free syphoning characteristics at low temperatures. The necessary viscosity requirement was obtained by adopting a viscosity index[80] of 85, combined with a

Regarding that difficult property, oiliness, it was thought that the results from dynamic testing

---

[79] When a plain bearing operated in the hydrodynamic zone, low friction was assured as figure 51 confirms, wherein a mineral oil and a fixed oil possessing similar viscosity could deliver almost identical coefficients. Indeed, for operation in this region contemporary engineers could specify a suitable lubricant from the mathematical formulae describing hydrodynamic lubrication. This theoretical approach was however impossible under conditions of mixed film and boundary lubrication because the friction characteristics were highly variable. In these zones, the required oil performance could only be obtained from trials of different oils followed by careful analysis of the resulting data.

[80] Viscosity index – All lubricating oils change in viscosity with changes in temperature becoming thicker when cooled and thinner when heated. However, there is a great difference in the way the various mineral oils behaved in this respect and the viscosity index (VI) quantifies the characteristics of the oil in this respect. The higher the VI of an oil, the less its viscosity changes with a given change in temperature. The viscosity index of a lubricating oil is affected by:-
    (a) the crude oil from which it is manufactured
    (b) the method used for refining
    (c) the existence of possible additives

It is calculated by comparing the viscosities of the sample oil, with those of a reference oil having a VI of 100. The viscosity index is improved considerably by mixing the oil with special additives so values of over 100 are now available. As a generalization, lubricating oils with a paraffinic base have a higher viscosity index than oils possessing a naphthenic base. The viscosity index is thus a useful value apart from the temperature-viscosity relationship, since it also serves as a means of identifying the crude oil feedstock. For a pure mineral oil, *i.e.* one without any additives to improve VI, a high viscosity index of, for instance 80-100 usually indicates an oil with a paraffinic base. A low viscosity index, say 0-40, normally indicates an oil having a naphthenic base, with VI between 40 and 80 often representing oil mixtures.

machines such as the Timken could be regarded as being reasonably representative of the property. This was despite the limitation that such machines could only divide the lubricants into the three main classes of increasingly superior oiliness – (a) mineral oils, (b) compounded oils containing fixed oils and highest of all (c) organically treated mineral oils *i.e.* EP additives. Furthermore, these machines could sometimes give results, which were somewhat erratic and did not necessarily establish a direct relationship between oiliness and the quantity of fatty oil.

The LNER had previously, in 1935, conducted some research into improving oiliness and the film strength of its lubricating oils. Initially, some thought was given to using chemical additives, but it was subsequently decided it would be better to rely on fixed oil compounding. While cocoanut oil possessed the highest boundary lubricating properties, it was unsuited to locomotive use, so refined rape oil was adopted because it ranked next and was free syphoning. Further research conducted on behalf of the company in the same year established that the maximum improvement in boundary lubrication was achieved when the compounded oil contained 20 per cent rape. However, as there was comparatively little gain above 15 per cent, the company's engineers decided in the interests of economy to adopt the latter proportion. When finalizing the precise blend of the 'W' oil, assistance was given by the wartime Lubricating Oil Pool, which also directed that supplies of the essential mineral oils, some of which were in short supply, were put at the disposal of the railways.

As stated at the beginning of this chapter, the LMS adopted the 'W' oil in 1943, applying it specifically to four locomotive classes fitted with highly loaded bearings. The company subsequently enjoyed a noticeable reduction in hot boxes, demonstrating that contrary to the findings of its 1937 investigation, the quality of the lubricating oil could indeed have a very serious impact on axlebox performance – a situation duly recorded[81]:-

"...which had given a marked improvement in hot boxes on the difficult engine classes."

and confirmed by Col Rudgard of the Operating Department[82]:-

"On the question of the improvement of the oil he agreed entirely with the Author, and very good results had been obtained on inside cylinder engines which were prone to hot box trouble. The improvement of the class of oil had definitely given much better results, and was doing what was required on the heavily-stressed bearings."

Mr J Hill[83] modestly wrote:-

"In authorising the use of 'W' oil the standard aimed at by the chief mechanical engineer was to secure by design the highest quality lubricant suitable for the particular work and it was gratifying to learn that an oil which was designed for high duty purposes had achieved its intended purposes of reducing the incidence of heated bearings under abnormally severe conditions; to what extent the improvement is due to the rape content or to the better mineral base was at present a matter for speculation; no lubricant could cope with mechanical conditions which tended to destroy the oil wedge or with faults in the supply systems."

Post war, with rape oil in short supply, the rape content of the 'W' oil was reduced to 10 per cent ('W10'), while the Great Western conducted trials using olein, but the experiment was abandoned without any worthwhile results being obtained. The LMS experimented with an oil it referred to as '2.OL', compounded with olein (2.0 per cent?) with an improved mineral base oil and with limited experience of it, Col Rudgard gave somewhat guarded support[84]:-

"...... did not think there was any cause to anticipate trouble from an increase of hot axles."

The company also trialled compounding using 2 per cent castor oil, but found it exhibited a tendency to settle[85] out into two layers. Possibly similar thoughts concerning rape oil availability, prompted the LNER into reconsidering the use of EP additives in straight mineral oils. These comprised chemical compounds of sulphur,

---

81 Mr E S Cox *Locomotive Axleboxes* I Loco E Paper 447 April 1944 p339.

82 Contribution made by Lieut-Col H Rudgard towards the discussion following
Mr E S Cox *Locomotive Axleboxes* I Loco E Paper 447 April 1944 p318.

83 Written contribution made by Mr J I Hill towards the discussion following
Mr E S Cox *Locomotive Axleboxes* I Loco E Paper 447 April 1944 p338.

84 Lt-Col H Rudgard *Organisation and Carrying-Out of Examinations and Repairs of Locomotives at Running Sheds in Relationship to Locomotive Performance and Availability* I Loco E Paper 464 January 1947 p153.

85 Castor oil is not easily mixed with mineral oils, at 50°F, the solubility is about 2 per cent, at 140°F about 20 per cent can be dissolved, but on cooling the two oils separate out forming two layers.

A Defence of the Midland/LMS Class 4 0-6-0

chlorine or phosphorous introduced individually, or in combination. The general concept is that the EP additives react with metals to form low friction surfaces once the local contact temperatures attain values in the range 300-400°F. In this sense, the term 'extreme pressure' is misleading since temperature is really the factor controlling the reaction process. EP additives are effective at temperatures at or above the values at which the metal soaps formed by the fatty acids in the fixed oil compounded oils become desorbed from the solid surfaces. Because the EP additives remain largely inactive below 300-400°F, they could offer little benefit in the white metalled bearings used in locomotives. The LNER compared an EP oil against an olein compounded engine oil on the motion and coupling rods of a pair of class N2 0-6-2Ts and against a rape compounded oil used similarly on class A4 4-6-2 N° 22 *Mallard*. The test results were mixed, the N2s were able to cope but not the Pacific, while the associated laboratory results demonstrated the superiority of rape compounded oil for load bearing and its freer syphoning. Essentially no current EP chemical additives available were found to be superior to rape or olein, hence their continued use, or as Mr Hill had expressed[86] it with prescience a few years previously:-

"What 'W' oil could do in improving bearing performance under overloaded conditions remained to be seen, but it probably represented the highest quality conventional oil possible at the moment and it was doubtful whether the future could produce anything much better, though the field of specially chemically treated oils remained to be explored, almost certainly in association with the research organisations of the petroleum industry."

Following its formation in 1948, British Railways rationalized the different oils it inherited from the 'Big Four' companies to produce a comprehensive range of suitable lubricants with those relevant to steam locomotives identified as N° 659, 660 and 661.

Item 4, from specification N° 660 for compounded oils can be seen to be very similar to the former 'W' oil developed by the LNER. Inspection of the viscosity change for this entry and reference to figure 76 reveals it reduced the least. Individually, this reduced change in viscosity allied with improved oiliness and syphoning plus an improved mineral oil feedstock represented small changes, but when combined and considered in conjunction with the steepness of the gradient of the mixed-film portion of the friction-ZN/P curve were sufficient to return a noticeably improved axlebox

Fig. 78 - Left-hand drive Class 4 0-6-0 N° 4526 passing through Mill Hill on the down slow with an express goods train with the continuous brake on not less than half of the vehicles.

---

86 Written contribution made by Mr J I Hill towards the discussion following
Mr E S Cox *Locomotive Axleboxes* I Loco E Paper 447 April 1944 p338.

Axleboxes, Bearing Metals and Lubricants

Table XXXV – Specification Nº 659 – Lubricating Oils for Locomotives (Mineral)

Item	Description	Sp. grav. at 60°F – max	Redwood viscosity Nº 1 seconds	Viscosity ratio – max	Closed flash point °F – min	Pour point °F – min	Asphaltenes % max	Organic acidity mg KOH/g max	Demulsification Nº max
1	Dark mineral lubricating oil for locomotives	0.935	@ 140°F 185 ± 3%	70/140°F 12	350	15	0.1	0.5	-
2	Red mineral lubricating oil for locomotives with enclosed valve gear	0.890	@ 140°F 110 ± 3%	70/140°F 12	390	15	Nil	0.1	300
3	Cylinder lubricating oil for saturated steam	0.945	@ 200°F 170-200	70/140°F 6	490	45	0.2	0.5	-
4	Cylinder lubricating oil (mineral) superheated steam	0.915	@ 200°F 220-240	70/140°F 4.5	510	45	0.1	0.5	-

The lubricating oils described in these specifications shall be mineral oils, free from suspended matter, mineral acidity, alkali, water, and other impurities.
The Nº 1 oil shall syphon satisfactorily through worsted trimming.
The Nº 2 oil shall be a high grade red mineral lubricating oil having good demulsification properties.
All tests shall be carried out by the methods described in the [then] current issue of the Institute of Petroleum Handbook, *Standard Methods for Testing Petroleum and its Products*.

Table XXXVI – Specification Nº 660 – Lubricating Oils for Locomotives (Compounded)

Item	Description	Composition	Per Cent by wght	Specific gravity at 60°F – not above	Redwood viscosity Nº 1 seconds	Viscosity ratio – max	Closed flash point °F – min	Asphaltenes % max	Pour point °F – min
1	Compounded engine lubricating oil	Mineral oil	98.5	0.935	@ 140°F 180 ± 3%	70/140°F 11.5	350	0.1	15
1		Olein	1.5						
2	Compounded engine lubricating oil	Mineral oil	97.5	0.935	@ 140°F 180 ± 3%	70/140°F 11.5	350	0.1	15
2		Rape oil	1.5						
3	Compounded engine lubricating oil	Mineral oil	90.0	0.935	@ 140°F 185 ± 3%	70/140°F 10	350	0.1	15
3		Rape oil	10.0						
4	Compounded engine lubricating oil	Mineral oil	85.0	0.915	@ 140°F 185 ± 3%	70/140°F 8.5	380	Nil	15
4		Rape oil	15.0						
5	Compounded cylinder lubricating oil for superheated steam	Mineral oil	97.0	0.915	@ 200°F 200-220	140/200°F 4.5	510	0.1	45
5		Acidless tallow oil	3.0						

The compounded lubricating oils described in these specifications shall comprise the stated compositions and shall be free from suspended matter, mineral acidity, alkali, water, and other impurities.
They shall not separate on standing and shall syphon satisfactorily through worsted trimming.
The organic acidity of the mineral oils used in the compounding shall not exceed .5mg/KOH/g of oil.
Rape oil used in the compounding of these oils shall have a free fatty content, as oleic acid, of not less than 95 per cent.
Acidless tallow oil used in the compounding of these oils shall have a free fatty acid content, as oleic acid, of not more than 1.0 per cent.
All tests shall be carried out by the methods described in the [then] current issue of the Institute of Petroleum Handbook, *Standard Methods for Testing Petroleum and its Products*.

Specification N° 661 – Oils for Compounding

Item 1 Olein	Item 2 Acidless Tallow Oil
The olein supplied shall have a free fatty acid content, as oleic acid, of not less than 95 per cent and shall remain completely fluid when maintained at a temperature of 45°F.	The oil shall have a free fatty acid content, expressed as oleic acid, of not more than 1.0 per cent. It shall become completely fluid when slowly warmed to 60°F with stirring and shall, on cooling, remain completely fluid after standing for 2 hours at 45°F.

Tables above taken from Mr P W Skelton *Steam Locomotive Lubrication – its Development and Practice* MIC Publications, Barrow-in-Furness 1997

performance. Certainly evidence such as figure 3 and tables VI to VIII, suggests that during BR days, the Class 4 0-6-0 does not seem to have been suffering unduly from poor availability.

Oil Delivery Arrangements

Beachamp Towers also carried out experiments into determining the optimum way of delivering oil onto a loaded journal, duly reported by Messers Deeley and Archbutt in *Lubrication and Lubricants*. He found delivering oil through a hole in the crown of the brass with a distribution oil groove or grooves was the *least* effective method. Moving the grooves further away from the crown increased the load a bearing could take without heating. He also investigated having no oil grooves in the brass, the lubricant being applied solely via pads pressed against the underside of the journal. The performance of this method was only exceeded if the lowest portion of the journal was allowed to dip into a bath of lubricant. In view of the performance demonstrated by pad lubrication contemporary engineers adopted it readily for their oil-lubricated rolling stock axleboxes. However, for their locomotive boxes, with one notable exception, they were far more circumspect, displaying a great reluctance to abandon the use of top-fed syphons or mechanical lubricators, although several did incorporate a small pad to serve as a back up or auxiliary lubrication method. This reluctance was not due to the innate conservatism of British locomotive engineers for there was a sound theoretical reason for not abandoning the introducing oil via the top of the bearing, apart from the potential dangers of badly designed oil pads highlighted by Mr Cox[87]:-

"This author recalls the packing of the underkeeps with oily waste at Horwich on coupled as well as bogie axleboxes, a process which was carried out in all good faith, oblivious of the fact that without any kind of supporting spring beneath it, the cotton waste subsided, after a short mileage out on the line, into a soggy mass which had lost all contact with the underside of the journal."

Even if the underkeep and pad was correct, although they might initially render some assistance when newly packed and clean towards maintaining the oil film in the event of a temporary lack of oil from the syphon, this insurance was apt to disappear completely over time through neglect, particularly if they were not readily accessible. The presence of collars on the axles, the closeness of crank webs and the arrangement of the spring attachment to the axlebox on traditionally designed inside-cylinder engines made the removal of keeps difficult without lifting the engine. In this situation, relying on the pad alone, where one was fitted would have been hazardous for its condition could not be easily and regularly ascertained by inspection. If neglected, the under keep accumulated dirt and water while the surface of the pad in contact with the journal became hard and glazed through retaining dirt and very fine white metal particles – in due course it ceased to function, quickly resulting in a hot box – hence the retention of the top feed[88]. Nevertheless, in the Midland loose brass box the crown lubrication was supplemented by a double spring pad placed in the keep, which pressed lightly against the underside of the journal. Mr Thorley[89] has recorded how

---

87 Mr E S Cox *Speaking of Steam* Ian Allan Shepperton 1971 p36.

Mr Harvey, who after training on the LNER worked on the Nigerian Railway also referred to waste packed axleboxes:-

"These were all but universal on the Nigerian Railway and tests were made there in 1938 proved that in order to saturate 10lb of cotton waste thoroughly, two days soaking in 12 gallons of warm axle oil was necessary. It was then allowed to drain for a further three days losing 8½ gallons of oil in the process. The result was a springy elastic material from which oil could be squeezed (although apparently dry) that did not drop away from the journal, unlike a soggy mass of undrained waste."

Mr D W Harvey *A Manual of Steam Locomotive Restoration and Preservation* David & Charles Newton Abbot 1980 p34.

88 A similar situation could also exist on more modern locomotives; the presence of the crank webs and eccentric on the leading coupled axle of the LMS 'Jubilee' class 4-6-0 meant the slide-out keep of the newly adopted standard Churchward/Stanier axlebox could not be applied.

89 Mr W G F Thorley *A Breath of Steam Vol 1* Ian Allan Ltd Shepperton 1975 pp132-3.

effective it could be in the case of ex-Midland Class 1 0-4-4T N° 1239, which albeit for a short while, worked successfully with the top feed to the leading left hand axlebox plugged and reliance placed solely on the auxiliary underpad feed.

In the absence of equivalent information regarding the operation of axleboxes in the mixed-film region, figure 79 shews a vertically loaded *fully* hydrodynamically lubricated fitted partial bearing, only something approximately approaching this will have occurred in a box. The experiments conducted by Beauchamp Tower and Professor Goodman[90] approximated to a carrying wheel axlebox since they concerned a *steady* load vertically applied to the bearing (or 'step') but tragically with the journal copiously lubricated allowing hydrodynamic operation. Possibly it was clearance or wear which prompted the different profiles observed by the experimenters, for Professor Goodman reported in his bedded partial bearing that small changes in the shape or fit of the bearing, as well as journal speed, bearing load and changes in oil temperature all had a very marked effect on the pressure profiles obtained. Ernest Ahrons provided a useful insight[91] into the behaviour of carrying wheel axleboxes:-

"One of the most interesting points in the Author's Paper is that as to the position of the oil holes with regard to the bearing; that is whether the oil should be introduced at the top, as is so frequently done, or at points down the sides. The experiments of Beauchamp-Tower and of Prof. Goodman showed that the oil should not be introduced at the zone of maximum pressure on the bearing. The zone of maximum pressure in a carrying axlebox is not far removed from the top, but somewhat on the 'off' side of the top, though at first sight the conditions would appear such that the point of maximum pressure is somewhat on the 'on' side. For the effort of the engine is transmitted in a carrying axlebox from the frame to the brass, which presses against the journal on the back or 'on' side. Nevertheless, in spite of these considerations, the wear of a carrying axlebox bearing appears to take place on the 'off' side, showing that the maximum pressure is on this side. Prof. Goodman (Proc. Manchester Association of Engineers, 1890) quoted a letter from the late Mr. William Stroudley, who stated that the occurrence of wear on the 'off' side had been noticed for many years. Apparently this peculiarity is due to the film of lubricant being drawn in on the 'on' side, so that it wedges the brass away from the journal, but when the film reaches the 'off' side, it is so thinned that contact between brass and journal takes place on the latter side.

It would therefore appear reasonable to place the oil holes well down the sides of carrying axles. The writer understands that the trailing axleboxes with outside bearings of the 'Atlantic' engines of one of the English main lines are supplied with oil in this way with the addition of a pad underneath.

The case of driving and coupled axleboxes is different, in that the fore and aft thrust and pull of the connecting rod causes the zone of maximum

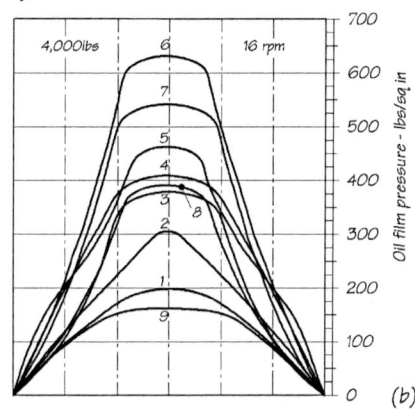

The bearing was 6 inches diameter by 3 inches long. oil *Castrol A*, load varied between 500lbs and 4,000lbs. In the above diagrams it was loaded to 4,000lbs giving a nominal bearing pressure of 222lbs/sq in. Figure *(a)* represents the cross-sectional pressure profiles through the bearing when running at 90° F, while in *(b)* are longitudinal section pressure profiles through the bearing when running at 60° F. The lower viscosity of the warmer oil has increased the maximum hydrodynamic pressure and thus altered the profiles. It seems highly likely that operation within the mixed-film region will have resulted in even greater changes in the very limited pressure profiles.

Fig. 79 - Pressure distribution in a fitted bearing - Professor Goodman

---

90 John Goodman, a former Whitworth Scholar, occupied the Chair of Engineering at Leeds University from 1890 to 1922. I believe he obtained his practical engineering training at Brighton under William Stroudley. He was certainly familiar with the latter's friction testing machine before later developing his own in 1895. Incidentally he also contributed the 'Goodman diagram' to fatigue analysis - a simplified technique that is still used today for alternating loads.

91 Mr E L Ahrons written contribution to the discussion following:-
Mr A E Kyffin *Notes on Axleboxes and Axlebox Guides* I Loco E Paper N° 108 1921 Journal N° 52 pp25-26.

pressure to alternate between both sides, and to be at points well down the sides. The alternating action between the journal and brass allows the oil to work round. It is probably for this reason that lubrication from the top has been so long used successfully."

To appreciate fully why top lubrication remained appropriate, particularly for inside cylinder engines, we should refer back to the forces that acted on an axlebox when in use, but more particularly the load line or *resultant* force.

In an inside cylinder engine having the conventional crank disposition, it acted for nearly half a revolution within a range of angles extending not more than 30° above the horizontal centre line, this effect is shewn in figures 71 and 73. It then rapidly reversed to produce a similar concentration of loading within a correspondingly small angular range on the opposite side of the bearing. In other words, the box took a pounding

high speed in a short cut-off. For then the axleboxes would have more nearly resembled those of carrying wheels, although factors such as regulator position, the presence or otherwise of the Anderson by-pass valves, together with the action of the balance weights in the wheels *etc*. will also have modified the load line so that its action will have remained variable throughout each revolution. The ever-changing action of the load line could result in it encroaching onto an oil groove if the latter was inappropriately placed thereby reducing the film thickness. Figure 80a indicates the ideal arrangement for a hydrodynamic bearing – again in the absence of information concerning mixed-film pressure profiles. In figures 80b and 80c are shewn the effects of interrupting the hydrodynamic pressure envelope by an oil groove – we may assume something along these lines occurred in a mixed-film lubricated axlebox although the hydraulic pressure would be nowhere

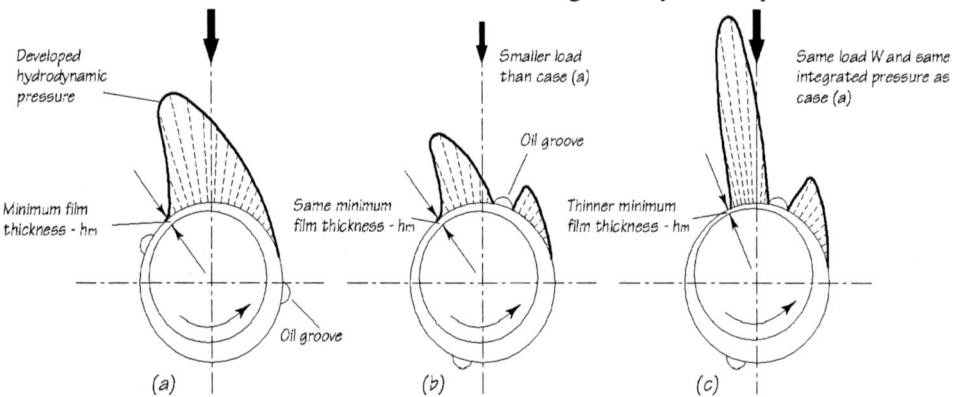

In the design of driving and coupled axleboxes, care was needed in determining the optimum positioning of the oil inlet grooves due to the varying position of the load vector when the engine was running. The oil groove positions should avoid loaded areas so that the maximum length of convergent oil film was available for the development of hydrodynamic pressure. If in operation the load line lies near to a groove then the load capacity of the bearing is reduced. Diagram (a) indicates a normal bearing whilst (b) and (c) demonstrate the effects of closer approach of the load line to a groove. If the same minimum film thickness h_m is to be obtained, then the load capacity of the bearing is reduced (b). Alternatively, if the same load is applied, then pressures will increase and the minimum film thickness h_m will be reduced (c), resulting in the bearing operating nearer to, or possibly beyond the limits of its materials.

Fig. 80 - Effect the location of oil grooves has on bearing load capacity

down near the horizontal centre line, and was only momentarily loaded on the vertical centre line. Incidentally, this varying load line action helped the establishment of a stable oil film soon after starting from rest; the carrying wheel axleboxes enjoyed no such assistance so conditions initially were correspondingly more onerous. Thus applying the oil to a driving wheel journal – be it via syphon trimming or mechanical lubricator – through a groove cut in the crown of the bearing did in these locomotives represent the zone of least pressure, although that position became less attractive if the engine was drifting or running at

near so great. If the same *mean film thickness* is to be retained, then the load on the bearing has to be reduced: alternatively, if the same load continues to be applied then the pressures increased due to the smaller area accompanied by a thinner minimum film thickness increasing the chance of metal-to-metal contact. Since in the mixed-film region, the film thickness is already very thin, the nett result is more asperity contact, greater wear and more heating. For optimum box performance, it is necessary to consider the load line pattern for each operating condition so that the optimum (or least detrimental) position for the oil grooves can be obtained.

While the engine was at rest, the bearings pressed downwards on the tops of the journals, so the commonly used transverse linear groove located in the crown of the bearing was unable to admit lubricant at all, as the oil could not enter against the bearing pressure. The Midland[92] effected an improvement by substituting an elliptical groove cut symmetrically about the vertical centre line for this enabled the oil feed to remain at the top while allowing oil to enter when the journal was stationary along with giving improved oil distribution when the engine was drifting. While this represented a useful compromise, research conducted later by the LMS into establishing the optimum location for oil delivery revealed because the brass strip at the crown was not wide enough to accommodate the whole of the groove, wear, and/or wiping of the white metal over into the groove, could occur – either action resulting in a reduced oil delivery. Experiments carried out by the LMS engineers suggested that a better compromise was obtained by returning to a transverse linear groove, but this time using a pair located symmetrically either side of the vertical, at an angle of 35-40 degrees depending on the diameter of the journal. Since they were located in portions of the brass less subject to loading, this was intended to overcome the risk of the lubrication being cut off through wear. However, once in every revolution of the journal, one of the grooves was in, or very close to, a zone of maximum pressure although in this situation oil was able to flow to its partner, which was therefore in a region of low pressure. However, the presence of the oil grooves effectively divided the brass into three pockets, which, as figure 80c suggests, was disruptive to the maintenance of the oil film. To counter this, the company's engineers then tried feeding the oil through a series of holes positioned on each side of the box on its horizontal centre line, which had the further advantage of enabling the white metal bearing surface to extend unbroken on either side down to within about 1½-1¾ inches of the horizontal centre line. While this arrangement of oil delivery was successful on outside cylinder classes, this was not the case with their inside cylinder siblings. In them oil delivery was being attempted in the region where bearing pressure was at or near its maximum value over much of the revolution, while in due course the delivery holes blocked, cutting off oil delivery, through smearing of the white metal over their openings as roll developed with wear. Accordingly, recourse was made to the interim arrangement with the oil delivered via a pair of grooves cut at 40° either side of the vertical centre line. In contrast the LNER adopted an arrangement reminiscent of Midland practice for the axleboxes of its inside cylinder engines[93]:-

"On the L.N.E.R. there had been very little trouble so far as their modern outside cylinder locomotives were concerned, but the heating of the boxes of the larger inside cylinder engines still frequently caused considerable trouble. At one time or another almost all the recognised forms of installing and lubrication had been used for driving boxes of these engines, but their latest design, and one which seemed to be giving good results, was a box with a machined oil groove 3/8in. wide and ¾in. deep in the crown of the box on the vertical centre line. The white metal is in pockets, leaving 1¾in. of bronze at the back and front above the horizontal centre line, and there is an inch bronze bar in which the oil-way was cut on the vertical centre line. Mechanical feed for the oil was used, and all boxes were provided with an Armstrong pad in the tray, giving an auxiliary under-feed lubrication."

After deciding where in the bearing the oil should enter, other equally important considerations were how much oil should be delivered and by what means. According to Harry Webster[94] of the time spent on locomotive repairs in Britain, overheated bearings probably represented one-half, and of these failures, the chief cause was insufficient lubrication. He commented:-

"It is perhaps a little odd that whilst from his earliest days every engineer is schooled in the principle that lubrication can only be effective whilst there is maintained an unbroken film of oil between two surfaces in contact, no authority seems to have laid down exactly what amount of oil is necessary under varying circumstances to meet that condition.

Thus so far as the locomotive is concerned, the writer has been unable to ascertain the minimum weight of oil per square inch of surface contact that is needed to

---

92 Mr R C Bond *The Design of a Locomotive Axlebox* paper delivered to Associate Section, Midland Railway Engineering Club 8th February 1923.

He thought the adoption of this oval groove, which the company used on its loose brass and manganese bronze boxes, was unusual.

93 Mr D D Grey contributing to the discussion following:-
Mr E S Cox *Locomotive Axleboxes* I Loco E Paper 447 April 1944 p318-9.

94 Mr H Webster *Locomotive Running Shed Practice* Oxford University Press 1947 p76.

ensure an unbroken oil film."

Locomotive engineers employed two methods of conveying the oil to the box, syphons had been the traditional solution but as the twentieth century commenced, presumably in response to the heavier piston loads, more and more locomotives were provided with mechanical lubrication.

Although syphon lubrication was very simple and extensively used, a major weakness was that the quantity of oil delivered could not be accurately controlled. The flow rate was affected by the characteristics of the oil, the material and number of trimmings, the height of the lift, ambient temperature *etc.*, while in any case the oil delivery was a function of time, which was not necessarily a reflection of the work being demanded of the locomotive. Further problems with trimming lubrication arose as engines were used more intensively. Once each engine ceased to be allocated a dedicated driver (or two), the beneficial work done by drivers to their regular charges on shed days ceased, consequently trimmings might not be so carefully made or adjusted, whilst oil reservoirs could be overlooked so they filled with water or dirt. Another factor was as the level of the oil in the box fell, so did the rate of feed and when keeping engines in traffic 16 hours on end, there was the danger of the supply falling to a rate that was too low to lubricate the box sufficiently.

The Midland practice of separate oil boxes was not followed by all companies, some instead arranged for large oil wells to be cast in the top of the axlebox. The slight warming of the box in service reduced the viscosity of the oil, thereby increasing the syphoning rate, which in turn provided, to a certain extent, an automatic regulation of oil feed to suit the work the engine was performing. Other companies filled these oil wells with a grease or oil too viscous to syphon at normal temperatures. If however, the box exhibited a tendency to run warm, the lubricant in the wells became more fluid and could syphon through to the bearing, thereby augmenting the main supply from a separate reservoir. Whether they were the main or emergency oil supplies, these arrangements had the disadvantage of being very inaccessible and liable to fill partially with water. The Midland considered that a separate oil reservoir suitably located to be a simpler and more efficient source of supply. Accordingly, it provided oil boxes fastened in an accessible position on the inside of the frames reasonably close under the boiler where they would be sheltered from the disturbing effects of air currents. The boxes contained three trimmings, the two outer ones supplied the horn faces while the middle one conveyed oil to the journal. In some classes including the Class 4 0-6-0, the bearing was supplied by means of an armoured flexible rubber hose that terminated at its lower end in a union screwed into the top of the axlebox, which connected via the two internal passages into the elliptical groove cut in the crown of the brass.

The height to which the oil could be lifted from a reservoir was affected by the fineness of the trimming material, so a cotton wick would lift higher than worsted – the limit for the latter being about 1¼ inches although lubricator boxes were made deeper than this to reduce water or dirt pick up. The quality of the wool or worsted also had a great influence on the *rate* at which oil was syphoned, as well as the more obvious effect of differing

Table XXXVII – Variation in the Delivery of Different Oils by Syphons Comprising Different Numbers of Strands

Hour	Temp °F	Number of strands	Quantity of oil syphoned – c. c.		
			Oil sample Nº 1	Oil sample Nº 2	Oil sample Nº 3
1	56	6	18	9	12
2	59		25	15	19
3	59		29	18	25
4	60		33	21	29
5	60		37	24	32
1	55	8	11	11	14
2	54		17	18	21
3	54		20	26	27
4	54		23	30	32
5	54		24	34	36
1	52	12	10	8	10
2	52		18	13	18
3	52		25	18	24
4	54		28	22	29
5	54		31	26	32
1	53	16	8	6	10
2	57		15	11	18
3	57		22	15	24
4	59		26	19	28
5	59		31	22	32

numbers of strands. However, reference to table XXXVII would suggest that the quantity of oil delivered was not in direct proportion to the number of strands in the tail. It also suggests a point of restriction could be reached if a large number of tails was crowded into the syphon tube. This restricted the oil flow, so the tail became in effect a plug trimming. These results demonstrate that different oils syphoned at different rates with the second sample, generally being the worst performing.

Mountford Deeley and Leonard Archbutt conducted some experiments exploring the syphoning properties of Berlin wool with two qualities of worsted. The oil was a mixture of a red mineral oil and rape under the same temperature and lift. These tests revealed the Berlin wool syphoned about twice as fast as the better worsted, and nearly three times faster than the poorer one. These results appear in figure 81 which shews the rapidity with which the rate of syphoning fell off as the lift increased.

regular and consistent flow of lubricant at a predetermined rate irrespective of the height of oil in the reservoir. The oil reservoir was made very wide in order to obtain the required capacity, while its depth was kept shallow since thereby the changes in oil level would be much reduced along with variations in the rate of delivery as it was consumed. It operated as a true syphon containing no trimmings thus eliminating another variable, while the oil could be observed as it passed through a nipple sized to give typically 10 to 11 drops per minute. It was used by the Midland on some of its largest passenger engines *e.g.* some of the '700', '999' and 'Compound' classes but not, judging from photographs, the Class 4.

Since the variation in the quantity of oil delivered was so wide with trimming syphons, and as the margin of tolerance reduced in the largest inside cylinder engines it is perhaps not surprising to find designers turned to mechanical lubrication in an attempt to obtain more consistent and predictable lubrication. Some however adopted mechanical

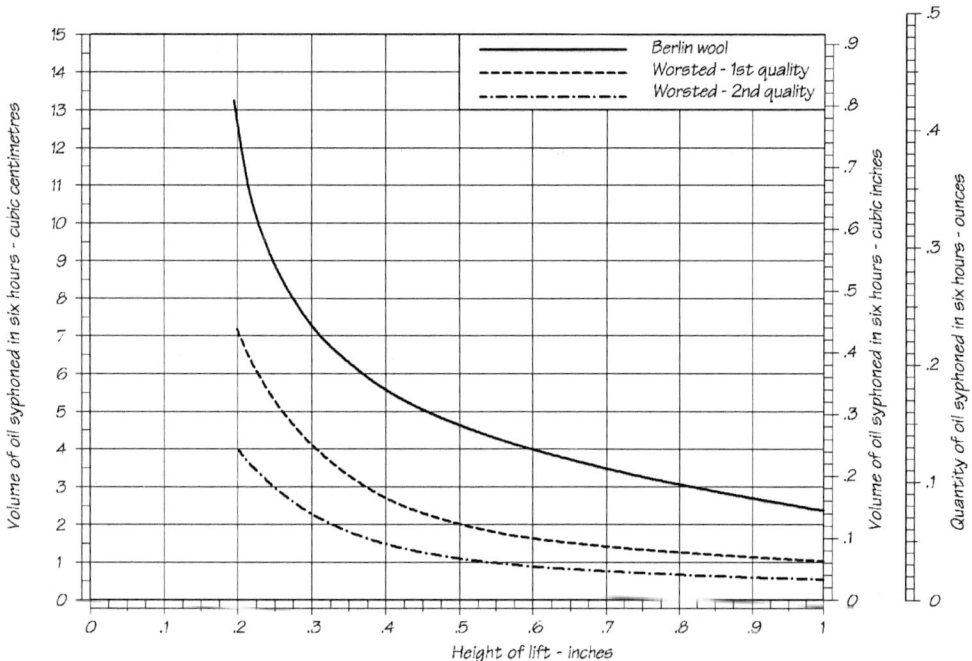

Comparison of single strands at almost constant temperature:- Oil used comprized a standard mixture of 90% Queen's Red engine oil and 10% rape oil.

The curves were drawn from the average of three series of tests using fresh syphons each time.
Range of temperature 13½ to 16°C (56¼ to 60¾°F)

Fig. 81 - Syphoning experiments

The *Valor* syphon lubricator (Geach's patent[95] - N° 7,511, March 1912), duly described by Messers Deeley and Archbutt, was designed to ensure a

lubrication as a means of saving oil, not least because, unlike a trimming, when the engine was stationary the delivery of oil stopped. It was not until 1918 however that the first 'Big Goods' N° 3852 and 3853, were provided as an experiment

---
[95] Mr L C Geach, the first Midland Superintendent of Motive Power, was the patentee.

with Silvertown[96] mechanical lubricators for the boxes; the same year for comparison N° 3877 was fitted with a Detroit[97] hydrostatic lubricator. The following year three more, N° 3887-9, were fitted with Silvertown lubricators. Both lubricator designs delivered oil at a constant rate for as long as oil remained in the reservoir, save that with a hydrostatic type the flow was time-based, and in this respect like trimming lubrication, took no account of speed or load. The testing of these two different lubricator designs suggests Derby had concerns over the consistency of the lubrication rate from the trimming feeds affecting axlebox performance. Presumably, mechanical lubrication was judged superior for this became the standard for future construction, but a sizeable minority (60 out of 192) of the Midland built engines were not modified until after 1923. A second mechanical lubricator was fitted adjacent the extant one provided for lubricating the cylinders and valves. Syphon trimmings were retained for lubricating the horn faces.

Each of the feeds from the Silvertown lubricator were individually adjustable by means of 'slip' thimbles, which effectively introduced a degree of lost motion into that pump's stroke. Each feed received 0.0156 cu in of oil per revolution of the drive shaft when fitted with 'slip' thimbles or say 2 oz per 100 miles. Substituting 'non-slip' thimbles ensured all of the pump's stroke was utilized for delivering oil, increasing it to 0.0276 cu in or 3½ oz per 100 miles. A further means of adjusting the output was provided by changing the settings of the lubricator driving gear. This entailed altering the angular movement given to the ratchet or clutchbox assembly by the drive for each revolution of the driving wheels. Alternative holes were provided in the lever on the clutchbox or else in one of the intermediate drive levers. Normally the increased oil delivery would be used for the first 1,000 miles following overhaul, but in May 1958, British Railways London Midland Region issued a memo (BR 358/16) giving the settings for the mechanical lubricator driving gear for ex-LMS classes. In the case of the Standard Class 4 the setting for both the cylinders and the axleboxes was to be on maximum - this setting may be confirmed by referring to figure 10. Mechanical lubrication presented the advantage, over the previous arrangements, in that that the rate of oil delivery became a function of engine speed. Albeit, if the lubricator was set to deliver sufficient oil under the worst conditions of working, say slogging heavily at 15 miles per hour, then it might be delivering an excess of oil at say 45 miles per hour, which would have helped generate a thicker film. Alternatively, referring to the ZN/P relationship N will have increased while P reduced, but the slightly greater oil delivery will have reduced the coefficient of friction by a small amount.

Mr Cox was of the opinion that conversion from syphon trimming oil feed to mechanical lubrication could rarely be justified since it only dealt with one of the many factors that affected bearing performance. While this was indeed the case, consistent and reliable oil delivery was undoubtedly one of the more important ones. Certainly, other engineers thought it was worthwhile to substitute mechanical oil feed in place of syphon feed, although interestingly James Clayton did not, nor incidentally did Oliver Bulleid who fitted syphon lubrication to the highly loaded boxes of his class Q1 0-6-0s. One company convinced of the worth of mechanical lubrication was the Great Northern, which started converting the heavily loaded axleboxes of Mr Ivatt's 0-8-0s from syphon lubrication in 1917, the year before the 'Big Goods'. Incidentally the same solution was later[98] applied to the N2 class 0-6-2T:-

> "The coupled wheel axleboxes were similar to those on the lighter N1 class engines, the journals being 7½in. diameter and 7in. long. Originally, lubrication was by means of an ordinary syphon trimming feed. In September 1922, No. 1736 was fitted with a second Wakefield No. 7 mechanical lubricator placed on the left-hand side just behind the leading splasher top. Less trouble and more economical oil consumption was experienced, so from 1926 onwards the remaining engines were similarly equipped."

With these improvements in mind, but before we leave this section on axleboxes, let us see some of

---

96 The Silvertown mechanical lubricator was designed and developed in 1911, being marketed by Gresham and Craven from 1923 – the patentees being Messers J E Anderson and S J Symes, Patent N° 28,851 December 1911. Mr Bond suggests the first versions may have had six-feeds only.

97 The Detroit lubricator was of the hydrostatic type fitted with a sight glass in each delivery. It incorporated a constant-head condensing chamber positioned above the oil reservoir. The weight of this head of water *i.e.* condensed steam furnished a constant driving force on the oil reservoir thereby giving a consistent and controllable oil delivery rate via manually adjustable needle valves to where it was needed.

98 Mr N Groves *Great Northern Locomotive History Vol 3b* RC&TS 1992 p78.

the remaining approaches that LMS engineers might have adopted in addressing the boxes fitted to the 'Big Goods'.

Improvements in Axlebox Performance

Since the axleboxes of an inside cylinder engine were inevitably more heavily loaded, this left the locomotive designer with four basic courses of action if he wished to reduce the number of hot boxes:-

> (a) reduce the loading on the boxes by reversing the crank position
> (b) reduce the loading on the boxes through adopting outside cylinders
> (c) give the bearings and associated parts extra attention
> (d) fit bearings of a different type that lasted longer or modify those fitted so that they lasted longer

There were serious disadvantages to *(a)* and it was perhaps not insignificant, that very few engineers were tempted to follow William Stroudley's lead, while some of those that did, quickly retreated from it. The Great Eastern also the Great Western in the time of William Dean, made a few applications; but when Charles Collet reset the cranks of many of his 56xx class 0-6-2Ts he made probably its most widespread application after Mr Stroudley. No reports appear to have survived regarding the performance of the few 'Big Goods' given this crank arrangement, maybe the LMS like most other users considered its disadvantages outweighed any improvement in axlebox life. Eric Langridge[99] briefly referred to the experiment remarking that no reduction in the heating of the right-hand driving axleboxes occurred - despite the significant reduction in their loading. As the engines with this crank arrangement were all in service before the introduction of the 'W' oil in 1943, this again points to factors other than simply box loading affecting performance.

The second option *(b)* was the path trod by Messers Ivatt, Riddles, Cox *et al*, but as well as being by far the most expensive solution it was not necessarily the most economical in the long term. Certainly, the larger bearings reduced maintenance requirements through running greater mileages, but in this instance, this was at the cost of heavier engines for the same power. Thus while this and other features may have reduced the demands on works and running shed maintenance, the penalty was that the additional weight meant the 'Big Goods' replacements consumed proportionately more coal, than had they remained inside cylinder.

Hitherto we have looked primarily at box design and operating characteristics, but the most important factor was *(c)* - the care and attention axleboxes received in the running sheds and works. After all there was only one fundamental reason for a hot box and that was the absence of an adequate oil film between the bearing and the journal in the region of the load. Of course the oil film might have been lost or broken-down for a number of reasons; Mr Phillipson[100] listed fifteen:-

> (i) insufficient or unsuitable supply of oil, especially when boxes were newly fitted
> (ii) dirty trimmings or pads
> (iii) foreign material – *e.g.* sand from sand boxes, or grit from ashpan on journal
> (iv) water in the oil box preventing the trimmings from syphoning
> (v) failure of mechanical lubricator
> (vi) broken, weak, or badly adjusted springs leading to excess weight on a box
> (vii) unequal adjustment of wedges
> (viii) opposite axleboxes out of alignment
> (ix) bad fitting of box to journal – not properly bedded down on crown, too tight on collars
> (x) axlebox too tight in horns
> (xi) failure of flexible pipes
> (xii) engine prematurely rostered for arduous duty after bearing refitted
> (xiii) dirty white metal
> (xiv) laminated white metal – defect in the metal, box too cold when re-metalled
> (xv) inferior lubricant, excessive lowering of viscosity due to high ambient temperatures

Of these, the majority may be seen to have been caused by poor or sloppy working practices, rather than any inherent weakness in the box design, although that certainly increased the propensity for heating through reducing the innate tolerance possessed by the axlebox towards such treatment or neglect. A situation commented on by one astute locomotive engineer[101]:-

---

99 Mr E Langridge *Under 10 CMEs Volume Two: C. E. Fairburn to J. F. Harrison* Oakwood Press Usk 2011 p169.

100 Mr E A Phillipson *Essays of a Locomotive Man* Locomotive Publishing C° London pp116-7

101 Contribution made by the chairman Mr L N Flatt to the discussion following:-

A Defence of the Midland/LMS Class 4 0-6-0

"As regards the hot box question, one member had stressed the importance of design and had gone so far as to state that the majority of our hot boxes were attributable to faulty design. Most of them, he thought, if they were honest with themselves, would agree that their present hot box figures could be very materially reduced without any modifications in design whatsoever. One railway in India maintained detailed statistics of hot boxes and an examination of those statistics from which it was possible to determine which axle and which box on that axle had given trouble on every individual engine – throughout the line – had shown that one locomotive might be a source of trouble consistently for several months and then be completely trouble-free for a period of five or six months. Similarly, another engine might be free from hot boxes for weeks and then be subject to an epidemic of them during a similar and following period. That, he thought, was clearly indicative of the necessity for greater individual attention in sheds rather than a modification in design."

Mr Harvey, shedmaster of Norwich, described[102] what form this greater individual attention took in the case of ex-LNER locomotives referring to the action his boss the motive power superintendent instigated in mid-1950:-

"Heated bearings continued to be problem at all depots and no further improvement in locomotive availability could be expected until their number had been drastically reduced.

The classes of engines most subject to hot boxes were those with inadequate bearing surfaces and a high piston loading, where any inadequacy in lubrication was bound to result in heating. Mr Parker tackled this problem by the introduction at all the principal depots of a special lubrication squad consisting of a fitter ('Put your best fitter on it, Harvey') and two mates, whose job it was regularly and thoroughly to overhaul the lubrication system of every locomotive as it came in for its shed day. Special tools were provided, a miniature pair of tongs, small enough to pass between wheel spokes for the extraction and subsequent re-insertion after cleaning of trimmings (renewed at three-monthly intervals) in axlebox oil wells. Syringes were provided for extracting of water from oil cups, oil wells and axlebox keeps – at the larger depots vacuum-operated extractors performed this operation more speedily. While the two mates responsible for making and keeping up a stock of trimmings were thus engaged, the fitter was busy searching for leaking and broken oil pipes, checking and adjusting mechanical lubricators, cleaning out and renewing ball valves and seatings as necessary in anti-carbonisers or atomisers.

In order to ensure that locomotives were properly lubricated by crews, a HQ lubrication inspector was appointed to visit depots and make spot checks of locomotive preparation. The result of these measures was a dramatic reduction in the number of heated bearings."

This leaves the fourth option, fit bearings that lasted longer and/or modify those fitted so that they lasted longer. LMS engineers were able to effect an improvement in axlebox performance under this heading through such action as superior finishing of the journals and bearings, elimination of hand scraping, the adoption of the 'W' oil *etc*. The beneficial impact these changes had on improving 'problem class axleboxes' was not widely publicised. Although Stanier style steel axleboxes, as mentioned previously, were fitted to many examples under order O/9105 - 300 engines had been so equipped by June 1938 - it effected no improvement over the Midland manganese design, continuing to require re-metalling at around 35,000 miles. The company also tried extending the white metal surface below the horizontal centre line thereby providing a continuation of the bearing surface beyond 180°. Three engines given cast steel/pressed brass axleboxes modified along these lines were inspected at intervals of 5,000 miles. After 35,000 miles, they had not suffered so much wear as the Stanier type steel/pressed brass type, but spreading of the white metal on the radius and instances of pock marks had nevertheless appeared. These defects were symptomatic of other weaknesses that a small increase in bearing area was unable to relieve although it permitted a reduction in wear rate. Incidentally, Mr W Rowland Chief Draughtsman of the Great Central had previously remarked[103] on the benefit of providing additional area below the centre-line:-

"In a modern inside cylinder engine the piston load can easily amount to 25 tons or more, whilst the spring load is usually somewhat about one quarter of this amount. The line of resultant pressure must therefore pass very close to the horizontal diameter of the axle even if the cylinders be horizontal, which is not always the case. Therefore the pressure over that part of the brass between the line of resultant pressure and the lower edge of the brass must be very high; in fact, a

---

Mr B S Sindhu *Some Experiences with Locomotive Utilization and Maintenance in an Indian Running Shed* I Loco E Paper 428 August 1939 p338.

102 Mr D W Harvey *Bill Harvey's 60 Years in Steam* David & Charles Newton Abbot 1986 pp164-5.

103 Mr W Rowland contributing to the discussion following the Manchester reading of the paper:-
Mr A E Kyffin Notes on Axleboxes and Axlebox Guides I Loco E Paper N° 108 Journal N° 52 p12.

pressure of as much as three tons per square inch towards the lower edge of the brass is quite usual in the case of a modern inside cylinder engine.

With outside cylinder engines even higher pressures than this occur, but as the coupling rods of outside cylinder engines take part of the piston load from the driving axlebox during a greater proportion of the stroke than they do in inside cylinder engines, the latter are generally more troubled by heating from this cause.

The remedy for the heating is simple and obvious as it consists in the provision of a bearing strip at the top of the keep below the horizontal centre line.

We adopt this course on the Great Central Railway for all inside cylinder engines having cylinders of over 19½in. diameter, and in consequence have considerably reduced the number of hot driving axleboxes. It seems strange that whilst designers of stationary and marine engines take every precaution to provide adequate bearing area to deal with the maximum load on the journal, the locomotive designer generally appears to regard piston thrust as non-existent and to confine his attention solely to meeting the far smaller spring load."

James Clayton[104] highlighted the fundamental weakness present in non-adjustable subsidiary bearing area namely that while it undoubtedly enabled the box to attain a higher mileage before attention was required, it was more awkward to restore once wear had occurred:-

"With regard to white-metal bearings underneath the axle, I do not see the force of that myself, because it will not be very long before the journals leave the bottom bearings."

Certainly, although these attempts ran counter to their preferred solution of *(b)* above nevertheless LMS engineers were able to improve the performance of existing bearings by providing more attention in the works. Roland Bond reported in 1953, in his Presidential Address to the Institution of Locomotive Engineers that the average mileage between general and intermediate repairs for all steam locomotives was then approximately 65,000 miles. This represented an increase of nearly 30 per cent over the preceding thirty years. One of the factors that helped effect this improvement was greater accuracy in the construction and repair of locomotives. Mr Scott[105] described the process adopted by the LMS to establish and then maintain the frames, cylinders and axleboxes were accurately aligned primarily in engines under repair. Interestingly, the engine that appeared in several of the diagrams illustrating the procedures was a Standard Class 4 Goods. When the axleboxes were called upon to operate nearer the limits of lubricant and bearing alloy, there was less tolerance for misalignment since the resulting errors inevitably loaded the bearings even further.

Although we have little evidence concerning the *direct* benefit this improved alignment conferred on the 'Big Goods' we may gain an insight in to what could be achieved by *(c)* above and *(d)*, if we look elsewhere starting with the sub-continent. Many of the standard locomotive designs running in India suffered quite severely from hot boxes through being fitted with bearings that were rather on the small side often compounded by the use of poor lubricants, but her engineers investigated and made considerable progress in reducing their incidence without fitting larger bearings. Some, like Mr D MacAulay[106] of the East Bengal Railway described what they did. The reduction in hot boxes came through a combination of additional care in the sheds and works together with the substitution in some cases of grease in place of formerly oil lubricated axleboxes:-

"Early in 1934 the E.B. Railway Suburban and Main Line Passenger Services, starting from and returning to Sealdah, were intensified and speeded up. The result was a spate of hot boxes; in fact, for one period of five months the luckless fitters of Narkeldanga shed were dealing with an average of 12 hot boxes a day, or 350 per month. As the total engine mileage of this shed averaged 400,000 per month, that meant that one box was experienced for roughly every 1,200 miles run.

It was at that time realized that something had to be done and that right rapidly. Monthly hot box meetings were accordingly introduced, presided over by Dy.C.M.E. (Running), and after various experiments grease lubricated boxes for driving wheels and oil lubricated boxes (of a type they called the "Victorian") for leading, trailing, bogie and radials, of all B.E.S.A. Passenger and Suburban engines were standardised, except for 0-6-0 goods engines which were provided with free feed grease lubricated boxes to all coupled

---

104 Mr J Clayton contributing to the discussion following the London reading of the paper:-
Mr A E Kyffin *Notes on Axleboxes and Axlebox Guides* I Loco E Paper Nº 108 Journal Nº 52 p48.
105 Mr J S Scott *The Lining-Up of Locomotive Frames,* *Cylinders and Axle-boxes* I Loco E Paper Nº 377 March 1937 Journal Nº 139.
106 Contribution made by Mr D MacAulay to the discussion following:-
Mr H P Renwick *Some Practical Reflections on Locomotive Axlebox Design* I Loco E Paper 423 Dec 1940 pp141-2

wheels, and I.R.S engines (although most the *(sic)* XB class engines were now fitted with the Franklin underfeed grease boxes on all their coupled wheels). Incidentally XB bogie boxes gave considerable trouble until they were converted to the Victorian system of oil lubrication, and the last statistics he saw regarding those engines were in December, 1937, when it was reported that they had run about 700,000 per hot bogie box.

Reverting to the hot box problem of Narkeldanga shed, he found from records that there were 38 hot boxes in September, 1936, the average mileage per hot box being 10,500 per hot box, a considerable improvement over the January, 1934, figures. The latest figures were as follows, for the half-year ending 31st December, 1939:-

2,396,124 engine miles were run and there were 54 hot boxes, equal to an average of nine hot boxes per month or 44,372 miles per hot box.

Actually, in December, 1939, there were only two hot boxes at Narkeldanga.

The total engines stationed at Chitpur goods shed ran an average of 160,000 of miles per month, and the average number of hot boxes experienced per month at that shed was in the neighbourhood of two. Practically all the engines belonging to that shed were on grease lubrication…

… In addition to standardising the boxes described above, steps were taken:-

1. To pay more attention to the correct alignment of frames and squaring up of horn blocks in shops.
2. Squaring and grinding up all bogie horns after checking on a surface table.
3. Burnishing of journals after grinding.
4. Burnishing of boxes after boring.
5. Substitution of No. 4 white metal by M.R. metal composed of:-

   Tin 84.2%
   Copper 5.3%
   Antimony ... 10.5%

6. More careful weighments.

Ninety-five per cent. of their boxes were cast steel with slip-in brasses, although lately they had commenced casting lead bronze bearing brasses (no white metal inserts) into steel shells for grease lubricated boxes."

Whether the M.R. above was a reference to *the* Midland Railway (or the Midland Railway of India) is unclear but what again appears is confirmation that a white metal having a high tin content and no lead (IRS N° 4 contained 2.5 per cent) improved bearing performance. Furthermore, there was no increase in the *size* of the bearings, despite it will be noted some of the affected engines being BESA SG type 0-6-0s which were a traditional British inside-cylinder plate-framed design, albeit broad gauge, but modified to grease lubrication on all coupled axles. Mr Sindhu[107] reported on the performance of a SG/C somewhat less extensively modified:-

"In February 1937, a design was developed for grease lubrication of coupled wheel bearings of engines having under-hung springs of the B.E.S.A. type. One 0-6-0 engine fitted with this method of lubrication on both driving axle boxes, covered over 57,000 miles from April 1937 to August 1938 on mail and express service without developing a hot bearing."

Mr Cox a keen adherent of contemporary USA practice ought to have been very familiar with the potential benefits of using grease lubricated leaded bronze bearings, for pioneered in America it enabled boxes size for size, to return superior load and wear characteristics. The grease was formed into U-shaped cakes that were lightly pressed via springs through a perforated plate, curved to match the radius of the axle, located against the underside of the journal. The grease was not forced onto the journal by spring pressure, but rather it was drawn through the holes in the perforated plate by the suction produced by the revolving journal. Although the practice was initially restricted to North America during the fifty years or so it was used, it was applied to thousands of locomotives, including many British built examples destined for service in India and Africa. The success of this practice depended on the adoption of the optimum grease and it is suspected ensuring that the frame was in good alignment. If the grease was too hard or possessed too high a flow point hot boxes would result, which in extreme cases due to the high temperatures involved resulted in axle failure. Nevertheless, although roller bearings were later adopted with great success from the early 'thirties, grease lubricated plain bearings remained in use in America and elsewhere until the end, while Mr M Sells, CME of the Nigerian and Rhodesian Railways considered their use eliminated hot

---

107 Mr B S Sindhu *Some Experiences with Locomotive Utilization and Maintenance in an Indian Running Shed* I Loco E Paper N° 428 August 1939 p308.
The BESA SG/C and SG/S were 5ft – 6ins gauge superheated 0-6-0s similar in size to a LMS Standard Goods, save their grate area, at 25 sq ft was a little larger. Cylinders 20ins × 26ins, boiler pressure 180lbs/sq in, wheels 5ft – 1½ins dia, weight 49 tons. Journals ≈8ins dia × 9ins long – diameter is approximate calculated from the known scrapping diameter of 6⅝ins and the allowance of 1¼ins wear for journals 7 to 8½ ins diameter originally.

bearings[108] and represented a saving in lubricant costs.

The Canadian Pacific Railway was somewhat unusual in terms of North American practice as it did not adopt roller bearings for its driving and coupled axleboxes, accordingly its 'Selkirk' 2-10-4s, built in three batches between 1929 and 1949, were all given grease lubricated plain driving boxes 12ins diameter and 14ins long. In the later examples of these engines, the 'Most Powerful Locomotives in the British Empire' as the Canadians proudly described them, the nominal bearing loading was 833lbs/sq in or about 7 per cent higher than a 'Big Goods'. On this basis, one feels that grease lubrication combined with a bronze bearing represented another possible avenue for the LMS to have explored – the Indian improvements described earlier had demonstrated its practicality in conjunction with inside cylinder engines. Mr Cox stated[109] that grease lubrication was considered from time to time, but courage failed, perhaps the LNER experience with grease lubrication dissuaded LMS engineers from experimenting with it.

The optimum solution to providing long-lived bearings on inside-cylinder engines was the adoption of roller bearings. For not only were they easily capable of carrying the bearing loads and could be made oil-tight but also the lack of wear ensured the transverse clearances were maintained to within a few thousandths of an inch throughout the life of the bearing significantly increasing tyre and crank pin lives. In a roller bearing, the outer race was secured to a housing that prevented it from turning, while the axle rotated the inner race thereby causing the rollers also to turn. Thus, each roller had two motions; it rotated on its axis and it also orbited around between the races. Since the cage rotated, a roller that was at the top at one instant was at the bottom the next. It was only at the top that the weight of the locomotive came onto the races and rollers, so that never more four or five rollers supported the load at any one time. A similar effect occurred when the bearing was subjected to piston loads, although the clearance that was taken up as the thrust reversed was very small. However, the heavy lateral thrusts were nominally borne by all of the rollers.

In 1930 the Timken Company, unable to convince American railroads to try its roller bearings ordered a demonstrator 4-8-4 locomotive from ALCO, which it had fitted with these bearings throughout. N° 1111 as it was identified, had a very low starting resistance – eleven ounces per ton – so low in fact that as a publicity stunt three Chicago female office workers reputedly pulled the engine a few feet by means of a rope. However, as Brian

---

108 Mr M P Sells *The Locomotive of To-day* Locomotive Publishing C° Ltd London 1951 p156.
An identical view referring to North American experience put forward by Mr N Shove in his paper *Grease Lubrication and Notes on the Working of Locomotives in Canada and the United States* I Loco E 1927.
Nigel Gresley, who chaired the meeting, however formed a completely different opinion on grease lubrication:-

"First of all, with regard to grease lubricated locomotives, I fitted up some seven or eight years ago an engine in this Country with grease lubrication, the whole of the appliances being supplied by the Franklin Co. in America, as I did not wish to do any pioneer work. They failed in one thing, namely, in not telling me there was to be no white metal, although I sent them drawings showing the white metal in the boxes. The thing was a failure; it was always running hot, and I got tired of it and rejected it. About two years ago, after the International Railway Congress, when there was a good deal of talk about the matter, and I was told good results were being obtained with grease, I arranged to fit another engine up, which has been done, and it has been now running for twelve months. The experience is that it has run hot again; it has been overheated two or three times and the journals have been cut. It is running fairly satisfactorily now, but there was no economy to speak of."

During the late 'thirties, the Southern Pacific Railroad made a limited return to oil lubrication in the case of some of its prestige passenger train hauling locomotives - the axleboxes were of the usual 'American' type without quarter bearings:-

"Putting the crown brasses on oil made it necessary to babbitt these brasses with a suitable bearing metal, which had to posses strength, a fair ductility, a fairly high melting point and not to be too easily deformed when under load. A high-tin babbitt, containing 85 per cent tin, 10 per cent antimony and 5 per cent copper, was selected for lining the crown and trailer brasses, while the hub faces were lined with Satco metal."

To ensure and maintain quality and consistency of its white metal, the company made its own babbitt from the purest grades of tin, antimony and copper:-

"To make this babbitt, the tin is first melted under a cover of charcoal, and when the temperature rises to 700 deg. F., the copper is added. At this point sal ammoniac is added which aids in cleaning up the oxides on the surface of the metal and causes the surface of the copper to tin, and once tinned it rapidly alloys with the tin above 750 deg. F.

It may be of interest to note that below 700 deg. F. the copper alloys slowly with tin, while at 800 deg. F. it is readily alloyed. Five per cent of copper in sheet form can be alloyed in approximately ten minutes. After the copper is all alloyed the antimony is added in small pieces about the size of a walnut, and the metal held between 800 and 850 deg. F., with frequent stirring until the antimony is alloyed, which will take a little longer than the case of the copper. The metal is then skimmed and poured into 25-lb. pigs and is stored for future use."

Mr H C Venter *Babbitting Locomotive Crown Brasses Railway Mechanical Engineer* September 1939 pp375-7.

109 Mr E S Cox *Speaking of Steam* Ian Allan Shepperton 1971 p84.

A Defence of the Midland/LMS Class 4 0-6-0

Reed[110] explained:-

"It was not the low specific resistance of N° 1111 that brought 22,000 roller-bearing axleboxes on Class 1 roads in the next 10 years. That was due to the lower lubrication cost and less attention required; and to the degree the elimination of wear enabled vital center *(sic)* distances to be kept within original tolerance limits between major shoppings cutting wear in other parts, keeping the riding qualities, and enabling the locomotive to be rostered for full tonnage and full speed duties right up to the time of overhaul."

The engine was later sold to the Northern Pacific Railroad and between 1930 and 1957, when it was withdrawn, it covered 2,125,000 miles. Being a 'one-off' Mr C P Atkins opined the locomotive probably retained most of its original major components, boiler, cylinders and especially its running gear. This side of the Atlantic, roller bearings were initially used on carrying axles, although the 'Turbomotive' was also provided with them on its driving axles while during the discussion[111] following Mr Cox's axlebox paper,

---

110 Mr B Reed *The American 4-8-4 Locomotive Profile N° 20* Profile Publications Ltd Windsor 1972 p175.

111 Contribution made by Mr J E Spear, to the discussion following:-
Mr E S Cox *Locomotive Axleboxes* I Loco E Paper N° 447 April 1944 p320.
The practice of fitting manganese steel faces on the surfaces of the axleboxes working against faces of the same material attached to the hornblocks was a well established practice in the USA where it was used in conjunction with roller bearings. The LMS however elected to apply the technique to plain axleboxes. Due to the extremely wear resistant surfaces that appeared due to work hardening of the matching faces high mileages could be run, furthermore, obviating the 1/8inch longitudinal movement that appeared in the conventional LMS axlebox/horblock wearing faces, had the bonus of reducing 'quarter slip'. This was the phenomenon where the tyres rotated in a series of jerks when the locomotive was engaged at heavy pulling at low speeds as the pistons reversed direction at the end of each stroke in both cylinders. The much reduced wear on the lateral faces of the axlebox and the horn ensured that riding quality did not deteriorate. A somewhat similar effect to quarter slip also obtained whenever the torque applied by the steam acting on the pistons momentarily, exceeded the adhesion.

As an aside, in contrast to the use of manganese liners, the German Reichsbahn adopted plastic liners:-

"To circumvent the shortage of non-ferrous metals, a plastic of the bakelite type was successfully used. It was light, very hard but had a tendency to crack when overloaded. It was formed from a compressed mixture of sawdust, shredded fabric and resin. The conditions necessary for satisfactory performance apparently were ample lubrication, medium loading and medium rubbing speed. It was successfully used as liners on axlebox horn slides, being secured by countersunk screws. No out-of-the-ordinary lubricant was required, and no machining, as the plastic parts can be pressed exactly to size within very fine limits."

Mr J Spear, an employee of Timken Ltd, advised that the Class 4 0-6-0 would be a suitable candidate:-

"Turning to the bearing problem on the Author's 0-6-0 inside cylinder locomotive referred to on pages 4 and 5 of the Paper, he would anticipate no difficulty in putting forward a suitable tapered roller bearing for the 8½in. diameter by 81/8in. long journal which the Author mentioned. It would be recalled that in Table I (*vide* fig. 73 - APT) the vertical load and resultant load on that journal were 6.75 tons and 25.9 tons respectively, a ratio of about 4:1. The Timken main journal bearings on the turbomotive engine were 10 13/16in. bore by 8in. long, and they were contained in an axlebox which was 10in. long overall, so that the proportions of the bearing were very similar to the proportions of a bearing which would fit the Author's locomotive journal. It was interesting that on the turbomotive engine the vertical and the resultant loads were 10.1 and 64.4 tons respectively, a ratio of 7:1 which was very much worse than the ratio for the 0-6-0 locomotive. It was realised of course, that the character of the forces arising in the two engines would be very different, but he felt confident that a roller bearing would stand up to the loading which the Author mentioned."

In effect he answered the final question posed at the end of the paper, namely could a roller bearing axlebox stand up to the severe loading conditions of a large inside cylinder engine, while giving extended mileage notwithstanding the limited space available on the crank axle? Despite Mr Spear's confidence, Mr Cox expressed concern citing the breathing and flexing that occurred in crank axles, however, due to the wartime conditions, nothing was done at the time. Their first European application to a crank axle was in 1945 when the Netherlands Railways applied SKF roller bearings to every axle of a batch of 15 three-cylinder 4-6-0s built in Sweden by Nohab. The roller bearing axlebox applied to the single throw crank axle was of the same vertical split type fitted two years later to the LP crank axles of two SNCF class 240P four-cylinder compound 4-8-0s. Later in the same year the LMS made a similar application to two of its 'Duchess' class 4-6-2s. The remaining members of this class, which could generate roughly 3,300 indicated horsepower, had plain bearings 10ins diameter and 97/8ins long giving a specific loading of 8.35 horsepower per square inch of projected bearing area. The French 4-8-0s, which also had divided drive, were capable

---

Mr F R Lawrence *Recent German Locomotive Practice* I Loco E Paper 471 April 1947.

Axleboxes, Bearing Metals and Lubricants

Axlebox is fitted with a single SKF spherical roller bearing and is arranged to split vertically with its halves held together by four fitted bolts. The cast steel box is arranged for an under hung spring as used on the Class 4 0-6-0 and is provided with manganese steel liners.

Fig. 82 - Crank axle fitted with a roller bearing axlebox

of generating 4,400 indicated horsepower yet had journals (plain or roller) only 220mm diameter by 225mm long (8.66ins dia × 8.86ins long) giving a substantially higher specific loading of 14.34. However, what perhaps is particularly relevant to this investigation is that the French bearings, *plain or roller*, were hardly larger than those fitted to a 'Big Goods' (8½ins dia × 81/8ins long), for an engine that was capable of, and expected to work very much harder. In fairness, Mr Cox was aware of this situation, for in a memorandum[112] written in 1934 and presumably intended for the eyes of William Stanier, he commented on some features of French locomotive engineering including their axleboxes:-

"Generally appear to be on the small side, and the axles are usually provided with collars. What is the type of box used, what are methods of lubrication and experience with hot boxes?"

It is interesting to record therefore when the LMS did first apply roller bearings to a crank axle it was to a pair of locomotives, whose larger diameter wheels would have promoted somewhat greater leverage than a Class 4 and therefore more flexing strains on the crank axle that so concerned Mr Cox in 1944. Further as principal express locomotives they were employed on services returning the highest values of *ZN/P* obtained in axleboxes, so *minimizing* the fund-amental advantage obtained from roller bearings – obtaining reliable operation within the low *ZN/P* portions of the friction curve – compare the friction profiles appearing in figures 52 and 53. This, allied with the lower bearing loading, is probably why these roller bearings and those for example fitted to the BR Class 7 4-6-2, did not demonstrate any clear advantage over their classmates fitted with plain bearings.

By the time of Mr Cox's axlebox paper, the LMS had progressed to welding in completely replacement sections of frame plate into a locomotive, thereby offering the opportunity for arranging for new inserts to accommodate roller bearings. Not only would this have enabled future cracking to be reduced or even 'designed out', but it also promised to maximize bearing life. Sadly, this opportunity to improve the performance the 'Big Goods' was missed, yet not all LMS engineers were averse to improving the class, for Dennis Monk[113], who was in the Development Office at Derby, remembers that around 1950 a scheme was developed for fitting roller bearing axleboxes to fifty Class 4s. Detailed drawings were produced and it is remotely possible one engine was so fitted at Crewe, but nothing further happened. Perhaps the expense incurred in this modification was too great when there were new BR Standards to be built while it may also have been the case that the benefits obtained from more appropriate lubricating oil together with better finishing of journal and bearing were deemed sufficient for what was by then a superseded class. The last thing that engineers would have wanted was for their latest baby to prove inferior!

---

112 Mr E S Cox *French Locomotives* memo to Chief Mechanical Engineer's Office March 1934.

113 Messers D Hunt, J Jennison, R Essery & F James *LMS Locomotive Profiles N° 10 The Standard Class 4 Goods 0-6-0s* Wild Swan Didcot. p57.

Appendix 4.1

Mr Michell's Method of Estimating the Oil Delivery Rate from Pad Lubrication

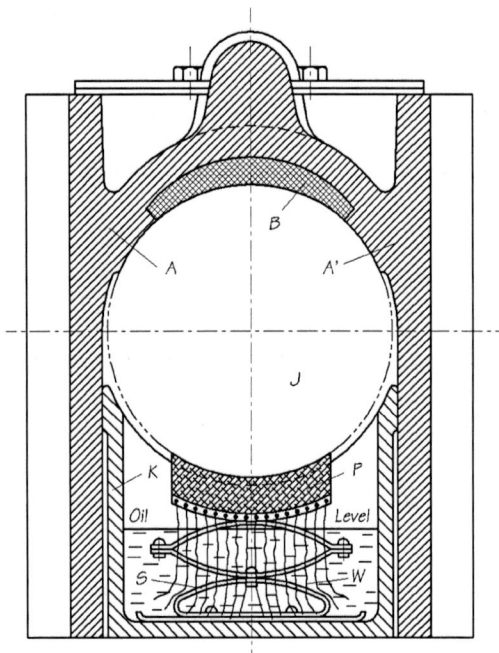

The diagram shews a simple form of axlebox suitable for a carrying axle. The journal *J* is in contact with the brass *B*, which was rigidly retained in the box. The brass *B* carries nominally a constant vertical load when running normally, but when braking the journal could make contact on the auxiliary surfaces *A* and *A'* present in the axlebox body beyond the ends of the brass. When passing over crossings and rail joints the brass and journal were liable to part company momentarily, thereby temporarily disrupting the oil film. The lubricant, oil in this instance, was contained in the keep *K*, which depending on the design could be readily removed for cleaning and inspection. Oil was raised from the keep to the journal by continuous capillary action (syphoning) by means of a pad *P* of porous material together with a wick *W*, attached to the underside of the pad. The wick was partially or wholly immersed in the lubricating oil with the whole assembly of pad and wick supported by and held in contact with the underside of the journal by a spring *S*.

Fig. 83 - Diagram of an axlebox

Anthony Michell estimated the quantity of oil needed to provide hydrodynamic lubrication while making up for the loss of oil escaping from the sides of a journal of the size typically fitted to a carriage or wagon axlebox was of the order of 3.66 cu ins/min.

The following approximate calculation, again by Mr Michell, reveals that a porous pad or similar device depending upon capillary action, yet sufficient compact to fit within an axlebox, was incapable of raising a viscous fluid such as lubricating oil at a high enough rate to provide hydrodynamic lubrication – ignoring of course the limited *capacity* of the keep.

The flow of liquid, relying on capillary forces, through a tube of radius a and length l, lifting to a height h, is given by:-

$$Q = \frac{\pi \times a^4 \times [(p1 - p2) - (\rho \times g \times h)]}{8 \times \mu \times l} \quad (i)$$

where:-
Q = quantity of oil delivered
$p1 - p2$ = the fall in pressure in the length of the tube
g = gravitational constant
ρ = density of the oil
μ = dynamic viscosity of the oil

Also, the fall in pressure corresponding to a capillary surface tension τ at the upper end of a tube, whose lower end is submerged, is given by:-

$$(p1 - p2) = \frac{2 \times \tau}{a} \quad (ii)$$

So, substituting (ii) into (i) above:-

$$Q = \frac{\pi \times a^4}{8 \times \mu \times l} \times \left[\frac{(2 \times \tau)}{a} - (\rho \times g \times h)\right] \quad (iii)$$

For the purposes of this calculation, a porous pad is regarded as being made up from a very large number of parallel capillary tubes conveying the oil. It is also the case, that the maximum oil delivery of a bundle of such tubes of a given total gross cross-sectional area A (which includes the walls of the tubes and the ineffective spaces present) is when the tubes are all vertical and thus of the minimum length necessary for the action and all of circular area.

Suppose that there are N tubes in the bundle, also the total area of all their bores ($N \times \pi \times a^2$), represents a certain fraction of the horizontal cross-sectional area of the pad, whence:-

$$(N \times \pi \times a^2) = k \times A \quad (iv)$$

where:-
k = ratio of the total area of the effective capillary pores to the cross-sectional area of the bundle

Substituting (iv) in (iii) above, and rearranging, gives the total oil raising capacity of the pad:-

$$\Sigma Q = (N \times Q)$$

$$= \frac{k \times A}{\pi \times a^2} \times \frac{\pi \times a^4}{8 \times \mu \times l} \times \frac{[(2 \times \tau) - (\rho \times g \times h)]}{a}$$

$$= \frac{k \times A}{8 \times \mu \times l} \times [(2 \times \tau \times a) - (\rho \times g \times h \times a^2)] \quad (v)$$

Differentiation of this expression with respect to *a* determines the optimum bore for the tubes, which will deliver the maximum quantity of oil for given values of *k*, *A* and the other fixed quantities. The radius is thus found to be:-

$$a = \frac{\tau}{(\rho \times g \times h)} \quad (vi)$$

Inserting this value of *a*, into equation (v) reveals the maximum possible flow:-

$$\Sigma Q = \frac{k \times A \times \tau^2}{8 \times \mu \times l} \times \left[\frac{2}{(\rho \times g \times h)} - \frac{1}{(\rho \times g \times h)} \right]$$

$$\Sigma Q = \frac{k \times A \times \tau^2}{8 \times \mu \times l \times \rho \times g \times h} \quad (vii)$$

Mr Michell opined it was hard to believe of pad where the ratio *k* exceeded about one-tenth – in the materials commonly used it was much smaller.

So for example, taking $k = 0.1$, $l = 4$ins, $h = 2$ins and A as 16 sq ins, adopting a rape oil of specific gravity 0.915 or 57.1lbs/cu ft, and viscosity of 200 seconds at 100°F, hence dynamic viscosity is about 40 centipoise or 0.0269 lbs/foot second, while the surface tension is 36.6 dyne/cm or 0.0807 lbs/sec². Whence the maximum quantity of oil lifted per second is found by substituting in equation (vii):-

$$\Sigma Q = \frac{.1 \times 16 \times .0807^2}{8 \times .0269 \times 4 \times 57.1 \times 32.2 \times 2}$$

$$\Sigma Q = 3.29 \times 10^{-6} \text{ cu ft/sec}$$

(i.e. 0.341 cu ins/min or 0.18 oz/min)

In his calculation Mr Michell used a typical mineral oil, and obtained a flow rate of 0.187 cu ins/min (or 0.097 oz/min), which he estimated was only about one-twentieth of the flow rate necessary for hydrodynamic lubrication. Substituting a pure rape oil, the freest syphoning of the oils commonly used in axlebox lubrication, has almost doubled the oil delivery, but nevertheless, it is still less than 10 per cent of the necessary oil flow, hence ordinary axleboxes operated in the boundary and mixed-film regions.

We may find practical support for Mr Michell's calculations from the results of some tests conducted by the National Malleable & Steel Castings Cº of Cleveland, Ohio, which compared the performance of its Isothermos with ordinary waste packed axleboxes. The results, which appear in figure 84, were obtained from a journal 5¼ins diameter by 10ins long carrying a load of 20,000lbs. The speed was equivalent to 60 miles per hour and both of the bearings were well run in. The oil-film pressures were measured at the centre of the bearings by a pressure gauge, while temperature readings were taken at the sides and near the rear of the bearings - presumably the temperature curves represent averaged values.

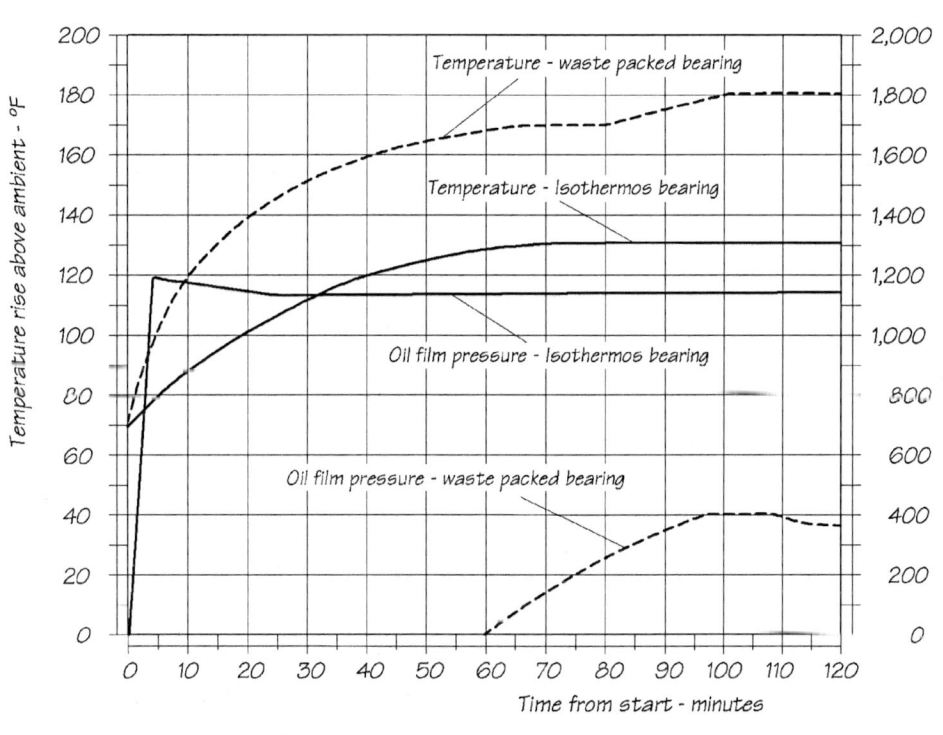

Fig. 84 - Typical oil film pressure and temperature curves for waste packed and Isothermos axleboxes

The curves record

the Isothermos axlebox had a stable oil-film pressure present within moments of the start of the test, conversely, the waste packed box had been running nearly 60 minutes before sufficient oil had been delivered to permit a film pressure to develop. Furthermore, from the bearing load and dimensions, the projected load on the bearing may be found to have been 381 lbs/sq in, but since the oil pressure was over 1,100 lbs/sq in, we may see from reference to Mr Tower's oil bath experiments that true hydrodynamic lubrication was being obtained. In contrast the case of the waste packed axlebox a central oil film pressure of just over 400 lbs/sq in suggests that very little or no hydrodynamic action was being generated, with the bearing operating instead within the mixed-film region, hence the resulting higher friction and the associated higher bearing temperature.

Figure 85 illustrates a National Isothermos axlebox, suitable for an American freight car or similar. This differs from other versions of the Isothermos box principally by virtue of the dirt-excluding fan located near the wheel seat end of the axle, in place of the more usual dust-shield. As the fan revolved, its blades created air turbulence which discouraged the entry of foreign matter into the axlebox and thence the oil reservoir.

In principle the axlebox is very straightforward; a 'dipper' or 'palette' bolted to the free end of the axle revolved with journal while the lowest point of its perimeter dipped into the oil reservoir or bath. As the palette revolved it continuously conveyed oil from the bottom of the axlebox upwards to the oil tray cast on the outer end of the bearing wedge. At low speeds the oil was dropped directly on to the tray, but at higher speeds, it was thrown to the top of the box whence it drained to the oil trough cast in the box and thence on to the oil tray. The oil was distributed along the length of the journal by means of grooves in the bearing. These grooves were provided with small reservoirs to retain oil when the vehicle was stationary. This way the journal was lubricated as soon as it started to move - as demonstrated by the curve.

The obturating (or oil-retaining) ring prevented the loss of oil through it creeping along the journal and past the dust-shield or dirt-excluding fan. Typically, at 25 miles per hour, the palette was delivering 3 to 4 gallons of oil per hour to the journal.

Performance - Two million locomotive tender-miles under maximum wheel and tender loading without a single hot box. Subsequently the design

Fig. 85 - A National Isothermos journal box. It produced lubrication comparable with an oil bath.

was used on many diesel and electric locomotives with an even better record.

One disadvantage of Isothermal (and similar) axleboxes was their greater weight compared to the ordinary type, which increased the unsprung mass. Likewise, although they enabled hydrodynamic lubrication to be established almost immediately after the journal started to rotate, they could do little to reduce the high starting friction which was also the chief disadvantage of plain bearings in axleboxes.

Chapter Five

Comparisons, Steaming and Performance

Why Double Heading was Not Necessarily a Disadvantage

Most people assume the Midland Railway was operating inefficiently when in its later years it double-headed many of its trains. While there can be some truth in this assertion in the case of passenger (and fast goods) trains, this was not necessarily the case with low speed goods and mineral trains – and coal traffic was the lifeblood of the company.

Three factors determined the weight of train an engine could pull over a given road:-

(i) The adhesion of the driving wheels had to exceed the maximum tractive effort it had to exert.

(ii) The size of the cylinders had to be big enough, in conjunction with the pressure, to generate the pull required when the train was starting from rest, running at low speed, and at the highest speeds demanded.

(iii) The boiler had to be capable of producing sufficient steam per hour to meet the demand of the cylinders.

These relationships are presented in figure 86a in which tractive effort has been plotted against speed and from this, the limits determined by the adhesion, cylinder and boiler capacity may be demonstrated. By adding a curve for the change in resistance of the engine and tender with speed, the drawbar pull available on a level road may be quantified as indicated by the shaded boundary. The effect of up and down grades was the subtraction or addition of a constant quantity to the level track resistance curve, albeit its precise value was determined by the gradient. Thus, the shaded area was reduced or augmented, according to whether the train was ascending or descending the gradient. Curves of constant horsepower appeared on the diagram as hyperbolas since:-

$$\text{Horsepower} = \frac{TE \times V}{375} \qquad (15)$$

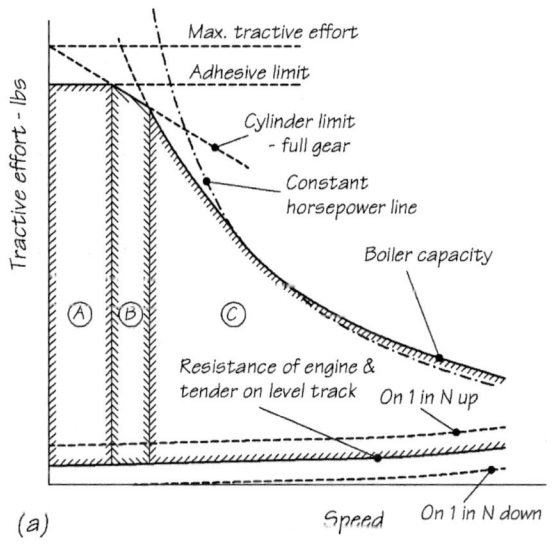

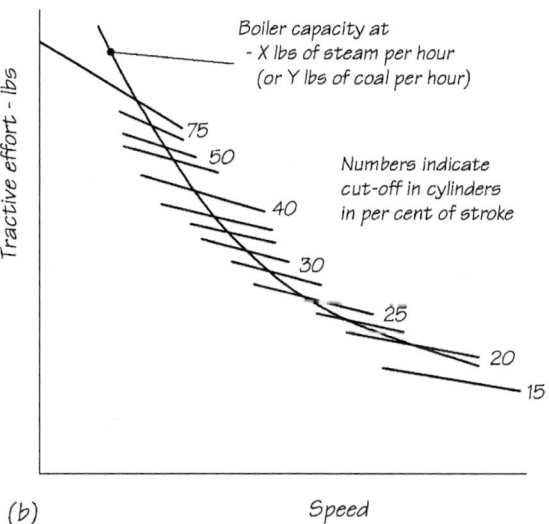

A - Zone where tractive effort limited by adhesive weight
B - Zone where tractive effort limited by cylinder capacity
C - Zone where tractive effort limited by boiler capacity

If the adhesive limit for dry rails (usually 600lbs/ton) appears above the maximum tractive effort *e.g.* as in the 'Big Goods', then zone A does not appear unless rails are greasy etc, so zone B extends to the ordinate as in *(b)* above.

Fig. 86 - Locomotive performance - speed against tractive effort

where:-
TE = tractive effort or pull – lbs
V = speed – mph

This then leads to a modification of the well known tractive effort formula:-

$$TE = \frac{n \times d^2 \times P_m \times s}{2 \times D} \quad (16)$$

where:-
TE = tractive effort – lbs
D = driving wheel diameter – ins
n = number of cylinders
P_m = mean effective pressure – lbs/sq in
d = cylinder diameter – ins
s = stroke – ins

To establish the starting tractive effort, it was usual to adopt a certain percentage of the boiler pressure, the standard was 85 per cent but other values were sometimes used. However, in the case of the tractive effort produced at speed, since the only variable in *(16)* above is *Pm*, the tractive effort becomes a function of its value (*i.e.* the mean effective pressure), which for any given engine depended on the steam chest pressure, the cut-off and the speed. Figure 86b shews how tractive effort varied with cut-off with speed, the regulator being full open and the steam rate constant. Thus, the limit of tractive effort with increasing speed for any particular cut-off was reached when the rising steam consumption of the cylinders equalled the maximum continuous steam output of the boiler. The curve describing the maximum steam rate therefore also recorded how far the tractive effort for any selected cut-off could be carried with rise in speed. Once the maximum steam rate had been reached and if further speed was required then this could only be obtained by reducing the cut-off; conversely with reducing speed the cut-off could be lengthened to gain more pull. To realise the maximum possible tractive effort from an engine demanded that its cut-off was continuously adjusted with every change in speed in order that the steam consumption of the cylinders exactly matched the maximum available steam output of the boiler[1].

Prior to the introduction of the 'Big Goods', both Samuel Johnson and Mountford Deeley had put forward 0-8-0 designs for hauling the Midland's immense London-bound coal traffic. Of the two schemes, Mr Johnson's came closest to fruition when ten engines were to have been built to order O/2694 of December 1903. The design was reminiscent of the North Eastern class T, presumably through the influence of John Smith, with outside cylinders 20ins diameter × 26ins stroke, driving onto the third axle. Wheels were 4ft - 7ins diameter spaced on a wheelbase of 6ft - 0ins × 5ft - 6ins × 6ft - 0ins; engine weight was estimated at 61½ tons. Most of the drawings had been completed, including general arrangement, frame arrangement, pipe and rod layout *etc.* when the order was cancelled in favour of more Class 3 0-6-0s. During the previous decade, at great expense, the Midland had quadrupled a large portion of its main line out of London, although the precise arrangement changed in places, for most of the route the passenger traffic was separated from the goods by the creation of dedicated up and down lines for the latter. However, it appears to have been 'under-engineered', because due to the use of weak short-span girder bridges on the line[2], the axle loading and weight per foot run of locomotive was compromised, while elsewhere on the system the lengths of lie-by sidings was limited. Thus, had Mr Johnson's eight-coupled locomotive been built it would have been restricted to the then current maximum mineral train length of 50 wagons, irrespective of the engine's actual capacity. Although there was a modest increase in wagon carrying capacity during the early years of the twentieth century, which permitted heavier trains for little or no increase in train length, after its recent heavy expenditure quadrupling, the Midland board was not receptive to upgrading the line[3] for the benefit of larger engines. Instead, it adopted the opposite view, that it was more

---

1 A somewhat similar effect may be observed in the frequent and small changes in cut-off made in Controlled Road Tests where the steam rate was maintained at a constant pre-determined value albeit normally less than the maximum.

2 Midland Railway locomotive engineers were particularly handicapped following the appointment of William Worthington as Engineer in 1905 until his retirement in 1915. He not only refused to sanction most of the Locomotive Department's schemes but also refused to say why! This presumably is why so many fruitless proposals appeared in that decade. Eventually it became the practice for the LDO to produce a bending moment diagram for any proposal and from this derive the equivalent uniformly distributed load values for various bridge spans which they then compared to Mr Worthinton's 1911 Bridge Curve, thereby ensuring their loadings did not cross the Engineer's Curve. The slope of this graph severely limited locomotive development on the Midland not least because the Engineer objected to wheel spacings closer than 8ft - 0ins × 8ft - 6ins.

3 I have seen a drawing of Elstree station dated 1912 suggesting that there was a proposal to sextuple the main line in the environs of London.

Table XXXVIII – Goods Derived Income as a Percentage of Gross Income

	LNWR	GWR	Midland	North Eastern	L&YR	Great Central
Total revenue (passengers, mails & goods)	£7,436,400	£6,526,758	£5,729,366	£4,521,867	£2,885,387	£1,931,370
Percentage derived from goods	59.2	55.8	68.7	67.4	59.2	69.5

sensible and economical in terms of infrastructure and locomotive costs to load its six-coupled engines up to their maximum permitted loading, which as we saw in the superheater trials was 50 wagons, and then in effect run two trains coupled together to reduce line occupancy. Later, albeit at great expense, the offending bridges were re-built by the LMS over a number of years so permitting heavier engines to be used.

Referring to figure 86 reveals that at starting and within the lower portion of the speed region that characterized much of mineral train working, the maximum pull the engine could generate was known as the cylinder limit. This was because the absolute maximum pull the engine could exert, which of course was obtained in full gear, was determined by the size of the cylinders i.e. cylinder volume, not by the steam output of the boiler which was far from its maximum. Since the physical constraints determining the upper limit of the diameter of the inside cylinders that could be fitted to a 0-6-0 also applied to a 0-8-0, consequently if the wheel diameter, steam circuit and boiler pressure of the two engines were identical, then the cylinder limit curves would also be the same. However, since a 0-8-0 was a larger and heavier locomotive then, apart from being somewhat more sure-footed through its greater adhesion, out on the main line it ought to haul a heavier train to justify its increased size, cost and weight, but the only way it could do that was by running in a later cut-off, so it would use its steam less expansively and therefore less efficiently. This was precisely the predicament that Henry Ivatt[4] found himself when accounting for the heavier coal consumption of his eight-coupled engines:-

"On 28th January, 1907 in his annual report to the Board, Ivatt stated that he had been asked by the General Manager Oliver Bury to say something about the coal consumption by the different classes (probably because there had been some adverse criticism of the 0-8-0 engines). He went on 'The consumption of the eight-coupled engines is very much higher than was the case with the six-coupled, but the eight-coupled take a load of 1,052 tons as compared with the 681 tons by six-coupled. The present consumption by the eight-coupled is 100 lb. per mile and of the six-coupled 60 lb., so the former burn seventy per cent more with an increased load of thirty per cent.'"

We may gain some measure of the effectiveness of the Midland's practice of double-heading its coal trains by using Mr Ivatt's figures. Had he instead used a pair of six-coupled engines they would have moved 1,362 tons at 120lbs/mile consumption or 0.0881lb per train ton-mile as opposed to his 0-8-0 which hauled 1,052 tons at 100lbs or 0.0951lb per ton-mile - a saving by the former of around 7½ per

Table XXXIX – Working Costs as a Percentage of Gross Income

Company	1909	1910	1911	1912
Great Western - large increase in route mileage	60.9	60.9	62.0	66.6
LNWR	62.6	61.5	62.5	63.4
L&SWR	59.6	59.4	60.0	62.1
Midland	60.0	59.0	61.0	60.4
North Eastern	~	~	62.4	61.8
Great Central	65.5	65.5	65.8	65.0
Great Eastern – serious floods 1912	~	~	60.75	64.3
Great Northern	63.1	62.7	62.5	63.8

cent. Furthermore, in that period immediately before the lamps went out over Europe the combined daily rate for a driver and fireman was less than the cost of the two tons of coal or so. Further support for this approach may be seen in tables[5] XXXVIII and XXXIX which suggest neither extensive double-heading nor operation with smaller locomotives than its peers – the usual criticism levelled at the Midland had a detrimental effect on the company's operating costs. In view of the immense coal traffic handled by the Midland - the percentages appearing in table XXXIX apply to the first six months of 1912 - if it had been moving this traffic inefficiently, then one assumes it would have adversely affected the working costs.

---

4 Mr N Groves *Great Northern Locomotive History Vol 3a* RC&TS 1990 pp37-38.

5 Mr O S Nock *British Steam Locomotives of the Twentieth Century Vol I* Patrick Stephens Ltd Cambridge 1983 p96.
Mr A Vaughan *Railwaymen, Politics and Money* John Murray Ltd London 1997 p 376.

A Defence of the Midland/LMS Class 4 0-6-0

In a conventional eight-coupled engine it was only through fitting more than two cylinders, or where the loading gauge permitted providing two larger diameter outside cylinders, could a greater pull be generated more efficiently, thereby allowing it to compete economically with a contemporary Edwardian 0-6-0 if the latter was provided with the maximum diameter cylinders. In this respect, the North Eastern Railway affords a cautionary tale with its three 0-8-0 classes. The T and T1 designs were both saturated with outside cylinders 20ins diameter × 26ins stroke, differing only in the former had piston valves and the T1 slide valves. The T2 class were superheated with similar sized cylinders, while the fifteen T3 also superheated, were given three cylinders 18½ins diameter × 26ins stroke. According to Ken Hoole[6] the T3 class was allowed to take loads 20 per cent above that allocated to the T, T1 and T2 engines. He opined that whilst the former were the company's most powerful goods engines, they were rather too powerful and their capacity was not exploited until BR days when they were used on Tyne Dock – Consett iron ore workings, a brief window of glory before they were replaced by BR Class 9 2-10-0s in 1962. However, larger or more cylinders increased the front end weight and overhang, consequently many engineers considered that the outside-cylinder 2-8-0 represented a more attractive solution than the inside cylinder 0-8-0, while offering opportunity for the pull to be increased although how practicable this was within the limited British loading gauge may be seen to have been a moot point.

Contemporaries and Successors

We should not overlook the fact that the Class 4 was not the last large 0-6-0 inside cylinder locomotive design to be built in Great Britain. Several similar six-coupled classes appeared either at the time of its introduction or soon afterwards *viz* Great Eastern '1150' class, GSWR '279' class, GNR J22 class etc., while the three remaining Big Four companies all produced new inside cylinder 0-6-0 designs. In the case of two of these companies their engines were considerably more powerful than the 'Big Goods'. It would be interesting to compare the frame and bearing performance of the Class 4 quantitatively with these and similar sized inside cylinder classes, but unfortunately, probably the best we can hope nowadays is a qualitative one. Nevertheless, we may surmise that the mileages LMS engineers experienced with the axleboxes fitted to the 'Big Goods' were not *that* unusual, even if some of the company's engineers might have given the impression they were. Had those critics of the Class 4 compared its axlebox performance with contemporary 0-6-0s of a similar size, they would have encountered a somewhat familiar story, although of course, such action would have reduced the impact of their criticism of the Class 4.

Very early in its life, the LNER was faced with a need for some more powerful 0-6-0s – at that time everybody's concept of a general purpose engine. Nigel Gresley however, thought otherwise and put forward a scheme based on a smaller version of the K3 class 2-6-0 with 5ft – 2ins coupled wheels and three cylinders 18ins × 26ins. The LNER board considered the design too expensive[7]:-

"Not surprisingly, authority for this rather extravagant design was withheld, and Gresley was forced to bring out an 0-6-0. Here he was making an error to be repeated in the fullness of time by Fowler and Bulleid: it was H G Ivatt years later who at last demonstrated that a modern 0-6-0 was "Not on," by producing an advantageous 2-cylinder 2-6-0, whose accessibility and reduced maintenance amply justified the higher first cost. The Gresley 0-6-0s, class "J.38" with 4 ft. 8 in. wheels, and "J.39" with 5 ft. 2 in. wheels, had large boilers, Stephenson valve-gear with 1½ in. lap, 8 in. piston valves, and 20 by 26 cylinders - with the attendant maintenance trouble on the driving axleboxes."

The reference to Sir Henry of course pertains specifically to the Standard Class 7 0-8-0, while Oliver Bulleid was responsible for the Q1 class 0-6-0. In his subsequent book *Bulleid of the Southern* son Anthony was far less critical of his father's design stating that none gave any serious trouble nor received any notable modification. A further factor present in all of these later classes was the adoption of large-lap valves, so drivers would have been encouraged to drive them with a shorter cut-off compared to the older engines. The more 'peaky' turning effect, which accompanies short cut-off working, would have exacerbated the near horizontal resultant load on their axle-boxes by virtue of the greater ratio between peak and mean pressures[8]. As we have seen, it is in the nature of the beast, that the axleboxes of an inside

---

6 Mr K Hoole *An Illustrated History of N.E.R. Locomotives* Oxford Publishing C° 1988.

7 Mr H A V Bulleid *Master Builders of Steam* Ian Allan Ltd London second edition 1983 p59.

cylinder engine are size for size, more heavily loaded than those fitted to an outside cylinder engine, while adding lap to the valves served to increase the power produced at higher speeds. Consequently short axlebox life was a fact-of-life experienced by others who built large-lap inside cylinder engines.

The class J39 did not fit into Edward Thompson's standardization plans even though the last examples did not appear until 1941 – the year he took over. Their large lap valves permitted these free-steaming engines to develop high power outputs at speed; as a result they were often put on fast goods trains and excursions although this resulted occasionally in overheated axleboxes and even dropped motion. The latter was because of certain weaknesses associated with the design of the crossheads compounded by the big end fastenings[9]:-

"A Stratford J39 engine arrived daily at Lowestoft from Goodmayes and worked the 3.50pm goods train back. With a tractive effort of 25,664 lb, the J39s, described when they appeared in 1926 as general service locomotives, were powerful, but most of them ran in dreadful condition and as we seldom received the same engines two days together my day shift fitters spent most of their time repairing them. Loss of a big end cotter on the way to Lowestoft was a common occurrence, often allowing the whole big end to work loose, which might well involve taking down the connecting rod and fitting new brasses; another frequent incident was the loss of the nut from a small end gudgeon pin, which allowed the pin to slide out of place until it struck some fixed part, bending the connecting rod, displacing the slide bars and generally smashing up the gear between the frames. The inside-cylinder design was unsuitable for such big engines, the forces developed when the massive parts were moving at speed being too much for the fastenings; unfortunately the LNER had 289 J39s in all and we had to endure and do our best with them but they were one of Gresley's less happy creations."

It is perhaps impish to record that of all the inside cylinder engines that appeared during Sir Nigel's time in charge of locomotive design, only the J38 and J39 represent his own work. The others were to a greater or lesser extent derived from the work of others, most notably that of Henry Ivatt. The Stephenson's valve gear fitted to classes J38 and J39 was developed from the short lap version fitted to John Robinson's 4-6-2Ts – later class A5 – a batch of which had been built at Darlington in 1925[10]. Despite this pedigree Mr Thompson chose the J11, a wholly Great Central design dating from 1901, which he proceeded to rebuild with large lap valves and longer valve travel in July 1942.

The axlebox performance of the two earlier powerful classes - 5F in the case of J39 and 6F for the J38 - could have been anticipated, particularly the wear. After all they were simply replicating in proportion to their smaller dimensions but similar specific bearing loads, the experience of New World engineers who had by then developed longer lasting boxes. Mr Bert Spencer, one of Nigel Gresley's inner circle, aware of this maintenance demand actively considered the way of improving[11] box performance tried six years earlier by the LMS with a handful of of its last Class 4s:-

"As originally constructed solid crank axles were fitted but on later engines built-up cranks were introduced. The engines have Stephenson valve gear operating 8 in. diameter piston valves with 1½ in. lap and a full gear cut-off of 75 per cent. Both classes have the normal disposition of coupling rods at 180° to the adjacent cranks and the maintenance of the driving axleboxes on such powerful inside cylinder types is consequently heavy. The possibility of reducing the loading of the driving axleboxes by placing the coupling rods on the same centres as the adjacent cranks is under consideration."

In the event this never happened and since the J39, the larger wheeled version of the slightly earlier J38, were both developments of the short-lap NER class P3 0-6-0 (LNER class J27)[12], it is somewhat ironic to record:-

"The flexibility of the 'J39s' was welcomed by the Operating Department, particularly in the North Eastern Area, but in the final days of steam when all that remained for 0-6-0s was short haul mineral trains, the more solid 'J27s' outlasted the 'J39s'."

Perhaps even more amusing to relate is that the J27

---

8 A longer cut-off reduced the ratio of peak (or admission pressure) to mean effective pressure, which prompted a more even turning moment giving less torque variation. At low speeds this made the locomotive less prone to slipping, while as a general rule, running with a longer cut-off at all speeds reduced the noise and vibration, as well as being kinder on the axleboxes, the crew and the valve gear.

9 Mr C H Hewison *From Shedmaster to Railway Inspectorate* David & Charles Newton Abbot 1981 p55.

10 Mr G Hughes *The Gresley Influence* Ian Allan Shepperton 1983 p105.

11 Mr B Spencer *The Development of LNER Locomotive Design 1923-1941* I Loco E Paper 465 March 1947 p174

12 Mr G Hughes *The Gresley Influence* Ian Allan Shepperton 1983 p77.

had a higher bearing load than either the J38 or J39 being roughly equal that of the LMS Standard Class 7 0-8-0! Nevertheless, the bulk of the 115 members of the J27 class 0-6-0s, built 1906-23, were withdrawn *after* the 289 examples of the J39 the LNER constructed from 1926 to 1941. Withdrawal of the former NER class commenced in March 1959 being complete in September 1967, but the first J39 disappeared in May 1959 with the class becoming extinct in December 1962. In contrast withdrawal of the smaller-wheeled J38 class, originally 35 strong, did not commence until December 1962 while the majority lasted until 1966-7, by which time they were 40 years old. Perhaps what this really demonstrates is that the operating people were willing to use 0-6-0s at the higher speeds that large-lap valves could readily deliver but if the design was not up to it this would result in problems. Thus the Q1 was satisfactory but the J39 suffered, conversely the J38 used like the J27 primarily at low speed survived.

Less commonly appreciated, is that at low speeds a large-lap engine could demonstrate no real water or fuel economy over its superheated short-lap equivalent unless, along with its normally higher working pressure, it was provided with a superheater that could provide really hot steam under those conditions. Thus just as the Standard 7 0-8-0 did not present any real advantage, neither did other later large-lap outside cylinder engines[13]:-

---

13 Contribution made by Mr J E Turner to the discussion following:-

Mr D R Carling *Locomotive Testing on British Railways* I Loco E Paper 497 1950 p566.

To which Mr Carling replied:-

"The Author replied to *Mr Turner* that they had not yet carried out, since nationalisation, tests with freight engines other than those in the interchange trials when the L.M.S. '8F' had been run in competition with the L.N.E.R. 'O1', the Great Western '2800' and the two 'Austerity' classes. They had had the 10-coupled 'Austerity' at Rugby, originally in connection with the acceptance trials of the plant.

Both 'Austerity' classes were due to be tested with the Mobile Testing Plant when this could be managed.

In the case of the '8F' something would probably be done in due course: To some extent, boiler results from the class 5 should be a very good guide to the '8F', which has almost the same boiler. It was possible that in the case that Mr Turner had mentioned the coal consumption of those engines might go down appreciably when the footplate staff became really familiar with them."

Unfortunately, the 8F boiler and the Class 5 boiler differed in one major respect - superheater area. In 1950, when scientific testing in Britain was in its early stages, it appears the importance of providing adequate superheater area, on goods engines was not generally appreciated, although this certainly was not the case with Continental locomotive engineers. When

"… asked whether much testing had been done on the plant of freight engines. The freight section was a vast field in which testing could be done and he had in mind the L.M.S. Standard class 8 freight engine. Some time ago, it was decided to dispose of the Standard 7s and they were replaced by the Standard class 8. The opinion of the enginemen was that, although they had grumbled at the 7s, they were sorry to lose them for the class 8, which was heavier on coal and no more powerful than the class 7."

This is a situation, which we will explore by proxy as it were, when later we compare the performance of LMS Standard class 4 and 8 locomotives hauling Toton to Brent coal trains.

Two of the modern large-lap classes, the LMS Standard 7 0-8-0 and the LNER J39, became extinct *before* the short-lap classes they were intended to replace, while the large- and short-lap versions of the J11/3 were withdrawn largely indiscriminately. Reference to the Availability and Productivity tables appearing in chapter two, record consistently lower values for these particular classes, than their pre-grouping predecessors achieved. While the axlebox performance of the 'Austin Sevens' is well documented other weakness present in the design, some seemingly due to the use of Walschaert's valve gear, appear not to be so well publicised. According to Mr Powell, eccentric strap wear was high and there was a long spell of trouble before the Second World War with the little ends overheating, while the crossheads shed gudgeon pins presumably with similar wrecking results on the valve gear as demonstrated by the J39s. Mr Cook reported the G7¾s boiler, for reasons unknown, incurred higher maintenance costs than

---

the 'Liberation' class 2-8-0 built by the Vulcan Foundry were first schemed out they were given a superheater of 580 sq ft in area, which represented 24 per cent of the evaporative heating surface (2,353 sq ft), and was considered capable of delivering a steam temperature of 600-650°F. These proportions were strongly criticised by the Continental engineers who demanded an *increase* in superheater proportions. The 32 flues were increased in number to 36 thereby giving a maximum steam temperature of 700°F, with the superheater becoming 660 sq ft or 29 per cent of an evaporative heating surface of 2,273 sq ft.

By 1959 when steam locomotive testing ceased sufficient evidence had accumulated about superheater performance to demonstrate its crucial importance. Yet in 1966, Mr Cox could still promote specious arguments suggesting the smaller superheater of the 8F class would enable that engine to deliver a superior performance over otherwise similar engines in terms of boiler, valves, cylinders etc - but fitted with *larger* superheaters. See for example *British Railways Standard Steam Locomotives* Ian Allan 1966 pp23-28.

the equivalent boilers[14] used on the LNWR engines, even allowing for the higher working pressure, while an operational weakness was the "lack of punch when getting away with a load" as Mr Nock expressed it. The full gear cut-off originally 73.7 per cent, was later increased to 74.7 per cent when the laps were *reduced* to *increase* the port openings; this contrasts with the 79.6 per cent full gear cut-off of the former LNWR G1/G2/GsA classes. Mr Cox mentioned in a memorandum to Mr Symes that the one foot longer wheelbase of the Standard 7 over the ex-LNWR 0-8-0s caused the 'Austin Sevens' difficulties when negotiating sharp curves in sidings coupled with some trouble in starting trains standing on sharp curves in certain yards *e.g.* Chilwell Sidings, Toton. This was also suspected of starting cracks in a number of solid crank axles, five in 1931, of which one broke completely. Mr Hardy[15] provided another instance of the expensive maintenance resulting from the use of Walschaert's gear of insufficient robustness to withstand the greater forces, at speed resulting from a longer valve travel[16], when wholly disposed in the cramped space between the frames of an inside cylinder locomotive. In the case of the sixty-two, class N7 0-6-2Ts Sir Nigel had built in 1927-8 with longer laps, the weak point being the valve spindles, which could bend at speed.

Turning to the Southern Railway, Mr Bulleid like Mr Coleman, was willing to remain with a traditional inside cylinder design, when he schemed out his very powerful class Q1 0-6-0 despite the behaviour of the LNER J38 and J39 classes, which ought to have been familiar to him during the fourteen years he was Sir Nigel's right-hand man. While, should he have been in any doubt, an earlier Southern 0-6-0 built by Richard Maunsell just before he assumed power, the class Q - 1½ins lap and 10ins diameter piston valves – might also have indicated[17] what could be in store:-

"However, it requires two eccentrics for each valve as compared to the normal single eccentric of the Walschaerts'*(sic)* gear. This can leave less room for substantial journals on the axle of inside cylinder locomotives and lead to the mechanical problems of wear occasioned by hard pulling at low speed for long periods, which usually manifests itself in hot boxes."

Mr Bulleid elected to retain Stephenson's valve gear for his Q1, four eccentrics notwithstanding or his experience of the J39 class, but as we have seen with the N7 and the 'Austin 7' longer laps, inside cylinders and Walschaert's gear had not necessarily proved a happy combination. The Q1 came in for criticism from certain quarters because inside cylinders were considered old-fashioned, however their use on an 0-6-0 was natural and resulted in a compact design which produced economy in operation and maintenance, furthermore despite their high loading, heating trouble in the axleboxes or the big-ends was not in practice a problem according to Bulleid junior. However, we may hear of Mr Bulleid senior's design reasoning from an address he delivered to Feltham locomotive men in November 1942, for he inferred he intended the Q1 to be *lighter* on maintenance than the Q. Perhaps he considered his vertical split design of axlebox would last longer, or maybe he simply thought the saving in fuel and superior power to weight ratio of a smaller lighter engine outweighed any minus due to extra axlebox maintenance. Along with explaining certain features of his Q1, such as fitting the largest boiler that he could against the background of a severe weight restriction, Mr Bulleid[18] clearly recognized the importance of obtaining a high power-to-weight ratio:-

---

14 Mr A F Cook *Raising Steam on the LMS* The Railway Correspondence & Travel Society 1999 pp83-84.

The LMS not only produced a revised version of the G7¾s boiler carried by the class, but also explored the possibility of fitting two different designs of taper boiler. Mr Cook refers in *Raising Steam on the LMS*, to a later report, stating the maintenance cost of the G7¾s boiler was higher than that of the equivalent LNWR boiler hence the redesign and the taper boiler design exercises. The first of the later was made in 1933, but never progressed beyond a sketch, the second in 1941 was given Job Nº 5246, and envisaged fitting a 3C boiler as carried by the Class 8 2-8-0. If this boiler change had proceeded would have demanded significant modifications to the engine, while the one-eighth larger grate would have offered a potential increase in power which would hardly have improved either axlebox or crosshead/valve gear component performance. It would seem that boiler and other maintenance costs *not* simply axlebox performance, were the reason why the class was withdrawn in large numbers between 1949 and 1951, although twenty lasted a further ten years.

15 Mr R H N Hardy *Steam in the Blood* Ian Allan Ltd Shepperton 1971 p150

16 The Great Western four cylinder classes and the LMS 'Princess Royal' were more successful in this respect, although subsequent LMS 4-6-2s had derived valve motion for the inside cylinders. In the 1950s a scheme was proposed to remove the inside valve gear from the 'Princess Royal' engines and to replace it with derived motion. It seems the proposal was primarily to overcome the frame problem rather than weaknesses in the inside gear, but *vide London Midland Fireman* p135.

17 Mr J E Chacksfield *Richard Maunsell : An Engineering Biography* The Oakwood Press (Usk) 1998 p145.

18 Mr H A V Bulleid *Bulleid of the Southern* Ian Allan Shepperton 1977 pp194-5.

A Defence of the Midland/LMS Class 4 0-6-0

"An engine was needed that would run over as much of the system as possible, that is to say, over all lines except unimportant branches. The Chief Engineer advised me that he could accept an engine not exceeding 54 tons, which could travel over 93 per cent of the track, and this figure was adopted as the limiting weight. The tender weight too was restricted to 39 tons 10 cwt (actual weight 38 tons).

The Q class met these limitations of weight. This class of engine had been giving good service. It has shown, however, that larger boiler capacity would be an advantage. Its motion could be improved, furthermore the cylinder design left something to be desired. We have here a good example of the difficulties of standardisation. The easy course would have been to build a further forty Qs, exactly like the others and this would have commended itself to the works, though hardly to the shed repair staff. A locomotive has a life of some forty years and obviously when improvements can be made they must be even at the cost of some additional increase in the stock of spares, but if attention is paid to the detail fittings to ensure they do not vary or are interchangeable, the drawbacks of additional types are minimised.

Having a maximum weight fixed, the next question to be settled was the boiler. The locomotive is a coal-burning machine and given reasonable design and an average fireman it may be said that the work done depends on the coal consumed. In other words, the boiler should be the largest that can be fitted so that the engine can do as much work as possible. The evaporative capacity is dependent on the grate area and the firebox heating surface and volume. A large volume is needed to ensure that the gases have time to burn, as the flame is extinguished as soon as it enters the tubes. A large heating surface is necessary to ensure that the maximum heat is transferred to the water. A point to remember is that no work is required to ensure the transfer, whereas any transfer through the tubes involves work in that the gases have to be drawn through the tubes. The largest firebox, as regards width at the top we can fit inside the Southern loading gauge is that of the 'Lord Nelson'. We had the press blocks required to press the various plates.

I therefore copied this design of box, the only dimension remaining to determine being the length of the grate and it was fixed to give 27 square feet.

The wheelbase was to be the same as for the Q class and the cylinders were to be in the same position. ......"

Some of these comments are pertinent to the 'Big Goods', for they refer to the class Q which designed under James Clayton's direction[19], was very much a Southern Railway development of the Midland 0-6-0 he had worked on previously, even down to adopting the same 8ft - 0ins × 8ft - 6ins wheelbase, a similar layout of indirect motion, albeit with 10ins diameter valves, and a certain reluctance to produce steam! Incidentally he had used that diameter valve combined with 1s/8ins of lap, when he rebuilt some SE&CR 4-4-0s of the D and E classes also against a strict weight limit, to form the D1 and E1 engines specifically to haul the Continental boat trains. These rebuilds proved very successful and worked loads of up to 300 tons. Thus, had the LMS engineers needed an example of how to effect improvements to their Class 4, they need have looked no further.

By the time of Sir William's arrival to the LMS in 1932 many of the class 2, 3 and 4 engines bequeathed to the company at its formation had been scrapped, but it was realized that replacements would be needed. However, there was no agreement between on one hand the designers and on the other the motive power people. The latter in the guise of David Urie and Harold Rudgard wanted direct replacements for the older engines - this extended so far as to include saturated boilers and slide valves. Mr Cox, who was against such solutions, suggested that the designers in the CME's department would not agree to making what essentially were cosmetic changes to pre-1900 designs, as had been done previously with the Class 2 0-4-4T introduced in 1931. Yet was this really as retrograde step as he implied? This is not to say the steam engine was incapable of improvement or that it should not have been, but rather recognition that until engineers could actually produce a locomotive that was a significant advance the sad fact is that modern designs intended for the lower levels of traffic were unable in everyday service to demonstrate much, if any, advance over their nineteenth century predecessors. The Great Western's designers recognised and accepted this so under Charles Collett adopted the practice of building twentieth century replicas of pre-1900

---

19 James Clayton came to the Midland initially at the behest of Cecil Paget to work in a private capacity as one of the two draughtsmen he had engaged to produce the drawings for this significant locomotive experiment – the other was Herbert Chambers later Chief Locomotive Draughtsman of the LMS. Mr Clayton joined the Midland Railway in 1905, and from 1907-14 was one of the two chief assistants to James Anderson when the latter was Chief Locomotive Draughtsman. He was thus intimately involved in all of the significant Derby projects of that period, including Mr Deeley's re-building of 4-4-0s, also the creation of the '483' class, the 'Big Goods' and the S&DJR 2-8-0s.

designs, hence for example the 2251 class 0-6-0, the 48xx 0-4-2T and the six-coupled 54xx and 57xx pannier tanks. Of these four examples *only* the tender engine was superheated and then very modestly. The omission of superheaters might appear strange, but unless the superheater was suitably proportioned, the engine able to 'warm up' and the steam rate maintained, then any superheat would be limited, furthermore, while steam temperature remained uncontrolled, obtaining adequate superheat at low steaming rates introduced the risk of excessive temperatures at higher steaming rates. The LNER in 1944 replaced the superheated boilers on J27s with saturated ones, presumably as a result of the engines by then being employed on more modest duties which compromised the superheat produced. There is evidence that discussions concerning the merits or otherwise of superheating small goods engines took place at a high level on the LMS. Mr Cook[20] referred to a report Derby Drawing Office produced in 1944 on the comparative costs of saturated and superheated engines on goods trains:-

"For Midland engines the comparison was based on the recorded coal consumption over the years 1936-8, and using the "booked loadings" (that is, the maximum loadings) for approximately level routes.

Comparing the Class 4 0-6-0 with G7S boiler with the Class 3 0-6-0 with G7 boiler, the superheated engine was rated at 1010 tons and the saturated at 850 tons, an advantage to the superheated one of 18.8%. The actual average coal consumption over the three years was 61.6 lb/mile for the superheated and 64.6 lb/mile for the saturated, a reduction of 4.8%. Combining the two, it was calculated that the coal consumption per ton mile (a favourite statistic, but a hazardous one) was 19% less for the superheated engine than for the saturated.

A similar calculation for the Midland Class 2 0-6-0 compared with the Class 4 showed that the superheated engine had an increase in booked loading of 42.3% for an increased coal consumption of only 12.6%.

A more convincing comparison was made on the LYR where two batches of 20 0-6-0s differing only in that one batch was superheated and the other saturated. A careful record was kept of the actual tonnage hauled by each engine over a period of two years. The results showed that the superheated engines had hauled an increased ton mileage of 22.6% compared with the saturated engines for an increased coal consumption of only 0.9%. Further calculations showed that the extra cost of the superheater was more than covered by the saving in the coal."

Superheater performance will be looked at later in a little more detail, but table III, which gives ten-year averaged coal consumption figures for ex-Lancashire & Yorkshire Class 3 superheated and saturated 0-6-0s confirms the superheated engines burned more. Unfortunately the loads are not recorded but the annual mileages being very similar perhaps suggests their usage was not that dissimilar. That in general service, as opposed to careful tests, there was little difference in coal consumption between saturated and superheated goods engines is lent support by the knowledge that at least two of the proposed Class 2 replacements produced by Mr Coleman in 1943 - DD 3714 and DD 3714A - were *saturated* 0-6-0s. This indecision about whether to use superheated or saturated boilers for these Class 2 engines also enveloped the Class 3 and 4 replacements, while the designs ranged even wider with schemes swinging between inside cylinder 0-6-0s, 2-4-2T and 0-6-2Ts and outside cylinder 2-6-0s, 2-6-2T and 2-4-2T.

For the fifteen years preceding the appearance of the Class 4 Mogul in 1947, LMS engineers, had with varying degrees of originality and it seems drive, schemed out a dozen and more replacements for the 'Big Goods'. Table XL, based on details[21] appearing in *Locomotive Panorama* records part of the chronology of the Class 4 replacement, wherein one-half of the proposals comprised 0-6-0s. The first example, which Mr Cox described as a simple re-boilering substituting a taper boiler in place of the parallel G7s boiler, appears to have been something more extensive, involving also, at the very least, new cylinders. Similarly, the scheme designated DD 3688, which he described as having bar frames, had plate frames - bar frames certainly appeared in several of the 2F designs *e.g.* DD 3711, DD3714 and DD3714A. Some of these proposals displayed considerable flair particularly the 0-6-0s; for along with these frame differences, many were schemed out on a 7ft - 9ins × 8ft - 0ins coupled wheelbase, a significant break with tradition. Different valve gears appeared including Allan straight link and a split arrangement of Walschaert's gear, with the combination lever and expansion link located between the frames driven via a rocker shaft by means of an externally located return crank. This latter arrangement would

---

20 Mr A F Cook *Raising Steam on the LMS* The Railway Correspondence & Travel Society 1999 pp176-7

21 Mr E S Cox *Locomotive Panorama Vol. I* Ian Allan Shepperton 1965 p145.

have permitted the cylinders to be located closer together, since eccentrics were no longer needed, thus enabling longer axleboxes to be fitted. The boilers on some designs were derived from a shortened version of the 4C boiler while in at least two schemes wide fireboxes extending over the rear coupled wheels were proposed. Externally some appear to have had their styling inspired in part at least by the both the J38 and the Q1 - *vide* figure 87. The initial attempts in 1937 to derive a 2-6-0 based on the taper-boiler 2-6-4T proved too heavy, while A F Cook referred to two further schemes that do not appear in the table. One was based on a modified 4C boiler *sans superheater*

persisted with the development of large-lap inside cylinder 0-6-0s as potential replacements for the 4F and although not recorded here, also for the 3F and 2F classes. This suggests that either he was ignorant of the heavier driving axlebox maintenance in an inside cylinder engine, which is highly unlikely or and far more probable like Oliver Bulleid, he considered it less of a handicap than did Mr Cox.

LMS locomotive policy seems to have been *very* fluid during the Second World War an opinion formed from the extensive changes Mr Coleman made in his recommendations to Sir William for

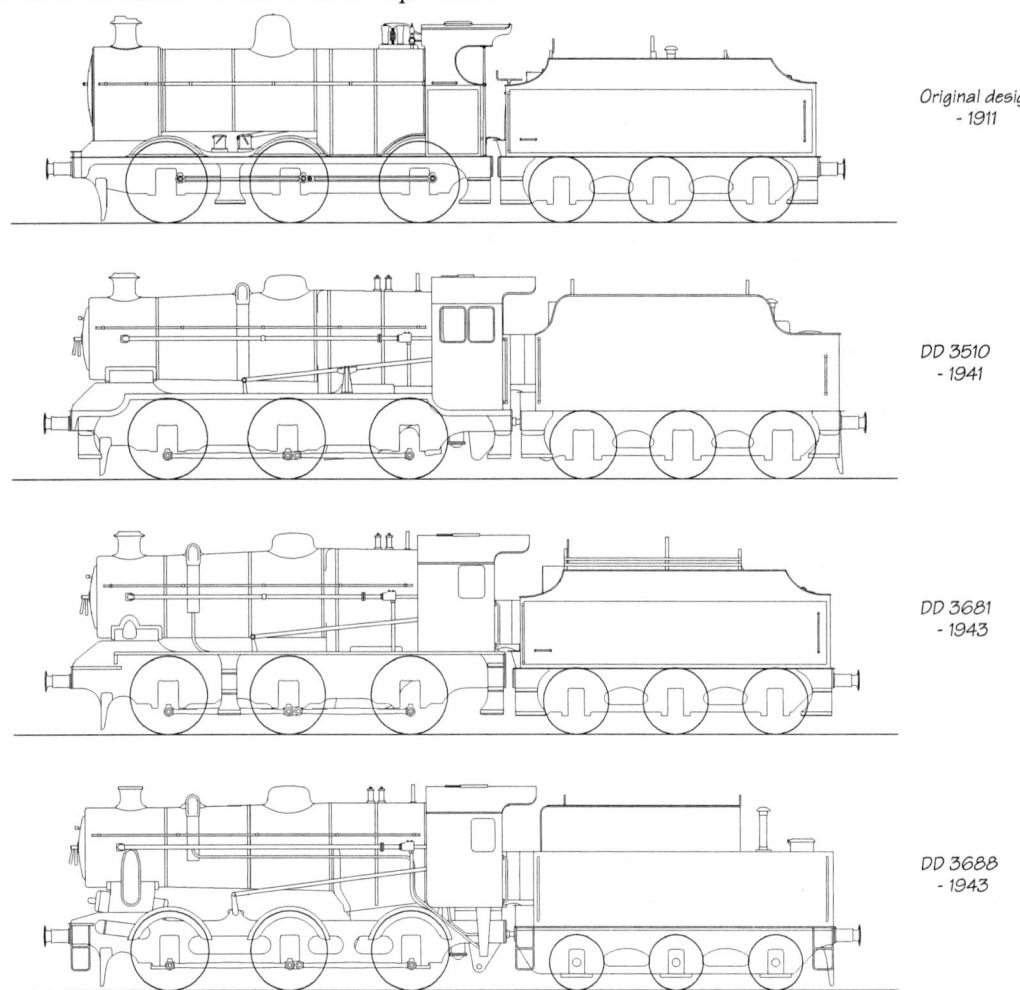

Fig. 87 - Examples of Mr Coleman's 0-6-0 replacement proposals for the Standard Class 4

with the tubes arranged as in the G7 boiler and carrying 185lbs/sq in working pressure, while an 0-6-0 proposal was produced with a round-topped firebox and 4ft - 11ins diameter wheels. Despite Mr Cox's criticism of the axlebox performance of the Standard Classes 7 and 4, we may see that well into the Second World War, Tom Coleman

the standard locomotive types needed post-war. In March 1942 he produced diagram DD 3605 which illustrated his proposal for twelve standard types. Seven were existing designs but one of the remaining five was a Class 4 inside cylinder 0-6-0 to DD 3510. Drawing DY 7376 dated 24th April 1942, shewed 12 steam classes and one diesel shunter. One example was again an 0-6-0, this time to DD 3526, but this was a *3F* carrying a taper-boiler. Subsequently in a later drawing, dated the last day of 1942, the extant 4F 0-6-0 was retained (incidentally along with the Garratt). In a later drawing dated 19th March 1943 two new 0-6-0 designs appeared amongst a total of ten classes - one a 4F and the other 2F.

The final decision concerning the 4F replacement was taken in November 1945 in a meeting both comprised one of Mr Cox's babies to figure in the post war LMS construction programme; conversely Mr Coleman remained wedded to an 0-6-0 for the same role. Of course, any perceived weaknesses in the 0-6-0 design would have strengthened the case for the 2-6-0 - in the event the only proposal from this list to appear. After commenting on the appearance of some of the rival schemes Mr Cox opined[24]:-

"Appearance apart, there is no doubt that an

Table XL – LMS Class 4 Replacement Development Chronology - *Locomotive Panorama Vol I*

Mr Cox's Description	Date	Diagram	Wheel arr'gt	Cylinders	Diving wheels	Boiler pressure lbs/sq in	Tractive effort lbs	Maximum axle loading	Total engine weight
Taper boiler on existing Fowler Standard engine	Dec 1932	EU 90	0-6-0	19" × 26"	5' ~ 3"	200	25,400	~	~
Modified version of 2-6-4 tank	May 1937	DE 48	2-6-0	18½" × 28"	5' ~ 6"	225	27,700	18 ~ 16	65 ~ 15
Modified version of 2-6-4 tank	May 1937	DE 51	2-6-0	18½" × 28"	5' ~ 6"	200	25,683	17 ~ 10	62 ~ 5
Direct adaption from 2-6-4 tank	1937	DRS 3518	2-6-0	19⅝" × 26"	5' ~ 9"	200	24,670	17 ~ 15	62 ~ 15
As first engine above. Raised footplate over rods.	1941	DD 3510	0-6-0	18¼" × 26"	5' ~ 0"*	200	24,530	17 ~ 10	50 ~ 2
As first engine above. Simplified footplate.	1943	DD 3681	0-6-0	18½" × 26"	4' ~ 11"	200	25,640	17 ~ 2	49 ~ 0
Bar frames, wide firebox, Allan valve gear and stovepipe chimney.	1943	DD 3688	0-6-0	17½" × 26"	4' ~ 11"	225	25,810	~	~
Tender version of Fairburn 2-6-4 tank. Straight footplate	1944	DD 3749	2-6-0	19⅝" × 26"	5' ~ 9"	200	24,670	18 ~ 00	62 ~ 15
Class 4 Mogul Nº 3000	1947	As built	2-6-0	17½" × 26"	5' ~ 3"	225	24,170	16 ~ 15	59 ~ 2

*This dimension calculated from the tractive effort figure appearing on DD 3510, Mr Cox gave the diameter as 4' ~ 11"

George Ivatt and Tom Coleman attended. Mr Ivatt has been accredited by several authors with making the decision that the new engine had to be a Mogul, yet as Mr Cook observed[22] the minutes to this meeting appear more vague containing a rather strange statement:-

"... having regard to the (Civil) Engineer's requirements which he put forward in 1937 for an engine of the 2-6-0 type which would be acceptable over all the present No 4 freight routes, it was decided to put forward (ie, to the Civil Engineer) an engine using a 4C boiler shortened both in firebox and in barrel working at 225lb pressure with 2-6-2 type cylinders and 5ft 3in diameter wheels."

If the Engineer had indeed requested a 2-6-0 in 1937 then why had so much effort been expended developing 0-6-0s? It also rather seems the Engineer was in effect determining locomotive policy. Mr Bond stated[23] from 1942 onwards, a Mogul derived from the Standard 4 2-6-4T

engine like this with its big valves and long lap gear could have been a very lively performer, far too lively for the good of the track. At 70 m.p.h. of which it would easily have been capable, its progress along the line, sawing wildly from side to side as is the wont of 0-6-0's *(sic)* at speed, would have been awesome to behold. Ivatt's wisdom and sure instinct was never so much in evidence as when he put an end to such flights of fancy and insisted upon the adoption of leading truck and outside cylinders for the new class 4 six-coupled engines. But if Ivatt had not been there ...?!!"

Yet the Great Western made much use of its '2251' class 0-6-0 in the Aberystwyth area and elsewhere hauling passenger trains sometimes in excess of 60 miles per hour[25], while Oliver Bulleid trod the same path. A few years before the appearance of the LMS Moguls, he had satisfied himself with regards the road-riding characteristics of his more powerful class Q1 0-6-0[26] as well as at the same

---

22 Mr A F Cook *Raising Steam on the LMS* The Railway Correspondence & Travel Society 1999 p174.

23 Mr R C Bond *A Lifetime with Locomotives* Goose & Son Cambridge 1975 pp160-3.

24 Mr E S Cox *Chronicles of Steam* Ian Allan London 1967 p139.

25 Mr J Chacksfield *C B Collet A Competent Successor* Oakwood Press Usk 2000 p97.

26 "The two inside cylinders had straight ports, moderate clearance volume and direct passages. The passages were given

time silencing his critics[27]:-

"Users of the Q1s took readily to them on account of their steaming and performance, though they asked pithy questions such as 'Are they safe when running tender-first at 70mph?' Bulleid said yes to this and then rode tender-first at 75mph to demonstrate, using engine No. C36, whose regulator and brake controls were duplicated on the fireman's side by a series of levers to assist reverse running. ....

In practice the engines were used well within their capacity and always had bags of reserve power. They were rather given to rolling at high speeds and

significantly further, for in his class Q1 he not only produced the most powerful example but also it carried a significantly larger boiler allied with a very good weight distribution. Indeed its superior power-to-weight ratio actually enabled it to compete against nominally larger 2-8-0 classes, thereby replicating the situation extant a generation or so earlier between the 0-6-0 and the 0-8-0. This superior performance was perhaps behind some of Mr Coleman's proposals, for example DD 3688 was to have been given a tractive effort of 25,810lbs and a grate area of 31.0 square feet. The

Table XLI – A Comparison between Contemporary Six- and Eight-Coupled Locomotives

		GWR 2251 0-6-0	SR Q 0-6-0	SR Q1 0-6-0	LNER J39 0-6-0	LNER J11/3 0-6-0	MR/LMS Class 4 0-6-0	LMS Class 8 2-8-0	WD 2-8-0	LMS/BR Class 4MT 2-6-0
Date of introduction		1930	1938	1942	1926	1942	1911	1935	1943	1947
Boiler pressure	lbs/sq in	200	200	230	180	180	175	225	225	225
Cylinders – bore	ins	17½	19	19	20	18½	20	18½	19	17½
- stroke	ins	24	26	26	26	26	26	28	28	26
Valves - type and diameter	ins	Flat	PV 10	PV 10	PV 8	PV 8	PV 8	PV 10	PV 10	PV 10
- lap	ins	15/16	1½	15/8	1½	15/8	1	1½	1½	1½
Driving wheel diameter	ft - ins	5 – 2	5 – 1	5 – 1	5 – 2	5 – 2	5 – 3	4 - 8½	4 - 8½	5 – 3
Combined heating surfaces	sq ft	1248	1432	1860	1670	1386	1404	1890	1991	1459
Firebox	sq ft	102	122	170	172	130	124	171	168	131
Tubes & flues	sq ft	1069	1125	1472	1226	1117	1034	1478	1512	1081
Superheater	sq ft	76	185	218	272	139	246	241	311	247
Grate area	sq ft	17.4	21.9	27	26	19.2	21.1	28.7	28.6	23
Tractive effort	lbs	20,155	26,160	30,080	25,664	21,959	24,555	32,438	34,215	24,172
Engine weight	tons	43½	49½	51¼	57¾	53¼	48¾	72	70¼	59¾
Tractive effort ÷ engine weight	lbs/ton	464	528	587	450	412	503	450	488	405
Tractive effort ÷ grate area	lbs/sq ft	1158	1190	1114	990	1144	1160	1130	1195	1051

The Great Western 2251 class 0-6-0 possibly had a shorter lap than the Victorian classes it replaced. According to J Maskelyne the 2301 class had 11/16ins lap although W A Tuplin states they were 15/16ins. I suspect the latter figure is the correct one.

were formally limited to 55 mph, though often timed quite a bit faster, confidently echoing the 75 mph trial"

Having carried out this demonstration into the acceptable running of a modern large-lap 0-6-0 in his typical flamboyant style Oliver Bulleid was content in the knowledge the engines could be used at speeds up to 75 mph but later commented that he never tried to see if it would do any more! Along with its speed capabilities, he had also demonstrated that the 0-6-0 could be developed

---

special attention so that the engines could be used for passenger working when wanted. The inside exhaust ensured a free escape and the back pressure was kept low by use of the multiple-jet blast pipe."
Mr S Day-Lewis *Bulleid Last Giant of Steam* George Allen & Unwin Hemel Hempstead second edition 1968 p209.
27 Mr H A V Bulleid *Bulleid of the Southern* Ian Allan Shepperton 1977 p74.

former was not too far behind the 32,440lbs of the Standard 8 2-8-0 while the grate area comfortably exceeded it suggesting that along with an increased ability to cope with poorer quality coals, that had the engine been effectively draughted it could have delivered a sparkling performance.

Table XLI compares a selection of 0-6-0s with two 2-8-0 classes along with the later LMS replacement for the 'Big Goods'. An approximate insight into how effective these designs were, may be obtained by introducing ratios – a practice employed by many locomotive engineers to a greater or lesser extent. Although their precise composition varied along with the importance that one might perhaps attach to a particular ratio. Some such as Cole's ratios, empirically derived from locomotive test data were undoubtedly able to predict engine performance reasonably accurately. Others, such as those used by Messers Fry, Poultney[28], Bulleid et al had perhaps a less solid scientific basis but were probably more widely used - certainly in Britain. Nevertheless as long as this caveat is remembered, they can fulfil a useful role when comparing locomotive classes.

The first of Mr Bulleid's ratios, shewn shaded in table XLI – tractive effort divided by engine weight – was intended to give a measure of the capital cost per pound of tractive effort. Good

per cent more than a 'Big Goods'. This additional weight, reduced the drawbar horsepower, which of course detracted from the haulage capacity of the engine, it also increased the coal consumption in lbs/dhp/hr. Even worse, in this respect was the Class 2MT 2-6-0 (376lbs/ton), which not only weighed roughly one-third more than the typical Victorian Class 2 0-6-0, but was even heavier than a Class 4 0-6-0. The extra coal that had to be burned in moving the engine reduced the benefit that its barely large-lap valves (15/16ins) could

Table XLII – Mr Bulleid's Locomotive Performance Analysis

		SR Q1	LMS 2-8-0	MR Class 4	Class 4MT
Tractive effort		30,000*	32,438	24,555	24,172
Weight of engine and tender		89t – 5c	125t – 3c	89t – 19c	101t – 18c
Engine and tender resistance	lbs/ton	12			
Resistance on 1 in 50	lbs/ton	44.8			
1 in 100	lbs/ton	22.4			
1 in 200	lbs/ton	11.2			
Total resistance on 1 in 50	lbs/ton	56.8			
1 in 100	lbs/ton	34.4			
1 in 50	lbs/ton	23.2			
Total resistance on 1 in 50	lbs	5070	7106	5109	5788
1 in 100	lbs	3070	4305	3094	3505
1 in 200	lbs	2070	2904	2087	2364
Available tractive effort behind tender on 1 in 50	lbs	24,930	25,332	19,446	18,384
1 in 100	lbs	26,930	28,133	21,461	20,667
1 in 200	lbs	27,930	29,534	22,468	21,808
Wagon resistance	lbs/ton	6			
Equivalent N° of 12 ton wagons at 16 tons gross on 1 in 50		31	31	24	23
1 in 100		59	62	47	45
1 in 200		101	107	82	79

*Mr Bulleid's value.
NB the engine weights are full working order and not the usual two-thirds fuel and water supplies. The table derived from *Bulleid of the Southern* with the last two columns added for comparison on the same basis.

locomotive design demands that the maximum power be obtained from the minimum weight, a lesson not shared by Oliver Bulleid's equivalents on the LMS who instead became wedded to the outside cylinder engine. The presence of outside cylinders and the necessary accompanying pony truck resulted in a significantly heavier engine suggesting less effective use of capital, whatever benefits they might have bestowed on the CME's maintenance budget. They also reduced the benefit of large lap valves since some of the saving in steam was squandered on moving the extra weight, the Class 4MT 2-6-0 weighed over 10 tons, or 20

bestow. The second ratio – tractive effort divided by the grate area – indicated the demand made on the fire (quasi-combustion efficiency) to support the tractive effort. This ratio, for the 'Big Goods' was very similar to most of the other 0-6-0s featured in this table, suggesting that the grate area in relationship to the work expected of the locomotive was fine and the problems with steaming were caused by a poor draughting system rather than insufficient grate area. An interesting point to reflect upon is that of the engines appearing in this table, the Great Western example had the shortest lap.

After observing his 'Austerity' Q1 was the most powerful 0-6-0 in the country, Oliver Bulleid then demonstrated its effectiveness by comparing its performance with that of the LMS Class 8 2-8-0, although he referred to it as a WD design, which at

---

28 See for example Mr Lawford Fry *Notes on the Comparison of Locomotive Dimensions* **Railway Mechanical Engineer** April 1921 and an earlier article in **The Engineer** October 13, 1911, also Mr E C Poultney *The Comparison of Dimensions and Proportions of British Locomotives* **Railway Mechanical Engineer** September and October 1921.

Table XLIII – Improvements in Steaming Capacity with Single Chimneys Following Testing Station Investigations – Post 1948

	Grate area - sq ft	Maximum steam rates - lbs/hr		Engine weight - tons	Steam production - lbs/sq ft	Steam production - lbs/ton
		Original	Modified			
GWR 'King' Class 4-6-0	34.3	25,000	30,000	89.0	875	337
GWR 'Castle' Class 4-6-0	29.4	20,000	26,000	79.85	884	326
GWR 'County' Class 4-6-0#	28.8	18,000	24,000	76.85	833	312
GWR 'Hall' Class 4-6-0	27.1	17,000	21,000	76.4	775	275
GWR 'Manor' Class 4-6-0	22.1	10,000	20,000	68.8	905	291
LMS 'Jubilee' Class 4-6-0	31.0	20,760	25,000	79.65	806	314
LMS 'Crab' Class 2-6-0	27.5	16,000	20,000	66.0	727	303
LMS Class 4 2-6-0	23.0	9,000	17,000	59.75	739	285
LMS Class 2 2-6-0	17.5	9,000	14,000	49.25	800	284
LMS Class 4 -0-6-0¶	21.1	~	19,000	48.75	900	390
LNER 'V2' Class 2-6-2	41.25	14,000	30,400	93.1	737	327
BR Standard 9 2-10-0	40.2	~	29,000	86.7	721	334

NB:- Exhaust steam injectors not in use. Different coals were used in these tests. The GWR express passenger classes usually received good quality Welsh coals, for the remaining passenger engines and all of the others the coal is believed to have been Blidworth.
\# Draughting improvement accompanied by tube plate changes
¶Mobile Test Units – not on stationary testing station

that time the majority were. The details appear in table XLII, however the opportunity has been taken to include the Standard Goods and the LMS/BR Class 4MT 2-6-0 produced by his brother-in-law. Comparing the two class 4 designs on this basis suggests there was little between them, with if anything the advantage lying with the older engine, a view given further support when we consider specific steam production rates. As the steam locomotive used steam as its motive fluid and from it created power, a crucial factor determining the maximum power that it could produce was therefore the maximum steam rate relative to its size. Admittedly, this is a rather coarse yardstick as it ignores the modifying effects that superheat temperature, back pressure, leakage etc. had on specific steam consumption, nevertheless it does give a good feel for the all-important power to weight ratio.

We may develop Mr Bulleid's approach of comparison ratios while inspecting the locomotives appearing in table XLIII all of which had had their draughting improved draughting by BR prior to testing. It reveals that the Class 4 0-6-0 returned the second highest specific steam production per square foot of grate area. As the steam rates appearing in this table, are from engines fed Blidworth or higher quality coals it may be taken as being an equitable comparison, accordingly we may conclude that the steep slope of the grate was not having very much detrimental effect. Furthermore, as the quantity of steam each could generate was a fundamental in deciding its indicated power output while its weight was a crucial factor in establishing its drawbar power, it is revealing to effect a comparison based on steam produced per ton of engine weight. We may see the 'Big Goods' generated the largest lbs/ton thus at the low speeds present in goods traffic we may see it represented an effective unit. At higher train speeds the weakness present in its short-lap valves would have become apparent, and from tests such as those carried out by the LNER with its A1 class 4-6-2, we find that large-lap valves brought savings of the order of 25 per cent in specific steam consumption at express speeds. Applying this factor to the Class 4 0-6-0 suggests that its specific rate of 390 lbs/ton should be reduced to 312lbs/ton to become roughly the equivalent of later large-lap engines, nevertheless this still represents a respectable value compared to them. This is particularly so when contrasted to the LMS/BR Class 4 2-6-0. Had all of the 4s been provided with this revised draughting rather than just the six(?) that were, the popular 'memory' of the 'Big Goods' might have been completely different, nonetheless Terry Essery was still able to write[29] about the original unmodified members:-

"Their basically robust construction had its Achilles heel but even so they earned a lot of revenue over a very long period and possibly missed true greatness by only a short head. The 7Fs *(sic)* front end, some adjustments to the draughting and improved axleboxes would probably have done the trick, but by the time this was appreciated, the design had been around too long and the class too numerous for major rebuilding to be considered. In spite of that, 4Fs were

---
[29] Mr T Essery *Steam Locomotives Compared* Atlantic Penryn 1966 p71.

never fully replaced by modern designs and continued to work right up until 1966 on BR while happily, four examples may still be seen drawing the crowds on preserved lines – which is not at all bad for an engine introduced in 1911."

Popular opinion as exemplified by this account by Mr Essery, is the Class 4 suffered because it was not fitted with large lap-valves – but is this really the case? Evidence from dynamometer carrriages certainly does not support this. The view appears to have arisen originally from a series of tests carried out between a LNWR G2 0-8-0 and one of the then new LMS Standard 7 0-8-0s and referred to by Mr Cox in *Locomotive Panorama Vol I*. Table XLIV records the relevant figures for these two engines using the more comprehensive data set out in the precursor, a paper[30] Mr E S Cox presented to the Institution of Locomotive Engineers in 1946. This reveals the large-lap engine returned a specific coal consumption of 2.8lbs/dhp/hr as opposed to 4.02lbs/dhp/hr from the older, short-lap one, which represents a saving in favour of the former of 30 per cent. This reduction, it will be appreciated had been obtained from similar weight locomotives, while the G7¾s boiler fitted to the Standard 7 0-8-0 was derived from that carried by the G2. This coal reduction was also nearly twice the saving a large-lap, *superheated* 2-6-4T had achieved over a short-lap, *saturated* 'Precursor Tank' working at a significantly lower boiler pressure. It was nearly one quarter as much again as that obtained by the LNER with its A1 class 4-6-2 - when the higher speeds and steam rates, plus the shorter cut-offs associated with express train operation meant the reduction in the throttling losses at admission due to the presence of large-lap valves were at their greatest. Table XLIV reveals that although the coal consumption of the 'Austin Seven' was indeed less, the steam it needed in order to generate each horsepower was almost the same as that used by the former LNWR machine. On this basis, the maximum improvement the presence of large-lap valves could effect in this particular comparison was a reduction of 5½ per cent. However, when we consider that the LMS engine carried a higher

Table XLIV – Performance Comparison between LMS Standard Class 7 0-8-0 and ex-LNWR G2 0-8-0 - Toton - Brent

		LMS 0-8-0	LNWR 0-8-0
Average weight of train	tons	900	940
Average running speed	mph	17.3	17.6
Coal:- Pounds per mile		53.9	79.0
Pounds per ton mile including engine		0.055	0.076
Pounds per drawbar horspower hour		2.8	4.02
Average pounds per sq ft of grate area per hour		39.4	59.0
Water:- Gallons per mile		46.1	50.0
Pounds per drawbar horsepower hour		24.0	25.4
Pounds per pound of coal		8.57	6.3

working pressure and six-ring piston valves, which will have reduced internal steam leakage compared to the Schmidt single ring piston valve fitted to the G2, the precise advantage *directly* attributable to the increased lap length was in all probability even less. It is only through comparing the specific steam consumption values, that we may establish the relative performance of the steam circuit possessed by one engine with that of another.

Although coal figures are commonly used, they are effectively one-step removed, since they also include the influence that boiler efficiency had on its value. This is particularly pertinent in these trials because the LMS Standard 7 boiler evaporated 36 per cent more water per pound of coal than its LNWR competitor. It was this superior *boiler* efficiency, which accounts for the overwhelming majority of the reduction in specific coal consumption, not the increased lap length, which enthusiasts undoubtedly influenced by Mr Cox, have blithely taken to be the reason. Reference to table III which records LMS ten-year consumption figures obtained from these two classes in service demonstrates the true position. Likewise, over the period 1933-5, the 'Austin 7' consumed 70.15lbs of coal per mile, while the ex-LNWR G2 and the ex-L&YR Class 31 0-8-0s, also power class 7 engines, burned 73.55lbs and 75.53lbs[31] respectively.

---

30 Mr E S Cox *A Modern Locomotive History - Ten Years Development on the LMS - 1923-1932* paper Nº 457 Journal I Loco E 1946 p125.

31 The 1933-35 consumption figures from the article *LMS Locomotive Operating Costs*

Mr J Reeves *LMS Journal Nº 7* Wild Swan Publications Ltd Didcot pp7-8.

Table XLV – Comparison in Goods Engine Performance LMS/BR Toton – Brent Up Loaded Mineral Trains

Year	Locomotive	Load tons	Route length miles	Running time mins	Average speed mph	Coal lbs/mile	Water galls/mile	Lbs/ton-mile (excluding engine)		Lbs/dhp		Evaporation lbs/lb
								coal	water	coal	water	
1925	LNWR G2 0-8-0	754	127.4	438.5	17.43	61.7	42.05	0.0818	0.5576	4.16	28.33	6.82
	MR Class 4 0-6-0	769	127.4	442.75	17.3	68.2	42.4	0.0886	0.5515	4.25	26.4	6.22
	MR Class 3 & Class 4 0-6-0s	1336	127.0	455.3	16.74	124.7	88.96	0.0934	0.6657	4.406	31.4	7.13
1927	LNWR G2 0-8-0	938	127.5	434.9	17.6	70.0	50.0	0.084	0.533	4.02	25.4	6.33
	S&DJR 2-8-0	927	127.3	435.1	17.6	80.6	60.8	0.087	0.656	4.37	32.9	7.54
§	LMS Class 7 0-8-0	900	~	~	17.3	53.9	46.10	0.060	0.512	2.8	24.0	8.57
1928	LMS Garratt 2-6-0 + 0-6-2	1556	128.0	504.6	15.22	143.9	97.7	0.093	0.628	3.86	26.22	6.96
	LMS Garratt 2-6-0 + 0-6-2	1423	128.1	479.8	16.01	128.7	88.3	0.090	0.621	3.81	26.13	6.62
	2off MR Class 4 0-6-0s	1484	128.0	448.3	17.13	118.9	92.9	0.08	0.626	3.63	28.41	6.81
	MR Class 3 & Class 4 0-6-0s	1353	127.6	441.4	17.35	118.9	94.8	0.088	0.701	3.74	29.85	6.43
1930	LMS Class 7 0-8-0 live steam injector	887	128.0	381.5	20.1	48.4	42.1	0.055	0.475	2.67	23.3	8.7
	LMS Class 7 0-8-0 ACFI feed heater	910	127.9	393.9	19.5	46.4	38.9	0.051	0.427	2.44	20.5	8.38
1931	LMS Garratt 2-6-0 + 0-6-2	1301	128.5	346.9	22.2	92.4	74.2	0.071	0.570	~	~	8.03
	LMS Garratt 2-6-0 + 0-6-2	1340	128.1	331.0	23.2	88.7	~	0.0662	~	3.37	~	~
1936	LMS Class 8 2-8-0	903	127.8	362.2	21.2	51.7	44.1	0.0573	0.488	2.89	24.6	8.51
	LMS Class 8 2-8-0	999	127.5	388.2	19.7	57.7	47.3	0.0578	0.473	2.92	23.9	8.18
	LMS Class 8 2-8-0	1070	127.6	401.1	19.1	66.3	51.0	0.062	0.477	3.03	22.8	7.69¶
1948	LNER O1 2-8-0	1061	127.8	440.3	17.4	73.0	54.4	0.069	0.513	3.37	25.14	7.46
	LNER O1 2-8-0	1080	127.8	525.5	14.6	84.0	64.77	0.0778	0.6	3.29	25.36	7.71
	LMS Class 8 2-8-0	1047	127.7	484.7	15.8	79.7	60.5	0.076	0.578	3.61	27.40	7.59
	LMS Class 8 2-8-0	*1080*	127.5	531.3	14.4	91.83	74.2	0.085	0.687	3.76	30.38	6.47
	WD 2-8-0	1091	128.0	440.7	17.4	84.4	62.9	0.077	0.577	3.6	26.82	7.45
	WD 2-8-0	*1080*	128.0	492.3	15.6	82.4	63.44	0.0763	0.587	3.67	28.26	7.70
	WD 2-10-0	1047	127.9	514.1	14.9	87.1	65.2	0.083	0.623	3.74	28.01	7.49
	WD 2-10-0	*1080*	127.9	508	15.1	86.45	66.22	0.080	0.613	4.01	30.72	7.66

* Load estimated – may not be exact.
§ Date not recorded by Mr Cox, presumably soon after building 1929 or 1930
¶ Quoted value; dividing per mile water by the per mile coal gives 7.52lb/lb.

Data taken from LMS dynamometer records, I Loco E, RTCS, Stanier '8Fs' at Work, British Standard Steam Locomotives Vol IV The 9F 2-10-0 Class, Mr C J Allen *The Locomotive Exchanges* Ian Allan London 2nd Edition 1950 and Mr O S Nock *The British Steam Locomotive 1925- 1965* Ian Allan London 1966.

Shaded entries represent large-lap locomotives. In this basic comparison, no allowances have been made for coal quality, which will have tended to favour the earlier tests, conversely, the later engines, used higher working pressures and were fitted with far less leaky piston valves as well in some cases exhaust steam injectors, which would have all been to their advantage. Thus the high specific steam consumption recorded by the S&DJR 2-8-0 performance *was no* due to short-lap valves *per se*, but symptomatic of the leakage past the Schmidt single broad ring and liner - the coal consumption of the 'Royal Scots' was found to have increased by typically 60-70 per cent from this cause - it was not discovered until 1930. The increase in specific steam consumption will have been equally significant.

At various times the LMS conducted tests on engines employed on Toton-Brent coal trains; in some cases short-lap and in others large-lap. In 1948, the newly formed British Railways repeated the exercise using a wider selection of engines on the same duty over the same road, differing only in that this time the contestants all possessed large-laps. Since these trials involved in-service dynamometer testing, they were subject to the vagaries inherent in the method such as delays in traffic, variations in speed *etc*. However, as a record of engine behaviour in service they are invaluable, for as they involved the same traffic at similar speeds over the same road they are directly comparable - table XLV summarizes the results. As with the tests between the 'Austin Seven' and the G2, if the large-lap engines were more efficient than their short-lap siblings, then they would have required less *steam* to produce each drawbar horsepower, because their superior steam circuit ought to have been able to use the steam more effectively. However, inspection reveals that there was little if any saving in steam, on the contrary, it is a little disconcerting to observe that in service a saturated 0-6-0 coupled to a superheated one - both of course short-lap – could use less steam than a modern superheated large-lap engine. That this was so was due to the innate nature and performance characteristics of the conventional steam locomotive, but essentially table XLV confirms that there was no real benefit from using large-lap valves on goods engines.

What saving the latter recorded in specific steam consumption may be explained by superior steam conditions or, and more importantly, by the reduced internal leakage present in the large-lap engines. They were provided with 6-ring piston valve heads compared to the Schmidt single broad ring carried by most of the short-lap engines. In April 1931 Mr Cox estimated the saving in coal (and therefore approximately water) through fitting these piston valve heads to have been 10 per cent. Applying this factor to say the water consumption of the Class 4 0-6-0 tested in 1925, means it would have fallen from 26.4lbs/dph/hr to 24lbs - not that different from the rates obtained from N° 8000 in 1936. Since the 0-6-0s were later provided with 4-ring piston valve heads, in practice they would have leaked slightly more, but there was little to gain from large-lap valves in this situation. Indeed had it been otherwise, then the Class 7 0-8-0 fitted with ACFI feed water heating should have become the standard goods engine! We might also reflect when comparing these performances, that the class producing the highest productivity per locomotive and crew on the basis of gross ton-mile per train hour, was the Garratt. This was primarily due to the low speeds present in mineral traffic so its four cylinders maximized the locomotive's cylinder limit, while being in effect an articulated tank engine gave it a high adhesion - *vide* figure 86.

Some Background Theory

Before we look into Class 4 performance in more depth, we ought to consider some of the factors influencing engine performance. The purity and relative simplicity of the steam locomotive makes for ready analysis but for this to be successful, we must allow for the three fundamental relationships, which describe its behaviour. The first is quite obvious being the boiler efficiency. Within the boiler, the working fluid underwent a change of state, entering as feed water drawn from the tank, but leaving as saturated or superheated steam. In either instance, this was accompanied by a considerable increase in its heat content (or enthalpy). Since this increase was always less than the heat content of the coal, the former divided by the latter revealed the efficiency of the boiler, values that could be estimated with a reasonable degree of accuracy. Very often in locomotive work, this ratio is not expressed in terms of the heat content of the water/steam relative to the coal, but more simply as the evaporation - pounds of water per pound of coal. This was an easier relationship to establish, but caution must attend its interpretation, since it takes no account of differences in superheat temperature or boiler pressure, both of which affected the enthalpy of the steam.

We may intuitively appreciate that a better designed locomotive would need less steam to produce each horsepower, *i.e.* its specific steam consumption (lbs/ihp/hr) would be smaller than that of a not so good engine. This is the second factor, however, to effect that judgement we must consider it in conjunction with the third factor, which establishes the theoretical consumption – a value that varied with the steam conditions. The Rankine (or cycle) efficiency, named in honour of William Rankine, may be defined at its simplest as the amount of heat energy theoretically available for conversion into work in each pound of steam divided by the heat energy necessary to turn one pound of boiler feed water into steam at boiler exit conditions[32]. Since the thermodynamic properties of water are available for all conditions of pressure and temperature, it is possible to establish the Rankine efficiency for any locomotive provided the steam conditions leaving the boiler and at the exhaust are known or may be estimated. The Rankine efficiency represents the maximum possible efficiency displayed by a perfect engine (or turbine) working between those same upper and lower limits.

Since real locomotives were not perfect we must allow for this imperfection, which we do by comparing their actual specific steam consumption with that of the consumption of the theoretical engine. The difference in the energy possessed by the steam when it left the boiler as opposed to what it should have possessed at the base of the blast-pipe assuming perfect expansion, is known as the 'theoretical heat drop'. This represented the maximum amount of heat energy that was available for conversion into work energy within the cylinders. If *all* of this energy was converted then the real engine would have had an *isentropic* efficiency of 100 per cent. In practice, because of design faults, certain inevitable compromises, internal leakage, condensation etc. the steam encountered between entering steam space in the boiler to leaving the blast-pipe ensured the isentropic efficiency was considerably less than this. If 2545[33] is divided by the theoretical heat drop, the dividend is the theoretical specific steam consumption in pounds per horsepower per hour. If this value is in turn divided by the actual steam consumption per horsepower returned by the engine, the result is the isentropic efficiency - sometimes referred to as the efficiency ratio. Typically, only between one-half and three-quarters of the theoretically available heat drop was actually converted into power - the rest was just 'lost'. However these losses were not a constant value, instead they were affected by engine speed and power output (*i.e.* steam flow rate).

The inclusion of the three factors given above, enables locomotive performance to be described mathematically by the following relationship:-

$$R\,E\,(\%) \times \frac{I\,E\,(\%)}{100} \times \frac{B\,E\,(\%)}{100}$$
$$= \text{The indicated thermal efficiency} \quad (17)$$
of the locomotive

where:-
R E = Rankine efficiency
I E = isentropic efficiency
B E = boiler efficiency

Whence a series of estimates may be made regarding a locomotive's performance:-

For example, consider a locomotive using saturated steam, employing a boiler pressure of 160lbs/sq in and with a back pressure of 5lbs/sq in[34], the Rankine efficiency corresponding to these steam conditions is 13.7%. Assuming it has an isentropic efficiency of 60% and a boiler efficiency of 75% thus:-

$$13.7\% \times \frac{60\%}{100} \times \frac{75\%}{100} = 6.2\%$$

Hence, this particular locomotive is working with a thermal indicated efficiency of 6.2%.

From this, we may establish its coal consumption. Firstly we must establish how much coal a 100% efficient engine would burn, which we do by dividing 2545 by the calorific value of the coal - if no figure is to hand assume 14,000 as a typical working value - and divide the dividend by the indicated thermal efficiency. The answer is the quantity of coal the locomotive will consume producing one indicated horsepower for one hour.

$$\frac{2545}{14000} \times \frac{100}{6.2} = 2.93 \text{ lb of coal per IHP per hour}$$

Thus, if at that moment we knew, or could estimate the locomotive was producing 400 indicated horsepower to pull itself and its train, it would therefore be consuming 1172 pounds of coal per hour – and if it was running at 50mph say 24lbs/mile.

From the three separate factors, we are able to determine:-

(i) Coal consumption relative to the work done - measured in pounds per indicated horsepower per hour - describes the overall efficiency of the locomotive.

(ii) Water consumption per indicated horsepower per hour which, when contrasted with the

---

[32] It was quite common practice when applying the Rankine cycle to steam reciprocating engines to adopt a modified version, which recognized that the cylinder was of finite size. Essentially, the expansion was considered to cease at the point of release rather than the back pressure. However, locomotives were variable speed machines, and at high speeds and/or short cut-offs the point of release was not discernible on indicator cards. Hence, for simplicity this 'modified' approach has been disregarded and the conventional 'turbine' version adopted.

[33] 2545BTU/hour is the thermal equivalent of one horsepower-hour.

[34] If the actual exhaust pressure is unknown, then 5 lbs/sq in is representative of the sort of average exhaust pressure, present when working the typical locomotive in its mid- to three-quarters power range. Such a back pressure was a necessary evil tolerated in order for the typical British design blast pipe arrangement, to generate sufficient draught for the boiler.

Table XLVI – Approximate Best Thermal Efficiencies of Various Steam Locomotives

		Representative saturated locomotive built c.1880	Representative superheated locomotive built c.1912	LMS 'Coronation' superheated 4-6-2 simple expansion	Chapelon superheated 4-8-0 compound expansion
Working pressure	lbs/sq in	160	180	250	295
Steam temperature	deg. F	371	580	615	750
Heat drop	BTU/lb	150.8	187	213.8	253
Rankine or cycle or theoretical efficiency	per cent	12.8	15.4	17.2	19.7
Specific steam consumption	lb/ihp/hr	16.9	13.6	11.9	10.0
Actual steam consumption	lb/ihp/hr	28.3	22.0	14.5	11.7
Cylinder efficiency	per cent	7.64	9.6	14.2	16.5
Isentropic efficiency (or efficiency ratio)	per cent	60	62	82	84
Boiler efficiency	per cent	68	75	76	78
Overall indicated thermal efficiency	per cent	5.2	7.2	10.7	12.9

theoretical consumption for the same initial and exhaust conditions, provides a measure of the engine/steam circuit efficiency.

(iii) Evaporation - pounds of water per pound of coal - when compared to the theoretical evaporation possible from a pound of coal provides a measure of the boiler efficiency.

Approaching data in this manner enables not only differences in the performance of one engine relative to another, to be quantified, but also to establish whether it was due to a higher Rankine efficiency, better steam utilisation or a superior boiler performance, thereby avoiding the elephant-trap Mr Cox fell into. Sir William Stanier[35] used a somewhat similar approach (table XLVI) to demonstrate the relative thermal efficiencies achieved at various stages in the development of the steam locomotive; starting in each case, with the Rankine or cycle efficiency, then the cylinder and boiler efficiencies and finishing with an overall indicated thermal efficiency for the complete locomotive. The example in the first column represents a saturated steam engine of the late nineteenth century, column 2 that of a typical superheated express engine of the period 1908-12 blessed with short lap valves. Columns 3 and 4 illustrate the performance standard achieved with simple and compound expansion by the time of the Second World War. Now without wishing to criticise Sir William, he was being a little misleading, with some of these figures. Sure, the *maximum* isentropic efficiencies obtainable from large-lap single expansion express engines such as his 'Coronation' class 4-6-2s were certainly of the order of 80 per cent, unfortunately, such values could only be obtained at the very highest express train speeds, wherein only a comparatively small proportion of the most modern locomotives spent only a comparatively small proportion of their working lives. Thus, although at high piston speeds these 4-6-2s and similar engines were able to return outstanding isentropic efficiencies this was not the case once their performance was averaged over the whole run. Consequently, even in express working where the potential gains were at their maximum, the improvement that could be attributed to long-travel valves was not as great as Sir William implied with mean isentropic efficiencies obtained in service being more typically around 75 per cent. While in the case of large-lap locomotives employed on humble goods duties, their isentropic efficiencies were lower still. In these circumstances, as will be seen, much of the perceived advantage of long-travel valves was in reality due to their higher Rankine efficiencies, combined with lower rates of internal steam leakage. Conversely, the isentropic efficiency he ascribed to the superheated short-lap engine could be comfortably exceeded by some examples employed on express passenger trains, while the French compound maintained its higher value over a much wider speed range than the simple expansion engines.

The cylinder efficiency appearing in table XLVI is the product of the Rankine efficiency and the isentropic efficiency, so it represents the combination of the first two terms of equation *(17)*.

---

35 Sir William Stanier *The Position of the Locomotive in Mechanical Engineering* Presidential Address I Mech E 1941 p52.

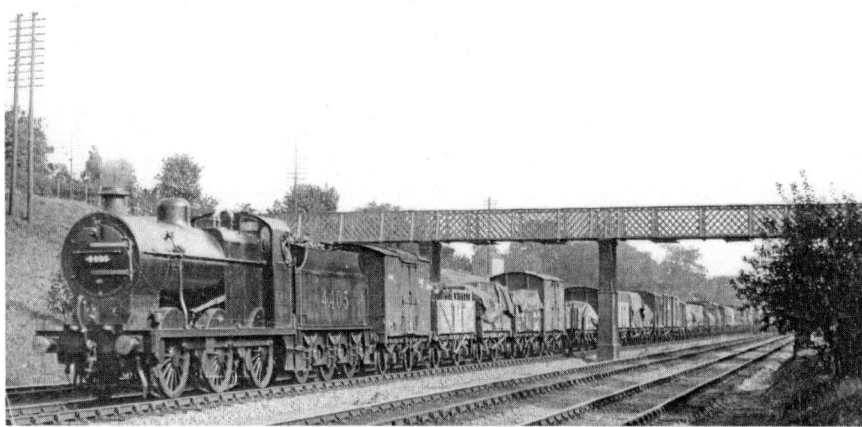

Fig. 88 - N° 4405 heading north on the down slow passes under the footbridge immediately north of Elstree station. According to the headlamp code the engine is hauling a through freight running not less than 15 miles without stopping.

this instance derived from *BR Bulletin N° 3 London Midland Region – Class 4, 2 Cyl., 2-6-0 Mixed Traffic Locomotive*. This plot records the variation in isentropic efficiency (or efficiency ratio) against indicated horsepower for variations in speed and cut-off. British Railways used a slightly different definition of Rankine efficiency from the one given earlier, since it took the expansion down to zero (gauge) pressure rather than the actual back pressure. There were further differences *i.e.* Rugby assumed the feedwater enthalpy was zero while Swindon afforded it a value. It does not matter which method is used provided it is applied *consistently* in any comparisons; serious errors will appear however should the results obtained from dissimilar methods be compared.

This was a common artifice used by locomotive engineers but some consider it misleading. In many ways isentropic efficiency is more representative of cylinder efficiency since it is telling us how effective the steam circuit was at converting the available heat drop into power. Whereas, when the two terms are considered together, it is not immediately apparent if the higher cylinder efficiency possessed by one class over that of another was due to a better designed steam circuit or simply because it carried a higher boiler pressure and/or superior superheat. This is something we shall return to later.

Figure 89 illustrates the change in isentropic efficiency for a modern large-lap locomotive, in

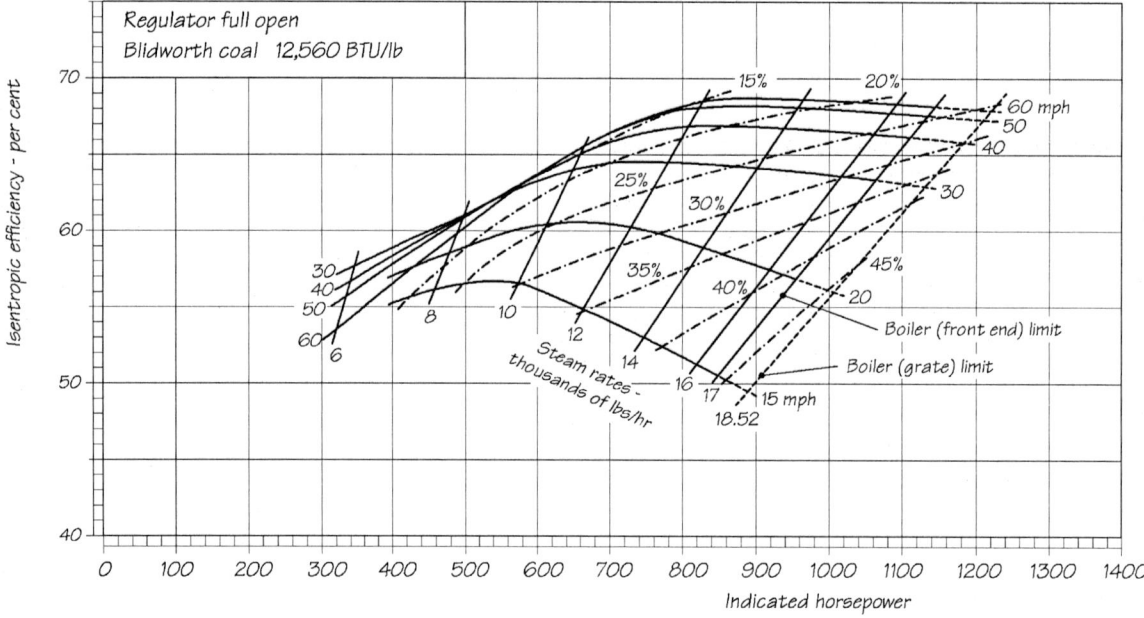

Fig. 89 - Example of the variation in isentropic efficiency - LMS Class 4MT 2-6-0 N° 43094

At its simplest the losses in the cylinder may be considered as being either time-based *i.e.* standing losses *e.g.* leakage past the piston valves and radiation loss or stroke based losses such as incomplete expansion, excessive compression, highback pressure, *etc*. At low power outputs, the loss of steam leaking past the pistons and piston

Comparisons, Steaming and Performance

Fig. 90 – Former Midland Class 4 0-6-0s Nº 3945 and 3946 with the ex-L&YR dynamometer carriage photographed on one of their runs – probably February 1928. It shews graphically what a 1,500-ton train looks like when composed of small capacity wagons as well as hinting at the skills needed to work it over an undulating road, while keeping it in one piece. It also suggests that working such trains with two engines was not necessarily as inefficient as might at first be thought.

valves formed its highest proportion of the total steam passing through the engine. The back pressure was low so compression would probably not be complete, further the engine would be running in a short cut-off giving considerable throttling of the steam at admission. Accordingly, all of these factors converged so the isentropic efficiency assumed a low value – in this instance in the region of 55-60 per cent – largely independent of speed, but it will be noted with the lowest value appearing at the highest speeds, as the cut-off was least.

For any speed, as the power output increased the isentropic efficiency rose because more steam was passing through the cylinders consequent upon the later cut-off so proportionately the standing losses reduced. The larger weight of steam passing through increased the back pressure so compression became more complete while the throttling reduced as the port opening increased resulting from the later cut-off. Having attained a peak value it then fell off consequent upon the longer cut-off needed to admit ever larger quantities of steam, which compromised the opportunity for the steam to expand, while the rise in back pressure reduced the Rankine efficiency. The highest isentropic efficiencies were attained when the engine was running at its fastest, in this particular example it peaked at around 68 per cent at 60 mph while producing about 850 indicated horsepower, conversely at 15 mph it peaked at about 57 per cent and 560 indicated horsepower. Whilst the isentropic efficiency of all locomotives followed this general format, there were quite noticeable variations between classes in the precise profiles of the curves and the maximum value value attained for any particular speed. Short-lap engines, had they been so comprehensively tested, would have demonstrated similar characteristics save their maximum isentropic efficiency values would have been lower, but at low speeds and power outputs the values would probably have not been that dissimilar.

Some limited superheat and back pressure figures were obtained from 'Big Goods' Nº 44030 when it was tested in 1954, whilst fitted with its original exhaust system. These curves suggest over the steam output range 10,000 to 13,000 pounds of steam per hour, the superheat temperature rose from 585°F to 595°F, while the back pressure increased from 0.75lbs/sq in to 1.62lbs. Assuming the intermediate values for 12,000lbs/hr and coupling them with Sir William Stanier's values for isentropic efficiency enables us to obtain approximate steam consumption rates:-

Steam conditions 175lbs/sq in 592°F	1318.8 BTU/lb
Exhaust steam conditions 1.28lbs/sq in	1104.3 BTU/lb
Theoretical heat drop	214.5 BTU/lb
Theoretical specific steam consumption	11.9 lbs/ihp/hr
Specific steam consumption adopting 55% isentropic efficiency	21.6 lbs/ihp/hr
Specific steam consumption adopting 60% isentropic efficiency	19.8 lbs/ihp/hr

From the theoretical steam consumption of 11.9lbs/ihp/hr, and assuming isentropic efficiencies of the order 55-60 per cent as being typical for a short-lap engine, gives for the actual specific steam consumption something the region of 20-22lbs/ihp/hr in round figures.

Mr Cox, who supervised several pre-war Toton-Brent dynamometer runs, has left us with a graphic account[36] of the working of coal trains on the latter road - it is from the last portion of which the following has been taken:-

"Away once more, the character of the route now changes, and our principle obstacles are the two long pull-ups and subsequent descents which separate us from our destination the first to Sharnbrook, and the second from Bedford to Leagrave. On the former the freight lines sheer away to the east separately from the passenger in order to keep the incline within the ruling grade of 1 in 200, but it is on the latter that we settle down to an hour's grind up the 17 miles to the top. This represents really hard work to come towards the end of the long day's work, and an average of 1,000 drawbar horsepower may well have to be exerted continuously with maximum tonnage trains hauled either by the Garratts or pairs of 0-6-0 engines."

A drawbar horsepower of 1,000 between two Class 4 engines is of course 500 from each but as the engines re-filled their tender tanks during the stop at Wellingborough and allowing for the gradient, it represented an equivalent drawbar horsepower of around 550. Since the horsepower necessary to drive each engine at 17 mph was probably in the region of 50-60, this meant each locomotive was developing 600 indicated horsepower or a little over, continuously for about an hour. Such outputs taking our estimated specific steam consumption of 20-22lbs/ihp/hr, necessitated steam production rates in the range 12,000-13,200 pounds per hour, but when we consider the cut-off for the climb was 42-45 per cent this estimate could be light. The later cut-off through reducing the expansion ratio will have lowered the isentropic efficiency by a small amount. Of course, this was the steaming rate obtained in everyday service, albeit of an hour's duration. It does not necessarily represent the maximum continuous output of the boiler and evidence will be presented that it was higher.

Incidentally, we may make these steam rate calculations another way since two tables in the original Toton-Brent reports highlighted the running of the loaded trains on the average gradients of 1 in 200 that occurred at three points in the journey. These snapshots have been reproduced as tables XLVII and XLVIII. Appearing in the second of these tables are estimates of the combustion rates maintained by the engines as they negotiated the sections. It is not clear how they were established as there was no specific facilities

Table XLVII - Toton - Brent Trials – Engine Performance on Grades 1925

			31/8/1925	2/9/1925	7/9/1925	
Date						
Engine Nº			574	3866	3866	3756
Engine type			G2	4F	4F	3F
Load Behind Tender		tons	753.75	768.8	1335.91	
Haringworth & Weldon Nth	Average boiler pressure through section	lbs/sq in	171	170	175	165
	Average position of the reversing gear in section‡		1½	5½	6	4
	Average regulator opening		0.5	0.6	0.3	0.6
	Average water level in the glass		0.8	1.0	0.9	0.9
	Average speed in the section	mph	13.72	12.2	10.92	
	Average drawbar horsepower in the section		451	419	698.9	
	Average drawbar pull in the section	lbs	12320	12880	23990	
Bedford & Leagrave	Average boiler pressure through section	lbs/sq in	175	170	175	170
	Average position of the reversing gear in section‡		1½	6	4	3
	Average regulator opening		0.5	0.7	0.3	0.5
	Average water level in the glass		0.9	0.9	1.0	1.0
	Average speed in the section	mph	14.42	15.88	14.3	
	Average drawbar horsepower in the section		424.7	487.35	749.8	
	Average drawbar pull in the section	lbs	11043	11726	19667	

‡Revolutions from mid-gear, in the case of the LNWR engine; notches in the case of the Midland engines.
Engine Nº 574   4½ revolutions from mid to full forward gear
Engine Nº 3866   12 notches from mid to full forward gear
Engine Nº 3756   7 notches from mid to full forward gear.

---

36 Mr E S Cox *Chronicles of Steam* - Ian Allan Shepperton 1967 pp 67-72

provided to record their values; presumably they were obtained by counting shovelsful of coal during the ascent. The experience of other testers, *e.g.*, Professor Lomonossoff and Dennis Carling, suggests 20 to 60 minutes was not really long enough periods obtain accurate combustion rate figures. If the coal was added at a rate that differed from the one at which it was burned then the surplus or deficit resulted in the firebed thickening or reducing. Nevertheless, with this qualification in mind, we have an approximate way of estimating the steam rate. Taking as a first example the figures for Nº 3945 and 3946 climbing between Bedford and Leagrave, the average drawbar power was 939. Assuming two-thirds supplies the engine and tender weight becomes 83.4 tons, so the equivalent drawbar horsepower is given by:-

$$939 + \frac{[2240 \times 83.4 \times 16.7 \times 2]}{200 \times 375} = 1022 \text{ edhp}$$

If each engine consumed, say 50 horsepower in driving itself, the combined indicated horsepower generated approximates to 1,120. The average evaporation the two engines over the whole run between Toton and Brent was 7.82lbs/lb. On the climbs it will have dropped off, let us assume to 7lbs/lb, so the estimated steam production was:-

$$[81.0 \times (21.1 \times 2) \times 7] = 23,900 \text{lbs/hr}$$

Giving a specific steam consumption of 20.3lbs/ihp/hr and tallying approximately with the lower of the two earlier estimates.

Two graphs appeared in the official report summarizing the 1928 series of dynamometer tests. The first shewed the variation in drawbar horsepower with speed, for the three combinations of locomotive/train used *viz* two Class 4 engines, one Class 4 engine and one Class 3 engine, and a 'Garratt' alone, on the normal schedule (average speed ≈17 mph). This graph therefore displayed three curves - one for each engine permutation. The second graph was derived from measurements

Table XLVIII - Toton - Brent Trials - Engine Performance on Grades 1928

	Date		23/2/1928	28/2/1928	4/3/1928
	Engine Nº		3945 3946	3756 3946	3945 3946
	Engine type		4F 4F	3F 4F	4F 4F
	Load Behind Tender	tons	1484.1	1353.0	1177.9
Gretton & Weldon North	Length of section	miles	3.64	3.64	3.64
	Average boiler pressure through section	lbs/sq in	175	175	175
	Average cut-off in section		42%	32% 45%	43%
	Estimated combustion rate in section	lbs/sq ft/hr	70.5	81.6	81.5
	Average booked speed in section		12.8	12.8	16.8
	Average speed in the section	mph	12.2	14.0	17.5
	Average drawbar horsepower in the section		819	923	920
	Maximum drawbar pull in section		27104	26208	22624
	Average drawbar pull in the section	lbs	25088	24640	19712
Wellingborough & Souldrop	Length of section	miles	7.81	7.81	7.81
	Average boiler pressure through section	lbs/sq in	175	175	175
	Average cut-off in section		42%	33% 48%	42%
	Estimated combustion rate in section	lbs/sq ft/hr	62.2	66.5	80.4
	Average booked speed in section		16.2	16.2	21.3
	Average speed in the section	mph	14.3	15.4	20.7
	Average drawbar horsepower in the section		722	751	907
	Maximum drawbar pull in section		28224	26208	24640
	Average drawbar pull in the section	lbs	19040	18368	16352
Bedford & Leagrave	Length of section	miles	17.19	17.19	17.19
	Average boiler pressure through section	lbs/sq in	175	175	175
	Average cut-off in section		44%	28% 45%	42%
	Estimated combustion rate in section	lbs/sq ft/hr	81.0	82.4	102.0
	Average booked speed in section		16.4	16.4	20.2
	Average speed in the section	mph	16.7	17.5	23.8
	Average drawbar horsepower in the section		939	930	1150
	Maximum drawbar pull in section		30464	25312	23968
	Average drawbar pull in the section	lbs	21056	19936	18144

A Defence of the Midland/LMS Class 4 0-6-0

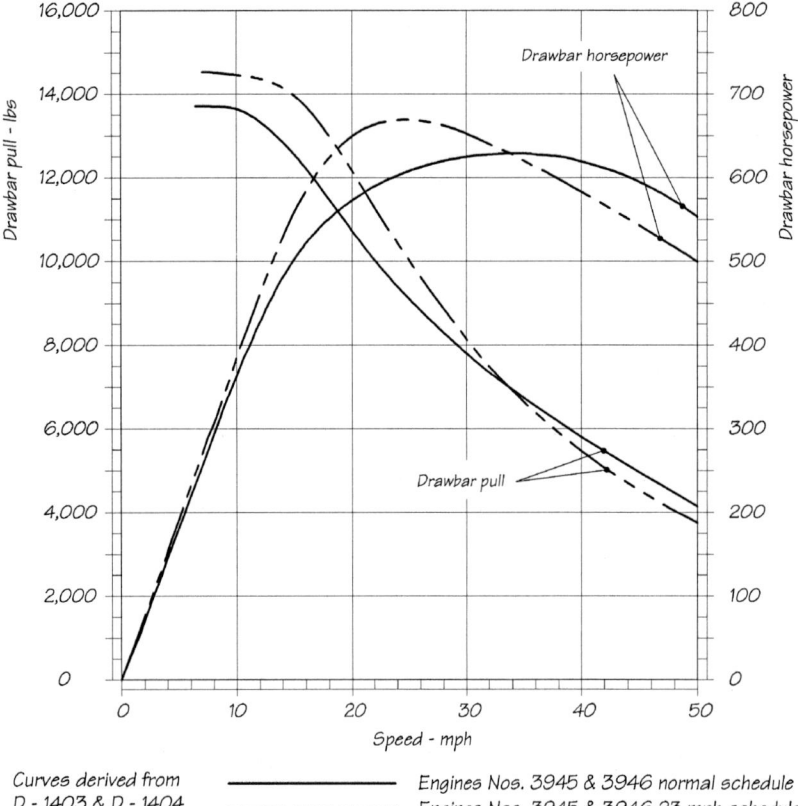

Curves derived from
D - 1403 & D - 1404

——————— Engines Nos. 3945 & 3946 normal schedule
— — — — Engines Nos. 3945 & 3946 23 mph schedule

Fig. 91 - Class 4 0-6-0, variation in drawbar horsepower and pull with speed

obtained on the runs made to a schedule, specially accelerated for the tests having an average speed of 23 mph. This series comprised only two curves representing a pair of Class 4 engines, and a 'Garratt'. In both instances the drawbar curves obtained from the double-headed trains employing two Class 4 engines have been 'halved' to realise the corresponding values for one engine working alone. These are shewn in figure 91, which also includes the associated drawbar pull or drawbar tractive effort. These curves demonstrate that the Class 4 Goods could generate around 670 drawbar horsepower at 24 miles per hour. For the engine to have driven itself at that speed would have demanded roughly 65-70 horsepower, so implying the corresponding indicated horsepower was around 740. Using the specific steam consumption given earlier of 20-22lbs/ihp/hr, this suggests a steam production in the range 14,800 to 16,300 pounds per hour.

Again as with the earlier estimate we have no information as to whether this power, although being the maximum recorded in this instance also represented the machine's absolute maximum continuous output. The values were obtained from tests designed to replicate the engines pulling their normal trains and working their 'normal' timetables rather than deliberate attempts to establish maximum outputs. Although Mr Cox's written report summarising the trials made no specific reference to these horsepower/speed curves, that in a way, is understandable; after all normally only out of the ordinary working deserves comment. The engines were simply performing the task for which they had been designed and one that they performed on a daily basis - the humdrum is not news. It is only because, alert to the forty odd years of barbs directed at the Class 4 Goods, we suddenly feel vindicated when we are able to demonstrate that the engines *could* do a worthwhile day's work.

Some considerable support for these power output estimates is provided by figure 92, which based on empirically derived data, compares the indicated performance curves for the 'Big Goods' and the G2 class 0-8-0. The figures were produced originally by LMS engineers in connexion with the development of the Rugby Testing Station just prior to the Second World War. The mean effective pressure values used in the table were derived from the 'Normal Curve' of mean effective pressure versus speed appearing in DD 3082. The LMS produced several of these plots during its lifetime whose principal use was for establishing the power classification of its locomotives, however, it is understood that this particular curve was the only one which was actually used. In the diagram the horsepower point values along with the tractive effort curves have been derived from the table, but the horsepower curves have been smoothed. When establishing the power class the capacity of the boiler was also considered basing its output on the grate area[37], but

---

37 The classification scheme comprised two calculations firstly the tractive effort was obtained at the piston speed associated with a speed of 50mph for passenger engines or 25mph for goods engines. The tractive effort was calculated using the conventional formula, but with the mean effective

Comparisons, Steaming and Performance

here, instead the engineers have concentrated on the tractive effort and horsepower performance. We may see that at 24 miles per hour the indicated power the LMS *believed* the 0-6-0 could deliver in normal running was about 860, which comfortably exceeds our earlier estimate of 740. This table also demonstrates the observation expressed earlier, namely the power output of an 0-8-0 need not necessarily be any higher than that of an 0-6-0 despite it being a physically larger machine.

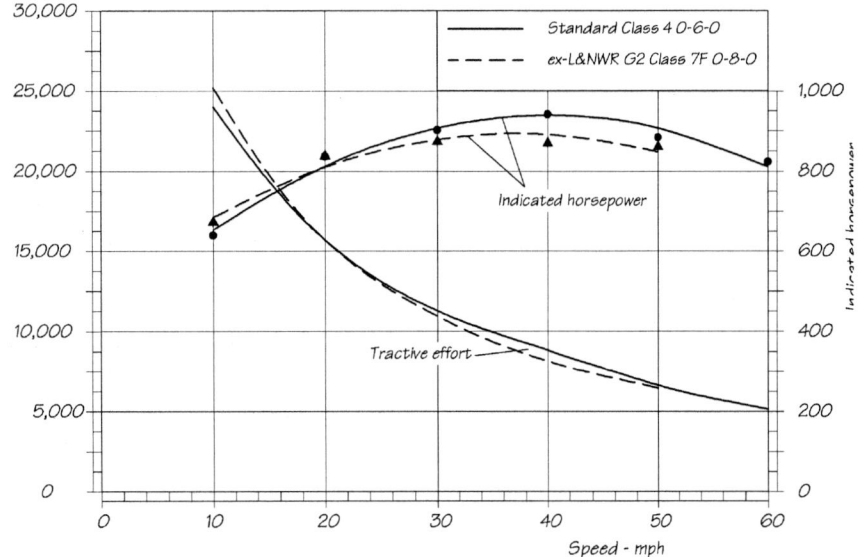

Class 4 0-6-0 - rated tractive effort 24,555lbs				Class G2 0-8-0 - rated tractive effort 28,043lbs			
Speed - mph	MEP as % of rated tractive effort	Tractive effort - lbs	Indicated horsepower	Speed - mph	MEP as % of rated tractive effort	Tractive effort - lbs	Indicated horsepower
10	98%	24,000	639	10	90%	25,200	672
20	64%	15,700	837	20	56%	15,700	838
30	46%	11,280	904	30	39%	10,940	873
40	36%	8,830	942	40	29%	8,140	869
50	27%	6,630	883	50	23%	6,450	860
60	21%	5,150	824				

Fig. 92 - LMS predicted indicated performance curves for Class 4 0-6-0 & G2 0-8-0 - Rugby Testing Station

Draughting and Steaming

We must now consider what appears from the crew's point of view was the major criticism of the Class 4, namely its reluctance to produce the required quantities of steam even with an experienced fireman. However, we must remember that these represent personal reminiscences often committed to paper several decades after they had been experienced. Furthermore, by the 'fifties, when most of those footplate men who have graced us with their memories were doing their firing, the great majority of engines in power class 4 comprised the 'Big Goods'. The only class 4 engine these authors were able to compare it with, was the new LMS/BR Class 4MT Mogul. In this respect, the latter presents a prime example of how the relative worth of a class can be given different values depending on the viewpoint of the writer. Thus Mr Higson, a former fireman, produced the following perceptive comment[38]:-

"It is curious that many of the modern small and medium-powered locomotives seemed inferior to their older counterparts. One could, of course only compare engines that were similar in power or that directly replaced older types, but this is not always a just comparison. However, one is hardly likely to impress an engine-crew with a machine, no matter how new and loaded with gadgets, that does not show up as well as the machine that has been displaced.

For example, neither of the two Ivatt designs of 2-6-0 were outstanding. The small 464xx 2-6-0s, despite their cab comforts and rocking grates, fell far short of the Midland or LYR Class 2F 0-6-0s in many other

---

pressure fraction derived from the curve substituted for the usual 85 per cent. The second calculation necessitated finding the boiler horsepower. A maximum hourly combustion rate of 130lbs/sq ft of grate was adopted, and it was assumed each pound of coal would evaporate 6.15lbs of water, giving 800lbs of steam per square foot of grate per hour. Then, assuming specific steam consumption figures of 20lbs/ihp/hr for superheated steam engines and 25lbs/ihp/hr for their saturated sisters, gave respective boiler horsepowers of 40 and 32 per sq ft of grate. The lower of the two values of cylinder tractive effort and boiler capacity determined the power class. Thus a G7s boiler with a grate area of 21.1sq ft had a boiler horsepower of 844; a G2's boiler at 23.6 sq ft returned 944.

38 Mr M F Higson *London Midland Fireman* Ian Allan Shepperton 1972 p43.

respects. Their ability to steam showed a limitation which was not apparent with the older engines. Further, they took longer to raise steam, a task which had to be accomplished with a fairly liberal use of the jet. The larger 430xx 2-6-0s were even less of a gift, and when one removed the 'frills' one found them less responsive than a good 4F 0-6-0. The steep inclination of the grate produced the same firing difficulties as with a 4F, and oscillation quickly worked the fire deep under the arch. In their original double-chimney condition they were ravenous beasties with two 'insides', half the fuel landing on top of the arch to provide a second fire, or vanishing through the tubes and out of the chimney."

Mr Nock[39], an experienced recorder of locomotive performance also supported the contention that the smaller 2-6-0 did not produce impressive a performance[40]:-

"In 1950 the new 2-6-0 engines were being used turn and turn about with the veteran ex-LNWR 18 inch 0-6-0s of Webb's design, non-superheated, and dating back to 1880. The new engines were dimensionally more powerful, having a nominal tractive effort of 17,400 lb against 14,000. They were, of course, much more comfortable to ride. But I cannot say I was particularly impressed by their hill climbing work, in comparison with the old LNWR 0-6-0s, seeing that a span of more than 60 years separated the two designs."

The final extract is from the pen of someone who served an engineering apprenticeship at Derby during Sir William's time before subsequently working for a number of years for Mr E S Cox. Mr Powell was not a man renowned for his approval of matters Midland, so let us contrast the views of the two previous writers with his recollection[41] of the LMS Class 2 2-6-0:-

"I do not think I can recall a class of locomotive which was so immediately and universally accepted by enginemen. They welcomed both the tender and tank versions with open arms, they worshipped the very rails they stood on - men who had staggered around the branches with Midland Class 2s and 0-6-0s, men used to L&YR radial tanks, or men weaned on L&NWR 'Cauliflowers'."

Given his somewhat caustic opinions of LMS

---

39 Mr O S Nock *British Locomotives of the 20th Century Vol II* Patrick Stephens Ltd Cambridge p216.

40 Following re-draughting on the Swindon model, N° 46413 was let loose on the Great Western main line with 15 bogies. Much has been made of this performance as proof of how good these engines were. Yet such a performance had for example been a *regular* feature on the Midland & Great Northern Joint using Class 1 saturated slide valve 4-4-0s.

41 Mr A J Powell *Living with London Midland Locomotives* Ian Allan 1977 pp48-50.

locomotive engineering prowess pre-Stanier, this comment perhaps makes his circumspect views of the larger Class 4 2-6-0 all the more significant. He referred to the dismal steaming of the double chimney version, and even admitted that with the single chimney version, steaming was only reasonably satisfactory, provided the fireman was careful. He then extolled the benefits of all their modern features before making a statement, which is perhaps more significant for what was omitted than for what was said:-

"From the drivers' point of view I think it would be fair to say that they appreciated their convenience and comfort, regarded them as a better tool for passenger work than a Class 4F 0-6-0, but inferior for real slogging freight work."

This observation lends support to the estimates in table XLII, that the Standard Freight had more pull available at low speeds; figure 89 records that the 2-6-0 could not run in 45 per cent cut-off at 15 miles per hour or faster. Now why, we might ask, should a locomotive designed in 1947 prove such a patchy advance on a locomotive design that had appeared in 1911? Well John Powell (*aka* '45671') has the answer ready to hand:-

"Alas, in their first form they were not the immediate success of their smaller sisters, nor did they ever fully become so. For that, a modicum of blame could be attached, believe it or not, to the Midland Railway. Its influence died hard!"

"The boiler was an entirely new design, and was excellently proportioned so far as the tubes, superheater and free gas areas were concerned ...

... but the grate was very steeply inclined, at a slope of about 1 in 4, the same as on the Class 4F 0-6-0 - this in 1947! - and a lot of trouble resulted from this."

An observation we might make, albeit one unlikely to be aired by Mr Powell, is the front portion of the 'broken backed' grate fitted to some of Sir William's boilers sloped at a steeper angle! In the case of the 3B boiler fitted to the Class 5 4-6-0 it was inclined at approximately 16¾° as opposed to the 14° slope of the G7s and this continued until 1957! Sloping grates undoubtedly could be more difficult to fire but that was *not* the prime cause of the firing trouble that some firemen experienced with the 'Big Goods', for consider the following concerning the ever popular[42] Class 3 0-6-0:-

"Compared with the 3F, the boiler of a 4F was

---

42 Mr M F Higson *London Midland Fireman* Ian Allan Shepperton 1972 p29.

not in the same class. In fact, if only the 3F had had more adhesive weight it could have licked a 4F any day. A 3F could be worked heavily with both injectors on, if needs be, a feat that I never managed with a 4F 0-6-0."

Since the G7 boiler fitted to the 3F and the G7s carried by the 4F were identical[43] even down to having the same design of brick arch and fire-bars differing *only* in the G7s being superheated, *if* the steaming problems experienced with the Class 4 were solely caused by the *slope* of its grate, then a similar effect *ought* to have manifested itself on the Class 3. Yet no author, as far as I am aware, has ever bemoaned the 3F ever for being short of steam, even at 60 mph, let alone for being the possessor of a steeply angled grate. Now this is not to say the grate angle did not cause some firemen difficulty when firing a 4 - that enough of them did is patent from their memoirs - but rather the real cause of their problems lay elsewhere and was perhaps an indication that the draughting of the Class 4 was not all that it could be.

In the case of the class 4MT 2-6-0, as Mr Higson stated, the slope of the grate did encourage the fire to work down to the front of the firebox. A situation experienced on the test engine, as the following[44] testifies, although the *cause* was symptomatic of a fault elsewhere in the design:-

"The speed range covered was 15 to 50 m.p.h. the upper limit being imposed by the effect of the mechanical disturbing forces on the fire. A major factor in this effect is considered to be the slope of the grate, which, being 1 in 4 continuous, is somewhat greater than usual."

"On the controlled road tests the effect of the mechanical disturbing forces were experienced also and to an extent that caused break-down in the coal-steam relationship when the speed was allowed to exceed 50 m.p.h. for more than a short time."

"On the road tests the engine was mechanically very noisy and violent oscillations were recorded when the speed reached and exceeded 60 m.p.h. This, however, does not accord with the general reputation of this class of engine in respect to riding qualities."

Let us not overlook that *all* of the small-boiler Midland 4-4-0s rebuilt in the early years of the twentieth century were also provided with H, G7 or G7s boilers, as well as the later LMS Standard 2P. These classes were expected to haul express trains typically at 50 mph and above, confirming the problem with the fire instability in the 4MT was not something inherently due to the slope of the grate *per se*.

Roughly, contemporary with these comments and to be considered in more detail later were some steaming tests[45] conducted on a pair of 4F 0-6-0s, prompted by the reputation the class had earned by the early 'fifties for poor steaming. Mr Rutherford referred to these tests in his article[46] about the Standard Class 4 Freight, together with the re-draughting that British Railways applied to these two engines and to the handful it subsequently modified:-

"The tests were carried out using the LMR Mobile Testing Plant on the Crewe - Holyhead line. The most remarkable result was with the re-draughted standard engine, whose maximum steaming was increased from 12,000 to 19,000 pounds per hour or 67% and the higher value held for nearly two hours on the road"

Incidentally, an increase in steam output from 12,000 to 19,000lbs/hr represents a gain of 58 per cent; a gain of 67 per cent was only achieved if the report's projected maximum steam output of 20,000lbs is adopted. It appears the engineers who wrote this report had no inkling of the performance Class 4s had produced in the past, such as those appearing in tables XLVII and XLVIII, for if they had, they would have realized that the engines *were* capable of evaporating far more than 12,000lbs/hr, and that some other factor – most likely coal – was severely compromising their performance. The report recorded that the coal used in the tests was very variable in quality with a high ash content. Interestingly, judging from photographs taken of Standard Class 4 Freight in action prior to the Second World War, when coal was undoubtedly of better quality, it is quite usual to see at least a wisp of steam escaping from the safety valves, suggesting that firemen in those days were not finding it that difficult to maintain full pressure.

---

43 The H boiler introduced in 1903, and fitted to the earliest examples of Class 3 0-6-0s, had the same grate angle, the boiler only differing from the G7 by virtue of it having a round topped firebox as opposed to the Belpaire firebox fitted to the G7 and G7s.

44 Bulletin Nº 3 *London Midland Region – Class 4, 2 Cyl., 2-6-0 Mixed Traffic Locomotive* British Railways October 1951.

45 BTC: *Report on Trials of LMR 0-6-0 Class 4F Freight Locomotives Fitted with Swirlyflo Boiler Tubes and Modified Draughting Arrangement.* Report L. 98 CM&EE Dept. Derby March 1954.

46 Mr M Rutherford *Masterpiece of Mediocrity – The 4F Saga* **Backtrack** June 1999 Vol 13 Nº6

A Defence of the Midland/LMS Class 4 0-6-0

In the face of such evidence, why had the Class 4 by the 1950s developed such a reputation for poor steaming and general feebleness? Since an example was never tested on the rollers at either Rugby or Swindon we cannot be certain, but the evidence suggests that most of the problems experienced[47] by footplatemen arose from its draughting, not from the engine portion as such:-

"The major problem with a 4F was steam; it would either steam or it would not."

Had LMS locomotive engineers post-war spent a bit of time/money/effort improving the draughting a lot of heartache could have been avoided. One might have thought of 772 reasons why this improvement should have been done, after all the class comprised approximately 10 per cent of the LMS locomotive stock – more than the Class 5 or the 8F Class 2-8-0 – but Mr Cox simply preferred to call it capricious[48] and avoid the issue. In locomotives where the free gas area through the barrel was a relatively large proportion of the grate area – 16.4 per cent in the case of the Midland G7s – a significant fraction of the total resistance the boiler presented to the flow of the combustion air/exhaust gases comprised the resistance of the firebed. Such proportions would make the engines more sensitive to coal quality since another way of considering the need for a large free gas area was because the limited draught poorly proportioned front-ends could produce was insufficient to cope with a higher resistance barrel[49]. This was the *real*

reasoning behind the LMS engineers[50] when they strove to obtain free gas areas of at least 15 per cent in their later designs:-

"... the contraction in diameter of the front tube plate due to the taper shape, plus the theory that the circulation arising from widely spaced tubes would help steaming, both resulted in a reduction in the total tube-free area through which the hot gases pass from the firebox to the smokebox. This value is vital to a boiler's performance, an area of 15% of the grate area represented free steaming, the area of 13% which this boiler had, imposed a severe upper limit to the ability to boil water."

Other than serving as a first approximation, there is no valid reason why expressing the barrel free gas area as a percentage of the grate area should serve as an accurate guide to boiler steam output *per se,* since a more efficient draughting system could cope with a higher resistance barrel. Indeed the free gas areas of André Chapelon's Pacifics varied between 10.8 and 11.4 per cent depending on the configuration of the superheater, while that of the G7s boiler at 16.4 per cent comfortably exceeded the LMS engineers' desire for 15 per cent yet its steaming was deemed capricious.

The resistance the firebed presented to the airflow passing through it, was partly affected by the damper setting and the free air space area through the grate, but its largest and most variable influence was the coal. Coals varied in their behaviour when heated on the grate, they could swell, coke, stick together or burst into small fragments. The ash in it might melt at the temperatures reached in the fire forming clinkers, or instead accumulate as a powder. To combat some of these effects the fireman might try to carry a thicker fire, which in turn presented a higher resistance, as would a fuel that was composed of smaller lumps. If a boiler, sans fire possessed a comparatively low resistance to gas flow, *i.e.* a free gas area say 15 per cent or above, then the *additional* resistance presented by the fire could assume a significant fraction of the *total* resistance; the magnitude of which was very much determined by fire depth, load, coal characteristics, fireman's skill etc. Should for example, the coal size be such

---

47 Mr M F Higson *London Midland Fireman* - Ian Allan 1977 pp28-9.

48 Mr R C Bond *Years of Transition* Presidential Address I Loco E Sept 1953 p455:-

"But the key to the whole situation, upon all else depends, is the ability of the boiler to deliver the steam required. A good steaming boiler can cover a multitude of sins – one that will not steam will rightly blacken the reputation of any locomotive. And thus a great deal of attention has been paid to boiler proportions, especially free area through the tubes and draught arrangements to ensure the maximum flow of air and products of combustion upon which good steaming largely depends."

An observation not it seems applicable to the Class 4 Standard Goods.

49 "Sometimes if your locomotive had just received a washout they were fine, the secret of a good steaming engine, was clean tubes, which you had after a washout had taken place. Some engines would steam with dirty tubes, but this certainly did not apply to the Class 4s."

Messers K Miles, J Hulme & F James *4F Reflections* **Midland Record Nº 4** Wild Swan Publications Ltd Didcot p43.

Whilst the presence of waterside scale and sludge will have reduced the heat transfer from the gases into the water their impact one feels ought to have affected all boilers roughly equally. It is suspected that it was soot and cinders in the flues

---

and tubes that particularly affected the steaming of the Class 4 0-6-0 through their presence increasing the resistance of the barrel to gas flow, or compromising the attainment of the full superheat temperature on which the performance of the engine depended.

50 Mr E S Cox *Locomotive Panorama Vol I* Ian Allan Shepperton 1974 p106.

that the fire packed down to form a high resistance bed, then this inevitably had a profound effect on the maximum gas flow that the draughting system could support. It might mean the front-end was unable to draw sufficient air through the fire to support the necessary combustion rate, with the result the engine would not steam so well on that particular coal.

At moderate rates of working, a higher resistance fire could be offset by opening the dampers wider than that needed with a better quality coal, thereby obtaining the same boiler resistance. Obviously, as the rate of firing was increased, this greater degree of damper opening had to be maintained, so when burning a poorer fuel the fully open position was reached at a lower steam output. Once this stage had been reached any further increase in output, would be accompanied by a shortage of air revealed by the presence of smoke, as the front-end draughting limit was attained for that particular coal. From this, it follows that those locomotives, which displayed the most severe reaction on being presented with a poorer diet, tended not to be good steamers *i.e.* in the driver's sense of being unable to maintain boiler pressure – essentially, they had a more restricted 'damper opening capacity' than a good steamer. Although all boilers exhibited a degree of sensitivity to coal quality/type/size, its extent was largely determined by the effectiveness of the draughting system.

The draughting of the 'Big Goods', in common with so many British locomotives, was poorer than it should or could have been. It was this weakness that prompted Mr Cox's comment, shared by others, about the steaming of the Class 4, but really this was recognition that a poorly draughted engine had less reserve to cope with the vagaries of different coal qualities and the higher resistance their use could incur. Even with the damper wide open, the higher firebed resistance reduced the quantity of air that could be pulled through the fire and with it the combustion rate possible. A situation that assumed greater significance in the 1950s when poorer quality coals compounded by inexperienced and/or disinterested firemen were facts of life. Poor steaming could occur of course even with good coal if the fireman attempted to carry too thick a fire. The traditional way of firing a Midland engine was to maintain a fairly thick fire at the back of the grate tapering it down so that it was just a few inches thick at the front. Under conditions of light steaming the available draught on a Class 4 was quite limited while the movement of the engine coupled with the slope of the grate made it difficult to keep the coal under the firedoor and prevent it from moving down the slope to the front. Since for equivalent steam rates the draught was lighter on a 'Big Goods' compared to a class 3F, the more successful firemen found it was better under these circumstances to carry a thinner fire, but not too thin so the damper opening pulled holes in it, and then to fire more frequently to ensure sufficient heat release.

As the impact of coal differences and coal sensitivity became more of a concern, British Railways conducted some tests at Rugby to explore these effects quantitatively. For example tests conducted on the re-draughted 'Jubilee' Nº 45722 - another class with a reputation for poor steaming - revealed when the engine was fired 4,435lb/hr of Blidworth coal (grade 2B), it had a front end limit of 25,000lb/hr of steam. Substituting Bestwood coal (grade 3B *i.e.* a goods traffic grade) meant a maximum of only 21,750lb/hr could be reliably obtained - a loss of over one-eighth. Part of this reduction in steam output was due to the lower calorific value of the latter coal, but the remainder was because the available draught could only support a firing rate of 4,219lb/hr. The inference being, that substituting a lower grade of coal reduced the capacity of the 'Jubilee' to that of a machine belonging to one power class lower, but supplied with medium grade coal. To put this further into perspective, had the comparison instead been between a grade 1A coal (*i.e.* express traffic grade calorific value around 13,700BTU/lb) and the 3B coal, the reduction in performance could conceivably have been the equivalent to *two* power classes.

Further examples of the impact the poorer coals had on engine performance appear in figure 93, which illustrates the evaporation curves for the WD 2-8-0 and 2-10-0 classes when burning Blidworth - a hard coal - and Blackwell (grade 3B) - a soft coal. Incidentally the WD 2-8-0 class was derived in large part from the LMS Standard Class 8. Steaming was considered satisfactory with Blidworth despite the highest rate of evaporation at which a balance could be continuously maintained between steam production and demand *i.e.* the 'front end limit' was only 19,500lbs/hour (271lbs/ton of engine weight). The Blackwell coal could not be burned satisfactorily for extended periods although a maximum steam rate of

A Defence of the Midland/LMS Class 4 0-6-0

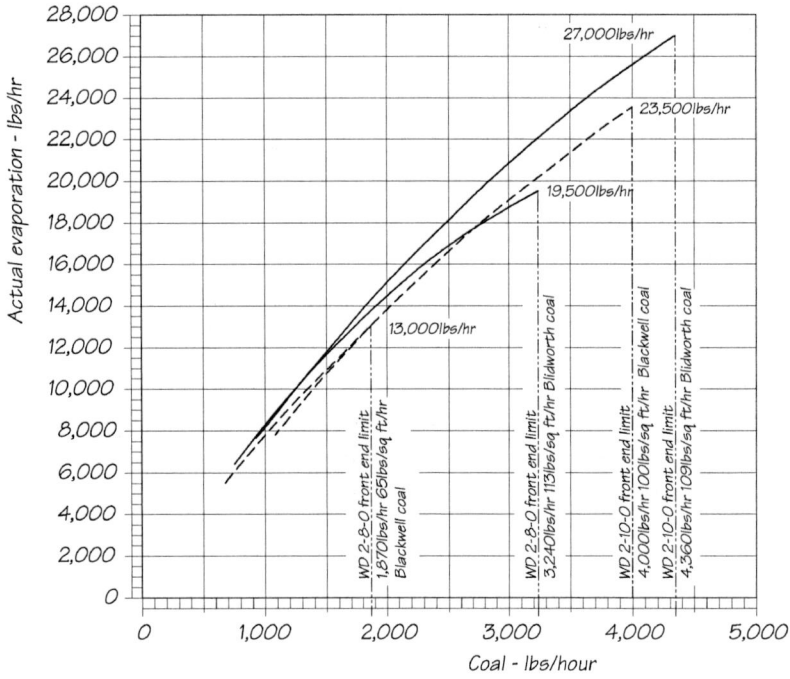

Fig. 93 - Actual evaporation comparisons WD Classes 2-8-0 and 2-10-0 when burning different coals

Johnson used a new form of petticoat pipe to most of his express passenger engines. The pipe was not directly attached to the chimney so did not present a smooth continuous surface with a bell-mouthed entry to the steam/gas stream. Rather it comprised a truncated cone separate from and located a few inches below the chimney. Other designers fitted more than one cone between the top of the blast-pipe and the inlet to the chimney. Mr C H Wingfield reported[51] that he thought that they would have little value, so to test his theory he made a model smokebox and found their inducing effect was insignificant, but when they were removed and the jet discharged into a plain chimney the vacuum was greatly increased. A finding supported by the practical experience of James Clayton who described[52] how the steaming of one class was improved by *removing* cones:-

13,000lbs/hr was sustained for 45 minutes. The coal quickly formed heavy deposits of non-porous clinker that adhered strongly to the firebars but the wide grate on the ten-coupled engine ensured a lower combustion rate enabling it to cope far better with the 3B coal.

Draughting inspired power losses of these orders were serious, yet if they were tolerated in modern express passenger and goods engines, what chance did a 'Big Goods' stand? Midland draughting, particularly the blast-pipe/chimney arrangement used on superheated engines, was probably even more feeble than the average British engine. The design had developed originally on saturated engines during Mr Deeley's time, but once superheaters were fitted, in line with Superheater Company advice, the blast-pipe cap diameter was reduced to compensate for the smaller steam flow needed for the same power output. Unfortunately altering the blast-pipe diameter will have affected the steam cone shape and its relationship with the chimney, particularly in respect of how effectively the latter was filled. Whilst this appears to have been of less consequence in the Midland built engines which carried a taller chimney, this was not necessarily the case, with the shorter chimneys fitted in LMS days.

When he adopted piston valves in the '90s, Mr

"I may tell you that at first the engines he has referred to were not good 'steamers'. The first experiments showed we had got something slightly wrong...

...We had also a cone in the chimney, as this was the practice based upon experience with other engines on the system, but the engines did not steam very well. First we removed the chimney cone altogether and left the main chimney plain. The steaming of the engines immediately improved by fifty per cent."

Edward Gass[53] reported that the removal of 'hoods' from some engines had had no discernible effect on steaming.

To modern eyes, not fitting a bell-mouthed petticoat pipe intuitively appears wrong, but we must remember in those days engineers were not

---

51 Messers F H Trevithick & P J Cowan *Some Effects of Superheating and Feed-Water Heating on Locomotive Working* I Mech E March 1913.

52 Mr J Maxwell Dunn *Locomotive Blast Pipes and Chimneys* I Loco E Paper N° 56 November 1917 p360

53 Mr E Gass *The Relation of Cylinder and Boiler Power to Locomotive Rating* Paper N° 73 I Loco E 1919 p290.

so clear in their understanding of fluid flow. Compare for example the aerodynamic form of a SE5a fighter, which was roughly a contemporary of these observations, with that displayed by the Supermarine Spitfire designed about 20 years later and more or less coincident with M Chapelon's zenith. Furthermore, designers were not necessarily cognizant of the contribution made by the chimney in gas stream capture many believing that it was due solely to the exposed jet within the smokebox.

With the 'Big Goods' hauling a decent sized train, burning good quality coal and enjoying a reasonable superheat the plain chimney provided with just a short parallel downward extension into the smokebox seemingly sufficed, judging from the safety valve evidence referred to earlier. Certainly, this arrangement, which appeared initially on the first member of the class N° 3835, fitted with a Derby superheater was maintained by the LMS – illustrated on general arrangement drawing 25-10238. In contrast, the Midland general arrangement drawing for the other 1911 build N° 3836, fitted with a Swindon superheater, which delivered steam at approximately 560°F or around 60°F lower, shews the engine fitted with a petticoat pipe. Since the Derby superheater arrangement proved superior, it was adopted with the associated draughting design. The absence of petticoat pipes, or at least the removal of cones, judging from an inspection of Midland general arrangement drawings, appears to have been a policy introduced early in the tenure of Mr Deeley continuing through to LMS days. Incidentally, drawings of these Class 4 draughting variants have been published[54]. Mr T Essery, who has considerable practical experience of the class, has described how the subsequent addition of a petticoat pipe significantly improved the steaming[55] of N° 43924 on the Keighley & Worth Valley Railway under the gentler operating conditions of the preservation scene:-

"In addition there was something not quite right with 4Fs (sic) draughting which left it deficient particularly when being worked lightly. I had this proved when firing one of the preserved examples some years ago and could not understand why it steamed so much better than any 4F I had encountered on BR. Apparently their firemen had experienced problems in this respect so their engineers had installed the modified chimney bell from an 8F and it worked so successfully that on the first run I could not stop it blowing off. It was a sobering thought to realise that such a simple modification might have saved firemen a lot of frustration over many years and made 4Fs the equal of 3Fs in terms of steaming."

Had the LMS chosen to improve the steaming of its Standard Class 4, it need look no further than at the arrangement it had provided for its parallel boiler 2-6-4 tank engines. These according to Terry Essery had first class draughting and never seemed to experience problems with maintaining a bright fire even when lightly worked. The 2-6-4T smokebox was the same diameter as that of the 0-6-0 and carried a chimney of similar height and diameter, differing only in that it had no capuchon and was provided with a 2ft diameter bellmouth (referred to by the LMS as a chimney base extension piece) extending 11½ins below the end of the chimney casting. The blast-pipe cap was 4¾ins diameter positioned 37/16ins below the boiler centre line as opposed to the 47/8ins diameter and approximate 1¾ins on the 0-6-0. This may have required a new stand pipe. Both barrels were provided with 21 large tubes 51/8ins diameter and 146 small tubes 1¾ins diameter giving identical free gas areas. The fact that pre-Nationalization engineers never elected to do so suggests either that they were ignorant of the daily trials and tribulations faced by Class 4 firemen, which does not speak very highly of their professionalism, or and more likely, it was not normally an issue.

There is one further aspect to be considered, albeit touched on briefly earlier, and that is the seemingly innocuous effect of chimney dimensions. In any series of nominally identical locomotives, there are always individual examples that were capable of giving that bit more than their siblings. The Class 4s were no different in this respect even if the contrast in the performance capability between the

---

54 Midland general arrangement drawings 11-8289 for N° 3836, and 11-8298, originally for N° 3835, but altered for N° 3837 onwards, together with LMS general arrangement drawing 25-10238 appear in Messers D Hunt, J Jennison, R Essery and F James *LMS Locomotive Profiles N° 10 The Standard Class 4 Goods 0-6-0s* Wild Swan Didcot.

N° 3835 - Mr OS Nock *British Locomotives of the 20th Century Vol 1* Patrick Stephens Ltd Cambridge 1983 p55

N° 3836 - Messers R J Essery & D Jenkinson *An Illustrated Review of Midland Locomotives Vol. 4* - Wild Swan Publications Ltd p166

Drawing N° 25-10238 - *Midland Record* Issue N° 2 Wild Swan Publications Ltd pp72-73

55 Mr T Essery *Steam Locomotives Compared* - Atlantic Transport Publishers 1996 pp70-71

best and the worst examples was perhaps more extreme. However, what made the class a little unusual was that footplatemen quickly learnt how to identify these 'stars' from the ground. The Midland Railway built examples were consistently considered better than the LMS built ones, a difference that was sufficiently great to prompt comment from almost everyone who worked with the Class 4. The following two extracts[56] will serve to illustrate the point:-

"My experience indicated that, on the whole, the older MR engines and Derby-built locomotives were better steamers and freer runners than those from Horwich or Crewe works, the 45xxx series being the most temperamental for steam. The best examples in the class were the few with tall chimneys (indicated by a blue circle on the cab sides) and they usually steamed very well indeed. The older MR engines were almost all shopped at Derby, and some drivers insisted that Derby set the valves differently from Crewe and Horwich. This may have been so, because I cannot believe that Derby supplied each 4F with a guardian angel or used any other magical persuasion!"

"One thing about the class '4s', which I cannot explain, was the fact that by and large the old Midland locomotives were generally better machines than the LMS standard locomotives, and the Derby built standard engines were superior to any of the others built post-1923."

For many years David Tee conducted interviews with retired enginemen and they again confirmed this to be the situation. Drivers may not always have been aware of the finer points of locomotive history, and as a consequence not described their charges in the terms most familiar to locomotive enthusiasts, but they knew a '38' or a '39' for example would steam and pull better than any of the later ones. Consequently, whenever sheds could arrange it, engines from those number series would be rostered for hauling excursion passenger trains. Since the '38' and '39' series of Class 4s were superior to the LMS built examples, but had no different exhaust system[57], the explanation for their superiority must lie elsewhere. It seems likely that this was, in part at least, simply because the chimney on these engines were generally taller than that fitted to the LMS version. An observation also supported by the comments of Ron Pennington a fireman at Rowsley in BR days who reported the Class 4 engines fitted with the tall Stanier pattern chimney, identified for route restriction purposes by a blue disk 3½ins diameter, were much freer steaming than their sisters fitted with shorter chimneys. The long chimneys used in the Victorian era had ensured considerable tolerance in the relative shapes and proportions of the draughting system, even if sometimes it meant the loss of some efficiency, but this latitude much reduced as chimneys became shorter. Most of the problems with poorly steaming locomotives appeared with the shorter chimneys of the twentieth century. The chimney was more than a mere conduit to ensure the escape of the exhaust steam and gases needing to be correctly sized and properly located relative to the blast-pipe. It had to be large enough to allow the entrained quantity of steam and gas to escape with the minimum of resistance, but if it were overly large, or if tapered it expanded too quickly, efficiency would be lost. The bottom of the chimney was in a region of sub-atmospheric pressure but its top was subjected to atmospheric pressure so it also had to act as a seal to prevent air from entering the smokebox. Suitably proportioned it also served as a means by which a portion of the kinetic energy present in the steam/gas stream could be converted into pressure, which increased the efficiency of the exhaust system through reducing the velocity of the escaping stream. The simplest way of achieving this was by arranging for the cross-section of the chimney to increase towards the top hence the reason for the tapered chimney that S O Ell adopted.

If the chimney was too short *i.e.* less than the optimum length for the rest of the draughting system, air might enter via a narrow annulus that formed between the mixed gas/steam stream and the chimney wall accompanied by flow reversal and significant turbulence, all of which served to compromise efficiency. To prevent this from occurring, designers usually attempted to arrange for the gas/stream stream to make contact with the upper portion of the chimney so as to effect a seal against the ingress of air [58]:-

"In regard to the 1 in. extra on the chimney

---

56 The first is from *London Midland Fireman* Mr M F Higson - Ian Allan 1977 p 130.
The second is from *An Illustrated Review of Midland Locomotives Vol. 1* Messers R J Essery & D Jenkinson - Wild Swan Publications p183

57 This of course ignores the handful of later 4Fs given modified exhausts, some of which were in the 438xx and 439xx series, because they were too few in number to have influenced shedmasters' decisions.

58 Mr D R Carling *Locomotive Testing on British Railways* I Loco E Paper Nº 497 September 1950 p589.

Comparisons, Steaming and Performance

Fig. 94 - 'Big Goods' N° 44030 one of the two engines tested on the Crewe - Holyhead line. Seen here much earlier in its career as LMS N° 4030 probably not that long after building at Derby in December 1924.

diameter, if that 1 in. were at the choke it might not matter so much, but if it were at the chimney top it would be fatal. That was why the 'class 2' 2-6-0 would not steam - the cone of steam would not fill the impinge on the walls of the chimney below the choke but, it must impinge on the walls of the chimney several inches below the top."

The chimney therefore had to be positioned the

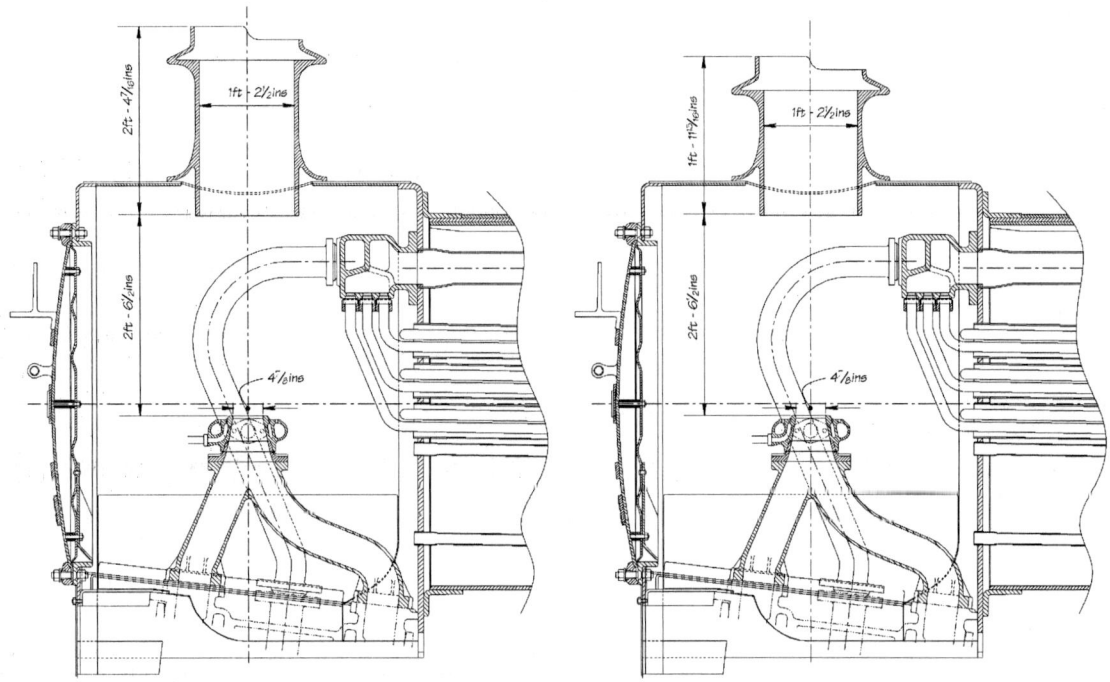

Fig 95 - Original Midland Railway and LMS short chimney draughting designs

chimney. Lowering the blast pipe would fill the chimney better, if it was practical to lower it sufficiently. It was very important with chimneys that the jet should not optimum distance above the blast-pipe cap so the expanding jet could enter and fill it with the minimum of disturbance. Should the expanding

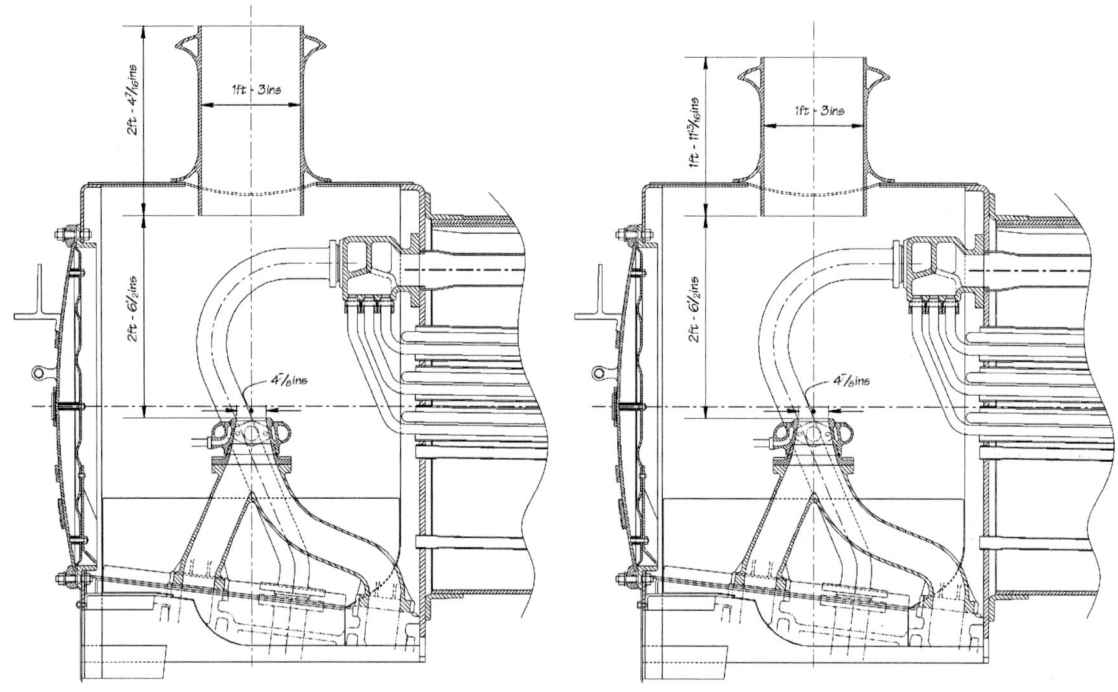

Fig 96 - Later LMS long and short chimney draughting designs

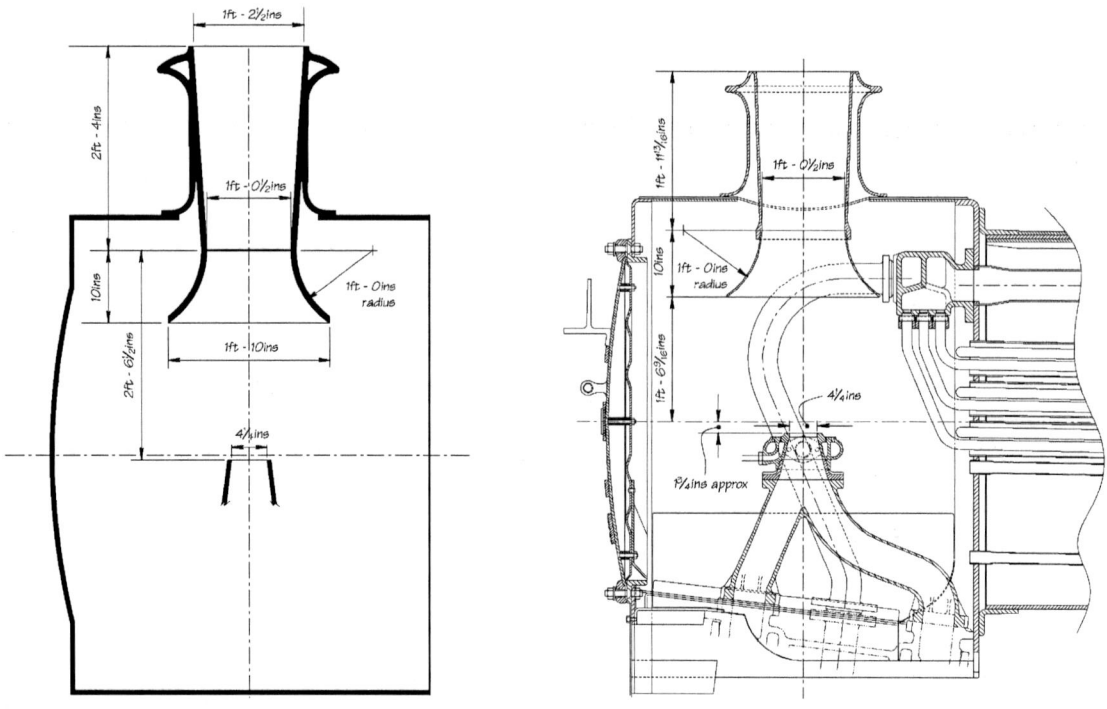

Fig 97 - British Railways modified draughting designs

steam/gas stream failed to completely fill the chimney at its top under say conditions of light steaming then the annulus would form allowing air to enter thereby reducing the vacuum within the smokebox. Introducing a bell-mouth entry to the base of the chimney increased its length slightly and improved the ingress of exhaust gases, which helped maintain or increase the smokebox vacuum.

Comparisons, Steaming and Performance

View shewing the inside the smokebox of the preserved Class 4 0-6-0 N° 43924 running on the Keighley and Worth Valley Railway. This is a replacement petticoat pipe fitted during the recent overhaul before the engine returned to traffic in the summer of 2011.

It will be seen that the bell mouth has been fabricated from a series of three truncated cones as it was found impossible to have a replacement petticoat rolled to replicate the Class 8 profile originally fitted following the locomotive's preservation. It was this latter petticoat that was referred to by Mr Terry Essery.

As might be anticipated the slight departure from a true curved surface has proved to be of no consequence with the enginemen reporting that the engine continues to steam very well indeed.

The new petticoat pipe sits lower in the smokebox and closer to the blast-pipe cap than either of the two BR designs appearing in figure 97 above. It is understood the inspiration for this revised design was derived from the work that Professor Goss carried out in America some years prior to the introduction of the 'Big Goods'.

Fig 98 - Replacement petticoat pipe fitted to Standard 4 N° 43924 - June 2011

Figures 95, 96 and 97 illustrate the six most important draughting arrangements used on the 'Big Goods'. Appearing in figure 95 is the original Midland Railway Deeley/Fowler pattern tall chimney design which was 1ft - 117/16ins long with a parallel bore 1ft - 2½ins diameter, while alongside is the standard initial LMS 1ft - 613/16ins chimney which was 45/8ins shorter but retaining the same internal diameter.

N° 44203 had both of the changes - Swirlyflo tubes as well as the improved draughting. The drawing illustrating the modified draughting appearing in the test report gave a chimney height of 1ft 113/16ins, while a photograph the author has seen of the re-draughted N° 44030 on the test train shews it also carrying a tall chimney, but the re-draughting drawing D54-22110 has a BR profile and a chimney height of 1ft 613/16ins, the nominal standard height for the class. Possibly this is the chimney seen here. It seems to have a similar profile to that appearing in D54-22110; David Tee who saw a few modified engines in service noted they had a distinctive sound.

Fig. 99 - N° 44203, the other engine tested on the Crewe - Holyhead line

Intuitively one can appreciate that the taller chimney was more likely to provide better sealing, particularly at lower steaming rates. Figure 96 shews the later LMS Stanier pattern chimneys that were fitted, the heights of the two varieties remained the same, but the internal diameter was increased by ½in to become 1ft - 3ins. In this design the internal profile of the chimney was now continuous to the top which perhaps offset the possibly detrimental effect the increase in diameter had. According to David Hunt from 1943 the short Stanier chimney was to become the standard but some tall chimneys were not replaced. BR later produced its own design of short chimney, which had a limited application but is not illustrated. The left hand diagram of figure 97 illustrates the modified draughting applied to N° 44203 and 44030, believed to have been created in each case by fitting a tapered liner to a tall Stanier chimney, maintaining the same height. This design incorporates a bell-mouth petticoat pipe coupled to the Swindon inspired 1 in 14 taper liner fitted to the chimney.

The former improved the entrance of the exhaust gases into the chimney while the latter change improved the conversion from kinetic energy into pressure. These modifications raised the efficiency of the system not only at lower steaming rates but also extended the engines' upper steaming capacity. However, the one major disadvantage of this design was that it necessitated a reduction in the diameter of the blast-pipe cap to 4¼ins. The right-hand draughting system in figure 97 is the one to drawing D54-22110, which Dennis Monk believed was intended to be fitted to the whole class. It will be noted that the chimney, which now has a BR inspired profile, retained the bell-mouth entrance and the 1 in 14 taper, but was reduced in height by 4 3/16ins, the other dimensions remaining largely unaltered. When N° 43850 returned to Westhouses after an overhaul at Horwich it sported a BR Standard 4 chimney and a petticoat - presumably to D54-22110. Mr Eric Riley recalled perhaps not surprisingly that it was a good steamer. It is not confirmed if all of the engines given BR profile chimneys also received petticoats.

Possibly air leakage, poor coal or both was responsible for the variation in the steaming British Railways crews reported in the 'Big Goods' but certainly the maximum evaporation of 12,000lbs/hr obtained from N° 44030 in 1953-4 while fitted with the original draughting would have limited the engine's output to within the range 545-600 indicated horsepower, at best only about three-quarters the power output anticipated by LMS engineers from Rugby Testing Station. Once N° 44030 was given the modified draughting system, it generated 19,000lbs/hr, giving a specific evaporation of 900lbs of superheated steam per square foot of grate area per hour - one of the highest specific steam production rates ever *measured* in Britain. This output while good for Britain, represents only 73 per cent of the 1,235lbs/sq ft achieved by André Chapelon with his 4-8-0 and his steam conditions were both superior, highlighting what further opportunity for development was missed. Nevertheless, just considering the impact the rise in steam output of N° 44030 had from 12,000lbs/hr to 19,000lbs, means that before modification it could only have generated a maximum power output roughly two-thirds what it could do in its re-draughted form. Extrapolating these estimates suggest the combined effect of a short chimney, poor coal and less skilled firemen might easily have reduced the maximum steam output by one-quarter or so below what was considered normal in the 'twenties and 'thirties, or indeed the performance engineers anticipated from Rugby - perhaps the equivalent of reducing them roughly into a Class 3 engine. In this situation and pulling a Class 4 load, the engine would have struggled - an outcome that is unlikely to have endeared the machine to its fireman.

Steam Circuit, Valve Diameter and Lap Length

The power a steam locomotive may develop is a function of the steam flow rate and the available heat drop. Although the latter in too many British locomotives *reduced* with increase in output, it necessarily follows high horsepowers are accompanied by high steam rates. Thus to produce twice the horsepower, will demand a more than doubling of the steam flow rate through the machine. However, the relationship describing the flow of fluids through pipes approximates to a square law, hence, if the flow rate is doubled the pressure drop will be roughly quadrupled. Consequently, as more power is demanded from a locomotive, the pressure drop experienced by the steam on its way to and from the cylinders increased, and with it the loss in isentropic efficiency. The effect increased flow rate had on loss of isentropic efficiency may be minimized by ensuring the whole steam circuit from the main steam pipe in the boiler, through the superheater elements, smokebox steam pipes, steam chest volume, ports and passages etc, all the way to the blast-pipe cap was as large as practicable. However, the individual drops in pressure the steam experienced as it negotiated each discrete section can never be avoided only minimized. Large steam circuits were a major contributor towards the sparkling performances that André Chapelon obtained from his locomotives; he always insisted that the cross-sectional area of his steam circuits was as large as careful design could accommodate. Indeed he believed the design of a steam locomotive ought to *start* with the laying out of the exhaust from the cylinders and the draughting arrangement.

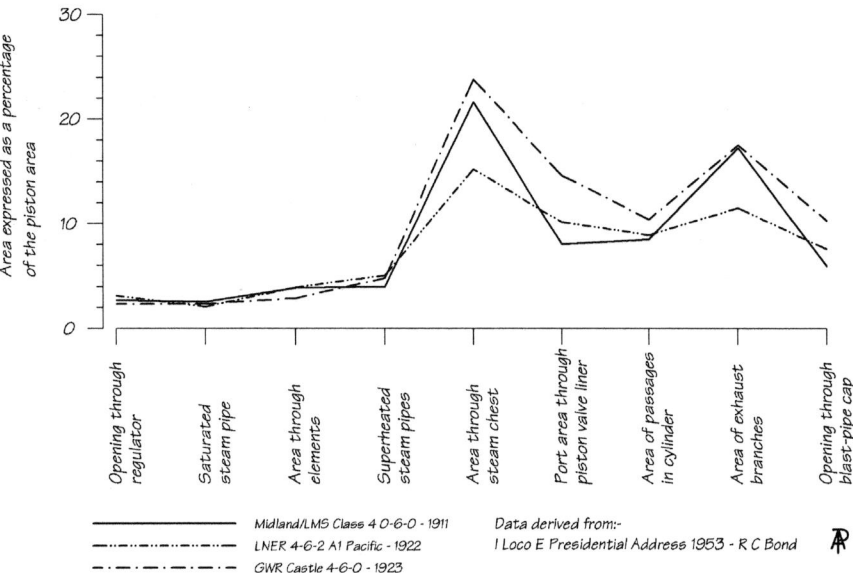

Fig. 100 - Relative sizes of common points in the steam circuit for a selection of locomotives

Since the 'Big Goods' was intended to be a goods and mineral locomotive we ought really to consider its performance primarily on that basis rather than the hauling of express goods and passenger traffic that sometimes it was called upon to do. Nevertheless, as figure 100 records, even though the engine was intended for lowly traffic, its steam circuit was not noticeably smaller in proportion to its cylinders that that of two later and very successful express passenger classes. The worst criticism compared to them is the diameter of its blast-pipe cap caused by the poorer geometry of its draughting system, which will have elevated its back pressure for equal steaming rates. Ironically, the Swindon-inspired improved draughting devised in BR days made this worse since it reduced the cap diameter yet further becoming 4¼ins diameter so it reduced from 5.9 per cent of piston area to become 4.5 per cent[59]. Remaining with the steam circuit, Mr Powell[60] and others, have criticized the smallness of the piston valves fitted to the Class 4 – 8ins diameter supplying 20ins diameter cylinders. Yet these two diameters were, for example, identical to those Nigel Gresley provided on his A1/A3 Pacifics, while most of the LNWR 'George the Fifth' class used valves 8ins feeding even larger cylinders at 20½ins diameter. Admittedly, both of these express engines carried longer laps, which increased the port openings for the same cut-off, while the latter class had double admission valves, but these were of little benefit in a goods engine. This was because in goods service the practice primarily of working heavier trains at lower speeds meant the reduced number of working strokes per minute permitted the steam to enter and leave the cylinders with sufficient freedom. Thus under these circumstances, large-lap engines offered no real advantage over the small laps associated with a traditionally designed steam circuit. Another way of considering this is since we know high-speed locomotive performance was significantly affected by the relative size of the piston valve and its associated port openings we might ask quite at what speed did it start to take effect? Professor Tuplin explored this relationship and produced a formula that predicted a speed range within which a given valve diameter, when combined with a selected cylinder diameter, would deliver its maximum power performance. For speeds below the lower limiting value cylinder performance would still be very good although power would be lower, conversely once the upper value was exceeded cylinder performance would drop away. As professional locomotive engineers have done

---

59 The GA for N° 3836 – the example fitted with a petticoat pipe and Swindon superheater – illustrates the engine with a 5ins diameter blast-pipe cap (6.25 per cent of piston area).

60 Mr A J Powell *Living with London Midland Locomotives* Ian Allan Shepperton 1977 – *vide* the caption to plate 6.

before us, we might criticise his formula for the factors it omitted and the assumptions he made, nevertheless as some of those engineers grudgingly admitted, albeit mostly privately, it did give answers reflective of locomotive performance.

For any chosen cut-off, the width of the port opening was proportional to the lap L of the valve, assuming a fixed ratio of lap to lead – usual in Walschaert's gear but not strictly true in the case of Stephenson's valve gear – and the length of the port was proportional to the diameter of the valve V. The time the valve was open to steam was proportional to engine speed while the latter, was in turn proportional to the diameter of the driving wheels D. Thus, the combined result of the extent of the port opening and the period for which it was open was proportional to the product DVL. The cylinder volume to be filled at any selected cut-off was proportional to the swept volume i.e. to $d^2 \times s$ where d was the diameter of the cylinder and s its stroke. The ratio of pressure built up in the cylinder to the pressure in the steam chest was dependent on the quantity of steam that could pass through the port relative to the size of the volume to be filled i.e. on the velocity at which steam could pass between the two. This was dependant on the velocity of wave propagation, which in steam was equal to about $35 \times \sqrt{(460 + T)}$ where T was the steam temperature in degrees Fahrenheit. This velocity was typically of the order of 1,200mph for the conditions pertaining in modern British locomotives, but Professor Tuplin found that the highest cylinder efficiency was attained when the steam velocity was between 27½ and 55 per cent of this maximum value. Incorporating all of these factors resulted in the following relationship:-

$$v = \frac{C \times D \times V \times L}{d^2 \times s} \qquad (18)$$

where:-
- v = lower or upper speed value – mph
- D = driving wheel diameter – ins
- V = valve diameter – ins
- L = lap – ins
- d = cylinder diameter – ins
- s = stroke – ins
- C = a constant having a value of 330 at the lower speed and 660 for the upper speed

The concept of an optimum valve size is useful because the steam could nether fill any cylinder instantaneously, nor could escape instantaneously when the valve opened to release. Thus, through defining a speed range within which the valve would be reasonably effective, presents a method of comparing the quality of different combinations of dimensions of valve, cylinder and driving wheel for different locomotives. With proper design, this valve speed range would coincide with the speed range that the locomotive was required to produce its maximum power. By way of example, the optimum speed range values for the Class 4 suggest 16-32 miles per hour, which as it happens was ideal for what was primarily intended to be – a goods and mineral engine, the equivalent speeds for the LMS Standard class 8 2-8-0 were 29 and 58mph. Since in mineral working even the highest powers were developed at low speed and usually when ascending banks, short-lap engines were able to admit sufficient steam without any really noticeable wire-drawing. Likewise, although the short-lap engine due to its lower working pressure might have to be worked in a somewhat later cut-off, provided the increase in admission period was modest, this was not necessarily as large a disadvantage as one might at first suppose. As recorded in figure 89, the peak isentropic efficiency attained at any speed, occurred neither at the shortest cut-off that the engine could be run in, nor at the highest steaming rate, so adopting a slightly longer cut-off might not seriously disadvantage the engine. Similarly, since the speed at which its steam circuit attained its maximum efficiency was lower in a short-lap engine, it meant that in slow speed traffic the machine was running nearer to its optimum speed. Further it was also helped by its smaller diameter valves which presented less of a leakage path. Reference to the isentropic efficiency curves appearing in figure 89 reveals that at low speeds and horsepowers, a large-lap engine, did not return as high an efficiency ratio as it would when running at higher speeds and power outputs. In fact, at the speeds involved in mineral and normal loose-coupled goods traffic, its isentropic efficiency will be seen to be similar to the estimate we used earlier for the 'Big Goods'.

For the steam to used as economically as possible necessitated that it had to be expanded to the maximum extent achievable within the cylinder and this demanded running in as short cut-off short a cut-off as possible. However, there were certain sound mechanical reasons for *not* running in the shortest practical cut-off, while in any case the scope for increasing the expansion ratio in a locomotive cylinder was compromised by the very necessary evil of clearance volume – the amount of free space present between the face of the piston at dead centre and the valve head. If a single expansion engine was running in a cut-off of 25 per cent and had a clearance volume of 7 per cent, the expansion ratio was not four, as might be assumed but a little over three. Indeed it was somewhat less than that, once the effect of release, which occurred before the end of the stroke, is considered. Due to the limited size of the cylinders that could be fitted - *vide* formulae *(15)* and *(16)* - this loss of expansion ratio increased whenever a longer cut-off was needed to raise the mean effective pressure and thus the higher tractive effort when say climbing a bank. Conversely, a later cut-off meant a larger port opening which all things being equal, helped reduce the throttling losses at admission.

The leakage past the piston valves, present all the time the regulator was open, was proportionately worse in slow speed traffic. Since the number of working strokes of the pistons was fewer at low speeds, the internal leakage loss assumed a higher fraction of the total steam flow rate through the machine. A somewhat similar effect occurred when the engine ran in very short cut-offs, but at higher speeds, which is one of the reasons why the most economical position of the link regarding specific steam consumption, was typically in the range 20-25 per cent.

Another factor was the amount of superheat present. Returning to table III again reveals the effect this had on ex-L&YR 0-6-0s, which under George Hughes' classification scheme of 1919 had been divided into three groups. With the exception of the older '928' class engines, the remaining saturated 0-6-0s, which were dimensionally similar formed the '27' class while all of the superheated 0-6-0s formed the '28' class. Since these latter two classes were rated power class 3 they could be used on identical duties, yet the superheated engines returned *higher* coal consumption[61]. We 'know' that a superheated engine ought to have been more efficient and therefore burned less coal than a saturated one, so how can this situation have arisen? If we assume the loads hauled by the engines averaged out to be the same, one influence could be the nature of the work since before a superheated engine could demonstrate its greater economy it had to 'warm up'. It might take, depending on superheater size and steam demand, ten, twenty or more minutes after starting before really hot steam started to enter the cylinders. If the engine was engaged on a roster that demanded frequent starting and stopping then the superheat temperature would have had little opportunity of attaining and maintaining a consistent value. Secondly because steam temperature was not controlled in a locomotive, it tended to assume a higher value as the rate of working or the steam demand increased. Thirdly, there was a *minimum* steam rate, whose value depended largely on the proportions of the boiler, before *any* superheat appeared, so operation near to that value meant little or no benefit was available from the superheater. Only if the demand placed on a superheated engine was sufficient to ensure that it was generating hot steam for a reasonable period of time could it deliver a more economical performance than the equivalent saturated engine. The deleterious effect that a lack of sufficient load had on a superheated engine could be compounded in the case of those examples, such as the ex-L&YR '28' class, which had been given larger cylinders (20½ins diameter) than their saturated siblings (18ins diameter), this could encourage running in too short a cut-off, a situation that would also reduce efficiency. As an extension of these observations, had those late LMS and early BR firemen who put fire on a Class 4 0-6-0 been performing that duty when the 'Big Goods' had been performing the heavier work they were employed on pre-War, then almost certainly a different opinion would have ensued.

Increasing the isentropic efficiency of a conventional engine included adopting smaller clearance volumes to ensure compression was complete, making release as late as possible, avoiding high back pressures, re-proportioning the superheater to produce hotter steam at lower steaming rates, reducing the internal leakage past the pistons and piston valves and improving the insulation of the cylinders to minimize the heat lost by radiation. A more radical solution would have been to have interposed reduction gearing between the cylinders and the driving wheels, something reminiscent of a traction engine. This way the cylinders would have made more working strokes for every revolution of the driving wheels. Sir Nigel Gresley seems to have been alert to this for he proposed a six-cylinder geared Uniflow vee engine with three vertical cylinders on each side of

---

61 This difference remained in 1933-5 although it had narrowed to 53.38lbs/mile and 53.28lbs respectively
Mr J Reeves *LMS Journal N° 7* Wild Swan Publications Ltd Didcot pp7-8.

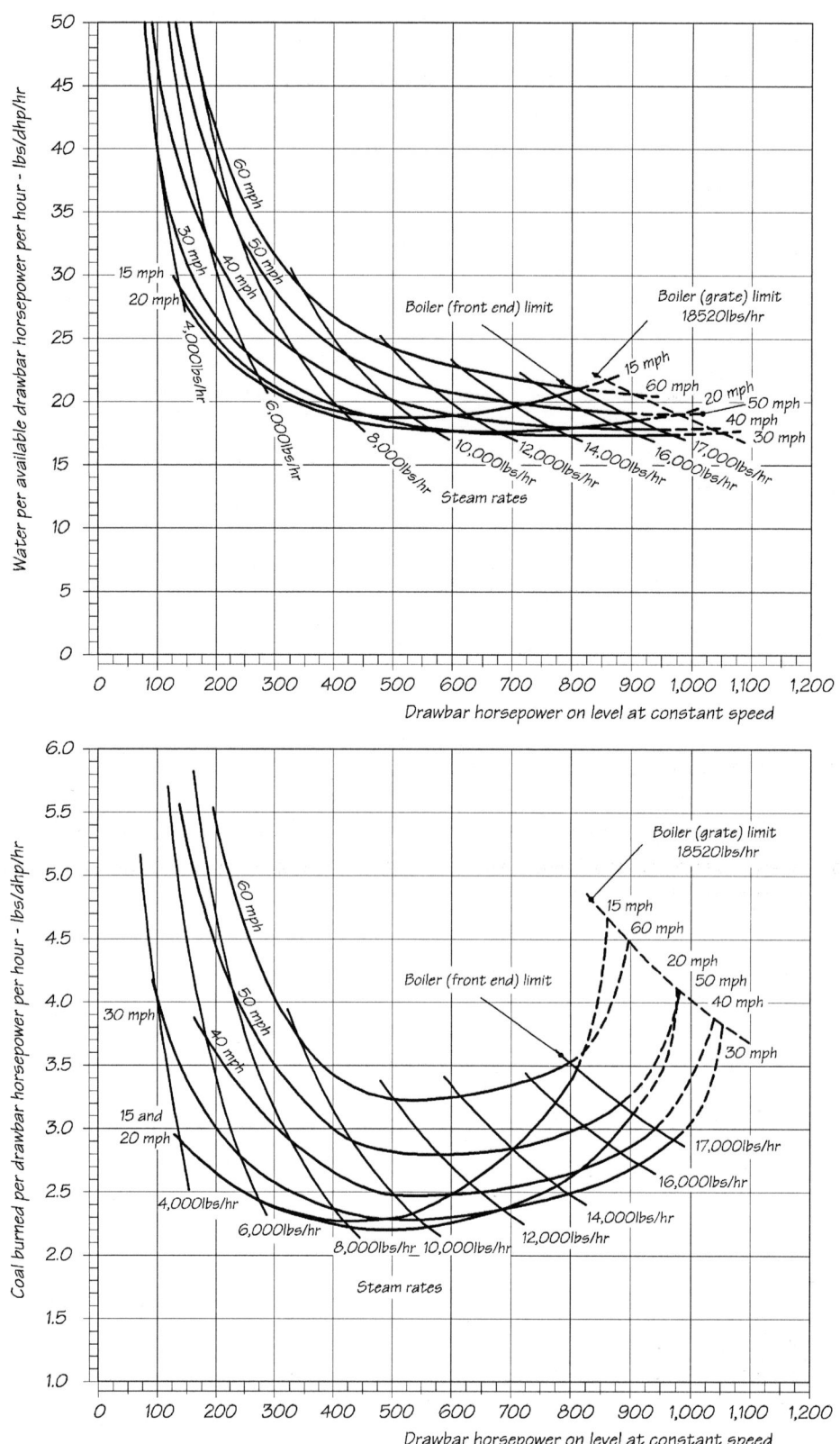

Fig. 101 - Drawbar water and coal consumption - Class 4MT Mogul No. 43094

the smokebox. This would have been a 4-4-0 of similar size to a class D49 but the provision of a suitable bevel-geared drive proved difficult to solve so unfortunately the project was abandoned.

Drawbar Performance

In several comparisons, we have expressed performance in terms of coal and water consumption per drawbar horsepower. These are examples of those deceptively simple measurements authors like to scatter amongst their writings to lend authority, but their value may become meaningless once they are extracted from the specific set of trials that gave rise to them. Hence although in many ways it is better to compare performance in terms of indicated power, unfortunately in practice only drawbar derived data is usually available. Accordingly since so many performance comparisons are based on drawbar consumption figures, we ought to be aware of some of its limitations.

Figure 101 illustrates the level track drawbar characteristics – power against specific consumption – of a BR Standard Class 4MT 2-6-0, actually obtained from an LMR example N° 43094 while on the stationary test plant at Swindon and from the associated controlled road tests for a range of different speeds whilst burning Blidworth coals. Contained in these diagrams are some important features of steam locomotive behaviour. Each speed curve follows a characteristic profile *V*- or *U*-shaped in the case of coal consumption with a tendency to assume a flatter *U*- or as in this example an *L*-shape for the steam consumption, but in neither case did the specific consumption assume a constant value for any speed or power output. When running light engine, the water or coal consumption was infinitely high because as no drawbar pull was exerted the water consumed and coal fired served merely to move the engine and mathematically, any number divide by zero results in infinity. Once however some small load was added to the engine, the specific consumption figures started to fall since drawbar power was now being produced, although they remained extremely high. As the locomotive was asked to produce more drawbar power through the addition of increased load, these specific figures fell, with the steam consumption eventually assuming an approximately constant value, before exhibiting a tendency to rise again. However, in the case of the coal consumption, this fell to a minimum value before quickly rising again as effectively the locomotive became overloaded, a situation that demanded uneconomic combustion rates. Where each curve attains its flattest portion represents the optimum load range for that particular engine and speed. Whilst each speed curve follows a generally similar shape, it will be appreciated they differed slightly from class to class, not only due to differences in their physical dimensions but also because a major factor influencing the precise profile of these curves was the power to weight ratio of the locomotive – dhp/ton. The lower this ratio was then effectively the narrower became the range of economical working which the engine could return at that particular speed resulting in a *V*-shaped curve. Furthermore, these curves assume that the engine was running on level track, so when the train was climbing a gradient it is necessary to add to the drawbar output, the power the locomotive absorbed in lifting its own weight against the pull of gravity. This corrected drawbar horsepower, referred to as the equivalent drawbar horsepower may be then applied to the diagrams to obtain the corresponding steam and coal consumption figures.

Since the drawbar horsepower exerted by a locomotive was the difference in magnitude between the indicated horsepower (or cylinder) horsepower and the power it absorbed in driving itself[62] it may be shewn that the indicated horsepower produced by an engine was primarily a function of the steam rate through it. The indicated power characteristic rose comparatively quickly from zero to attain a maximum value, following which it displayed relatively little sensitivity to further increase in engine speed[63]. Conversely, the horsepower it absorbed in driving itself was a function of its speed, weight and resistance. Combining these two dissimilar effects meant that at low speeds cylinder capacity and piston speed served to limit drawbar power. As no Class 4 0-6-0 was tested on a stationary testing station it is not possible to provide an equivalent set of curves to those forming figure 101.

Although the locomotive testing station at Rugby was originally a joint LNER/LMS venture, both companies invested in constant speed testing, so

---

[62] To be strictly correct the horsepower absorbed by the locomotive was the difference between the 'rail horsepower' and the drawbar horsepower. The rail horsepower was in turn slightly smaller that the indicated horsepower by the amount absorbed in overcoming the engine friction. However, in an effort not to complicate the subject unnecessarily rail horsepower and indicated horsepower have been assumed as being one and the same.

[63] This is when it is considered on the basis of constant steam flow rate from the boiler (variable cut-off); when the cut-off is constant, the curves approximate to a parabola, because the steam flow rate falls off with rise in speed.

A Defence of the Midland/LMS Class 4 0-6-0

the drawbar characteristics could be determined. In the case of the green engine company this took the form of the test locomotive dragging the specially modified counter-pressure locomotive with the ex-NER dynamometer carriage separating the two over flat main lines in Yorkshire. Due to a lack of sufficiently level portions of main line of adequate length the LMS had to adopt a more sophisticated approach. This resulted in the Mobile Test Plant, which authorized in 1936, had been designed by Dr H I Andrews of the LMS Research Department assisted by the CME. This plant was to comprise a new dynamometer carriage, a special tender and three Mobile Test Units. Each of the latter braking units contained four 375 horsepower generators driven by the road wheels and whose output was dissipated via air-cooled resistors. Varying the excitation of the generators, and thus the power they absorbed, enabled the speed of the train to be kept at a selected value to within very fine limits irrespective of gradients up or down, or the influence of curves. The object of the mobile testing plant was two-fold; firstly to control the working of the engine so that constant conditions were obtained, *i.e.* replicating the same testing method used on the Continent despite the gradients and curves; secondly to measure the various characteristics of its performance under those conditions. The former was obtained by setting the engine controls in pre-determined positions and including in the train one or more of the Mobile Test Units. The electric rheostat braking of the unit(s) was automatically controlled so as to maintain the speed exactly constant under all conditions, while the second objective was met by equipping the dynamometer carriage with the remote cylinder indicating equipment and chemical apparatus for analysis of the smokebox gases in addition to the usual dynamometer carriage instruments.

For a normal constant speed test the intention was that the test locomotive would be attached to the special tender followed by the dynamometer carriage and an appropriate number of the braking units. On starting the train would accelerate freely to the desired speed at which point the electric braking would be gradually introduced, the automatic control initiated and the speed maintained exactly at the specified rate. Engine cut-off and regulator opening would be set in the test positions and time allowed for stable conditions to appear. Once stability had been achieved, readings were to be made over a fixed period of time during which every effort was made to avoid affecting the engine. The mean of the readings taken over this period represented one point on the performance curve of the locomotive. The procedure for determining the full characteristics of an engine, was to run a number of tests at one particular speed but using different cut-offs, enabling the corresponding tractive efforts and efficiencies to be obtained. The cut-off would be gradually increased until the boiler was no longer able to maintain its full pressure, which represented the point of maximum evaporation for that particular speed. This process would then be repeated for a selection of speeds. Graphs would then be produced of steam consumption against speed for various cut-offs also tractive force against speed for the same range of cut-offs. By joining the appropriate points, curves of constant cut-off and constant specific evaporation could be obtained with the results displayed in the form of a tractive effort - speed chart as shewn in figure 86b. Points derived when running in the full gear cut-off gave the cylinder limit of the engine and the diagram would be completed by the addition of the adhesive limit. The three test units were not quite complete as the situation in Europe rapidly deteriorated during the summer of 1939, but Unit

Fig. 102 - Standard 4 0-6-0 Nº 4542, seen here in LMS days. This engine was used to haul the first Mobile Test Unit trials conducted during May and June 1939.

N° 1 was sufficiently advanced to be used in an initial series of tests, presumably intended to check and commission the vehicle and hone procedures, rather than to obtain a record of locomotive performance *per se*. It was hauled by Standard 4 0-6-0 N° 4542 between Derby, Burton on Trent and Leicester - the results from these runs appear in table XLIX. Inspection of these demonstrate that close and consistent control was being obtained over drawbar power - presumably Dynamometer Car N° 1 was used to obtain the horsepower-hour values.

According to Professor Lomonosoff, who essentially introduced the concept of constant speed testing about forty years previously, only about 20-30 minutes of stable running was needed to establish the steam consumption rate. However considerably longer was needed before an accurate assessment could be made of the fuel rate due to the impact that errors in ensuring that the same quantity of coal lay on the grate[64] at the end of the test period as had been present when the trial had started. It was realized at the time that the accuracy of the results also depended very much on the skill of the fireman and possibly an important part of these initial tests was to ensure the fireman could fire consistently and reliably. Details of the coal used including its calorific value appear not to have survived, likewise how it was delivered to the fireman. The special tender was to have contained 3 tons of coal made up in one hundred weight sacks for use during the test period with the start of each sack signalled to the dynamometer carriage by the assistant fireman as he emptied the bag onto the firing plate. These arrangements for recording coal and water consumption were not the Great Western's 'Summation of Increments' and so lacked the self-checking control inherent in the method. That technique was not adopted until post-1948, so despite the speed and horsepower (and cut-off) having been kept constant, the lowest coal figure recorded in the table was three-quarters the highest while the lowest water about four-fifths the highest - perhaps not that bad for a first attempt.

Dynamometer Car N° 3 was specially designed to form an integral part of this LMS testing regime, but it was not finished before the outbreak of the Second World War. After these few runs all of this test equipment was stored and put to one side, not to re-emerge until some time after the end of hostilities. Dynamometer Car N° 3 was originally to have been fitted with an electric (*i.e.* remote recording) indicator housed within a dark room located immediately behind the instrument recording room. Connexions from the front of the engine would allow indicator cards to be taken from any cylinder or valve chest at will. It appears this was not fitted, for certainly when the vehicle was completed it was provided with a Farnborough type remote recording indicator similar to that used at the Rugby Testing Station.

These runs recording N° 4542 hauling Unit N° 1 represent one of the handful of tests conducted as the plant was originally intended to be used. In another series of Class 4 trials we will encounter two of the units used in conjunction with the road test method adopted post-nationalisation. This was when they were used in a series of runs exploring the effects adopting tubes possessing superior heat transfer characteristics and improved draughting could effect on the class' performance. This series of tests conducted under the auspices of British Railways was based on the former Great Western practice of maintaining a constant steam rate through the engine. In this system cut-off and speed would normally be varied as necessary to keep the steam flow constant, so although in this particular series the Mobile Test Unit vehicles enabled the speed also to be kept constant, this was not an absolute condition requirement of the new testing method; in this instance their primary role was to provide an artificial load.

Before that however we must explore some traditional *variable* speed testing of the 'Big Goods' and other goods engines. In these, interposing a dynamometer carriage between the engine and its train enabled speed, drawbar pull and the number of units of work done to be recorded on a moving chart. These tests were carried out under ordinary running conditions on the line so the speed varied from point to point according to the natural variation of gradients, other traffic etc. Consequently, the results, usually summarized as the coal and water consumed per drawbar horsepower hour, gave a result which was an *average* of all of the changing conditions experienced throughout the run, but nevertheless it presented an accurate picture of the engine's *in-service* performance on that duty.

---

64 As part of its 'testing package' the LMS also developed a self-weighing grate precisely to overcome this problem. Unfortunately Dr Andrews was unable to develop it to the point where it would give consistent and reliable readings.

Table XLIX - Performance Data Obtained from Class 4 0-6-0 N° 4542 Using Mobile Test Unit N° 1 - 1939

Route		15th May	16th May	17th May	18th May	19th May	5th June	6th June	7th June	8th June	9th June	19th June	20th June	21st June	22nd June	23rd June
							Derby - Burton on Trent - Leicester									
Test miles		58.12	52.81	34.68	35.41	35.89	29.44	27.84	34.79	34.55	35.30	33.62	34.83	33.30	34.08	34.30
Test time	- mins	118.58	108.08	71.25	72.75	74.92	60.50	56.66	72.0	70.58	71.83	68.25	71.16	67.0	69.0	71.33
Average speed	- mph	29.45	29.30	29.20	29.20	28.80	29.20	29.50	29.40	29.30	29.50	29.60	29.40	29.80	29.65	28.85
Work done	- horsepower-minutes	49956	44865	29910	30540	31500	24210	23670	30390	30330	30735	27180	29310	27570	27765	28605
Work done	- horsepower-hours	832.6	747.75	511.8 / 498.5	521.4 / 509.0	535.8 / 525.0	418.4 / 403.5	394.5	519.6 / 506.5	517.7 / 505.5	524.55 / 512.25	466.2 / 453.0	501.1 / 488.5	477.5 / 459.5	479.0 / 462.75	491.2 / 476.75
HP hours per test mile		14.3	14.1	14.78 / 14.3	14.7 / 14.4	14.95 / 14.6	14.2 / 13.7	14.17	14.91 / 14.59	15.0 / 14.65	14.85 / 14.5	13.85 / 13.45	14.3 / 14.0	14.32 / 13.8	14.03 / 13.58	14.31 / 13.9
Average drawbar horsepower		421.3	415.1	*430.1* / 419.8	*430.0* / 422.7	*429.1* / 420.4	*414.9* / 400.2	417.8	*433.0* / 422.1	*440.1* / 429.7	*438.2* / 427.9	*409.8* / 398.2	*422.5* / 411.9	*427.6* / 411.5	*416.5* / 402.4	*413.2* / 401.0
Coal total weight	- lbs	3307	2807	1722	1783	1778	1326	1588	1660	1598	1658	1610	1568	1539	1592	1511
Coal consumption	- lbs/mile	56.8	52.6	49.7	50.3	49.5	45.0	57.0	47.75	46.3	47.0	47.8	45.0	46.2	46.8	44.1
Coal consumption	- lbs/dhp/hr	3.98	3.76	3.37	3.42	3.32	3.17	4.02	3.20	3.08	3.16	3.46	3.13	3.22	3.33	3.08
Firing rate	- lbs/sq ft/hr	79.3	73.7	68.7	69.6	67.5	62.25	79.5	65.6	64.3	65.6	67.2	62.7	65.3	65.6	60.25
Number of shovelfuls		246	221	139	156	153	~	~	~	~	~	~	~	~	~	~
Average weight per shovelful	- lbs	13.45	13.3	12.4	11.42	11.6	~	~	~	~	~	~	~	~	~	~
Water total quantity	- gallons	2435	1795	1245	1235	1365	1020	1085	1395	1390	1320	1140	1220	1164	1212	1253
Water consumption	- galls/test mile	41.8	34.0	35.9	35.2	38.1	34.6	38.9	40.2	40.3	37.4	33.9	35.0	35.0	35.6	36.5
Water consumption	- lbs/dhp/hr	29.2	24.0	24.3	23.7	25.4	24.4	27.5	26.9	26.85	25.2	24.4	24.4	24.4	25.3	25.5
		7.35	6.4	25.0	24.3	26.0	25.3		27.5	27.5	25.75	25.2	25.0	25.3	26.2	26.25
Evaporation lbs water/lb of coal				7.23	6.92	7.7	7.7	6.84	8.4	8.7	7.97	7.08	7.8	7.57	7.62	8.3

Shaded entry did not appear in original data and has been calculated from the work done *i.e.* (horsepower-minutes ÷ test time minutes)
Entries in italic print are the values corrected for gradient, thus in the case of the drawbar horsepower values they represent equivalent drawbar horsepower (edhp) figures.
The difference in height between the start and finish of each run appears to have been obtained from the barometric height formula, from which knowing the length of the run, the mean gradient could be obtained and thence the edhp.

Comparisons, Steaming and Performance

In April 1959 such a series of variable speed trials was conducted with an ex-LMS Class 5 4-6-0 hauling Class D goods trains with the ex-Lancashire & Yorkshire dynamometer carriage recording the data between Rowsley and Cheadle Heath. Following these tests, it was recommended that either the existing timings should be modified, or if the timings were to remain, then the loads should be altered. Although, at the time, most of the Class D goods trains on this section of line were worked by Class 4 0-6-0s, none was tested. Instead the results from the Class 5 were applied 'proportionately' to determine the recommended 0-6-0 loadings. It is not clear on what basis they were calculated, but it appears they had over estimated the Standard Goods' capabilities, so later in the

quality coal was used which clinkered. Generally, the coal, which was not identified, was of the quality normally used for Class D goods and comprised approximately 25 per cent lumps and 75 per cent smalls and fines. A summary of the results appears in tables LI and LII, while figures 105 and 106 are records of the drawbar pull and speed curves, boiler water level and pressure together with the lapsed times for two of the runs - one for each direction. It is not clear how the steam rates quoted on the diagrams were obtained. It is suspected they may simply represent the quantity of water drawn from the tank divided by the time. The height of the water in the tender tank could be ascertained in the dynamometer carriage, giving a continuous check on consumption during the run.

Fig. 103 - Class 4F 0-6-0 N° 44481, the locomotive which took part in the Class 'D' express goods train trials between Rowsley-Peak Forest and Cheadle Heath-Peak Forest in November 1959. This engine was quite a late survivor not being withdrawn until November 1964.

same year another series of tests[65] was instigated this time using a 'Big Goods'.

The same engine, N° 44481, then allocated to Walton-on-the-Hill although worked in all cases by Rowsley enginemen, was used throughout the tests, hauling the following reduced loaded trains:-

(i) 1-10am (Mondays excepted) Class D
    Rowsley - Walton

(ii) 8-00pm (Saturdays excepted) Class D
    Huskisson - Walton

Eight runs were made, four in each direction. The report stated the engine was in good mechanical condition and steamed freely at all times, with the single exception of the first run when a poor

These tests have been referred to previously[66], indeed part of the report was quoted:-

"It is apparent from these tests that even with the reduced loadings the locomotive could not maintain the point to point running times. High rates of steaming for this type of boiler were attained although these were invariably achieved at the expense of boiler water level or steam pressure and the engine was worked at heavy cut-offs. Even so insufficient power was being developed at the drawbar to enable time to be kept. Consequently the loadings were varied to ascertain a suitable weight of train which could be hauled without loss of time."

The report concluded:-

"The tests showed that the power output of the Class 4F 0-6-0 locomotive was rather lower than was

---

65 BTC: *Test with ex-LMS Class 4F 0-6-0 Locomotive on Class 'D' Express Freight Trains Rowsley-Cheadle Heath* Report L. 129 CM&EE Dept. Derby November 1959

66 Mr M Rutherford *Masterpiece of Mediocrity – The 4F Saga* **Backtrack** June 1999 Vol 13 N° 6

originally estimated. They are really unsuitable for working Class 'D' freight trains between Rowsley and Cheadle Heath, but if there is no alternative motive power the loadings should be restricted as under

a) Rowsley - Peak Forest North 26 wagons of goods

b) Cheadle Heath - Peak Forest North 24 wagons of goods"

However, we might question, on the evidence presented in the report, that the 'Big Goods' was unsuitable for the task and instead opine it was the initial (derived) loadings of April 1959 that were inappropriate. The length of the test runs, over which the dynamometer recorded data was taken was restricted to about three-quarters of an hour in one direction and an hour in the other, furthermore, in both instances, the engine was starting from rest. As we have seen previously, the main reason for the 'Big Goods' being a class 4 engine was due to it being fitted with a superheater. Superheat temperature in a steam locomotive was not controlled, instead it 'floated' attaining a value that was determined by the rate of working of the engine. Furthermore, after a period of rest there was a delay after starting before the temperature attained its maximum value associated with that steam rate. According to George Hughes[67] should one of his superheated 0-6-0s suffer a stoppage of four minutes duration, the temperature of the elements fell to the saturation temperature. He mentioned in the same paper, that the superheat obtained was 270°F giving a steam temperature of 650°F. A steam temperature of 600°F was obtained about four minutes after opening the regulator, after which it slowly increased to 650°F, but was prevented from rising further by the damper opening. A few years later Nigel Gresley stated[68] that to get a steam temperature of 600°F in an ordinary goods engine (*i.e.* 0-6-0) not fitted with dampers, which by then he no longer used, took about five minutes after starting from rest.

Figure 104 illustrates the rise in steam temperature recorded in a Western Australian Government Railway class Fs 4-8-0. The plot of steam temperature against time curve for this WAGR locomotive appearing in the absence of the equivalent curve for the 'Big Goods'. Although superheat temperature was affected by a number of factors apart from simply the element area present as will be demonstrated later when comparing the G7s and the 4D boilers, nonetheless this curve may perhaps serve give a rough feel for how the 0-6-0 boiler responded remembering its evaporative surface was 6 per cent larger, superheat area 34 per cent larger, while its grate was 12 per cent bigger than those of the narrow gauge engine. The larger grate area tended to reduce the superheat because it lowered the intensity of combustion for similar

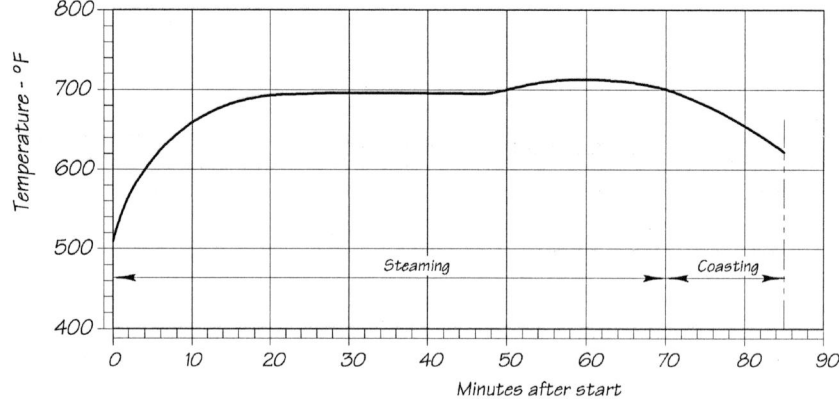

The WAGR Class Fs 4-8-0, introduced in 1912, was a 3ft 6ins gauge locomotive having the following dimensions - driving wheels 3ft 6½ins diameter, cylinders 17ins × 23ins, evaporative heating surface 1097sq ft, superheater 183sq ft, grate area 18.8sq ft, 175lbs/sq in working pressure, weight 55.5 tons and a tractive effort of 23,265lbs.

Test was conducted in June 1952 between Midland Junction and Chidlow. Unfortunately, no details of the load were given but it may be seen that something approaching stable steam temperature was not attained until over twenty minutes following a start.

Fig. 104 - Variation in steam temperature with time - WAGR Class Fs 4-8-0

steam rates. The impact of superheater surface was more subtle since its impact did not depend simply on the area but also on it being suitably proportioned, so although the area of the 4D superheater was slightly smaller than that of the G7s its better proportions enabled it to deliver hotter steam at equal steam rates.

Inspecting the final portion of the Rowsely - Peak

---

67 Mr G Hughes *Compounding and Superheating in Horwich Locomotives* I Mech E March 1910 pp437 & 495

68 Contribution made by Nigel Gresley to the discussion following the presentation by Sir Henry Fowler of his paper

Superheating Steam in Locomotives vol 196 Proc I Civil E 1914 p140.

Forest trace appearing in figure 106 reveals that reasonably stable conditions of pull and speed were obtained during the final stage of the climb to Peak Forest thereby enabling some approximate performance calculations to be be attempted. Ignoring for simplicity the effects the minor changes in speed will have made on resistance, over that portion of the chart, engine N° 44481 was generating a drawbar pull of around 10,200lbs, while running at about 22 miles per hour, which is equivalent to 600 drawbar horsepower. However, the engine was climbing a gradient of 1 in 90 at the time, so assuming two-thirds coal and water supplies and thus an engine and tender weight of 83.4 tons, this is an equivalent drawbar horsepower of 720. Once the horsepower absorbed in driving N° 44481 is considered, the engine was probably producing something close to 800 indicated horsepower. Such a power estimate suggests the 'official' steam rate quoted on the chart of 12,600lbs/hr was an underestimate and that the actual steam production during that final portion of the run, even allowing for a well warmed superheater, was nearer 15,000lbs/hour.

Since this has been judged a poor performance, we might compare it with what a WD 'Austerity' class 2-8-0 could have done, a class selected simply because it was one of the tiny handful of goods engines that were comprehensively tested in Great Britain. From figure 107 the front-end limited drawbar output for this engine at 22 miles per hour and on level track was about 1,010 horsepower, giving a corresponding pull of 17,200lbs. Since, under the same conditions of fuel and water supplies the locomotive would have weighed 115.3 tons, the maximum drawbar pull it could have exerted on the bank would have been about 14,300lbs or say 840 horsepower. Scaling up from the 301 tons hauled by the 0-6-0, this would give a gross train weight of 40 per cent more or say 422 tons.

Table L summarizes the differences in performance between the two classes and suggests that that of the 'Big Goods' was fully the equal of a locomotive designed thirty years later. It also suggests that some of the findings in the report might reasonably be questioned, although one point to consider is that the 4F performance was not sustained for at least one hour, which was the case when the 2-8-0 was tested. The report mentioned that the 0-6-0 could not maintain boiler pressure or water level during periods of maximum effort, but we know had the commitment been there this could have been addressed by a minor change to the draughting. An opinion that is supported by the higher outputs obtained later from N° 44030, which *were* maintained for periods of around *two* hours in length, while further support is lent by .the climbs recorded in the 1920s on the Bedford-Leagrave section appearing in tables XLVII and XLVIII, which were of approximately one hour's duration. Indeed the power output/speed entries for March 1928 were roughly comparable. Both tables reveal, with one exception full boiler pressure was maintained on these climbs, while in the one engine where it was not, the pressure was light, by only 5lbs. Only the 1925 series of tests recorded the water level but it too was maintained well up in the glass suggesting the boiler was not finding the demand made on it was more than it could sustain continuously It might also be helpful to bear in mind, when considering the changes in the height of the water level recorded in figures 105 and 106, that the actual visible portion of gauge glass in a G7 boiler was quite limited being only about five inches in total. Perhaps the firemen on N° 44481 were content for the pressure and water level to fall a little as the engine neared the summit safe in the knowledge that once it had passed, the steam demand would drop away. Allowing the water to fall a little beforehand would let the injector absorb the resulting rise in pressure.

Table L – Comparison Between ex-LMS Class 4F 0-6-0 and WD Austerity Class 8F 2-8-0

		Class 4F 0-6-0	WD 2-8-0
Engine weight	tons	48.75	70.25
Drawbar horsepower (level)		720	1,010
Drawbar horsepower per ton		14.8	14.4
Tractive effort	lbs	24,555	34,215
Drawbar pull at 22mph on the bank	lbs	10,200	14,300
Drawbar pull ÷ tractive effort		0.415	0.418
Drawbar pull at 22mph on the level	lbs	12,273	17,216
Drawbar pull ÷ tractive effort		0.50	0.50
Weight of train	tons	301	422
Weight of train ÷ weight of engine		6.17	6.01

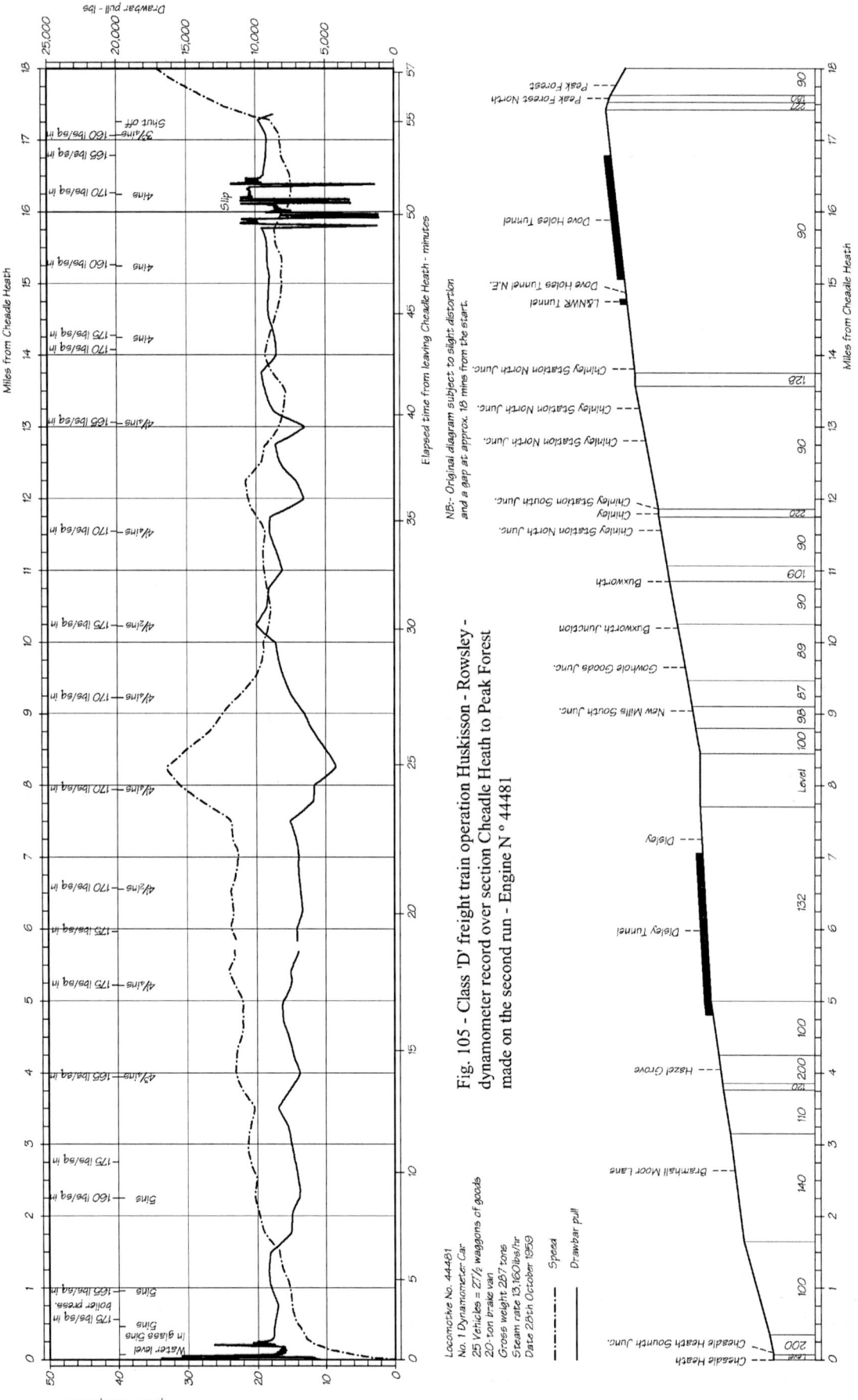

Fig. 105 - Class 'D' freight train operation Huskisson - Rowsley - dynamometer record over section Cheadle Heath to Peak Forest made on the second run - Engine N° 44481

Table LI – 8.00 pm (Saturdays excepted) Class 'D' Freight Trains Huskisson - Rowsley

	Date	26.10.59		Rail	Wet		Date	28.10.59		Rail	Dry
	Driver	J Thraves		Load	23 equal to 25 goods		Driver	G Hallam		Load	25 equal to 27½ goods
	Fireman	J Bond		Gross tonnage	264 approx.		Fireman	J Bond		Gross tonnage	287 approx.
	Weather	Heavy rain		Steam rate	9,900lbs/hr		Weather	Fine		Steam rate	13,160lbs/hr
	Wind	Fresh westerly					Wind	Negligible			

		Running Times		Point to point		Remarks	Running Times		Point to point		
		Schedule	Actual	Booked	Actual		Schedule	Actual	Booked	Actual	
Cheadle Heath Sth Junc.	Dep	11.12 pm	11.40 pm				11.12 pm	11.42½ pm			
New Mills South Junc.	Pass	11.40 pm	12.12 am	28	32	Poor quality coal caused very bad steaming.	11.40 pm	11.9½ pm	28	27	
Chinley	Pass	11.49 pm	12.23 am	9	11		11.49 pm	11.18 pm	9	8½	
Dove Holes Tunnel North End	Pass	Midnight	12.35½ am	11	12½		Midnight	11.29 pm	11	11	Severe slipping in Dove Holes Tunnel.
Peak Forest North	Pass	12.08 am	12.47 am	8	11½		12.08 am	11.38 pm	8	9	

	Date	2.11.59		Rail	Wet		Date	4.11.59		Rail	Dry
	Driver	B Kenworthy		Load	27 equal to 31 goods		Driver	H J Walker		Load	21 equal to 22 goods
	Fireman	M Lane		Gross tonnage	325 approx.		Fireman	F B Halesbrook		Gross tonnage	245 approx.
	Weather	Rainy		Steam rate	11,760lbs/hr		Weather	Fine		Steam rate	11,120lbs/hr
	Wind	Light south east					Wind	Light northerly			

		Running Times		Point to point		Remarks	Running Times		Point to point		
		Schedule	Actual	Booked	Actual		Schedule	Actual	Booked	Actual	
Cheadle Heath Sth Junc.	Dep	11.12 pm	11.29 pm			Bad slip in Disley Tunnel Goods line at Chinley South Junc. Stood at Chapel 12.16½ to 12.21. Almost brought to stand at Dove Holes.	11.12 pm	11.02 pm			
New Mills South Junc	Pass	11.40 pm	11.58 am	28	29		11.40 pm	11.25½ pm	28	23½	
Chinley	Pass	11.49 pm	12.8 am	9	10		11.49 pm	11.34 pm	9	8½	Very severe slipping in Dove Holes Tunnel. Speed down to 6mph for nearly one mile.
Dove Holes Tunnel North End	Pass	Midnight	12.28 am	11	20		Midnight	11.45 pm	11	11	
Peak Forest North	Pass	12.08 am	12.38½ am	8	10½		12.08 am	11.57 pm	8	12	

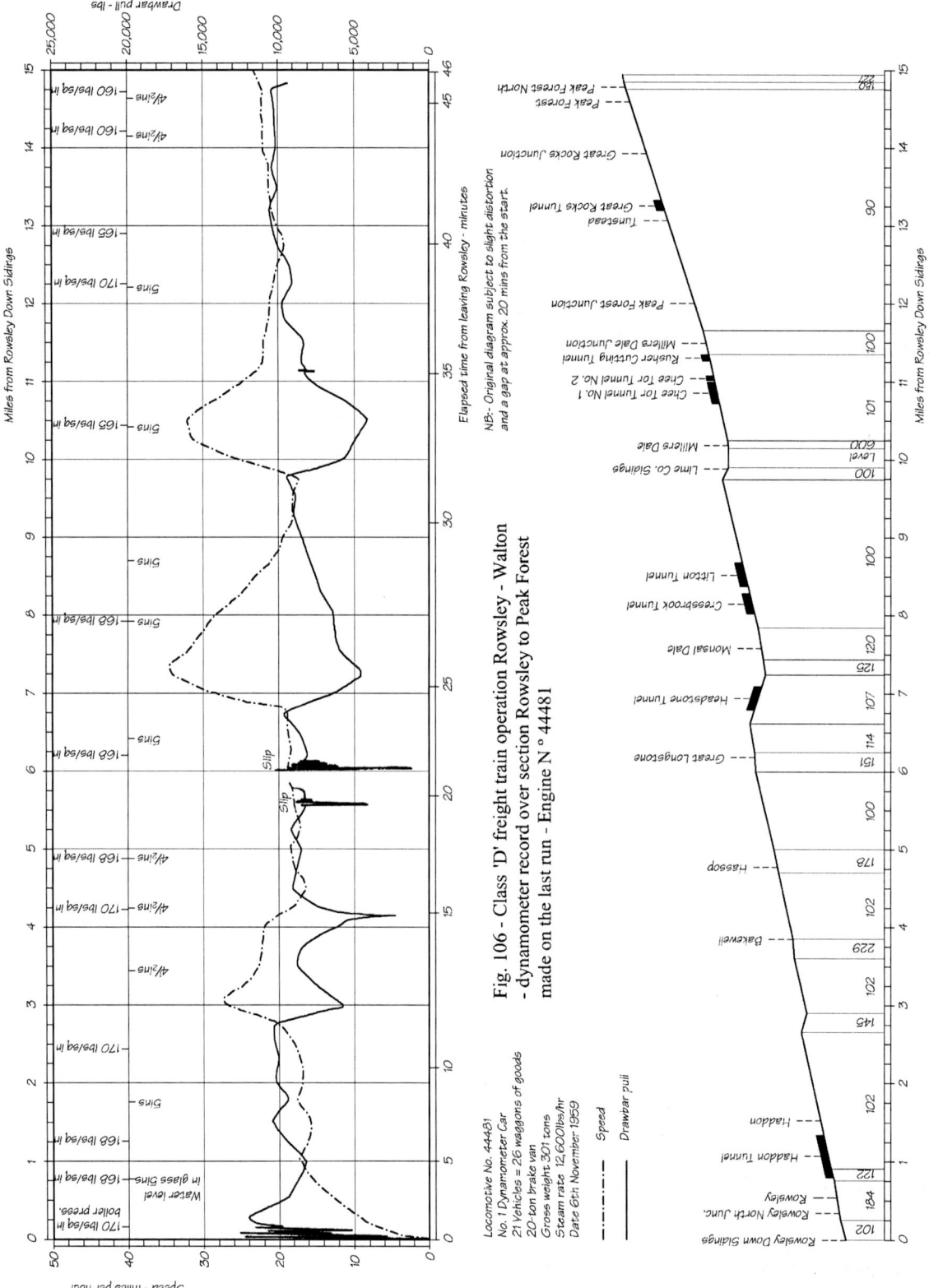

Fig. 106 - Class 'D' freight train operation Rowsley - Walton - dynamometer record over section Rowsley to Peak Forest made on the last run - Engine N° 44481

Table LII – 1.10 am (Mondays excepted) Class 'D' Freight Trains Rowsley - Walton

Date	28.10.59		Rail	Dry	Date	30.10.59	Rail	Greasy

28.10.59

Date	28.10.59		Rail	Dry	
Driver	E Jilbert		Load	23 equal to 28¼ goods	
Fireman	F R Hawley		Gross tonnage	314 approx.	
Weather	Fine		Steam rate	13,800lbs/hr	
Wind	Negligible				

		Running Times		Point to point		Remarks
		Schedule	Actual	Booked	Actual	
Rowsley Down Sidings	Dep	1.10 am	1.09 am		3½	Slipped badly drawing out sidings. Slipped Headstone Tunnel
Rowsley North Junction	Pass	1.14 am	1.12½ am	4	32½	
Millers Dale	Pass	1.41 am	1.45 am	27	15	
Peak Forest North	Pass	1.54 am	2.00 am	13		

30.10.59

Date	30.10.59		Rail	Greasy	
Driver	E Jilbert		Load	23 equal to 27 goods	
Fireman	F R Hawley		Gross tonnage	344 approx.	
Weather	Rain		Steam rate	12,000lbs/hr	
Wind	Negligible				

		Running Times		Point to point		Remarks
		Schedule	Actual	Booked	Actual	
Rowsley Down Sidings	Dep	1.10 am	1.04 am		6	Slipping experienced in most tunnels. Some time lost due to this.
Rowsley North Junction	Pass	1.14 am	1.10 am	4	40	
Millers Dale	Pass	1.41 am	1.50 am	27	17	
Peak Forest North	Pass	1.54 am	2.07 am	13		

4.11.59

Date	4.11.59		Rail	Dry	
Driver	G Taylor		Load	25 equal to 32½ goods	
Fireman	F R Thraves		Gross tonnage	358 approx.	
Weather	Fine and freezing		Steam rate	12,660lbs/hr	
Wind	Negligible				

		Running Times		Point to point		Remarks
		Schedule	Actual	Booked	Actual	
Rowsley Down Sidings	Dep	1.10 am	1.15½ am		4	Severe slipping in most tunnels.
Rowsley North Junction	Pass	1.14 am	1.19½ am	4	38	
Millers Dale	Pass	1.41 am	1.57½ am	27	16	
Peak Forest North	Pass	1.54 am	2.13½ am	13		

6.11.59

Date	6.11.59		Rail	Greasy	
Driver	G Taylor		Load	21 equal to 26 goods	
Fireman	F R Thraves		Gross tonnage	301 approx.	
Weather	Frosty, fog patches		Steam rate	12,600lbs/hr	
Wind	Negligible				

		Running Times		Point to point		Remarks
		Schedule	Actual	Booked	Actual	
Rowsley Down Sidings	Dep	1.10 am	1.07 am		4	
Rowsley North Junction	Pass	1.14 am	1.11 am	4	31	
Millers Dale	Pass	1.41 am	1.42 am	27	13	
Peak Forest North	Pass	1.54 am	1.55 am	13		

Table LIII – Sample LMS Dynamometer Car Tests Toton – Brent Up Loaded Coal Trains – Short-lap Engines

	Train				31/8/25 0-8-0 G2 Nº 574	2/9/25 0-6-0 4F Nº 3866	Nº 3 & Nº 4 Class 7/9/25 0-6-0 Nº 3756 & 3866	2 × Nº 4 Class 31/1/28 Garratt Nº 4998	2 × Nº 4 Class 2/2/28 Garratt Nº 4998	2 × Nº 4 Class 23/2/28 0-6-0 Nº 3945 & 3946	Nº 3 & Nº 4 Class 7/2/28 Garratt Nº 4998	Nº 3 & Nº 4 Class 28/2/28 0-6-0 Nº 3756 & 3946	1200 Tons 19/2/28 Garratt Nº 4998	1200 Tons 4/3/28 0-6-0 Nº 3945 & 3946
	Date													
	Class													
	Engine													
a	Weight of engine (two-thirds coal & water)			tons	96.29	81.12	159.64	139.72	139.72	166.82	139.72	161.93	139.72	166.82
b	Weight of train (with dynamometer car)			tons	753.75	768.8	1335.91	*	1556.3	1484.15	1422.75	1353.05	—	1177.9
c	Total weight of engine, car and train			tons	850.04	849.92	1495.55	*	1696.02	1650.97	1562.47	1514.98	¶	1344.7
d	Train miles				127.36	127.37	127.03	128.27	127.96	127.96	128.14	127.58	127.53	127.57
e	Ton-miles excluding engine				95990	97920	169710	193781	199144	189912	182311	172622	149997	150265
f	Ton-miles including engine				108260	108260	189980	211703	217023	211258	200275	193281	167815	171546
g	Running time			mins	438.48	442.75	455.33	525.7	504.6	448.3	479.8	441.4	324.8	323.0
h	Time including stops in minutes				518.43	524.83	521.55	632.5	580.8	510.7	553.8	512.8	377.4	379.0
i	Average speed			mph	17.43	17.3	16.74	14.64	15.22	17.13	16.01	17.35	23.56	23.7
j	Maximum speed			mph	35.0	36.0	39.5	39.0	37.5	38.5	37.5	37.0	44.0	44.0
k	Average drawbar pull			lbs	7753	8348	14753	18928	18234	16666	16867	15859	13664	14291
l	Maximum drawbar pull			lbs	13754	15752	26544	36736	33040	31360	29792	26880	26432	32480
m	Total work done by engine in horsepower-minutes				113411.7	122733	215766	297562	286038	251118	259942	243144	205155	214074
n	Total work done by engine in horsepower-hours				1890.2	2045.55	3596.1	4959.4	4767.3	4185.3	4332.4	4052.4	3419.2	3567.9
o	Average drawbar horsepower				332.6	363.1	611.4	692.2	714	737.0	707.5	723.8	855.2	881.8
p	Maximum drawbar horsepower				682.0	621.0	896.0	1046	1020	1255	1112	1165	1238	1337
q	Horsepower hours per train mile				14.85	16.06	28.3	38.67	37.26	42.2	33.8	31.76	26.81	27.96
r	Horsepower minutes per ton mile (excluding engine)				1.18	1.25	1.27	1.54	1.44	1.32	1.43	1.41	1.37	1.42
s	**Coal:-** Weight burnt in pounds (excluding shed duties)				7856	8681	15843	18353	18415	15214	16488	15164	12380	13334
t	Pounds per train mile				61.7	68.2	124.7	143.1	143.9	118.9	128.7	118.9	97.1	104.5
u	Pounds per ton mile excluding engine				0.0818	0.0886	0.0934	0.095	0.093	0.08	0.090	0.088	0.082	0.089
v	Pounds per ton mile including engine				0.0726	0.0802	0.0833	0.087	0.085	0.072	0.082	0.078	0.074	0.078
w	Pounds per drawbar horsepower hour				4.16	4.25	4.406	3.70	3.86	3.63	3.81	3.74	3.62	3.74
x	Average per hour including stops			tons	0.406	0.443	0.814	0.777	0.780	0.798	0.797	0.792	0.879	0.942
y	Average per hour excluding stops			tons	0.48	0.523	0.932	0.935	0.977	0.909	0.920	0.920	1.021	1.106
z	Avge per sq ft of grate area per hour excluding stops			lbs	45.55	55.8	49.47	47.1	49.2	48.3	46.7	48.8	51.4	58.7
A	**Water:-** Gallons consumed				5355	5400	11300	13364	12500	11890	11320	12095	8575	10185
B	Gallons per train mile				42.05	42.4	88.96	104.2	97.7	92.9	88.3	94.8	67.2	79.8
C	Pounds per ton mile excluding engine				0.5576	0.5515	0.6657	0.690	0.628	0.626	0.621	0.701	0.572	0.678
D	Pounds per ton mile including engine				0.4947	0.4988	0.5947	0.631	0.576	0.563	0.565	0.626	0.511	0.594
E	Pounds per drawbar horsepower hour				28.33	26.4	31.4	26.95	26.22	28.41	26.13	29.85	25.08	28.55
F	Pounds per pound of coal				6.82	6.22	7.13	7.28	6.79	7.82	6.87	7.98	6.93	7.64
G	Pounds per sq ft of evap. heating surface per hour				4.41	6.33	6.43	7.14	6.96	6.81	6.62	6.43	7.41	8.1

Weight of train (with dynamometer car) - *1536.3 tons for 10 miles, 1519.6 tons for 40 miles then 1502.9 tons for 78 miles - ¶1184.6 tons for 61 miles then 1168.4 tons for 67 miles

Total weight of engine, car and train – *1676.1 tons for 10 miles, 1659.4 tons for 40 miles then 1642.7 tons for 78 miles - ¶1324.4 tons for 61 miles then 1308.1 tons for 67 miles

Table LIV – Sample LMS Dynamometer Car Tests Toton - Brent Up Loaded Coal Trains – Large-lap Engines

			LMS 8F 2-8-0 417 Nº 48400	LMS 8F 2-8-0 417 Nº 48189	LNER O1 2-8-0 417 Nº 63789	LNER O1 2-8-0 417 Nº 63789	WD 2-8-0 417 Nº 63169	WD 2-8-0 417 Nº 63169	WD 2-10-0 417 Nº 73776	WD 2-10-0 417 Nº 73776
	Class / Schedule / Engine	mins								
a	Weight of engine (two-thirds coal & water)	tons	116.2	116.2	113.65	113.65	115.3	115.3	123.35	123.35
b	Weight of train (with dynamometer car)	tons	1080	1047	1080	1061	1091	1080	1047	1080
c	Total weight of engine, car and train	tons	1196	1163.2	1194	1174.7	1206.3	1195	1170.4	1203
d	Train miles		127.5	127.5	127.8	127.8	128.0	128.0	127.85	127.85
e	Ton-miles excluding engine		137700	133493	138024	135596	139648	138240	133859	138078
f	Ton-miles including engine		152490	148308	152593	150127	144756	152960	149636	153848
g	Running time	mins	531.3	484.2	525.5	440.3	441.4	492.3	514.8	508.0
h	Time including stops in minutes		~	~	~	~	~	~	~	~
i	Average speed	mph	14.4	15.8	14.6	17.4	17.4	15.6	14.9	15.1
j	Maximum speed	mph	~	~	~	~	~	~	~	~
k	Average drawbar pull	lbs	≈12970	≈12290	≈13716	≈11552	≈12091	≈11971	≈12534	≈12169
l	Maximum drawbar pull	lbs	~	~	~	~	~	~	~	~
m	Total work done by engine in horsepower-minutes		186853	168901	195889	165955	180062	172431	178678	165372
n	Total work done by engine in horsepower-hours		3114.2	2815.0	3264.8	2765.9	3001.0	2873.9	2978.0	2756.2
o	Average drawbar horsepower		498	518	534	536	561	498	498	490
p	Maximum drawbar horsepower		~	~	~	~	~	~	~	~
q	Horsepower hours per train mile		24.42	22.08	25.55	21.64	23.44	22.45	23.29	21.56
r	Horsepower minutes per ton mile (excluding engine)		1.36	1.23	1.42	1.22	1.29	1.25	1.33	1.20
s	Coal:- Weight burnt in pounds (excluding shed duties)		11708	10162	10735	9329	10803	10547	11138	11053
t	Pounds per train mile		91.83	79.70	84.0	73.0	84.4	82.4	87.12	86.45
u	Pounds per ton mile excluding engine		0.085	0.0761	0.0778	0.0688	0.0774	0.0763	0.0832	0.0800
v	Pounds per ton mile including engine		0.077	0.0685	0.0704	0.0621	0.0700	0.0690	0.0744	0.0719
w	Pounds per drawbar horsepower hour		3.76	3.61	3.29	3.37	3.6	3.67	3.74	4.01
x	Average per hour including stops	tons	~	~	~	~	~	~	~	~
y	Average per hour excluding stops	tons	0.590	0.562	0.547	0.567	0.656	0.574	0.580	0.583
z	Avge per sq ft of grate area per hour excluding stops	lbs	46.16	43.95	44.0	45.5	51.35	44.95	32.45	32.63
A	Water:- Gallons consumed		9460	7713	8277	6959	8048	8121	8342	8467
B	Gallons per train mile		74.2	60.49	64.77	54.45	62.88	63.44	65.25	66.22
C	Pounds per ton mile excluding engine		0.687	0.578	0.600	0.513	0.576	0.587	0.623	0.613
D	Pounds per ton mile including engine		0.620	0.520	0.542	0.464	0.521	0.531	0.558	0.550
E	Pounds per drawbar horsepower hour		30.38	27.40	25.36	25.14	26.82	28.26	28.01	30.72
F	Pounds per pound of coal		8.08	7.59	7.71	7.46	7.45	7.70	7.49	7.66
G	Pounds per sq ft of evap. heating surface per hour		6.48	5.79	5.69	5.70	6.51	5.89	4.98	5.13

A Defence of the Midland/LMS Class 4 0-6-0

Brief reference has previously been made to the several series of dynamometer tests conducted by the LMS and later BR on the former Midland main line between Toton and Brent. The earliest of these were conducted to ascertain which of the competing classes were capable of doing the required work with the greatest economy, while other trials were to demonstrate the superiority of the latest design. Nevertheless in every case, whatever their final purpose, each trial had the primary objective of ascertaining the comparative coal, water and oil consumptions of the different competing engines, or combinations of engine, hauling loaded southbound coal trains to London, and their corresponding down empties. In each direct comparison, the locomotives were run over the same route, at the same timings hauling similar weight trains, whilst burning the same grade of coal. Only the weather condition from day to day was left as an uncontrolled variable

Ignoring whatever the LMS and British Railways hoped to draw from them, for us they have bequeathed valuable data from which, we can obtain some insight into 'Big Goods' performance. Extracts from the original LMS dynamometer carriage test result summary sheets appear in table LIII. In this respect, we are following in the footsteps of Mr Cox who also used such data to demonstrate that the Class 4 was less efficient. Examples appeared in his paper[69] *A Modern Locomotive History* and subsequently in an expanded version in *Chronicles of Steam*. In both instances, some of his tabulated figures are incorrect, for they differ from those present in the original test results. In this respect, it is intriguing to record that the errors all conspired to shew the weaker candidate in a poorer light. Perhaps this was simply a case of genuine mistake in noting down figures, unfortunately, sometimes Mr Cox could be deliberately misleading in his opinions, so one cannot be certain if these errors were introduced accidentally or not. The shaded entries represent additional, calculations performed on the original data, simply in order to present as consistent a format as possible. Thus the 1925 tests did not have a line G, conversely the 1928 series did not have the values represented by lines x, y and C.

As these test results were obtained from a dynamometer carriage, they contain certain quirks that are inherent in its use. One of which concerns the value of the average drawbar horsepower. An engine may only produce drawbar horsepower when it is exerting a pull. Now it will always exert such a pull when it is accelerating its train, when it is climbing a gradient and, providing it is not coasting, when it is travelling on level track. Conversely, when it is descending a gradient it may be producing no pull at all and therefore no drawbar horsepower even though the train is still moving[70]. In this situation, the engine continued to burn coal, and may even have used a breath of steam to drive itself, and thus still produced indicated horsepower. When coasting or braking, the engine will have been producing neither drawbar nor indicated horsepower – an observation introduced, as a caution regarding the weight locomotive enthusiasts might sensibly apply to abridged dynamometer test results. Since the line from Toton to Brent contained both uphill and downhill sections their presence had an impact on the recorded performance, which is why caution must be exercised when comparing dynamometer test results obtained from one route with those obtained from another even if all of the other factors remained unchanged. By way of example, sufficient information is presented in table LIII to obtain the 'average' drawbar horsepower by several methods:-

(i) Firstly, for each of these results, there is a line o denoting the average drawbar horsepower as recorded in the dynamometer carriage.

(ii) However a value for the average drawbar horsepower may be obtained from the product of the average speed (line i) and the average drawbar pull (line k) divided by 375.

---

69 Mr E S Cox *A Modern Locomeotive History -Ten Years Development on the LMS - 1923-1932* paper N° 457 Journal I Loco E 1946 p100. also Mr E S Cox *Chronicles of Steam* Ian Allan London 1967 p76.

70 This admittedly is a simplification. Negotiating down grades with double-headed loose-coupled trains comprising 90 wagons weighing 1500 tons and nearly one-third of a mile long demanded enginemanship and teamwork of a very high order. Eliminating the slack - something around 45 feet - out of such a train on a down gradient in readiness for the attack on the next rise while avoiding parting the train, knocking the guard off his feet or exceeding the speed limit took concentration from both drivers. Yet this was mere bagatelle compared to the situation be it braking or pulling when a long train straddled more than one up and down section when some of the three-link couplings would be tight and others slack. On the shorter saw tooth gradients the engines would be set in mid-gear with a full open regulator; the drivers wound their reversers a fraction of a turn at a time as the most sensitive means available for the steady and gradual application of power as the couplings sorted themselves out before it was possible to resume steady pulling.

(iii) Thirdly, there is the official method; thus if the total work done by the engine in horsepower minutes (line *m*) is divided by the running time (line *g*) a certain value for the average drawbar horsepower is obtained.

(iv) Finally we may obtain the official value if the product of the coal consumption per mile (line *t*) and the average speed (line *i*) is divided by the coal consumption per drawbar horsepower (line *w*).

These last two entries confirm this was the method locomotive engineers used to analyse their results.

minutes by the average drawbar horsepower obtained by method *(i)* reveals the length or proportion of the journey over which the engine was exerting a pull. If the line was comparatively level or completely uphill over the trial portion then we would expect this ratio *(line ix)* to be unity or close to it. If however the road undulated then the fraction would be less than unity because for a portion of the journey the locomotive was able to make use of gravity. From this we may draw a further observation, if over the same road while

Table LV – Summary of the Various Drawbar Horsepower Calculations Derived From Short-Lap Engines Used on Toton–Brent Coal Trains

	Engine		Nº 574	Nº 3866	Nº 3756 & 3866	Nº 3945 & 3946	Nº 3756 & 3946	Nº 3945 & 3946
i	Average drawbar horsepower	*(line o)*	332.6	363.1	611.4	737.0	723.8	881.8
ii	Average drawbar horsepower	*{(line k × line i) ÷ 375}*	360.3	385.1	658.6	761.3	733.8	903.2
iii	Official average drawbar horsepower	*(line m ÷ line g)*	258.6	277.2	473.9	560.2	550.8	662.8
iv	Official average dhp (by coal)	*{(line t × line i) ÷ line w}*	256.5	277.6	473.8	561.0	551.6	662.2
v	Ratio (ii ÷ i)		1.083	1.061	1.077	1.033	1.014	1.024
vi	Total work done - horsepower-minutes	*(lime m)*	113412	122733	215766	251118	243144	214074
vii	Running time - minutes	*(line g)*	438.48	442.75	455.33	448.3	441.4	323.0
viii	Time dhp generated - minutes	*(line m ÷ line o)*	340.99	338.0	325.9	340.73	335.93	242.77
ix	Ratio (viii ÷ vii)		0.777	0.763	0.775	0.760	0.761	0.752
x	Average speed	mph	17.43	17.3	16.74	17.13	17.35	23.7

Average value of *(line ix)*, excluding the high speed run (shaded) is 0.767

Table LV summarises these different methods. The average horsepower determined from method *(ii)* only exceeded by a few per cent the average horsepower obtained from line *o* i.e. method *(i)*. However, on a line with grades in both directions, the line *o* average drawbar horsepower will always well exceed the official value revealed by method *(iii)* because the latter is based on the total running time. Although the regulator openings and cut-off employed over the whole journey would have been recorded by the footplate observer, we do not have those details so we are unable to state exactly when the locomotive was producing drawbar horsepower and when it was not. Nevertheless we may establish approximately the proportion of the time the locomotive spent actually pulling its train. Since the route included sections of falling gradient when the engine produced no (or very little) drawbar horsepower, the average horsepower obtained by *(i)* or *(ii)* represents the mean power produced during the periods when it was actually *pulling* its train. Thus, we may appreciate by dividing the total work done in horsepower-

hauling nominally similar train, speed etc, competing locomotives returned differing values for this ratio then the one with the lowest value was able to exploit gravity the most perhaps through slightly freer running vehicles.

Inspection of the average drawbar horsepower values revealed by the different methods for each locomotive of combination, *i.e.* line ix, suggests through their relative consistency, that similar techniques were employed by the drivers in the way they controlled their charges on the Toton-Brent road. This in turn provides us with an operating profile that we may extrapolate with a reasonable degree of confidence to other Toton-Brent loose-coupled coal trains, namely those obtained in 1948, following the formation of British Railways, and which appear in table LIV. Five representative engines drawn from four modern goods classes were run *viz*; LNER O1 2-8-0, Austerity or WD 2-8-0 and 2-10-0 together with their LMS 8F 2-8-0 precursor. Each engine made two up and two down trips giving a total of sixteen runs; the GWR 28xx 2-8-0, which was used on trials conducted elsewhere, would have fouled the Midland loading gauge so did not run. In the case of the LMS 8F, two locomotives were used in this series of tests, N° 48400 and N° 48189, although there appears to be some slight confusion as to the specific engine used on each run. Mr Nock stated that N° 48400 worked the first down and up trips. Mr Allen merely states that the test series started with N° 48400 but as it was in poor mechanical condition and priming badly N° 48189 was substituted, however he does provide dates:-

"Between Brent and Toton, on the London Midland Region, delays were so serious that on one only of sixteen runs was the booked time kept. The engine concerned was LMR Class 8F N° 48189 on June 29th which took 339.8 minutes as against 340 minutes allowed. Coming up, the same engine lost 67.7 minutes on July 2nd and N° 48400 lost 114.3 minutes on June 30th."

"...while on the single run on which time was kept (Class 8F N° 48189 on June 29th), there were three out-of-course slowings only and two unbooked stops from which speed had to be recovered."

them, as previously being indicated by an unshaded entry. The shaded areas represent calculations performed on the published data so as to construct, as far as possible, the equivalent table, following the format presented earlier for the 1925 and 1928 series of tests. According to Mr Allen, all of the up trains left Toton with between 1060 and 1100 tons, although on some runs the loads were reduced slightly en-route to a minimum of 1030 tons. For the purposes of this comparison, where it has been possible to identify the correct load it has been included, but for the others an average load of 1080 tons has been assumed. Since the lowest load of 1030 tons recorded by Mr Allen does not appear, this means the assumed weights will be erroneous in at least one instance resulting in a slight inaccuracy, nevertheless this is held to be of minor importance, since the primary purpose for this table is to illustrate what were the actual locomotive efficiencies achieved in service.

Mr Allen reported, quoting from the official report, that N° 48400 had been worked with up to full regulator both on the level and uphill, with cut-offs

Table LVI – Summary of the Various Drawbar Horsepower Calculations Derived from Large-Lap Engines Used on Toton–Brent Coal Trains

	Engine		LMS 8F		LNER O1		WD 2-8-0		WD 2-10-0
i	Average drawbar horsepower	(line o)	498	518	534	536	561	498	498	490
ii	Average drawbar horsepower {(line k × line i) ÷ 375}		~	~	~	~	~	~	~
iii	Official average drawbar horsepower (line m ÷ line g)		~	~	~	~	~	~	~
iv	Official average dhp (by coal) {(line t × line i) ÷ line w}		351.7	348.8	372.8	376.9	407.9	350.3	347.1	325.5
v	Ratio (ii ÷ i)		~	~	~	~	~	~	~
vi	Total work done - horsepower-minutes	(lime m)	186853	168901	195889	165955	180062	172431	178678	165372
vii	Running time - minutes	(line g)	531.3	484.2	525.5	440.3	441.4	492.3	514.8	508.0
viii	Time dhp generated - minutes	(line m ÷ line o)	375.2	326.1	366.8	309.6	321.0	346.2	358.8	337.5
ix	Ratio (viii ÷ vii)		0.706	0.673	0.698	0.703	0.727	0.703	0.697	0.664
x	Average speed	mph	14.4	15.8	14.6	17.4	17.4	15.6	14.9	15.1

Average value of (line vi) is 0.696. This ratio is a little smaller than in table LV due it is assumed to the slightly lower resistance of the trains, which probably contained a higher proportion of wagons fitted with oil lubricated axleboxes.

The manner in which Mr Nock's table is laid out implies that this trip was worked by N° 48400, but be that as it may. These four sets of results are representative of locomotive working as it existed in the Britain of 1948 - the beginning of the period, which many enthusiasts hold to be the high noon of steam locomotive operation in this realm.

The figures appearing in table LIV are derived from three books[71], with data taken directly from

at a maximum of 47 per cent, while N° 48189 was not allowed more than half regulator, with cut-offs ranging from 18 per cent on the level to 45 per cent uphill. With the exception of the priming incidents, both locomotives were credited with maintaining pressure and water level well.

Now according to conventional theory, a large-lap long-travel engine should consume less water and

---

71 Mr C J Allen *The Locomotive Exchanges* Ian Allan London 2nd Edition 1950

Mr O S Nock *The British Steam Locomotive 1925-1965* Ian Allan London 1966

Messers J Walford & P Harrison *British Railways Standard Steam Locomotives Vol IV – The 9F 2-10-0 Class* RCTS 2008

Comparisons, Steaming and Performance

thence less coal, per drawbar horsepower yet in these examples the specific consumption figures do not demonstrate a convincing improvement over that of a Class 4. But if we recall from earlier, plotting coal consumption expressed in lb/dhp/hr power produces a 'bath-tub' curve. Every engine's fuel consumption therefore becomes a minimum at the load that is the optimum for that particular locomotive and road combination. Obviously, it is important to load locomotives correctly for the task in hand, avoiding either, under- or overloading them, as this will unduly affect the consumption figures, even if the engines were of equal efficiency. For example, a 'Royal Scot' class 4-6-0, hauling 420 tons would have been pulling 3½ times its own weight, but a Class 2 4-4-0 hauling say 220 tons would have been pulling around 2½ times its own weight. If we assume, as was commonly done for 'quick calculations', that the resistance per ton of the engine was twice that of the carriages, we will find, for the 4-6-0, that the work recorded by the dynamometer carriage was 64 per cent of the work done in the cylinders. However, in the 4-4-0 the drawbar work only represented 52 per cent of the cylinder work, thus, even if the two engines were of identical efficiency, the Class 2 would have recorded a higher coal consumption in lb/dhp/hr than the 'Royal Scot'.

performances demanded of the Class 4 0-6-0 and the Class 8 2-8-0 were indeed comparable. These probably represent as fair a set of comparisons that can be drawn short of actually running the two classes on test together, or by devising a *very* sophisticated computer program.

Although the coal consumption figures for the Class 4 0-6-0 and the Class 8 2-8-0 were not that dissimilar there were several other factors that may, or may not, have influenced this situation apart from the length of the valve lap. Undoubtedly, the coals used in the tests differed to a greater or lesser extent with the properties they displayed on the grate possibly having as large an impact as their calorific values. Perhaps the coal used in 1928 possessed a higher calorific value, but the higher firing rate and smaller grate will have reduced combustion efficiency, while the coal may have had a greater or lesser tendency to be picked up in the draught. Finally there is the not unimportant factor of boiler efficiency, accordingly it is for these reasons that it is more revealing to compare these engines in terms of their specific *steam* consumption per drawbar horsepower hour. As in the earlier comparison between the 0-8-0s, there was only a very small saving in this respect in favour of the 2-8-0 and possibly this was indeed simply a reflection of the nominally superior steam circuit fitted to the 8F. Since the Standard Class 8

Table LVII – Summary of the Relative Locomotive Loadings - Toton–Brent Coal Trains

Engine	Tractive effort - lbs	Engine weight - tons	Total train weight - tons	Mean dhp *(line o)*	Mean dhp ÷ engine w'ght - dhp/ton	Train weight less engine weight - tons	Ratio of train to engine weight	TE ÷ total train weight - lbs/ton
MR/LMS Class 4 0-6-0	24,555	48.75	849.92	363.1	7.46	801.17	16.4	28.9
			825.49	368.5	7.56	776.74	15.9	29.7
LNWR G2 class 0-8-0	28,043	62.0	850.04	332.6	5.36	788.04	12.7	33.0
LMS 8F Class 2-8-0	32,438	70.5	1196.0	498	7.06	1125.5	16.0	27.1
			1163.2	518	7.35	1092.7	15.5	27.9
LNER class O1 2-8-0	35,520	73.3	1194.0	534	7.29	1120.7	15.3	29.7
			1174.7	536	7.31	1101.4	15.0	30.2
WD Austerity 2-8-0	34,215	70.25	1206.3	561	7.99	1136.05	16.2	28.4
			1195.0	498	7.09	1124.75	16.0	28.6
WD Austerity 2-10-0	34,215	78.3	1170.4	498	6.36	1092.1	13.9	29.2
			1203.0	490	6.26	1124.7	14.4	28.4

In the case of these Toton – Brent trials it will be seen that with the exception of the WD 2-10-0 and the LNWR G2, whether the engines are compared on the basis of train weight divided by engine weight or tractive effort divided by total train weight, the ratios were very similar. Thus assured we may assume without too much error the

would have shewn a distinct advantage had the speeds been much higher, the important thing is to appreciate that in mineral and low speed goods work it was of no advantage because under these circumstances a traditionally designed valve gear could return a similar performance. Consequently, any improvement a more modern engine

A Defence of the Midland/LMS Class 4 0-6-0

demonstrated was through it having superior steam conditions, reduced internal leakage, etc. together with perhaps the addition of feed water heating. The 8F was certainly fitted with an exhaust steam

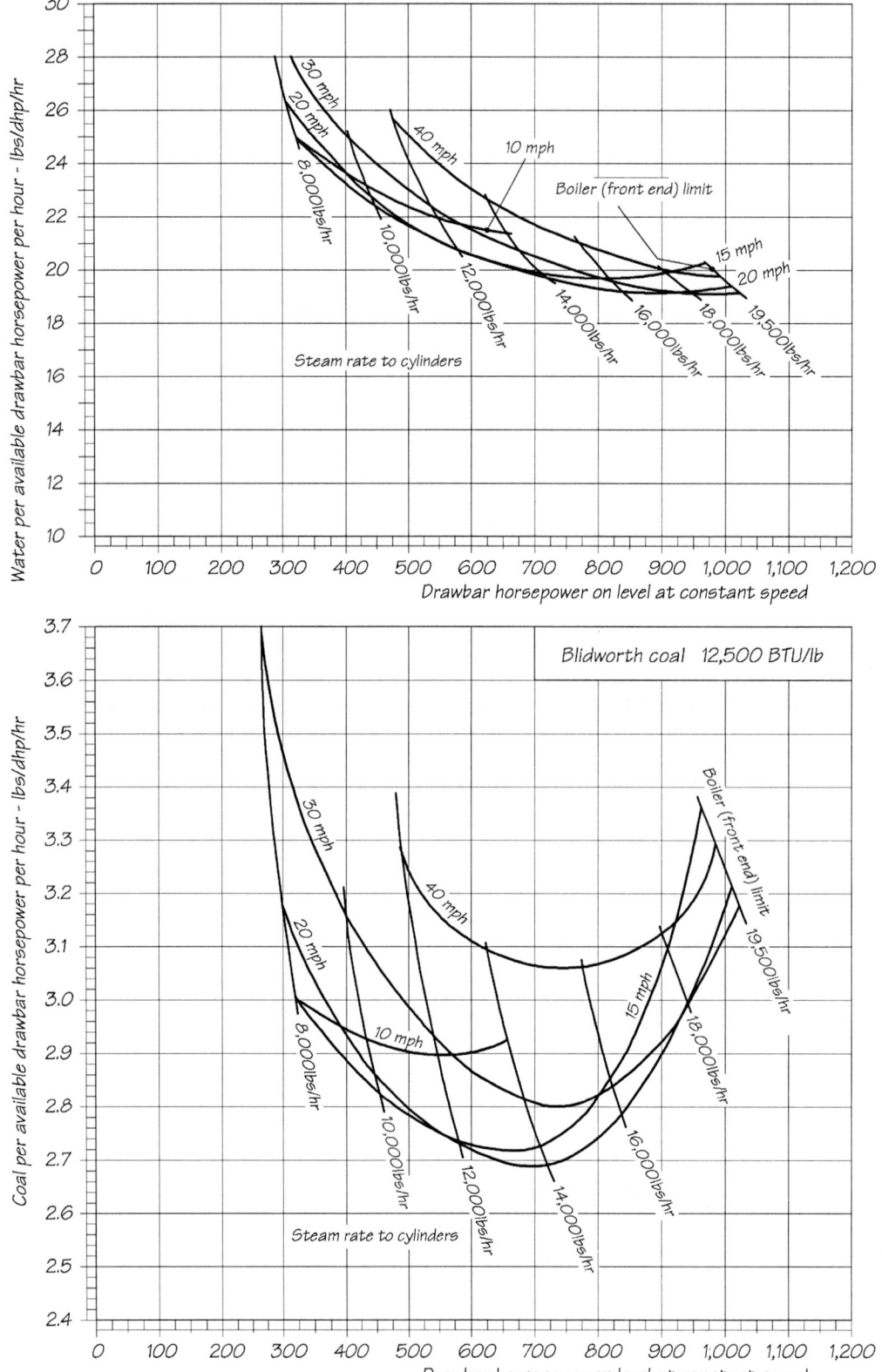

Fig. 107 - Drawbar steam and coal consumption - WD Class 8F 2-8-0 Nº 90464

Comparisons, Steaming and Performance

injector but it is not clear if it was used in these tests although given the low firing rates it is probable that even if it was, the benefits would have been small.

Rugby tests conducted on Class 5 N° 44765 fitted with a 3B boiler carrying 28 flues, during the second half of 1950 recorded steam temperatures in the range of 590-610°F at around 12-14,000 pounds of steam per hour. Since the superheater fitted to the 2-8-0 was smaller than that fitted to the

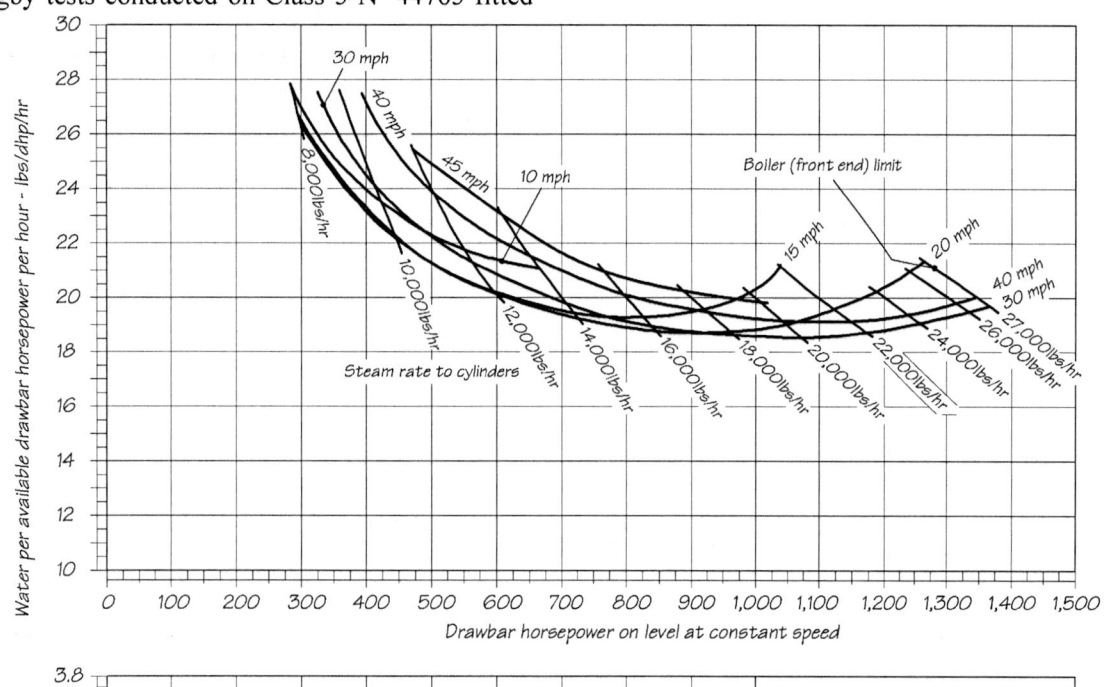

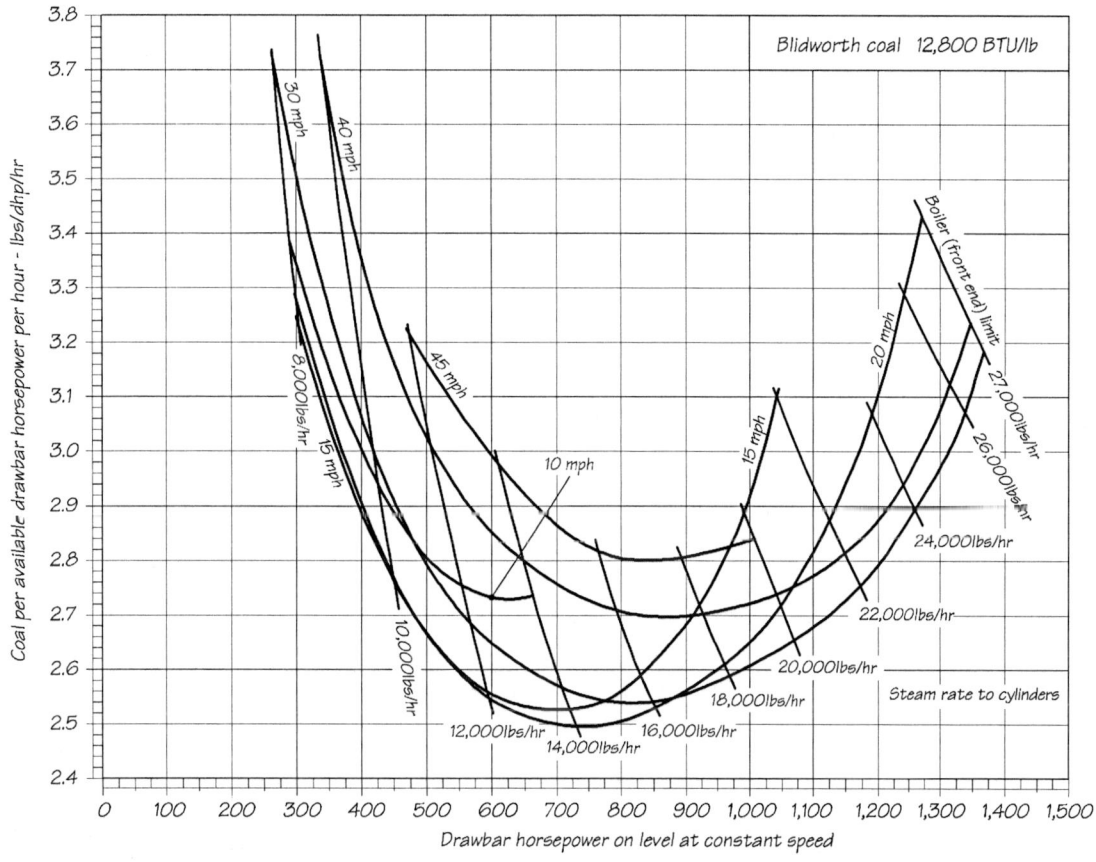

Fig. 108 - Drawbar steam and coal consumption - WD Class 8F 2-10-0 N° 90772

A Defence of the Midland/LMS Class 4 0-6-0

4-6-0 in otherwise very similar boilers, we might reasonably assume its steam temperature would have been lower. Taking a value of 550°F and assuming a 5lbs/sq in back pressure gives a theoretical heat drop and steam consumption of 207.9BTU/lb and 12.24lbs/ihp/h[72] respectively – or only a little smaller than that of the 'Big Goods'. Having increased the boiler maintenance demands by virtue of adopting an extra 50lbs/sq in working pressure, the potential advantage of the higher pressure on locomotive economy was largely lost through providing insufficient superheater area – refer to the earlier footnote regarding the relative superheater performance of the 3B and 3C boilers. The two WD engines had larger superheaters but neither was fitted with an exhaust steam injector, but they are also interesting for they represent the only examples of the engines used on these tests that had been fully tested *Bulletin Nº 7 Performance & Efficiency Tests WD 2-10-0 & 2-8-0 Freight Locomotives*. Drawbar characteristic curves of both classes appear in figures 107 and 108 and these may be used in conjunction with the figures from the Toton–Brent run. The starting point is the average drawbar horsepower values recorded in *line o* of table LVI, which represents the mean power the engines produced when hauling their trains. However, the engines only produced this power for around 70 per cent of the journey, although during those periods they will have been consuming coal and water at roughly the rates recorded by the performance curves if the effect of the nett mean gradient between Toton and Brent is disregarded. However, while the engines were running they were burning coal and consuming water for the whole journey. We may allow for this albeit approximately by adopting the approach used for the average horsepower values. Thus the specific fuel and water consumption figures corresponding to the mean drawbar horsepower values for the run are read from figures 107 and 108 before being divided by the values obtained in the tests - table LIV. This results in another series of factors which for convenience are summarized in table LVIII.

Despite the objections that might be applied to this

Table LVIII – Comparison Between Recorded and Estimated DHP Figures

			WD 2-8-0		WD 2-10-0	
			Run 1	Run 2	Run 1	Run 2
a	Average drawbar horsepower	(line o)	561	498	498	490
b	Drawbar horsepower by coal	{(line t × line i) ÷ line w}	407.9	350.3	347.1	325.5
c	Ratio		0.727	0.703	0.697	0.664
d	Coal consumption from results (table LIV)	lbs/dhp/hr	3.6	3.67	3.74	4.01
e	Water consumption from results (table LIV)	lbs/dhp/hr	26.82	28.26	28.01	30.72
f	Coal consumption from graph (figures 107 & 108)	lbs/dhp/hr	2.745	2.78	2.67	2.68
g	Water consumption from graph (figures 107 & 108)	lbs/dhp/hr	20.95	21.7	21.3	21.4
h	Ratio (f ÷ d)		0.76	0.76	0.71	0.67
i	Ratio (g ÷ e)		0.78	0.77	0.76	0.70

technique it does give a simple way of anticipating the *in-service* fuel and water consumption values from the drawbar characteristic curves. However, it should only be considered a first approximation while the above factors are only applicable to this *particular* combination of road and traffic. With these provisos this technique affords us a way of comparing a Class 4MT 2-6-0 with a Standard Class 4 Freight, had one of the former been available for use in the 1928 series of trials. From figure 101 the corresponding water rate for an average drawbar power of 368 at 17 mph was about 19lbs/dhp/hr. The ratio of the weight of the engine to its train, at 14.3, was close to that of the 2-10-0, so adopting a factor of 0.76 for the water consumption - line *(i)* from table LVIII - gives 25lbs/dhp/hr as opposed to the 28.4lbs obtained from Nº 3945 and 3946. In the case of the coal consumption, this smaller demand for steam will have reduced the demand for coal - the corresponding figures being 3.0lbs/dhp/hr and 3.63lbs if we remain with the same factor (the 2-10

---

72 Early dynamometer tests with the Standard 8 2-8-0, which always carried 21 flues, revealed steam temperatures of about 500°F. On the above basis, this would give a specific steam consumption of around 12.75lbs/ihp/hr. Steam temperature was reportedly raised only slightly by fitting larger diameter elements, so our figure of 550°F is unlikely to be an overestimate.

The importance of having sufficient superheat is demonstrated by some trials made in October 1934 with Class 5 Nº 5036 fitted with a 14-element superheater hauling the 2-55pm Camden to Carlisle fitted goods train – FF1 to Crewe and FF2 thence to Carlisle (Fitted Goods Nº 1 and Fitted Goods Nº 2 in Midland parlance). The dynamometer records revealed higher coal and water consumption figures than those recorded from either Horwich Moguls or 'Big Goods'. Subsequent tests in March 1935 on Sheffield to Carlisle fitted goods trains supported these findings. Low superheat allied with possibly a heavier engine relative to the work demanded had negated the benefits of large-lap valves at a higher running speed.

suffered delays which will have affected the coal consumption far more than steam). Whilst these figures support an advantage in favour of the 2-6-0, unless everything was equal other than the length of the valve laps, a reduced steam and coal consumption cannot be attributed to large-lap valves. For example, disregarding the error inherent in selecting appropriate factors, the consumption of the 0-6-0s might have been artificially raised through internal leakage past their Schmidt piston valve rings. The superheater fitted to the Mogul was particularly effective, which promoting a higher Rankine efficiency - hotter steam at a higher pressure - will inevitably have reduced the specific water and coal consumption figures irrespective of the valve design. However, with this technique we are unable to estimate by how much the better steam conditions were improving the 2-6-0, furthermore as will be demonstrated later, some of the performance data for this engine is suspect putting the machine in better light.

The Class 4 0-6-0 and the Class 4MT 2-6-0 Compared

This performance comparison between the 4MT Mogul and the 'Big Goods' may be pursued in greater detail by extrapolating from data obtained when a pair of the latter[73] was tested at constant, albeit a slightly higher speed, in early British Railways days. Quoting from the report:-

"The original object of these trials was to compare the performance of a locomotive fitted with 'Swirlyflo' small tubes with that of a locomotive of the same class fitted with standard tubes. It was considered that 'Swirlyflo' tubes would be most effective when applied to a comparatively small boiler. L.M.R. Class 4 Freight 0-6-0 engines were selected, the decision to employ them also being influenced by their poor steaming characteristics.

Several engines of this class were due to be experimentally fitted with a modified draughting arrangement; the opportunity was therefore taken to conduct a further series of trials with the two test engines modified accordingly."

N° 44203 was fitted with 'Swirlyflo' tubes, with the control engine N° 44030 retaining conventional small tubes. The 'Swirlyflo' tube had a three-lobed cross-section, reminiscent of the club symbol on a playing card but without the foot, which was then twisted in a slow helix lengthwise - they were one of several patent tube designs of the period, another being the 'Sinuflo'. These designs were marketed as improving steam production through the enhanced heat transfer they promised. After the first series of tests had been completed, both engines were then provided with Swindon-inspired improved front ends and the tests repeated.

The trials were conducted between Crewe and Holyhead over the period October 1953 to January 1954 using the ex-LMS N° 3 Dynamometer Car and Mobile Test Units N° 1 and 2. The main instrument room in the dynamometer car accommodated the control desk for the Mobile Test Units along with the recording table which provided a continuous record of speed, drawbar pull, horsepower etc. Various multi-point thermometers, draught gauges etc. were also housed in this room. The carriage also included a smaller room known as the indicator compartment that contained a Farnborough indicator which provided indicator cards on a crank angle base, whilst another compartment held apparatus for continuous sampling and analysis of the smokebox gases during tests. It appears no indicator cards were taken from the engines during these trials. In use the Mobile Test Units automatically maintained a constant speed by varying the resistance they presented to the engine in accordance with the road. The resistance reduced when the ensemble was climbing a gradient but increased when it was descending. There were three units in total, which could be used singularly, in pairs as here, or all three together, according to the speed and braking force required for each controlled trial. Control was applied from the dynamometer car and the speed could be regulated by hand regulation or automatically. Normally for each controlled test the gear would be set to give the required cut-off and with the speed and boiler pressure kept constant, this likewise implied a constant steam flow rate to the cylinders and thus a constant horsepower output. This in turn implied constant firing and feed water rates. In practice, slight changes would be made in gear setting from

---

73 BTC: *Report on Trials of LMR 0-6-0 Class 4F Freight Locomotives Fitted with Swirlyflo Boiler Tubes and Modified Draughting Arrangement.* Report L.98 CM&EE Dept. Derby March 1954.

Ralph Ingham thinks the tests were not to improve the Class 4 *per se,* but rather to use a known indifferent steamer to test the properties of the 'Swirlyflo' tubes which were subsequently used in the carriage warming steam generators fitted to diesel locomotives. They were a common (standard?) feature of Spanner vertical boilers which were used on some diesels.

time to time in accordance with the indication of the steam flow meter to compensate for small fluctuations in boiler pressure. The cut-off was increased by stages from test to test until the maximum sustained rate of evaporation was reached. The 'Summation of Increments' method as developed at Swindon was used to determine water and firing rates. The test coal was loaded onto the tender in one hundredweight bags with each being recorded on a graph by noting the time the instant when the fireman completed the consumption of that bag. Concurrently the corresponding particulars of the amount of feed water injected into the boiler were taken. As the test progressed, the coal and water consumption figures were plotted on a time base. The validity of a test was established when it was possible to draw fair straight lines through the points on the graph, while the gradients of the lines established the coal and water rates in pounds/hour.

The order of the testing was:-

(i) Engine Nº 44203 fitted with 'Swirlyflo' small tubes and standard draughting.

(ii) Engine Nº 44030 fitted with standard tubes and draughting.

(iii) Engine Nº 44030 fitted with standard tubes and modified draughting.

(iv) Engine Nº 44203 fitted with 'Swirlyflo' small tubes and modified draughting.

The tests were conducted at a constant speed of 33 miles per hour, which in the majority of the runs yielded a test duration of two hours. During each run, continuous records were made of speed, drawbar pull and horsepower, smokebox vacuum and various temperatures *e.g.* exhaust gases and superheat. The engines burned Blidworth coals but the report commented the fuel, derived from three consignments was very inconsistent in quality; the calorific value varied between 11,000BTU/lb and 12,500BTU. The main reason for this variation was held to have been caused by differences in the ash content in the batches, which ranged from 5 per cent to as much as 15 per cent.

Despite these trials not having been conducted on a stationary plant, nor being as comprehensive as those associated with the WD 2-10-0 and 2-8-0 classes, they nevertheless enable a comparison to be made with the Class 4MT 2-6-0, the nominal successor to the 'Big Goods'. Accordingly, some of the data obtained from tests (ii) and (iii) above has been extracted for that purpose. As they are not directly relevant to this comparison, no further reference will be made to the results obtained from the 'Swirlyflo' fitted engine other than to record the maximum evaporation rate with the standard front-end was raised from 12,000 to 13,000 pounds of steam per hour by the use of these tubes.

In the case of the test series with the modified draughting, the highest steam production rate was with the standard tubes - 19,000 pounds per hour compared with 17,320 pounds for the 'Swirlyflo' tubes. The smaller free area through the 146 of the latter, which replaced the 146 ordinary small tubes, resulted in a 17 per cent reduction in the free gas area through the barrel prompted by their non-circular cross-section and thicker walls. The

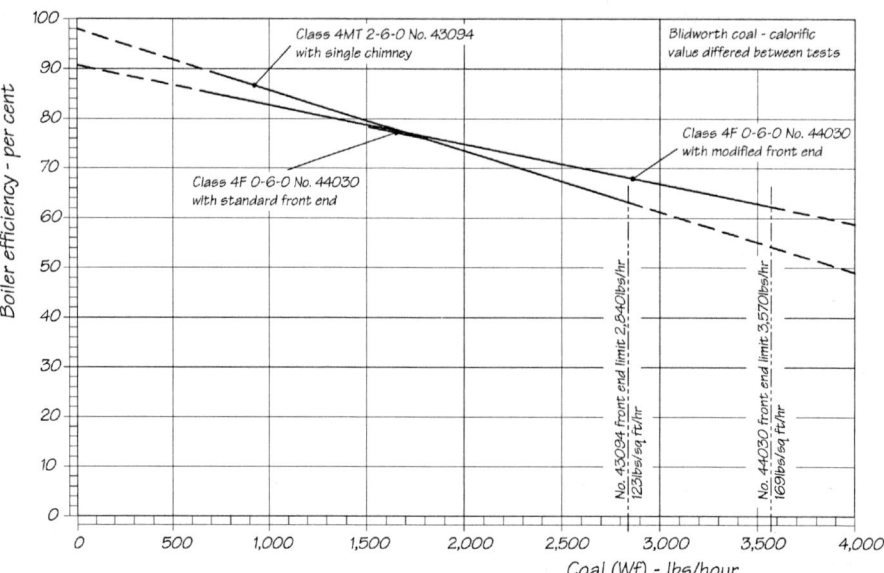

Approximate boiler efficiency curves:-
Class 4MT 2-6-0 $h = 98 - .01225 W_f$
Class 4 0-6-0 (modified front end) $h = 90.75 - .007985 W_f$

When tested, No. 43094 was specially provided with a back damper, which gave a more even distribution of air over the grate. Its adjustment was far less critical than the front damper and its effect was to reduce the loss of coal from the grate especially in the middle and low ranges of the firing rate.

Fig. 109 - Boiler efficiency comparison between 4MT 2-6-0 and 4F 0-6-0

temperature of the gas exiting the 'Swirlyflo' tubes was approximately 200°F lower than that leaving the standard tubes over a wide range of working.

Also appearing in figure 109 is the boiler efficiency curve for the Mogul Class 4MT N° 43094 tested at Swindon. This latter boiler - LMS

Table LIX - Maximum Evaporation Rates - G7s Boiler

Locomotive and configuration	Maximum test rate lbs/hr	Estimated maximum evaporation rates - lbs/hr		Increase on standard engine	
		Actual	Equivalent	Actual	Equivalent
N° 44030 - Standard tubes and smokebox	12,000	12,000	16,420	Standard	Standard
N° 44030 - Standard tubes and modified smokebox	19,000	20,000	27,520	66.7%	67.5%
N° 44203 - Swirlyflo tubes and standard smokebox	12,500	13,000	17,720	8.3%	7.9%
N° 44203 - Swirlyflo tubes and modified smokebox	17,320	18,000	24,720	50.0%	50.5%

Whilst this might infer a superior heat transfer, because it was accompanied by an increased superheat temperature, it more probably suggests the higher barrel resistance the 'Swirlyflo' tubes presented, encouraged an enhanced gas flow through the flues.

Figure 109 records the variation in boiler efficiency with change in firing rate for engine N° 44030, both when carrying its original draughting system and after it had received the modified front-end. As commonly occurred when the draughting system was improved on the Swindon model, the boiler efficiency curve was not significantly displaced, or if it was, it was within the scatter present in locomotive tests, so in effect the original curve was simply extended to a higher firing rate supported by the enhanced draughting capacity. The report commented on there being a fair degree of scatter present in the boiler efficiency values, which was considered primarily to have been caused by the variations in the calorific value of the coal rather than through inaccuracies in collecting the data. The curves represent the best mean line drawn through the appropriate series of values. It will be seen that a very slight gain, say one per cent, has been suggested for the modified draughting, but as this is within the range of experimental error inherent in boiler efficiency tests, the modified draughting curve has been assumed to be equally valid for the original arrangement. The report mentioned that both engines steamed very freely with their modified draughting before continuing:-

"There was no appreciable tendency to pull the fire from the front of the grate, and very little spark throwing was experienced, except at high steam rates outside the normal operating range of this class of engine."

4D - returned a higher efficiency at the lower firing rates, but at the higher rates it was less efficient than the G7s carried by the Class 4. The cause of the lower efficiency at higher steam outputs as both were burning nominally the same coal, was a larger coal loss rate (*i.e.* a higher value for *Wf*) prompted by a less even air flow pattern through the fire. This in turn being due in part to having a larger free area through the firebars and the 2-6-0's rougher riding characteristics. According to Bulletin N° 3, the Mogul exhibited a tendency for its fire to move forward, also a more even air distribution was obtained over the grate *after* an experimentally fitted back damper was provided and used, in preference to the extant front one. Its adjustment was much less critical in affecting the coal loss from the grate, particularly within the middle and bottom firing rates. The efficiency curve for the 4D boiler was based on the use of this damper, however, it appears this modification was probably not fitted to the remaining members of the class. Certainly the preserved example, N° 43106 carries a front damper only, never having been fitted with a rear one and if, as seems likely, this was the situation with the rest, then this efficiency curve represents an overestimate of the capability of the Mogul. Some notes concerning the make-up of boiler efficiency together with the impact the extent and proportions of the heating surfaces, including *S/A* ratios, had on its value, appear in Appendix 5.2 at the end of this chapter.

Table LIX summarises the maximum evaporation rates obtained from N° 44030 and 44203, while figure 110 compares the actual evaporation characteristics of the former engine when carrying the modified draughting with that of N° 43094. The grate limit of the G7s boiler carried by N° 44030 when fitted with the modified front end was

A Defence of the Midland/LMS Class 4 0-6-0

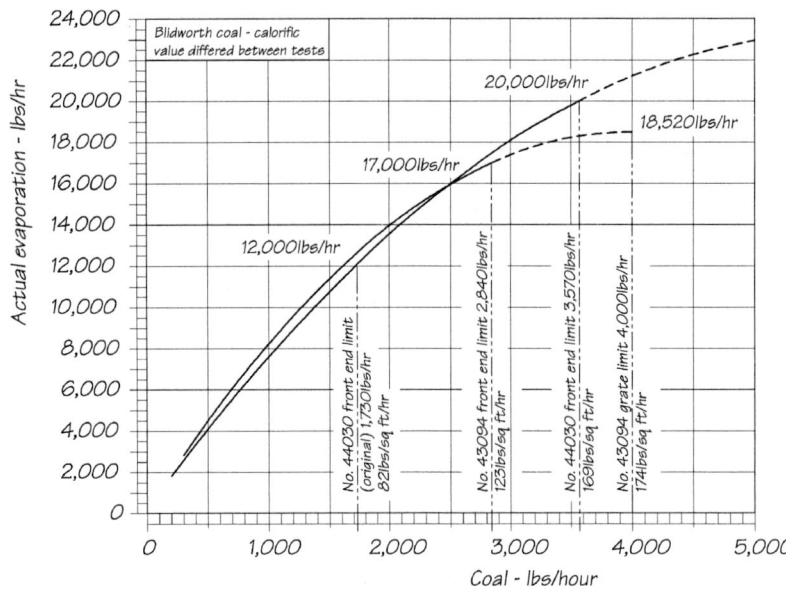

The grate limit represents the ultimate steam output possible from a boiler. At this limit no increase in steam production is possible with increase in firing rate even if the air necessary for combustion could be supplied. The front end draughting limit is the highest evaporation at which a balance can be continuously maintained between steam production and demand without excessive smoke formation through the presence of sufficient excess air etc.

Although both locomotives burned Blidworth coals the calorific value of the samples used in N° 44030 averaged 11,950BTU/lb while that fed to N° 43094 was higher at 12,560BTU/lb. Hence the evaporation curve of the latter engine is 5 per cent high for strict comparison. When the modified front end was used on N° 44030 (standard tube arrangement) the maximum sustained evaporation rose from 12,000lbs/hr to 19,000lbs/hr - an increase of 58.3 per cent. The report estimated that a maximum rate of 20,000lbs/hr was attainable without adversely affecting the boiler efficiency.

Fig. 110 - Actual evaporation comparison between 4MT 2-6-0 and 4F 0-6-0

approximately 5,700lbs/hr giving a corresponding firing rate of 270lbs/sq ft/hr and an associated absolute maximum evaporation of 23,300lbs/hr. The diagram records that the 4D boiler produced slightly more steam at all firing rates almost up to its front end maximum of 17,000lbs/hr. However, there was a difference in standardized calorific values adopted in these two series of tests - 12,560BTU/lb in the case of the Mogul but only 11,950BTU/lb for the 0-6-0. If this is allowed for, and taking the calorific value of the coal adopted for the 4D boiler as being more representative of the 12,600-12,800BTU/lb normally accredited to Blidworth coals, then the evaporation curve of the 0-6-0 should be increased in the ratio of the calorific values, *i.e.* 12,560 ÷ 11,950 or say 5 per cent, which lends further support to the estimated maximum evaporation of 20,000lbs/hr being attainable. If this correction is applied, it will result in the evaporation curve for the 4D appearing below that of the G7s. Nevertheless, because the 4D boiler was absorbing more of the heat in the coal, by virtue of its higher efficiency for about half of its range, we may see by comparing the two diagrams appearing in figure 111 that the superheat temperature of the 2-6-0 was considerably higher than that of the 'Big Goods' for the same steam rates. This pair of diagrams illustrate some further interesting aspects of boiler performance, for example the superheat temperature of N° 44030 was higher when the engine carried its modified blast-pipe, then in its original condition. The revised design could draw more air through the fire and the resulting enhanced gas flow raised the steam temperature through superior heat transfer although the temperature of the gases passing through the flues increased very little. Heat liberated to the superheater elements is proportional to the product of the gas flow rate, the heat transfer coefficient, which itself is a function of the flow rate, and the difference in temperature between the entering and exiting gases. If we assume more or less similar firebox exit temperatures, which will be approximately true, then primarily the increase in the first two terms sufficed to raise the superheat.

The second diagram appearing in figure 111 illustrates the impact that three distinct coals, with their associated differing exhaust gas quantities and composition, could effect on the superheat and tube exit temperatures; in this case on the 'Doodlebug'. Of these three coals, Blidworth produced the highest superheat for any steam rate. Comparing the two diagrams reveals that in the case of the 4D boiler, the temperature of the gases exiting the flues was higher than that leaving the small tubes, which is the opposite of the position with the parallel boiler. This was prompted by the higher resistance the small tubes presented to gas flow compared to the flues, following Mr Ivatt's adoption of 15/8ins diameter in place of the 1¾ins

Comparisons, Steaming and Performance

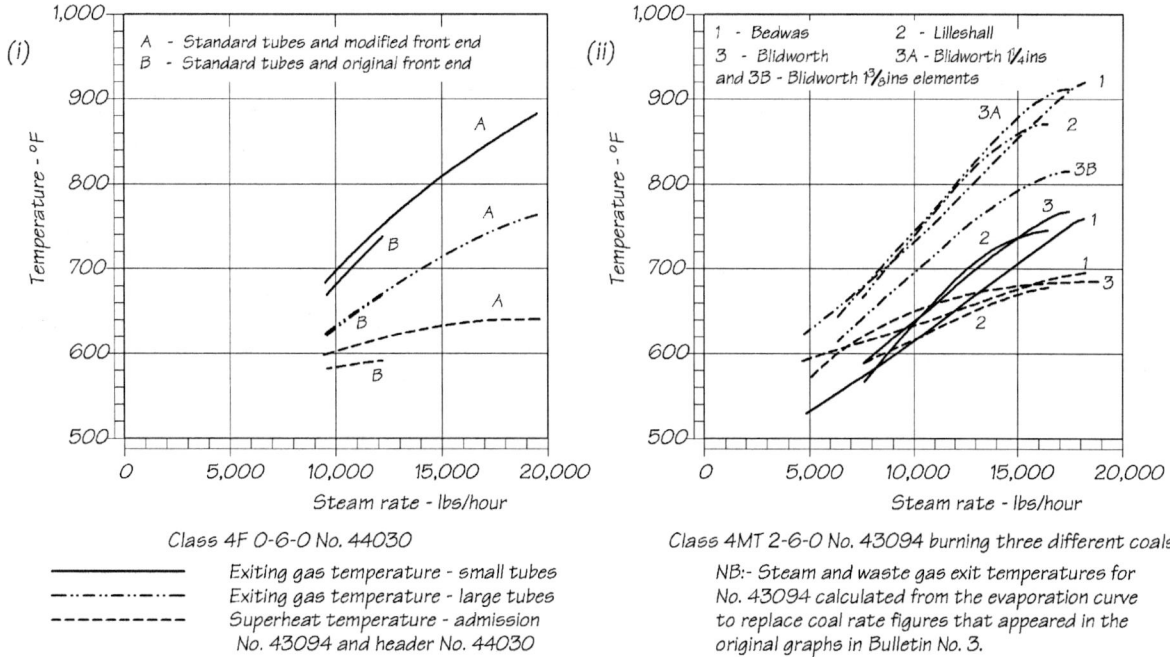

Fig. 111 - Comparison in boiler superheat and tube exit temperatures

tubes used in the G7s. While Nº 43094 was at Swindon, some runs were carried out with 13/8ins diameter elements substituted for the 1¼ins diameter ones standard in the class. The increased resistance the flues now presented to the gases resulted in a lower flue gas exit temperature, but no difference was discerned in superheat temperature.

Figure 113 demonstrates the impact the modified draughting system fitted to Nº 44030 had on the smokebox vacuum when burning the Blidworth coals provided. The original front end draughting curve could only sustain steaming rates between 9,000 and 13,000 pounds per hour with this fuel. At 12,000lbs/hr the draught was about 2½ inches of water, however, with the modified system it increased to 3.3 inches; some or all of which would have been available to compensate for the effects that poorer coals might have on steaming.

The three curves appearing in next comparison - figure 114 - explore the rise in back pressure with increase in steam rate. In the case of Nº 44030 there are two curves present, a short one shewing the position when it carried its original exhaust and a longer curve encompassing a wider range of steam rates once it had been given the modified front end. Comparing the two curves shews when the engine carried its Midland designed exhaust, it ran with a significantly lower back pressure. This

Fig. 112 - 'Big Goods' Nº 43937 late in its career with one of its nominal replacements Class 4MT 2-6-0 Nº 43156 alongside. Notice how more massive the Mogul appears compared to the 0-6-0, the inevitable outcome of its extra 20 per cent greater weight.

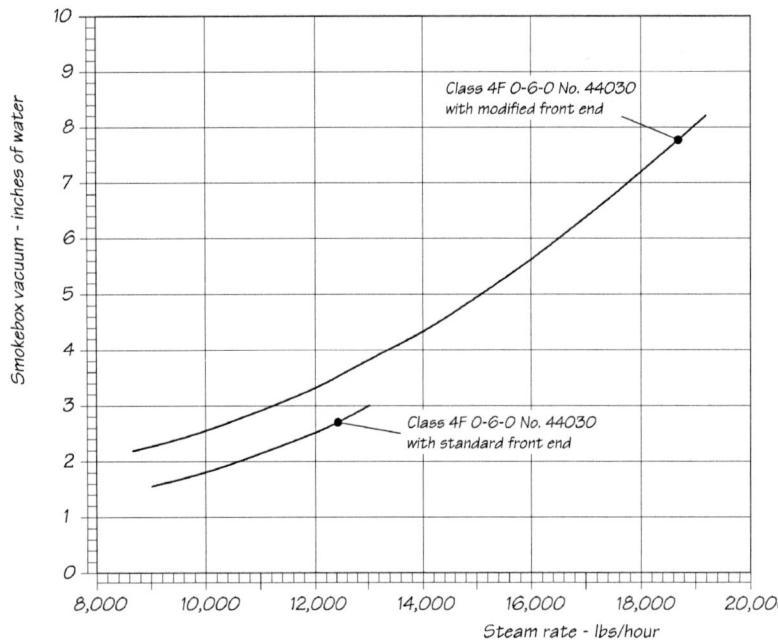

Fig. 113 - Variation in smokebox vacuum with steam rate - Class 4F 0-6-0

was about 1¼lbs/sq in, with a steam rate of 12,000lbs/hr but once the revised draughting design had been fitted it rose to 2.4lbs/sq in for the same steam flow. This increase in back pressure was simply because an integral part of the improved draughting necessitated its blast-pipe cap being reduced in diameter from 4⅞ins to 4¼ins. Contrasted with these two curves is the one for the 4MT which was provided with a cap 4⅜ins diameter. Although the positions where the pressure was measured differed in the two engines, so accordingly they will not be *directly* equivalent, nevertheless, at the highest steam rates we may see the 2-6-0 enjoyed a lower back pressure.

From figure 111, we found for the same steam flow rates the superheat temper-ature in N° 43094 was higher than that obtained in N° 44030. This, when combined with its higher working pressure, ensured the enthalpy of the steam at entry to its cylinders was larger than that pertaining in the 0-6-0. Although at the lower steam rates, the back pressure was slightly higher in the 'Doodlebug' this situation reversed once the steam rate exceeded 14,000 pounds per hour. Furthermore, for rates above that figure the back pressures were noticeably higher in the 'Big Goods' than in the other engine. Interestingly, when these two effects are combined - steam conditions at entry and exit from the cylinders - we find the 2-6-0 *always* enjoyed a larger heat drop at the same steam rates.

Appearing in figure 115 is the plot of drawbar horsepower against steam consumption at a constant speed of 33 miles per hour for N° 44030 when carrying its modified front end. The short curve records the performance of the engine when it was fitted with the standard draughting. Although the range of steam rates for the latter was limited, we may see that at the lower rates the modified design could provide a slightly higher drawbar power through a superior specific steam consumption. It is assumed this had been prompted by the gain from the higher superheat that the revised exhaust created more than offset the greater back

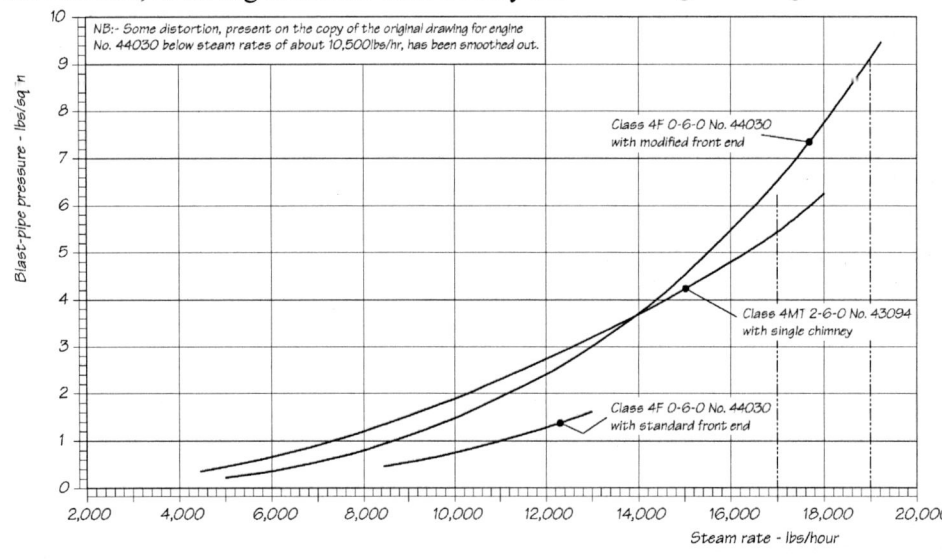

Fig. 114 - Variation in back pressure with steam rate - 4MT 2-6-0 and 4F 0-6-0

pressure its restricted blast-pipe cap diameter had given rise to. Conversely, at a steam rate of 13,000 pounds per hour, this advantage had nearly disappeared. This suggests, that if with good high quality coal the *original* front end could indeed have supported steam rates of c.16,000 pounds per hour, then the engine would have produced slightly more power. At these higher steam rates, the greater rise in back pressure of the modified exhaust was more than negating the positive

that the 2-6-0 used hotter steam supplied at higher pressure which it was able to expand, certainly at the higher rates, to a lower back pressure. These superior steam conditions at supply and exhaust gave the 2-6-0 a higher Rankine efficiency, so it *ought* to have required less steam irrespective of the length of its valve lap. This is demonstrated by the two additional curves appearing in figure 116, which represent the 30 miles per hour steam consumption curves obtained from the WD 2-8-0 and 2-10-0 classes. Although these engines also possessed large-laps valves combined with 225lbs/sq in working pressure, their superheat temperatures were more modest being reminiscent of those obtaining in the 0-6-0. Inspection reveals that for drawbar powers below about 625 the Standard Goods required less steam per drawbar horsepower than the eight-coupled engine and below 500 horsepower, less than the 2-10-0. The cylinders, valve gear and valve events were the same in the two WD classes, yet it was the heavier 2-10-0 which returned the lower specific steam consumption

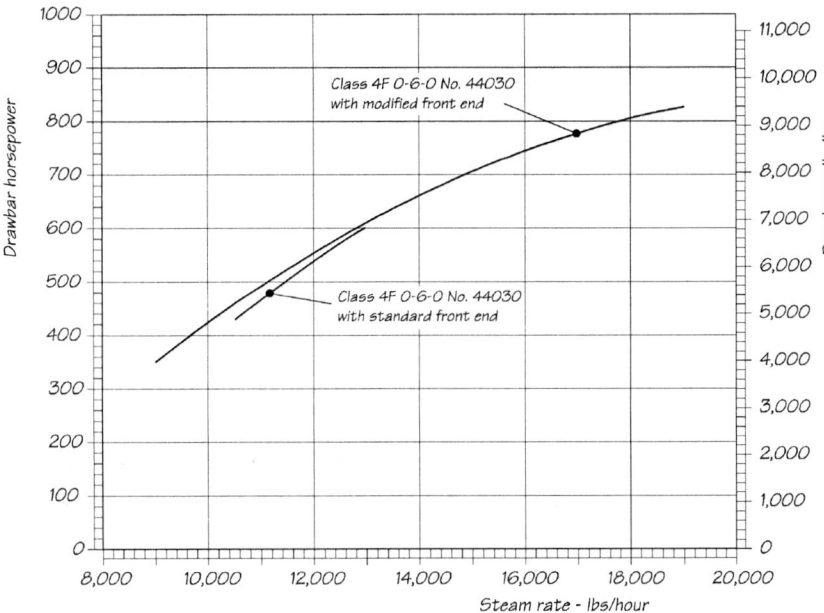

Fig. 115 - Variation in drawbar horsepower with steam rate at constant speed of 33 mph

benefit the enhanced steam temperature could effect. At the maximum steam rate of 19,000 pounds per hour obtained with the revised front end, the drawbar horsepower was 827 giving a specific steam consumption of nearly 23 pounds per drawbar horsepower per hour. This was considerably higher than the equivalent figure obtained from the Mogul.

For convenience, and to make the next comparison easier, the specific steam consumption curves for the 0-6-0 and the 2-6-0 are compared in figure 116. This has been achieved by replicating the 30mph curve appearing in figure 101 for the Mogul and in the case of the 0-6-0 deriving the necessary plotting points from the curve present in figure 115. There is considerable economy in steam demonstrated by the 2-6-0, since the older engine needed approximately 20 per cent more steam to produce each drawbar horsepower. However, before we assume this to be a vindication of the presence of large-lap valves we must remember

for outputs above about 300 drawbar horsepower. For equal steam rates there was little difference in the superheat between them but what advantage there was, was enjoyed by the 2-8-0. As more horsepower was demanded from the 0-6-0 and the 2-10-0, their specific steam consumption curves commenced to rise upwards suggesting that the increased power was starting to become uneconomical and could only be obtained from a sacrifice in efficiency. Had the 2-8-0 been able to steam at higher rates then its characteristic curve would have followed a similar trajectory to that of the 2-10-0. In this respect, the obviously superior performance returned by the Mogul particularly the flatness of its curve for drawbar horsepowers in excess of say 700/800, does make one harbour a doubt or two about their accuracy - *vide* the variation in the horsepower absorbed in driving the Mogul at 30 miles per hour appearing in table LX, along with some comments concerning the accuracy of some of the test data for this engine -

these observations are expanded further in Appendix 5.1.

Whatever the true situation, we may compensate for the benefits conferred by a superior Rankine efficiency possessed by the Mogul, if instead we consider the two Class 4 locomotives in terms of their isentropic efficiencies. If now the 2-6-0 was consuming less steam for each drawbar horsepower because of superior steam circuit, longer-lap valves, bigger ports, etc. then it will have returned a higher isentropic efficiency. This comparison is explored in tables LX and LXI using data derived from the diagrams presented so far, wherein it will be seen that over most of the range there was little variation in the isentropic efficiencies returned by the two locomotives. This is shewn graphically in figure 117, where the isentropic efficiencies returned at constant speed by the Mogul and the 'Big Goods' are compared on two basis - steam rate through each machine and indicated horsepower output. Comparing the latter curve for the 2-6-0 with the equivalent one appearing in figure 89 reveals that adopting the back pressure as the lower limit for the Rankine efficiency has had the effect of increasing the value of the isentropic efficiency because the theoretical heat drop has reduced in size. These curves are with the regulator full open so giving the highest steam chest pressure, and it will be seen that in both instances the isentropic efficiency exhibited a modest rise to assume a maximum value although its change over the operating range of each engine was quite small. As we have already seen the reason for the profile of these curves is because they represent the combined effect of two fundamental factors. Firstly there were the 'standing losses' which existed the whole time the regulator was open, these losses included steam leakage past the piston valve heads, and secondly the 'power based' losses that were a function of the steam demand of the engine, principally its speed and the cut-off it was running in.

When the engine was producing only a small amount of power, it would have been run in a short cut-off. In this situation the throttling effect at admission was greatest, the back pressure was low so compression was most likely incomplete, while the leakage, particularly that past the piston valves assumed its highest proportion of the total steam passing through the engine. Keeping the same speed, but increasing the power necessitated a longer cut-off. Although this reduced the expansion ratio of the steam, it also reduced the wire-drawing at admission, while the higher steam rate helped increase compression. Likewise, with more steam passing through the cylinders meant the radiation loss from the cylinders became proportionately smaller as did the fraction of steam that leaked past the valves. The nett outcome of these individual effects was a small gain in the isentropic efficiency. However, once the cut-off exceeded a certain length the gain in isentropic efficiency ceased and instead started to fall. Primarily the loss of expansion ratio caused by the later cut-off, coupled possibly in due course with too much compression, ensured the steam was being used less efficiently than before. Steam leaving the cylinder at release was now doing so at a significantly higher pressure than the back pressure.

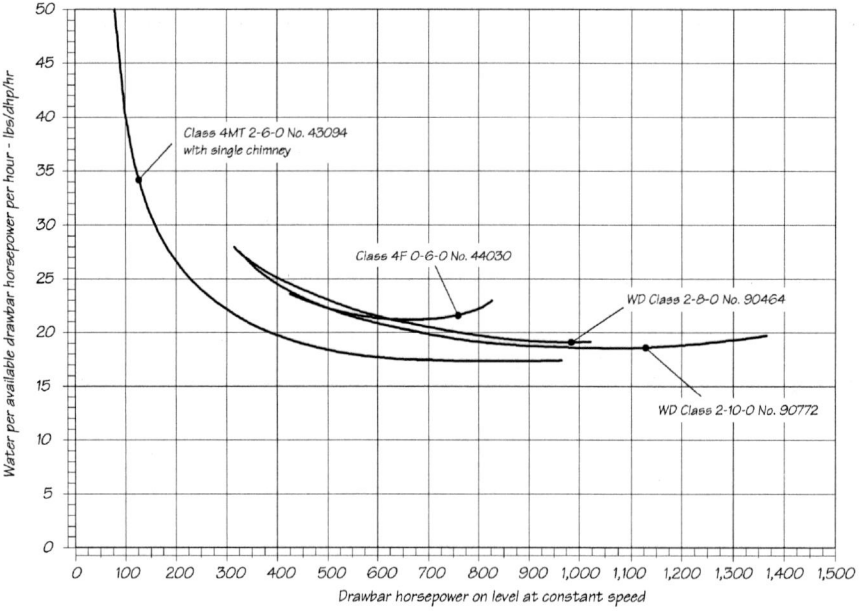

Fig. 116 - Classes 4 0-6-0 and 4MT 2-6-0 also WD Classes 2-8-0 and 2-10-0

Table LX - Performance Analysis of Class 4MT 2-6-0 N° 43094

C1	C2	C3	C4	C5	C6	C7	C8	C9	C10	C11	C12	C13	C14	C15	C16
Steam rate - lbs/hr	Steam temperature - °F	Enthalpy of superheated steam - BTU/lb	Exhaust pressure - lbs/sq in	Enthalpy of exhaust steam - BTU/lb	Heat drop - BTU/lb	Specific steam consumption - lbs/ihp/hr	Drawbar horsepower	Indicated horsepower	Horsepower to drive engine	Actual steam consumption - lbs/ihp	Rankine efficiency - per cent	Isentropic efficiency - per cent	Cylinder efficiency - per cent	Drawbar steam consumption - lbs/dhp/hr	DHP per ton of engine weight
6,000	593.4	1315.6	0.661	1082.7	232.9	10.93	253	346	93	17.34	18.12	63.03	11.42	23.72	4.28
8,000	626.5	1333.1	1.202	1096.1	237.0	10.74	407	499	92	16.03	18.19	67.00	12.19	19.66	6.89
10,000	649.8	1345.4	1.892	1106.6	238.8	10.66	561	649	88	15.41	18.15	69.18	12.56	17.83	9.48
12,000	665.6	1353.7	2.731	1115.1	238.6	10.67	682	780	98	15.38	18.03	69.38	12.51	17.6	11.54
14,000	676.4	1359.3	3.688	1122.3	237.0	10.74	794	902	108	15.52	17.83	69.2	12.34	17.63	13.43
16,000	682.5	1362.5	4.797	1128.5	234.0	10.88	910	1016	106	15.75	17.56	69.08	12.13	17.58	15.4
17,000	684.1	1363.3	5.436	1131.3	232.0	10.97	966	1063	97	15.99	17.4	68.61	11.94	17.6	16.35

C1 - Steam rate selected from graph
C2 - For each steam rate, the corresponding steam temperature determined from figure 111. Values quoted to one decimal position for accuracy.
C3 - Enthalpy (or heat content) of the steam leaving the superheater, corresponding to temperature in C2 and a steam pressure of 225lbs/sq in (gauge). In practice there would be a small pressure drop of c. 5lbs/sq in as steam negotiated the superheater. Since its value is unknown, it has been ignored - doing so will slightly reduce isentropic efficiency.
C4 - For each steam rate, the corresponding back pressure determined from figure 114. Values quoted to three decimal positions for accuracy.
C5 - Enthalpy (or heat content) of the exhaust leaving, corresponding to pressure in C4 and assuming perfect expansion (*i.e.* no change in entropy) from inlet condition C3.
C6 - The difference in enthalpy across the cylinders *i.e.* (C3 - C5).
C7 - The quotient obtained from (2545 ÷ C6).
C8 - Drawbar horsepower output obtained from figure 101 corresponding to selected steam rate C1.
C9 - Indicated horsepower output obtained from figure 89 corresponding to selected steam rate C1 at 30mph.
C10 - Difference between indicated horsepower and drawbar horsepower thus revealing power consumed in driving engine *i.e.* (C9 - C8). Value should sensibly be the same suggesting errors in the original data and the original diagrams, and/or their redrafting and interpretation for these purposes - *vide* Appendix 5.1.
C11 - The quotient obtained from (C1 ÷ C9).
C12 - Heat drop of the steam theoretically available for conversion into work, divided by the heat absorbed to generate that quantity of steam *i.e.* 100 × [(C6) ÷ (C3 - 30)] where 30BTU/lb represent heat in boiler feed water at assumed tender tank temperature of 62°F.
C13 - The product of 100 and theoretical indicated specific steam consumption divided by the actual indicated specific steam consumption *i.e.* (100 × C7) ÷ C11.
C14 - The product obtained from (C12 × C13)
C15 - The quotient obtained from (C1 ÷ C8).
C16 - The quotient obtained from (C8 ÷ 59.1), where 59.1 is the weight, in tons, of a 4MT 2-6-0 (engine only) in working order.

Table LXI - Performance Analysis of Class 4 0-6-0 N° 44030 with Standard Tubes and Modified Draughting

C1	C2	C3	C4	C5	C6	C7	C8	C9	C10	C11	C12	C13	C14	C15	C16
Steam rate - lbs/hr	Steam temperature - °F	Enthalpy of superheated steam - BTU/lb	Exhaust pressure - lbs/sq in	Enthalpy of exhaust steam - BTU/lb	Heat drop - BTU/lb	Specific steam consumption - lbs/ihp/hr	Drawbar horsepower	Horsepower to drive engine	Indicated horsepower	Actual steam consumption - lbs/ihp	Rankine efficiency - per cent	Isentropic efficiency - per cent	Cylinder efficiency - per cent	Drawbar steam consumption - lbs/dhp/hr	DHP per ton of engine weight
10,000	602.6	1324.2	1.481	1108.6	215.6	11.8	424	97	521	19.19	16.66	61.49	10.24	23.58	8.7
11,000	609.8	1327.9	1.926	1112.9	215.0	11.84	492	97	589	18.68	16.57	63.38	10.50	22.36	10.09
12,000	616.7	1331.5	2.105	1115.9	215.6	11.8	554	97	651	18.43	16.57	64.03	10.61	21.66	11.36
13,000	623.2	1334.8	2.999	1121.7	213.1	11.94	611	97	708	18.36	16.33	65.03	10.62	21.28	12.53
14,000	628.2	1337.4	3.706	1126.1	211.3	12.04	661	97	758	18.47	16.16	65.19	10.53	21.18	13.56
15,000	632.7	1339.7	4.524	1130.7	209.0	12.18	706	97	803	18.68	15.96	65.20	10.41	21.25	14.48
16,000	636.2	1341.6	5.475	1135.3	206.3	12.34	745	97	842	19.00	15.73	64.95	10.22	21.48	15.28
17,000	638.7	1342.8	6.524	1139.8	203.0	12.54	778	97	875	19.43	15.46	64.54	9.98	21.85	15.96
18,000	639.8	1343.4	7.755	1144.4	199.0	12.79	806	97	903	19.93	15.15	64.17	9.72	22.33	16.53
19,000	640.2	1343.6	9.135	1148.9	194.7	13.07	827	97	924	20.56	14.82	63.57	9.42	22.97	16.96

C1 - Steam rate selected from graph
C2 - For each steam rate, the corresponding steam temperature determined from figure 111. Values quoted to one decimal position for accuracy.
C3 - Enthalpy (or heat content) of the steam leaving the superheater, corresponding to temperature in C2 and a steam pressure of 175lbs/sq in (gauge). In practice there would be a small pressure drop of c. 5lbs/sq in as steam negotiated the superheater. Since its value is unknown, it has been ignored - doing so will slightly reduce isentropic efficiency.
C4 - For each steam rate, the corresponding back pressure determined from figure 114. Values quoted to three decimal positions for accuracy.
C5 - Enthalpy (or heat content) of the exhaust leaving, corresponding to pressure in C4 and assuming perfect expansion (*i.e.* no change in entropy) from inlet condition C3.
C6 - The difference in enthalpy across the cylinders *i.e.* (C3 - C5).
C7 - The quotient obtained from (2545 ÷ C6).
C8 - Drawbar horsepower output obtained from C10 of table LX.
C9 - Mean value obtained from C10 of table LX. Underestimates of horsepower to drive engine will reduce isentropic efficiency, conversely overestimates will increase it.
C10 - Total of drawbar horsepower and horsepower consumed in driving engine *i.e.* (C8 + C9).
C11 - The quotient obtained from (C1 ÷ C10).
C12 - Heat drop of the steam theoretically available for conversion into work, divided by the heat absorbed to generate that quantity of steam *i.e.* 100 × [(C6) ÷ (C3 - 30)] where 30BTU/lb represent heat in boiler feed water at assumed tender tank temperature of 62°F.
C13 - The product of 100 and theoretical indicated specific steam consumption divided by the actual indicated specific steam consumption *i.e.* (100 × C7) ÷ C11.
C14 - The product obtained from (C12 × C13)
C15 - The quotient obtained from (C1 ÷ C8)
C16 - The quotient obtained from (C8 ÷ 48.75), where 48.75 is the weight, in tons, of a 4F 0-6-0 (engine only) in working order.

The cut-off at which the maximum isentropic efficiency appeared varied with the speed of the locomotive. At the lowest speeds, to ensure sufficient steam was passing through the machine to offset the leakage losses meant it appeared at a comparatively late cut-off, which in turn meant it peaked at a lower maximum value. Conversely, the faster the engine was going the shorter was the cut-

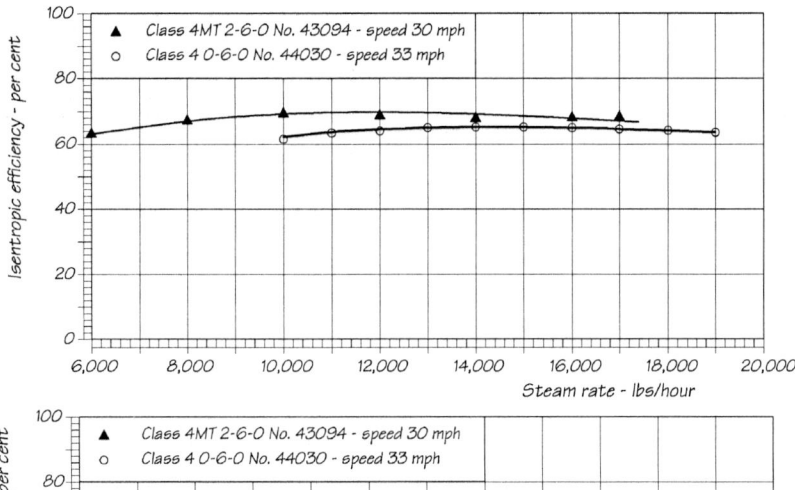

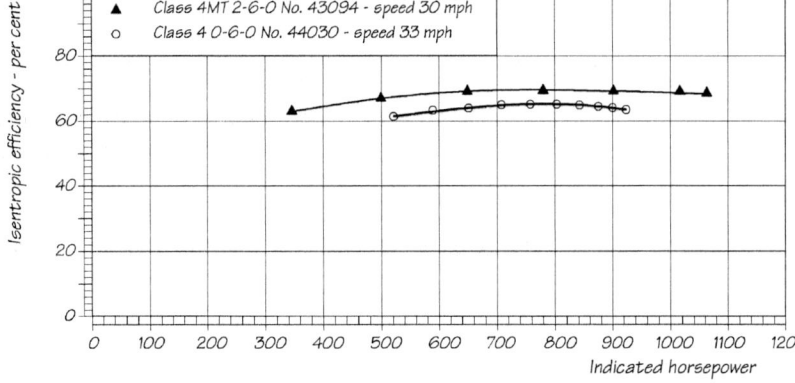

Fig. 117 - Variation in isentropic efficiency - LMS Class 4 0-6-0 & 4MT 2-6-0

off at which the maximum isentropic efficiency appeared and the higher the value it attained. It is for these reasons primarily that the maximum economy did not appear at the shortest cut-off the engine could be run in and typically in passenger service, it appeared somewhere in the range 20 to 25 per cent cut-off.

Of course there is another way of driving a steam engine and this involves running with a partially open regulator and a longer cut-off. This is commonly, but erroneously, considered always to have been a less efficient way of driving a locomotive than with a fully opened regulator at all times and the power output adjusted on the gear. Under certain circumstances, principally when low power outputs are required, it can actually be a more efficient way than with a full-open regulator

coupled with too short a cut-off. This is explored in more detail by the author in another volume[74], but we may for now gain sufficient insight if we remember that the leakage across the heads of the piston valves was determined by the difference between the steam chest pressure and the exhaust pressure. When the regulator was shut in, then this pressure differential was reduced and with it the leakage loss. Of course a partially open regulator incurred a throttling loss, but this might be no larger than the loss which occurred when full steam chest pressure steam was wire-drawn as it tried to enter the cylinder through the very small port opening associated with a gear that was well linked up. Running with a later cut-off reduced the expansion ratio but it also reduced the wire-drawing. With both short-lap and large-lap, engines the nett result of these opposing effects was a gain in steam economy when running with a partially open regulator at low power outputs *i.e.* a gain in isentropic efficiency.

The curves for the 'Doodlebug' were derived from data collected at 30 miles per hour, while those for the 0-6-0 pertain to when it was running at 33 mph. Consequently, the short-lap engine is being compared under a slight disadvantage, nevertheless the difference in isentropic efficiencies *i.e.* the advantage possessed by the 4MT was quite modest. This advantage may well have been even smaller when it is remembered the horsepower values appearing in column 9 of table LXI are an averaged figure derived from the variable values taken from the 2-6-0. In this instance, due to the method of calculation from the drawbar horsepower, any underestimate of the horsepower absorbed in driving the 0-6-0 will similarly underestimate its isentropic efficiency.

Whilst at higher speeds, this slight advantage in

---

74 *An Introduction to Large-Lap Valves and their Use on the LMS* Crimson Lake Aberystwyth 2008.

favour of the Mogul will have become greater, this was not the case with slower speed traffic. Since the speeds employed in Toton-Brent coal trains averaged around 17 miles per hour, the difference in the isentropic efficiency of the 2-6-0 over that of the 0-6-0 would have been much reduced. In other words the short-lap valve gear and the smaller ports and port openings of the 0-6-0 were having very little impact on the efficiency with which the machine could convert heat into work. Equally importantly, it was effecting this conversion with an efficiency that was only a little lower than that of the 2-6-0. Thus, even at 33 miles per hour, largely as Professor Tuplin's formula predicted, the valve lap and cylinder design of the 0-6-0 was adequate, so there was little to be gained from the presence of large-lap valves in locomotives running at that speed or even a little higher.

A finding supported by the locomotive practice followed by the Great Western during the 1920s and 1930s, which elected to introduce modernized replacements for worn-out Victorian engines, with the prototypes for these new classes dating back in some instances to the Armstrong era. The new machines might have carried a higher working pressure combined in some instances with superheaters, but they were all short lap, some even retained flat valves (15/16ins lap) located between the cylinders. Yet when that same practice was adopted on the LMS, with for example the Class 2 0-4-4T - lap increased from 1inch to 1 1/8ins, but the use of second-hand boilers precluded raising the working pressure or superheating - the result attracted ridicule from certain professional engineers, who really *ought* to have known better. Unfortunately their erroneous views have been picked up and subsequently frequently repeated by legions of steam locomotive enthusiasts.

Earlier using a rather crude method we estimated the possible performance that a Class 4MT 2-6-0 might have produced on a Toton-Brent coal train had the class existed in 1928. We can now repeat the exercise with somewhat greater precision, albeit for a speed of 33 miles per hour, and predict how a Standard Class 4 0-6-0 would have performed had it been provided with a boiler pressed to 225lbs/sq in and given revised tube ratios arranged to raise the superheat. In other words had the superior steam conditions present in the Mogul also been enjoyed by the 'Big Goods' thereby eliminating the in-built thermodynamic advantage possessed by the 2-6-0 by virtue of its superior steam quality. The results of this exercise appear in table LXII.

The starting point of the analysis is the assumption the available *theoretical* heat drops and associated specific steam consumption values of the hypothetical 0-6-0 would have been the same as those for the 2-6-0 at the same steam flow rates. This of course necessitates that the back pressure experienced by the Class 4 would have been the same as that in the Mogul. In practice the largest factor determining the size of the back pressure was the blast-pipe cap diameter, not as is commonly assumed port opening to exhaust or even the cross-sectional area of the passages. Although the pressure drop through the latter was important, the steam flow rate through them in a two-cylinder simple was only one-quarter the rate through the blast-pipe. The pressure drop experienced by a fluid passing through a pipe is determined by the flow rate raised to a power, which under the conditions present in a steam locomotive, assumes a value typically of about 1.9. Whence and assuming the cross sectional area through a passage was equal to the area through the blast pipe:-

$$\text{Pressure drop} = \frac{(\text{Steam flow rate through passages})^{1.9}}{(\text{Steam flow rate through blast pipe})^{1.9}} \quad (19)$$

$$= \frac{(0.25)^{1.9}}{(1)^{1.9}} = 0.072$$

Thus, the pressure drop through the passages would have been only one-fourteenth the size of that of the blast-pipe. In practice, their cross sectional area was larger, but when linked up the port may not have opened fully which induced a throttling action on the steam passing through, nevertheless as figure 118 confirms the pressure drop was roughly in line with this estimate.

Conversely when the fluid flow rate is kept constant, the pressure drop is determined by the pipe diameter raised to the power of approximately 4.75. Consequently even the small reduction in the blast-pipe cap diameter from 47/8ins to 41/8ins would have a significant impact on the back pressure:-

$$\text{Pressure drop} = \frac{(\text{New pipe diameter})^{4.75}}{(\text{Original pipe diameter})^{4.75}} \quad (20)$$

$$= \frac{(41/8)^{4.75}}{(47/8)^{4.75}} = 2.2$$

Thus the reduction in diameter theoretically will

have increased the back pressure by a factor of 2.2. In practice, due to other effects such as the different steam conditions the rise may not be so high, nevertheless figure 114 reveals at a steam rate of say 11,000 pounds per hour the back pressure nearly doubled. Hence the dominating influence that blast-pipe cap diameter had in determining the back pressure.

Figure 118 records the contribution that each portion of the exhaust circuit made towards creating the total back pressure acting on the pistons. Although these curves were derived from a large-lap engine, believed to have been 'Jubilee' N° 45722, they will also apply in general format at least, to a short-lap engines such as the 'Big Goods'. Whilst the magnitude of the pressure drops in the passages, the blast-pipe branch pipes and that through the blast-pipe cap for a given steam rate would have differed, the overwhelming cause of the back pressure in a short-lap engine would still have been the diameter of the last named resistance. Indeed, the presence of short-lap valves usually had little to no effect on the back pressure, the reason for this being their main impact was through restricting the quantity of steam that could *enter* the cylinder. Indeed it is quite conceivable the pressure drops in the exhaust system up to the blast-pipe cap in many short-lap engines were lower than those in a large-lap engine if only because the cross-sectional areas of the latter, in Britain at least, were not increased in size commensurate with the enhanced steam flow that their larger port openings *to steam* permitted.

Of course in adopting the same back pressures in our hypothetical 0-6-0 as those present in the 2-6-0 we are assuming that the rebuild could be arranged to steam adequately with a blast-pipe cap 4 3/8ins diameter. Nevertheless this is not an unreasonable assumption given the increase in performance Terry Essery experienced with N° 43924 when a petticoat pipe was simply added to the base of the chimney while retaining the standard 4 7/8ins diameter cap.

In our theoretical rebuilding we may allow for the Class 4 engine's poorer steam circuit in the analysis by applying the isentropic efficiencies associated with the 0-6-0 at a particular steam flow rate to the Rankine specific steam consumption

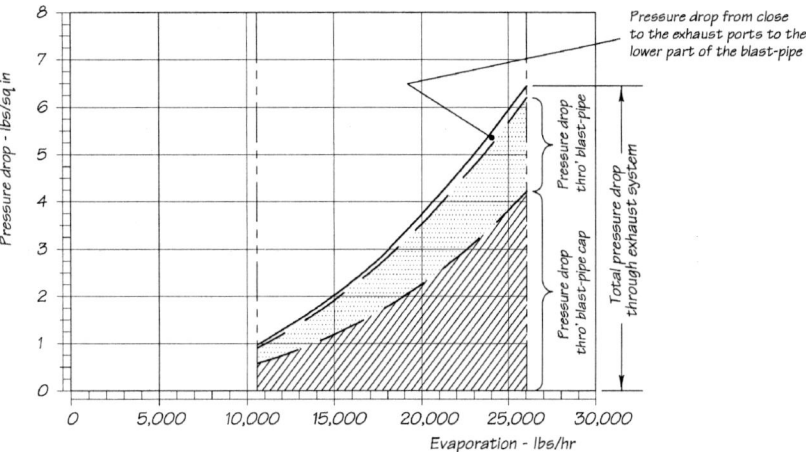

Fig. 118 - Pressure drop through the exhaust system for various steam flow rates shewing the contribution made by the various portions. Curves obtained from an unidentified engine tested at Rugby but possibly 5XP class 4-6-0 No. 45722.

figures obtained from the 2-6-0 for the corresponding steam rates. This will not be strictly correct since the value of the isentropic efficiency, which is a measure of the losses in the system, is also affected slightly by the steam conditions. Thus hotter steam at a higher pressure possesses slightly different flow characteristics from somewhat cooler steam at lower pressure. However, for our modest increase in steam conditions from 175lbs/sq in to 225lbs/sq in accompanied by a rise in temperature of about 50°F the properties, such as specific volume are not that dissimilar, suggesting we might assume similar flow characteristics. There would also be corresponding changes within the cylinder *e.g.* leakage rate, lower heat transfer and a slight adjustment to the cut-offs to obtain the same steam flow rates. Nevertheless, the most important factor determining the magnitude of the isentropic efficiency for any steam rate was the relative sizes of the steam circuit from the boiler to the steam chest, steam chest volume, port openings to steam and exhaust and its size downstream of the cylinders. So with this proviso but armed with the knowledge that this approach was one of the techniques André Chapelon used when he schemed out his rebuilds and accurately predicted their performance while they were still on the drawing board, we may proceed.

Inspection of table LXII reveals that at a steam rate

of 17,000 pounds per hour our hypothetical 0-6-0 rebuild would have produced around one-eighth more drawbar horsepower per ton of engine weight than the 2-6-0. This it will be appreciated is despite the retention of short-lap valves. Comparing the performance figures for the rebuilt and original 0-6-0s reveals the same drawbar horsepower could have been produced from roughly 10 per cent less steam. While reference to figure 116 suggests a 'Big Goods' rebuilt along these lines would have returned a specific drawbar consumption roughly half-way between a 'Doodlebug' and the WD 2-10-0. These estimates again support the viewpoint expressed earlier by Terry Essery, namely that the Class 4 0-6-0 was a basically sound design and given a few simple modifications could have been substantially developed and turned into one of the all time greats.

Table LXII – Predicted Performance of a Hypothetical Rebuilding of a Standard Class 4 Goods

C1	C2	C3	C4	C5	C6	C7
Steam rate - lbs/hr	Rankine specific steam consumption - lbs/ihp/hr	Isentropic efficiency - per cent	Indicated horsepower	Drawbar horsepower	Estimated specific steam consumptions - lbs/dhp/hr	dhp/ton of engine weight
10,000	10.66	61.49	577	480	20.8	9.85
12,000	10.67	64.03	720	623	19.26	12.78
14,000	10.74	65.19	850	753	18.59	15.45
16,000	10.88	64.95	955	858	18.64	17.60
17,000	10.97	64.54	1000	903	18.83	18.52

C2 - Derived from the Class 4MT 2-6-0 steam conditions *i.e.* boiler pressure, superheat and exhaust pressure
C3 - Isentropic efficiency derived from 'Big Goods' performance corresponding to C1
C4 - Indicated horsepower obtained from [(steam rate ÷ C2) × (C3 ÷ 100)]
C5 - Drawbar horsepower obtained from C4 less 97, where 97 represents the assumed horsepower absorbed in driving the engine
C6 - The quotient obtained from (C1 ÷ C5)
C7 - The quotient obtained from (C8 ÷ 48.75), where 48.75 is the weight, in tons, of a 4F 0-6-0 (engine only) in working order.

Their Performance Glimpsed from Shed and Footplate

In too many cases writers have concentrated on the shortcomings of the Class 4, without mentioning they were also present in many other classes, some far more modern, or giving credit for the positive benefits the 'Big Goods' possessed. We should not overlook the class was multiplied very soon after the formation of the LMS because at the time it was considered the best available, nor should we dismiss the impact reluctant and/or unfamiliar crews could wrought on the reputation of a class. Unfortunately at that time of their introduction the previous *status quo* of the old companies had been shattered and locomotive crews did tend to be amongst the *most* conservative of men. Several writers remarked how unpopular they were on the Western and Central Divisions, in this respect it is interesting that the Northern Division was far more welcoming. Given Crewe's attitude at the time in respect of how the Grouping had turned out, probably no Derby-designed product would have pleased black-engine men, while in *My Life with Locomotives*[75] Eric Mason (*aka* 'Rivington') has recorded a similar reluctance amongst former Lancashire and Yorkshire men:-

"... no amount of persuasion would induce the men to get interested in the L.M.S. standard class 4 0-6-0 engines when they began to filter through soon after 1923."

"We must now see what happened on the introduction of standard engines. It was not to be expected that the advent of Midland Railway standard engines would be hailed with shouts of delight and approval. Early in 1923 small-sized Midland engines of the 2-4-0 and 0-6-0 types by Kirtley and Johnson worked into Manchester from the Normanton direction. The outside frame coupling rods of the former engineer's designs came in for a lot of light-hearted comment from local railwaymen, and one wag asked a Midland driver if it was true that when the engine got short of steam he and his mate leaned over the sides of the cab and helped to push the rods round with their hands! Needless to say this feeble witticism was not too obviously appreciated by the party at whom it was directed. It was not until much later that the class 4 freight engines began to be turned out in such numbers that enabled some to be allocated to former L. & Y. sheds.

---

75 Rivington *My Life With Locomotives* Ian Allan London 1962 pp83, 128-129 & 130.

At the shed for which I was responsible, two engines of this class, Nos. 4474 and 4541, were the first of the so-called engines to come into the fold. They had a very mixed reception; fitters examined the detail fittings and made note of the strap and cotter big ends, which had gone out on all but shunting engines years ago. Boilermakers said very little except that it would probably take over a week to straighten the front buffer beam should the engine by mischance happen to run into something with rather more vigour than discretion. Their estimate proved to be somewhat conservative, and in later years it was a job seldom undertaken at a shed. Everyone was confused by the resemblance between the tender handbrake handle and the water pickup handle, and this I may say persisted: at least thirty years later it was still possible to find instances of a fireman screwing down the water pickup handle thinking it was the handbrake, and then, on finding out his mistake, had omitted to lift it up again after properly securing the engine in the shed, with the result that the water pickup mouthpiece fouled the first crossing when the engine was moved again. To add to the confusion some of the class had right hand drive and some had left hand drive, with corresponding alterations to the tender gear.

Finally the enginemen came to the inquest and wanted to know what the engines failed with. They were not long in finding this out, as one of the most vulnerable points in the earlier engines was the Fowler-Anderson bypass valve. Simply described, this fitting was an arrangement for preventing excessive back pressure in the cylinders when the engine was running with steam shut off. It consisted of a pipe connecting the front and back ends of the cylinders, in the middle of which was an automatic valve which closed the bypass when steam was on and the engine working, the closing being effected by steam at boiler pressure being admitted to the underside of the valve. These valves used to break with distressing frequency, and even when the stipulated examination period was shortened they were still regarded with suspicion. When a valve did break the engine was a complete failure, as both ends of the cylinder were receiving boiler steam which escaped through the open ports and up the chimney with a resounding roar."

"These 'Standard Fours', as they were called, were intended to do quite a lot of passenger work as well as roadside jobs, and old L.&Y. men, used to Joy's valve gear and not at first appreciating the different handling required, would try and run them with the running gear notched up, with the result that we had big end trouble. In any case this would probably have caught us up before long, as the bearing surfaces were quite inadequate for the hammering the engines got on heavy specials.

Another weak point was the oil feed to the coupled axles leaking and causing hot boxes: the arrangement of oil pipe adapters would work loose through the bearing-down of the engine on the springs, which caused them - the adaptors - to strike the main frame at the top of the hornplate gap."

Implicit in this criticism is that the strap and cotter big end was old-fashioned; certainly the design was old, but it was used by the majority of the pre-grouping companies; it was also very reliable when set up correctly. All of the then LMS standard engines fitted with inside cylinders were provided with this type of big end including incidentally those produced later[76] by William Stanier, so in this respect it was the Lancashire & Yorkshire that was out of step, since only comparatively few of the old companies had adopted the bolted or marine type. One major disadvantage of the marine type was that it tended to be less rigid while the bolts were sometimes overtightened. Big ends were stripped at regular intervals for examination and unless reassembled with care could promote a failure that the examination was intended to prevent. This applied to both designs although there would have been a steep learning curve for L&Y fitters not least through some of the remedial measures they found suitable for the strap and cotter big ends of shunting engines could not be applied to main line engines. The reputed deficiency in big end area is interesting especially when it is considered it was larger on the Class 4 than George Hughes had provided on his four-cylinder 4-6-0s, which at the time were the company's principal express engines. Perhaps the problem experienced by L&Y fitters was same as Mr Burgess recalled, a difficulty in coping with the generously curved surfaces that formed the bearing of a Midland solid forged crankaxle.

The brake and water scoop columns were located according to a strict convention on Fowler-type tenders. The hand brake was positioned on the fireman's side, *i.e.* on the left-hand side of the tender on a right-hand drive engine and visa versa. In addition, the scoop was provided with a cast iron label located alongside its column. Furthermore, when tenders were swapped between engines, the water scoop and brake linkages were altered as necessary to maintain the convention. However the withdrawal of some Standard Class 7

---

76 The oil box fitted to the inside big end strap on the earliest 'Jubilees' Nº 5552-5654 proved to have insufficient capacity; Midland Division allocated engines being particularly prone to trouble. Under Job Nº 5304 their connecting rods were, for a time at least, fitted with a Midland big end strap to drawing 06-6103.

Mr R Townsin *The Jubilee 4-6-0's* RCTS 2006 p172.

0-8-0s in 1949-50 released Fowler tenders that were transferred to 165 4Fs running with older style former Midland tenders. The Job instruction highlighted the 0-6-0s were right-hand drive whereas the 0-8-0s were left-hand drive consequently the hand brake and water scoop columns were therefore mismatched. When the tenders were reallocated, instead of swapping over the operating linkages as had previously been done to avoid confusion, it was decided instead that the columns were to be clearly labelled with their function in white letters. This though was around 20-25 years after the first Standard Class 4s had been places in Eric Mason's charge[77].

In *Breath of Steam* William Thorley gave a completely opposite opinion concerning the by-pass valves stating they were no problem if conscientiously inspected and maintained. This, like the failure of the oil feed to the axleboxes appears to have been prompted, let us say, through unfamiliarity with the class. The lubrication failure being a side effect resulting from spring failure. Laminated spring performance was poor throughout the life of the LMS with spring changing a continuous chore at running sheds. E S Cox estimated in 1946 that the life of the average bearing spring was less than eighteen months. It was probably not helped by the excessive axlebox/horn clearances the company tolerated which tended to loosen the spring buckle.

Due to the wholesale replacement policy pursued earlier by the LMS, by the 1950s the majority of the ex-LMS Standard locomotives a driver would have encountered were considered to be large-lap. This was not the case with the other regions making up British Railways where a higher proportion of short-lap engines remained in service, some still hauling important traffic, while in the case of the Great Western many of them were modern locomotives. With large-lap engines drivers were encouraged to adopt full regulator as far as possible making any necessary adjustments in power by altering the cut-off. In contrast the traditional method of driving short-lap engines, which presumably would have been more familiar to drivers on the other regions, even the younger ones, was to make greater use of the regulator for effecting power adjustments. Whilst the former method is the theoretically correct method, since it should result in the maximum economy, unfortunately for a variety of reasons, as we have seen *all* real steam locomotives, to a greater or lesser extent, departed from this thermodynamic theoretical ideal. Thus, driving engines in the traditional manner including modern large-lap ones (depending principally on the power output required) *did not* automatically result in an increased coal or water consumption. In the case of the short-lap engines it was better to put the gear in the position the engine liked best as Henry Ivatt once expressed it and then to adjust the regulator opening - as a former Class 4 driver recollected:-

"When I began to work as a driver from Derby, we had a Midland driver conducting us, and he recommended that we wound the reverser back one and half turns and varied the regulator opening as may be necessary depending upon the road, I found this worked very well indeed, it gave a sharper blast which helped the engine to steam. If you turned the screw back any more the engine started to strangle itself."

Terry Essery reported in the 'Big Goods' first valve working would normally provide all the power needed.

One suspects that some of the criticisms regarding the poor performance of the class, and for that matter that of the Class 2 4-4-0, was not wholly the fault of the engine as such, but rather was prompted by drivers operating them in too short a cut-off. A generation or more earlier both classes had been significant players on the Midland and the LMS. Apart from former Midland and Somerset & Dorset enginemen, ex-GSWR drivers for example also got on well with the 4-4-0, while there are occasional performance records[78], obtained when they were handled sympathetically, which belie the common perception. Despite the

---

77 Similar confusion appeared on the LNER when for example tenders were swapped between new A3 class 4-6-2s, which were built left-hand drive, with converted A1 4-6-2s which retained right-hand drive.

78 Messers J Walford & P Harrison *British Railways Standard Steam Locomotives Vol IV – The 9F 2-10-0 Class* RTCS 2008 p249.

O S Nock referred to the Class 2 4-4-0s doing yeoman service as pilots, running at 55 per cent cut-off and full regulator accompanied by loud exhausts- - *vide British Locomotives from the Footplate* Ian Allan 1950. These contradict the modern misconception of the poor train engine having to *push* its ancient pilot as well as haul its train.

Or consider the following:-

"The poor performance of the early Jubilees lead for a short time to such sights as the 10.23 non-stop leaving Bedford behind a Leicester 2P 4-4-0 whilst the following 10.38 stopping train was graced with a Kentish Town 5XP 4-6-0."

Mr G Goslin *The London Extension of the Midland Railway* Irwell Press Caernarfon 1994 p36

Class 4 having been intended for mineral traffic, in capable hands they were found to be quite lively engines which encouraged their use on mixed traffic or fast goods trains. George Bushell[79] has referred to a 'Big Goods', which whilst not taxing in terms of haulage demands - three carriages - did require smart running by the engine:-

> "My first experience on this working was on the p.m. turn with 3967 which was kept on this turn as far as possible. I had Jimmie Winsall, check number 23, as my driver. Jimmie was a white-haired frail-looking old fellow, but there was nothing frail about the way he handled that train. He was also reputed to be the only driver at the shed to own a motor-car. He instructed me to fill the firebox right up all over. It was as well that I did so. We left the station, slowed for the curve on the loop line over the river, slowed again for the curve on the L.N.W.R. line, stopped in London Road station, then Jimmie really got cracking, non-stop till we slowed for the curve at Hardingstone Junction and then up the branch to John Street which was a small terminal station. All I could do was to stand gripping the beading round the cut-out in the cab side as 3967 rocked and rolled its way at a speed which was far greater than anything that I had travelled at on the footplate before. The time allowed for the 13 miles was seventeen minutes - which was quite good considering the three junctions in such a short distance."

Even in their twilight years they could still be seen hauling local passenger and parcels traffic, excursions etc[80]:-

> "Strangely enough, my finest trip over this line was with a 4F 0-6-0 hauling a twenty-coach empty stock train which we took over at Skipton to work through to Morcambe. Nº 44207, one of the tall-chimney 4Fs from Holbeck shed, with exhaust steam injector, pounded her way from Skipton up to Clapham without any fuss at all."

Although short-lap valves coupled with small diameter driving wheels was not the ideal speed combination, Terry Essery suggests they would happily haul passenger trains of 200 tons or so at 50 miles per hour while running in a cut-off of 35 per cent. Ron Pennington was of the opinion that the engines were not given to fast running, a view supported by Ken Stokes who considered them no speed king with 55 to 60mph being their normal limit. But this is understandable since the piston speeds on the 0-6-0 being around 30 per cent higher than those of a 4-4-0 for the same train speeds, which would have significantly reduced the mean effective pressure in the black engines. Nevertheless when called upon, they were readily able to attain their diameter speed (*i.e.* 63 miles per hour) - a traditional rule-of-thumb performance applied when all engines were short-lap. The five examples built new for the Somerset & Dorset Joint were highly regarded as good express passenger locomotives, although with the fearsome gradients the speeds were necessarily lower than elsewhere - apparently the engines were classified[81] as '5P4G'. Perhaps we might therefore conclude that it was not so much that a Class 4 could not actually make a fast passenger run *per se*, but rather that the occasions when they did so were few and far between. Some of their work on express goods trains pre-War also lends credence to this observation. Professor Tuplin recorded in *Midland Steam* how an LMS built example reached 80 miles per hour in 1963, when in an emergency it took a 300-ton express from Appleby to Carlisle - admittedly if this proves nothing else, it confirms, like many other 'racers' they could run fast downhill! Elsewhere, he identified the engine as having been Nº 44386 hauling the 'Waverley' express 30¾ miles in 34½ minutes start to stop with the maximum speed occurring near New Biggin. A few further examples of Standard Class 4 0-6-0s pulling expresses and excursions are mentioned in *LMS Locomotive Profiles Nº 10*[82].

Since many former footplatemen have commented that a Class 4 was a poor tool when used on jobs that either by design or through line congestion involved progress marked by a series of cold starts from lie-by sidings and the like, we might explore the performance of its superheater. Although it has not been possible to plot the speed at which steam temperature rose; a few accurate steam flow rates together with their corresponding temperatures does permit the profile of a locomotive's superheat

---

79 Mr G Bushell *LMS Locoman Wellingborough Footplate Memories* Bradford Barton Truro pp80-81.

80 Mr M F Higson *London Midland Fireman* Ian Allan Shepperton 1972 p27.

81 Messers R J Essery & G Toms *The Midland 'Big Goods' and LMS Standard Class 4s* **British Railway Journal** Nº 19 1987 p430.

Using the LMS standard power classification a Class 5 express engine was capable of producing a tractive effort of 3.5 to 4 tons at 50mph, which is the equivalent of 1045-1195 indicated horsepower. The table accompanying figure 92 suggests the engines could produce 883 horsepower at that speed which almost made them Class 4 passenger 3.0 to 3.5 tons tractive effort or 896-1045 horsepower, although the boiler capacity was light. I assume this was a local S&DJR variation.

82 Messers D Hunt, J Jennison, R Essery & F James *LMS Locomotive Profiles Nº 10 The Standard Class 4 Goods 0-6-0s* Wild Swan Didcot.

temperature curve to be established normally to an accuracy within 5-10°F. Such an analysis has been conducted on the 'Big Goods' when fitted with its original draughting system using figures derived from N° 44030, with the result appearing in figure

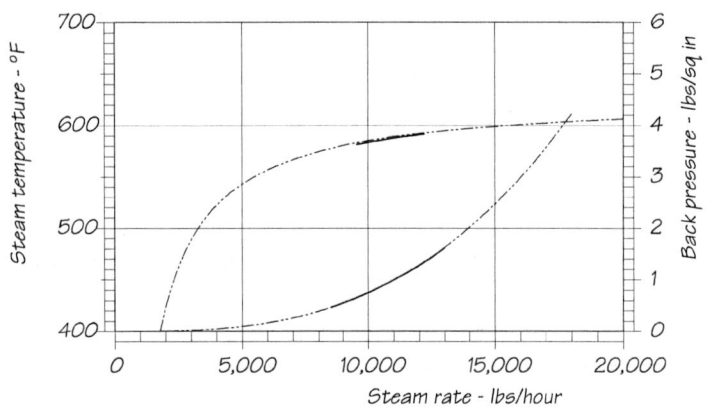

Thick lines - Recorded superheat and back pressure curves
Thin lines - Predicted superheat and back pressure curves

Fig. 119 - Predicted superheat temperature and back pressure curves for a 'Big Goods' carrying its original draughting system

119. Also included in this diagram for interest is the corresponding back pressure curve derived from the same engine. Inspection of this latter curve reveals that for the complete steaming range of N° 44030, its back pressure was lower than that of N° 43094 as recorded in figure 114. In other words the short-lap engine had a lower back pressure than a more modern large-lap engine. This is further supporting evidence of the author's belief the weakness with short-lap engines was not the size of their port openings at exhaust, but rather their smaller port openings to steam reduced the quantity of steam that could enter the cylinder particularly at speed. Hence it is suggested the common explanation that it was restricted exhaust port openings once the cut-off was reduced to below say 30-35 per cent which compromised the free running of short-lap engines is erroneous. Rather it was the reduced port openings to steam as the engine was linked up, which when combined with higher speeds, meant they were too small and open for too short a period of time that was causing the apparent sluggishness due to a lack of power. Power generation in a steam locomotive is proportional to the product of steam flow rate and heat drop - compromise either and the output will be similarly affected. Hence the wisdom of not shortening the cut-off too much and instead making power adjustments via regulator opening.

The superheat curve suggests that there would be no superheat at all for steam rates a little under 2,000lbs/hour, while following its appearance and a rate of say 6,000lbs/hr the steam temperature did not rise above 550°F. From that steam rate up to the maximum the temperature rose more slowly to assume eventually a maximum value of a little over 600°F. Sir Henry Fowler reported a steam temperature of 620°F in 1913, a difference assuming boilers of similar states of cleanliness, possibly prompted by the different combustion characteristics of the coal used in his Toton - Brent tests - a conclusion supported by the different superheat temperatures obtained in the 4MT when given different coal - *vide* figure 111[83]. However, in his contribution to the discussion following Richard Wagner's paper[84], Sir Henry gave 393 as the *S/A* ratio for the flue and element combination, which suggests the Midland used longer elements - *vide* table LXIII. Incidentally, at the higher steam rates the Standard Class 4 superheater performance was roughly the equivalent to that obtained from a Class 5 fitted with 28 flues and noticeably superior to a Class 8F.

One criticism that frequently appears in many footplateman's memoirs of a Standard 4 was the appearance of fine ash into the cab. This appears to have been first aired in 1931 when in the June of

---

[83] N° 3835 had a superheater damper during its trials but this would have been fully open when running to give maximum steam temperature.

It was still the practice to incorporate smokebox dampers to protect the element return bends when the Midland first experimented with superheating. However, Derby soon found when the dampers were shut the elements quickly lost their heat and took some time to regain it. This loss of heat and the tardiness of its restoration initially militated against the use of superheated steam on goods and stopping trains. It led the Midland to introduce, for a while, automatic damper control gear which could be set for either long-distance ('fast' position) or stopping work ('slow' position). In the fast position, the dampers worked in the normal way, when steam was off they were shut and visa versa. When the damper control gear was set in the slow position, the dampers remained open even when the regulator was closed, provided the blower was not opened too far. If the blower was put on above a pre-determined limit, steam from its supply pipe closed the dampers.

[84] Dr R Wagner *Some New Developments of the Stephenson Boiler* I Loco E Paper N° 253 September 1929.

that year the CME stated he had received complaints about excessive quantities of ash appearing in the cabs of a few classes. In common with most Midland designs the Class 4 was provided with a generous sized ashpan approximately 3 feet wide and around 24 inches deep at the front and deeper still at its rear. There was a single centrally-pivoted damper fitted at the front about 20 inches high. In line with all of the later Derby designs the ashpan was fitted with a perimeter flange provided with a number of holes, through which passed a number of slotted studs protruding from the ring. The ashpan was secured quite loosely to the underside of the foundation ring by means of cotters passed through these slots.

George Bushell was of the opinion the ash escaped via the gap between the flange around the perimeter of the ashpan and the foundation ring due to the scoop action of an open damper. Others considered it fell out of the ashpan via the open damper door being dislodged by the movement of the engine, whereupon it was entrained in the air before being carried up into the cab, entering via the largish gap that existed between the front of the boiler and the dragbox on either side of the central boiler steady. Ken Stokes stated it occurred when running at any sort of speed with the regulator shut.

What is rarely mentioned is that at the time three Midland/LMS Standard Classes were afflicted with this problem - *viz* the Compound, 2P 4-4-0s and the 'Big Goods'. In each case these classes were provided with a heat shield spaced a short distance off the rear end plate of the ashpan. This plate was intended to protect the trailing axleboxes from heat radiated from the ashpan by acting as a channel to guide cold air between itself and the ashpan. However this narrow but wide passage, whose upper end terminated near the gap referred to earlier, acted as a conduit for ash. Under NWO 2446, the heat shields were shortened in an attempt to cure the problem - it was unsuccessful. The next attempt was in June 1946 when under Job Nº 5452 a revised design of heat shield incorporating a curved baffle plate was fitted however complaints continued to be made. In due course engineers came up with yet another solution, which they considered was caused by the steam brake, issuing Job Nº 5587 in October 1950 *'Elimination of Dirt in Locomotive Cabs.'* The instruction describing the problem:-

"In order to prevent the entry of fine ash into the cabs of certain engines, it has been agreed that a flange should be brazed to the existing brake discharge pipe. This has been proved by experiment to overcome the trouble, about which complaints have been made by footplate staff."

Following the adoption by the Midland of the steam brake, with the exception of the configuration adopted on the first one or two classes, the waste steam from the brake cylinder was arranged to discharge via a perforated 'silencer' into the ashpan - the original discharge had been through the cab roof via a plain pipe but was quickly altered because of the noise. Operation of the steam brake therefore disturbed ash in the ashpan which in these three classes alone could then find ready access into the cab. The Standard Class 4 being a goods engine would tend to be worse affected by this problem than either of the two passenger classes since it made more frequent brake applications during the course of a journey, particularly when hauling loose-coupled trains, which perhaps is why most of the criticism by footplatemen has been directed towards the six-coupled engine. It took nearly eight years to modify all of the engines involved as they passed through the shops with the job reported as complete in August 1958, although whether this modification actually cured the problem is unclear, some enginemen maintained that it did not. Of course, by the time the job was started the first Compounds had been in service 45 years and the other two classes for 39 and 38 years - while other classes fitted with heat shields *e.g.* the '999' class and the '700' class 4-4-0s had gone or were almost extinct. Maybe this dilatoriness indicates the importance the powers-that-be attended to such matters, or simply it is also reflective of the deterioration in maintenance and operational standards[85] that had occurred over those years. For as John Hulme observed:-

"If all the footboards were in place, you had a dust-free ride, ..."

Mike Higson, an experienced fireman of the early British Railways period also referred to the presence of this gap when giving his opinion[86] of the Class 4:-

"All 4Fs had two features in common, a gap

---

85 It was not unknown for shed staff employed in the 1950s even to smash up the wooden seats provided in cabs using them as a source of firewood for lighting up engines.

86 Mr M F Higson *London Midland Fireman* Ian Allan Shepperton 1972 p131.

between the floor and the firebox back-plate which caused clouds of dust to swirl up when the engine was moving, despite wedges of sacks and old clothing stuffed in to block this space, and a roof gutter which deflected the rain in a stream down one's neck or back. However, comfort was of secondary importance on the 4F, for the going was generally a full-time occupation. Personally I learned to treat the 4F with the greatest of respect. If circumstances allowed, I built the fire up very carefully, mainly under the door, and kept firing at frequent intervals, about four shovelsful at a time. Firing too heavily only caused the firebox to choke with smoke and a heavy black fug to roll out of the chimney while steam pressure fell rapidly. The grate was so inclined that coal needed do no more than just get inside the door, with a little placed down each side. At best, the fire could be so thin at the front as to be literally hopping about on the grate, but this was hard to achieve, and with poor coal the front of the grate soon became clogged with dirt and steaming became impaired.

The parallel boilers of these engines seemed more susceptible to dirt and priming than did taper boilers - this goes for all MR-type parallel boilers - and the method of boiler feed delivery was more cooling than top feed. The ancillary fittings - blower, steam heat supply and injectors - were a great drain on the boiler and working a passenger train with a 4F 0-6-0 was quite an experience. They rode quite well, however, and MR men usually adored them, defending them at every stage. Other men put up with them or despised them, and LNW men much preferred their 0-8-0s. All in all, the 4F was a most controversial engine, which personally I found to be too temperamental and unreliable."

As a complete contrast to Mr Higson, in a conversation with the author, Eric Riley considered the 'Big Goods' to have been a superb locomotive and that Midland enginemen largely knew how to drive them "not linked up too much" and fire them "good back on and thin at the front" - skills not necessarily mastered by men on the other Divisions hence the problems.

When used regularly on heavy mineral traffic the permitted wear allowed in the boxes, particularly the trailing ones could result in them becoming rough as confirmed by George Bushell, while Terry Essery has provided more details[87] concerning their

---

87 Mr G Bushell *LMS Locoman Wellingborough Footplate Memories* Bradford Barton Truro p79.
Mr T Essery *Steam Locomotives Compared* - Atlantic Transport Publishers 1996 pp70.
Mr Essery seems to suggest Job Nº 5587 had not cured the ash problem since according to him the ingress of ash remained a problem. Unfortunately as none of these reminiscences give specific dates and the work took so long to complete it is difficult to be certain.

riding-

"Working back from Cricklewood the next day with 4237 on the 9.5 empties, I found out just how rough a rigid wheelbase loco could be when driven hard and fast. I knew enough about '4s' to get away with a good start, but when we started rocking and rolling at speed, I found it difficult to keep my feet."

"Approaching 60 mph the ride became very lively indeed, with the high pitched boiler seeming to add a rolling motion to at times quite vicious lateral oscillations and harsh vertical movements."

This description of their road-riding is reminiscent of the comments Mr Cox had made, which it will be recalled were directed at *all* 0-6-0s at speed, while this rolling behaviour was certainly also present in the Q1 0-6-0, another class with a high-pitched boiler 9ft - 2ins against 8ft - 6ins, but it did not unduly discourage Southern men or for that matter those on the LNER or Great Western with *their* 0-6-0s.

Mike Higson thought they rode reasonably but LMS fireman D Wilson[88] held a different opinion, although it should be remembered he was writing during the dying months of the Second World War when maintenance standards had been allowed to drop. This was especially the case in the Northern Division according to Eric Langridge, combined in some cases with the adoption of inferior materials[89], practices which undoubtedly will have

---

88 Comments appearing in *Railway Magazine* July/August 1945 pp 235-6.

89 Perhaps the classic instance in the case of the Standard Class 4 stemming from the substitution of poor quality material were the crankpin fractures the class suffered from for a period, referred to by Mr Powell in *Living with London Midland Locomotives*:-

"The 4Fs - everyone at Derby knew them as the 'Big Goods'! - had another endearing habit, that of snapping off outside crankpins, usually the driving ones. The coupling journals were, if I remember rightly, no more than 3¾ in diameter, and if the engine got anything of a slip when pulling heard and then one pair of wheels got a grip to stop it, off would come a crankpin like a crisp carrot, more or less flush with the wheel boss, and showing a sizeable fatigue flaw. The answer was plain to see - bigger pins. But that would have required new coupling rods, and the cure would probably have been more costly than the disease."

Crankpin failures only became prevalent during the '40s and '50s. Initially it was thought to have been due to roll in the axleboxes allowing a 'snatch'. Nevertheless Job Nº 5724, issued in August 1954, authorised fifty engines to be fitted with new coupling rods which allowed larger crankpins to be fitted, although it seems doubtful if many were modified. Due to the larger diameter coupling rod bosses, small coupling rod slasher were needed, which made it a particularly expensive modification. Concurrently, Mr Powell's colleague Dennis Monk, investigated the problem discovering during the War

affected the ride. In response to a critique of Sir Nigel Gresley's designs expressed in the *Railway Magazine* by some LNER enginemen, Fireman Wilson defended the J39, which he considered to be one of the handiest 0-6-0 designs and noticeably superior to the 'Big Goods':-

> "Their large side-window cabs, are in sharp contrast to those of the L.M.S.R. class '4' 0-6-0s, which are absolutely devoid of comfort for the men. On a wet day their short roofs leak at every bolt hole, while the dirt and ashes from the ashpan blow right up between the firebox and the floor-boards. The brick arch is too low at the front end for comfortable firing and after they have been out of the shops for a month or two, the side to side motion that they acquire is terrible."

He directed some further ire at certain weaknesses he saw present in other LMS classes:-

> "In his experience as a fireman, most L.M.S.R. engines, except those with a bogie or pony truck under the cab, as the 2-6-4 tanks and the Pacifics, can be very rough-riding when due for the shops."

The lateral and longitudinal wear that appeared in the axleboxes, particularly those on the trailing coupled wheels, which tended to be the worst affected, was the primary cause of this rough riding. The LMS practice of providing white metal rubbing rubbing surfaces to the horns and the back of the wheels, whilst easy to apply, machine and fit, was not very long lived. Under the pounding it received, particularly on goods engines slogging heavy mineral trains, fore and aft wear of 1/16ins could quickly develop giving a thoroughly uncomfortable axlebox thump, reduced spring life and accelerated wear in the coupling rod bushes.

---

and following Austerity period, crankpins had been machined from reclaimed tender axles. This steel was unsuitable, so when the heat treated steel (grade 13F) he specified was substituted it appears the problem was cured, which seems reasonable since apart from isolated incidences, it had not been a problem pre-war. The precautionary practice of re-metalling axleboxes at 30-36,000 miles, which had been introduced to reduce roll was also stopped.

That this problem was primarily caused through injudicious materials selection is suggested by the following quotation from *Under 10 CMEs Volume One: Dugald Drummond to W A Stanier*. Mr Langridge was intimately involved with the design of the LMS Standard Class 7 0-8-0, and demonstrates the pins were of large enough section:-

> "... the big-end loading indicated that a '4F' 0-6-0 bearing would fit the bill and the axle loading again compared favourably with the '4F', so that '4F' axles and spring gear appeared adequate for the 0-8-0. The outside coupling rods, being calculated against buckling by the force to slip the wheels, could also be to the '4F' section; the middle rod would have to be heavier as it must be strong enough to slip both intermediate and trailing wheels."

Sideways wear would be exacerbated by the somewhat spasmodic lubrication present that would inevitably also attract dirt.

After commenting on the LMS use of single-ended regulators, the LNER equivalent could be worked from either side of the cab, Mr Wilson continued:-

> "The class '5' 4-6-0s are very hot in summer, rough-riding when worked on the large port of the regulator-valve, and have an inadequate seat for the fireman."

The *Railway Magazine* observed that while an LNER fireman had had little positive to say in favour of the bucket seats provided for the crews, Mr Wilson thought such comforts would be appreciated by LMS locomotive crews.

What perhaps these comments and others like them really tell us is that if the fireman or driver, for whatever reasons had taken a dislike to a locomotive class then that was likely to remain his firm opinion. Since the 'Big Goods' has earned a reputation as being a 'difficult' class which did not take any prisoners, perhaps it is simply human nature for many of those locomotive crews who having had bad trips with them preferred to direct blame and their venom on the engine rather than accept their inadequacy might in any way be part of the problem.

For an example of a more enlightened approach made around this time, let us consult another future author, Terry Essery's older brother Robert[90] who had recently become acquainted with the 'Big Goods':-

> "However, the run to Water Orton introduced me to the class '4' goods engine. Love them or hate them, you couldn't as a Midland Division man, ignore them - there were too many in service for that, at first, and for a long time I hated them. They were difficult to fire, or rather to maintain with a good head of steam, and I just couldn't get the hang of them. No wonder they were disliked by the majority of non Midland LMS locomotive crews. Mind you, I could claim that it wasn't all my fault. Once I went onto the main line, my first driver was Charlie Smith, and his idea of driving was to run with the locomotive 'wound back'. This in itself reduced the exhaust draw on the fire and that didn't help since I usually had too thick a fire. Nevertheless, we sometimes had good trips with class '4s'."

---

90 Messers R J Essery & D Jenkinson *An Illustrated Review of Midland Locomotives Vol. 1* - Wild Swan Publications p180.

A Defence of the Midland/LMS Class 4 0-6-0

A year or so later[91] and with a different driver:-

"During our first week, we relieved a set of Gloucester men at Bromsgrove with a Bristol-Washwood Heath through freight. I climbed on board and the Gloucester fireman said 'She's a good 'un' - and that was that. I opened the firedoors and some of the fire fell onto the footplate. The locomotive was N° 43940 and it was fitted with the Midland type of firedoors. I had never seen a class 4's fire made up like this. It rose up and I couldn't see the top of it. It was a mountain of hot burned through fire. I now know there was virtually nothing down at the front, with the fire sloping down from the apex, which left space between the fire and the bottom of the brick arch as well as leaving sufficient space to clear the deflector plate. Naturally, the back corners were well packed up.

While I was trying to grasp all this, the signals came off and whistling up we were away. Discarding the inclination to 'put some fire on' (note the expression - not 'put some coal on'), I 'boxed her up' (closed the firehole doors), left a little space for 'top air' (secondary air), and decided to see what happened. I adjusted the injector and as we went up the bank the needle stayed 'on the red line', so much so that I tapped the boiler pressure gauge just because I didn't believe it, and somehow had formed the theory that the needle was stuck. 'Glued to the red line' was a common expression but not with a class '4'- impossible! Impossible or not, it was actually happening and, whilst the remainder of that journey is somewhat blurred in my memory, I do recall breasting the summit of Blackwell and, as my mate eased up, the safety valves lifted."

"We disposed of the locomotive and went home. It made me think. Maybe this was the way to fire the class '4'."

He then described a return working Washwood Heath to Bristol - crew change at Gloucester - in which he allowed himself plenty of time before departure to prepare the fire which he built up in a similar manner:-

"This trip marked a new beginning for me with the class '4Fs' and, whilst it would be untrue to say that never again was I in trouble with them, at least I understood them and my successful runs by far outnumbered the 'rough trips' of the past."

Whilst the class was difficult to fire they were not as bad as some would have us believe, a point reinforced by Terry Essery[92] who also had a lot of experience firing Class 4s:-

"... for a higher level of skill was certainly demanded. Perhaps concentration would be a better term because provided one applied all the basic principles with care and consistency, adequate steaming could be anticipated; but the least lapse would soon be seen on the pressure gauge. I found that, in general, rather thinner fire beds than would be carried with a 3F were preferable since the lighter draught was better able to keep them bright. The same profile would be used and firing over the bottom flap of Midland doors or the combustion plate found with sliding doors helped to maintain furnace temperature."

While Ken Stokes[93] confirmed they needed forethought in firing:-

"They could be indifferent steamers and always required care in firing, no heavy fire, well up at the back of the box and down the sides. It was to ask for trouble if coal was shot to the front of the firebox...

... And yet I liked the 4F for each one represented a challenge; they required full boiler pressure, for if it dropped by even 20 pounds the performance was adversely affected."

Robert Essery opined the fundamental problem with a 'Big Goods' was that should the fireman get into trouble, he had no easy solution to hand. Most other engines allowed the fireman to mortgage the boiler *i.e.* permitting the water level to fall in order to allow the pressure to rally, but this procedure did not really exist with a Class 4. If the boiler pressure started to fall it would continue to do so since a fall in pressure implied insufficient heat release and this will have affected the superheat temperature, which in turn increased the demand for steam, thereby starting a vicious circle that could only be relieved by a drop in steam demand:-

"The fact was that once the needle started to go back it would continue to do so. Nevertheless, they would continue to run and I have worked between Burton and Birmingham, hauling a coal train with a class '4F' with less than 100 lbs on the clock and the water in the bottom nut! We didn't keep time but we kept going."

In order for steam pressure to be maintained the necessary heat release has to be present in the firebox. The official or approved method of ensuring this was by firing 'little and often', but many steam locomotives would go if fired 'lots and occasionally'. There are instances of runs with 'Duchess' class 4-6-2s where the fireman would put on fifty or more shovelsful in one go and then sat down for quite a long while before repeating

---

91 Ibid p180.

92 Mr T Essery *Steam Locomotives Compared* - Atlantic Transport Publishers 1996 p71.

93 Mr K Stokes *Both Sides of the Footplate* Bradford Barton Truro pp32-3.

the exercise. If the engine had sufficient mastery of the load, or perhaps too little was demanded of it, then firemen could adopt such an approach. Under these circumstances the firebed would vary quite considerably in thickness, while with 'little and often' approach this variation would be reduced. The diametric situation was present in mechanical stoked locomotives for the coal was introduced continuously in a manner somewhat akin to burning oil. In effect firing was maintained at or very close to the rate of combustion permitting very thin and thus low resistance firebeds to be adopted.

Given reasonable coal, the main problem faced by firemen of 4Fs appears to have been estimating with sufficient accuracy the anticipated demand for steam. Over estimating it meant an excess of fuel slowly built up in the firebed increasing its resistance to the available draught. Conversely, if he misjudged it the other way then a hole would appear in his fire. Either effect reduced the heat release rate and with it the steam rate that could be maintained. Many years ago, when the author was a fireman on narrow gauge engines he remembers being told early in his firing experience that anybody could fire a big engine all you had to do was keep shovelling, but the closer the engine's capacity was matched to its load the more skill and anticipation was needed as the margin for error became so much smaller.

George Bushell[94], referring to his second year as a passed cleaner at Wellingborough, a few years before the Second World War, and who spent quite a bit of his footplate career on Class 4s, confirms preparation, observation and anticipation were very necessary skills to cultivate:-

"The year 1937 started off very well for me for in the first month I logged 23 firing turns. These included several lodging turns to Toton, mainly with 3F or 4F 0-6-0s. Although the '4s' were so numerous, they were not very free steaming and to get the best results one had to take advantage of every opportunity, either to slip an extra drop of water into the boiler, or get some more fire built up on a slight downgrade. In fact one had to watch them carefully and try to be one step in front all the time. When going out to work on a train, best results were obtained if the fire was built up in the back of the firebox by placing each piece of coal in by hand, and the pieces mustn't be too big either, not over 6". In this way, a large porous mass of fuel would be ready with plenty of air spaces through it to develop a lot of heat soon after starting. Also, with a good head of water, the engine could travel several miles before it was necessary to start feeding water in with the injector. By this time, the superheater tubes would have warmed through and also the large mass of the cylinder and steam chest block. All these factors affected the consumption of fuel and water. Away to a good start like this, one could confidently expect to have a good trip on a 4F. Thereafter firing three shovelsful along each side of the firebox and one under the door; never firing until the smoke had cleared, with a slight pause for the coke residue to reach its highest temperature. A lot of people who have never experienced the pleasure of travelling on the footplate of a locomotive when working hard will not know that under these conditions, the interior of the firebox becomes a mass of yellow flame, almost like looking at the sun. Once under way, it is impossible to know what the fire bed is looking like, and an efficient fireman carries a mental picture of it, aiming fresh coal in the places he thinks it ought to go, bearing in mind the characteristics of the grate and how hard the engine is working. If things start to go wrong and pressure begins to slip for no reason, the shovel could be used upside down to deflect a stream of clear air through the flame to examine the bed of fire. Sometimes too much coal had worked its way under the brick arch or the fire had burnt thin or the fire would be too thick all over. Gradually, over the years, one built up a store of experience which was essential to make almost every trip a successful one."

Keith Terry[95], who was based at Bushbury, admitted in his reminiscences that it took him a long time before he felt confident as a fireman. Indeed it was not achieved until he had passed through the freight links and had entered the top link firing the London expresses, as the following extracts explain:-

"The larger '4F' 0-6-0s, also based on a Midland Railway design, were not so free steaming as their smaller sister engines, and I had great difficulty maintaining anywhere near a full head of steam on these locomotives."

"The underlying theme of this book so far has been my inability to master the art of correctly managing a steam engine's boiler, notwithstanding my enthusiasm for steam engines. I knew where to place the coal in the firebox, and I could handle and swing a shovel as deftly as anyone else. It was that infernal timing; I just did not seem able to get it right."

"Then it hit me, I was now doing the exact opposite to what I had been doing all those years in the freight links, and I now knew where I had been going

---

94 Mr G Bushell *LMS Locoman Wellingborough Footplate Memories* Bradford Barton Truro pp78-79.

95 Mr K Terry *On the Footplate at Busbury 1947-1962 An Engineman's Tale* The Oakwood Press 2006 pp118-9, p151 & pp 154-5.

A Defence of the Midland/LMS Class 4 0-6-0

wrong. It was the timing, which from this point on I was to get exactly right. I was now truly master of the job, and now I could manage a steam engine's boiler as well as any one else. Strange to relate that, apart from the scanty advice afforded us at the Walsall lectures, and the the time Ernie told me of the shallow firebox carried by *Quebec*, I never once received any advice on where I was going wrong. However, I did glean one tip, although it was not expressed directly to myself. I just happened to overhear a group of drivers talking. One man said that, "To successfully fire an engine on the London expresses then, 'knowing the road' was half the battle.'"

Perhaps this, or similar goes part of the way at least to explaining the diametrically extreme opinions that crews could adopt when considering the 'Big Goods'. Midland men were inevitably more familiar and comfortable with the technique but Western and Central Division crews had been used to firing physically larger eight-coupled engines formerly used on the mineral and goods duties typically now being given to Standard Class 4 0-6-0s. The other engines, apart from the benefit of familiarity also had perhaps greater tolerance towards firing errors. Furthermore and perhaps equally significant is that LNWR and L&YR engines had level grates, not steeply sloping ones coupled with 'sensitive' draughting, which underlines the earlier comment that much of the trouble was simply because Western and Central Division men had no idea how to fire them nor it seems were they that disposed to learn.

The more effectively a locomotive was draughted the more reserve it possessed for overcoming defects that would have had a less effective example booked for being short of steam, but perhaps the most important benefit was from the fireman's point of view. An engine that steamed more freely meant that full pressure and water level could be maintained more easily, with the results not being so critically dependent on his skills.

Reference has been made to the perceived variation in performance enginemen reported between the different batches or even between individual engines. The following dating from the early British Railways period and related by Ken Stokes, by which time he was an inspector, demonstrates what the class could do[96] when everything came together:-

"The 7.0 p.m. Wicker - Carlisle fitted was a most important duty, loading to 45 vans every night. I was instructed to do three successive weeks on this train which, at the time, was worked by Grimesthorpe men to Leeds (Engine Shed Junction) then Leeds men to Skipton South Junction, with Carlisle men forward from there. At this period, a wide variety of power was used; from 5XPs to, on one occasion a 4F (which was probably the best 4F I ever came across, fortunately). Of course, the loading was reduced for the 0-6-0 - but it was so good an engine that when we got to Skipton and filled the tank, I suggested to the Carlisle fireman when he got on board (he was only a youngster and not likely to have seen many other 4Fs) that he could ride in the brake van and I would do the firing. The driver agreed with this, so off we went. I fired according to the book, wasting no water, and the needle was on the mark the whole way. As this engine was not fitted with a scoop, the driver and I discussed stopping for water but in the event we did not do so - the water being well down when we arrived at Durran Hill. But we made it comfortably and I don't think any other 4F would have done."

The real tragedy for the class and for its enginemen is that as the above extract demonstrates fundamentally the Standard Class 4 was a sound and competent design. If *one* example could produce such a performance then *all* of the other class members ought to have been capable of working to a similar standard. The basic laws of physics are immutable, they do not vary from one engine builder to another or for that matter from one running shed or works to another even if perhaps the skills and aptitude by which they were applied might!

Before concluding this chapter let us cross the footplate as it were and consider the very high opinion that Driver Charlie Harrison had of the Class 4 0-6-0s which he used to take on the London fitted trains. He was a highly respected Rowsley driver, not just by his colleagues but also by Control, so his statements should be valued, especially in view of the type of traffic and the road to which he was referring, starting with Nº 44046:-

"... was a typical Derby 4 ... it were a snooter! I'd had it on the Londons that week, every trip. I don't think we were overdone for load, y'know; probably two or three short, but she were boss of them all t'time. Just like being on my holidays."

"We had some good 4s at Rowsley when you think about it: I liked 'em every time we had one. You take 4564, 4565 and 4566, they were like sewing machines. getting them on t'Londons, it were a doddle - I'd sooner've had them than t'Crabs."

---

96 Mr K Stokes *Both Sides of the Footplate* Bradford Barton Truro pp100-101.

Not perhaps the usual opinion one hears expressed about the 'Big Goods', but certainly it supports the view that the capability and reliability of the class was not as bad as some *post*-war locomotive crews and writers have tended to present. What perhaps makes these comments even more interesting is that Driver Harrison was an ex-North Western man who had started at Buxton, moved to Oldham before coming to Rowsley, thus he had not been imbued from his days as a cleaner with any innate ideas of Midland superiority, but rather had formed that opinion on the basis of his experience. Secondly, another Rowsley driver Syd Curzon said that many drivers preferred the 'Number Fours' to the 'Crabs' because the smaller wheels gave better braking, especially on loose-coupled trains.

Comment has been made previously about the skills drivers needed to work, successfully heavy loose-coupled trains; to work them double-headed demanded even more, not least in how the drivers arranged to share the work of hauling and braking between their two engines. Unfortunately not much appears to have been recorded on this aspect with regards to any of the combinations of engines used in this way on the Midland main-line, let alone concerning Standard Class 4 Goods, but the following extract[97], although representing highly unusual behaviour provides an amusing note on which to end this chapter - and it did involve a pair of 'Big Goods' :-

"The following week, I was called on at 8|15 for a special to Manton. We were second engine on a double-header from Corby, the engines being both 4F 0-6-0s. The train was a long one, even by Midland standards, as it was 88 tube wagons - equal to 133 ordinary wagons. The driver of the leading engine was Stan Keilor, who had transferred from Willesden to Wellingborough for promotion. He was a thin man with a limp and had a rugged leathery face. Judge our surprise when struggling up the 1 in 167 through Glaston Tunnel, Stan appeared through the dark swirling smoke and steam on *our* engine gesticulating to Albert Charters, my driver, for him to open our regulator a bit more. And then he vanished in the darkness back to his own footplate! Stan must have come along the tender side on the three-inch angle, hanging on to the beading along the top of the tender and stepped across the three-foot gap between the engines... This was something cleaners would quite happily do in the comfort of a loco shed, but not in the dark and smoke of about the worst tunnel in our area! At Manton, another two engines were waiting to take our train from us to Peterborough, which was in the opposite direction but there was a brake van at each end. All the way back to Wellingborough, Albert Charters - who was a stolid individual - kept marvelling at Stan's daredevil acrobatics...."

---

97 Mr G Bushell *LMS Locoman Wellingborough Footplate Memories* Bradford Barton Truro pp99-100.

A Defence of the Midland/LMS Class 4 0-6-0

Appendix 5.1

Observations Concerning the Accuracy of the 4MT 2-6-0 Test Results
- Performance and Efficiency Tests BR Bulletin N° 3

Column 10 of table LX records the horsepower necessary to drive Class 4MT 2-6-0 N° 43094 at a speed of 30 miles per hour, determined by subtracting the drawbar horsepower from the indicated power. This, we might anticipate should sensibly be a constant figure if we disregard the very small effect caused by the changes in compression as the steam rate through the machine altered in response to changes in cut-off. However, inspection of the figures in column 10, which were obtained from the 30 mph curves appearing in figures 89 and 101 for the selected steam rates reveals the absorbed horsepower values ranging from 88 to 108, a tolerance amounting to almost 20 per cent. This is beyond the variation we might expect from a rise in compression - a view confirmed by the highest absorbed power not appearing when the steam rate had attained its maximum value. A variation of 20 per cent is really too large for the most likely cause for the discrepancy - errors in plotting the smoothed curves or to be more precise in the choice of the plotting points Swindon used to generate the indicated and drawbar horsepower curves. Thus we must conclude that one or both of these curves is incorrect.

In practice below about 25-30 miles per hour the resistance of a locomotive did not vary that much with change in speed, so a common and convenient simplification, which introduces little loss in accuracy is to assume it is a constant value. Oliver Bulleid used this artifice, adopting a value of 12lbs/ton as demonstrated in table LXII. Some years later, accurate resistance tests conducted by BR on Class 5 4-6-0 N° 44764[98] confirmed that it rose only slightly from around 13½ to 14½lbs/ton for a rise in engine speed from 10 to 30 miles per hour. Values deduced from other BR Performance & Efficiency Test Bulletins suggest similar profiles

---

[98] Dr H I Andrews *The Measurement of Train Resistance* Paper 531 I Loco E February 1954.

albeit with the values being a little higher. Accordingly for the horsepower estimates appearing earlier in this book, a constant value of 14lbs/ton has been adopted. Applying this figure to the Class 4MT suggests the horsepower needed to drive the engine and tender weighing 94 tons (based on 2/3 supplies) would have been 105.

The normal testing practice used by Swindon, where N° 43094 was tested, was to determine the indicated characteristics first, which necessitated a period of running on the stationary test plant, during the course of which typically 1,000 indicator diagrams would be taken. This series of tests was then followed by a series of Controlled Road Tests which enabled the drawbar characteristics to be established. If the indicated horsepower figures are the more accurate, as is possibly more likely to be the case, then the drawbar power values should be approximately 105 less than the former.

The bulletin recording the performance of N° 43094 appeared in October 1951 and it is known that some of the early Rugby tests were of a lower standard of accuracy than the testing staff were able to achieve later as they learned their craft. However since this engine was tested at Swindon where the experimenters already had far more experience of the test procedures, not least through having developed them, we might conclude that by then they should have been attaining a higher level of accuracy. Nevertheless they experienced difficulty when testing this engine to obtain the 60 miles per hour curves.

Bulletin N° 3 reported that the speed range covered was 15 to 50 miles per hour, with the upper limit being imposed by the effect the rough riding of the engine had on the fire. These mechanical disturbing forces were also experienced during the road tests to an extent such that they caused a breakdown in the coal-steam relationship when the speed was allowed to exceed 50 miles per hour for more than a short time. Apparently this was overcome for testing purposes by increasing the load relative to the steam rate and by allowing the brakes to drag on some down gradients whilst the steam rate to the cylinders was maintained. How successful this approach was is not certain, nevertheless performance curves for 60 miles per hour duly appeared in the bulletin.

The locomotive was tested with three different coals, Blidworth, Bedwas and Lilleshall and their

Comparisons, Steaming and Performance

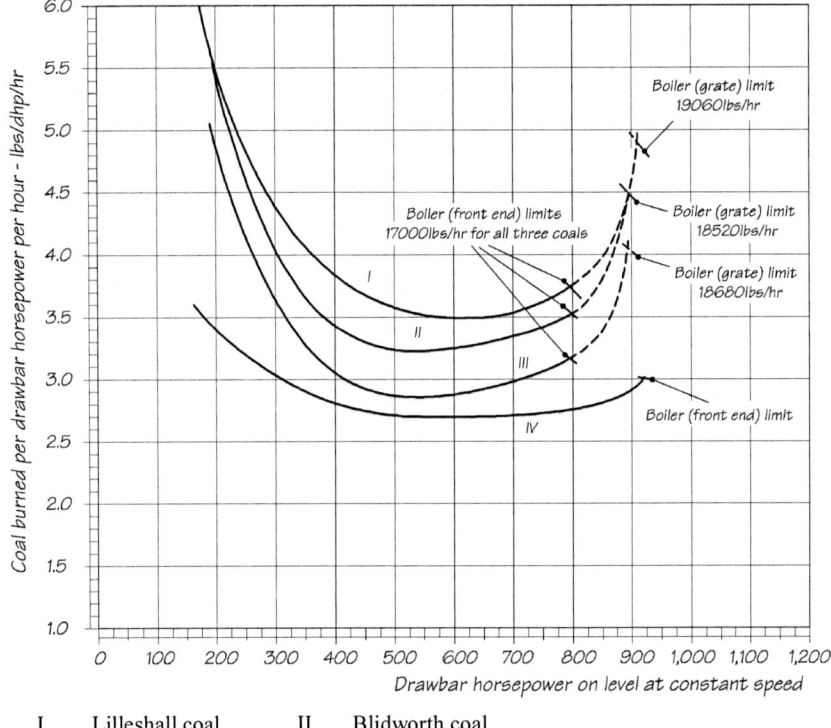

I   Lilleshall coal   II   Blidworth coal
III   Bedwas coal   IV   Curve taken from figure 23 of Mr Cox's paper

Fig. 120 - Variation in coal consumption against drawbar horsepower whilst running at a constant speed of 60 miles per hour - Class 4MT 2-6-0 N° 43094.

different calorific values and combustion characteristics affected the drawbar coal consumption. Accordingly, three sets of coal consumption/drawbar horsepower curves appeared in the Bulletin each covering a similar number of speeds ranging from 15 to 60 miles per hour. An example of one of these diagrams with the engine burning Blidworth coals appears as figure 101. The 60 miles per hour curve from this diagram has been transferred to form figure 120 along with the corresponding 60 miles per hour curves for the remaining two coals. However, also appearing in figure 120 is a curve taken from Mr Cox's book *Locomotive Panorama Vol. II* p92, or its earlier appearance as figure 23 in *Experiences with British Railways Standard Locomotives* I Loco E Paper 532 March 1954 also by Mr E S Cox.

This latter diagram, thus dating from nearly 2½ years after the appearance of Bulletin N° 3, purported in its original format to record the minimum coal consumption figures of five BR Standard locomotive classes *viz* Class 2 2-6-0, Class 4 2-6-0, Class 4 4-6-0, Class 5 4-6-0 and Class 7 4-6-2. For these comparison curves to be valid the engines had to be burning the same coal, the only common coal used in all of these latter classes was Blidworth coal. For our purposes only the curve representing the larger Mogul appears in figure 120. Inspection reveals that this latter curve not only differs from the Blidworth curve that appeared in the Bulletin but also it exhibits a different profile from either of the other two, yet these were the only coals used in the Class 4 Mogul tests. A similar comparison process conducted on the Class 7 and the Class 5 curves with those appearing in their respective bulletins has revealed a similar situation. It is not clear why Mr Cox's curves, which shew the locomotives in a considerably better light, should differ from those appearing in the respective official Test Bulletins.

One further unknown concerns the efficiency curve for the 4D boiler appearing in figure 109, which the Bulletin recorded was based on the use of a specially provided rear damper, however, it appears this was not a modification fitted to the remaining members of the class. Accordingly this curve represents an overestimate of the capability of the Mogul. This unique damper provision, the observed variation in the magnitude of the horsepower absorbed by the locomotive when driving it at for example 30 miles per hour, coupled with the difficulty the testers experienced in obtaining the 60 miles per hour performance curves, plus the presence of a different, albeit later fuel consumption curve claiming to represent the same information, must inevitably cast certain reservations over the accuracy of the data forming Bulletin N° 3.

Appendix 5.2

Some Observations Concerning Boiler Proportions and Performance

The fundamental performance parameter of the locomotive boiler is its thermal efficiency (*i.e.* the heat taken up by the boiler in evaporation and superheating expressed as a percentage of the heating value in the coal fired), which followed a linear profile over the practical working range of the engine. This in turn was formed from two further linear relationships, the absorption efficiency (*i.e.* the proportion of the heat available that actually went to make steam) and the combustion efficiency (*i.e.* the proportion of the fuel that was actually burned as opposed to that fired). It had been known for a long time that not all of the coal fired was burnt but around 1920 an accurate method was developed to quantify it. Prior to then, because the coal loss had been grossly underestimated, it was assumed the absorption efficiency fell off with rise in output but in fact it remained more or less constant, so the significant drop in boiler efficiency recorded for example in figure 109 was overwhelmingly prompted by a fall in combustion efficiency.

These relationships were established using data derived from locomotive testing stations. Other figures from this same sources used in an investigation conducted a little earlier, enabled the interdependent relationships between free gas area, heating surface, evaporation and boiler efficiency to be finally unravelled, albeit qualitatively. These may be briefly summarized:-

(i) An increase in heating surface, while keeping the same free gas area, necessitates an increase in tube length. This may slightly raise boiler efficiency but the evaporation will be increased only very slightly, if at all, as the greater resistance the longer tubes present to the gases may prevent an increase in the amount of gas passing through the barrel.

(ii) An increase in free gas area without an increase in heating surface means a larger number of shorter tubes. Any significant change in this direction will considerably increase the evaporation because the enlarged free gas area combined with reduced tube resistance enables a greatly enhanced mass of air to pass through the boiler for the same draught, although shortening the tubes may entail a slight reduction in boiler efficiency.

(iii) When a boiler is working below its maximum output, then the free gas area is less important than is indicated above. If a boiler having a maximum firing rate of x lbs/sq ft/hr of grate area is fired at say 2/3x lbs, then with an efficient draughting system it would be possible to block up around 20 per cent of the tubes and still draw the same amount of combustion air through the boiler. Despite the 20 per cent reduction in free gas area, the combustion rate would be maintained at the same rate while the efficiency of heat absorption in the tubes would be affected only to the extent of 1 or 2 per cent. With the number of tubes reduced the quantity of gas passing through them is necessarily increased. This results in a corresponding increase in the rate of heat transfer so the total amount absorbed is practically the same in spite of the considerable reduction in heating surface[99]. Furthermore, the effect the plugged tubes may have in modifying the combustion air flow pattern through the grate might even improve the combustion efficiency.

Until the appearance of locomotive testing stations, boiler design had of perforce largely been an empirical process, although some hardy souls had attempted to obtain worthwhile data from road tests it was fraught with difficulty. A combined approach was adopted by Adolphe Henry of the Paris Lyons Mediterranean Railway who from 1885 to 1890 arranged for tests to be conducted on the road and on stationary locomotive boilers to determine the effects tube length and plain and ribbed tubes had on the evaporative power and boiler efficiency. It was then well known that with the same grate area, number and diameter of tubes, the boiler efficiency might rise with longer tubes but the evaporative power appeared to reduce. Mr Henry wanted to establish if the improved boiler efficiency compensated for the increased weight and reduced evaporation, or alternatively if boiler efficiency should be sacrificed to obtain a lighter engine and greater power? At the time many

---

99 This is possibly an avenue the operators of preserved locomotives might wish to explore. Plugging say one-quarter or even more of the small tubes would force a larger portion of the exhaust gases through the flues thereby raising the superheat. Any loss in boiler efficiency would be small, while it would be more than made offset by the gain in engine performance – the least efficient part of the machine.

engineers, either through tradition and/or observation, used tube length/diameter ratios in the range 80-100. These trials largely supported this practice while lifting a curtain on how changes in tube diameter affected the draught demand but it is suspected adopting a *specific L/D* ratio was not then a design tool. Subsequently the testing station at Altoona *did* suggest the optimum proportion for the small tubes was a *L/D* ratio of 102-113 (*i.e.* 15ft for 2ins tubes and 19ft for 2¼ins tubes). This is known to have featured in Derby design practice post-Grouping.

In line with (i) above, as tubes increased in length it was confirmed the quantity of steam each one generated reduced due to the higher resistance their longer length presented to the exhaust gas flow. For a longer tube to make proportionately the same quantity of steam as a shorter one of the same diameter (*i.e.* lbs/ft of tube length), required that the draught be increased by a considerable amount. This was simply so that a sufficiently enhanced mass of gas would be induced to flow along the tube. Since the tubes serve two roles – heat transfer *and* as a conduit for the waste gases Altoona presented these *L/D* ratios as an acceptable compromise.

This dual function featured in a paper[100] Dr Richard Wagner delivered to the I Loco E in which he described how through adopting a *L/D* of 100, or as he expressed it a *S/A* of 400 – these being the same[101] – and applying this ratio to *both* the small tubes and the superheater flues/elements in one or two boilers, he had obtained an improvement in performance. This was subsequently seized on by LMS engineers as a design tool. Unfortunately it would appear Dr Wagner obtained his improvements primarily by luck for whilst *S/A* ratios do have some relevance in heat transfer it is not that significant under the conditions pertaining in locomotive barrels. Likewise, arranging identical *S/A* ratios for the flues and small tubes *does not* ensure they present identical resistances to gas flow.

During the thirty-six years' long period between the introduction of the 'Big Goods' and the 'Doodlebug', experimenters into heat transfer theory had made considerable progress, including that present within boiler tubes. Furthermore, although not yet complete it was certainly sufficiently advanced by the early 1930s for practical application - a development it seems that was overlooked by many locomotive engineers. Indeed those on the LMS were advised by a non-locomotive boiler designer[102] in 1938 that tubular heat transfer *and* tube resistance depended on a good many other things than simple *S/A* ratios but some seemingly chose to ignore this advice. So, while Mr Cox admitted in the same year to harbouring some doubts about the method, he nevertheless was unable to abandon the technique, retaining it, postwar for his BR Standards. Unfortunately, it resulted in heavy boilers, limited superheat and lower than possible steam outputs. In contrast, whomsoever[103] it was who designed the 4D and 7 boilers used on Mr Ivatt's 2-6-0 classes, appears to have given it less importance for their tube ratios exhibit significantly different values.

The LMS championed the necessity of a free gas area through the barrel of 15 per cent in order for an engine to steam, yet plenty of other boiler designs could out steam them with lower fractions so we must also question this finding. The quantity of exhaust gas produced (lbs/hr) is roughly 1.6-1.75 times the steam flow so it necessarily follows that high steaming rates result in lots of gas while lower rates far less. Since an engine was designed to fulfil a desired duty, this necessitated a certain steam rate and thus an accompanying gas flow. If the free gas area is large, then the resistance the barrel presents to gas flow will be low but so will

---

100 Dr R Wagner *Some New Developments of the Stephenson Boiler* I Loco E Paper N° 253 September 1929.

101 The *L/D* ratio is simply the length L of the small tube in inches divided by its internal diameter D also in inches. Conversely in the S/A ratio S is the total area in contact with the waste gases and A is the free area available for gas flow through the tube.

So for a small tube S is given by $(\pi \times D \times L)$
and A by $[(\pi \times D^2) \div 4]$
whence:-
$$S/A = (\pi \times D \times L) \div [(\pi \times D^2) \div 4] = \frac{4 \times L}{D}$$

---

102 Messrs M M Loubser & E S Cox *Locomotive Boiler Design - Theory and Practice* I Loco E Paper N° 388 January 1938 pp 412 & 413.

103 Presumably this change was initiated under the direct instruction of Mr Coleman, or at the very least with his tacit agreement. Incidentally of the three proposed Class 4 0-6-0 designs illustrated in figure 87, DD 3510 drawn in 1941, had 1¾in tubes × 12swg and 10ft - 9in between tubeplates, which would have given a *S/A* ratio of 335 ignoring the thicknesses of the plates. For DD 3681 of 1943 the distance between tubeplates remained the same but the tubes were to be 15/8in × 12swg, giving a *S/A* of 364, while DD 3688, also of 1943 the tube dimensions remained the same but the distance between tubeplates was increased to 11ft - 4in giving a *S/A* of 384. All three proposals were to have 21 flues.

the gas velocity and this reduces the heat transfer rate but the latter is offset by the larger heating surface area present. Conversely if the free gas area is small, then the heat transfer rate is improved, which compensates for the reduced heating surface area, but at the expense of a higher resistance - all generally as per (i) and (ii) above.

of it. As the efficiency of the front end improves so the free gas area through the barrel can be reduced, for the same gas flow rate, improving combustion efficiency as well as the heat transfer effect, thereby enabling a smaller, lighter boiler to be fitted.

It may be demonstrated that the resistance a barrel

Table LXIII – Comparison in Boiler Proportions and Performance at their Front End Draughting Limits

		G7s	4D	BR4
Coal fired (Blidworth)	lbs/hr	3,570	2,840	3,250
Steam production	lbs/hr	19,000	17,000	19,600
Steam temperature	°F	640	684	643
Boiler efficiency	per cent	64	63	62*
Steam production	lbs/hr per sq ft of grate	900	739	734
Steam production	lbs/hr per sq ft of evap. surface	16.4	13.9	13.6
Steam production	lbs/hr per sq ft of total free gas area	5,476	4,462	5,185
Firing rate	lbs/hr per sq ft of grate	169.2	123.5	121.7
Tubular heating surface	sq ft	1034	1090	1301
Firebox heating surface	sq ft	124	131	143
Total heating surface	sq ft	1158	1221	1444
Superheater surface	sq ft	246	231	258
Grate area	sq ft	21.1	23.0	26.7
Heating surface ÷ grate area		54.9	53.1	54.1
Length between tubeplates		10ft - 10½ins	10ft - 10½ins	13ft - 0ins
Tubes	large	21 × 5 1/8 ins	24 × 5 1/8 ins	21 × 5 1/8 ins
	small	146 × 1¾ ins	156 × 1 5/8 ins	157 × 1¾ ins
	elements	1½ ins	1¼ ins†	1 3/8 ins
S/A ratios¶	flues	357	274	368
	small tubes	342	374	405
Free gas areas	flues sq ft	1.58	2.11	1.74
	small tubes sq ft	1.89	1.70	2.04
	total area sq ft	3.47	3.81	3.78
Flue free gas area as percentage of total free gas area		45.5	55.4	46.0
Free gas area as percentage of grate area		16.4	16.6	14.2

*This value taken from table V *Experiences with British Railways Standard Locomotives* by E S Cox I Loco E Paper Nº 532. In table XVII appearing in *British Standard Steam Locomotives* Ian Allan 1966 also by E S Cox, it had fallen to 61 per cent.

†During testing at Swindon, as a trial, elements increased to 1 3/8 ins diameter and S/A ratio increased to 290. This had no discernible impact on boiler efficiency or superheat temperature.

¶ S/A ratios for G7s from *Report on Trials of LMR 0-6-0 Class 4F Freight Locomotives Fitted with Swirlyflo Boiler Tubes and Modified Draughting Arrangement*; for the 4D from *Raising Steam on the LMS* and for the BR4 *British Standard Steam Locomotives*.

If the draughting system was of a poor design – as many LMS ones were – then the barrel and grate resistances had to be kept down so that enough air could be drawn through the fire, to enable the boiler to generate steam at the rate the cylinders needed it for the engine to do the work demanded

presents to gas flow is *very* much influenced by the tube diameter and number. However, for a chosen percentage of free gas area and a constant *S/A* ratio (small tubes), barrel resistance becomes largely the same for equal total gas flow rates, which is probably why after the debacle over the 'Jubilees'

LMS engineers placed such emphasis on these two ratios. Having established 15 per cent free gas area *and a S/A* of 400 worked satisfactorily within the capacity of their draughting designs they found these ratios could then be applied to other boilers with a reasonable level of confidence - subject to sufficient flues being provided. Hence presumably the adoption by LMS engineers of another 'iffy' design ratio - the fraction of the free area through the flues as a proportion of the total free gas area. Although important it is not the whole answer as the performance of the Swindon superheater fitted to N° 3836 demonstrated.

Tubular heating surface can be shewn to be very good at transferring the available heat, consequently almost any combination of tube diameter and number will return an acceptable performance; the more so when it is considered that the tubes only transferred a portion of the total heat released in the firebox. So whilst small diameter tubes are more effective at transferring heat, the gain is not as great as one might imagine. Consequently, a limited number of larger diameter tubes does not really 'lose' very much absorption efficiency. As a corollary of this, whilst adopting patent tubes such as the 'Swirlyflo', or the Serve internally ribbed tubes tested by Adolphe Henry, effected an improvement in heat transfer, it was not large, while their heat transferring profiles gave them a higher resistance to gas flow as well as making them awkward to install and clean. When this very small gain in absorption efficiency was set against the deleterious impact on boiler efficiency made by the fall in combustion efficiency, their disadvantages outweighed the gain hence they never really became popular in Britain.

When an engine is running in its lower power outputs most of the steam is liberated within the firebox with comparatively little from the indirect surfaces, but as the steam demand rises then the fraction of the steam generated in the barrel increases. The ratio typically changes from around 2/3 : 1/3 to become ½ : ½, or in locomotives having particularly high steam outputs perhaps 1/3 : 2/3. For saturated engines this effect is of no consequence but this is far from the case with superheated ones. The low gas rates associated with low steam flows means a high proportion of the available heat is absorbed in the firebox so the gases have a comparatively low temperature when they enter the barrel. If the small tubes, as in the G7s, have a lower resistance than the flues then the superheat will be even lower than it need be.

It is revealing to compare the performance of the re-draughted G7s and 4D boilers at their respective front end draughting limits[104], for the former represents one of the last designs that of perforce had to be proportioned largely empirically, while furthermore superheating was in its infancy. Conversely when the latter was designed the heat transfer theory was comprehensive and accurate. This comparison appears in table LXIII, but for completeness the equivalent figures for an even later class 4 boiler, the BR4 carried by the BR Standard Class 4 4-6-0, have been included. This represents a similar sized boiler designed by Mr Cox based on the concept of adopting *S/A* ratios of 400[105] for the flues and small tubes, within the constraints of standard commercially available tube diameters:-

"Wagner confirmed that there is an optimum relationship between resistance to flow of gases and heat absorption capacity when the free cross sectional area of the tube is about one four-hundredth of the total swept surface. Containing four 1 3/8-in. diameter superheater element tubes, the 5 1/8-in. diameter flue produces this best condition for a length between tubeplates of about 14ft. typical of an average 4-6-0. For shorter tubes there is not enough gas resistance and boiler efficiency is lost. For longer tubes which can vary from 17 to 22 ft. in 'Pacific' locomotives, resistance to the flow of gases along the large tubes is restricted, and in particular, superheat temperatures tend to be lower than they ought for greatest cylinder efficiency."

Table LXIII reveals that despite having the smallest grate area and the least evaporative heating surface, the G7s produced the second

---

104 Since the grate limit represents the ultimate maximum steam output attainable from a given combination of boiler, draughting system and coal, this might be considered a fairer comparison basis than the draughting limit. The latter was to some extent subjective since it relied on opinion whereas the grate limit is mathematically definable.

	C1	C2	C3	C4	C5	C6
	Grate limit steam lbs/hr	Grate limit coal lb/hr	Draughting limit steam lbs/hr	C3 ÷ C1	C1 ÷ C2	C5 ÷ C4
G7	23,300	5,700	19,000	81.5%	4.09	5.02
4D	18,500	4,000	17,000	91.8%	4.63	5.04
BR4	22,490	5,078	19,600	87.1%	4.43	5.08

However, this table reveals the front end draughting limit for the G7 was set at a lower fraction of the grate limit steam output than in the other two so basing the comparison on front end values is not penalizing the more modern boilers.

105 Mr E S Cox *British Standard Steam Locomotives* Ian Allan Shepperton 1966 pp74-7.

highest steam output. Furthermore, although the thermal efficiencies of the three boilers are very close, it is the G7s which was the highest. So, despite having the highest firing rate, it was able to retain a superior combustion efficiency than either of the two modern boilers. This is demonstrated by the steeper slope of the boiler efficiency curve for the 4D boiler appearing in figure 109. Its greater unburned coal loss reduced the combustion efficiency with the result the equivalent boiler efficiency was reached at a lower firing rate. A similar effect may be seen to have occurred in the BR4 boiler, wherein its maximum specific steam generation rate per square foot of grate was obtained at a very similar firing rate to the 4D.

Unfortunately, it has not been possible to establish weights for these three boilers, but comparing the dimensions appearing in table LXIII confirms the BR4 boiler will have been the heaviest of the three. While the 4D and the G7 probably did not differ that much in weight, it is suspected the taper boiler design was a little heavier - the saving from the tapered barrel being more than offset by the larger firebox. Although the absence of weight figures prevents a quantitative comparison, nevertheless it is clear from the above reasoning that the G7 boiler will have produced the largest quantity of steam per ton of boiler weight.

If the superheat temperatures for the G7s and 4D boilers are compared for the same steam rates, in every case the taper boiler delivered considerably hotter steam – this is even more pronounced at the lower rates. This it will be noted is despite its flue/element combination having a S/A ratio just over two-thirds of the 'optimum' 400. The main reason for this being the flues presented a lower resistance than the small tubes so they received proportionately more of the gas. The G7s flue/element combination had a S/A ratio of about 400 with a lower ratio for the small tubes, while the converse is the case with the BR4, but both delivered almost identical steam temperatures at very similar steam rates. The higher combustion rate, caused by the smaller grate for equal steam rates, largely offsetting the more restricted flues with their slightly larger elements.

Even though the 4D possessed tube ratios very different from those of the BR4, the specific steam release rates per square foot of heating surface for the two boilers are almost identical, and this is also despite it having the least evaporative heating surface relative to grate area. These comparisons confirm that attempting to predict heat transfer and thus boiler performance, simply in terms of the proportions of the tubular surface was a pointless exercise *unless* it was considered in conjunction with the exhaust gas flow. Furthermore, the impact that the presence of an extra foot or two on the end of a tube had on the total heat transferred was neither here nor there. Provided the resistance of the boiler was within the capacity of the front end at the desired steaming rate, and the superheater surface sufficient and correctly proportioned, then it was *far* more important to reduce the fall in combustion efficiency as far as possible. Worrying about trying to obtain one or two per cent extra gain in heat transfer through adopting the 'correct' tube ratios seems laughable when the same designer was willing to accept a drop ten or twenty times larger in combustion efficiency. Nevertheless a boiler designed nearly forty years earlier, whilst far from solving the problem did nonetheless return a noticeably superior performance.

Chapter Six

Some Final Thoughts and Summary

Whilst the 'Big Goods' was not one of the finest locomotive classes to grace the rails of Britain it was however very far from being the poorest, although to read some commentators' views one could be mistaken for believing it to have been the worst designed locomotive ever and that it should never have been built. Had this really been the case, we must wonder quite how powerless and/or incompetent were the first three Chief Mechanical Engineers of the LMS who allowed the class to be multiplied, unmodified until it represented 10 per cent of the company's locomotive stock - another view is that its performance was not as black as some would have us believe. Indeed it seems far more reasonable to believe those engineers in the Operating Department who requested more Class 4s and those in the Chief Mechanical Engineer's department who agreed to their production made that decision because they thought the locomotives would well serve the new company, after having determined the class' performance from comparison tests.

Other critics of the 'Big Goods' take the view because other railways had introduced 0-8-0s or even 2-8-0s by the time of its appearance, Derby should not have been so 'timorous' in its response. Contrary to the opinions of some, the purpose of engine designers was not to keep up with the 'locomotive Jones' although that certainly occurred on occasions, but rather to produce machines which complied with the restraints of the Engineer while meeting the traffic and route requirements of the Operating Department.

No doubt, had the need been there, or perhaps the LMS been less awash with money for its scrap and build policy, some improvement might have occurred, but instead, it seems later engineers preferred to criticise the machine, thereby providing themselves with the excuse for building a completely new replacement. Perhaps this criticism of the Class 4 *et al* would have been more fairly justified if the locomotives built to replace them had been shining paragons of the craft of the locomotive engineer - sadly, they were not. Furthermore, the development of the successor to the Class 4 0-6-0 Freight was a long drawn out affair with a gestation period of ten years. From this we might observe that for all its faults, it was not until 1947 that LMS locomotive designers had proved capable of producing a replacement engine which possessed sufficient power, lightness and route availability to satisfy the operating people and the Engineer, to become the nominal successor to a design introduced thirty-six years earlier.

The following summarizes the main criticisms of the Midland/LMS Class 4 0-6-0; most it will be observed individually are comparatively minor, and could have been addressed quite simply, had the will been present:-

Frame cracking: Although the engine had a tendency to crack its frame, so did many, more modern classes, many of which could develop cracks more extensively and at a faster rate. Furthermore, in the case of some, particularly the pure LMS designs and derivatives, this was after considerable study into its causes, yet, applying the lessons had not produced a frame immune from cracking. This was understandable, since steam locomotive engineers did not have access to the necessary design tools to prevent it from occurring. In view of this, it does therefore appear rather unfair for LMS and BR engineers, and others, to criticize a design made two, three or even four decades earlier when the knowledge regarding the causes of frame cracking was even less thorough. This is particularly so when their own efforts were no better and in some cases considerably worse.

On the last day of 1947 the LMS handed over to the embryonic British Railways 7,805 steam engines, of these 772 comprised Standard Class 4 0-6-0s, yet the frame of these engines remained the 1911 design. Contrast this with the then 742 extant members of the Class 5, whose frame design had undergone considerable revision and modification. Indeed it was the predilection for frame cracking exhibited by so many of William Stanier's newly introduced classes that initiated the major investigation into the causes and the extent of the problem.

Axleboxes: While these were small by later standards *i.e.* when compared to those that could be fitted to outside cylinder engines, this was not the *real* reason for their poorer performance. The evidence is there demonstrating that engines fitted with similarly, or even more heavily loaded bearings, running on other companies, fared better.

Mr Cox demonstrated that in 1930, one important non-standard LMS class of inside-cylinder goods engine had returned a hot-box performance - one every ten years - that was identical to that obtained from the Stanier-box fitted to the taper boiler classes. This achievement demonstrates the error in assuming it was bearing size alone that automatically determined a propensity for hot boxes. The statistics also suggest that hot driving wheel axleboxes was a problem that became more troublesome under the LMS but it was one largely of its own making. Changing the white metal, plus poor re-metalling techniques in sheds, together with a less than optimum choice of lubricating oils all served to worsen the situation on the LMS. Later, improved finishing techniques coupled with an improved oil certainly increased their life as well as reducing the incidence of hot boxes. Thus, by the time of British Railways incidences of hot boxes had fallen right away becoming much rarer - yet the bearings themselves were not increased in size nor at the time had the work demanded of the class significantly reduced.

As the tables appearing earlier reveal 4F class members were returning annual mileages typically 85-90 per cent of those obtained from Standard Class 8 2-8-0s - the other principal ex-LMS goods locomotive class. This does not seem a bad effort, similarly, this improved axlebox performance also ensured less axlebox wear and deterioration in service. Consequently workshop attention that had been demanded typically at 30,000 miles during the 'twenties and early 'thirties had by BR days been roughly doubled. As figure 3 reveals, although as to be expected the mileages between repairs were higher for 8F 2-8-0s compared to the 4Fs, nevertheless 40 per cent of the eight-coupled engines ran 60,000 miles *or less*, before entering the works for an Intermediate following a General while 54 per cent of the six-coupled engines ran 50,000-60,000 miles *or more*. By the 1950s, having corrected the mistakes introduced earlier and combined them with improved workshop techniques ensured that these slightly shorter mileages between workshop visits were simply because the bearings wore out quicker due to their smaller size. They were not due to a reduced technical performance.

Size for size Class 4 axlebox performance was comparable proportionately to that obtained from the 8F. Indeed, we ought really point out that high mileages were obtained from LMS and BR Standard locomotives fitted with Stanier-axleboxes not because the engines were fitted with wonderful bearings but *rather* it was because the engines concerned were not producing power outputs commensurate with their size. Thus, modern locomotives running elsewhere in the world and shod with designs of plain axlebox similar to, or even nominally better than the LMS Stanier-box, could require attention at mileages as low as 25,000-30,000 miles. On that basis, one could argue that LMS and BR engineers had not obtained economic use of capital, since in their desire to reduce maintenance costs, they had produced engines that were were larger and heavier than they need otherwise have been, thereby increasing their fuel and water costs.

Availability and productivity/utilization figures together with the annual mileages obtained infer the 'Big Goods' were reliable and cost effective, but due to their nominal replacement by new classes this meant that a scheme to provide them with roller bearings - the optimum solution - was not deemed worthwhile. Nevertheless, in the mid-1950s a handful of examples were provided with manganese steel liners to their axleboxes, which confirms bearing mileages had improved sufficiently to give the experiment some credence, but this modification would have been better combined with roller bearings.

Steam utilization: Despite the carping, there was nothing wrong with the Class 4 valve *events* indeed Mr Ivatt subsequently altered the LMS three-cylinder valve events so that they more closely resembled them! Not only did he *reduce* their lap length while increasing the lead, in order to *increase* the port opening but also he returned more or less, to the Midland Railway's favoured lap:lead ratio of four. While in the case of his Class 5 4-6-0 built with outside Stephenson's valve gear the valve events were more or less identical with those of the Class 4, differing only in that the port openings to exhaust were proportionately smaller. In all of these outside cylinder classes the port openings to steam were larger for equivalent cut-offs than those in the 'Big Goods' simply because of the longer lap.

The presence of short-lap valves compromised steam economy and performance for high speed traffic, but the class had been designed for goods and mineral traffic so although it was also found suitable for fitted freights, local speed passenger and excursions, unless it spent a sufficiently high proportion of its time on such higher speed traffic, there was probably little benefit to be gained from fitting large-lap valves. Whilst consideration appears to have been given to such a modification, it did not proceed. The ex-LMS locomotive designers whose stars shone post-war opined that the speed of fitted freight trains was such that the 0-6-0 was no longer suitable and that engines in possession of a leading pony truck or even a bogie were more appropriate, although the Southern Railway thought otherwise.

Steam production: The 'Big Goods' was introduced to haul the Midland Railway's immense coal traffic, under which circumstances, it would have generated plenty of *hot* steam. Essentially it was only the gain in enthalpy obtained from superheating that gave the engine its class 4 rating - the larger diameter cylinders were primarily to accommodate a sufficient mass of the hotter *less dense* steam. Smaller loads, frequent starts and stops also poorer quality coal would all have affected its performance for the worse. If that was going to be their lot, then Dr Geisel's superheater booster, which comprised a loosely pivoted baffle in front of the small tubes might have been worth investigating. It represented a cheaper alternative to the optimum one of altering flue and small tube diameters and numbers.

The steaming difficulties could have been overcome by attention to the draughting/exhaust system. That such a large class of engines could be left with so reduced a steaming capacity in the face of poorer coal, says a great deal about the abilities and misplaced priorities of certain locomotive engineers. The draughting could readily and very cheaply been improved - certainly for far less money than the contemplated changes associated with increasing the lap length even if the latter had been restricted to when new cylinders were required.

Bad as draughting design could be on the LMS, which tended to be rather hit-or-miss witness the fiasco that accompanied the first few 'Doodlebugs', nevertheless, some improvement could have been effected if only perhaps by the simple expedient of adopting the draughting design of the parallel boiler 2-6-4T. Not only would an improved front-end have given it more of a reserve to cope with poorer coal, but also the resulting increased quantity of steam, would have helped offset its poorer steam economy at speed. There is a hint of this in the superior power-to-weight ratio of Nº 44030 compared to Nº 43094.

Modifications: The class was, post-1928, provided with four-ring piston valves in place of the original Schmidt single broad ring, which reduced the internal steam leakage. Exhaust steam injectors were tried but later abandoned - feed water heaters demonstrate their greatest saving in fuel when the locomotive is being worked consistently near its maximum output. In this respect following the introduction of newer, larger engines, it is likely exhaust steam injectors made less impact on Class 4 economy following Sir William's arrival, but by the same token they were probably no more effective on for example the Class 8 2-8-0.

For regular use on high speed work a modest improvement could have been effected in the steam circuit, which it will be recalled was not noticeably smaller, in proportion to its cylinder diameter, than that of two contemporary express locomotives. Nevertheless its weakest features could have been cheaply overcome - increasing the diameter of the superheated steam pipes, revising the porting in the piston valve liners, and possibly streamlining the valve heads. A useful further halfway house might simply have been a modest increase in valve lap by say 1/8ins or 3/16ins, which could have been accommodated by shortening the eccentric rods and substituting launch type expansion links. To increase the lap further would probably have necessitated a revised cylinder design.

Tragically, for the steam locomotive, particularly in the land of its birth, fitting large-lap valves and superheaters represented more or less the pinnacle of its technical development. Unfortunately, the poor understanding of locomotive performance demonstrated by some designers, or perhaps simply the determination to incorporate certain pet 'hobby-horses' into the design, was such that they were able to destroy much of benefit, which even these modest improvements could bestow. For example, ignoring whatever benefit fitting the replacements built in the 'thirties and later with carrying wheels and outside cylinders was meant to achieve through easier maintenance and better riding, one downside was they increased engine weight, while the locomotives themselves produced no more power.

Whilst a Class 4 0-6-0 needed more steam to produce each horsepower, at low speeds this was primarily because of its lower steam pressure and superheat conditions with very little due to its smaller steam circuit. However, it was a considerably lighter engine, thus once allowance is made for the horsepower required to drive the heavier Class 4MT 2-6-0 is considered, the advantage the latter's superior steam circuit presented was less than one might at first suppose. Along with this we must remember that some of the published test data for the 'Doodlebug' is suspect appearing to shew the locomotive in a better light. A conclusion that is confirmed to some extent by the comments made by several footplatemen to the effect the Mogul was no better than a good Standard Freight. Incidentally there was a precedence for this data manipulation in the case of at least one other BR Standard class. Michael Rutherford advised that the 'best' test results were used as the plotting points for the charts recording the Class 7 4-6-2 thereby giving the locomotive in its Performance and Efficiency Bulletin a most optimistic performance. At the time Mr Cox was both in charge of locomotive testing *and* responsible for the design of these classes.

When we consider the poor return on capital investment that so many more modern classes actually represented, is it any surprise that 'despised' locomotive classes, such as the Midland/LMS Class 2 or the 'Big Goods' lasted so long? However challenging they might have been to their crews in comparison to more modern locomotives, from the viewpoint of the bean counters, there was no difference. The new modern replacement locomotives, due to inherent design defects, and/or their unsuitable power-to-weight ratio in respect of their duties, meant that frequently they were unable to demonstrate any real economical or financial advantage over these *pre-grouping* designs.

As Cuthbert Pounder[1], a director and Chief Technical Engineer of Harland & Wolff Ltd observed, albeit in connexion with marine engine building:-

"Engineering is, first and last, a commercial business. The similarity between building and selling an engine, and making and selling a pair of shoes, may be disguised and overlaid, but, at root, the two things are the same. The engineering works, with its complicated plant, its many trades and its technical officers has, in the last analysis, kinship with the shoemaker, who, taking his raw material, fashions it into a pair of shoes and sells them over the counter. Shoes are sold on suitability, durability, price and so on; so is a power plant. The end is precisely the same; it is only the means to that end which are different. All this may be obvious, but nevertheless it is hard to get technical men to appreciate - in their bones, so to speak - the commercial aspect of their work. In design offices, men - especially those whose cast of mind tends to the academical - are apt to become so absorbed in their problems as to mistake the means for the end. In the works, men with the super-organizing complex commit the same error."

Perhaps in time, once the steam locomotive has receded further into history, there will be more objective and considered appraisals made of its development under the auspices of the LMS derived from the Midland Railway's legacy - as opposed to the current simple acceptance by enthusiasts of the criticism prompted by others, possibly with personal axes to grind. The outcome of these, the author ventures to suggest, may come as a surprise to a great many people.

---

1 Mr C C Pounder *Human Problems in Marine Engineering* Trans I Mar E March 1960.